Doctrine for the Lady of the Renaissance

Doctrine for the
Lady of the Renaissance

RUTH KELSO

Foreword by
Katharine M. Rogers

University of Illinois Press
Urbana and Chicago

© 1956, 1978 by the Board of Trustees of the University of Illinois
Manufactured in the United States of America
C 5 4 3

This book is printed on acid-free paper.

Library of Congress Cataloging-in-Publication Data
Kelso, Ruth, 1885–
Doctrine for the lady of the Renaissance.
Bibliography: p.
Includes index.
1. Women—History—Renaissance, 1450–1600. I. Title.
HQ1148.K4   1978
301.41'2'09024   78-2487
ISBN 0-252-00693-3

To Hardin Craig

WITH ADMIRATION AND GRATITUDE

Foreword

Ruth Kelso's *Doctrine for the Lady of the Renaissance*, originally published more than twenty years ago, is a landmark in the historical study of women, not only for its comprehensive account of Renaissance views on the lady, but for its recognition that she was in many ways excluded from the freedom and enlightenment characteristic of the period. Covering western European writers on women from 1400 to 1600, Kelso provides an invaluable survey of Renaissance ideals and specific recommendations for education and conduct. Concerned with theory rather than practice, she indicates the range of opinion on such matters as the extent to which an unmarried lady should manifest bashfulness, the question of whether girls should study poetry or rhetoric, and the degree of pleasure permissible in the marriage bed (a husband who made love to his wife passionately might awaken unchaste desires in her). There are ample materials in this book for the study of Renaissance thinking about woman's potential and limitations and her proper behavior as daughter, wife, love object, lady in waiting, or ruler.

Kelso demonstrates that, contrary to conventional assumptions, the Renaissance had remarkably little effect in loosening traditional restrictions on women. While the Renaissance gentleman was exhorted to develop his capacities freely and in every direction, the lady "turns out to be merely a wife." Her virtues were defined in terms of what filled her husband's needs. First of these was chastity, rarely mentioned in connection with gentlemen. Rigorous training in this all-important quality dominated her education, and brought with it as safeguards bashfulness, passivity, and seclusion from experience. Any intellectual pursuit had to be rejected if it seemed to imperil chastity, and even the most liberal writers excluded certain branches of learning on this ground. Luis Vives, the most influential authority on women's education in the sixteenth century, ruled out the study of logic and history and declared it shockingly immodest for marriageable women to go about socially, converse with men, speak eloquently, or love the man they intended to marry.

Study or any other form of self-development was subordinated to wifehood, the only vocation open to women (apart from the convent). The Renaissance concept of the wife's role came intact from St. Paul and the Fathers of the early Church: obedience was a wife's first duty, and patience, humility, and fidelity were enjoined regardless of how her husband treated her. Even the idealized love of the Renaissance, which would seem to exalt women, was, Kelso points out, male-centered: the lover's feelings for his lady were fully expressed, but nothing was said of hers for him. Some writers even extended this one-sidedness to a proof that women were inferior to men because it is more noble to love than to be loved. In short, the standards set up for women and men were different in almost every respect. The virtues recommended to even the greatest lady were adapted to her feminine nature: humility, peace-making, sobriety, chastity, obedience to her husband and constant solicitude for his well-being.

Though Kelso includes much evidence of restrictive attitudes in her book, she does not condemn them so explicitly as would an author writing today. Moreover, in contrasting Renaissance doctrine for the lady and the gentleman, she lays most stress on the fact that the gentleman was clearly distinguished from men of lower social class, while the lady was not. This point in itself is not significant, at least for modern readers, unless it is related to the persistent tendency to stereotype women as men are not stereotyped, to assume that their supposedly female attributes make them more alike than any possible differences could distinguish them. The main point, surely, is not that Renaissance authors reduced all ladies to women, but that they reduced all women to a narrowly defined role. The lady, being a mere woman, was to develop only in accordance with male needs, while the gentleman was to fulfill himself by expanding his potentialities to the utmost. As long as chastity and obedience were considered far more important than active virtues or mental development, all women had to be restricted in their education and their sphere for action. Since they were still regarded as mere helpmates, any opportunities offered them had to be justified in terms of their usefulness to men. While learning was assumed to be good for men, even relatively feminist authors found it necessary to justify it for women by arguing that education need not interfere with their chastity, modesty, or household duties.

This tendency to define women in terms of roles that meet the needs of men may help to account for a discrepancy that Kelso leaves unexplained. Despite the enormous emphasis on chastity in wives, which included absolute fidelity in thought as well as act, women were idealized as the objects of extramarital love and were expected to respond to the devotion of their lovers. Renaissance writers rarely attempted to reconcile the ideals of wife and mistress, generally looking at women from one angle or the other. This may have been easier to manage because men, seeing women as fillers of various functions rather than as independent human beings, did not find it necessary to form a consistent ideal for their total development. Unlike the gentleman, the lady existed primarily in relationship to others, each of whom defined her in terms of his own requirements.

In any case there was nothing new in the contradiction between Renaissance ideals for wife and mistress, which springs directly from the medieval cult of courtly love with its sharp separation of love from marriage. Renaissance attitudes can best be understood in their historical context, which Kelso does not supply. Love poetry, written mainly by men, has always tended to focus on the man's feelings and to reduce the woman to an often depersonalized love object. At no time was this more apparent than in the late Middle Ages, when Dante poured out love for a woman whom he never knew well and who was already dead. Beatrice is a symbol, a construction of man's fantasy, rather than a human being in a reciprocal relationship. A tradition such as this may apparently exalt woman as the object of love, but it has no effect on her actual status. It can coexist comfortably with restrictive marriage, and did so in the Middle Ages and the Renaissance alike.

Renaissance writers' anxiety about educating women and insistence on wifely subjection simply illustrate the prevailing tendency of our culture, both before and since their time, to center on the male and to limit women. True, it is surprising that the far-ranging changes of the Renaissance—the broadened speculation, the questioning of old ways of thinking, the emphasis upon joy and fulfillment in this world—had such small influence upon the position of one half of the human species. Evidently it would take even more profound changes to shake fundamental assumptions about relationships between the sexes, to overcome man's need to keep woman in an ancillary position, and to justify this subordination by maintaining that she is differently qualified from, even if possibly not inferior to, himself.

Only now are scholars beginning to write social history with a full analysis and questioning of the patriarchal assumptions underlying our culture. One of the best examples is Joan Kelly-Gadol's essay "Did Women Have a Renaissance?" in the anthology *Becoming Visible*.[1] Through analysis of Baldassar Castiglione, she explores the ways women, despite "the professed parity of noblewomen and men in *The Courtier*," were reduced to passivity and a "merely decorative role." Another recent anthology, *Not in God's Image*,[2] includes several sec-

[1] *Becoming Visible: Women in European History*, ed. Renate Bridenthal and Claudia Koonz (Boston: Houghton Mifflin, 1977). This book contains several other interesting essays on women of this period, all written with clear feminist awareness.

[2] *Not in God's Image: A History of Women in Europe from the Greeks to the Nineteenth Century*, ed. Julia O'Faolain and Lauro Martines (New York: Harper and Row, 1973).

tions on the Renaissance in its excellent collection of original source material.

Further information about the lives of Renaissance women may be found in two classical older works, Louis B. Wright's *Middle-Class Culture in Elizabethan England* (1935) and Carroll Camden's *The Elizabethan Woman* (1952). Camden's work gives a full picture of women's daily life, though it overestimates their degree of emancipation. Wright's chapters on "Instruction in Domestic Relations" and "The Popular Controversy over Woman" show that middle-class views on women were remarkably like the aristocratic ones described by Kelso. The same may be said of the middle-class Puritans whose attitude is described in William and Malleville Haller's "The Puritan Art of Love."[3] The best recent account of the social position of women, providing a useful background for the theories Kelso discusses, is Pearl Hogrefe's *Tudor Women: Commoners and Queens* (1975). It is filled with fascinating details and organized around the ways in which women managed to transcend the limitations imposed upon them by moral theory and the law, although it does not compare with Kelso's book in thoroughness of coverage.

Kelso's *Doctrine for the Lady of the Renaissance* stands without rival as an amply detailed account of Renaissance ideas of what a lady should be. Despite the development in feminist thinking since it was originally published in 1956, a development which would have produced some changes in emphasis and more organized analysis, her work remains an indispensable source book. It not only brings together background material necessary for scholars of the Renaissance, but provides a foundation for study of attitudes toward women in later times and, through its illustrations from one period, insight into assumptions about women that are engrained in our culture.

New York, N.Y., November, 1977   KATHARINE M. ROGERS

---

[3] William and Malleville Haller, "The Puritan Art of Love," *Huntington Library Quarterly*, V (1941-42), 235-72.

Preface

Because of the nature of this book some explanation of the use of quotation marks and references is needed. Everything in the book, except a few gratuitous remarks of my own, has been taken from others, usually not in long summaries or quotations but in snippets, from this and that author, which had to be woven into coherent discourse. The problem has been peculiarly vexatious since obviously it has been impossible to put quotation marks around each phrase or to indicate all gaps by asterisks. For short passages I have used quotation marks only when the words are particularly significant and interesting and the translation close. The longer passages taken from single authors are usually condensations and rearrangements of the original, therefore not strictly eligible for quotation marks, and have been left with only some comment of my own to indicate their closeness to the original. In a few instances, where the passage is long, unbroken by references to the author, and of some special dramatic value, I have enclosed it in quotation marks to set it off even though I may have tampered with order and content. To sum up, when quotation marks are used the words belong to their author; where there are no quotation marks the words still belong to someone else except when clearly my own ideas are being expressed.

The references have been placed at the end of the text and numbered rather with respect to topics than to particular authors. With an eye to readability I have worked to reduce the sprinkle of distracting little numerals to the lowest count compatible with clearness and exactness. Sprinkle is perhaps too thin a word for what threatened to look rather like the proverbial "thick as spatter." So I have devised for my notes what is first of all an outline of the contents of each chapter, and in general have represented only each topic or sub-topic with a numeral. The system has for the most part brought the numerals, placed at the end of paragraphs, close enough to make identification of references for particular authors easy. Where the list of references under a numeral is long, and where the passage from an author is some pages in length, and especially where the same author has been cited more than once in the discussion, I have assigned numerals to items within a sub-topic. It is the multiplicity of authors from which this work has been drawn that has reduced me to using this not quite orthodox system of numbering, but I hope that only a little more patience is required to find the reference wanted.

The multiplicity of authors also presented another problem both in composition and in references. I felt obliged to reduce as much as possible direct citing of authors, most of them bound to be little known, who were all saying pretty much the same thing on any given topic, and saying it in a very ordinary fashion. There are whole sections where there seemed no occasion to mention names, but the sources are duly listed in the notes. Where names have been mentioned they have been in most chapters only a small part of the authorities needed to establish the generalization. In the main the authors following a numbered author bear out the same point for which he was cited, but it should also be taken for granted that they are likely to cover other points under the topic. It has been this consideration that in part made me reluctant to tag a particular author as belonging to a particular idea. Besides, I look on these lists of authorities, more importantly perhaps, as furnishing substantial evidence for the implication of the whole book, that generalization concerning the lady of the renaissance over a long stretch of time and many countries is justified. Additional material may be found by consulting the subject index for the bibliography.

Lack of references to secondary sources is sure to be noted, and I should like to say a word about that. At the beginning of my study I sought for books on the subject of women of the renaissance. The books that I found were of little help to my purpose—a consideration of theory only, for they usually dealt with historic figures and in covering centuries down to modern times they were forced to be very sketchy on any one century. Then, as what seemed to be the best method of handling my material emerged, merely summarization, I abandoned systematic search for secondary material. What came my way was based on far fewer authors than I had read, and subject at times to correction because of that very fact, as when the claim was made that the books on love are negligible for serious study of ideals because they were all addressed to courtesans—on the ground of Tullia d'Aragona's disputed dialogue, *Della Infinità d'Amore*. I have done so at my peril of course, but the mere summarizing has taken too long; others will have to undertake amplification, interpretation, and correction.

Finally, I should like to record here my indebtedness and gratitude to the patient and courteous attendants in the libraries where I have had the good fortune to work, particularly in the Library of the British Museum, who pulled out the hundreds of volumes I called for, many of them more than once, and many only to be rejected. I am particularly grateful to Madame de la Fontinelle of the Bibliothèque Nationale of Paris, without whose generous help scores of books would not have been available at all. Two men have not lived to see through the toil of composition, but I should like to express here my sense of loss and my gratitude to Doctor W. L. Bullock for substantial contribution in its early stages to the bibliography out of his own library, and to Doctor H. S. V. Jones for the unfailing confidence and encouragement shown until his death, the memory of which has helped in the years since.

Urbana, Illinois, May 15, 1953   RUTH KELSO

Contents

CHAPTER ONE : *Introduction*

The renaissance argued, as if much hung on the answer, whether the word "man" covers both sexes of the human race. The question seems to rise again when one contemplates the result of prolonged search in the realm of ideals for a portrait of the renaissance lady. To state the conclusion roundly, there was no such thing as the lady so far as theory went, no formulated ideal for the lady as such, distinguished either from the gentleman or from any other woman. That many books of a theoretical sort were written for and on the lady the list appended to this volume furnishes ample evidence, but beyond the dedications to ladies, duchesses, or queens, the contents, it is scarcely an exaggeration to affirm, apply to the whole sex rather than to any favored section of it. The lady, shall we venture to say, turns out to be merely a wife. Most of this book will serve for proof of this conclusion.

The original impulse for this study came from my conviction, at the close of my work on *The Doctrine of the English Gentleman in the Sixteenth Century*, that I would not have the whole ideal picture until I explored the rest of the literature intended for the instruction of members of the privileged classes. The existence of a wife and child, to be sure, was in no way predicated by the assumptions that produced the gentleman. He existed in his own right, in England to serve the state, in Italy almost entirely for his own sake—the cultivation of perfection alone posed as the chief end of man. But since he was given advice more or less perfunctorily on his domestic duties, choice of wife, education of children and handling of servants, and on love-making, lifted by Platonizing Italians to the art of all arts, the lady had to be supposed. What would a study of treatises on the lady contribute toward rounding out the fragmentary picture suggested by these glimpses, and also toward completing the doctrine of gentility itself? The character of the results of this study is at first discouraging and puzzling. One knows of course, from the historians and poets particularly, that ladies, resplendent in figure, cultivated in mind, able in action, existed in the renaissance, fit mates for their lords and more than adequate substitutes for them, at need. But the actual renaissance gentleman was as well served by the theorists as by historians and poets. Lose all other record of him than the theorists furnish and we could reconstruct him to the life from their ideal portraits. It is not so with the lady. The emphasis is placed so overwhelmingly on the good wife within the walls of her house, whatever her rank, that the few exceptions affording some glimpse of the reality would do no more than merely ruffle the mind of the searcher with a slight doubt as to whether he had the whole picture. Why this correspondence between theory and practice in the one case, and this gap, or more adequately this chasm, in the other? One is free to speculate. Perhaps it is most significantly taken as merely an illustration of how theory must lag behind practice, and how in this instance especially men were reluctant to admit the fact that, after all, women are a part of the human race.

So the first answer to discouragement is that the lady did exist in actuality though not in theory. And the second answer is that the ideal man so elaborately set forth by the renaissance under the title of gentleman is in essence and in effect the human ideal, the ideal of man in the generic sense. In the renaissance, so far as the highborn woman shared the work of men, as administrator of estates or kingdoms, leader in war, and so forth, she was ruled by the same standards as men. What was not granted to her was the common right to share. Circumstances alone gave her that power—the death or absence of her husband, the inheritance of a title through lack of a male heir, or, as in nunneries, the lack of competition from men. Theory went only so far as to make some occasional slight suggestion that high birth placed her above the lot of ordinary women by making her a prince.

What started out to be an appendix has, however, turned out to be a book, for if the doctrine of gentility gains little from a survey of these treatises written about the lady, the gentleman does gain a wife, and analysis of the treatises is important to show whatever they reveal of renaissance ideals of human conduct. Again, as in my earlier study of the gentleman, I shall confine myself to theoretical treatises; there is God's plenty, as Chaucer's miller would put it, of the sort of thing they do furnish to fill a book. There is all the greater need for a study of history and fiction if a full portrait of the renaissance lady is to be achieved, but again that is not the task undertaken here. The shape imposed on the book by the material leaves much to be desired, and I should like to outline briefly the difficulties one encounters in trying to come at just what was the ideal set up by the renaissance for the lady.

First of all, there is not one portrait but several which cannot by any superimposing of one upon the other be combined into a composite, single portrait. These books about women concern roughly four subjects, the war of the sexes, the training and duties of the wife, love and beauty, and the court. From the first can be gathered what the renaissance thought about woman's position in the scheme of things; from the second comes almost all that is said about the bringing up of a girl and vocations for women; from the third, a peculiar theory about the function of women in the business of love; from the fourth, specialized instructions for the lady who serves or rules a court. From each can be drawn a portrait. The four overlap, but if the overlapping were taken for the renaissance ideal woman, she would lose the little each portrait shows of differentiation from the common run of women. The purposes of these writers are too disparate and the elements too antithetic to each other; they have no central figure in common as the writers on the gentleman have. I have thought it practicable only to leave each a distinct ideal, reducing synthesis to a meager pointing out of resemblances and differences. The result is not the building up steadily from start to finish of an integrated ideal, as was the case with the gentleman, but a series of fresh starts and stops.

Another difficulty lies in the lack of definitions for the lady. There was endless effort to define the terms gentility, nobility, and derivatives. Collections of such definitions, popular with lawyers from the middle ages on, turn out on inspection to concern only men and their sons. "Ingenui" does mean children, and an unwary reader might conclude that no differentiation between sons and daughters was intended, as none for the most part was explicitly made. But the few direct references to women, to their lack of nobility except in their fathers and husbands, their incapacity to transmit it to husbands or children, their meager rights due to rank, make it clear that implicit in all discussions of rank is their applicability only to the masculine sex. "Ingenui" means sons. Daughters and wives are definable only by indirection. The concept of the term lady is vaguer therefore than the concept of gentleman. One gains the impression of a type emerging with the middle ages and continuing unchanged through the renaissance. The wife of a knight was a lady, and so was the wife of a renaissance gentleman. The gentleman differed considerably from the knight, but their wives would not have found much to wonder at in each other, once they got below such matters as dress and table manners. At best the ideal quality of the term lady never had the serious import of gentleman. Both have been more and more indiscriminately bestowed since the decline of classes, but lady lost long ago almost all its ideal meaning, where even today gentleman with due precaution may be used as a general term of approbation.

Neither did the theory of the favored class help to distinguish the lady from the inferior sort of womankind, or of mankind for that matter. The fundamental assumption of the whole ideal of gentility was that some must rule and some be ruled. The first law of woman, as we shall see, was submission and obedience, exemplified in the beginning and for all time by our Mother Eve. Theory does not divide women into two groups, the rulers and the ruled, and prescribe to each a different set of laws on the basis of that relationship. Practice did just that, but not theory. Theory said that all women must be ruled. As a result of this leveling, the scope of this discussion becomes extremely limited. Occupations which filled books especially addressed to gentlemen encompassed government, war, the learned professions, agriculture, and commerce; but for women only one occupation was recommended—housewifery. Education for the gentleman was a wide-flung subject, involving all that was called liberal and drawing on the best pedagogical advice of the time. Education for the lady looked to her proficiency in domestic affairs and what in moral and religious training would keep her safely concerned only with them. As far as theory goes, the lady would seem not to have been considered a part of the favored class.

A special difficulty arose for me because I was interested primarily in English ideals, and there are not enough books from which to generalize about the English lady. I have been forced, as my title indicates, to attempt for my general scheme a composite portrait for the renaissance, using whatever material has come to hand, chiefly Italian and French in origin. It seems like veering from Scylla only to fall into Charybdis, but so fundamentally does most of what everybody says, regardless of nationality, seem to be what men have always been saying about women that, with due precaution, generalization for Europe seemed wiser than generalization solely for England. The slant is still English in that I am writing primarily for English-speaking readers.

Accepting, however, the limitations and the dangers imposed by the subject, and the shape it has assumed, there still remained the most vexing problem of all, the method of handling the material, material taken from two centuries, roughly between 1400 and 1600. I thought first merely to synthesize in my own words, then to illustrate from life, compare with modern instances, and interpret. But as every writer knows, there is a stubborn life about one's subject that will assert its will and bend intentions to another end. The fabric of thought woven by those renaissance minds on the subject of women's virtues and the paths they should take presents so much variety in little space that summary would reduce to bare platitudes and squeeze all the life out. The subject of humility would be reduced from pages to a short paragraph. To do mere justice to the theme I was driven to become a joiner of other men's sayings into a patchwork of as much design and coherence as possible. It was the only way to save for the modern reader the color and feel and spice of these old books. And then with terms and turns of phrases that inevitably produce an old-fashioned effect, the introduction of modern instances and comments in the language of today was to introduce incongruous patches and break whatever spell of an older time might be building up. So I have restrained all such impulses to brief analyses of what I take to be the general significance of the material, usually placed at the end of each chapter. The book is therefore not my own, and has been infinitely harder to write than if it were.

CHAPTER TWO : *Women in the Scheme of Things*

Christine de Pisan was sitting one day in her little cell, she tells us, wearied with her studies, and for relief picked up a book, a recent present, which she found to be Matheolus' scandalous attack on women. Forced soon to desist from reading because of licentiousness of both matter and language, she was set to musing how it is that so many men educated and uneducated say and write so many slanders against women. Not only one or two, or this Matheolus of no reputation with more of his kind, but generally all philosophers, poets, and rhetoricians before they end their treatises find occasion to blame women and agree in assuming that the nature of women is inclined wholly to evil. Deeply concerned, she began to examine herself as a natural woman and many other women well known to her, not only princesses and other great ladies but ordinary gentlewomen as well who had confided in her, in order to test with strict impartiality the truth of this charge. Search as she might, she could not see that such conceptions of the essential nature of women were justified. But she had no sooner come to this conclusion than the great flood of sayings and proverbs recurred to her and swept her into despair that, after all, God had made a foul thing when he made woman, and she broke into lament, so she says, that God had not made her to be born into this world of the masculine gender, to the end that all her inclinations might have been to serve him better and that she should not have erred in anything and might have been of as great perfection as they say men be. Here, however, reason again came to her aid. She should not let mere plurality of strange opinions beguile her. Scholars disagree and are mistaken, poets make up fables that mean the opposite of what they say, perhaps Matheolus and Jean de Meun are of that sort. So she concludes, "Know well that all these evil sayings of women in general hurt the sayers and not the women."[1]

Thus Christine records the occasion for taking up her pen in 1404 (it was not the first or last time) to defend women against their slanderers. And thus may be introduced two famous protagonists in an ancient debate that took on something of formal shape in the middle ages, raged full tilt through the sixteenth and seventeenth centuries, continued spasmodically in similar fashion through the eighteenth century, and still, it must be admitted, is going on in the twentieth. Vituperation of women seems always, as far back as we have any record, to have been a manly sport. Nor was it ever confined to any one region or class. Folk tales notoriously make women the butt of their satire, and Scheherazade's bedtime stories are one long penance for women's infidelity. But it took the middle ages to produce the phenomenon called the war of the sexes, in which, at its height in the sixteenth century, recognized traducers and champions charged and countercharged, often changing sides and even fighting on both sides at once.

Out of this war must come the material for determining as well as we can what place in the scheme of things the lady was assigned by renaissance opinion. Here the war itself is not of direct importance, but something of its course and fashion had better be shown as a background for the sharply contrasting values placed upon women, that is, the favored section of them, in comparison with men.

At first the poets, or more often mere poetasters, were the chief participators, and poured forth verses of a highly satiric or as highly laudatory character. They were still doing it well into the seventeenth century—witness Jacques Olivier's *Alphabet of Women's Imperfections and Malice* of 1617, which ran into fourteen reprintings during the century and one more in 1730. In the sixteenth century this dispute over women's capacity and probity became the subject also of serious prose treatises, chiefly on the side of women. Good examples are those of Maggio, Bruni, Torquato Tasso, and Bronzini, among the Italian; Bouchard, Agrippa, Billon, and Mademoiselle de Gournay, Montaigne's protégée, among the French; and Nicholas Breton among the English. Other prose forms than the straight treatise were common in this century: the dialogue, much favored by the Italians, Biondo, Speroni, and Zinano, for example; the dream, already used by Christine; the extended list of questions and answers, like Landi's, in his case heavily weighted against women; letters such as Hélisenne de Crenne's. One will also expect to find material on the subject in places not specifically labeled attack or defense. Many of the books on marriage and love arraign or defend women. Fusco's *La Vedova*, for example, is actually a defense of the prudence of women. Orazio Lombardelli has occasion to condemn women in general in the course of instructions on the proper behavior of young men. There he lays down the general precept that conversation with all sorts of women is to be avoided because of human frailty, this time, however, quite impartially the frailty of both young men and young women.[2]

It seems to have been almost impossible to write without partisanship on any subject involving women. Detraction was the vogue from courtier to cobbler, said William Heale of Exeter College, Oxford, rising to the defense of women when some of his own group in 1608 went so far as to support in public the legality of wife-beating on the ground of women's questionable morality, their incapacity for learning, and therefore their worthiness of blows.[3]

Why vituperation of women should have been popular for so long will probably never be completely explainable. The puzzle lies not only in the volume but in the violence and unreasonableness of the language used and in the often high and serious character of the defamers. Both sides offered explanations, the offenders more often averring noble intentions to warn unwary young men away from the snares of evil women, or to reform evil women themselves, or merely to furnish salutary lessons to good women.[4] The results seem at times to have surprised these officious reformers. Jacques Olivier, having stirred up a hornet's nest by his *Alphabet*, indignantly protested that he had not thought any eulogists of women would object to his candor in exposing vice, thus actually aligning themselves with vice, and promised "a stroke of the currycomb" for these idolators of Cupid and Venus. Aiming only to do women good, he had exposed evils first to prepare for the inculcation of virtues later; by blaming vices in the bad he had thought to make the virtues of the good shine brighter and to give pleasure to the good, who by this mirror of the faults of others may correct their own imperfections.[5] The trouble with such apologists for themselves, as Lucrezia Marinella pointed out, was that though they intended to condemn only the bad, by saying nothing about the good, or only a little, they seemed to condemn all.[6] Some even, like Domenico Bruni, who wrote to defend women, were severely reprimanded because they repeated the old charges before proceeding to the defense, as aid to refutation, they said, by revealing its strength in contrast. And there was no denying that the repetition served to perpetuate the charges and even to spread them among readers who would not have looked at the direct attacks because of their scurrility.[7]

The champions of women thought they saw truer explanations for the wholesale slander of women in such motives as disappointment in love, or surfeit of love, or desire for vengeance or for domination, or envy even, or mere delight in evil-speaking. Or it was suggested that many youths practiced their pens on this worn theme merely for sport to make a show of wit, or perhaps it was the old device of charging others with one's own vices to cover faults and doing it first.[8]

Praise of women seems to have come not so often spontaneously as in answer to attack, but the motives of those who rose to defense were likewise mixed. Some wrote out of sincere belief in women's essential goodness and desire to expose the falsity of the charges against the whole sex, not like many, said Vincenzo Maggio, who take up the subject merely to make known to the world the acuteness of their wit in being able to treat copiously something that appears humble and low, in the same way as men eulogize the fly, ague, and baldness.[9] More seriously some churchmen spoke out to defend innocence, they said, or to show the glory of God in this his most perfect creation, most proper subjects for them. Some professed personal reasons, like Hélisenne de Crenne, who said that her husband called her and all women deceitful and unfaithful, and charged them with deliberately ensnaring men through their beauty, and she must therefore defend the maligned. Or it might have been a matter of civic pride. The knight no longer rode out to do battle against any heretic who denied the supremacy of his lady, but charged with his pen to defend the superior beauty and excellent qualities of the ladies of his city against similar claimants for other cities. Scarcely a city in Italy or France, it seems, lacked an eager eulogist of her ladies. Or a few felt that men themselves were maligned by these slanderers of women, who wrote as if all men agreed that all women are evil, certainly much inferior to men, and hence any man who served his lady must be considered to debase himself.[10]

A frequent motive obviously was to please a patron, whose own qualities can be easily inferred from the praise meted out to the sex in general, or who may in the dedication be directly presented with a bundle of virtues, like the Duchess of Ferrara, who was given by her pensioner Garzoni the beauty of a Bathsheba, the chastity of a Susanna, the wisdom of a Judith, the piety of a Magdalene, and so on. Most flattering of all, perhaps, was Torquato Tasso, who absolved the Duchess of Mantua from the restrictions of merely feminine virtues, and gave her the large and manly virtues suitable to her high birth in the House of Savoy and her present exalted position.[11]

Little of the burden of defense was borne by the women themselves, as Torquato noted in his defense of marriage against his brother's attack. He hoped some eloquent gentlewoman would come to the rescue.[12] Laura Terracina about the middle of the century had grown angry that she alone of her sex was speaking out, and had larded her commentary on *Orlando Furioso* with caustic reproaches to those who think of women so vilely.[13] The most outstanding advocate of her sex was Christine de Pisan, already cited, herself a refutation of all the charges, as contemporaries and successors long noted. With dignity and firmness not untouched by humor she refuted the slanderers, particularly rallying those scholars who bring up their batteries munitioned from Adam, David, Samson, Solomon, in French and Latin, night and day, to blast women for deceiving them. Aren't men rather the deceivers, running after crowds of women indiscriminately? Why does it take so much art and wit and great subtlety to bring women to their will, as Ovid and Jean de Meun make out, if women are so frail and variable? But it is men that write the books, concluded Christine, and women don't pay much attention to what they read against themselves and their morals.[14] Another Frenchwoman two centuries later retorted more sharply and even bitterly against those who trumpet in the streets that women lack dignity, aptitude, temperament, and organs to rise to the worth of men, judging in their ignorance that all worth must be measured in terms of the male and that the highest excellence women can reach is to resemble the common run of men. Braver than Hercules these men indeed, who in place of only a dozen monsters slain in a dozen combats overthrow half the world with a single word.[15] The rest who took up their pens against traducers can be counted on one's fingers.

Further evidence on how women felt about the matter is furnished by two incidents arising out of the publication of certain diatribes. In Turin in 1521, reported François de Billon in 1555, a man named Nevizzano had been so brainless as to publish an attack on marriage, in Latin to be sure, under the euphonious title, *Silva Nuptialis*. The ladies of the city, when they understood its libelous character, at once banished the author in disgrace from their company. Some time after he did win the repeal of his sentence, but only on his knees, wearing on his forehead as a visible sign of his repentance these two verses:

> Rusticus est verè qui turpis dicit de muliere,
> Nam scimus verè, quod omnes sumus de muliere.

"This Latin rhyme shouldn't be held ridiculous," commented Billon, "for although it was not made by a too prudent person, it was made at least by a man fit for heavenly aspiration as very chaste indeed, considering that after this incident and up to his death he could never find a woman, however old she might be, to make his bed for him, and gossip of this affair has not yet died away in this region."[16]

The other incident is reported by Cristoforo Bronzini of Giuseppe Passi, a member of the Accademia de' Signori Informi of Ravenna, who seems to have found himself in even more of a pickle. The ladies of Ravenna were so offended by his *I Donneschi Diffetti*, delivered before the Academy and published in Venice in 1599, that they showed ill will not only toward Passi but toward the whole Academy, as if all its members in one had intended the outrage. Nor was the wrath in their soft bosoms easily assuaged. Passi was still publishing in 1603 little compositions intended to make amends for his offense; the Academy voted to publish the lecture of Giacomo Sasso upon a sonnet of Bernardo Tasso's, in which Sasso discourses not only upon the beauty and gracious manners of the ladies, but also upon their great courage, dignity, and nobility; and Muzio Manfredi of the Academy of Parma, long a champion of women, published in 1602, in praise and honor of the ladies of Ravenna and to the shame and confusion of their adversary, a series of a hundred sonnets to as many ladies (named alphabetically, he explains, so that none could boast of precedence or grieve at depression).[17]

Why was the subject so important is the question that arises in one's mind, as the extravagance, volume, and continuance of discussion indicate? Guesses are our only recourse. For some reason, in the sixteenth century more than before, men's eyes were sharply focused on the differences between men and women—looks, moral character, capacities, power, position in society, obvious differences to be sure, whatever one may think of their actual significance. I am inclined to set down this sharpening for one thing to the leavening that brought so many other changes to the renaissance, the rediscovery of ancient thought and the resulting spread of education. The education of the gentleman was no longer considered a matter merely of skill at arms and courtly manners, but a pretty solid acquisition of book learning was prescribed for him. If for gentlemen, then for gentlewomen too, as the long lists of learned ladies testify. This stirring at the top was working gradually down through lower levels of society, like the bourgeois group in Lyons led by Louise Labé in the middle of the sixteenth century. It was a disturbing phenomenon, this rising interest of women in the world of books and their demand for education, certain to increase suspicion and antagonism. It may well be suspected that the flood of satire and the other flood of advice to wives on marriage, modeled on St. Paul's pattern, rose in the renaissance in part from alarm that women were breaking out of bounds and needed to be kept or set back in their place. The facts of life—women's inferiority to men in position and power, their dependence upon men for protection and support, their ignorance—were in the way to be flouted and therefore in need of explanation, iteration, and defense. The currency of this bold type of attack and defense lasted until well toward the time when systematic education for women was becoming a fact, and today when all the professions are open to women in the western world, though prejudice and resentment still hamper their progress, the worth of women is no longer discussed after the old fashion. Men and women may be said now to have accepted in part, at least, a revised set of the facts of life.

Up to this point our concern has been with the accompanying circumstances of the debate upon the relative merits of men and women rather than with the debate itself, in order to suggest the conditions and the atmosphere in which the debate was carried on. We must believe that under the extravagance of expression there was a real antagonism and that it rose from disagreement as to where women belonged in the general scheme of things and what were the special rights and privileges that men were born to. With that assumption the literature of the quarrel takes on serious import, and an examination of it becomes inescapable in a broad study of the ideal for the renaissance lady. In it must be found, as has been said, whatever answer there is to the question, what was her position in the scheme of things.

Four attitudes can be distinguished in this confused debate. Some thought woman at best a necessary evil, some admitted her good in a limited and humble way but of inferior value compared to men, some took her as good and necessary equally with men, and some claimed superiority for her over men. All together set up a certain ideal picture of the renaissance lady that can be compared with the other pictures drawn from books on other subjects.

One approaches the slough of vilification of women at his peril; once thoroughly in he would find it a long and tedious job to get out. But for the sake of the clarification of other aspects that the derogatory view furnishes, I am going to take the risk of slipping in too far for balance, and survey as briefly as I may for my purpose the methods and charges of renaissance writers who found woman thoroughly evil and at best a mere biological necessity.

The necessity is obvious enough, so obvious that the most inveterate enemies of woman had to admit, though grudgingly, that the current setup made her indispensable for the continuance of the human race. Some were so bold as to suggest that God might well have improved the method of propagation to eliminate woman altogether. The extent of the evil in women may not be entirely clear to our age, since we seem not to be putting as much thought on the subject as our predecessors. But candor and ingenuity can go a long way to prove that when you have said "woman" you have said all the evil possible. Three other sayings were current that more specifically mark the boundaries: nothing in the world is worse than a woman, however good she may be; the wickedness of a man is better than the goodness of a woman; and if the world could be maintained without women, men would live like God himself—three notable sayings, comments Guazzo.

To descend to a few of the details drawn indiscriminately from the Bible, ancient philosophers, and medieval physiology by renaissance philosophers, churchmen, courtiers, poets, and scribblers of every sort. The nature of woman had to be crooked for she was made from Adam's expendable rib, which, unfortunately for her, was crooked. Her warping was shown in the pride that refused to serve Adam as she was created to do and urged her to rule, and the discontent that aspired to divinity. Nature, taking over after the creation, goes on making women, but always by mistake. Her intention is to create men, since she aims at perfection, but some weakness or error reduces her product only too often to a woman. The elements in this woman are badly mixed; humidity and cold prevail over heat and dryness with the result that she is timid, even cowardly, by disposition and shrinks from the great exploits that make the name of man glorious. Built in frailer fashion than man, her body is not apt for great toil and exertion, and her brain power is small to suit. Hence lacking reason to guide her, she is governed by her passions alone. With this chart we are prepared to hear of "the nine thousand, nine hundred, and ninety-nine forms of malice" that plague the world in the shape of women. Like a blotter she has absorbed them all. Beginning with the Seven Deadly Sins the catalogue runs to great length by division and subdivision, but only the most frequently repeated need listing here: licentiousness, instability, disloyalty, intractability to God's express commands, drunkenness and gluttony, pride, vanity, avarice, greed, seditiousness, quarrelsomeness, vindictiveness, and evidently the most irritating of all, talkativeness. To end with the favorite summary of weary cataloguers: if all the seas were ink, land and fields parchment, trees pens, and all who know how to write were to write without ceasing, all the evil in women could not be expressed.[18]

These charges were commonly supported by examples, authorities, and epithets. The examples were drawn from the Bible, ancient mythology and history, and, rarely, from contemporary history, the argument being that all women were like Semiramis, Clytemnestra, Dido, the Queen of Sheba, Cleopatra, Hippolyta, Sappho, Judith, Aspasia, and Zenobia. Oddly enough most of these examples appeared in the list for defense also. Lists of authorities were equally popular in the renaissance—Aristotle, Democritus, Simonides, Euripides, Thucydides, Juvenal, St. Ambrose, St. Jerome, St. Augustine, Matheolus, Jean de Meun, Boccaccio, Rabelais, Luis Vives, to name a few, a motley crew, some of whom would have stared to find themselves in such company. Occasionally distrust and weariness of the endless repetition of examples and authorities was shown. Le Fevre thought examples of no weight, because if you have Vashti who suffered for her pride you also have Esther, and if you have Eve there is the Virgin Mary. Another skeptic on the value of examples, like a good strategist, first weakens them by division and then picks them off. There are four sorts of bad women, says our anonymous Italian: first those excessively bad like Jezebel—but some men are worse; next those who sin thoughtlessly rather than maliciously, like Bathsheba and Helen—but it is then the fault of the men who tempted them; then those who sin through the negligence of men who could prevent them, as in domestic dissensions; finally, those who sin by example set by men, as in superfluity of ornament, extravagance, licentiousness of dress. As for authorities, Brinon found odious the indiscriminate mixture of sacred and profane in the cloud of witnesses evoked by his kind, and promised to avoid it as much as possible by drawing on the poets. More independent still, Taillemont said some thought it strange that he had not cited great authorities, but he did not wish to take the clothing of another and felt that he was merely fortunate to have his opinions conformable to the judgment of others.

Epithets and particularly metaphors seem to have possessed great efficacy in the demolition of woman's character. A dialogue by Michelangelo Biondo well illustrates this method. The speakers are Nifo, well known author of a book on the courtier, and his pupil Socrates. "What is woman?" asks Socrates. Nifo answers, smoke because she is bitter, obscure, and black; vain shadow because lacking firmness she is full of vanity, greedy for honor and praise and boastful of what is not hers; a fury because she has an overwhelming desire for everything beyond reason and if injured burns for revenge; the embodiment of pride—no animal in the world has so great a desire to excel and to know too much, or so great an envy; a sea full of winds destructive to man, and confusion. "Who rules her then?" asks Socrates. No law, rein, or reason rules her, is the answer. Neither smoke, shadow, pride, or sea has law, and therefore she has none, but is governed like the fox who is sly, the wolf eager for prey, the sow caring only to grow fat, the kite, the mule, the dog. Unbridled will guides her. Deceit is the art that conquers all the seven liberal arts. Poison is the food she serves; worldly pomp her only study. With words, winks, songs, smiles, and glances she subdues the great heart of man, and for his love returns infamy, death, pain, and tears. Thus were epithets given the weight of proof by those who belonged to the school of Simonides.

Other proofs of women's natural inferiority were found in her subjection to men, her economic and legal dependency, and her exclusion from the professions and all public offices. Such facts served for sound evidence of her incapacity. The partiality of women themselves for sons and their supposed longing to be men, even of lower rank than their own, was turned against them as an admission of the superiority of the male. Christine had an answer, as we shall see. It is unnecessary, however, to pursue the subject further, since it must be clear that according to this gloomy view of women practically nothing can be said for her on the credit side. She shares with other female animals the burden of reproducing her kind. Beyond that the semihuman traits that lift her above them only enable her to trick, harass, and destroy men. Whether many men actually believed all this, except perhaps in moments of exasperation, one may well doubt, even though many expressed themselves so. This extreme view of woman has been presented here only for the sake of completeness, and to give a reason for the opposite extreme. It does show in a negative fashion what some men would have wished women to be.[19]

The vehemence and numbers of the traducers of women roused many to defense. Domenichi must have spoken for most when he exclaimed, "O immortal God, where shall I begin my argument? The good name of woman is attacked at every point, and wounded by great calumnies. So heavy and so diverse are the charges perpetually made that I do not know on what side they are most imperiled. And so I stand in great doubt what to take up first to relieve their distress." According to their own temperament these defenders answered the charges point by point.[20] They divided on the question of comparability to men, some holding woman inferior, however good, others holding them equal or even superior in their gifts, but they agreed on the essential goodness of woman's nature as on the essential goodness of man's.

"All women evil?" asks William Heale. Then how deceived were Plutarch, Chaucer, St. Jerome, St. Gregory. As well argue all men evil as all women, an untenable position in either case for we are told God saw that all his creation was good. Other defenders cited experience against the charge of depravity. In general women do submit to their husbands, bear patiently everything laid upon them, and then praise their tyrants even when many wish for death rather than the life they lead at their husband's will. Besides, far the greater number are content with one man, while a man so content is considered a fool by most men; and if, as even some defenders believed, they are naturally more concupiscent, then all the more praise to them. The seclusion and greater leisure of women cannot rightly be assumed to lead them easily to sin, as so many charged; idleness may work that way for a bad disposition, but to a good disposition leisure is an aid to virtue through prayers, the reading of good books, and good conversation. As for the long lists of women notorious for their crimes, they may be matched with men, and on the other side historians have always been unfair to women, not only exaggerating their evil deeds and misinterpreting their good, but for the most part keeping silence about women who show manly courage and high heart.[21]

The argument that restrictions imposed on women by law implied moral and mental incapacity was emphatically denied. Bruni takes them up one by one. Prohibition from public and legal offices rests on the unsuitability to decorum and chastity of women's mingling freely with a multitude of persons in a public place, as is necessary in public actions. Incapacity is not to be inferred, since jurisconsults rule that hereditary accession to a kingdom or title by a woman gives her the right to rule. Women's capacity is admitted also by their legal right to stand in their own causes, their children's, or their relatives. Prohibition from power over her own children rests on the impossibility of children's serving two masters, but she is granted guardianship over her own children, though not over others, thus admitting capability. Prohibition from remarriage within a year rests on sense, for she might bear a child in that year whose paternity would be in doubt and then succession would be clouded. Prohibition from testifying in wills and capital cases is based on care for the honor of women. Hate and enmity follow witnesses, and women are too busy with bearing and rearing children to give time. Civil laws are based on civil and reasonable grounds and are not intended to degrade women but to protect them. This is all the more true of canon and divine law. The prohibition from ecclesiastical offices implies no derogation of woman, but looks to the majesty and essential character of the creator, who created his like to represent him on earth, man. Woman he made to be a companion to man. Finally, the laws rule against women because they are made without their wish, consent, knowledge, or opposition. The fact imputes no blame, any more than if women had done the same to men. These are some of Bruni's instances, drawn from Roman law. Laws varied in different countries, but in general these restrictions and others like them in written and unwritten law would be found in all the countries of western Europe.[22]

Such was the turn given to defense of women against the general charge of fundamental evil. In specific charges the accusers were met usually with a reversal of the point to the advantage of women.

If Genesis in the hands of detractors seems to have given the case of women away, it furnished in the hands of friends even better proof of their worth. Priority of creation does not make Adam the crown of creation—quite the contrary. God, looking on Adam, saw that he was useless by himself and so he made Eve, his masterpiece therefore, as the last of creation necessarily his best, else God is said to go from perfect to imperfect, which is unthinkable. Some even denied any point in the order of creation. Taillemont said he was amused by those who begin at the beginning and argue from Adam made in God's image. Which image do they mean, body or soul? If they reply "body," what beasts they are, since Genesis says that God is a spirit. If they reply "soul," then woman's is as good as man's since made of the same essence. Their bodies also are made of the same four elements, have the same life, feeling, and reason. Whether first or last makes no difference. Indeed there is no first or last act of God, since God foresees the whole from the beginning, and the first in intention is the last in execution. Anyway, according to this argument of priority the animals, created before man, would be more perfect than he. As for the argument on original substance, the defenders ignored the crooked shape of Adam's rib and its unimportant, even dispensable, part of man's anatomy (but how subtract a rib without marring the perfection of Adam—or wasn't he made perfect in the beginning?) and glorified its composition. Adam was made of the raw stuff, common dirt, but his rib from which Eve was made furnished refined material, animate and purified. Also, if woman was created imperfect, it would be the fault either of the maker or of the material. It is blasphemy to assume God capable of imperfection, and if the material is at fault, the argument admits man's imperfection, since woman was made of him. Hence woman must be conceded as perfect as man in her original creation.[23]

Then what about the temptation and fall? Wasn't the woman tempted first as the weaker, didn't she seduce Adam into eating the fruit too, and isn't she therefore the never-to-be-punished-enough cause of our ruin? The answers are many, but chiefly run to this tune. Satan approached Eve first, knowing her more difficult to deceive than Adam, and counting on having Adam if he could get Eve. She was completely deceived and ate the forbidden fruit, not out of gluttony but out of her desire for more knowledge, a noble motive. Eager to share her supposed gain she urged

Adam to eat too, but not, so far as the Bible shows, resorting to deceit or seductive charms as means of persuasion. Adam knew just what he was doing, but Eve sinned ignorantly, tempted by the wiliest and most malicious of creatures. Adam had free will, and if he had not sinned mankind would not have lost Paradise. Therefore Adam, the theologians said, is responsible for our ruin. We have sinned in Adam, said Paul, not we have sinned in Eve. Again, if the greatness of the sin is to be measured by the punishment, man's punishment is the greater, St. Ambrose said, because Eve was punished in herself alone, while for Adam the whole earth was cursed with barrenness and he must toil for daily bread. Woman's pain, moreover, is forgotten in her child, and her subjection to man is the subjection of a reasonable creature under the laws of marriage, that is, under contracts as between equals, not the subjection of servant to master, or child to parent. Therefore the circumstances of the temptation and fall give no support to the charges of woman's original frailty or condemnation to servitude. Indeed there were not lacking bold souls to quote St. Gregory's alleged argument that the greatest good came to the world through sin, which woman introduced into the world. If Eve had not sinned, the impotence of Satan would never have been revealed, to the soverign glory of God—"O happy sinner who has merited so great a redeemer."[24]

In similar fashion other arguments were turned from reproaches to advantages. Woman's temperament, in which the humid and cold humors admittedly prevail, should not be made a reproach, for both men and women have all four humors in common, and only relatively can the humid and cold be said to dominate women, and the hot and dry men, and that not always in the same degree. Grant that the nature of heat, providing it is not excessive, is to be more quick and lively and better disposed toward every kind of activity. Yet nature has ordered each temperament for the special office assigned, and woman's is better for bearing and nurturing children because of its greater humidity even though it is more cold. Moreover, the dominating heat and dryness of men's temperament, which drives them on to great exploits, also breeds more ardent passions, the enemies of reason. Therefore women, of the opposite temperament, are more likely to have the mean amount necessary for activity of the mind. Their heat being more modified by humidity, they are less hasty, not so quick to feel anger, and hence more considered in their judgments. The argument has many ramifications, too many and too wire-drawn to be covered here.

Bodily weakness so often charged against women as proof of mental weakness could likewise be turned to her advantage. When men boast of their physical strength they are only exalting what they share with animals and what is more appropriate to animals than to reasonable creatures, nor is such strength always to man's advantage, as one can see in the cases of Hercules and Samson. The argument logically can end only in proving porters more noble than gentlemen, and beasts more noble than men. Besides, from any standard of beauty the body of woman is more perfect than man's in every way, and in its refinement even a more suitable instrument for the soul to use. Certainly in dexterity and agility there is nothing to choose between men and women. Their physical differences are all accidental, not essential.[25]

Woman, therefore, her defenders argued, cannot be called an imperfect animal produced by chance through some error of nature. The divine image is perfect in her and in man equally, and the same portion of soul is in both. In all that marks the species human she is equally complete and perfect with him. One man cannot be more wholly man than another, or the male more perfect in substance than the female, for both belong to the same species: man. Or, as Marie de Gournay asked leave to put it, nothing is more like a cat in a window than a cat.

This is the ground for the second view of woman's place in the scheme of things, that she was created for a particular purpose with special attributes that make her as perfect to do her work as man to do his. In the performance of her part in the propagation and continuance of the human species, she has no excuse for not going as worthily as man to the ultimate end of happiness. This view restores dignity to women, and even leaves room for favorable comparison with men. In the domestic realm how many mothers of families, exclaims one of these moderate admirers, have been known to preserve their houses from ruin, or restore one already ruined in fame or wealth when loss or default of husbands threw the responsibility on them. How many have lived the life of celibacy with the greatest praise. How many even surpass their husbands in fame and honor.[26]

In this second view, however, the goodness of woman's nature does not give her equality with man, for she lacks his natural capacity for command and is therefore rightfully subject to him in both private and public affairs. Luis Vives puts the case as well as any man. He must be listed among the friends of women, for he takes them seriously; grants to them the same nature—"the woman is even as man is, a reasonable creature, and hath a flexible witte both to good and evil, the which with use and counsell maye be altered and turned"; argues for their need of education (though he would severely limit its range); sharply rebukes those who argue woman's nature evil because a few women are so; and prescribes from husbands gentle and kindly, though firm, treatment of their wives. But this he has to say of the difference between the two. Nature "hath geven unto man a noble, a high & a diligent minde to be busye and occupied abroad, to gayne & to bring home to their wives & familie, to rule them & their children, and also all their household. And to the woman nature hath geven a fearful, a covetous, & an humble mind to be subject unto man, & to kepe that he doeth gayne." And again, "We must remember that women are so feble and weake of nature, that thei nother in mind nor yet with the body can sustaine nor beare that is heavy and grevious." Without blame but without remedy, woman is inferior to man in her very creation and therefore quite naturally and rightly to be ruled by him. Inferiority must mean subjection in a philosophy based on hierarchies, heavenly, earthly, human. No longer a necessary evil, but a necessary good, woman has been formed to play her part, as man his, to yield obedience as an inescapable condition for the performance of her duty and the realization of her perfection. This was the prevailing belief, which of course fitted existing conditions.[27]

Doubts, however, were stirring in the minds of renaissance men and women as to the eternal fitness of things as they were, and stout protest was finding expression against injustice in the accepted rule of man over woman. The appeal to God's wisdom or the laws seemed to some protestors highly inadequate grounds for taking her subjection as necessary or just. Since God gave men free will, they argued, not all the effects of creation can be taken as good and willed by Him. Laws made by men share their imperfection and are often unjust, particularly so in prohibiting public offices to women. The apparent incapacity of women for other than domestic duties rests on their lack of education. If allowed in the schools they would show the same excellence as men. An Italian who signs himself merely a humble lover thus eloquently paints the whole situation: "Instead of teaching women good and praiseworthy arts we turn them to mechanic exercises. In place of paper and ink we give them needle and thread. Where it would be just to treat them as companions and consorts in grave and important deliberations, we condemn them innocent to low and unworthy cares. By God, sirs, imagine for the brief space of an hour that men were living a new but not impossible way contrary to precedent, no longer in schools among learned people or among those skilled in military exercises but forcibly shut up idle in the little circuits of their chambers for months, and years, and ages, even until death, passing the time in low and unworthy occupations with servants similarly low. Such a picture well in mind, imagine for yourselves what by proof poor women can know. Then think how important it is to engage from the beginning in noble affairs and high exercises, also how iron rusts unused, how virtue itself is no other than custom and habit. Behold a boy child destined to the mastery of arms. As he grows his mind is set on arms; he cares only for them, works at them, thinks of nothing else. Who doesn't know that he will be able to become a brave and expert soldier, but not a musician or painter? There is no exercise or art either mechanic or liberal which does not demand much study and continual diligence, and most especially in one who, not contented with a certain mediocrity, desires to reach some degree of excellence. Or supposing a father wants his son to be a merchant, though the boy is set on studies. With what prayers, persuasions, arts, deceits, injurious words, threats, even torture does he break him of his first desires and to his own will, with loss of natural vigor, weakened and conquered. O evil and wicked custom that men lead their lives at the will of another. So much the more must be lamented that very few women are not subjected to the violence of such harsh usage, their industry turned into sad idleness, and their good works changed into trifles and lies. The ladies should take no offence at hearing their good care of the family and diligent management of the house called trifles and lies. These things are good in themselves, but low and vile in respect to those who do them, born to greater undertakings." Nor is he speaking here, he adds, of sailing, cultivating the soil, merchandising, and the like, but of speculation, philosophy, and such exercises of the mind.[28]

It is just these common beliefs of the times, argues Billon, that corrupt women: that they should be kept idle in the house as if incapable of higher education, and that they should be subjected to the rule of matrimonial jealousy or of nuns, and prohibited public office by law. He would not deny the necessity for order, superiority and inferiority in sexes, estates, and persons, but the humility that God requires of all from lowest to highest would end this old and odious war of the two sexes and all these disputes and sharp restrictions of feminine liberty. Aristotle, so often quoted against women, thanked God he was a man rather than a woman, not because he thought women lower and less perfect than men, but because he would not have had a chance to become so learned. Short shrift was given by such advocates to the attempts to convict women of this damaging inferiority out of their own mouths. They would not prefer sons to daughters, said Christine, if their happiness didn't depend on gratifying their husbands' desire for them, and how mistaken men are in setting such store by sons and undervaluing daughters. Because of the dowry necessary to marry a daughter, sons are supposed to be less expensive to launch, but in fact they are fully as expensive if education, meeting their necessary expenses, and getting them started in business or a profession are counted, likely to amount to a greater sum than any dowry. Fathers, hearing so much about the frailty of daughters and desiring so greatly to get them safely off their own hands into the hands of a husband, forget all the trouble and sorrow that the wild ways of young men cost them, and the bad treatment, neglect, and envy natural in the young toward those who stand in the way of ambition, where daughters commonly are a comfort. There were even some to question whether women do prefer to bear male children. Canoniero much later claimed that in reality they wish to bear female because they suffer less with them. As for the charge that women of high rank would prefer to be men even of much lower rank, this is not, said Domenichi, from desire of perfection, boasted to exist better in the lowest man than in the highest woman, but from desire to free themselves from the tyranny of men of all ranks wrongly imposed.[29]

The third view holds that the sexes are equal not only in bodily substance and soul but in capacities of every sort. Firenzuola furnishes a general statement of this common humanity in his *Dialogo delle Bellezze*. Women, he says, are as noble as men, as wise, as apt in exercise of the moral and speculative intelligence, as apt also for mechanic performance and knowledge, and possess the same virtues. The differences between them arise from the domestic offices that women in their modesty have assumed, just as differences appear between the philosopher and artisan, doctor and merchant in the working of their minds. Finally, to quote directly, "We are one and the same thing, of the same perfection; you have to seek us and love us, and we have to seek you and love you; you without us are nothing, and we without you are nothing; in you is our perfection, in us is yours." There were many to agree with Firenzuola. In their defenses of women Dardano states at the beginning that he intends to prove that if women ought not to be preferred to men in virtues, they are not inferior; Bruni closes with these words, "And so we conclude both sexes in perfection, in virtue, and in every other noble and worthy quality to be equal;" and Marie de Gournay is content to claim equality between the sexes, she says, because nature must be as much opposed to superiority as to inferiority, or unlike every other species the human race is not one but two. An Englishman, Tofte, translating Varchi's work on jealousy, is moved to insert a marginal note when Varchi raises the question of whether men or women are more given to that vice, and shies from answering: "Woman is of one and the self-same substance with man, is what man is, onely so much more imperfect, as she is created the weaker vessel. . . . A modern writer concluding thus:

> Women to men are equall every way,
> And like infirmities (in both) doe stay.
> Wee Men are Women, Women are Wee Men,
> What difference is twixt us and Women then?"

To quote one more such comment, Taillemont has this to say. "In sense, judgment, and reason, ready wit, are they not as able as men? Does not one see by experience the fruit some have produced, and are producing still, with the little instruction allowed them; if not always as generally as men, it is necessary to blame custom alone, which is only to know how to sew and manage their house. So much is this to their prejudice that if they were instructed in letters as men are, I dare well promise for them the advantage, and certainly it is a great shame that so many fine wits are not employed in better business than those to which the tyranny of men have assigned them, for then they would know by experience what I say to be true, and there would be no need to allege the sciences and virtues of an infinite crowd of women who are and have been, and whom for the sake of brevity I do not wish to recite."

There was one man to represent dramatically the logical conclusion from all of this. Zinano's lover, somewhat to the surprise of his beloved, discourses eloquently and ingeniously on the claim women have to the high title masculine. His beloved replies, "How then can I fail to despise myself, knowing womanly nobility to be so great that it can be compared with masculine valor and yet seeing women so subjected to men? Isn't it enough for men to have deprived us of consulates, dignities, kingdoms, priesthoods, and all the various ranks of glory, that they still wish to make us slaves? Happy Marguerite of Austria who not only disdains to be subject but like famous heroes seeks various adventures in government and arms, desirous of ruling. Happy other great women, but how unhappy we others because we cannot I will not say rule but even hope to possess liberty, that precious gift of God, and to be free to exercise our own capacities so that we may become famous. The more wretched that we do not even know the reason."[30]

The fourth view, that women are superior to men, may be taken as a natural reaction to the wholesale negations of the vituperators, but apotheosis in turn results in absurdities and needs to detain us only long enough to show to what lengths praise could go in that age of extremes. After making the most out of a crowd of little points, the exalters of women went on to sweeping claims like these. The superior fineness, delicacy, softness, and beauty of woman's body argues her superior fitness for all the loftier activities of human beings, and Aristotle's argument that men with muscular bodies are naturally intended by nature to be slaves to others more inclined to prudence, contemplation, and command only prove men born to be slaves and women to be their masters. Since love is a desire for beauty, a man must love a woman for her incomparable beauty and seek perfection in her. Without her he is incomplete. She, on the other hand, possessing perfection does not seek it in another, but loves herself first and desires to be sought by men only because of her beauty. Men themselves admit women's superiority; even among soldiers, who sell themselves for a little money, where find one who will not confess some woman the patron of his heart and queen of his will, and say that women are more perfect than men? Compare women and men: the young woman is modest, truthful, pious, the young man insolent, imprudent, irreligious; the middle-aged woman is honest, chaste, retired, the middle-aged man intemperate, greedy, malicious; the old woman is a good manager of a house, but the old man lacks judgment.

Or may one detect a sly purpose of satire by indirection in some of these apotheoses, as when Pont-Aymerie, entitling his defense, *Paradox Apologetique, ou il est Fidelement Demonstré que la Femme est Boucoup Plus Parfaicte que l'Homme en Toute Action de Virtu*, explains that he calls his treatise a paradox because that is what other men do their best to prove, but he actually takes it for truth and intends to support it against all comers. And in fact he does go as far as a man may: "Oh most happye sexe," to use the words of a contemporary translator, "if it were lawfull for me to speake, as Plato did [or rather a fool reported by Plato], who thanked the gods for making him a man, and not a beast; so could I have wished, that I had been created a woman, having attayned to such knowledge of feminine perfections;" and to clinch the matter he concludes, "I may well say, with a million of our elders, that there is sixe and thirty severall beauties in one woman, and hardly any one in a man: for he is the true anatomy of natures imperfections, yea, the very image of her weaknesse, as a woman may justly tearme herselfe, the perfect mirrour of her virtues."[31]

Perhaps we are to take all such gentlemen as having their tongues in their cheeks, but to close the account of these extremists, each bent apparently on depressing the one sex in order to exalt the other and on concentrating all virtues and capacities in one, we should take note of one attempt to answer the question judiciously. Girolamo Camerata wrote a book on the true nature of honor, which he defined as esteem and good opinion coming from a person who knows the merit of the honored. The controversy over superiority between the sexes becomes of some moment if one is to bestow honor fitly when it is due. After a survey of the arguments on both sides he applies two tests to determine which set outweighs the other, what actually now is, and what ought or could be if there were no obstacle. Certainly we see men engaged in the liberal and important mechanical arts—philosophy, medicine, law, war, government, administration—and women with but rare exceptions only in some inferior and less important arts. In these occupations men show themselves more possessed of the great virtues than women, and thus, though at the same time they show themselves more vicious than women in assassination, theft, treason, heresy, and so forth, they are more worthy of honor. So much for what is. As for what should or could be, he seeks the answer in the humors. Men, hot and dry in comparison with women, are bold and spirited in action, superior to women in these respects, and more able to endure fatigue. Thus they have been able to reduce women to the servile arts. But if we consider the more temperate complexion of women, who are thereby more stable, chaste, healthy, long lived, they surpass men in disposition to understand all the disciplines of the intellect. Since all knowledge comes through the senses, and they have by nature senses more temperate than men, it must even be assumed that their intellect is more perfect. The conclusion is then that men are to be preferred in arms, business, activities, and women in letters and speculative pursuits, so far as disposition goes. On the more difficult point of relative merit, since both have imperfections and perfections, Camerata comes finally to this cautious answer: considering how women are gifted by nature with a temperate complexion that disposes them to the understanding of letters and contemplative studies and to great moral virtues, it can be concluded that if either is more perfect it is the woman.[32]

The renaissance was full of a sense of the dignity of man, his essential goodness and the greatness of his powers. Circumstances, some obscure impregnation of races, not of merely scattered individuals, brought once more such a flowering of human genius and burst of energy that men found their ideal in the lordly Greek rather than in the lowly Jesus. The perfection of man was a favorite theme of the age, and if that usually meant the perfection of men alone, some of the more thoughtful men of particularly the last half of the sixteenth century, as we have just seen, accepted "man" as covering the whole of the human race, and wrote these long discourses on the perfection of women, partly as answers to detractors, partly as a variation on their favorite theme, praise of man.

I should now like to put together the portrait of the perfect woman, the lady, that is to be drawn not only from the sober commendations but also from the exaggerations and distortions created by the argumentative mood of those who loved her too much and those who misprized. In renaissance theory woman's place in the scheme of things depends primarily upon the qualifications seen in her or assigned to her. They have all been mentioned in one way or another but need putting together with further comment by way of reservations, distinctions, definitions. The renaissance habitually found much to say on both sides, even on what may seem a simple matter to us today, and after long following their labyrinthine ways one comes to think them right and us wrong: nothing is so simple as it seems.

Well, what are the qualities that renaissance writers praised most frequently as constituting perfection for women? First of all, beauty will have to be assumed, the chief good of the body, requisite for perfect happiness and all other perfection, moral and intellectual. Since it was discussed at much greater length in connection with love, I will leave the analysis of its parts and force to the chapter on the lady in love. Far the greatest concern here must be with moral qualities, listed with variations by almost every defender of women. The lists do not materially differ during the two hundred years that this study may be considered to cover, nor does it seem to matter whether a man or a woman is speaking. Christine de Pisan at the very beginning of the fifteenth century, Philippe Bouton toward the end of that century, Moderata Fonta at the end of the sixteenth century, and Francisco della Chiesa in 1620 praise in women humility, sweetness, simplicity, peaceableness, kindness, piety, temperance, obedience, patience, charitableness, and the like. The emphasis remains on the gentler, more passive aspects of human nature, rather than on the more aggressive, positive aspects.[33] The quality most frequently praised is chastity. Enough could not be said of it as the foundation of womanly worth. Let a woman have chastity, she has all. Let her lack chastity and she has nothing. Especially was this held true of noblewomen. Chastity in them shines the more glorious as they are more in peril of dishonor and more open to temptation than women of low place, being delicate in constitution, nourished on food that leads to lascivious thoughts, lacking endurance for sustained and onerous toil, where the woman of low birth is more robust, more enduring of toil, fed on plain, unexciting food. Valor and learning increase the honor of a noblewoman, but if she lacks chastity she lacks everything and cannot be called honored. Credit for chastity, indeed, was rated according to circumstances, from the most imperfect chastity of those who do not sin for lack of chance or for fear of husbands, revealed by change in behavior after the death of husbands, or the uncertain chastity of those who are chaste in deeds and reputation but lascivious in words, gestures, bearing, to the chastity of those who have a special, supreme chastity that goes beyond the common, less perfect chastity of the ordinary run of women.[34]

Little attempt was made to define or describe this queen of all virtues, as Brinon called it. Writers occasionally insisted that purity of mind, that is freedom from carnal desire, was the first requisite, and bodily purity only the outward sign. Brinon pointed out that customs vary in different countries, what is unchaste in one being regarded as chaste in another. That it might present variety in combination with other desires was shown by one writer in an analysis of several heroines famous for chastity. Lucretia was chaste, but desirous at the same time of a reputation for chastity; hence her decision to yield to Tarquin in order to be able to clear herself afterward by denouncing him, at the same time expiating her forced sin by not surviving its discovery. Susanna, on the other hand, in accord with Christian teaching, preferred to be held unchaste and be unjustly punished rather than commit sin. Judith was like Susanna, but where Susanna was occupied with domestic cares, inexperienced beyond them, simple, endangered by chance, Judith was concerned with the welfare of her nation and showed both matronly and political qualities; she would risk both chastity and reputation for a public gain. Saint Agnes at the age of twelve could meet great dangers with a man's heart and mature mind, but she did not desire life like Susanna, or fear shame like Lucretia, or seek danger like Judith, but desired solely to die and be with Jesus. In these instances purity of mind seems to be the quality of chastity most prized, since all, though they might have lost bodily chastity, would still have been renowned as heroines, and all with Lucretia would still have been praised for chastity.[35]

Why should this one virtue have been singled out as so important for women when so unimportant for men? Even in the ideal set down for the gentleman this chastity is not included among the virtues required of him. Temperance, continence, yes, but not chastity, though Spenser can be cited as having dedicated a whole book to chastity as one of the twelve moral virtues that make a gentleman. And, there, significantly enough one must think, the representative of chastity is a lady knight. No doubt the ascetic ideal fostered by the church had something to do with the emphasis on chastity for women, but then why not for men? I venture to suggest here what I shall refer to later on, that the ideal set up for the lady is essentially Christian in its character, and the ideal for the gentleman essentially pagan. Therefore even men who were most minded to accept women as having equal powers with themselves saw them still governed by a different conception of morality, or at least a different emphasis upon certain elements in that morality. Back of that conception lies, of course, a tangle of social, economic, and political facts and ideas that I shall not attempt to analyze except to point out that chief of all the conditions that fixed the terms of a woman's existence was the fact that she was the property of someone, usually a husband. Ownership implies special rights not shared by other people, and the reason frankly given for guarding so jealously the virginity of a girl before marriage and exclusive enjoyment of her by her husband afterward was the desire to insure a man heirs of his own body for the continuance of his race. Where estates and titles were in question the legitimacy of heirs easily assumed paramount importance.

Four other virtues were much praised in women chiefly as handmaids to chastity, without which chastity itself could not be preserved. These are modesty, humility, constancy, and most of all temperance. Modesty governs behavior, carriage of the body, use of the eyes, gestures, and the choice and wearing of clothes, in such a manner as to reveal a pure mind, and not to incite, though unwittingly, unchaste thoughts in others. Humility helps the woman to avoid that great vice of pride, greater in women than in men, and to moderate the violence and immodesty of men. Constancy, passive constancy that means endurance, wards off temptation. For women temperance means almost wholly restraint in eating and drinking. The restraint belongs to them because modesty, sobriety, and chastity itself come from it. The contrast between men and women in this matter, Pont-Aymerie said, was glaring; one could run all over Germany, the empire of drunkards, and not find a single woman touched with drunkenness, or even showing that she has had too much. Those answer foolishly, he added, who say, "But then it is not suitable for a woman to drink too much." Men are no more permitted evil than women, though they approve in themselves what they find evil in women, and subject women to laws they would never observe themselves, driven by jealousy, avarice, depraved conscience, and pride. Here may be added still another virtue, which was infrequently mentioned but taken to underlie all the others, piety. Praised by some as the greatest of all virtues it was claimed to belong pre-eminently to women for their devotion to religious exercises, their hope and faith and patience under affliction, and their piety and charity for the poor.[36]

Piety and all the virtues noted so far relate essentially to the inner life of the individual, shaping character with reference to an ideal for the self alone, without concern for other people. All of them belong as much to the recluse in her cell as to the woman of the world, and form the core to which the other standards of behavior are referred. The rest of the virtues, which may be viewed as particularly appropriate to the lady under certain circumstances, look outward and concern her relation to others. They are praised for softening the lot of men, binding families together, and allowing the woman to show herself in her most appealing guise, tender, gracious, and generous.

First among them is what we may call humanity, named variously by the renaissance love, desire to please, kindness, pity, or helpfulness. Primarily, since the sphere of woman's action was domestic, she was praised for exercising her humanity on the members of her family, showing her devotion and benevolence first to her parents, and then, after marriage, to her husband and children in her care for their bodily necessities. As one admirer who calls himself Vigoureux put it, "Women are secluded in their homes, see and converse only with their husbands, care only to please them, turn only to them a smiling face at the risk of seeming rude to others, all because their kindness and their sweetness carries them to the point where each is happy providing only that she is loved and cherished by her husband. What greater kindness can one ask of a woman than this, that though created as a companion for man, by divine law one with him and neither subject to the other, and though as capable of ruling and counseling as he, nevertheless she is subject to him under the color of human laws which give the governing to men and not to women." Her sweetness shows even in her face, and her readiness to weep, said Christine, is only another proof of the goodness of her heart. Tears were of course scorned as a sign of great weakness in men, and women's tendency to let them fall on every occasion, big or little, was often used against them. Puttenham, as well as Christine, came to their defense. "For Ladies and women to weepe and shed teares at every little greefe, it is nothing uncomely, but rather a signe of much good nature & meeknes of minde, a most decent propertie for that sexe; and therefore they be for the more part more devout and charitable, and greater gevers of almes than men, and zealous relievers of prisoners, and beseechers of pardons, and such like parts of commiseration. Yea they be more than so too: for by the common proverbe, a woman will weepe for pitie to see a gosling goe barefoote." Praise of pity and humanity thus leads to praise of liberality, in which virtue, Billon went so far as to claim, women are comparable to men. But a little scrutiny shows that what was called liberality in women was really not the liberality praised in men.[37]

Giving on a grand scale as evidence of superiority in wealth and position, and as a means of building up support from superiors, equals, and inferiors was much recommended to princes, lords, and gentlemen of substance, with elaborate advice on why, when, and how to give. Liberality became magnificence when occasions which conserved the honor and dignity of the state, such as public events, investiture of magistrates, honoring of kings and princes, or private affairs like weddings, banquets, and the entertainment of foreigners, were concerned. For ladies, however, there was no recommendation of magnificence, and liberality was almost entirely confined to almsgiving. Out of the goodness of her heart, not the calculation of her head, she was urged to give to the lowly poor, to needy gentlemen, to prisoners of the Saracens, to the support of holy orders and poor priests and other servants of God, and to other like claimants who could not make return in kind; and such giving was highly praised as most becoming to women and more often found in them than in men. The charge of avarice often leveled at them by their detractors rested only on the strait way, Christine said, in which wives were kept by husbands either poor or prodigal. If men are wasters wives must hold on to what they have for their own and their children's sake. Even so they readily give alms. It is men, she says, who turn avaricious after they have spent all they have.[38]

Courtesy must be included in this list because it is mentioned among the virtues required of women, but where it spread so wide and fair a sail for gentlemen it shrinks, like liberality, to something smaller for ladies. Very little, indeed, is said about it for them. Spenser in defining courtesy assigns it to both men and women.

> What vertue is so fitting for a knight,
> Or for a Ladie, whom a knight should love,
> As Curtesie, to beare themselves aright
> To all of each degree, as doth behove?
> For whether they be placed high above

> Or low beneath, yet ought they well to know
> Their good, that none them rightly may reprove
> Of rudenesse, for not yelding what they owe:
> Great skill it is such duties timely to bestow.

It is this heedful measuring of manners by ranks that is commended specially to ladies when showing hospitality to their guests. Courtesy puts on a more gracious aspect when lovers are considered, but we will leave discussion of that until we come to that very special world.[39]

Courage, known as valor, fortitude, and magnanimity, was assigned to women as well as men, but with disagreement as to its kind and degree. Physical courage, though at times claimed for them, was usually cried down as of little worth since tyranny, outrage, and crime are the results of it. The valor necessary in war is not so necessary to them as to men, and indeed their fear and abhorrence of war count as a virtue in them. But moral courage, the sort that endures miseries and pain and restrains the most brutal desires, they need and are generally agreed to have in abundance—witness their patient endurance of their husbands' evil ways, particularly the intemperance in eating and drinking which turns men into lascivious beasts. Magnanimity, the princely form of courage which marked the superior man in every action and thought, was also occasionally granted women, but with a difference. Chasseneux praised women for magnanimity, using queens for his examples, but he defined their magnanimity as fortitude, wisdom, and industry, and then by going on to name the other virtues for which women may be praised—chastity, beauty, mercy, liberality and devotion—he shows that he is not describing exactly the same thing that Bacon meant when he summed up magnanimity as consisting "in contempt of peril; in contempt of profit, and in meriting of the times wherein one liveth." Only under special circumstances demanding that a woman play a man's part was commended in her all the courage of mind and body required to acquit herself as splendidly as he.[40]

What about justice, the great and shining virtue without which, Elyot said, no gentleman could be commended? Justice was not denied to women though it was not emphasized as necessary, and indeed was rarely mentioned. Exactly what was meant by it as a quality of women is therefore not easy to determine, but to judge from two passages it had, as one might expect, a private and not a public application. Capella says that justice is not separated from charity, that is almsgiving, in which women excel as they excel in the virtues that proceed from justice, innocence, religion, piety, friendship, affection, and humanity. Certainly they are not robbers, murderers, and usurpers, the great sinners against justice that men are. Mori was not attempting to describe justice, but when he calls women more just, upright, regulated, obedient to law, and restrained from every vice than men are, he seems to suggest that justice means chiefly abiding by the law. For men justice was self-maintained, put among the virtues applied to public good, and called the foundation of power, present in all the virtues else they diminish in value. Justice would seem to be in men what chastity is in women.[41]

Prudence is another virtue assumed and praised in women, but because it was not made as controversial as other points not much was said about it by their defenders. It is set down here last because it is both a moral and an intellectual virtue, moral as necessary for the proper operation of the moral virtues, intellectual as first of all concerned with the working of the mind. It could easily be accepted as a conspicuous and suitable virtue of women because it was distinguished from the great powers of the mind—logical, imaginative, speculative, inventive, all of which need training by liberal studies—as natural wit applied to practical affairs. This ability to advise and foresee and govern wisely was clearly displayed in household management, too clearly in the opinion of some negligent husbands, remarked Christine, who accused their wives of being too busy, as if they would be mistress and show themselves wiser than their husbands. Nevertheless, by general agreement, conservation of what has been acquired and the government of the house belong to women and are well accomplished only through prudence. How badly off a house is without a woman to run it, Capella suggested, you can learn by observing the difference between courts which are under a woman and those which are not. Such prudence also is necessary for the instruction of children and the counseling of husbands, who would do better, many said, if they would more often seek and follow advice from their wives. The aptness of women in household exercises, admitted by all, belongs to prudence. Nor should such exercises be looked on as ignoble works of poverty, most admirers said, because noble and rich women employ them to escape idleness and also to know how to better govern their servants. The success of widows in managing their affairs was also pointed out as proof of woman's natural wisdom, revealed clearly only when she stands alone and makes her own choice. Dispute over the prudence of women arises, said Capella, only if the common opinion is accepted that prudence consists wholly in knowing how to find a plan in some emergency, men being credited with natural ability to act more quickly than women; but not to act so wisely, he thought, since men lack the subtlety that belongs to woman's colder, less active, but more penetrating, nature. This is therefore for him too narrow ground on which to base comparison. The prudence that is recommended for men, necessary in public affairs, a corrective of too much study of books, the result of experience in affairs, is a different story that is seldom told for women, even by their most fervent, and at the same time sober, admirers.

The prudence described above by its working is the prudence of the perfect woman, seen as a specially feminine virtue, and given full scope within the walls of her house. It shades off into industry.[42]

Yet, however restricted and orthodox a view was presented of certain commonly praised virtues in women, these men of the renaissance were ready to derive woman's true greatness and equality with men from her intellectual gifts, her capacity to profit by the study of books, to engage in speculation on high matters, and to invent, the greatest gift of all. Men and women have equally perfect minds, they said, and at times women may show themselves even sharper, clearer, and abler in wit than men. One might expect them to have greater capacity for learning, we have already heard some of their defenders suggesting, if greater delicacy of body and greater beauty mean anything. A less robust body, demanding less of the strong foods that send disturbing vapors to the brain, and capable of repose instead of burning for action, is more suited to the practice of contemplation; and beauty of the exterior must indicate beauty within, both of soul and mind. But the point was not insisted on. The differences in this respect apparent between men and women in general, were often assigned to differences in education and occupation. Christine summed the case up well for all: If little girls were put to school like boys they would learn as perfectly and master all the arts and sciences as well, and perhaps more women than men would do so, for women understand less only because they are kept at home and do not go to so many places. Yet hampered as they were by all sorts of restrictions, disbelief in their capacity, lack of opportunity for serious education, and confinement at home, women were shown to deserve credit for impressive achievement in letters on the same plane as men. The Italians, especially, busied themselves compiling long lists of learned ladies of ancient and modern times, in which were almost sure to appear Corinna, Sappho, Cornelia, Aspasia, Eustochium and Marcella the friends of St. Jerome, Isotta Novarolla, Costanza Sforza, Battista Malatesta, Vittoria Colonna, Laura Terracina, Marguerite of Navarre, often Christine de Pisan, the daughters of Sir Thomas More, and, if the author could overcome his hatred of heresy, Elizabeth of England.[43]

These then were the moral and intellectual qualities praised in women: chastity—supported by modesty, humility, constancy, temperance, and piety—humanity, courtesy, courage, justice, prudence, and learning. Add beauty and the image of womanly perfection appears, as the more thoughtful and restrained advocates of her worth presented it in this controversy. The intention was to show equality between men and women without essential differences, or, as Torquato Tasso averred, without any differences at all. All the virtues flourish in both, he concluded, and the same virtue shows the same in both, with different colors in different individuals, as courage shows differently in Achilles and Ajax. Any further degree of difference is ascribable to inequalities in external conditions rather than to differences in species; there is after all only one human race. Set women over against men for comparison, said Billon, and by their own worth they assume equal importance as moral and intellectual beings. The work of the world must be done by all the members of it together. If division of labor has been given—to women the care of the household and to men the provision of the means of maintenance and the regulation and protection of human society—it is without invidious labels of inferior and superior, since both are equally necessary. Piccolomini explained that he had principally considered the felicity of man in his book on the bringing up of the nobly born, because in so doing he really included the felicity of women, the virtue and felicity of the woman being necessary to the full perfection of civil life. What accommodation of his advice to her particular needs is necessary can be easily made. Though all the virtues belong to both, in their use some have come to be more especially assigned to men, and some to women, and in his treatment of family government he will show why the philosophers do not assign to woman all that is suitable to man, though she is fitted for all the operations performed usually by him, as many examples prove. The assignment of woman to the domestic end is perfectly natural and necessary because of her function in bearing and nourishing children. Her more delicate frame and more gentle disposition specially fit her for this, as they unfit her to endure the strenuous exercises and turmoil of public life.[44]

This is the general view of where women ideally belonged. It does not preclude, as we see, granting them the mental capacity to perform all the offices of men, or deny them the right to use that capacity as leisure and opportunity and necessity allow. There were none, however, to argue that she should have equal opportunity and equal reward for her effort. The real feminist was still to be born.

This debate over the relative merits of men and women, it should be explicitly stated, concerned in reality a class and not all mankind. I have been using almost altogether the terms men and women, as my authors do, but the argument, even when couched in the most general way, was addressed to the world of ladies and gentlemen. All defenders of women from their vituperators assumed that ladies were the objects of attack. Examples were drawn by both sides only from the upper classes, queens, duchesses, and at the lowest, gentlewomen. Only a few times was the wall breached to admit a glimpse of the vast majority of women, the toilers, another race born to serve. Marinella argued against the general assumption of women's inferior physical strength by calling attention to the plebeian women in the country and city who endure the toil of men. It is exercise that does it. Two writers, Bruni in 1552 and Bronzini in 1625, go farther and argue a common humanity at some point, not only in men and women of high birth but in women both of high and low birth, and in women and men of low birth. Here is the passage from Bruni. "The charge of lightness against women cannot be accepted as true if we observe how every woman according to her station attends as every man to taking care of what belongs to her. We see a shoemaker, a tailor, a smith, a market-gardener, and others of the lowest occupations attending each to his own business, not caring for states, or pomps, or greatnesses, or honors, or affairs of government, or other like things which would divert them from their intention. Just so it happens to lowborn women who according to their station, devote themselves, some to sewing, some to cooking, some to weaving, and some to other domestic cares, along with care of the house, bringing up their children, preserving family possessions, and other similar exercises, which everybody knows are appropriate and peculiar to poor women. When we go higher and look at what women have done in all the affairs of life—government, arts, oratory, war, politics, we find them equal to the men in their achievements." Bronzini, after extolling the virtues of ladies exemplified in Leonora di Toledo, wife of Cosimo de' Medici, in terms equally applicable to men, went on to say, "Nor in this do we omit the women of low condition from their humble share of honor because to their sole care household matters are committed, not having any greater exercises suitable to them; and if indeed we wish to speak further of the lowborn, we will find them not in any part inferior to or different in quality from their husbands. They are intent on low and rude occupations as their husbands are, and besides they attend to the education of their children, to the daily care of the house, to conservation of domestic possessions, which things are of great moment, of much greater effect and much greater consideration and utility than are the simple operations of the artisans and laborers that their husbands are. And through this we see clearly that whether in a state of greatness, as is the lady, or in a middle, or low, or rude state (as we say), not for this are the women to be reputed of lesser rank, lesser valor, lesser virtue or perfection than men." Thus both imply, though they do not state, a common humanity in women of both high and low birth. Such juxtaposition of the two is very rare indeed. Christine could dwell at some length on women of the lower orders, for she discussed the duties of bakers' and farmers' wives, as well as of princesses, but broad as her interest and experience was, she went no lower than mean gentlewomen in her examination of woman's essential character. As a rule, somewhere along the way, in the dedication to a queen or duchess, or in phrases indicating the rank of the group under consideration—such as, "born to greater undertakings" than household arts, or in reference to the scale of that household or to choices that only the possession of rank and wealth allows—these writers on women's character reveal that they have in mind only members of the favored group.[45]

When the renaissance, however, raised the question of the place of the lady in the scheme of things, it clearly viewed her in a very different light from the gentleman. The gentleman as a member of the favored class was compared to the rest of undifferentiated mankind in order to show wherein his special worth and superiority lay. The result is well summed up in this passage from a mid-sixteenth-century handbook for gentlemen: "Lyke as the rose in beauty passeth al other flowers and is an ornament and settyng forth of the place wher it groweth and so by the excellencye that nature hath geven, it leadeth a mans eye soner to the aspecte and beholdyng of it then of other flowers, so ought a gentleman by hys conditions, qualities, and good behaviour to excell all other sortes of men, and by that his excellencye to set forth and adorn the whole company emong whom he shall happen for to be; and therby to leade the eye of mans affection to love him before others for hys vertue sake."[46] Nobody who wanted to distinguish him thought of comparing him with the lady, but only with other men of lesser fortune and worth. In contrast, nobody, in order to distinguish the lady, thought of comparing her with other women of lesser worth. She finds her place in society only in comparison with the gentleman within the favored class to which they both belong. This is a comparison of sexes, not of classes, and tends more and more to concern a vertical division that runs through all society, obliterating class lines.

As a result of this difference in point of view little was said, with respect to women, on that subject much discussed for men, nobility, or gentility (the terms were interchangeable). One must not be misled by such titles as Domenichi's *La Nobilta della Donne*, or Agrippa's *De Nobilitate & Praecellentia Foeminei Sexus*. Here nobility is used in the broad sense of excellence, honor, merit, and not in the narrow legal sense of rank or quality conferred by birth, or by personal achievement recognized by the king, or just by long-continued living in the manner of a gentleman, as in the *De Nobilitate's* of the lawyers, or in any discussion relating to men. Most of what was written about the nobility of women in this special sense is to be found tucked away in these works of the lawyers. In effect, what was said practically denied to women essential nobility in their own right; at least with the exception of the top ranks theirs was a weaker and dimmed quality. Princesses, duchesses, perhaps those of a step or two lower, were in a class by themselves and might not lose their birthright by marriage beneath them—at least in theory.

The first general principle applied by the lawyers was that women assumed the rank of their husbands. Thus a lowborn woman was ennobled by marriage with a nobleman, retained his rank as a widow, and still belonged to his family and house unless she remarried or chose to return to her father (in that case of course carrying her dowry with her). This nobility that depended on a husband was lost by remarriage with a man of lower birth. On the other hand, if a woman of high birth married with a plebeian she did not ennoble him but lost her own nobility, and their children followed the condition of the father. If later she married a noble she acquired nobility again through him, not by her birth. The second principle was that nobility by birth was of more force than nobility by marriage, because it gave the lady in her own right the privileges that belonged to her house, as far as they applied to women. That might mean no diminution, for when women fell heir to kingdoms or great titles they assumed the full prerogatives of any male heir. But then, said Sir Thomas Smith, it is blood and not sex that is regarded, and the safety and peace of the realm, not the weakness of the ruler, there always being sage counselors at hand to supply all defects. What Sir Thomas really thought about women in office he had just made clear. Only freemen are considered as subjects and citizens in the English commonwealth, he said, and not bondmen who can bear no rule or jurisdiction over freemen, or women, made by nature to keep house and nourish their family and children, and not to meddle with matters abroad or bear office any more than children or infants. The third principle concerned the power of a woman to transmit nobility to her sons. In accordance with the rule that she lost her own nobility in marrying a plebeian and her children followed their father it would appear that she could not. Yet it was recognized that a son born of a noble mother though ignoble father had more nobility than one that was not, just as it was recognized that a son born of both a noble father and a noble mother had more perfect nobility than one born of a base mother. If both parents are noble, the nobility of the mother combined with that of the father can be said to operate, but if the father is ignoble his ignobility is dominant over the nobility of the mother.[47]

In England there seems to have been more inclination in the renaissance to allow the transmission of nobility by the mother. Robert Glover, Somerset herald, an authority on all matters connected with genealogy, and heraldic arms and orders, supported this conclusion. His works, all in Latin, were not published in his lifetime, but edited, supplemented, translated, and printed by his nephew Thomas Milles. The following passage comes from *The Catalogue of Honor*, 1610. "I have franklie affirmed Nobilitie to discend from the father unto the children, & what if I should say the same force to be in the mothers nobilitie also? Surely, both reason, and the opinion of Doctors, and aunciuent Customes also, will be present for the defence of this cause. If Nobilitie draw any thing naturall at all from the Parents, almost the whole constitution of the Childe, is to be geven unto the Mother. It hath also such shape (if we may believe Phylosophers) as the mother conceiveth, together with the seed. For first, it taketh life from the mother, it taketh likewise nourishment of and from the mother, encreasing from the Mother, and in briefe by the consent of all men, it together with the spirite and vitall humour draweth from the Mother, affections, Vertues and vices. And that such power is in the Mother, it is manifest by the Precepts of Phisitions, who commaund Parents to be most carefull to what Nurses they put their children to be nursed. In briefe, if the Vertue of the Father be in the children to be reverenced, why should not the Mothers be also? The manner of the Sex, doth neither diminish nor encrease Nobilitie, which is for it selfe to be desired. Nay, in tender women it seemeth to have both more admiration and grace. It is of a certain Lawyer well written; that amongst the causes for which the honour and dignity of persons is encreased or diminished, that is of others the lightest, which is drawne from the difference of the Sexe." Customs in Greece, Asia, and Rome, he continues, not unknown in England held in more favor the nobility of the mother than the father. Englishmen, for instance, have sometimes taken the names of their mothers as more noble. Sidney comes to mind here, who found a special spur to noble actions in his mother's rank, because hers was higher than his father's.

This nobility under discussion was not merely a label of rank, as can be seen, but implied the qualities that nobility in the general sense covers. Its operation is described thus by Francisco India, writing on the gifts necessary for the perfect gentleman. Nobility, that is the accident of high birth, is one of the gifts of fortune necessary for the perfection and happiness of man. United to a good constitution it is called the virtue of race, it nourishes and wonderfully preserves the true seeds of virtue, inclining the possessor always to the performance of illustrious and glorious actions and rendering him apt, by nature, to produce posterity inclined to similar actions. There is nothing here that the defenders of the equality of men and women would not subscribe to. In a definition of nobility which involves a particular act to raise the rank of the individual can be seen better the gap between the two sexes in their capacity for nobility. "Nobility politicall," says Glover, "is a dignity bestowed by Soveraigne Grace, upon Persons of Vertue or hability, for life, or forever, whereby a Man exempted and raised by Degrees, becomes lawfully preferred above the vulgar People, the better to do service, to the King and Commonwealth." Was ever a woman thus ennobled?[48]

A woman, then, born above the common lot, labors under a disability not known to her brother. She achieves nobility in the first place only by birth, never by her own great deeds as he can. She can lose her position by marriage beneath her, as he does not, and she cannot then transmit to her children the condition to which she was born. Her brother's place in the scheme of things is clear; he is a member of a favored class in his own right.

Her place is in reality contingent upon her husband's, so far as rank, power, and influence are concerned. So far as womanly worth is concerned, like any wife and mother of a family, she furnishes the other half of a working partnership. And in this respect the theory of the lady is the theory of woman without consideration of rank.

Neither do the human qualities assigned to the lady, which furnish so much of the material for the quarrel over the relation of men to women, actually differentiate her from the woman of low birth. The same difficulty is met here as in the case of the gentleman. If nobility rests upon the exercise of virtues it is hard to see any essential test for the difference between gentleman or plebeian. Justice, prudence, courtesy, liberality, temperance, courage—these were the virtues chiefly prescribed for the gentleman. But something more was needed to justify his claim to special privilege, since plebeians exercised such virtues too. The difficulty was recognized by the renaissance and some attempt was made to distinguish gentle from plebeian virtues by separating the virtues into public and private virtues, or by intensifying the degree of virtue required for responsible position in society. For the lady no such effort was made by her defenders, since there was no interest in defining her position in the favored class. Not only does she exhibit the same virtues as any good woman, but the emphasis falls in her catalogue on the virtues primarily of value in the domestic sphere—chastity, humility, obedience, constancy, patience, piety, temperance, kindness, prudence in household management, and fortitude under affliction. Courtesy, a virtue belonging chiefly outside the house where varieties of people meet; liberality, concerned with maintaining one's superiority; courage, necessary to great exploits; and justice, which also belongs to the wide world, together with the wisdom that comes from experience and serious study, are all, at one time or another, included as praiseworthy in the lady, but they are not, as they were for the gentleman, the basic stuff of her character, and many, even of her most ardent defenders, do not mention them at all.

The moral ideal for the lady is essentially Christian, as I have said, as that for the gentleman is essentially pagan. For him the ideal is self-expansion and realization. He is to develop to the utmost every power that he has, and direct every action with the proud consciousness of his elevation above the crowd not only in position but in worth. All his virtues are turned to insure his pre-eminence, enhance his authority, the essence of Aristotelian magnanimity. For the lady the direct opposite is prescribed. The eminently Christian virtues of chastity, humility, piety, and patience under suffering and wrong, are the necessary virtues. That is, the suppression and negation of self is urged upon her, even by those that love and admire her most, as will appear still more clearly in the recommendations for her upbringing and education.

We do have, however, in these qualities, the whole list of them, a picture of the renaissance lady which makes her, as her admirers intended, comparable in some degree at least with the gentleman. If she still remains a figure incomplete unless joined to his, she appears worthily framed for her place beside him (or is it a few paces behind), with some of the qualities necessary for acting in his place lightly sketched in.

CHAPTER THREE : *Training*

The renaissance seems to have paid little attention by way of formal treatise to the training and education of women. Luis Vives says in his preface to his *Instruction of a Christian Woman* that he is the first to treat of the information and bringing up of a Christian woman, for though Xenophon, Aristotle, and Plato have said many things about a woman's office, and Saints Cyprian, Jerome, and Augustine have treated of maids and widows, they have done so rather by way of exhorting them to a certain kind of reading than by way of teaching them. They confine themselves to praising chastity, which is a goodly thing and fitting for such gifted and holy men to do, but they give very few precepts and rules on how to live. He therefore intends to compile rules for living, and though he has divided them up as they apply more particularly to maids, wives, and widows, each will have to read the whole book to get all that pertains to herself. This is 1523. In 1545 Ludovico Dolce, no doubt surveying the Italian scene only, remarked that though many have written on how to know and train a horse, none before him have written on how a young woman ought to be brought up, in spite of the fact that nothing is more necessary to the repose of mortals than to teach virtue and chaste habits to women. He could not have been expected to know Francesco Barberino's long treatise in verse on the subject, written in the last years of the thirteenth century but never printed until 1815. By 1586 Stefano Guazzo, in his dialogue on the honor of women, was saying there are volumes on the bringing up of a girl, and therefore no need for him to go over the ground in order to show how immaculate chastity, on which the honor of women chiefly depends, is to be acquired and preserved, more than to enumerate the chief means—sobriety, avoidance of idleness, restraint of the senses and speech, especially idle talk, and avoidance of occasions for dalliance and of deceitful lovers. The catalogue of discoverable books up to 1625 on the training and education of women is still a short one compared to that for the gentleman, but since almost everything written on or for women embraced exhortations, warnings, and examples concerning these same points, a rather indiscriminate survey might easily have led to Guazzo's conclusion. The fact remains that the training for girls, particularly their formal education, must be drawn from a few books devoted to the subject, and scattered references elsewhere. Most writers on the training and education of youth thought it not worth their while to spend any time on girls, though occasionally a chapter or so in a discussion of general education for boys considered briefly what was suitable for girls, and one such writer, Silvio Antoniano, claimed that all he said applied proportionately to girls, so far as the state and condition of their sex allowed.

Even Vives and others who wrote especially for women sound condescending toward their subject. Vives explains in his preface that for easy and frequent reading he has been brief, using few examples and staying within his purpose by not treating generally of vice and virtue, "a large feeld to walke in." "Moreover," he adds in defense of his brevity, "though the precepts for men be innumerable: yet women may be informed with few words. For men must be occupied both at home & abroad, both in their owne matters and for the common weale. Therefore it cannot bee declared in fewe bookes, but in many and long, how they shall handle themselves in so many and divers thinges. As for a woman shee hath no charge to see to, but her honestie and chastitie. Wherefore when she is reformed of that, shee is sufficiently appointed." Others write, they say, to aid feminine fragility and promise not to use big words, or excuse their use of the vernacular by their desire to be better understood or read more widely.

Despite the paucity of material it has seemed wise to attempt to differentiate between training and education, although either word might cover both. Education has been especially connected with the systematic study of books for so long, and in the early treatises for boys did mean so nearly only that, that it is convenient to set out by itself what was said on booklearning for women in order to sharpen the contrast between the two. Besides, the problem of organization, difficult at best because of the great variety of subjects in the domestic realm, has been considerably simplified by the division. Therefore this chapter covers every side of the bringing up of a girl except formal studies.[1]

As a succinct guide to the course recommended for the early training of women we may start with Dolce's declaration quoted above: nothing is more necessary to the repose of mortals than to teach virtue and chaste habits to women. For carrying on this training of daughters the mother was chiefly responsible, though the ultimate responsibility rested with the father, who was admonished that he must oversee her work at every point lest she be too indulgent or negligent. Of course if she proved wise and diligent, he would need to give less attention to details. Care for providing wholesome surroundings and forming good habits, it was thought, could not be taken too early. Hence the oft-repeated advice that the mother should nurse her baby herself, for the sake of the health and disposition of the child, and the love between them that such an office fosters; and if she could not, then a nurse should be chosen as nearly as possible like her in temperament and habits. When the child needs them she should be given playmates of her own age, preferably only girls, always watched over by the mother, nurse, or some other chaste woman. For amusement she should play games that represent the whole of life, and introduce her to particularly chaste women. Miniature household utensils should be put into her hands to teach the use of them and inspire a desire for them. Stories are good for her, but only chaste and exemplary tales that teach love of God, reverence to her mother, and the virtues belonging to women. From the first she should see and hear only what will lead to chaste habits, thoughts, and actions. Extremely important for this end is the example set in speech and actions by her elders, her father and mother and all those in special charge of her. Too often before she can talk she will hear amorous and lascivious verses which will stay in her memory. The songs of servants particularly will bear watching, and certainly bad servants and all kitchen servants should be kept away from her.

Correction of faults and likewise reward for good behavior so that the child can learn to hate the one and love the other is a paramount duty of the mother, or the reliable matron who has charge of her and who may even be preferable to the mother in this respect, since only too often the mother is blinded with love or too careless to discharge such a serious duty well. The mother or matron, knowing what is to be feared and hoped in a maid, will observe her inclinations, foster what is good, and try to eliminate what is bad. Instruction will be lightened with pleasantness, because tender children cannot be assumed to have the powers of intellect which allow prolonged concentration on more serious matters. The lighter errors of childhood merit some indulgence, and the child, accustomed to smiling faces full of lovable grace, when she must be corrected, can be made to know by only a sober face that she has been reproved. Threatening words and frowns should be used as the last resort, only rarely and briefly, else they are not effective. But when such severity brings a troubled look to the child's face, revealing great terror, smiles and serenity should return and harsh words turn into gentle instruction to calm her mind and remove her terror. Above all blows will be avoided as brutal punishment unsuitable to the mind of the gentleborn.

This correction with mildness was the particular office of the mother in distinction to the father. Both were warned against excessive affection, harmful because it makes them yield to the child against her own good, but each was assigned a special role in the bringing up of daughters. The father had to consider his home a little state of which he was the ruler. As a father, he ought not to be so severe with his children that he loses the character of father, but at the same time he must take care not to be so gentle as to cease to be the ruler. Of the two extremes severity, however, was held safer than mildness, since too much liberty corrupts children. How far that severity might advisedly go is revealed by Silvio Antoniano's warning to the father not to turn a cheerful face to his daughter, lest by his indulgence she become bold enough to do what she would not do if she had proper paternal fear, and lest his caresses should accustom her to a certain amount of familiarity with men by which she would lose, little by little, the fear of shame which is like a wall to a chaste woman. He has no intention, he adds, to persuade that the father ought to wear a continuously angry face, but that he should retain his gravity and not reveal a certain tenderness of love, dangerous particularly to daughters. The extreme severity with which both fathers and mothers could treat their children is a matter of record, notably Roger Ascham's account of finding Lady Jane Gray at her book instead of out hunting with her family.

To the mother, then, according to the best advice, belonged the special office of softening the necessary rigor of paternal authority with the tenderness of her maternal love, and a softer manner in admonishing with more perseverance and patience than the father usually shows. This applies to sons as well as daughters, who will both show more tender love toward their mother and be more disposed to listen to her. Except in their infancy and early childhood the mother had more care of her daughters than her sons, though if a good mother she could always have a great part in the bringing up of all her children.[2]

The first lesson that the little girl must learn, all agreed, is to love goodness, particularly chastity, and to hate evil. There was some debate as to the best way to teach her. Some thought it necessary to show bad as well as good in order to make the child recognize the good and desire it; but others, like Vives, thought it wrong to teach evil because not even to know evil is a more sure, profitable, and happy state. Most writers evidently believed that girls especially should come late to knowledge of evil, for they prescribed close confinement at home, away from feasts and public entertainments and even from windows that allow them to see everything going on in the street and to be seen openly by youths full of licentiousness. Church-going was held perilous also, but since even girls must go to church advisers had to be content to send them to the nearest by the shortest way, and always in the company of mother or other staid older person.

That other great danger to chastity, books, could be met only by severely restrictive measures. It was a pity, some thought, that girls should learn to read at all, and they would have them taught late. But learn girls would, and then they should be given examples and lives of famous and virtuous ladies, out of the Bible and other histories ancient and modern. Never should they be set to learn by heart what Salter calls the "bookes, ballades, Songes, sonettes, and Ditties of daliance," which so many unwise fathers give their daughters for their first books. If all reading that softens the mind and endangers morals cannot be prohibited, at least anything that would make her unworthy of herself and her rank should be. Many a book, it was charged, under covers studded with gold and gems, and even under color of religion, teaches low and corrupt habits. In every way the child must be guarded against learning unclean, wanton words, together with uncomely gestures and movements of the body, even in innocence, because she will use the same when older, unaware and often against her will. And especially parents must avoid approving any such behavior, by words, laugh, or look, kiss and embrace, for she will repeat what she thinks pleases.[3]

With childhood distinctly behind, the girl, writers pointed out, begins to think and feel for herself, and her training must become even more strictly an effort to inculcate in her the virtues appropriate and necessary to her. More needs to be said here, therefore, about some of the virtues discussed in the preceding chapter, for we are viewing them now as the problem of fathers and mothers to teach and preserve in their daughters. In the effort to frame a dream of perfect womanhood, ideal qualities detached from daily realities were, in the main, the only consideration, where it is a practical question now of shaping the means to produce a woman suited to limited purposes, the offices of wife, mother, and mistress of a household. Besides, where before the talk was of adults, here it is of immature youth, hardly out of childhood when they are handed over to husbands, and purposely left, some recommended, still largely unformed and even largely uninstructed in what the wife should know, because the husband would then be free to mold his young wife into the pattern he desired. The account of the education of women therefore continues into the chapter on marriage where, with further instruction and experience, the woman shaped from her birth by prudent parents takes her rightful place as the working partner of her husband.

It is already obvious that every consideration from the first turns upon the central demand of chastity, the great virtue of woman, so judged by women as well as men. Mrs. Dorothy Leigh, one of the few women who spoke for themselves, bore witness on this point. Facing early death she wrote a little book of advice for her three small sons, chiefly on religion but touching on other matters. She was particularly anxious that they should bring up their children well and advised that they begin by giving good names to their children—Philip, Elizabeth, James, Anna, John, and Susanna. Over Susanna she paused for comment on the chastity which that name should inspire the bearer to preserve: "Whoso is truly chaste, is free from idlenesse, and from all vaine delights, full of humility, and all good christian virtues; who is chaste, is not given to pride in apparell, nor any vanity, but is alwaies either reading, meditating, or practising some good thing which she hath learned in the Scripture." The need for constant care she went on to describe. "Man said once, the woman which though gavest me, beguiled me, and I did eate. But wee women may now say, that men lye in waite every where to deceive us, as the elders did to deceive Susanna. Wherefore let us bee, as shee was, chast, watchfull, and wary, keeping company with mayds. Once Judas betrayed his Master with a kisse, and repented it: but now men, like Judas, betray their Mystresses with a kisse, and repent it not: but laugh and rejoyce, that they have brought sinne and shame to her that trusted in them. The onely way to avoid all which, is to bee chaste with Susanna, and being women, to imbrace that virtue, which being placed in a woman, is most commendable," and for gentlewomen in particular, others added, an ornament and a grace.[4]

There is little direct advice on how to teach chastity, except to recommend such reading as will show what it is and inspire emulation; the lives of chaste virgins and renowned ladies who lived virtuously, but not the lives of Aspasia, Cleopatra, Semiramis, and a lot of other famous women dear to defenders of women for capacity as great as men's, but highly suspect on all true womanly counts. The girl and her companions can then be led into sober conversation about such serious matters, but lest young minds should grow fatigate—to use Sir Thomas Elyot's word—the wise mother, or whoever is in charge, will lighten the serious with ingenious questions and witty arguments. The chief safeguard for chastity was said to be the impulse, in the young especially, to fear shame, called shamefastness or bashfulness, which is described thus by Barnaby Rich: "Nature hath ordained in all good and vertuous women this affection of shamefastnes, which serveth as a restraint to withhold them from those artificiall abillimentes that do either smell of vanitie or breed suspect of honesty: for Bashfulnes is it that moderates their thoughts, makes them modest in their speaches, temperate in their actions, and warie in all there deliberations."[5] Most writers are content to recommend shamefastness to women, the young especially, without warning of excess, seeing in it a corrective to pride and desire for honor and public fame. An Italian, however, was more anxious over the danger of running into the fault of unseemly and foolish shamefastness, which, he said, under the habit of custom and nature continues into ripe years with occasion for great reproof. Too much boldness is a serious fault, but fearfulness or shamefastness—and here we will let Bruto speak in his own words as translated by Salter—"where it is needelesse, is a pointe of greate follie, fitter for babes to use, then suche a one as I wishe our Maiden to bee, that delighteth to decke her minde by this *Mirrhor*, therefore restrainyng these two extremities, if any commit offence proper to yong age, let them be shamefast, onely in acknowledging their fault and not otherwise, and so not beeying obstinate in denying, thei shewe greate signe of amendemente. And sure there can not bee a greater chasticement, then the same that suche a one shall conceive. Likewise where it behoveth her to shewe her vertue, she shall bee readie but

not to bolde, and by a sodaine blushyng, whiche immediatly will over-
spread her lillie cheekes with roseat read, she shall shewe that she beareth
in her breaste a reverente harte, farre separated from infamous and re-
prochfull shame. In suche wise I saie, she shall with a cherefull countenaunce, and a well tempered gravitie, castyng her eyes to the yearth, shewe
of her selfe that whiche neverthelesse, although she knowes it will redounde
to her praise and commendation, she would willingly dissemble and faine
not to care for. With this commendable confidence, when it behoves her
through request to recite any Psalme, or other Spirituall song, or godlie
sentence, she shall set her selfe forthe to doe it with a milde refusall, yet
altogether voide of undecent affectyng."[6] Other good stays recommended
for chastity were simplicity of mind, best preserved by severe restriction
of reading, wisdom as to the bounds within which restraint should be
practiced, and majesty in face and actions to prevent evil solicitation. All
these the girl's training will be framed to cultivate, in ways brought out
later with reference to deportment, dress, and other matters.[7]

Among the important lessons that the girl must learn, obedience held
a high place. It must indeed underwrite all the other virtues, and it belonged as much to the wife as to the little child. Woman's whole life was
a lesson in submission to the will of another. Obedience, to win praise, had
to be complete, unquestioning, and included the acceptance of correction,
even blows, in all humility, subjection, fear, sweetness, and patience without provoking either parents or, later, husband by talking back, babbling,
or running away. For as all reiterated, God has commanded silence and
entire subjection from women. The end or crown of this training in obedience would come with the daughter's acceptance of her parents' choice of
a husband for her. She should do so because parents know better what is
for the good of their daughter than she can possibly know. If she, rejecting
their counsel and even command, makes a secret marriage for pleasure,
she must expect that such a husband will suspect her of inchastity and
never have confidence in her, and she may look to have such love suddenly
lost and turned to hate. Not that parents have a right, or are other than
most unwise, to force a husband of their choice upon an unwilling daughter.
She may protest if for some fault or vice she cannot love their choice, and
withhold her consent, but without some special reason to object she should
bow to their superior wisdom. Even more unquestioning would have to be
her obedience to her husband, for on that depends the happiness of all the
rest of her life.[8]

Humility, then, it can be seen, is another important lesson, though it
is more often assumed than directly discussed, perhaps because it must
be taken for granted as one of the supreme virtues of Christian life. When
it is specifically recommended the terms are religious, as in this passage
from Bruto, given in its English dress. "Also she (the Matron) shall inforce

her to be humble, and lowly of harte, because that humilitie is not onely a Christian and civile vertue, but the verie Foundacion and Pilloure of all Christian and civile verteous, for it engendreth in us, the knowledge of our selves (as muche as our weaknesse maie or can conprehende) and therefore it wil give her the understandyng of gods Sapience, Bountie, and Puissance (whiche she ought to know to be infinite, not only in creatyng the whole world by admirable ordynance of nothyng, and fillyng and garnishyng it with greate varietie of all thinges, but in conservyng it in the same beying by eternall and devine Providence) and it will not only shewe her that all that whiche maie be in a yong Maiden, but all that whiche maie be in Kinges and Emperours, and all that whiche was in them that in tyme paste sprounge out of the *Licio, Portico,* or *Accademia* with fame and renowne to bee wise, in comparison of that whiche God maie or can, and esteeming all that whiche by anie maner of meanes maie in us have the name of bounty and goodnesse compared to that of gods, is moste abhominable wickednesse."

Even renaissance conceptions of morality for the girl in her father's house are thus narrow and one-sided. Most that is said on the topic concerns these few qualities, all of which are made to turn around the one great, necessary virtue of chastity. There can be no question that in a world where daughters must be disposed of and where the first condition of acceptablility to a husband (unless it may be the dowry, the cynic might say) is virginity, parents did well to spare no pains to enforce the lesson by every means in their power, and then to set strict guard upon the movements of their daughters, lest temptation overcome training and even natural inclination. Religious training was not ignored as a powerful bulwark to chastity, but little was said about it beyond prescription of simple piety, true love of God, prayer, and humility, which teach fundamental lessons of service, goodness, and admiration for virtue rather than for things of this world. Dolce boiled down to two the lessons that a girl of gentle birth must learn, religion and the management of a household; he said, as all said, constant devotion alone can prevent sinful thoughts that may lead to sinful deeds, and household activities prevent idleness, feared as the nurse of all evil in a group that commonly found no business in life except the problem of finding ways to spend leisure hours.[9]

Chiefly on this ground mothers were advised to train their daughters in all the household arts, but there were other good reasons. Such knowledge would be an aid in managing the household when girls came to marry, in pleasing husband and friends with special dishes, in winning renown for skills most appropriate to women, and even in helping the mother while they were growing up. This training, Vives thought, should begin as soon as children were able to learn anything; he would set no particular age, four, five, or seven, the nature of the child must decide that, nor

should parents, out of inordinate affection, postpone beginning for fear
of sickness. "I will meddle heere," he added, "with no low matters, lest
I should seeme to make much adoo about things that be too simple for
my purpose. But I would in no wise that a woman shoulde be ignoraunt
in those feates, that must be done by hand, no, not though shee be a
Princesse or a Queene."

The most unquestioned housewifely art for the gentlewoman of any
rank was needlework, with spinning and weaving still recommended though
obviously out of fashion since advisers spoke of them as a cause already
lost. There were many books of designs for embroidery and fine needlework
of every sort. One published in England in 1596, called *A Booke of Curious
and Strange Inventions*, was dedicated by the printer to the Lady Isabell
Dowager of Rutland for "the singular vertue wherewith God hath graced
you, and therewithal the excellent knowledge you have in Needleworkes."
The whole argument was then set forth in verses that may be condensed
to this: woman's strength is unequal to the strenuous toil by which men
show their wit, but with the needle, in silk and in gold, their white hands
may reveal their own sharp and pregnant wit; great knowledge, pains,
and skill are required to win the prize in needlework, which is a suitable
employment for all women, queens and noble ladies as well as maids of
low degree who by their skill and fame often come to be companions of
noble ladies and even teachers of the daughter of a king and thus raise
their own rank. With such works, the renaissance thought, women rendered themselves more beautiful and famous.

Next in favor as an art worthy a lady's accomplishment was cookery.
That it was not beneath the notice of people of high degree is evidenced
in a cook book of 1597 which contains three recipes for keeping lard, "after
my Lord Ferries way, my Lady Westone Brownes way and my Lady
Marquesse Dorsets way." The girl should be taught cookery, sober and
measurable, said Vives, that she may prepare for her family, especially
if sick, what will please them more than if dressed by servants. "Let no
body loath the name of the kitchen; namely being a thing very necessary,
without the which neither sicke folkes can amend nor whole folkes live."
The other parts of keeping a house should be taught also, adorning a room,
making a bed, arranging furniture, even sweeping, for humility and useful
exercise. Only with such skill herself can the lady know the offices of her
servants, both men and women, and be able to note carefully how well
they put the halls and chambers in order, or how quickly they dispatch
the feasts or care for the storerooms. Then she can better issue commands
and reprove with authority, and by her very presence she will spur ambition and desire to do well. Those who say that sewing, cooking, weaving,
and spinning are base exercises performed because of poverty and not out
of fitness to the sex, are merely ignorant, for, setting all other reasons

aside, noble, rich, and great women must occupy themselves in such matters to avoid idleness. How else can such persons fill up their time profitably, asked Vives. Talk and musing are not good because talk is only too likely to be light and lead to worse, and "woman's thought is swift and for the most part unstable, walking and wandering out from home." Reading is best, he admitted, but she cannot read all the time, and she must not be idle. Besides, by domestic and practical duties she is held aloof from much company, a desirable effect since in a crowd it is harder to avoid vices and corrupting habits.[10]

On daily regime for the girl there was much grave advice concerning food, drink, and clothes, and all such matters involving hygiene for the body as well as health for the soul. Sobriety is the ruling virtue here. Food, all agreed, should be moderate and plain, not spiced and delicate, and should be eaten sparingly. Until marriage, Vives advised, much fasting is good, not to the point of enfeebling the body, but in order to restrain it and "quench the heat of youth." If possible he would recommend complete abstinence from wine and allow only pure water. If, however, the stomach will not stand water, then ale or much diluted wine can be allowed, enough to digest food and not inflame bodies. Modesty, silence, and chastity all hang on temperance in food and drink. In line with such austerity was the advice that the girl's bed should not be very soft, but clean, and she should be allowed only enough sleep for health, not enough for softening and weakening her body and mind. Clothes also should not be overdelicate, but clean, unadorned with jewels, and unperfumed, to the enhancement of her modesty, humility, and chastity. Since extravagance in personal adornment is the particular fault of women, the good mother restrains her daughter and teaches how ugly it is for a chaste gentlewoman to dress like a prostitute who learns a different way every day of tricking herself out after the latest fashion to set off her beauty, when the true adornments of a wife will be chastity, modesty, truth, silence, sobriety, love of husband and children, knowledge of how to conserve goods, spend wisely, and the like. "But here peradventure," imagines Vives, "some dangerous dame would answer that with her quick answers hath gotten a name of wisdom: we must doe some thing for our birth and gentle bloud, & possessions." The answer to that if she is a Christian is that she speaks out of devilish pride and not out of Christian humility. Then perhaps she will say, "Wee must needes doe some thinges for the use of the worlde and customes." To that Vives would ask whose custom, a wise man's or a foolish? If an evil custom has arisen, a Christian woman should be the first to reject it and others will follow. Women put on rich dress only to seem fairer and entice men to great risk of chastity. Beauty has brought many to sin. If silk, cloth of gold and silver, precious stones and gems are taken from a woman, she will more easily be kept at home. Let her wear clean woollen and coarse linen, wash her face, comb her hair, and look in the glass only to see that her head is clean and neat. Particularly she should be allowed no men's apparel lest she think she has his courage—when has this protest not been voiced?

As for any attempt to improve on God's handiwork, the girl should be content with natural beauty. If she lacks that and hopes, by paint particularly, lotions, false hair, and all the other tricks, to seem beautiful and attract a husband, she is very foolish, for the effect on her husband when he sees her in her chemise or without paint—does she expect to go to bed with it—will be disillusionment and loss of love. Better never marry than seek to attract a man who delights more in a painted face than in her natural one. Besides it is wrong to desire to be fairer than God made her; she defiles his work by trying to change what he has made. Beyond all that the habit of painting is detrimental to the body; the skin wrinkles sooner, and health is affected by the white lead, quicksilver, and soaps. Every man of virtue will value her more for virtues than for beauty.[11]

Much as all advisers would seem to have preferred to keep all girls, and women too, strictly at home, safe from sights that would put worldly and flighty ideas into their heads, and from the observation of men, tempted and offering temptation, they recognized the impossibility of turning the house into such a prison, and admitted the necessity of occasionally going abroad, if only to church. The rule was to go out as seldom as possible, because of the danger. Vives more than any other writer considers just what the reasons are for thus curbing the freedom of women, and how the girl can be trained to minimize the dangers. The principal reason, he says, is that whenever she goes among people she is under "judgement & extreme perill of her beautie, honestie, demurenes, witte, shamefastnes, and vertue." Nothing is more fragile than the fame and reputation of a woman, nothing in more danger of injury, because people require perfection of her and at the same time are suspicious of her and ready to slander her. Once uttered, a slander is practically everlasting. The impossibility of seeming perfect enough to escape criticism he illustrates in this passage: "If thou talke little in companie folkes thinke thou canst but little good: if thou speake much, they recken thee light: if thou speak uncunningly, they count thee dul witted: if thou speake cunningly thou shalt be counted but a shrew: if thou answere not quickly, thou shalt be called proude or ill brought up: if thou answere they shall saye thou wilt bee soone overcome: if thou sit with demure countenaunce: thou art called a dissembler: if thou make much moving, they will call thee foolish: if thou looke on any side, then will they saye, thy minde is there: if thou laugh when any man laugheth, though thou doo it not of purpose, straight they will say thou hast a fantasie unto the man and his sayings, and that it were no greate maisterie to winne thee." The Greeks were right; the best woman is the one least talked about either in praise or dispraise. "A woman shoulde be kept close, nor be knowen of many, for it is a token of no great chastity or good name, to be knowen of many, or be songed about in the Citie in songs, or to be marked or maimed by any notable marke, as white, lame, gogle eyed, little, great, fat, maimed, or stutting."

Well, Vives continues, she must at times venture out; let her go, but prepare her mind beforehand as if she were to fight. Strengthen her against assaults on chastity by teaching her that all she will see is vanity and giving her lessons on vice. Have her dress modestly. Let her walk not too fast or too slow. In company let her be sober in face and movements of her body, not looking much at men or thinking that they look at her. Some maids have the idea that every man looks and speaks only of them. Twenty may be sitting in a row; let a man pass by and they all laugh at once, pretending to laugh at something one of them is doing or saying, but it is only because each one thinks herself "so wonderous faire & goodly to se & behold." There should be no unreasonable laughing—the sign of a very light and dissolute mind. Only a fool would laugh back at young men that laugh toward her.

The dangers of company were constantly harped on, and, almost by common consent, public affairs beyond church services were proscribed for the well-brought-up girl. To quote Vives again because, unlike the rest who are content to forbid, he explains the reasons for such prohibitions: At feasts, he says, "What gard of chastitie can there be, where the mayd is desired with so many eyes, where so many faces looketh upon her, and againe shee upon so many? She must needs fire some, and her selfe also to be fired againe, and shee be not a stone. Moreover there is layd great nourishment unto that heate, by the reason of meat and drincke of the feast, and talking, touching, groping, & plucking, & many other wanton poynts, where unto that unbridled Bacchus gyveth lybertye and boldnesse. What minde can bee pure and holy amonge all this geare, & not spoted with any thought of luste . . . I dare be bolde to say, that fewe young women, after they begyn to waxe to womans state, come from feasts, and banquets, and resorte of men with safe minds. But some be taken with eloquence, some with pretines of bodye, some with one propertie, & some with other: which a young woman shall finde in a great multytude of men, set lyke nettes. And it is an harde thing to scape uncaught with these thinges, whereunto shee is some thing inclined already. How much were it better not to love this jeoperdye, than to perish in it as the wise man saith; Verilye my mind is, & I trowe Christes too, that maides should be kept at home, and not goe a broad, except it be to heare divine service, and that wel covered, lest they either give or take occasion of snaring. A Christian maid ought to have nothing a doe with wedding feasts, banquets, and resortings of men. Finally, what mine opinion is concerning young women you may know by that, that I would not have yong boyes brought unto feasts, both because it hurteth the strength & the health of the child, in the time of growing: and because that feasts be the springs of great and many vices, be they never so sober & moderate."[12]

Further advice on manners of a somewhat more specific character may be picked up here and there to fill in the picture. The cardinal rule for women's behavior at all times was to avoid calling attention to themselves. First as to general bearing, management of the body. The girl must be trained to stand quietly, feet together, without meaningless movements of head, shoulders, hands, and feet. In the street especially she should walk with medium steps, slowly, but not too slowly lest she be taken to be loitering for a purpose. At table she should sit erect with feet and knees together, to be known as a virgin and not a prostitute, her eyes cast down, not gazing about to see who is eating and what, except when she is serving or correcting those younger than herself. She should eat daintily and so chastely that food is not seen in her mouth or her teeth more than is necessary. It is shameful to make her mouth a sack with exaggerated movements of her lips. Her face should be grave and her eyes habitually lowered for the sake of humility and modesty, even to the point, one extremist would go, of leaving no chance for anyone to accuse her of ever having looked in the face of her father, mother, and brothers, much less of anyone else, from the age of seven. Downcast eyes are the feature most stressed, with the exception perhaps of the bridled tongue, because as Barberino long before explained, through the eye one's mind is revealed to others, and she is wise who keeps such knowledge to herself; only a little look can discover a great love. Also through the eyes chiefly enters the knowledge of worldly things, distracting at least, if not damaging, to virtue. In her face should appear kindness, humility, shame, without pride. She should be taught to show herself gentle and sweet to her company, to honor them, and to be liberal and courteous not only to equals but to inferiors—virtues that will bring small praise, but some reproach if they are lacking. When she speaks she must take care to whom, where, when, and of whom.[13]

But the art of speech for the girl, and the woman as well, was reduced for the most part to one simple rule: Silence. "For there is nothing," wrote an English clergyman for his daughters, "that doth so commend, avaunce, set forthe, adourne, decke, trim, and garnish a maid, as silence. And this noble vertue may the virgins learne of that most holy, pure and glorious virgin Mary, which, when she eyther hard or saw any worthy and notable thing, blabbed it not oute straight wais to her gossips, as the manner of women is at thys present day, but being silent, she kept al thos sayinges seacreat, and pondered them in her hart."[14]

For a little embroidery on this general pattern we can draw impartially on an Italian, a Frenchman, and another Englishman. Rare, slow, and low, advises the Italian, should be the speech of the girl, who will use her mouth to hide her tongue and teeth when speaking, and when silent will close her lips with all due and natural humility, without any unnatural movements, such as biting or gnawing the tongue or lips. Laughter is most objectionable because it shows the teeth. The Frenchman writing expressly for girls who want to marry tells them to reply humbly and in sweetness mixed with gravity and adorned with prudence, weighing their words, that nothing may be superfluous, ambiguous, ill-intended, crude, or derogatory to virginal shame. Then everyone will praise them through admiration for their little speaking and good speaking, and someone will want to marry them. The promise of a husband on this one good point is supported by the Englishman's declaration: "What others would request or desire in their Wives or Mistresses, I know not; but my nature so much abhorreth a Woman of much tongue as I had rather have her infected with any of the seaven deadly Sinnes, then to be counted a notorious Scold: and therefore,

A Womans Tongue that is as swift as thought,
Is ever bad, and she herself starke Nought:
But shee that seldome speakes and mildly then,
Is a rare Pearle amongst all other Women.
Maides must be seene, not heard, or selde or never,
O may I such one wed, if I, wed ever.[15]

After all what has a woman to say that can delight a man? She can only complain, weep, threaten, or tell empty stories, or what the cook has prepared, what she has dreamed, how many eggs the hen laid, or what her other lover does for her, no pleasure but torment." Thus concludes the misogynist in prescribing silence. One friend, Thomas Artus, Sieur d'Embry, coming rather late in our period, did challenge this universal prescription of silence for women, as purely negative advice. Education is the thing, the only way to teach the girl the proper use of language and to furnish her with things to say. After all a girl of rank can be recognized by her wise words. Everything is open to abuse; silence as well as speech, for it can cover up boldness and give a license to men to say things to the ignorant which would be withheld if the woman were well read.[16]

The maid is warned on all sides against the behavior that endangers her chastity but little specific advice is offered on how to deal with actual situations forced on her by importunate lovers, which might happen, even in Italy where girls seem to have been much more secluded than in France or England. Bouchet went into the matter more particularly than anyone else. The proper technique is first of all not to listen to any young man who begins saying foolish things. If she listens, or holds any conversation with him, he will think her heart is gained. She should go off but not as if angry, or he will speak evil of her and say something has gone to her

head. Of course if she has to repulse evil men, she will show her scorn
vigorously, but ordinarily a proud rebuff is only too likely to cause further
trouble, not only by arousing pique and desire for revenge, but by fostering
pride in her. She must guard against pride—not even chastity is pleasing
to God unless joined to humility, a recognition of her weakness and need
of God's help—and a fear to offend. Women who are chaste of eye, heart,
and body but stained with pride have been known to presume too much
on their good character and thereby fall into public infamy. A maid must
trust in God, pray him to preserve her in all integrity, and look out that
by overconfidence she does not lose all at a banquet, feast, or dance. She
should never, if possible, find herself alone in secret places with men, either
old or young, and never indulge in sinful kisses, for they lead toward
worse; even if the kissers get no more they will ridicule her in prose and
verse. Let her reserve her kisses for her relatives at the proper time and
place, and, ultimately, for her husband, especially when they have been
long separated. One last caution—she must reject rondeaux, lays, ballads,
all sweet sayings which overcome the heart, and all gifts from men sick
with love. "There is in Fraunce & Spaine," wrote Vives, "a good saying.
A woman that giveth a gyfte, giveth hir selfe: a woman that taketh a
gifte, selleth her selfe."[17]

What amusements then is the maid to have? That she should have some
recreation was grudgingly granted by the more liberal planners of her
bringing up, but the list of prohibitions is much longer than of permissions.
Here is one from an evangelical minister named Eustorg de Beaulieu, who
wrote his little book of advice for his niece Magdaleine, the daughter of a
noble mother of the house of Turenne. Listen to no vulgar tales, he tells
her, worldly follies, salacious suggestions; as a guard against what might
lead to lubricity, avoid worldly farces, dice and card games, dances and
other pastimes of a dissolute character, books on love or other profane
writings, in short, anything that might cause carnal desire; go to no banquets, and don't run about the streets from house to house to gossip; if
music is desired, listen to hymns. That pretty well sums up current opinion
on the negative side. For actual recreation Vives would allow the maid and
her companions, virgins like herself, innocent games of ball in gardens and
orchards far from the sight of men, and other pastimes of similar nature.
But she should spend most of her leisure time in holy reading and conversation, no talk even of dancing, feasting, or pleasures, lest she be moved with
some false color of delight. Even when alone in her chamber our maid must
not be frivolous and idle. As a rule, let her work, read, and pray.

Dancing and music, though under deep suspicion with the moralists,
were open to some debate. Vives records his unqualified disapproval of
the dances of the day, particularly the vault. "What good doth all that
dancing of young women holden up on men's arms, that they may hop the

higher?" he asks and complains that girls can dance all night but are unable to walk to the next church. To this serious-minded man it was perhaps the importance given by women to dancing that was most objectionable. "It is a world to see," he continues, "how demurely & sadly some sit, beholding them that dance and what gesture, pase, and moving of the body, & with what sober footings some of them dance. Where in also a man may spie a gret part of their folly, that go about to handle such a foolish thing so sadly: neither see them selves have a matter in hand without any wisedome, neither any thing worthie." Bouchet, though he too advises staying in the house as much as possible to guard against temptation, yet more realistically adds, if a girl must go to a wedding or feast, let her dance an honest dance. More wholeheartedly an English physician, John Jones, on the authority of Sir Thomas Elyot, Erasmus and others, recommends among sports and pastimes "comely dancing for preserving the healthy spirits as also for strengthening the sound bodie, using only that kind of Musicke called Dorios, where neyther deformitie is practised, nor wantonnesse enticed, but rather these virtues (as sheweth Erasmus and Fuchsius) as prudence, modestie, sobrietie and policie in Bargenets, Pavons, Galiardes, Sturgions and Roundes only." Then, surprisingly enough for the reader of many renaissance treatises on women, he concludes, "Other exercises, as walking, running easily at Bace, at grinstole ball, boules, riding on horseback, wagon, chariot, coach etc. I wil omitte, partlye bycause it may be gathered, which according to everye degree be honest, meane, and moderate," the only time surely when such physical exercises are even mentioned in connection with women.

Music, though admittedly one of the liberal arts, fell under the disapproval of most as another inflamer of passions and excuse for public display of beauty and skill. Under the name of virtue, they said, it carries grave and important evils, especially at banquets, where rich food has already loosened the mind. Some would not allow the girl to be trained to play or sing at all, even though they granted that most people thought it an ornament and grace to a girl of gentle birth to master both arts. Others would have her taught but only for private use as recreation and consolation in times of sorrow, trouble, and anxiety, or as a pastime in vacant hours if she has nothing better to do. Then she will play or sing at the proper time and place, and always modestly and not to be heard. Or rarely, admitting the pressure of custom, one may be found to advise that when this girl of gentle birth must sing in public she will sing chaste songs in a low voice and without oblique looks, but with reverence and shame in her face.[18]

It is obvious that with increasing opportunity and variety of activity allowed the older girl, increasing responsibility would fall upon the mother to guard her daughter from all possible sources of contamination. Ideally she would keep her by her side, and supervise every part of her life. Since that might be impossible, especially for a mother of high rank, she would take great pains in the choice of a wise and trustworthy woman to supplement her care. Undesirable company would be the prime concern: first of all men, not only strangers and outsiders but even close relatives in the shape of young men; then women, "young gossips who under coverture of gentilitie, gallant attire, and costly ornaments, or (whiche is most infectious) under fained Religion and honestie doe hide corrupte and wicked maners," and, also, strange women who seek opportunity to speak to girls under pretext of sewing, work, and other such things. In such an important matter as a girl's chastity, says Antoniano, some suspicion of neighbors and servants is advisable, not with rash judgment or in condemnation of anyone, but to show the caution that belongs to elders who know how great is the simplicity and fragility of that sex, and how clever are the deceits of plotters. House servants presented a serious problem, and were to be carefully chosen for seriousness and plainness, but, even at the best, were to have little to do with the daughters of the house, men servants nothing at all.[19]

Thus the girl in her father's house would grow to marriageable age, habituated to modest and discreet behavior, in which pert looks, roving eyes, loud laughing and babbling, were abhorrent. Still happy and pleasant she would have learned to show a modest and shy face, to keep her eyes down, her whole body composed, to speak only when questioned and then to reply humbly and briefly. Desiring only to please God and her parents, she would have learned the lesson of complete obedience and subdued all wayward and rebellious impulses, and in her own heart would hold virginity her chief jewel until time to surrender it to a husband as the most precious gift she could bring to him. As the chief means to preserve her from temptation she would prize industry and seek to improve her skill in household arts. Temperate in all things, she would abstain from wine and rich and delicate foods, and likewise elaborate clothing, as things that undermine health, increase vanity, and incite passions dangerous to chastity. All the more to guard her chastity she would not desire to run abroad, even greatly to go to church, but would prefer the seclusion of her home and her mother's protecting presence. Not to be unfurnished within she would have read, and pondered well, holy books, works containing examples of good women, and whatever else might teach her how to be truly virtuous. Her answers, then, when her elders questioned her, might be prudent and gain her praise, though always she would be far off from any desire to display what she knew. Always she would remember that for a woman, and a woman of rank, it is not enough to be merely virtuous, but the height of perfection must be her aim.

Thus accoutered and shaped to the pattern of the wife all men desire, she may hope, if at moments she allows herself to glance at the future, for a husband, young, handsome, rich, healthy, and good, such a one as her parents in their love and wisdom will provide for her. If she is wholly orthodox, of course, she will avoid such straying thoughts. It is not becoming to her even to desire marriage, Vives sternly warns her, and how much less to show her longing. At most he would allow her to pray for such a husband as will not hinder virtuous living. What Vives, along with all advisers, thought about the necessity of the maid's entire submission to her parents in the choice of a husband has already been surveyed. Obedience, her greatest virtue next to chastity, took care of that. Vives, however, was, if anything, more concerned over what he seemed to consider a peculiarly contemporary attitude. "Now afore I make an end of this booke," he wrote, "I will answere unto a mad and frantike opinion, which both maids and wives have, and all the common people in generall, that thinke it expedient for maids, that are come to lawfull age of marriage, to bee seene oft abroad amonge people, goodly and jukedly arrayed, and to keepe company & communication with men, to be eloquent in speech, and cunning in dansing and singing: yea and to love him aforehand, whome they intende to marry: for so they saye, they shall the more lightly meete with a bargaine." Point by point he answered, as he had already, these foolish arguments of a too easily misled sex.

If a girl cannot marry without infecting her mind and endangering chastity, she had better not marry. How can she avoid danger, if not disaster and a tarnished reputation, if she recklessly seeks the company of men abroad, instead of preserving the only two things a man seeking a wife cares about, a chaste body and good fame by staying at home? Men will think she can hardly keep her purity if they meet her in every corner. She will be more attractive if heard about than seen. As for the lure of rich clothing, if it is used to conceal faults, hatred will be the result when the truth is known, and besides, rather than an attraction it may prove a deterrent. He could name various maids in England and Spain who could never get married because men were put off by their costly apparel, afraid of their extravagance. Eloquence in a maid and all her other arts of pleasing men in company are no such commendations as they seem, for though men will praise her to her face for her merry talk, jolly dancing, pleasant play, and good manners, they do so only because they wish to have her at their pleasure, none will want such for a wife. "But and the foolishe maides could heare what men speake afterwardes among themselves one unto an other, without dissimulation: then should they know in deed how hartely they praised them, and liked them: they should understand then, that when the men called them mery conceited, they ment they were bablers, and chatters: and when they called them lustie tyres, they ment they were light minded: and where they called them welnurtured, they ment they were wanton." Some few may marry by such behavior but most do not. And those who do need not look for a good life with a husband got by wiles and crafts.

As for love before marriage, the whole idea is abhorrent to Vives. He has heard that in England young men have given up women they were seeking in marriage merely because the women said they could not love them. Such men cannot even see how unchaste these women are. Should a woman love her husband because she is used to his love before marriage, instead of because he is united to her by God's laws? Such is the way of drabs and harlots. These, however, are to be taken as incredible exceptions. The girl that shows love for the young man she is to marry may rather look for suspicion on his part, that she is as ready to show anyone else the same, having no more reason to love him than others. All the love that should be kept in marriage is spent before. There is a common saying that they that marry for love shall lead their life in sorrow; love will not last that is not nourished with honest loving. Therefore, Vives concludes, it is not expedient to make marriages by love beforehand.[20]

The fundamental pattern is the same from century to century, for all ranks. To go no farther back than Francesco Barberino, who began around 1290 to compose his regime for women, the first treatise of its kind, he claimed, though there had been many for men. He intended to write clearly, he said, in order that every woman might take it to heart, and he meant every woman, for he addressed the daughters of each rank in turn, emperors or kings, dukes and other lords, gentlemen of arms, judges, doctors of repute, other gentlemen, through the lower ranks of better-to-do farmers and the like, to the poor farmer, artificer, and laborer. Advice grows shorter as he descends because he can simply counsel those of lower station to adapt to their own needs what he has said for their betters, and he finally gives up differentiation when he reaches the subject of the age of readiness for marriage, his observations, warnings, and general instructions being easily applied by each to her rank. Little adaptation would seem to have been necessary, for the plight of the girl waiting for marriage, from twelve onward Barberino set the age, could not have varied much with rank if the proper behavior of a girl at all times was observed—modest, unassuming, self-effacing, shrinking from drawing attention to herself by the slightest flutter of an eyelid, shift of foot, or movement of a finger, the rules are familiar. Barberino tried to show some differences based on rank, but in effect, as he admitted in summing up, the rules apply only more strictly and narrowly to the highest born because faults appear worse and the penalty is more severe as rank rises. Other writers, most notably Vives, except for some suggestion of wealth in the size of the establishment, the number of servants employed, the richness of food or clothing that might be had if wanted, the time that might be spent in idleness instead of industry, the banquets and dances that might be attended, give no hint that there may be any difference in training between girls of high parentage and low. In fact all these luxuries that belong by right to the highborn are specifically ruled out for their daughters.[21]

For what, then, as Guazzo asked, is the lady to be honored, that is, set above the rest of womankind? Men engage in arms and letters to win renown; women for all practical purposes are shut out from such roads to fame. His answer is that the two virtues of chastity and good management of the household, well joined, are enough to enable a woman truly to be called honored. A peasant, however, may have both; how is one to be more honored than the other by such marks? It was the old stumbling block to accepting the morally desirable definition of nobility as based not on birth but on virtue. Well, in the first place, Guazzo explained, "magnanimous and gentle," dearly loved titles, can be applied to everything possessed by the few, to the common human virtues seen in the high but not, to the same extent, seen in the low. In fact virtue is not the same in all cases, but is greater as it shows in greater contrast. Thus more esteem is due to the chastity of a beautiful young woman than to the chastity of an old and ugly woman, because the one is tempted and the other is not. So for the noble woman, whose chastity is so much the more worthy and glorious as she is more subject to the peril of dishonor than the peasant, through the delicacy of her complexion, the quality of her food, her inability to endure fatigue, and other circumstances, where the peasant is more robust, more enduring of toil, and less fed on foods that raise lascivious thoughts. Accomplishment in arms or letters, and some women have been seen even to excel men in such unwonted exercises, can add to a woman's honor, but without chastity there is no honor possible for her, and with it there is honor, though all else be lacking. Therefore let fathers prefer to have their daughters unlearned and chaste, even ugly and chaste, rather than preeminent in beauty, and famous for deeds more appropriate to men. All of which amounts again to saying that there is at bottom no real difference between the ends for which girls of gentle birth and their lowlier sisters are trained—so far as renaissance theory goes. If one is seeking, therefore, for some mark by which to distinguish the women of the upper classes from the women of the lower, it is clearly not to be found in the generally recommended training of the girl born even to the highest rank.[22]

CHAPTER FOUR : *Studies*

However narrow the aims set for the training of a girl, still the renaissance could not fail to raise the question of formal studies as a part of that training—it would not have been the renaissance if it had failed. But the free, bright world into which we step when it is a question of education for boys vanishes on consideration of girls, and we move in an atmosphere of doubt, timidity, fear, and niggardly concession. Vergerius, one of the first of renaissance schoolmasters, thus defines the studies prescribed for the sons of noblemen: "We call those studies *liberal* which are worthy of a free man; those studies by which we attain and practice virtue and wisdom; that education which calls forth, trains and develops those highest gifts of body and of mind which ennoble men, and which are rightly judged to rank next in dignity to virtue only." Then he goes on to list the chief subjects that may be included under the name of liberal studies. He gives the first place to history for its attractiveness and its utility, of equal appeal to the scholar and the statesman; next comes moral philosophy, the purpose of which is to teach men the secret of true freedom; then eloquence, by which the truths of history and philosophy are set forth in such a way as to bring conviction to differing minds, and to which grammar, logic, and rhetoric are of prime importance; then poetry which belongs chiefly to leisure, and music as a healthy recreation for the moral and spiritual nature; arithmetic and geometry, weighty because they possess a peculiar element of certainty; astronomy, that lifts us into the clear calm of the upper air; and finally natural science, delightful and profitable to youth. Freedom, expansion of powers, recreation, and delight are the lures to tempt boys to arduous effort in mastery of the product of the world's best minds.[1]

What do we find when we look at renaissance ideas on liberal education for girls? We meet at once with difficulty in determining any single general plan that can be labeled the renaissance ideal of education for girls, first of all because material is scanty and generalization therefore difficult, and secondly because the available schemes range all the way from negation to something comparable to what was generally agreed upon for boys. The best that can be done seems to be to show the extremes, and then settle on the middle ground as probably nearest to anything that can be called a general ideal for girls. Opinion was still pretty much in the state recorded by this bit of dialogue. The inquiring father, having listened to arguments for education, concludes, "I perceive now plainly, that the sonnes are to be instructed very carefully, but in the meantime, what shal become of the daughters?" His informant replies, "Jesus Syrach saith: If thou have daughters, keepe their bodies, and shew not a cheerful countenance towards them. Marrie thy daughter, and so shalt thou performe a weightie matter: but give her to a man of understanding." We will begin with the attitude nearest to this, at the bottom of the scale.[2]

As we have seen in the preceding chapter, the training of the girl for her destined occupation of marriage was aimed at suppressing all individuality, fostering both fear of offense and complete dependence upon the will of her husband for all her comforts, and contentedness to live within the orbit of the house furnished her, occupying herself only with domestic tasks. Clearly nothing in the description of liberal studies for boys suits such aims, but rather the opposite effect is to be looked for. There is a passage from Bruto which so well shows the usual grounds given for denying altogether a liberal education to women that it is worth reproducing at length. The quotation is taken from Salter's translation.

"I am therefore of this advise, that it not mete nor convenient for a Maiden to be taught or trayned up in learnyng of humaine artes, in whome a vertuous demeanour & honest behaviour, would be a more sightlier ornament, then the light or vaine glorie of learnyng, for in learnyng and studiyng of the artes there are twoo thynges finallie proposed unto us, that is recreation and profitte, touchyng profitte, that is not to bee looked for, at the handes of her that is geven us for a companion in our labours, but rather every woman ought wholelie to be active and diligent about the governement of her housholde and familie, and touchyng recreation by learnyng that cannot bee graunted her, without greate daunger and offence to the beautie and brightnesse of her mynde; seying then that the governement of estates and publike weales are not committed into the handes of women, neyther that it is lawfull or convenient for them to wright lawes, by whiche men should bee ruled and governed, as Draco, Licurgus, and Numa Pompilius did, neither as professours of Science and facultie, to teache in Schooles the wisedome of Lawes and Philosophie, and seeing also that in such studies, as yeldeth recreation and pleasure, there is no lesse daunger, that they will as well learne to be subtile and shamelesse Lovers, as connyng and skilfull writers, of Ditties, Sonnettes, Epigrames, and Ballades, let them be restrained to the care and governement of a familie, and teache them to bee envious in following those, that by true vertue have made little accoumpt of those, that to the prejudice of their good names, have beene desirous to bee reputed Diotimes, Aspaties, Sapphoes, and Corinnes. For suche as compare the small profit of learnynge with the greate hurt and domage that commeth to them by the same shall soon perceive (although that they remaine obstinate therein) how far more convenient the Distaffe, and Spindle,

Nedle and Thimble were for them with a good and honest reputation, then the skill of well using a penne or wrighting a loftie vearce with diffame and dishonour, if in the same there be more erudition then vertue."

There is a noticeable difference here in the ground for objection between writers interested in general depreciation of the worth of women and those concerned with their bringing up. Bruto does not base his argument on the alleged incapacity for learning, so familiar in the diatribes, but on the unsuitability of such learning to the vocation ordained for women. Incapacity would have been an unsafe argument against the free pursuit of liberal studies, especially in Italy where so many women were holding courts, writing, and even disputing in public debates. This state of affairs he reveals when he rebukes parents for their indiscretion in believing that moral and natural philosophy are necessary for their young daughters, and that honor comes to them for being thought well learned, since, on the contrary, such studies bring knowledge of the evils that belong to human life and of our own inclination to vice, a knowledge not at all requisite in young women. No wise father will ever take example from Sappho, or hold it safe that his tender daughters of fragile nature display themselves boldly in theaters and public spectacles to contend for glory and pre-eminence in letters. For women, Bruto concludes, fame and honor are not dependent upon learning; history both ancient and modern is full of the noble deeds done by rare and excellent ladies famous for their courage and chastity and without learning. We meet elsewhere with further criticism of current practice. Girls and boys, warned Antoniano, should not be taught together under the same masters the languages, speaking, and writing poetry. What utility can follow for public good or the good of little girls? Since the feminine sex is vain by nature it will become more proud and desire to be master in the house, against St. Paul's precepts. Also there is danger in having girls of rare gifts and accomplishment introduced to learned men, as parents are fond of doing, because occasion is offered for forming attachments, especially by means of beautiful compositions. Conformity of minds and studies softens minds and nourishes hidden flames. Hence the good father of a family should be content that his daughter knows how to say the office of the Holy Virgin and read the lives of saints and some spiritual books, and for the rest, to attend to spinning and sewing and other womanly exercises praised in the Scriptures. Commonly speaking, it is better for women to content themselves with the duties of their sex and leave the men to theirs, since presumably they have all they can manage in attaining the skill necessary to run their households well. Besides, with learning they are sure to become more talkative, hence less careful of honor, which is better preserved by silence than by words, and also more apt in deceit. Opposition to educating girls on the same lines as boys was thus based on occupational grounds. All of which is in accord with renaissance belief in the freedom conferred by studies; a mind liberally trained is not easily subdued to the will of another, or shut within a narrow round of interests. Open the door of the cage and the bird is almost certain to fly out.[3]

Further evidence of the deep distrust of learning in women is furnished by women themselves in their apologies for breaking into fields held to belong so exclusively to men. Mrs. Dorothy Leigh bears witness to this fear. She wrote her little book of advice to her three sons first of all, she says, because of her motherly love for them that made her forget herself, and if one sentence helps them she does not care what others may think. "Neither must you, my sonnes," she feels it necessary to add, "when you come to bee of judgement, blame mee for writing to you, since Nature telleth me, that I cannot long bee heere to speake unto you, and this my minde will continue long after me in writing." Her second reason for writing is that she hopes to inspire them to write for their children: "For where I saw the great mercy of God toward you, in making you men, and placing you amongst the wise: where you may learne the true written Word of God, which is the pathway of all happinesse, and which will bring you to the chiefe Citie new Jerusalem: and the seven liberall Sciences, whereby you shall have at least a superficiall sight in all things: I thought it fit to give you good example, and by writing to intreate you, that when it shall please God to give both vertue and grace with your learning, hee having made you men, that you may write & speake the Word of God, without offending any, that then you would remember to write a booke unto your children of the right and true way to happiness which may remaine with them and theirs forever." Then she sets down a third reason—"to encourage women (who, I feare, will blush at my boldnesse) not to be ashamed to shew their infirmities, but to give men the first and chiefe place: yet let us labour to come in the second."

Madeleine Des Roches also felt it necessary to defend herself, but in particular against the opposition of women, who, as always in matters of common belief, share with men the prejudices of the times even against themselves. She addresses the prefatory letter of her first works to ladies, to explain that she is publishing her compositions to show her friendship for them. She hopes they will not be so uncharitable as to advise that the great ornament of women is silence, which can cover faults of tongue and understanding, because it is her opinion that though silence can prevent shame it cannot increase honor. Only speech separates us from beasts. She, like Dorothy Leigh, urges women to employ their pens in learned works, particularly in defense of themselves against their accusers.

In other terms but to the same effect, Margaret Tyler, having been urged to translate a romance from the Spanish, makes this same need for defense her apology. If men dedicate their works to women, she reasons, then women may read them, and so discourse upon them, and then why not undertake a translation, "being a matter of more heede then of deep invention or exquisite learning." "Whatsomever the truth is, whether that women may not at al discourse in learning, for men lay in their claim to be sole possessioners of knowledge, or whether they may in som maner that is by limitation or appointment in some kinde of learning, my perswasion hath been thus, that it is all one for a woman to pen a story, as for a man to addresse his story to a woman."[4]

Many voices, both men's and women's, were raised against this distrust of liberal education for women, and in behalf of even the necessity of such learning. The most notable came from the little group of men in England at the beginning of the sixteenth century, Sir Thomas More's circle, who believed in women and who worked for their liberation by precept and practice. Learning and morals go together, insisted Sir Thomas, in a letter to Mr. Gunnel, the tutor of his daughters, "Nor do I think that it affects the harvest, that a man or woman has sown the seed. If they are worthy of being ranked with the human race, if they are distinguished by reason from beasts; that learning, by which the reason is cultivated, is equally suitable to both. Both of them, if the seed of good principles be sown in them, equally produce the germs of virtue. But if the female soil be in its nature stubborn, and more productive of weeds than fruits, it ought, in my opinion, to be more diligently cultivated with learning and good instruction, to correct by industry the defects of nature. These were the opinions of the most wise and virtuous men of antiquity. To omit others, I shall only mention the venerable names of Jerome and Augustine, who not only exhorted the most illustrious matrons the most admired virgins to apply themselves to learning, but also assisted their progress, by diligently explaining to them the most abstruse parts of the scriptures; and wrote to young women letters so full of erudition as to be barely intelligible to many men who profess themselves extremely erudite. My dear Gunnel, make my daughters acquainted with the works of these excellent men."[5] More and Vives were agreed on this point. It is a foolish idea, wrote Vives, that learning will increase evil, when, on the contrary, precepts for living and good examples are keepers of chastity and purity. If a woman does evil in spite of these, what would she be with no learning at all? A mind set upon learning will abhor lust and light pleasures. For examples, he adds, consider the daughters of Sir Thomas More, Margaret, Elizabeth, and Cecilia, all learned women, and good at the same time.[6]

Another witness, both to the excellence of the training and accomplishment of More's daughters and to enthusiasm for the extension of the new learning to women as well as men, was Richard Hyrde, a young friend and disciple of More. Hyrde wrote a preface to Margaret's translation of Erasmus' little treatise on the Lord's Prayer, in which he runs over the chief arguments for the education of women, and ends with a eulogy of Margaret. He protests against the common practice of trying to condemn Greek and

Latin literature on the score of its craft and eloquence, which is to turn the chief virtues of these tongues into vices. As for the evil effect on women, which most men argue is exclusively theirs because of their frailty, the accusers either don't care what they say or are jealous, for women are as constant and discreet as men, "if one looks at them with an even eye." It is men that trespass in the pursuit of women, not women in the pursuit of men, and women, not men, that are ashamed if caught, and if learning causes evil then men must sin more than women because they are freer, meet more occasions, and are less restrained. Latin and Greek works are as little hurtful as English and French, which women read if they will, and are far better for it. A current charge that with Greek and Latin women would talk more boldly with priests and friars, Hyrde felt too frivolous to answer, except with the jest, reminiscent of More's free tongue, that there is no better way to keep a wife safe from them than to teach her the old tongues because little do priests and friars—that is the worst of them—know of Greek and Latin, and most of them fly from the sound as fast as from beggars. Margaret herself, he says, is living proof of what good learning does when surely rooted, for in her conversation, way of life, and serious bearing, she furnishes an example of prudent, humble, and wifely behavior, and of every Christian virtue, "with whiche she hath with Goddes helpe endevoured her selfe no lesse to garnisshe her soul, than it hath lyked his goodnesse with lovely beauty and comelynesse to garnysshe and sette out her body." Great advantages have, beyond doubt, come to her. Her husband's delight in her learning, and the comfort and pleasure they both enjoy from the sharing of it, is a delight no unlearned couple can either take together or imagine.

How deeply this Richard Hyrde felt on the subject is illustrated again in the prefatory letter that he wrote for his own translation of Vives' *Instruction of a Christian Woman*. He wished, he said, that either women in every country knew Latin or the book were translated into every tongue. He had to wonder again, as often before, at the unreasonableness of men who never cease to complain of women's faults and yet, having everything in their hands, do little to bring women up more successfully, and even purposely keep them from the learning that might help them to better themselves.[7]

Such protests and arguments were made elsewhere than in England, but we will content ourselves here with one more, by Charlotte de Brachart, who in livelier fashion echoes Hyrde's protests, and knows exactly how to account for the absurdity in men that mystifies him. Astonishment takes her, she says, at the perversity of a large part of the world in wishing to forbid the attainment of virtue to those who, by laborious study, wish to make themselves capable of it. How can learning, if it has nothing evil in itself, produce evil effects in a soul happily born, or, in a soul inclined to evil, will it not more often lessen rather than augment its malignity? It is a popular error to think that letters lead human minds to evil designs, or render their execution easier. The fact is, she continues, men wish to claim learning as peculiar to themselves and forbid it to the sex they call fragile. Women ought to keep their old simplicity, they say, not knowing that simplicity belongs in the heart and conscience and not in the mind. It must be pure envy on the part of men, who see how, with only a little pains, women surpass them in reasoning capacity, prudence, control of the passions, and would surpass them in solid judgment and capacity for all great and high enterprises if they were not tyrannically deprived of all means of practising the sciences. "There," she finishes, "that's how I look at it, in the firm belief that these gentlemen would like to see us plain imbeciles so that we could serve as shadows to set off better their fine wits."[8]

In the renaissance, the most thoughtful writers on the subject, accepting the belief of the Greeks that morality needs knowledge to develop and fortify the good disposition born in us, saw no difference between men and women in disposition, or in capacity for instruction, and prescribed liberal studies for girls as well as boys, though with reservations.

The second great argument against education of women, that it would interfere in various ways with the duties of marriage, also met vigorous denial. Madeleine Des Roches, herself a wife and mother, saw no incompatibility, but, rather, definite advantages, which she runs over briefly: knowledge of Xenophon's *Economics* is as useful to women in the management of a home as to men in their affairs; the Bible teaches wives how to obey husbands in the proper spirit; moral philosophy shows them how to guide themselves aright, how to value honor and to fear shame; some knowledge of law and medicine enables them to aid their families and neighbors; their own learning enables them to teach their children more easily the fear of God, and of father and mother; true learning teaches humility, which will render them less presumptuous toward their husbands, for it is ignorance that makes wives and mothers boast that they know more than they do, and think their daughters should know only what will serve for love and avarice; and last of all, if widowhood is their lot their learning will help them to live chastely without husbands, like Laura Terracina and many other modern examples.[9]

Sir Thomas Elyot in his urbane *Defence of Good Women* puts into the mouth of Zenobia, now a prisoner, arguments for not marrying off a girl until she has time to learn what will aid her in marriage and widowhood, when she will carry on her husband's work. Her father kept her at her studies, she is made to say, until she was twenty, and between sixteen and twenty she learned such lessons as she would never have known had she married earlier: Philosophy taught her prudence; constancy; justice, which means honoring husbands next after God by due obedience, and refraining from doing anything unseemly; fortitude, which keeps a woman constant in resisting passions and in sustaining afflictions patiently; and temperance, which is woman's chief virtue, teaching her to use a just moderation in her words and deeds, so that she knows when to speak and when to be silent, when to keep herself occupied and when to be merry. All this, she learned, is to be wisely measured to the will of her husband, unless he is bent on what she must seriously condemn, and then she should seem rather to give him wise counsel than to appear disobedient or stubborn. The profit of her learning showed in all things. During her husband's lifetime she was able to avoid what displeased him and to do what delighted him. In hunting and other pastimes her learning taught her such circumspection that no suspicion of dissolute appetite fell on her, and yet never was her learning held in derision by any honest man. After her husband's death she found her learning a great treasure in governing the realm. With enemies on all sides she determined to act quickly and endure patiently the outcome. To keep the name of woman from contempt she avoided womanish behavior. She sat among her nobles and counselors, heard others speak first and then gave her opinion in accord with good sense. She chose honest servants. She went often among the people with her children, reminding them of the liberty and honor they had had under her husband, and exhorting them to fidelity. She visited the whole realm, rebuilt fortresses, made munitions, and caused good laws to be published and executed. And she saw her kingdom increase through her good government. Now she rules her passions as the Romans rule her. "To the which wisedome and policie," she concludes, "I attained by the study of noble philosophy."[10]

It was also argued that prospects for marriage improved with increase of learning, even in the case of girls of lower parentage. An Englishman goes especially into this aspect of the question. If parents are of high birth and position and their daughters show promise, a careful education may bring about many commendable results. Young maidens well trained are soon sought in honorable matches because their qualities will correspond to their state, and their wisdom promises help in procuring the common good of the house, not to speak of "what frute the common weale may reape, by such witts so worthily advaunced." Likewise, even though parents may be of inferior birth, if their daughters have natural ability and from the very first reveal that some singular quality is likely to ensue from their training, hope may grow great that the choice of some great match may fall on such maidens so excellently qualified. This hope may fail because great personages do not always have such good judgment, nor do young maidens always have such good fortune, but the maidens remain the gainers in that they have the qualities to comfort their mediocrity, and the great ones take the losses for not having had the judgment to set forth their nobility.[11]

This Englishman was Richard Mulcaster, the first head of the Merchant Taylors School of London. In 1581 appeared his *Positions*, an examination into the underlying principles of education. It seems worth while to present here his ideas on education for women, partly because he gives some idea of where opinion moved during the century, and also because as a pedagogue (or educator if you please) he gives a more systematic analysis of the question. He was aware that people would think it odd, if not reprehensible, that in a book devoted to the education of boys he should stoop to consider girls, but since he began with the first elementary school where little girls were trained, he does not see, he says, how he could seem not to see them, and he spends one chapter out of forty-five on the particular questions raised by girls. He would, however, make it plain that though he considers both it is with a difference. Boys must come first because the male is naturally more worthy and more employed in public affairs, and education must therefore be planned first for their use. For girls studies must always be merely accessory, but since they are mortal and reasonable creatures and destined to be the mates and sometimes by law the mistresses of men, they should share in education that comes from books, that they may play their parts well. He saw four reasons for setting young girls to learning. First, it is the custom to allow them to learn in England where they are admitted to elementary schools though not, by custom, to grammar schools or the universities; private opinion, therefore, should not be opposed. Second, duty commands men to see them well brought up, if soundness of mind and body is to be sought in the mothers of their children. Third, they have the natural ability to profit by learning, and show themselves capable of achieving excellence in studies without neglecting their duties in marriage, indeed, rather to the adornment of those offices. Fourth, the excellent results in women who have been well trained shows that they deserve the best training, as Queen Elizabeth and many English gentlewomen demonstrate.

The limitations on the training of women will be set by their occupations. The young maiden destined for marriage will be trained in obedience to her husband and in the other qualities required; if making a living is in point, then she must be taught a trade; if her birth or position call for capacity to adorn and honor it, then she is to have the best education suited to her; "Princely maidens above all," he concludes, "bycause occasion of their height standes in neede of such giftes, both to honour themselves, and to discharge the duetie, which the countries, committed to their hands, do daily call for, and besides what matche is more honorable, then when desert for rare qualities, doth joine it selfe, with highnesse in degree? . . . The greater borne Ladyes and gentlewymen, as they are to enjoy the benefit of this education most, so they have best meanes to prosecute it best, being neither restrained in wealth, but to have the best teachers, and greatest helpes: neither abridged in time but to ply all at full." Certainly leisure for study and the means to pay for books and teachers were two requirements that would automatically exclude from consideration those who were poor or pressed by household affairs.

What little opinion was expressed on the subject agreed on denying education to women of low rank as out of keeping with their everyday concerns, or severely limiting it to their limited leisure. Considerable light on the whole matter is thrown by a letter D'Aubigné wrote to his daughters at the end of the sixteenth century. He evidently had a lively set who were pushing him harder than was quite comfortable. He concedes that he doesn't blame their desire to study with their brothers, and he doesn't want to discourage them, but at the same time he doesn't really want to encourage them. For he has observed that almost always such learning is useless to girls of middle rank like theirs, and often proves harmful by so puffing up the heart that scorn of housekeeping and of poverty results. The only women he would wish to encourage to undergo the labor of learning are princesses, who are obliged by their rank to assume the care, knowledge, adequacy, deeds, and authority of men. In them knowledge can succeed, as in Queen Elizabeth. But like the indulgent father that he is, he announces that their brother is bringing them his abridgement of logic, which he charges them to use only among themselves and not on persons who are their companions and superiors. They had better conceal the art and its terms, and never use such arguments on their husbands, when they get them—far too dangerous. He must, however, have undone all his cautions, for he spends most of the space in this long letter describing in glowing terms the accomplishments of several learned ladies of the century, beginning with Marguerite of Navarre and ending with his grandmother, whose copy of Basil annotated in her own hand is his cherished possession. Evidently he does not, as some did, place restrictions on the studies suitable for queens and princesses.[12]

Such are the grounds on which men who favored some sort of liberal education for women of the upper classes argued against the general position taken by Bruto, that learning would be a detriment to such women, that it would threaten moral degeneration and cultivate scorn of the humble duties to which they were born, for the queen, no less than the mechanic's wife, owed obedience to her husband. When it comes to prescribing studies for women, however, there is general agreement with Bruto that the desired effects are sound moral habits and the prudence needed to perform worthily their duties in the vocation of marriage.

Bruto himself felt compelled to yield a point or two for the girl nobly born. Much as he would have liked to forbid teaching girls to read, he had to admit that, though the evil day might be postponed, no one could prevent a girl from learning to read for herself, and therefore control must be instituted over the books she reads to see that they are chaste, clean, and Christian. Since everything has been translated, let her read, beside the Holy Scriptures, Plutarch on famous women of ancient times, Boccaccio on those of his own times, and others on those of today, books that are pro-

vided with pleasing and beautiful pictures of virtuous and pious women
which can influence the minds of tender and delicate girls; also the Christian poets, Prudentius, Prosperus, Giuvencus, and many others, which she
will understand the better for not reading the loves of Ovid, Catullus,
Propertius, Tibullus, Vergil's *Dido and Aeneas*, and Homer's adulteries
and loves of gods and men; and such philosophers as Zeno and Chrysippus,
who will teach her well enough, he adds ironically, to defend the doctrines
of Epicurus too, if parents are so ambitious as to want to see their daughter
disputing in the schools. Plato's *Symposium* he particularly forbids. Finally
she will be kept by a wise father from all amorous verses, fables, and tales
like Boccaccio's, "which are read and regarded by us more for their beauty
of style and speaking, and for beautiful meter and harmony of words, well
selected, noble, and significant, then for their matter." In these recommendations Bruto has stuck consistently to his intent, that girls shall read
only what is chaste, clean, and Christian, and read it in their native tongue.
The great ancient classics are banned except for certain philosophers.
Reading for edification solely is the aim.

There is no breadth in Bruto's list and none could be expected. How do
studies for women fare at the hands of those who may be expected to be
more liberal? The range varies. Bouchet praised women as creatures to be
honored equally with men and advocated their right to read and even
present the results of their reading in books. He, however, would strictly
confine their reading to moral books in the vernacular. No one could then
reasonably object to such reading, he argued, for what difference is there
whether one hears or reads a sermon or exhortation. This may be labeled
the minimum program, a very low minimum, apparently, though Bouchet
does not specify what goods books he would include. Is it even lower than
Bruto's? Bouchet goes on to exclude the Holy Scriptures because certain
passages are dangerous to women and simple, unlettered men, who read
according to the letter. He had published some years before a little manual
of the doctrine necessary to fight the vices and come ultimately to salvation,
in order to divert women and girls, he said, from further reading of the translation into French of the Old and New Testaments. With his restriction of
reading to the vernacular Bouchet raises the highly controversial point of
the learned languages. The acquirement of Latin and Greek was under
deepest suspicion in some circles, even in the case of boys, because they
opened the way to literature so superior to anything in the vernacular that
their "craft and eloquence," it was feared, would be all the more likely,
insidiously, to inflame women, weak and variable, to vice, and to destroy
that simplicity which should be the chief quality of a virtuous girl's mind.
There is nothing more hateful in a free girl, says one writer on the training
of virgins, than cunning, and a shrewd and acute mind, in which you see
deceit, inconstancy, and variability, and nothing that more alienates good

men than too much subtlety in a girl in place of candor and shame, the true signs of a prudent mind in women. Bouchet and Bruto would keep the evil in check by not teaching these dangerous tongues. Of course as the sixteenth century wore on translations of the old classics increased until the learning of Latin or Greek was no longer the sole key to liberal studies. But those who wanted a solid foundation for learning prescribed at least Latin and often Greek too.[13]

Bouchet and his kind, then, are only a degree above those who actually deny all training of the mind to women. What reading they allow has solely the purpose of religious and moral instruction of the simplest and most restricted sort. Bouchet even suggests it as a much better occupation, able to be carried out in the seclusion of their homes, than engaging in the vain and idle talk of men and women in mixed assemblies. For contrast we may set alongside him the recommendations of Leonardo Bruni written early in the fifteenth century in the form of a letter to Battista Malatesta. Here we will see the most liberal advice that has come to my notice, which can serve as a sort of measure for the rest. He is considering, he says, a student of high aspiration and ability who finds interest in every form of liberal study. But even he, on the threshold of building a program for such a student, has to stop to impose certain limitations because it is a woman's part that he is considering. Thus arithmetic, geometry, and astronomy in their more subtle and obscure reaches will not repay a woman the effort needed to master them. Rhetoric also, though more doubtfully, should be excluded because it is wholly inappropriate for women to study delivery, the proper place to throw out an arm or vigorously raise the voice, or any part of the craft of public adddress in debates or court trials or controversies of any sort, which belong to men.

What studies, then, shall he prescribe for a Christian woman of high gifts and aims? There is first of all the field of religion and morals, not only as presented in sacred literature—and whoever studies Augustine, Jerome, Lactantius, will learn a very great deal about matter and style—but as contained in the great works of Greek and Roman philosophers on the virtues, continence, temperance, modesty, justice, and courage, and their relation to happiness. The nature of happiness itself is discussed from three points of view by Epicurus, Zeno, and Aristotle. Such subjects furnish material for debates and literary exercises. To supplement or ornament these, other kinds of literature should be studied too, chief among them history, oratory, and poetry, which are all the more to be urged upon her because they also assist and illustrate the supreme studies of religion and our duties in the world. Last of all, to enable us to make effective use of what we know, we must add the power of expression, that is, proficiency in literary form.

Bruni then goes on to explain in considerable detail the advantages to be gained from these studies. He is the more explicit not only because he is supporting the appropriateness of women's undertaking serious accomplishment in these fields, but because he is defending classical learning itself from those who were still trying to suppress it as dangerous doctrine against the Christian faith. The result is the freest interpretation to be found that views the capacities and needs of women.

History comes first, he says, because it lets us understand our past, and thus gives foresight into the future, and furnishes us a store of examples of moral precepts. Livy, Tacitus, Sallust, and Caesar for his fine style, are to be prized. But then he must in this matter fit his argument a little more closely to women. They may read history with the greatest expectation of success because it is easy to learn, presenting no subtlety and raising no question, consisting wholly in the narration of the simplest matters of fact which, once grasped by the kind of mind under consideration, are fixed in the memory for good. Then the great orators of antiquity are to be studied, for they extoll virtues and condemn vices, praise well-doing and scorn evildoing, and they furnish us with instruments we may use in speaking and writing—a wealth of words, forcefulness in style, the ornaments of words and sentences which elevate speech. The poets, especially, should be read and known. The greatest men read poetry, among them Aristotle, who quotes so often the verses of Homer, Hesiod, Pindar, Euripides, and others, that he seems to have been no less studious of them than of the philosophers, Plato likewise, Cicero, Seneca, and no less Augustine, Jerome, Lactantius, and Boethius. For in the poets are to be found life and manners, nature, the principles and causes of generation, as it were, the seeds of all knowledge, and also great authority on account of their wise opinions and their beauty, splendor, and elegance. Since he is writing for a woman, he says, he will impose some restrictions. There are degrees of worth in the poets. If something less than modest comes from a comedy writer or some vice is too openly exposed by a satirist, he would wish this woman to pass him by. But the excellence of mind of which he has been speaking will be lacking unless it comes from a knowledge of a great variety of things. Therefore much must be seen and read, poets, philosophers, orators, historians, and all the rest. For thus comes such a fullness and sufficiency that we seem amply furnished, varied, and beautified, and never wanting or crude. Letters without knowledge of things are sterile and empty, and knowledge, however great, if it lacks the splendor added by letters seems obscure. Finally, it must be remembered that these great writers of the past are to be studied because they assist and illustrate the supreme studies, religion and morals.[14]

One is moving here in a world comparatively free. There is a minimum of reference to the limited sphere of action enjoyed by women, and only one slight suggestion that women's mental equipment may be less than men's, though it is not quite clear whether women have any more cause than his-

torians to bridle at Bruni's description of history. The same sort of restrictions in the reading of comedy and satire were recommended in the
case of boys, though the comparison may be of little point here because
Bruni seems to be considering more than the early training of girls. Even the
emphasis on religion and morals is not to be taken as too peculiarly an
adaptation to women, since studies for their own sake were never recommended even to men of the ruling class, being feared as deterrents to action.
Studies were praised, it is true, as good to occupy leisure time, particularly
for purposes of entering into social affairs—composition for elegant entertainment in courts and academies, material and style for conversation—
but this is the nearest to cultivation for their own sake that they are proposed, and then not with regard to the main business of life, soldiering or
ruling.

We have to go to the mid-sixteenth century for the next example of extended advice on education for women, contained in a book on the general
upbringing of women, not in a special treatise on education alone; Ludovico
Dolce also believes in studies for women and prescribes a substantial program. Knowledge of Latin is necessary, he thinks, for reading both old and
modern books; Greek he is not dogmatic about, but it may be left out as
putting too heavy a load on the shoulders of women. For ancient writers
he recommends Plato, Seneca, all the philosophers of good effect, Vergil,
the parts of Horace that are more chaste and moral, Cicero, and the historians. Among moderns he includes Petrarch for examples of the most
honest and chaste love in beautiful poetry, Dante for an excellent summary
of Christian philosophy, Bembo's works, Sannazzaro's *Arcadia*, Speroni's
moral and elegant dialogues, and Castiglione's *Courtier*, from which, in his
judgment, can be learned all the virtues and the good and chaste habits
which belong to a gentlewoman, and at the same time a way of speaking
which if not altogether Tuscan, at least is pure, distinguished, and without
any affectation. Here we have considerable breadth of studies; the aim, like
Bruni's, is especially the production of virtue, and Dolce narrows virtue to
the one virtue of chastity because he agrees with many others that
without chastity a woman lacks every other virtue. He does, however,
admit ornament as an end of studies for women as well as men, and he also
advises them as occupation for idle hours to avoid temptation.[15]

Bouchet, Bruni, and Dolce, however, because they are either too high or
too low, do not seem to represent the broadest theory of education for
women that may be taken to have won any general acceptance. We shall
have to go to England for the Spanish author that seems to have been most
influential in shaping opinion in England and on the continent for the
greater part of the sixteenth century. Vives wrote his *De Institutione Feminae Christianae* while still tutor to Queen Catherine and the Princess Mary,
and dedicated it to the Queen, saying that in it he had drawn a portrait of

her for the Princess to copy. This little book, first published in 1523, went through something over forty editions and translations before the end of the century. The English, Dutch, French, Germans, Italians, and Spanish knew it in their native tongue, coming fairly to realize Hyrde's wish. Hyrde dedicated his own translation to the Queen, and there relates how he took it to Sir Thomas More, whose advice he was accustomed to seek on all important matters, and found More already so enthusiastic about the book that he intended to take time to translate it himself because of its great value and also as a tribute to the Queen for the great interest she had in "the vertuous education of the womenkynde of this realme." Glad to find the work already done More took the translation to read it over and correct it. This English translation was reprinted half a dozen times during the century. So strong is More's and Hyrde's approval that we must be justified in looking on Vives as the spokesman for More's group on this subject.[16]

Vives' ideas on the content of education for girls are to be found chiefly in the two chapters devoted to the subject in *The Instruction of a Christian Woman*, but also in the briefer, parallel passages in *The Office of a Husband*, and in the outline of studies for girls prepared for the tutor of Princess Mary, and usually published with a similar list for boys made out for young Mountjoy. We are already familiar with the general principle by which studies are to be selected: "The studie of wisedome: which doth instruct their manners, and infourme their living, and teacheth them the way of good and holy life." Since women do not need all the sorts of knowledge that men do, to govern, and teach, and go abroad among men, Vives rules that grammar, logic, and history should be left to men. Eloquence he does not greatly care for, he says in his *Instruction for Women*, and women don't need it, but he will not condemn what Quintilian and Jerome so praise in Cornelia and Hortensia; and in supporting the capacity of women to learn he has cited the often-mentioned learned women of the past to praise them for their accomplishments, and among them Hortensia. "Hortensia," he says, "the daughter of Hortensius the oratour, did so resemble her Fathers eloquence, that she made an oration unto the judges of the citie for the women: which Oration the successors of that time did read, not onely as a commendation and praise of womens eloquence, but also to learn cunning of it as well of Cicero or Demosthenes orations . . . and in St. Jeromes time all holy Women were very well learned. Would God that now a days, many olde men were able to bee compared unto them in cunning," and he goes on to that tune at some length. But in his *Office of a Husband*, where perhaps he feels freer to say all that he thinks about learning in petticoats, he forgets all this praise of eloquence in women, and rather ill-naturedly snaps at the Cornelians, Mutians, and Hortensians who are praised for eloquence, not because they had learned an art and could speak of many things eloquently, but because they were able to say a few things purely, without pain and labor, from listening to their fathers. Nowadays, he adds as a final rap, women are called eloquent if they can entertain with a "vayne confabulation."

What about books then—which are to be read and which are not? Certainly not the romances that treat of war and love. Vives is explicit on the subject of romances, those farragoes of lies which tell how one man kills twenty men by himself, another thirty, another wounded with a hundred wounds and left dead rises up again and on the next day, cured and strong, overcomes two giants and goes off loaded with more gold, silver, and precious stones than a galley could carry. What madness to take pleasure in these books, in which moreover the only wit is a few words of wanton lust spoken to persuade a woman to yield to illicit love. He would have the laws put down such foul books and he furnishes a list to start with from Spain, France, and England. Boccaccio's tales and all like his are of course specifically forbidden. The Greek and Latin poets are not for women either. Ovid himself, said Vives, would not have one that intended to be chaste touch the wittiest and most learned—Calimachus, Anacreon, Sappho, Tibullus, and Propertius. And Ovid must be added to the list, so much more dangerous than Homer and Hesiod, whom Plato banished from his commonwealth and almost all these later lawgivers would banish from the world of women. Women should beware of all these books as of serpents and snakes, and if any delights in them and won't give them up and loathes good books she should be kept from all reading until she forgets how—"if it can be done." Poetry, fables, romances, and ribald songs are hurtful to both men and women, making them wily and crafty, stirring up covetousness, anger, envy, and beastly desire.

What the virtuous woman should read are good and holy books—the Old and New Testaments, the works of the Church Fathers, Jerome, Cyprian, Augustine, Ambrose, Hilary, Gregory—which will make her more virtuous, but not books on divinity, which will make her contentious. Women also have a great need of the moral part of philosophy that teaches how to subdue passions and quiet the tempest of their minds. Excellent for this are Plato, Cicero, Seneca, Plutarch, Valerius Maximus for examples, Aristotle, and Xenophon; and among moderns there are Paulus Vergerius and Francisco Filelfo. If a woman delights in verses, let her read the Christian poets—Prudentius, Ararus, Sedulius, Juvencus—either in Latin or the vulgar tongue.

Vives' list for the Princess Mary, is not strikingly different, adding some of Erasmus' works—his *Institution of a Prince* most appropriately, More's *Utopia*, and history, lightly drawn from Justinus, Florus, and Valerius Maximus. Cautious as all this winnowing shows Vives to be, he has to provide one further check to possible straying: let a woman always follow the advice of wise and learned men, never trust her own judgment. More generously Thomas Artus, prescribing also the sober, elevating kinds of knowledge, lightly dismisses doubts. "What if, in crossing the great garden of the Muses, they find something more delightful than this substantial fruit? Let them taste by way of experiment, but not linger. A well-born girl will always know how to discriminate."

This program of studies for the woman obviously of the leisure class looks decidedly meager compared to anything recommended for the gentleman—Vives' list for Mountjoy includes the Roman historians, poets, and agricultural writers, and the famous names among the Greek poets, historians, philosophers, and orators. But to do it justice, one must view it also against the whole background of the still recommended confinement of women to the home, and their training only for domestic duties. How much wider the door was that Vives opened for women, even by his narrow view of their need and use for learning, can be well measured by the enthusiasm of More and Hyrde for his *Instruction of the Christian Woman*. More went far beyond Vives in his attitude toward the education of his daughters, setting no such limits as Vives did, agreeing with their tutor that the lofty and aspiring genius of his dear Margaret ought not to be curbed. But he could welcome Vives' serious attitude toward women and his prescription of solid training in liberal studies, not in translation, for the advance that it marked in educational ideals for women.[17]

That these ideals worked like leaven through the century may be taken for granted if only from the constant reprinting and translation of Vives' book. If not directly influential with Ascham and Mulcaster, it must have helped to create the pedagogical atmosphere in which they lived and from which they drew similar ideas. Ascham himself does not treat of the education of women, though his well-known, laudatory account of the accomplishments of Queen Elizabeth and Lady Jane Grey clearly implies a liberal attitude toward classical studies for women, and as tutor to Elizabeth he must have applied the methods that he describes in the *Schoolmaster* for teaching Latin to gentlemen. Mulcaster includes no specific list of authors or studies for girls, no doubt leaving tutors to choose from his prescriptions for boys. He does, like everybody else, bar geometry, law, medicine, and divinity, except such parts as are needed for virtuous living. In his summing up of the equipment for a gentlewoman he is more explicit than elsewhere: "And is not a young gentlewoman, thinke you, thoroughly furnished, which can reade plainly and distinctly, write faire and swiftly, sing clear and sweetely, play wel and finely, understand and speake the learned languages, and those toungues also which the time most embraseth, with some Logicall help to chop, and some Rhetoricke to brave. Besides the matter which is gathered, while these tounges be either learned, or lookt on, as wordes must have seates, no less than rayment bodies. Were it any argument of an unfurnished maiden, besides these qualities to draw cleane in good propor-

tion, and with good symmetrie? Now if she be an honest woman, and a good
housewife to, were she not worth the wishing, and worthy the shyryving?
And yet such there be, and such we know. Or is it likely that her children
shalbe a whit the worse brought up, if she be a Laelia, an Hortensia, or a
Cornelia, which were so endued and noted for so doing?" But all of this
adds up to less in solidity of acquirement than the general tone of his
chapter would lead one to expect.[18]

No writer considered thus far seems to have thought much about modern
languages as a necessary part of a well-educated woman's knowledge. That
some were thinking about it is evidenced in some verses commending Peter
Erondelle's *French Garden: for English Ladyes and Gentlewomen to walk in.*

> Swift Erondell, why hast thou been so slowe,
> Whose nature is to bring the Sommer in?
> Why hast thou let the balefull winter blowe,
> Ere thou to chaunt thy native tunes begin?
> Thy braine replenish't, and thy fethers grow'ne,
> Why is thy worth and worke so long unknowne?
>
> Ladies have long'd to match old Holliband,
> That they with men might parle out their parte:
> Their wittes are rare, and they have tongues at hand,
> Of Nature full, their onely want is Arte:
> Where former age regarded not their neede,
> Before all others thou hast done the deede.
>
> S.D.

A little address to the reader informs us that nothing of this sort had been
done for women especially, except *The French Alphabet*, scarcely a page and
therefore almost worthless. Such lack seemed strange to the writer, since
English ladies are "as studious and of as pregnant spirits, quicke conceites
and ingeniositie, as of any other country whatsoever." Erondelle's book has
been compiled for those of judgment and capacity only. Likewise training
in their own tongue, except for some references to good models for Italian
already quoted, is not given consideration. A passage from Puttenham's
Arte of English Poesie reveals again some thought on the matter, with a hint
of how some ladies, and gentlemen too, might look on such programs as we
have been considering. Chapter X of Book III is headed, "A division of
figures, and how they serve in exornation of language." It is chiefly intended, says Puttenham "for the learning of Ladies and young Gentlewomen, or idle Courtiers, desirous to become skilful in their owne mother
tongue, and for their private recreation to make now & then ditties of
pleasure, thinking for our parte none other science so fit for them & the
place as that which teacheth *beau semblant*, the chiefe profession aswell of
Courting as of poesie: since to such manner of mindes nothing is more
combersome then tedious doctrines and schollarly methodes of discipline,

we have in our owne conceit devised a new and strange modell of this arte, fitter to please the Court then the schoole."[19]

Beyond such matters as have been noted writers on the education of women rarely go, particularly on the more practical aspects of education. Mulcaster again is an exception. Who should be trained and at what age training should begin, he would leave parents to decide, not by years, but by "ripeness of witte to conceive without tiring, and strength of bodie to travell without wearying." Commonly, he says, the schooling of girls lasts only to thirteen or fourteen, so little time that much work must be done to have any show for it afterward. If parents can allow a long continuation of study, a different plan is needed. No public provision is made for the training of girls, except what teachers make in consultation with parents. They can be sent to the elementary school at first and later trained at home, or receive all their training privately at home, according to the means and desire of parents, who must show diligence in providing what is necessary. On the question of whether men or women should be chosen to teach girls there is more frequent comment. Those who did not take education seriously of course prescribed women for safety. Even Vives prefers a woman, holy and learned, but he accepts a man if he is either well aged or very good and happily married. Mulcaster concedes women are fittest in some respects, but evidently prefers men, who "frame them best, and with good regard to some circumstances will bring them up excellently well, especially if their parentes be either of learning to judge, or of authoritie to command, or of both, to do both, as experience hath taught us in those, which have proved so well."[20]

By way of summary on renaissance theory regarding the proper education for girls of the ruling class obviously not much can be said. In general it was assumed that a liberal education would have to be based on sound knowledge of Latin, and possibly Greek. The one secular field all agreed on as suitable for women was moral philosophy as a buttress for the Scriptures and the Church Fathers. The study most frequently prohibited was poetry because it was assumed most dangerous to chastity, but it had its advocates, as we have seen. History and oratory might likewise be prohibited as outside the concerns of the good woman, but both were admitted as proper studies for the achievement of virtue. Rhetoric was under suspicion as leading to vain exhibitions of mere verbal skill, clashing most of all with the desired unobtrusiveness of a woman who held her tongue. And yet effective control of language was advocated in order that when a woman spoke it might be to the point and persuasively. Apparently such skill was to be gained from the reading of good authors rather than from the sytematic study of the art of speech. At best the material is particularly meager on this subject of the liberal education of women, probably because the whole question was still in a highly tentative and unformed state, and also because, in practice, under favorable conditions of rank and wealth girls were tutored along with their brothers and studied the same things in the same way. It is, however, I think, quite clear that the whole subject in Italy as well as in France and England was viewed generally with great suspicion and handled gingerly with an eye always on the image of woman as a creature, if not of limited powers, at least of limited sphere, and with the assumption that nothing must be allowed in the training of her mind that would encourage or enable her to compete on even ground with men. This general assumption is implicit in everything that was said on the training and education of women, in the limited aim set for their education even by their most ardent supporters, in the restrictions on subjects and books, and most of all in the almost total absence of reference to the professions. Most writers evidently thought it unnecessary to prohibit occupations so obviously unsuitable for women. The few who mention the possibility are likely to shudder away from the thought, Filogenio from the picture of a woman in armor covered with blood, though he believes that if brought up like a man she would fight as well; Vives from the thought of all the harm a woman teaching in the schools might do by spreading through her authority the false opinions that she would surely form because of her frailty, weak discretion, and credulity, "which thing our first mother Eve sheweth, whom the Devil caught with a light argument."[21]

What we see in these two centuries that cover the renaissance, from its flourishing in Italy, through its development in France and in England, to its decay in all three countries, is merely the faint stirrings of a new conception of women as fully human. At the same time there were stirring ideas about men that ultimately were to shape into the belief that common men, too, are fully human. Curiously enough both currents rise in the favored classes, and both have to do somehow or other with education. When the knight turned into a gentleman the most important part of his training was his instruction in the liberal arts and sciences, to enable him to play a distinguished part in the courts of the renaissance and to carry on his civic duties, which increasingly outweighed his military duties. And thus the door was opened wider and wider to the poor man's son to achieve office and distinction by more serious application to his studies, until we see today the practical extinction of classes founded upon birth. It is commonly shared education that has shaped for men the dream and the realization of democracy. Far more slowly and inconspicuously, with long setbacks, has the other half of the human race, women, attained its majority, and only as opportunity for education as liberal as men's has become a fact. The development of democracy, so feeble in its beginnings, so slow, so painful, so precarious, so incomplete as yet, is after all only the growth to maturity of the whole human race. We are a long way yet from that maturity, but looking backward to 1600 we can see how far we have come even if we consider only the change in views on how and why women should be educated.

CHAPTER FIVE : *Vocation*

The training of the well-born girl was directed in every respect, as we have seen, toward fitting her to become a wife. In renaissance theory it is true to say, only one vocation, marriage, was proposed for the lady. Occasional reference to a choice before the girl, or rather before her father, between marriage and dedication to the church was made, only to be dismissed as extremely limited in possible practice because of the small chance of the girl's fitness for the nun's life, and also because of more important, material considerations, for in fact the lady is purely a secular figure. The great final business of parents of daughters may be said to have been to provide husbands, and thereby relieve themselves of responsibility. Marriage alone was held the proper vocation for woman mainly because she was fitted only to learn the duties that belonged to her as a sort of junior partner to her husband. There she could without blame fulfill the whole law of her being. No single condition set so clearly and inescapably the terms of woman's existence as the clamping down upon her of this single destiny. The perfect man, as Castiglione set the pattern for a century, was the courtier, resplendent with all the highest human powers and graces, to which only a court could give full scope. The perfect woman, in general renaissance theory, was the wife, married to a man well born and virtuous, and shining in her restricted realm with her own qualities, but only like the moon, with reflected light.

What we have to examine, therefore, is the institution of Christian marriage as it was understood in the renaissance, with special reference to the lady—so far as it seems to have taken any account of differences in rank. The only novelty in this study will be the application of a narrow range of religious and moral tests and practical requirements to the proud and lofty, with small distinction from the duties preached to the low and humble.

Marriage, by definition, was a joining by God of a man and a woman into one body, mind, and will, with the consent of the two and under the approval of those responsible for them. The purposes of marriage were held to be the preservation of the race, mutual aid and comfort, and avoidance of sin, the first usually receiving the most emphasis. The pattern of a wife that fits into this institution can be better seen if we consider first the part that men were supposed to play in the domestic world, the terms that they exacted, and the climate they created, since the whole institution of marriage was deemed to exist as a way of life or a problem primarily for men. The wife was essential to the institution, but what role she should fill and what sort of life it might be for her was not fundamentally within her will or choice. First of all, for men, who were free to choose, the question of whether to marry or not had point and was endlessly argued from many angles. Objections to marriage ranged from the faults of women to the inescapable restrictions on a man's freedom, the troublesomeness of children, the greatly increased expense for house, food, comings and goings, salaries of nurses, servants, tutors, and dowries, and the general increase of cares. Not least important was the natural reluctance of a superior being to accept as his companion a creature of such trivial or even despicable traits as a woman.

On the other side various weighty reasons were urged for sober consideration. First, there is the great dignity of the married state, ordained by God, and honored by civil laws which prefer the married man to the unmarried in offices. Next, only through matrimony may a man provide himself with heirs of his own body to his name and estates, and realize thereby such immortality as he may well view with the deepest satisfaction. Through his children also he may increase his substance and power by alliances with other families, in which well-placed daughters especially may be of great value, many times over the price of dowries. Indeed, with rise in rank the legitimacy of a man's children assumed such importance that at times the whole pattern of the lady's existence seems to have been framed in order to assure her husband that her children were his own. From the point of view of society also the propagation of the human race within marriage was held of the greatest importance because the quality of citizens must deteriorate in illegitimate children who are by nature disposed to evil, and who have no certain father and of necessity a bad mother. Legitimate children are more disposed by nature to goodness, especially to chastity, more seriously brought up, and more spurred on to full achievement by the feeling that the virtues of their illustrious ancestors draw all eyes to them. The most practical advantage in marriage was the aid and comfort that a carefully chosen wife could be. With her to take charge of affairs indoors, since her interests are identical with his, a man may trust her to preserve his goods, even increase them, and use them economically for the well-being of the whole household. No man of considerable possessions and external affairs can hope to manage domestic affairs well, or to find servants, even the best, adquate and trustworthy. Last of the great arguments for marriage was the possibility of thus living a better regulated life, for outside of a few souls gifted with chastity, men could not hope for purity and peace except in marriage. Let it be granted, then, that marriage has its own pains and anxieties, yet if a man chooses to marry, he finds himself freed from many cares and enjoying in their stead sweet satisfactions that only wife and children can furnish. The cares that are unavoidable are lightened by sharing them with one whose whole thought is for him. Thus ran the argument to persuade the young man to conserve by marriage his health, strength, property, and reputation, in short, his happiness. The champions of marriage in spite of its drawbacks still praised it as the best life available for men, against those who would adopt instead celibacy, or solitariness, or worst of all a life in sin.[1]

If one is to marry, choice of a wife is the next great question, and much advice was proffered, with occasional warning against expectation of too much perfection in any one woman. The three points most often mentioned were physical appearance, age, and moral character, next birth and fortune, now and then others like temperament, health, and education, with varying emphasis according to the chief concern of the wife-hunter. To avoid repetition the points that lie within the choice and the will of the woman herself and form a part of the pattern the lady, as a wife, should seek to copy will be left for the description of her. The rest rather belong to the framework into which she must fit and seem to need some attention here.

Concerning birth, it was said in general that the gentleman should seek a wife of equal rank. Superiority in rank, with the wealth and powerful connections implied, might make a wife independent, proud, scornful, exacting, and extravagant. The balance of power would almost surely shift from husband to wife with all the inconveniences and dangers involved in such an unnatural relation. As for marriage with a woman of inferior rank, only gentlemen of the higher degrees might possibly ignore the certain disadvantages for the sake of special advantages, usually financial. Rank alone, however, should not govern the choice of a family into which to marry. The ways of living and habits of all the connections are important, for marriages can be wrecked by union with a family of proud, quarrelsome, litigious, ill-willed men, or with such as by their poverty or bad management, or lack of enterprise only furnish a whole new house to support.[2]

Next among what may be called adventitious qualifications, wealth may be considered, not as important as some people thought, but not to be neglected. The amorists liked to argue against the whole system of the dowry as the certain prevention of love in marriage, for by reducing marriage to a cold, commercial proposition, it provided a justification for supplementing the husband with a lover. In general, serious advice urged both the need of the dowry to help support a greatly increased household, and the justice of having the wife share the financial burden not merely of supporting, but of enhancing the prestige of the family in whose welfare she had an interest equal to her husband's. Wealth is necessary for great enterprises, for gifts that, well placed, bring gratitude and love and advancement for children, and for the education of those children in liberal studies, if they are to be equal to their opportunities. But due regard for the mean dictated dowries that are mediocre, certain, and immediately available as more desirable than great sums of uncertain payment, especially if likely to increase the husband's difficulty in controlling his wife. Tiraqueau had a good deal to say on this last point. Neither out of greed nor ambition should a man take a wife with a great dowry, for with it she gains freedom and buys power, and reduces him to slavery, or to poverty by excessive demands out of her pride. Mutual love, benevolence, and peace, he reasonably added, are greatly promoted by equality of station, both in wealth and rank, for then the wife, not daring to refuse anything, is loving and obedient. In all candor it had to be admitted, of course, that many wives inferior in birth and wealth, if proud by nature and greedy of domination, would try to usurp power over their husbands, thus overturning all law and order—divine, natural, and civil, but they could and must be restrained.[3]

As for age, by common consent preference fell on youth, for these reasons especially: A girl would accept more willingly the instructions of her husband, and with better spirit try to apply his corrections to the remedy of her faults; also she would be more adaptable to new habits and ways of living. But not too green a youth, since some ripeness was desirable for more wisdom and understanding, and also for the production of more robust children. Implicit in this argument for youth is the assumption that the prospective husband has reached maturity so as to give him sufficient knowledge and experience to frame his young wife wisely. He should not be too old, however, lest he should be so weakened that he himself will impair the robustness of his children, and be unable to guide them in childhood and see them grow to manhood, and also lest he be unable to satisfy his young wife. A wife of the same age, or older, might think to take over control of the house, and especially if older she would seem to have reached old age while her husband was young. It is best that they should come to old age together when their passions are dying, which will be likely if there is ten years' advantage on the husband's side. Implicit also in the argument for youth is preference for a virgin to a widow, not only on the score of malleability but of devotion. Women were generally thought to love most the man that they marry first because they more easily take on his habits and love more passionately.[4]

Shall a man seek a beautiful wife? Most writers saw in the question, or professed to see a dilemma: if a wife is beautiful, her husband will enjoy her but must fear sharing her with others; if she is ugly, he cannot enjoy her himself though secure from fear of competitors. The solution usually advised was to seek mediocrity, enough beauty to escape boredom and temptation elsewhere, and to promise comely children, but not so much as to cause suspicion and worry. After all a man wins no praise if he marries beauty only for pleasure. But beauty had the preference, for it is among the good things of life and therefore, as Barbaro said, there is no need to labor the point. A man will have a beautiful wife—if he can find one. Also the Platonists could argue that beauty of body is an index to beauty in the soul, the beginning of love. The danger that beauty will inflame other men may be viewed philosophically, for at the same time it may be seen as a great stirrer-up and fortifier of a husband's love. As Guazzo said, "If wives be not amiable in other men's eyes, surelye their husbands wil never make great account of them: for a man careth not to possesse that thing, which no man coveteth not to have." The prudent husband, more-over, takes measures to make his wife immune to temptation by seeing that she is content, esteeming her, showing her that he holds nobody more dear, and gathering often the fruit of a mutual love. There was something found to be said, however, even in behalf of an unattractive wife. Beauty and goodness may be assumed to belong together, but it does not follow that ugliness and evil are companions. The wife conscious of her lack of physical appeal will take all the more care to please; her beauty will show in her virtue, the one essential thing for a happy marriage. Experience only too often proves that beauty in a wife does not always have its de-sired results; it is no assurance of beautiful children or of content for the husband since it does not prevent desire for others—man at heart craving variety.

What type of beauty is to be favored in a wife is little discussed, and that contradictorily, as advisers were thinking of pleasure or procreation. Trotto, considering the first, recommends small size because nature takes more pains to perfect little things, proportions are more easily observed, and the eye takes in details more completely. Just for that reason Barbaro prefers for procreation good size, a small woman seeming more fitted for pleasure than for the office of creating heirs, but he holds out for one detail, beautiful hair, for he cannot imagine Mars in love with a shaved Venus. More particularly, Alberti says that beauty in a wife does not rest in the charms and refinement of the face but rather in a tall and well-formed body, not too thin or too heavy, fresh and lively in color and active, well designed to carry and produce beautiful children. The general proposition of what constitutes beauty must be left for the chapter on love.[5]

Such then were the chief external considerations urged upon the man seeking a wife, to which of course were added moral conditions. Since perfection cannot be expected he must judiciously weigh one advan-tage against another and choose where the soundest are to be found. Some thought disparity in years and rank, forced consent, and lack of dowry to weigh heavily against any other advantages, while others saw more evil in too great wealth, or the extremes of beauty and ugliness, and in the vices of deceit and avarice. The wisest, it was said, would think nobility, chastity, and youth quite enough, lack of wealth of no weight against these, and beauty desirable only because it makes all the other qualities desirable.[6]

Marriage, admittedly, was a grave decision for a man to make, not only because he was committing himself, for the rest of his life presumably, to whatever lot fortune and his choice of a wife brought him, but because he must himself assume heavy responsibilities for the welfare of his household. Since the duties assigned to the husband show more clearly the framework within which the wife has to shape herself, and explain and even prescribe the duties which belong to her, we must pursue further this analysis of what the renaissance prescribed, with inexhaustible zeal, as the husband's part, before we can come directly to the portrayal of the wife.

The first duty of the husband, writers agree almost without exception, is the exercise of authority. The argument runs like this. Through Adam God conferred upon the man the headship in marriage. All order or prospect of order in human society depends upon his exercising this divinely appointed duty, for he represents God here, in perfection of understanding, judgment, and reason, and though he erred in Adam he still surpasses the woman in strength of mind and body, and is bound to show such natural virtues in the government of his wife and household. He may rule with strictness and severity as some advise, or with gentleness and persuasion as most recommend, but there must be no question that he rules. Disorder in the house, enmity between husband and wife, arises only when men do not know how to command and women therefore do not know how to obey at the same time that they do not know how to govern. The blame rests squarely on the shoulders of the husbands if through laziness or indulgence toward their wives, or fear of their wives' superiority in nobility and wealth, or too much love of their wives they fail to exercise this authority.

The nature of this authority, it was conceded, must be clearly understood, since it was open to great abuse. By marriage a woman puts herself at the mercy of her husband, having given herself and her dowry to him, and is bound to love and obey him as long as she lives, but his authority over her is not the master's over the servant, but rather the older brother's over the younger, or the king's over the vassal. The desired end is peace, attainable only if he uses his power with courtesy, gentleness, and prudence, for he must win the confidence and willing obedience of his wife, a difficult task admittedly because women, like everyone else, love liberty and resent authority. Therefore, a husband loving his wife as himself should govern with love for her own good. That some uneasiness accompanied this advice of moderation and pleasantness creeps out here and there in a warning to wives not to misread the absence of severity.[7]

With the husband's assumption of authority went also responsibility for the performance of his wife; he cannot neglect his duty to teach her all that she needs to know to please him and promote good will between them. First lessons seem to have concerned proper attitudes toward her husband with special emphasis on what is his due as her superior. Also he will have to teach her household management, however well instructed in such matters she may have become under her mother's tutelage, for it must be assumed that she will be stepping into an organized, long-established house and must learn its ways, the ways that please him. Since the salvation of her soul must be held specially in his charge, religious and moral instruction is also his duty. Vives summed up thus his advice to husbands on this point: "A woman should know herself, her origin and purpose, and what Christ's religion is, without the whiche nothing can be well done nor justlye. But yet it muste be religion and no superstition; to the ende she maye knowe what difference there is betweene them. Religion doth make them verye simple and good, and superstition verye hypocrytes & molestious." On the subject of books Lombardelli, the husband who so painstakingly and minutely instructed his young wife in her whole duty to man, furnished a list sufficient, he said, for the time being. In general, only religious books, no poetry of love and battles, examples, lives of the saints, spiritual instruction recommended by her mother and husband; in particular, Vives on the Christian woman, Giovan Gerson's *Dispregio del Mondo* and Diego Stella's *Dispregio della Vanità*, St. Gregory's dialogue, and two or three others. Then at last, said Erasmus by way of encouragement no doubt to both teacher and pupil, when the woman knows herself transformed by the instruction of her husband, and compares herself with what she was before, she will begin to say to herself, "O happy me who fell to such a husband. What a beast would I have been unless he had instructed me." Now she will begin not only to make him her choice as a husband, but to honor him as a preceptor, and to reverence him as a father, or to put it more Christianly, to venerate God in her husband. So she will rightly despise the purple, gold, and gems of the world and prize the true ornaments of chastity, modesty, sobriety, and kindness to the poor, and prefer books to licentious gatherings, feasts, and the sessions with loquacious women from which no woman, however good, but returns worse to her house.[8]

The husband then will go as far as may be consistent with his dignity, and the expectation he may rightly have of co-operation from his wife to make her into the prudent and contented partner necessary to the success of their marriage. But if she is faulty and especially if she persists in disappointing his hopes and rejects the ways toward peace that he points out to her, whether because of ignorance, slowness to learn, or recalcitrance, he carries the further responsibility of correcting her faults and even punishing her if necessary, to secure obedience. Much advice was offered on this point. Forbearance with minor faults should be the first rule, for considering the miserable condition of women, subject to illness, weak of mind, far less experienced and instructed than men, subservient to men all their lives, who would be so cruel as not to pity rather than blame them and so wink at many of their faults (which are indeed allowed to their frailty but forbidden men), in conversation, dress, and attention to personal appearance.

Faults that call for correction, however, must be firmly handled, though always with regard to their seriousness and the attitude of the wife. If she is chaste and humble the husband should warn her pleasantly without anger when she fails at times, rather by way of instruction than reproof, and if she blushes he should consider her punished enough. If, however, she is proud, rude, rebellious, and quick tempered he should reprove even the lesser faults more severely and show by his stern face that he is much displeased with her words and bearing and will not endure them. Sharp words and threats should ordinarily be reserved either for persistent repetition of faults or more serious faults. As a last resort against misdoing that risks damnation of the soul, or shame for the wife or husband, or danger, some advised application of the stick, others warned never on any provocation to strike a wife or she will never love him perfectly. Striking angers a good woman and makes a bad woman worse, agree Christine and Bouchet and many others. To beat or not to beat was not in fact a mere academic question. The prerogative of corporal punishment belonged without question to all husbands whatever their rank, carrying with it some conviction of its necessity as the only efficacious cure for certain evils inherent in women. An old piece of doggerel put the case succinctly:

> A woman, a dog, and a walnut tree,
> The more you beat 'em, the better they be;

and a curious passage in a book of dialogues in Italian and English, put out by a professor of Italian in London, seems to intend hearty support of this doctrine, though one may doubt how far to accept it literally. "Observe my English Gentleman," says our Benvenuto, "that blowes have a wonderfull prerogative in the feminine sex; for if shee be a bad woman, there is no more proper plaister to mend her, then this: but if (which is a rare chance) she be good, to dust her often, hath in it, a singular, unknowne, and as it were an inscrutable vertue to make her much better: and to reduce her, if possible to perfection." Support for the doctrine may be found in still higher circles about the same time, 1612. Dr. William Gager, graduate of Oxford, famous Latinist, playwright, and churchman, defended in public the proposition that it was lawful for husbands to beat their wives. How far he went in recommending the practice is not clear, for his argument apparently has not been preserved, but that he went too far is clear in that another clergyman, William Heale, published a defense of women against Dr. Gager, pricked on to it evidently by an outraged wife, for he dedicates his book "To the Ladie M. H. the cause of this treatise."[9]

Most advisers are against wife-beating. If good example, kindness, constancy, and patience, they say, will not win a wife to better ways, beating certainly will not. Even Tiraqueau, who had a reputation for severity against wives, and held that the laws do admit moderate blows, would have none of them. Much is permitted by laws and canons, he says, which is still vicious and unsuitable. Blows turn love to hate and lead wives to hope for the death of their husbands. The wise and great have either ignored the faults of their wives or gently corrected them. That should be the rule for all, and example will accomplish more than anything else. The higher the rank, the more sensitive and noble the soul, the greater the gifts of mind, then the more necessary judicious and gentle treatment. Vives, writing always, one must suppose, with his royal and noble patrons in mind, cautions the husbands of such thus: "Ther are in noble women as ther is among men, certayne excellente motions of the mynde: the whyche to those that be not wyse, and doe marcke the thynge but slenderlye, seme to come of arrogancye and pryde. Nor these ought not utterly to be kept under, and cleane extinguished, for without theym they canne not approche nor come to that hyghe and memorable ornament, that exciteth and moveth man to marvaile and to prayse & extolle them." Such women should not be sharply rebuked but gently drawn from faults.[10]

In general the behavior of a husband toward his wife in public and in private should be loving and considerate. Going about with rigid face and averted eyes, issuing commands, is a mistaken idea of how authority is to be maintained. Rather he should show an amiable countenance, accepting kindly what she does out of wifely good will, commending what is well done, returning courtesies, readily granting requests, and not exacting all that is possible. There is no abasement of a man in such deference to a woman, coming as it does voluntarily from a superior as a token of kindness, favor, and honor to his wife. Ahasuerus lost no royal dignity in extending his scepter to Esther. In private particularly, a husband should unbend; especially if his wife is young and he somewhat old, let him borrow some turns of youth, lay aside his wise old age and live in joy, laugh, and joke—chastely of course. Daily conversation should be simple and intimate, about their common affairs—the house, children, necessary provisions—and general topics such as virtue, manners, and the errors of common people, with some mixture of outside matters and even merry report of such things as happen to friends and neighbors. Just as men rejoice in knowledge so women, since they are kept close within the house, greatly desire to hear what is done abroad, and judicious gratifying of this natural appetite will

lessen their coveting to go abroad themselves. Never to talk over household matters or discuss subjects within his wife's understanding, or bring
in outside news, is to be cruel to a fellow creature who is largely dependent
upon him for refreshment of this sort. At times also he should seek her
counsel, for though the counsel of a woman is weak, fragile, infirm as
women themselves are weak and lacking in reason and intellect, yet even
such at times say things strongly to the purpose, and ought not to be
scorned by the best of men. Nor are women of wisdom entirely lacking,
by whose counsel men better even their own affairs. But since women are
loquacious and least silent and faithful in secrets, husbands should seek
their advice only in affairs that would not be a danger or inconvenience
even if made public. Christine de Pisan like others, however, put the blame
for betrayed secrets on a husband who did not well consider what kind of
wife he had, since not all women are wise, any more than all men are.
No one should be surprised, she said, if a fool betrays him, but a good and
wise wife deserves his confidence.

A husband should never quarrel with his wife if he wishes to preserve
peace. But if he does quarrel, Canoniero warns, "he should take care that
she never suspects in anything he says, even in jest, the least criticism of
the beauty she thinks is hers, either natural or artificial, for she will support with patience any other blame, as Lodovico Vives says, except that."
Likewise he should find no fault in what she considers herself proficient,
singing, embroidery, and so forth, for there he strikes home. It is possible,
however, to reprove her in wrath by saying things that sound well in the
ears of wives and can be attributed to praise, as if he calls her proud, she
will think herself magnanimous, if cruel—modest, if stubborn—inviolable.
If a husband avoids quarreling and cherishes his wife tenderly she will
love him in return, and out of this mutual love comes peace and quiet.[11]

On the greatest intimacy of all most advisers had a good deal to say,
particularly on the necessity of remembering that marriage was intended
for the procreation of children, and in case of need for the avoidance of
fornication. The great danger, men were warned, was that the girl who
came to the marriage bed a virgin in body and mind might become de-
bauched by the excesses and lack of modesty of her own husband. A husband who inflames his wife is to blame if afterwards she admits a lover.
Most writers assumed, like Tasso, that women are naturally libidinous and
no less inclined to venery than men. Since it is the husband's duty to
preserve in his wife the chastity that belongs to a wife, resembling as
closely as possible the chastity of a virgin, he must treat her as a husband
and not as a lover, that is, not as an adulterer who cherishes a mistress,
but as one who has in his keeping a being useful and delightful. For that,
good judgment and not mere passion is necessary. Many writers would
have eliminated all pleasure from the marital act if they could, and went

so far even as to recommend methods that insure the least possible satisfaction to the wife. In this respect, however, such advisers as Vives, Tasso, and Bouchet, more humane in their attitude toward women, though advising restraint, left room for unhampered, mutual pleasure as one of the great arguments for married life. Tasso conceded that at first a married pair might be admitted to be lovers, but he would have them speedily reform, for the embracings of husband and wife should be like the suppers of well-dieted men where pleasure is the more increased by temperance. Vives more explicitly recommended that "The solaces & pleasures of those which are marryed, must be rare and sober . . . as though they went aboute to seke a refreshynge onelye of theyr cares and labours, and not a mayntaynynge and a continuance of theyr cupidities and bodelye pleasures. And the woman in semblable maner muste be at these pastymes, that as she is partaker of the travell and payne, she maye lykewyse rejoyse in theyr recreations, that beynge therwith refreshed, she maye be the more able to sustayne and beare the burden." Bouchet, too, advised there was no solace such as that of a man and his wife together in the bed of honor, where is to be found the pleasure of chaste love, sweet and assured, without danger or fear, a merit and not an offense toward God. The husband's duty is to please and satisfy his wife, and the wife's duty is the same, in order to ward off temptation to either to transgress the law of marriage. Both are blamable if they refuse, unless there is adultery, or severe illness, or both may wish to desist, having made a vow to keep chastity. Husband and wife may be allowed to take their pleasure for delight only, when neither generation nor avoidance of fornication furnish a reason, for they commit only a venial offense and not a mortal sin by so doing (like drinking wine beyond thirst for pleasure at a meal or away from the table), so long as excess is avoided. The husband, for the sake of his health, was urged to use moderation, especially if somewhat along in years; with excess his eyes and nerves will suffer as Avicene says, and also his stomach, and he will age quickly. Appetite often exceeds power, he was warned, and one frequently sees men who marry beautiful women, especially old men, die soon after marriage, even suddenly. Women who wish their husbands to live long with them will bridle their desires.[12]

Human nature is frail, however, and excesses are only too likely to threaten the peace and understanding that are desirable between husband and wife, through an excessively passionate nature or jealousy in the husband, and through indiscretion if not evil intention on the part of the wife. The palliative measures recommended by some seem excessive. Fausto da Longiano frankly advises that if the husband cannot find satisfaction with his wife without offending decency, he might better seek a vent for his passion elsewhere rather than misuse his wife. Nor should his wife take it ill, providing he is found with a woman of evil life and low condition. She should consider that through shame and the respect he bears her, he has wished rather to have someone else share in his violence and lasciviousness. Jealousy, a vice of excess also, comes from loving too much and fearing too much the loss of what one loves. It starts often for no reason except that the husband wants to possess his beloved, his wife, wholly, see every deed, hear every word and thought, and is offended by every act contrary to his pleasure. Then he becomes suspicious of everyone, unable to concentrate without interruption by this frenzy. Nor is there any cure for him; if his wife adorns herself, it is to please someone else; if she does not adorn herself, she is trying to deceive him in order to have a better chance to injure him by allaying suspicions; whoever praises her or blames her has designs; even presents made to him are bribes to share her. He watches incessantly, unable to sleep or eat, and can take no joy in beauty that can be enjoyed by others. Such is this monstrous love, the reverse of all that a continent husband should feel for his wife. When it comes to recommending measures against this lamentable condition some advisers threw on the wife the burden of giving no cause for jealousy in the first place, and if it arises, of allaying it by discreet behavior. Others held it impossible to forestall suspicion from the start, a crucial period, for the simple girl taken from her father's house without experience cannot have the judgment needed. The man just married should know that women long for praise, especially of their beauty, and therefore readily show kindness to anyone that appears affectionate and disposed to praise them. The easiest way for the husband to seize his young wife's mind is to praise her beauty and gentility himself. If she is not wholly circumspect with others, out of her inexperience, he should avoid jealousy like the plague, for if roused it will make him wretched before he can taste the sweetness of marriage. He should even go so far the other way that not for any reason will he show doubt of his wife's fidelity, either by keeping her too close at home, or denying her all company, though he will skillfully, without her knowledge, take care that the entertainments and her company are honest. She has cause for complaint if she sees that he doubts her faith, and for revenge may break faith. Even if he has good reason to suspect her fidelity, he should avoid prying, for if he finds what he fears and lets her know, there will be never a cure for the breach. Other measures are to be taken. Discreet third parties may better effect reform. As the English translation of a little treatise on governance of a family put it, "A noble herte / and hygh gentyll mynde / wyll never serche of womens maters. A shrewe wyll soner be corrected by smylynge or laughyng / than by a staffe / or strokes. The best way to kepe a woman good / is gentyll intrety and never to let her know that she is suspecte / and ever to be counceyled & informed with lovyng maner."[13]

Two things especially worked against acceptance of this highly sensible advice on the proper way to handle wifely fidelity. One was the current scorn and ridicule of the deceived husband, and the other was a man's need to know that his heirs were of his own body. In general it was assumed that a wife's infidelity brought shame and degradation to her husband, however upright and innocent of wrong against her he might be. The cuckold—when has he not been—was fair game for sport, and infinite were the jests passed upon this "horned" species of man. Protest was not lacking, however. Giovanni Battista Modio, after speculating on the origin of horns for the deceived husband, and on why soldiers seem to wear them more frequently than scholars, finally comes to the conclusion that it is only false opinion that attaches disgrace to the wearing of horns. The shame of a woman, choosing evil of her own will, cannot obscure the honor of a man, which is wholly within his keeping. An Englishman states the conclusion in these terms. "The more discretion a man hath, the less shall hee bee troubled with these frantike fits: and seeing, as a certain noble Gentleman sayth, the Honour of a true heroique spirit dependeth not upon the carriage or behavior of a woman, I see no reason why the better sort should take this false playing of their Wives so much at the heart as they doe; especially, when it is their Destinie, and not Desert to be so used. Montaigne, that brave French Baron, being of this minde; for saith he, the Gallantest men in the world, as Lucullus, Caesar, Anthony, Cato, and such like Worthies, were all cuckolds; yea, and (which was more) knew it, although they made no stirre about it: neither was there in all that time but one Gull, and Coxcombe, and that was Lepidus, that dyed with the anguish thereof. Read the third Chapter of the third Booke of the foresayd Montaigne's Essayes, and he will satisfie you at large in this poynt." But if a man must feel assured that the family name and possessions would go to his own legitimate son, he could hardly take so philosophically either the possibility or the certainty that his children were not his own.[14]

Thus, in brief, a gentleman on marrying will seek to form and maintain an establishment that will promise him as stable a life as man may hope for in this world, under as advantageous conditions as may be, to enable him to play the part in society fitted to his birth, talents, and connections. In this unequal partnership of marriage he holds the dominant place, and bears the ultimate responsibility. His wife works with him for their mutual benefit, and he is bound to recognize her valuable contribution to his welfare and pleasure and the continuation of his line, and accord her the honor belonging to one so closely associated with him. To regard her as a servant and treat her as such because she deals with menial matters and even performs menial tasks for him is a degradation and injury not only to her but to himself. Trotto's dialogue boldly raises the point. Antonio objects that women, who wish to be called good and wise, seem always to be occupied in low things—keeping silent, enduring their husbands, looking after children and the kitchen. Astemio answers: admit these offices vile, they are yet so necessary that more important matters cannot go on without them, and therefore they are not less important than the offices of men. Besides, women advise their husbands and run the house if the men are absent or disabled. Women well born and well brought up, are of the greatest aid to country, husband, and family. The husband therefore owes his wife benevolence, tender and faithful love, provision of needful things, wise government, good instruction, protection and honor.[15]

In the light of these duties of the husband, his purposes in seeking the yoke of marriage, and his expectations from his wife, the portrait of the perfect wife can now be comprehensibly drawn. We may well begin where we began with the man, with the question of whether to marry, though it loses most of its significance now. For the well-born girl it was assumed that the choice between marrying and not marrying was not as for the man the choice between assuming the responsibility of a family and remaining free to lead her life as she pleased, but at most the choice between two vocations, marriage and the religious life. The girl in her father's house had no recognized, permanent status; there must be found for her if possible another means of support. According to theory this choice was hers, and parents were admonished to search diligently for signs of fitness for one or the other vocation, that they might make no mistake even in taking her word. Only the clearest indications of aversion to marriage and undoubted fitness for dedication to the service of God alone should allow parents to consent to such a disposal of their daughter. Almost without question, however, among Catholics as well as Protestants, marriage was assumed to be the destined lot of a girl. Argument on choice was therefore superfluous in the first place. For men marriage seems generally to have been looked on as a necessary choice between evils, the commodities, however, outweighing the drawbacks because of the great utility of a wife. For women the case was frankly admitted to be entirely different. "Certainly no man will envy the condition of a wife," said Erasmus, "if he observes what is true, that all the goods of marriage belong rather to the husband than the wife." She must marry out of hard necessity. The praise of marriage that often does accompany exposition of wifely duties usually merely points out the gratification that comes to wives from performance of duty, and the hope for reward in the next world, all the greater in proportion to the tribulation endured here. Or women are assured that it is impossible for them to reduce human emotions to perfection and escape calumny, no matter how carefully they conduct themselves, and therefore life with an honest marital companion is preferable to the only alternative for them, a life of tedious solitude. The comfort of matrimony is to be found in having with one husband one body, one mind, one house, one table, one bed, and the assurance of being together until death, where all other companionship is uncertain of duration.[16]

Advice on the kind of husband to look for was usually addressed to fathers, in whose hands lay complete power over the disposal of their daughters. More often they were warned against the mates they should not choose for their daughters. Fusco ran over what seem to have been the mistakes commonly made. If a father marries his simple, innocent child to a man poor in judgment and reason, who will teach her the things she does not understand, how to show modesty in success, and to comfort in adversity, and who will counsel her in either? Or if he marries her to a proud man, what conversation can she have with him, being gentle, humble, and pious by nature, as most women are, and he full of wrath? She will come to hate him and by contradicting will make him hate her. There will be no chance for agreement and pleasing companionship, but greater perils will continually fall on her innocent head. Worst of all, a father who gives his daughter, noble, beautiful, well brought up and virtuous, to an old man, crippled, brutish, ignoble, stinking or diseased, or to a jester, whorer, or tormentor, dooms her to a long and troublesome pain, perpetual affliction, disease, irreparable wrong, and atrocious death; he might better have drowned her. Rather it is for the father not to regard always wealth, birth, ambition, and his worldly interests in marrying his daughter, but to put himself in her place in order to judge more rightly what husband will be good for her all her life. Although she, an inexperienced virgin, can not well judge for herself in this matter, yet perhaps for her own satisfaction she would know better than her experienced father what to do. At least he should consult her mother. Without conformity of character and habits, said Taillemont, a man of the same mind as Fusco on the wrongs done to women by men's usurpation of rule over them, there can be no marriage according to God and reason. What folly then to give daughters to men they have never seen. Three things he would have before marriage, the necessary foundation for all marriages—knowledge of each other, reciprocal friendship, and voluntary consent. After marriage what they have should be in common, mutual tolerance and aid should cement their partnership, neither one living off the pain and sweat of the other or pretending to mastery.[17]

However the choice of a husband was made, on marriage the girl passed out of the control of her father into the hands of her husband, who thereafter had sole responsibility for her. As his duty toward her rested on the predication of his superiority to her in strength and wisdom, so her duty toward him rested on the assumption of her inferiority and necessary subjection to him. And as his authority needed definition, so her subjection calls for explanation. A most satisfactorily explicit handling of the subject may be found in William Gouge's *Domesticall Duties*, all the more impressive, shall we say, because he was an Englishman writing for English-women, who were noted in Europe for their freedom. The book consists of sermons delivered during his incumbency of Blackfriars parish somewhere between 1608 and 1622, the date of publication. It is dedicated to "The Right Honourable, Right Worshipful, and other my beloved Parishioners," with the opening self-gratulation, "If noble Birth, high Honour, great Estate, true Piety, bountifull Charity, good Esteeme of God's word and Ministers, and in particular, intire love of the Author, be inducements to choose a Patron for his worke, I, for my part, need not goe farre for a Patron. In mine owne parish are all these." As a matter of fact he had found himself in hot water for his exposition of wifely subjection, umbrage having been taken, he recalls in his preface, at his particular application of the general rule to specific duties. In protest and excuse Gouge explains that though he had declared what a wife was bound to perform in the extreme subjection God had decreed for her, if her husband chose to exact the extreme due to his authority, he should not have been taken to mean that a husband might or ought to exact the extreme, and that a wife was bound to do all that was set down as her duty whether the husband performed his duty or not. When he came to the husband's duties he had shown the limits to which he should go, so that if he were wise and con-scientious his wife would have no just cause to complain of her subjection. "That which maketh a wives yoake heavy and hard," he added, "is an husbands abuse of his authority: and more pressing his wives duties, then performing his owne." We should set down here, however, the uttermost reaches of the subjection he prescribed for wives to their husbands, for these wives included the high born as well as the low.

Gouge was not considering the legal aspects of the matter—nor was the lawyer Tiraqueau for that matter—but rather the religious, moral, and natural aspects. The man is the wife's head, he began, the wife her hus-band's body. Her submission to her husband is voluntary because he is her head and therefore worthy, as Christ is worthy the submission of the church. The wife's first duty must be to acknowledge her husband as superior and respect his superiority, since God has commanded her sub-jection. That is the whole matter in a nutshell. It is a fault in many wives, he continued with what seems like temerity, that they think themselves in every way as good as their husbands because of the very small difference between them; but that little is enough for disparity. By taking a husband a woman advances him over her, so that a man of low rank is superior to a noble wife, a servant married to his mistress superior to her; even if he is a drunkard, glutton, swaggerer, and swearer, and she is sober and re-ligious, she must count him her superior and worthy of a husband's honor. The evil quality of his heart does not deprive him of the civil honor God has given him. To put it the most extreme way, in Gouge's own words,

"Though an husband in regard of evill qualities may carrie the Image of the devill, yet in regard of his place and office he beareth the Image of God; so doe Magistrates in the commonwealth, Ministers in the Church, parents and masters in the familie."

In spite of the resentment these lessons aroused, no doubt in the Right Honourable and Right Worshipful particularly, he had not changed his mind or his manners when he came to publication for he went on to give a sharp nip to rebellious wives. Some wives, he said, think they could subject themselves to any husband except their own, a worse fault than the other, which could proceed from ignorance, of thinking themselves as good as their husbands. "But for a wife who knoweth and acknowledgeth the generall, that a husband is above his wife, to imagine that she her selfe is not inferiour to her husband, ariseth from monstrous selfe-conceit, and intolerable arrogancy, as if she her selfe were above her owne sex, and more than a woman." In their arrogancy some women even marry men of lower rank on purpose to rule them, and old women marry boys for the same reason. Against the reverence due husbands in outward action as well as inward thought, wives show an intolerable familiarity in manners and specially in speech. For the decorous "Husband" they use "Brother," "Cosen," Friend"—a step lower they address him with "Sweet," "Sweeting," "Heart," "Love," "Joy" and even descend to "Ducke," "Chicke," "Pigsnie." They not only use their given names, John, Thomas, William, unseemly enough, but contract them much more to the form by which servants are usually addressed. As for "Grub," and "Rogue," though given not in passion but in ordinary speech, he is ashamed to name them. How can anyone tell he is a husband? "Such tokens of familiarity as are not withall tokens of subjection and reverence are unbeseeming a wife, because they swerve from that marke." Wives instead should think humbly of themselves in regard to their sex and its weakness. Even if endowed with any gift above ordinary women, they should note their own infirmities as perhaps worse than the infirmities of others. Extreme as these statements are, they can be accepted as the fundamental general view of the proper relation between the wife and her husband. Thus William Gouge simply echoes the ideas prevailing in all of Christian Europe from the first about the position of wives, whatever their rank.[18]

It should go without saying that this neat disposal of wives did not entirely escape attack from both men and women as tyranny of the worst sort, but even though their voices are quite lost in the chorus on subjection, it is only fair to give the defenders of wives a brief hearing. The question is again the nature of women, since subjection was squarely based on the assumption of inherent weakness of body and mind. The lawyer Tiraqueau came to hold a prominent position in the sixteenth century among the depressors of wives and then, in general, among the enemies of women, though he may well have been surprised to find himself thus labeled. Lawyer-like, he was apparently only trying to codify marriage laws, rules, and customs, drawing impartially on Christian saints, Greek and Roman philosophers, historians and poets, modern as well as ancient, and of course the jurisconsults of the past and present. But he did follow the opinion of the majority that women are by nature weaker in body than men and far inferior in mind, and hence the first law of marriage, subjection. His friend, Amaury Bouchard, felt constrained to set matters right and wrote a little book called *The Defence of Women against Andreas Tiraqueau.* After examining pretty much the same set of authorities, Bouchard delivers himself of this advice: "Your conclusion must be tempered, Andreas, I think, which you can base only on false assumptions. From citations from your authors you assert women far inferior to men in body and mind when you ought to make them equal. Therefore, not like servants should wives be subjected to husbands, as seems to you to follow your premise. St. Paul really settles that. We are not commanded to forsake father and mother in order to cleave to a slave, man or woman. Neither slave nor servant strives to know the will of his master, whose slightest word is law. You yourself claim that a man should seek a wife among equals and of similar character since likeness is the greatest cause of love, nor do the interpreters of the law even consider marriage between unequals. What similarity is there between servant and master? Moreover true love is said to be the foster-child of liberty. Whoever fears hates. Joannes Faber, our countryman, in his commentaries on civil laws not unlearnedly wrote, whoever concedes power to the husband over his wife raises hate in the wife toward her husband, compulsion destroying love. Since all living things seek liberty the woman more than others will be resentful of servitude. The wise legislator not wishing to see the will of the woman broken does not call her a slave or add her to her husband's household servants but makes her a companion, a word how alien to rule." The main stream, however, was set to firm belief in the husband's right and duty to rule his family.[19]

We can now proceed to look at the qualities of the wife, prescribed to fit the demands and needs of the husband. Obviously, from the premise of subjection, the most important virtue of the woman as a wife is obedience. Upon that was made to hang all the peace and happiness of a household. The sharpest confirmation of the truth of this generalization may be felt, perhaps, in the recommendation of it that a husband gave as a first lesson to his newly wedded wife. One is tempted to read between the lines that sixteen-year-old Delia, not having readily enough accepted the overlordship of her husband, Orazio Lombardelli, had been left alone in the country to ponder well what her behavior was to be. From the city, where he says he has been delayed by various duties, he sends her his admonitions on the duty of a married woman, in which she will particularly note the steps which appear most needful to her. His lessons begin with the following passage. Let her rivet closely in her mind that by God's order and no merit of her own she has been provided with such a husband as himself, that is, a man of equal rank to herself, who has until death to love, cherish, defend, teach, and govern her in place of father, mother, brother or tutor. She must be contented, or offend God and risk punishment. She ought to hold herself very happy to have to obey a worthy person, for as the head adorns the body, the prince the city, the gem the ring, so the husband adorns the wife, and she should obey not only when he commands but when he doesn't. She need not expect many happy days unless she wishes to be modest, pleasing, kind, and lovable, but she may expect to enjoy every sweet thing if she will be tractable to her husband, for she may well believe that if he has known how to write of the duties of the married woman, he has known also how to stamp on his heart the duties of the good husband.

Short of disobedience to God's commands obedience meant complete surrender of the woman's will and desires to her husband's wishes. Vives himself furnished the measure by which to estimate the full meaning of wifely devotion, accepted, exacted, praised by men, and voluntarily, dutifully, willingly granted by the perfect wife. If Vives' account of Clara Vaudere's marriage to a husband nearly thirty years older and early decaying with syphilis, as she learned on her wedding night, were not so long and so harrowing to modern minds, I should like to quote it here. But he has nothing but praise for her twenty-years' selfless nursing of a man more than half dead from the beginning, to whom she bore eight children, and for whose death she had such grief as she might have had for a husband "young, whole, faire, lusty, and rich." Neither she nor her children ever became infected, Vives reports. "Whereby a man may clearly perceive, howe muche their holinesse and vertue is worth that love their husbands with al their harts as duty is, which doubtlesse God will never leave unrewarded." Vives knew well the whole story for he took as wife one of Clara's daughters. It should be noted here, however, that Vives was not indifferent to the risks that a wife ran for herself and her children if she married a diseased man. He is one of the few who thought to set down health as one of the first considerations in choice of a mate.

Let this discussion of obedience close, however, on a more moderate, and to the age itself, more generally acceptable note. Here is Erasmus' arresting counsel to the wife who finds obedience a hard lesson, especially to an exacting and stern husband. Let her think this austerity wholesome for the family, even if at times bitter. Nature has given it to the male to carry on the struggle for a living that he must undertake for wife and children. Would the wife want this masculine fierceness to be lacking when affairs demand a strong man? In danger would she prefer a monkey to a lion? "Serve then your lion, accommodating yourself to his manners, avoiding exasperating his wrath. Think within yourself, where you are the lion, I am the lioness; where you are master, I am mistress." By obedience, in truth, the good wife rules the husband. "All of a wife's care," said Fausto da Longiano, "is to know the habits and ways of her husband and be obedient, not hard, not difficult, not vexing, but composed, pleasant, merry, and gracious."[20]

The rest of the wifely virtues in reality are included in the first. An obedient wife will, of course, be chaste and modest, having no eye, ear, word, or desire for any other man than her husband; she will be patient under all possible burdens that God and her husband can lay upon her; she will not chatter when her husband wishes to talk or be silent; she will love him, with all his faults, and conform her manners to his; she will dress in accordance with his wishes; she will diligently look after his house and children, and will therefore not plague him by wanting to gad about; she will, in short, do everything as he would command her without waiting for commands and with good will and grace. But since the whole lesson of obedience has obviously many parts, we will consider separately under the name of virtue or duty those that raised most discussion.

Next to simple obedience chastity is probably the most frequently mentioned requirement of a wife, and is often given first place. According to Vives the two greatest points in a married woman are love and chastity. Love she will find after she enters her husband's house, and it should prove a great love, because in him for the rest of her life are her father, mother, brothers, and sisters, all that she held dear as her protectors, benefactors, and companions. Chastity, however, which includes much more than virginity, she brings with her from her father's house as her greatest gift to her husband. To the wife it becomes a more important thing than to the unmarried woman, for if she is unchaste the offense multiplies, now not only against God and her parents, but against her husband and her children, her vows and the church, the laws, society, and her country. What was meant by chastity in the wife, as distinguished from chastity in the unmarried woman, must be more particularly examined here. Most of all, it meant fidelity to husband, not only in act but in thought as well, and not only in fact but in seeming. A wife who raises evil hopes in other men by light behavior—too much laughter, too much agitation of body, immodest clothing, roving looks, careless speech—incurs serious blame no matter how innocent her intention. Worst of all, she arouses suspicion in her husband and then jealousy with risk of destruction of the home. She must guard herself at every point to preserve herself against the merest breath of suspicion of inchastity. Her safest defense lies in preserving a chaste mind, nor can a woman merit the title chaste unless her thoughts match her actions. She must not harbor evil desires, for desire can, little by little, corrupt a sincere mind unawares. Therefore she must avoid all occasions for evil thoughts, especially idleness, keeping herself busy within doors for the benefit of her household, praying often, reading only books that inculcate goodness, and shunning public affairs where she must inevitably see and hear something unchaste. Her mind must be set so well in a habit of chastity that when by chance she hears some unchaste word or sees some unchaste sight and is unable to retire, she is so collected in herself that she shows herself not to have seen or understood any dishonesty or to take any account of it. Yet the rule must still be moderation, wrote Pietro Belmonte for his daughter on her behavior after marriage. Chastity is not shown by being more rigid, discourteous, and rough than others. Happiness is fitting for youth and should appear in her laughter, her movements, her voice, but always with modesty and due regard for her company and her state. In all her actions she should leave others in doubt which is greater in her, chastity, humility of look, temperance, beauty of laugh, gentleness, sweetness of thought, gravity of speech, dignity in walking, majesty in standing, courtesy, and charm of manners.

No simple matter, evidently, was this guarding of reputation by the wife anxious for her own and her husband's good name. One finally comes indeed to feel that it was a sort of pitched battle between a woman and the rest of her world, including at times even her husband, a world of Peeping Toms on the alert to catch her off guard. It is of course a question of a young wife, young and beautiful. Husbands were admonished, as we have seen, of the heavy duty that lay upon them to keep their wives from temptation and opportunity to sully their chastity, but so difficult is external control of the behavior of human beings that some writers openly conceded that a husband might just as well act as if his wife were faithful, because if she were determined on deceiving him she would find a way, no matter what measures he took to check her. Women, as well as men, argued that the surest way to preserve chastity in them was to show confidence, because jealous suspicion incites women to wrong-doing, where if they were left free and shown confidence they would resist temptation for their own glory and in return of their husband's kindness. There was no better guard to her honor than a woman's own will and disposition. Some men, as already noted, thought this thorny problem could be solved by not taking a beautiful wife, but where did beauty end and ugliness begin, and when could a man or woman be trusted to recognize the line?[21]

The supreme importance of chastity to a woman was most clearly shown in its linking with honor. In women honor and chastity were exchangeable terms. Honor for both men and women was something external, a good name, for men a reputation for excellency in many things, for women only in one thing, chastity. But the difference went further, for if a man's honor was impugned, either justly or unjustly, he could seek redress in the duel, but a woman, though wrongly accused, could only hide her shame in perpetual seclusion. All the more it behooved her, then, to guard her honor from all stain from the beginning. Another difference showed in the place chastity was given among the virtues prescribed for men and women. From first in the roll for women it holds so little importance for men as almost to be said to hold no place at all. Chastity was usually just left out, or it might be merely mentioned. I have run across only one real discussion of this difference, which though overlong is deserving of space for its rarity.

It occurs among Benvenuto's "exquisite dialogues in Italian and English," composed for instruction and diversion. The speakers agree that chastity has been enjoined upon both men and women by divine law and then one makes the following observations. In respect to this it seems entirely repugnant to reason that Italians should keep their wives with so much care, circumspection, and jealousy and yet themselves have their necks altogether free from this yoke, especially when everyone knows that a man incurs infamy in adultery just as in transgression against justice, for there is no denying that he does break the oath of matrimony. There is, however, a difference between consorting with an unmarried and a married woman. In the first case he deserves blame, as has been said, but he doesn't lose honor since he injures no one except his own wife. In the second case, whether married or unmarried himself, he is dishonored in that he sins against temperance, and against justice also, by injuring another man's honor—a thing more precious than any other outward good. In well-governed cities adultery, therefore, is more heavily punished than theft. The evil of the times is shown only too well in that all over Europe men boast of their adulteries and are not punished. His listener here raises a pertinent question: if a man loses honor only when he accompanies with a married woman, may we say also that a married woman is infamous only when she offends with a married man and not when with an unmarried. The answer can be foreseen. The cases are entirely different; a married woman would sin worse than a man, first because she would stain her husband's honor as well as her own; second, because subject to man she inflicts the greater injury of an inferior upon a superior; third, to use Benvenuto's words, "because shee may bring into her Husbands house strange children, to wipe her husbands owne childrens nose of their share in his goods, and falsifie all whatsoever, so as not being honest, it will be hard to know which was Georges, and which was Martinses sonne; and therefore we read that a very poore woman being almost at the point of death, and her husband lamenting for the great burthen of children, which was like to lye upon him, his sicke wife replied: good husband doe not feare, nor take thought, for such a sonne of mine was such a Gentlemans, the other of such a Lord, the other of such a Merchant, the fourth was one of my servants: when the youngest of all, who though he were very young, yet he could understand and speake well, falling upon his knees, said: Oh loving Mother, appoint mee a very good Father."

Perhaps we should not go to dialogues concocted to teach a foreign tongue to home-bred English for instruction in moral attitudes, but it would not be difficult to collect elsewhere the scraps from which Benvenuto Italiano shrewdly wove his exposition of inchastity in men and women. One further scrap may be added to these differences. Shamefastness, fear of offense, so highly recommended to women as the preserver of chastity, is in a woman, Belmonte said in his advice to his daughter, what reason is in men, a guide to action, a curb to impulses. Now reason makes a man reasonable and sociable: if he loses it he merely ceases to be reasonable. But let a woman lose shame, and she ceases to be a woman. The result of all this Spontone notes with some complacency: not sharing wholly in the virtues and goodness of men, women, in their eagerness for praise, work hard to surpass them in minor virtues, cleanness of face, ornaments of head and clothing, affability in words, graciousness in jesting, ingenuity in the most subtle works of the needle and similar things. With the escape of blame they buy good opinion.

There is one more requirement for perfect chastity. A wife may belong wholly to her husband in fact and in desire, and bear an unclouded reputation, and still she may sin against chastity when alone with her husband. Preservation of chastity in their relation to each other must be the work of both. Our painstaking Trotto carefully admonished the wife: with her husband she should never pass the bounds of sweetness, or approach lasciviousness, or she will arouse suspicion, harm him, and lose his love. Even in the most secret caresses she ought to be true to her reputation and not offer herself to her husband like a bold prostitute. It is for her to remain bound to show restraint as a chaste wife.[22]

Something more may be said here of that other great virtue in women, silence, already described for girls. The wise wife, wrote Trotto, never contradicts, even if right, never opposes, disputes, blames, interrupts, or answers back if chided. Silence is a great preserver of love in husbands, who thus are not plagued by idle words but are listened to reverently when they wish to speak, whose anger is not aroused or increased by the sharp words of that most unnatural animal, a wife who wishes to conquer, and whose hearts are free of the suspicion and jealousy sure to kindle at the sight of a wife conversing readily with strangers, foppish young men, princes and lords of higher rank—not too reluctant to command favors— and even the lower sort, hucksters, merchants, and the like. Let a wife remember, added Vives, that it is no shame for a woman to hold her peace. Yet of course the silent wife is not to be a dumb wife. Life is not so simple for her as for the maid. Occasions arise when she must speak, out of courtesy to her husband's guests, or desire to counsel her husband, or even necessity to avoid the suspicion that her very silence may cause, especially if she hesitates when he asks a question. In more detail this is the advice that Barbaro gave to ladies on their speech. "Let them reply modestly to their husbands when called upon to do so; let them return salutations; and when place and occasion offer let them speak to the point so briefly that they may be thought to be reluctant rather than eager to open their mouths, and may be praised for their brevity in serious speech rather than for their lengthy eloquence. Speech in public, especially with strangers, is not suitable to women, whose voice is not less to be dreaded than their nakedness, since habits and emotions are easily betrayed in speech. Indeed silence is often praised in the wisest men, though some contemporary, who need not be named, commends it only in those who have no wit to obtain applause, or prudence to obtain authority, or eloquence to gain repute. This, however, would admit certain women to speech along with men, when though sometimes expedient for them, it is in general alien to the chastity, discretion, and constancy of a matron. By silence indeed women achieve the fame of eloquence." Even in the company of women only, restrictions are almost as severe. Braithwait, in his *English Gentlewoman*, published somewhat past our limits, speaks as well for his predecessors' desires on this point as Barbaro for him, more than two hundred years before. "Touching the subject of your discourse," he says to his gentlewomen, "when opportunity shall exact it of you, and without touch of immodesty expect it from you; make choyce of such arguments as may best improve your knowledge in household affaires, and other private employments. To discourse of State-matters, will not become your auditory: nor to dispute of high poynts of Divinity, will it sort well with women of your quality. These Shee-clarkes many times broach strange opinions, which, as they understand them not themselves, so they labour to intangle others of equall understanding to themselves."

Men seem to have greatly feared woman's meddling with theological matters, no doubt viewing with misgiving the extremes to which women, in their lack of balance, might carry the advice to read diligently the Holy Scriptures and the writings of the Church Fathers and other godly men, though carefully warned to read for help to their frailty and not for speculation. There was a common saying, said Guazzo, that a young man should not talk like an old man, or a woman like a man. Practically no differentiation was attempted in these general treatises on marriage and wives between educated and uneducated women. Silence is good for all of them: against inchastity always lurking in free conversation in mixed companies, against idleness fostered by chatter, against presumption blown up out of ignorance, and against invasion of husbands' peace and prerogatives.[23]

Prudence, or discretion, was another prescribed virtue, regarded as much needed by wives in solving the practical problems of everyday life. To judge from emphasis, the most practical problem of everyday life was the handling of husbands in difficult situations, including the bestowal of counsel when wifely wisdom sufficed. The usual picture of husbands, here men of high birth in their domestic setting, is not attractive. They were reproached for acting the tyrant at home in mistaken exercise of their superiority conferred by nature, law, and custom, whereas that very superiority should teach them gentleness, kindness, patience, and courtesy toward those weaker and inferior beings so dependent upon them. Or as Lombardelli put it, if the well-born wife will not do wrong willfully, or unintentionally, or through love, but from good habits and ready affection will always act with merit, then her husband, since man by nature is noble and does not endure being surpassed, will do as much again for his wife. Fortunate indeed was a woman, said Vives, if her husband was good, most unfortunate if he was bad, but in either case her duty was to love, honor, and obey him in all honest things.

The more difficult a husband might prove to be, exhibiting faults and even vices that threaten to destroy mutual happiness and security, the greater would be her opportunity for showing her prudence. For the time wisely enduring wrongs and displeasure, due either to her fault or his defect, and remembering that men have more freedom than women to sin as well as to act nobly, she will set herself patiently and sweetly to learn how to solve her problem, with careful reference to what she knows of his habits, disposition, and state. Among the lesser faults anger was most frequently mentioned, and she was advised to begin by avoiding occasion for anger through strict obedience to his commands and compliance with his wishes, which she will discover, if possible, before he needs to mention them. When he is angry she will soothe him with patience, humility, and repentance if she herself is at fault, and if not, never at the time will she lay the blame on him. She will not at any time provoke him to worse attacks by arguing with him, nor will she ever, under any provocation, treat him with scorn. When the time seems favorable, she will courteously and gently and as impersonally as possible acquaint him with his fault, suggesting, if it has been committed in the presence of others, that this or that can be said of him which would not be to his honor. But she should not do this often, and should be well assured before she attempts correction. If he only grows angry she will desist, having done her duty, and will put up with what cannot be mended.[24]

The other fault that is specially singled out is jealousy. We have seen what advice was offered the husband himself on its control; the wife too cannot escape responsibility for avoiding occasion to arouse or feel it. Vives has a good deal to say to her on the subject. "Verilie it is a sore vexation and agonie," he warns her, "and a verie cruell tyrannie, which as long as it raigneth and rageth in the Husbands heart, let the wife never hope to have peace. It were better for them both to bee dead, than anie of them to fall into jealousie, but especiallie the man." She should work with all her power to prevent it by never saying or doing anything that may arouse suspicion in him. Here follows most of the advice already recorded with this special application. If suspicion does arise, in her chastity and love without dissimulation must lie her hope for a cure. As for jealousy in herself, if strong and disturbing, she must seek a remedy in remembering that, as her lord, her husband may do what she may not, bound like her by God's law to be chaste but not by the laws of the world, and that he lives in more liberty than she. If wise she will refuse to listen to anyone who wants to speak ill of her husband. The worst thing she can do is to quarrel with him or leave him because of his mistresses, for she only throws him more into their power and causes public gossip—a worse thing for a woman than any kind of pain she may endure with him. In truth any grudge she may bear for his lying with other women should be taken as mere fantasy of bodily pleasure and not love. By displeasure she will provoke him the more, and the sooner reclaim him by her patience, especially when he comes to compare her gentle manners with his mistress's unreasonable pride. Rather she should dissemble all knowledge of his infidelities and even act before the world so as to destroy all suspicion of her discontent as did the wife Vives praises, who hearing that her husband was in danger from the husband and relatives of his mistress had him bring her home and yielded to her first place in all things, showing no sign of what she thought except that she was much in church and in prayer. At the end of a year, won by her beauty and goodness, superior in all respects to his mistress's, her husband put his mistress away and set his love on his wife again. Thus the faults of the husband give occasion to the wife to show fortitude and greatness of heart, by which some wives have won immortal fame.[25]

One more question that concerns a wife's prudence or discretion. Should she be expected or allowed to offer her husband advice on his own affairs, a very different matter from the domestic concerns hitherto considered. It is to be feared that common opinion agreed with the advice fathered upon Marcus Aurelius in commonplace books: "Hardy is that woman that dare geve counsaile to a man, but he is more hardy that taketh it of a woman, he is a foole that taketh it, and he is more foolish that asketh it, and he is most foolishe that fulfilleth it." Few there are who talk about "wise" wives, and the scope of women's wisdom, when it is allotted to them, is obviously narrow and centered on the husband in his domestic role. He is their book, and what they are to learn there, Valerio, by no means a complete depressor of women, says, by way of summary, consists in knowing themselves, their weakness, their consequent subjection, the great importance to them of honor, their need of all the reason, discretion, moderation, and foresight they can muster to foresee and prevent possible evils. Some hardy advisers, however, held that husbands should seek counsel from wives as prudent as they were supposed to marry, and that those prudent wives were to feel themselves bound to give such counsel as they could conceive. Ordinarily wise wives would not offer it without being asked, but in the case of serious need they should volunteer, taking great care to choose a favorable time, and in all humility venturing their opinions, like Chaucer's Prudence, an example of the wisdom, tact, and humility that the wise husband should look to find in his wife. Secrecy would of course have to be a part of this prudence. No taunt was ever more frequently hurled at women than incapacity for secrecy, from the wife of Midas down, but sober renaissance defenders of women denied any ground for such a charge with plentiful examples of women secret to heroic degrees. Lombardelli assumes Delia can be secret when he advises her not to tell whatever he tells her in confidence, and Vives says that a well-taught wife will keep her husband's secrets and give comfort and counsel.[26]

Love may be set down next as a most important virtue for the wife because it serves as a motivating force behind the other virtues, in fact behind the wife's whole existence. It is conjugal love that seeks the husband's exaltation through her resignation. Let her love her husband next to God, advice runs, with such zeal, faith, and grace that she may not be found wanting in diligence, benevolence, and reverence toward him. Let her love him not for his riches, or beauty, or strength, or nobility, or for carnal pleasure, but for his modesty, prudence, sober speaking, and the like, in obedience only to God's command. Let her show him clearly that she does love him by losing no chance to reveal her love and avoiding everything that might arouse suspicion. She should be glad or sorry as he is, and be of the same mind as far as possible. Even by her frugality and industry in his interest can she show her love. Then may not the wife who thus loves and cherishes her husband expect the same love and consideration from him? She must, however, use good judgment lest in her zeal she arouse the suspicion that she seeks to avoid. Too much cheerfulness may arouse question; too much soberness may breed boredom and drive him to seek relief elsewhere. It is her part to love constantly and allow no infirmity in his mind or body to change her love. If he should through some fault in her, or ignorance or perversity on his part, seem to have lost his love of her, she should not despair but hope to regain it by continued effort to please. Chaste love is of the soul, and takes time for growth; it is not made without long acquaintance, by the union of souls, wills, manners, and affection. Therefore how much wrong people do, either men or women, who try to force it by philters or enchantments, so dangerous to the health and sanity of the beloved, and so fleeting.

There is something of ambiguity about the discussions of love as it should be between husband and wife. For the husband, as we have seen, love is treated almost altogether as a problem of physical relations, the conjugal duty of sexual intercourse. For the wife love is obviously a matter of social relations, nearer to friendship, that is related to the performance of the offices of friendship. In assigning these helpful offices to the wife, writers occasionally recommended them also to the husband as reciprocal duties, but without placing any special emphasis on his share. The physical side of married love from the wife's point of view is almost wholly ignored, except for an occasional reference to her duty to help realize one of the great purposes of matrimony, the avoidance of adultery. It is made obvious elsewhere that most writers feared that in performing this duty too much passion might be aroused, endangering the wife's chastity, and counseled the husband especially against excess even to the point of deprecating pleasure. There were, however, a few eulogists of marriage who pointed out advantages in this love over illicit love, in that it is more chaste, free, strong, beautiful, and secure, and who even go so far as to advise the wife to work to preserve and increase passion in her husband by willingly and zealously seeking to enjoy it, and by taking thought of her appearance. More realistically than most, these recognized the advantage beauty gave to a wife in holding a husband. The beauty she has she should take all necessary care to preserve and enhance, and thus avoid making the mistake of thinking she has more than God gave her, and if she lacks beauty, she can at least improve every part. Since beautiful clothing sets off beauty, she should spend much thought on dressing appropriately to herself and her rank, and, most of all, pleasingly to her husband.[27]

Last among the virtues that are specially required of the wife I have placed modesty because it touches on one side or another all the other virtues. Given such a wide application it becomes vague in meaning, but impossible to ignore because it is held so important for wives that at times it seems to top the rest. Honored by everyone, Barbaro says, modesty is most pleasing to husbands because chastity itself depends upon it. No woman can be counted wholly chaste, we have been told repeatedly, if a breath of suspicion falls on her, and suspicion rises from just the visible things that modesty is to rule. Let a woman be immodest in behavior, talk, and dress, and she will be suspected of grave faults since she brings temptation to herself as well as others. Just what is modesty? The meaning of the word must largely be inferred. It is often loosely used as a synonym for other virtues, particularly chastity, and then seems to have no meaning of its own. In so far as it has a special sense it appears to have meant chiefly a kind of timidity, that is, a shrinking from drawing attention to oneself, a desire to be inconspicuous, a fear of adverse comment, or to give it positive force and a more praiseworthy connotation, moderation. Some do define it as moderation. Cabei calls it the virtue which has power to moderate the passions of the soul and exterior operations also; Belmonte defines it as moderation in all things, dress, recreation, behavior to associates, in keeping with honor and state. From its general use one would judge Belmonte more exact in applying it only to external things, as suggested above. Occasionally modesty appears coupled with another virtue which seems to be intended rather as a synonym than an addition. Thus Spontone says that *modesty and generous shame* belong to woman, and Fausto da Longiano that the *modest and temperate* woman clothes herself with chastity. The idea of restraint is at least emphasized. More reliably, however, the meaning of modesty is to be drawn from the occasions and affairs in which it was recommended.

To take a few examples—nothing assists love in marriage, says Tillier, more than modesty, for no matter what the behavior of the husband his libertinage can be corrected with a calm eye, a measured step, and a firm gesture. Much was said about the face that the wife should turn to her husband at home. Lombardelli directs his wife when in his presence to show a face tranquil and happy, for a laughing, lascivious, or changing and disturbed face is sign of an evil mind, particularly if she laughs when he is sad. When he asks her any question, she must answer simply and at once, to avoid any unpleasant suspicion as to what she may be thinking. Others warn the wife that it is even more important if she is to escape the attentions of lightminded men abroad to. control the expression of her face. Her eyes should be cast down, the clearest sign of modesty, not roving around boldly meeting the gaze of men. Her expression should call for no remark, but her features be composed, undistorted by twisting of her lips, or pouting, or laughing boisterously, a fault in everyone but especially a sign of levity, if not lasciviousness, in women. This is not to forbid laughter, some relent, which should reveal her contented state, but to warn her to laugh with modesty, that is, with little movement of her face and body, low tone, and rarity, to show her sincerity not her vanity. So her carriage should at all times be firm, her walk slow and dignified, not mincing or too hasty, her hands quiet, gestures few and restrained. Walking or standing she should guard against falling into any affectations or unsuitable habits. If she is careless in any of these matters, lightness is charged and great harm may ensue both to herself and her husband. The most frequent advice on going abroad was of course to go abroad seldom, even less than maids who seem to be seeking husbands, Vives adds surprisingly, perhaps an English touch. She is unfortunate if she has business abroad, and should be old or middle-aged. If young, she will have to be courteous, but without flattery, and she may better lose money than chastity. When she must be abroad, he finishes, she should show no sign of presumption, disdain, or dainty stomach, by words, countenance, or pace, but she should be simple, forthright, demure, sober, tempered, and spiced with shamefastness. Thus modesty will guide her behavior, preserving her from vanity, reckless exposure of herself to misunderstanding, and ill repute. Transgression in a woman received more severe blame than in a man, as was plainly set down in the book of rules for anchoresses, who were instructed in confession to say: "I am a woman, and ought by right to have been more modest than to speak as I have spoken, or to do as I have done. Therefore my sin is greater in me than in a man because it was more unbecoming to me."

The decisions of husbands had no small bearing on their wives' behavior. Moderate advisers recommended a judicious relaxing of the generally accepted rule that a woman's place was in the house attending to her business. The house should not be a prison. Out of regard for the natural desire in youth for recreation the husband should occasionally entertain his young wife with public spectacles, feasts, weddings, and the like where assured of their honest character, and he should allow her to go to assemblies of honest women without following or watching her. Of course her own circumspection would largely determine the freedom he could allow her.[28]

How wives should dress themselves agitated many minds as a serious problem connected with women. Whole books were devoted to the subject, more space, however, being given to blaming women for extravagance and immodesty (the two went naturally together) in dress, ornaments, and use of cosmetics than in setting down principles for guidance. Most advice ignored the problems for women of high birth by telling them to stay at home where temptation for display is lacking, to dress simply in clothes fit for domestic duties and at their gayest only for the husband's eye, but modestly even so, not to arouse concupiscence in him. Beyond that the most important considerations were cleanliness in dress and person, not merely of face and hands, orderliness in keeping of hair, and restraint in wearing of ornaments. Husbands themselves should not be so foolish as to want to deck wives out in finery only to have them go about to show off with corresponding neglect of duties at home.

The subject of painting stirred up a good deal of heat. For what or for whom should a wife paint? If painting within reason was permissible to the girl not yet furnished with a husband and therefore anxious to present as attractive an appearance as possible, the argument was no longer applicable to the married woman, who had no acceptable incentive to attract the eyes of men. Modesty forbade her to wish for attention from others than her husband, religion forbade her to try to improve on what God had given her, thus painting to please herself was sheer vanity and therefore displeasing to God. If nothing else, concern for her health should hold her from using the highly dangerous concoctions of poisonous and filthy things that were offered women silly enough to think that they could improve on natural beauty if they had it, or decrease natural defects if it was their lot to be less than beautiful. As for pleasing her husband, "Make thy soul gay with vertue," said Vives, "and he shall kiss thee for thy beauty." Lombardelli, to quote a man writing to his wife, forbade rouge and all cosmetics to Delia because of the harm done by deceiving men, the scandal reflected on upbringing when wives show too much devotion to themselves, and the loss of time and neglect of duties. Such was the unvarnished, uncompromising advice commonly given to wives without consideration of rank.

A few writers, more realistic than most, advised that birth, income, occasion, and most of all her husband's wishes should govern a wife's dressing, painting, and adorning of herself with jewels. Barbaro with his usual good sense ruled that the wellborn should not dress meanly if able to dress better since moderate adornment reveals the husband's rank, wealth, and position, and less than that serves as a derogation to him in that people expect his wife to have ways of living and manners corresponding to his. Even Vives allowed some concession to the times and a husband's wishes, a part of the wife's due obedience, though he thought the husband unwise to favor costly dress and painting as only too likely to endanger chastity by fostering vanity and inviting other men to desire her.[29]

These then are the qualities that seem to have been most highly and frequently recommened in wives: obedience, chastity, silence, discretion, love, and modesty. One would have expected to find humility and piety, too, but they were in fact seldom more than named, rather, one may judge, because they are so necessary as to be taken for granted than because they were deemed unimportant. The good wife, said Trotto briefly, is humble toward her husband and toward all whom he honors and loves, his parents and relatives, dear to him before she was. The highly religious character of the reading prescribed for wives indicates that piety was largely assumed to underlie and guide all other virtues, though few writers explicitly prescribe it, and, one may remark, reverence seems to have been a word appropriated almost exclusively by husbands. Belmonte summed up religious duties for his daughter newly married thus: she should spend an hour each day in private at prayers for peace and concord with her husband, and for the health of his relatives and peace with them—in private, not in public lest she be suspected of hypocrisy if she seemed too devout; she should attend mass and other divine offices silently; and with her husband she should give alms generously. To all these other virtues some took pains to show that pleasantness should be added if a wife was to hold and increase the love of her husband. "The wife should couple and binde her husbande unto her everie daye more and more, with her pleasant & gentle conditions," wrote Vives. "For nothing doth more draw & entice unto it, than doth pleasant conditions & sweet speech. A wise woman should have in mind merry tales, & histories (howbeit yet honest) wherewith she may refresh her husband, & make him merry when he is weary. And also shee shall learn precepts of wisdome to exhort him unto vertue, or draw him from vice with all, and some sage sentences against the assaults and rages of both fortunes, both to plucke downe her husbands stomacke, if hee be proud of prosperity and wealth: and comfort and heart him, if he be stricken in heaviness with adversitie. . . . And againe the wife shall make her husband a counsail of al her sorrowes and cares: so that they bee meete to tell a wiseman of. Shee shall take him onelie for her companion & talking felow, counsellour, master, and Lorde, and utter unto him al her thoughts, and rest in him. For these thinges make love and concorde.''[30]

Since the wife was admonished that it was her duty not only to cultivate the virtues necessary to her and appropriate to her nature, but also to search for the faults inherent in women's weakness and infirmity and to eradicate those she found in herself, we had better record advice on the reverse side of the wifely image. In general the faults of wives are the opposite of their virtues. The most serious faults that men would have women avoid seem to have been pride and wrath. Pride was singled out particularly because it led to the insolence of striving for supremacy over husbands, that is over men, a great peril even to states; witness, shuddered Capaccio, the horrible example of Elizabeth of England, whose pride fed by power led her, to her ignominy and shame, to desire to supersede the authority of the Apostolic Chair, and to imbrue herself in the blood of so many martyrs. Of less import may be thought the other manifestations of pride in women's common habit of exulting in their beauty, or their family connections, or wealth, all in no way a mark of their own worth or a product of their own efforts, and in the great value they set on every little blast of honor paid them by titles, precedence in place, and small favors. Vives reads wives a severe lecture on the lightmindedness shown in this lack of perspective. To be sure men go out of their way to prefer women in the best place in the house or in the highest seat, pay them compliments, bestow gifts of gold, silver, precious stones, fine clothes, but not, as women think, out of reverence for them. Only because they see women greedy for such small things and deeply hurt by small offenses do men give these signs of honor as toys to children to keep them from crying. No man thinks a woman more honorable because honored in these ways by men, but counts men courteous and gentle for doing what pleases so much at so little cost. Among themselves men make great sport over women's foolishness on this point. In truth women do not understand honor, that it is becoming to deserve it, not to covet it, and they should be ashamed to receive what their worth does not match. Anger likewise was a fault found particularly common in women, charged with being more quickly aroused than men and less easily reconciled, partly because they are shut up and lack variety of scene and fresh matter to fill their minds. They should, therefore, bridle their tongues, warned Vives, so full are they of wrath that there is no measure to their chiding and scolding. He had had to wonder at the intemperance of tongue of otherwise good and honest women, and had had to be ashamed for them.

One list of faults should be included, partly for its corroboration of the preceding, and partly for the query it raises. Lombardelli advised his wife to avoid pride, boasts, desire to surpass others, anger, fierceness, bravado, cruelty, violence—more becoming to soldiers and prostitutes than to ladies —and not to use oaths without great cause. What passionate depths had he already glimpsed in his Delia, or is he merely providing for all contingencies? It is hard to know exactly what to do with this piece of advice, so incongruous with the lighter view usually taken of women's faults, as at their worst the product of their natural weakness. Vives, less severe in advising husbands on wives than in his instructions to women, goes so far as to suggest that men should not wish women different, for after all, their weakness is necessary if they are to submit to being ordered about by men. If they had wit and strength they would strive to rule. Their loquacity, within measure, is sometimes pleasing to men when wearied with public and private affairs, and with it they teach their children to talk and do other things suitable to that age, to which the nobility of man would not stoop. Their envy and rivalry if not in excess "sharpens their vertues and qualities, and the domestical diligence and custody of their behaviour." Even superstition is not intolerable so long as it does not extinguish true religion—in fact he does not commend the woman who doesn't incline to superstition out of her great zeal for religion, unless she is one of those absolute and perfect matrons.[31]

The wife thus framed and disposed, full of the virtues prized by husbands, and free of the faults equally detested, can scarcely fail to please her husband. If she is to play her role adequately, however, in the partnership of marriage, much is still required of her in the skills necessary to the care of a family: the management of the house, the direction of servants, and the rearing of children. Division of authority for these practical, domestic ends was recommended by all writers. Without question outside affairs belong to the man, the management of his estates and his profession or business, through which he provides the means to support his family. For such purposes he has been made strong and courageous to bear the weight of toil for public and private good. Also without question belongs to him the general ordering of domestic affairs, such as the choice of site for his house, the building of it and appointment within of quarters for each purpose— women's rooms, servants' quarters, guest rooms, kitchens, storage rooms for clothes, arms, food—the choice and training of servants, the entertainment of friends and strangers, and the style of daily life. But for the minute details of executing the various duties he should have not time or inclination but should hand over responsibility for them to his wife, who has been made timid and delicate of spirit and inferior in strength expressly for such business, to stay continually in the house, diligently preserve what he has brought in, bear the tedium, squeamishness, and trouble found in the heaviness, the birth, and bringing up of infants. The head of the house must of course reserve final authority in himself, but he should delegate to his wife enough to relieve himself of matters which belong to women rather than to men, and also to assure her of his confidence in her. Each then should assume that it is unseemly and a disgrace when either usurps the place of the other.[32]

The part that belonged to the wife in household management, as was foreseen in her training, included supervision of all the many activities within doors, knowledge of how each operation is carried out, and even ability to perform many of the tasks herself. Her aim will be a well-ordered house, everything in place to be at hand when needed, everything needful supplied. She must look after the food that is brought in, store it in appropriate places, use it when ready, and preserve what is perishable and cannot be eaten at once. Likewise she must keep in suitable places, free from dust and moths, the clothing, linen, tapestries, and so forth. Since she has charge of the purchasing and dispensing of goods within the house, the apportioning of expenditure is largely in her hands, and to her falls the keeping of accounts. With due regard to the dignity of the family, she will not be niggardly in seeing that everything necessary is furnished, but frugality and foresight are needed here, thought for the future, for the losses that may come, and for old age when endurance fails, to guide the judgment and restrain expense. Even when her husband urges spending, she must work for the good of the family and not spend merely to feed vanity and ostentation. In almsgiving, however, she must allow generous donations, and approve also whatever her husband wishes to give for religious uses. All the more important operations and arrangements must of course be made in accordance with her husband's directions and wishes, but she will not run to him about matters that she should be able to settle for herself. She cannot expect him to descend to minutiae: cooking ordinary food, preserving, alleviating the thirst of gentlemen, keeping count of the washing and kitchen ware, visiting the cellar, granary, garden, poultry yard, sewing and spinning for use and ornament, all strictly women's business. If she attends to these things with diligence and zeal he is to consider only whether she can with reason be called virtuous and honored and himself happy and glorious, deeming such a wife worthy the title of patron and lady.[33]

It is to be noted again that little attempt was made to distinguish in household economy between the noblewoman of a large establishment and the lady of a lesser one, or scarcely between the lady and the poor man's wife. Torquato Tasso, one of the few to take account of differences between the higher and lower, said that the lady of high rank should occasionally set her hand to some work, not in the kitchen for that would soil her clothes and was not the business of a noble matron, but appropriately at her wheel and loom. The farther off she is from noble estate, however, the more she should busy herself with meaner work. Barbaro, likewise, laid down the general rule that women of the highest nobility should not be employed in the lowest tasks, but by adding the provision, unless in emergency such as sickness or sudden guests, he obviously assumed that even they should be able to perform the lowest taks. There was common agreement with Tasso and Vives, already quoted on the subject in relation to the training of girls, that the needle, spindle, and loom were exercises that belonged to ladies just as much as arms and letters belonged to gentlemen, and were important not only against the dreaded idleness, so fertile in offering temptation to evil, but for the substantial contribution to the family goods that could be made by the production of clothing. An Englishman even found cause for national pride in such accomplishments. "The labours that be both decent and profitable for gentlewomen," said John Jones, physician, "are these, most meete in my minde, and also in daylye use with many, as spinning of Wooll on the greate compasse Wheele, and on the rocke or distaffe, wherewith I would not that any should be so daintie, as to be offended thereat but rather to commende and use them as an ornament, and benefit of god bestowed upon oure flourishing countrey, surpassing all our princely neyghbours." No highborn lady, therefore, should scorn such occupations.[34]

The most important care of the wife, however, is looking after the welfare of the people of her household. Their comfort, health, happiness are in her hands, and particularly in illness she will show her diligence, for nothing, said Trotto, so restores and benefits both body and mind as the loving-kindness of a cheerful wife or mother. Skill in the preparation of food and simple home remedies for the common ills is essential if she is going to meet their needs. Markham thoroughly agreed, and among the virtues of the English country housewife he declared "the first and most principall to bee a perfect skill and knowledge in Cookery, together with all the secrets belonging to the same; because it is a duety really belonging to the woman, and shee that is utterly ignorant therein, may not by the lawes of strikt justice challenge the freedome of marriage, because indeed shee can then but performe halfe her vow; for she may love and obey, but shee cannot serve and keepe him with that true duetie which is ever expected." The Italian prescribed simply food that is always tasty, delicate, and wholesome. The Englishman is more specific, and English. "Let her dyet be wholesome and cleanly, prepared at due howers, and cookt with care and diligence, let it be rather to satisfie nature then our own affections, and apter to kill hunger then revive new appetites, let it proceede more from the provision of her owne yarde, then the furniture of the markets; and let it be rather esteemed for the familiar acquaintance shee hath with it, then for the strangenesse and raritie it bringeth from other countries." And if she is to be a good cook "shee must be cleanly both in body and garments, she must have a quicke eye, a curious nose, a perfect taste and a ready care (she must not be butter fingered, sweet-toothed, nor faint hearted); for the first will let everything fall, the second will consume what it should encrease, and the last will loose time with too much nicenesse."

Only less important in Markham's opinion was "a physicall kinde of knowledge, how to administer many wholsome receits or medicines for the good of their healthes, as well to prevent the first occasion of sicknesse, as to take away the effects and will of the same when it hath made seazure on the body," and Vives advised the housewife to see that her closet is well stored with medicines and salves of her own making so that she will not have to send often for a physician or buy everything of an apothecary. But some apprehension existed over possible undesirable results of such advice. Vives, with due regard for the women's modesty, chastity, and mental inadequacy, cautioned, "I would she should learne, rather by the experience of sad and wise women, than of the counsel of any phisition dwelling nigh about: and have them diligently written in some litle booke, and not in the great volumes of physick." Markham is also uneasy, though on a different ground. "Indeed we must confesse that the depth and secrets of this most excellent art of phisicke, is farre beyond the capacitie of the most skilfull weoman, as lodging only in the brest of the learned Professors, yet that our hous-wife may from them receive some ordinary rules, and medicines which may availe for the benefit of her familie, is (in our common experience) no derogation at all to that worthy Science. Neither doe I intend here to leade her minde with all the Symptoones, accidents, and effects which goe before or after every sicknesse, as though I would have her to assume the name of a Practitioner, but only relate unto her some approved medicines and old doctrines which have beene gathered together, and delivered by common experience, for the curing of those ordinary sicknesses which daily perturb the health of Men and Women.[35]

A great deal was said about the duties of the prudent matron toward the servants of the household. First of all she was to have respect for these human beings who served her, because they are human, that is, reasonable creatures, and Christian. They are children of God, as she is, and if they serve Him more truly than she does, they will have a higher place in heaven than she. Accept that they are born to obey and have as their peculiar gift the capacity of receiving and executing commands willingly, yet they are not to be scorned as beasts. They are able to care for themselves, and as free men, not serfs, they become servants to make their living that way, or to learn an art, or craft, or science. Poverty and lack of knowledge commonly make men servants, and sometimes it is seen that fortune and not nature has decreed their lowly lot, since some become able assistants and even advisers of their employers, coming at times to great honors and estates through their loyal service.

The mistress's duties in overseeing her servants concern every aspect of their lives. She provides sufficient food and clothing suitable to the rank of the family, and when they are sick she personally sees that they are well taken care of. She apportions their work according to their abilities, taking care not to impose on them what they are unfitted to do. She sets them an example of industry herself by doing more work than they and showing greater usefulness. She encourages them with praise and judicious rewards, but if necessary she points out their faults, and reproves them reasonably without anger. She must of course without fear exact obedience from them, but by quiet and gentle rule rather than by rigorousness. Chiding, scolding, all the more railing and brawling, are hindrances and entirely unbecoming to her dignity. Think, said Alberti to his young wife, of her distorted appearance when angry, contorted mouth, rolling eyes, and threatening hands, and then keep her voice low, admonish with sweetness, and command with reason as if used to command; through her wisdom, seriousness, and gravity of words and sentences she will gain from them the love and reverence due a mother rather than the fear inspired by a mistress. She should try to hold servants long in service, obedient to her and her husband, kind to the children, and friendly to each other. To this end selection in the first place should be most carefully made on the basis of good qualities, such as good and moderate mind, good birth, sufficient ability to reason and talk for the service appointed, temperance, and above all piety. Then frequent change will be unnecessary, which can be disastrous since discontented, discharged servants spread tales of defects. The good opinion of servants is desirable for they are most believed by the crowd, who make up the greater part of a city. Even if a lady does not care for their praise, she should fear not a little their blame.

With her men servants she will maintain due reserve, not conversing much with them or allowing them to play or dally with her, nor will she be over-pleasant or merry of speech. She must take care that they do not misinterpret her words and actions, and if they show signs of licentiousness she must have them dismissed, but not in such a way as to make them enemies of the house, lest they spread lying reports and bring all to ruin. She will therefore spend most of her time with her maids for whose welfare, instruction, and conduct she is more especially responsible. By staying with them she can keep them all busy and chaste, and instruct them. She must herself set them an example by her own way of life, not above working with them even in the kitchen dressing meat, as Vives has said, and spinning, weaving, and sewing so that things will be better done. She must vigilantly oversee them so that there may be no secrets in their way of life, and if they show any inclination to vice she must find remedies, or if any persist dismiss them, since the mistress is judged according to her servants.

Servants themselves are occasionally admonished. Loyalty, diligence, soberness, and chastity are enjoined upon them. They should keep secrets, be obedient, humbly acknowledge faults, refrain from talking back, seek to please with all their power, never saying "I don't know," but finding out how to do the service requested, keep an open and cheerful face, love their masters and never contradict their ladies but give service equally to both, weep and rejoice with them, avoid flattery but show that they desire the honor and profit of both, be gracious and truthful to children, keep body and clothes clean, sow no dissension among fellows, or frequent taverns or games, sleep a moderate amount, and give strict account of everything entrusted to them. Such loyal service may lead to honor and the position of master in their turn. So Bouchet summed up his advice, writing, he said, not out of high learning but experience. The pattern, one will observe, is not so different from that for a wife.[36]

To the mistress of the house as the dispenser of comfort and food naturally falls the chief responsibility for the entertainment of visitors. Kindness and desire to please and honor each according to rank are her aims. When her guest is a man she will meet him with a cheerful look and gracious welcome, and converse circumspectly with him on suitable subjects, not on serving or cooking, which do not belong to men, nor on law and war which do not belong to women. She will order everything without a lot of ostentation and fuss, not scorning to overlook preparations in the kitchen in order to present him an abundance of the best foods. She will not do as some, make a lot of protestations and a great fuss about seats and footstools, and such a rattle of dishes and cutlery that he is prepared for a feast and gets a badly cooked and served meal. On his departure she will show all possible courtesies, accompanying him to the top or the bottom of the stairs according to his merit, and sending her greetings to his family. In general the same considerations hold when her guest is a woman, except that there is more freedom and less respect. Conversation, however, should not be mere chatter and endless details about their houses and husbands, and tedious fault-finding with everything; but with reserve she should try to converse on delightful and pleasing subjects. Of course if her guest insists on long speeches which she cannot check, she will have to endure patiently. She should exert herself to please her women visitors, not after greetings plant herself in a chair and remain there, but see to the fire and windows, take them to the gardens, show the house or anything new and beautiful, so as to reveal her gentility and familiarity and not her pride. She must provide refreshments. If someone has brought a small child she should caress him and give him a little present as a sign of love, not wealth. Little gifts like this sometimes cause great friendship. In her turn she will have to visit those who call on her, either in the order of merit, or in the order in which they called on her. In their houses she will not change her seat unless invited by her hostess, nor will she go uninvited to other parts of the house. For conversation she will always have something pleasing to say, never speak anything but good of others, and avoid lies and curiosity.

Such, then, are in brief the duties of the wife as the mistress of the house. If she performs them with care and skill to the utmost of her ability, she will deserve the benediction of all men expressed in Barnaby Rich's words, "The certain markes of a vertuous woman is to be a good huswife."[37]

One more role remains for the wife to play, that of mother. It was taken for granted that married women would want children, one of the three fundamental purposes of marriage being the propagation of children, sometimes set first, sometimes second to the other purposes. Women generally seem to have needed reproof not for desire to escape maternity, but for overdisappointment at not having children. Lombardelli wrote his young wife that she must learn how to serve and bring up children well, and added, if she should have no children she must submit to God's will. Bouchet made children the chief end of marriage, but like Lombardelli advised that people should not fret if they lack children, for it is God's plan for them. In compensation they are then at liberty to think of all the grief, pain, and labor that they have escaped. Vives much more explicitly went into the subject in his *Instruction of a Christian Woman.* He cannot see, he said, the reason for this great desire women have to bear children. Why want to be a mother?

He explored the possible reasons. Is it to replenish the world? Can't that be done without a particular woman's bearing a little beast or two? Can't God fill his own house as he wills, even by turning stones into people? Or perhaps the reason is fear of reproach for barrenness. She should remember that she is a Christian woman, not living under the old law which said, "Cursed be that woman in Israel that is barren." The new law of Christ prefers virginity above marriage and her Lord says, "Woe be unto women, that be great with children; and blessed be they that be barren: blessed be the wombes that beare not, and the breasts that give not sucke." It may be that God intends her for one of these blessed women. Or is it desire to see a child come of her own body? Will he be of any other fashion than other children? She has all the children of the city and all Christian children to bear motherly love to. Let her think them all hers.

Then why desire children? If mothers could see in one picture all the cares and sorrows caused by children, none would be so greedy of them, but fear them as death and hate them like venomous serpents. What joy can be had in them? Only tediousness and pain and toil and grief when they are young; as they grow older only fear what way they will take; if they are evil only lasting sorrow and if good only perpetual fear lest they die, or are harmed, or go away, or become changed. If she has many children she has all the more care, and just one gone astray wipes out all the joy in the others. So far he has been thinking of sons. As for daughters, what a torment of care to keep them, and what pain in marrying them off. Few fathers and mothers see good children of their own, for true goodness is never without wisdom which comes only in discreet years. Then fathers and mothers are gone.

Finally Vives had a word for those who, believing their barrenness to come of some other cause than themselves, think to find a remedy in desperate measures. Let barren women believe the cause lies in themselves and not in their husbands, as is more likely either by nature or by the will of God. Nature brings forth few barren men and many barren women, very wisely since there is more loss in the barrenness of men. If a woman is barren by nature she can never conceive and acts against nature and grace if she tries. If it is God's act that there shall be no children, then prayer is the only remedy. Search for any other is superfluous and also cursed. But when she asks God for a child, let her ask for a good child, or she might better have no child at all.

None painted the displeasures of having children more vividly than Vives. One must think of the Queen for whom he wrote the book in 1523, whose long disappointment in failing to provide Henry with a male heir was nearing its climax in divorce. Was he providing thoughts to comfort her specially, as well as all other women in her predicament? For whatever the law of the new Gospel said, the law of men still laid a heavy curse upon the wife who bore her husband no children, particularly no sons. What was all the painful care for, that was taken first of all by parents of the upper classes especially to keep their daughter chaste until she could be handed over to her husband, and then by her husband to keep her for himself, if not to assure a man true heirs of his own body? And what were all the pains for, which were taken to match rank to rank and fortune to fortune, if not for the benefit of succeeding generations that only the wife could furnish in the legitimate line? And what was all the insistence for, in the teaching of both sons and daughters, that passionate love either before or after marriage had no place in the choice of a mate or in the serious business of marriage, and that parental consent must be had under pain of God's curse for disobedience, if not for the same reasons? The European wife needed to fear barrenness, and the higher her rank, the greater the fear and the peril.

Therefore much was written on the duties of even the highborn wife toward her children. Vives, forgetting all the harsh things he had just said about having children, proceeded with understanding and even tenderness to advise such a woman as he has predicated on how to bring up her children in health and goodness, and particularly in goodness. Children are all a mother's treasure, he softened to say now, and therefore in keeping them no labor is to be refused, for indeed "Love shall make all laboure light and easie."[38]

First, a good deal of stress was laid by all writers on the advisability of the mother's nursing her baby whenever possible, and especially the noble and well-born mother because her milk was more delicate than a nurse's of low rank and more suitable for the breeding of fine gentlemen. A Frenchman even dedicated his Latin poem on the topic to the king, explaining that though it might seem on the face of it too low and common a matter to be presented to such a monarch, Henry IV, yet even he ought to be interested in the preservation of children since they served him later in arms, letters, commerce, and other vocations, and their survival depended on their early care. If it was impossible for the mother to nurse her children, and an Englishman realistically declared that the mothers of every rank cannot always nurse their children in England, "Let Syr Thomas More affirme it to be never so usuall with every dame in Utopia," then she must select with great care a healthy, virtuous nurse lest her child be corrupted in body and mind by impure nourishment. Nor were the pleasures of the mother who nursed her child neglected. Vives at the beginning of the section on the upbringing of a maid wrote, "And the Mother may more truely reckon her daughter her owne, whom shee hath not onely borne in her wombe and brought into the worlde, but also hath carried still in her arms of a Babe, unto whome shee hath given teat, whom she hath nourished with her owne bloud, whose steps she hath cherished in her lappe and hath chearefully accepted and kissed the first laughes, and first hath joyfully heard the stammering of it, coveting to speake, and hath holden hard to her breast, praying God to prosper it." If such joy accompanies the care of a baby daughter, how much more may it be the reward of a mother with her baby son.[39]

Next to the physical care of her children, and even more important in the eyes of the humanists, was the mother's charge with the education of her children, her sons up to seven and her daughters until they left home.

The importance of these early years was fully recognized in setting habits of speech, manners, morals, and religious beliefs. If the mother has learning, said Vives, and he fully intended that those brought up by his book should have it, "let her teach her little children her selfe that they may have all one, both for their Mother, their Nurse, and their teacher. And that they may love her also the more and learne with better courage and more speede, by the meanes of the love that their teacher hath toward them." She needs to study continually the books of wise men, if not for her own sake, for her children's, that she may teach and make them good. A baby's only skill is imitation, and his habits and information are taken from his mother, who, therefore, has more of a part than men think in forming the characters of their children, either for good or for evil. Particularly stress was laid on training in speech—pronunciation, vocabulary and manner, the almost ineradicable marks of position or origin in an aristocratic society. It was one of the strongest reasons for not turning gently born children over to nurses, from whom in their most impressionable years they must inevitably learn a debased form of speech to their later embarrassment and even detriment. The aim should be to develop, as Trotto put it, a tongue proper, distinct with words of common usage, civil, not flattering, or affected with unusual syllables and accents, but with sound and pure eloquence. It should be the mother therefore that sets her children's habits of speech, taking great care not to use any blunt or rude speech and to insist on proper pronunciation. "Children will learne no speach better, nor more plainlye expresse, than they wil their mothers," said Vives; "they runne unto their Mother, and ask her advise in all thinges: they enquire every thinge of her: whatsoever she answeareth, they beleeve and regard and take it even for the Gospel." A habit of talking little should also be inculcated, at this time in both boys and girls, for children and youth should be for the most part silent in the presence of their elders, and when addressed reply with courtesy and brevity. Vives recommended that the mother very early read her children pleasant stories that commend virtue and rebuke vice, so that before the child knows what is good and bad he will love virtue and hate vice and become like those he hears his mother approve. She should repeat over and over again the praise of virtue and dispraise of vice and to that purpose have some holy sayings and precepts commonly in use which will stick by repetition. Right opinions and religion should be poured into their minds: to despise riches, power, honor, pomp, nobility, beauty as vain things, and to love justice, devotion, holiness, continence, knowledge, meekness, mercy, charity. Manners, too, were the mother's task to teach, based on reverence for parents, honor to all elders, and no scorn for the poor, or pride. To support all by example children should be given as companions wise men, prudent women, and children of their own age likewise well brought up.

Maternal discipline will have to find some middle ground between too much license and too much fear through demanding servile obedience. Children should not be allowed too much liberty lest they fall into vices from which it will be hard to win them. "Specially the daughters," warned Vives, "should be handled without any cherishing. For cherishing marreth the sonnes, but it utterly destroyeth the daughters. And men bee made worse with over much libertie, but the women be made ungratious: for they bee so set uppon pleasures and fantasies, that except they be well bridled and kept under, they runne headlong into a thousand mischiefs." Punishment should not be prevented by love. The mother should never laugh at any deed of a child that is lewd, shameful, naughty, wanton, or pert, or kiss him for them, but correct him instead and show disapproval. An embrace and a kiss should be the reward for well doing. Children should be loved but not idolized, and love even on the mother's side should be partly hidden lest they take advantage to do what they like. Nor should the mother teach them to love her too much while they still do not know what love is. For a picture of a mother approved in this respect we can take Vives' account of his own. "No mother loved her childe better than mine did me: nor any childe did ever lesse perceive himselfe loved of his mother than I. She never lightly laughed upon mee, she never cockered me: and yet when I had bin three or four daies out of hir house shee wist not where, shee was almost sore sicke: & when I was come home, I could not perceive that ever she longed for me. Therefore was there no body that I did more flee, or was more loth to come nigh, than my mother, when I was a child; but after I came to young mans estate, there was no body whome I delighted more to have in sight: whose memory now I have in reverence, and as oft as shee commeth to my remembrance, I embrace hir within my mind and thought, when I cannot with my body."[40]

These, then, are the virtues and the duties required for perfection in the renaissance wife and lady. For a summary of such a woman moving capably in her own special sphere we cannot do better than quote from careful Markham: "To conclude, our english Hus-wife must be of chast thought, stout courage, patient, untyred, watchfull, diligent, witty, pleasant, constant in friendship, full of good neigbour-hood, wise in discourse but not frequent therein, sharpe and quicke of speech, but not bitter or talkative, secret in her affaires, comfortable in her counsailes, and generally skilfull in all the worthy knowledges which doe belong to her vocation." Trotto, from whom we have frequently quoted, when he viewed his creation was moved to this impassioned apostrophe, "O family well governed, O goods well preserved, O wealth usefully spent. O most happy marital love, O matron well worthy the name of mother of the family who so well knows how to govern and to fill the office to which heaven has destined her."

What reward may this pattern of all the virtues that bring content and well-being to the family expect? There is agreement on this point among the men: the true wife's reward is that in the end she can hope to gain eternal happiness in recompense for having obediently served God under the yoke of matrimony. So Lombardelli assured his sixteen-year-old bride after pointing out the hard road she must bend her will to follow, not dreaming how short that road was to be for her. In a letter to his uncle, appended to his book, he reports the loss of this wife with a little son, a terrible blow to her father, relatives, friends, and himself. For Delia in spite of her youth, nineteen, was an exemplar of goodness, sober in judgment, truly devout, modest in conversation, agreeable to all the members of the family, more or less according to their rank, skillful in household management, such, in sum, as not only he who had lost her, but all who knew her, mourned and piously confided to God for her blameless life, and the good signs in her illness and death. In this world even, if the true wife lives to be old, she should reap some benefit, and Vives advised husbands to deal with her then as with old and faithful servants. If an old horse or ox is freed from labor, bondmen are made free, old soldiers are pensioned, how much more ought an old wife to be treated with honor. For now she no longer needs the restraint of her husband's authority, since her agitations and troubles of mind are over, and she is wiser with age and experience. Certainly her labor must be lightened. "Begynne nowe therfore to make her equal with thy selfe, & counsel with her about thy matters whether they be great or smal, for so shal she recyve the frute & reward of her obedience, to be a mistres, the whiche was so long thy servaunt." To the wife he holds forth the prospect that when old she will be held as an example for the young and will rule her husband by obedience so that he will have her in great authority. For herself let her set her mind on heaven and do holy works.

Again to emphasize how the sort of advice to wives rehearsed in this chapter was held to be appropriately addressed to the lady even of very high rank, we can observe how Luigini finished his portrait of the "perfect, beautiful, gifted, and adorned lady." What about the needle, distaff, and wheel, do they belong only to low, mechanic, and plebeian females? After citing noteworthy examples of women of high rank who have sewed, spun, and cooked, he draws the conclusion that they belong to all women both high and low, but where the poor find only utility in these arts, the rich, noble and beautiful lady wins honor alone. What else ought the highborn lady to prize? "How sweet it is," he ends, "to hear of some gentlewoman—she does this, she says that, she delights in knowing everything that belongs to the perfection of the feminine and womanly sex, and wishes never to know what can be harmful to her essential worth and honor."[41]

Consideration of the state of wives often led to concern for the possible eventuality of widowhood, which in general opinion constituted practically a kind of rebirth. The woman, standing out free from the governance of a a husband, from anybody's governance, and therefore freer than before marriage when she was under the control of her father or guardian, has a choice to make for herself. Shall she, or shall she not remarry? Her whole future way of life depends on her answer. Diverse advisers said diverse things ranging all the way from Savonarola's portrait of the true widow completely secluded from worldly matters, to Christine de Pisan's soundly practical solutions for the predicaments of widows both of princely and lower ranks when they had to face alone a world particularly harsh to the defenseless. That at the heart of Christianity, as it took shape in early times, there was something opposed to marriage crops out even more strongly in the problem of the widow than in the first consideration of whether parents should find a husband for their daughter or dedicate her to the church. Both laymen and churchmen, except for a few of the Protestant position,

began their advice concerning women with the admission that virginity was
the highest state realizable by human beings. So speedily do both set that
aside to entertain the proposition of marriage that they leave, unintentionally perhaps, the impression of having paid mere lip service to a pious ideal,
but the reader must concede that the first choice naturally cannot be pressed
in a book on the duties of a wife. If a girl had no natural inclination to become a religious, her parents were advised to enter her as early as possible
into the honorable state of matrimony to preserve her from sin. If the wife,
however, became a widow, the case was in general different. If God removed
her husband, and she had well served the ends of marriage, then the opportunity to serve Him better, more single-mindedly, and to exercise the
great virtue of continence should not be lost. This seems to be the preferred
answer, certainly by all who viewed marriage and wives as primarily, in the
inscrutable will of God, the means of producing and maintaining the human
race.

To illustrate how complicated a problem the widow really had, it may be
worth while to summarize Savonarola's analysis. He divides widows into
true, good, and bad. They may be either good or bad whether they decide
to remarry or not. They are good when they want to remarry because they
recognize their lack of God's gift of chastity. They are then in peril, especially if very young, and should remarry. They are bad if they decide to
remarry because of desire, avarice, pride, or any other unworthy motive.
Likewise they are bad even when they decide not to remarry, if their motive
is not the service of chastity and God but worldly things, lack of dowry,
fear of a bad husband, love of children or riches, or a desire to please themselves. Widows who remain widows are praiseworthy in varying degrees if
their primary motive is the service of chastity and God even though they
do not devote themselves wholly to it. Some feel that they are not free to
leave their children, or parents, and do not want to leave them. Every service such give to their family for love of God wins eternal reward, and they
should not be separated from these duties. More praiseworthy, however,
are those who would like to be free of all worldly cares but are hampered
in some way. Most praiseworthy of all are those who are given to contemplation day and night, whose chief aim is to serve God in purity of heart,
and who to that end root out all earthly affection, reveal their state of grace
by signs of weariness of this world, great desire for the next, delight in reading and hearing God's word and in prayer, and at times by their feeling of
internal inspiration. Such to Savonarola are true widows.

His reasons for preferring widowhood are those commonly urged, all
religious in bearing. 1. The widow is free from the laws of a husband, which
really divide her into two parts. The wife must think first of her husband,
who may even be bad and not allow her to serve God, who wants the whole

heart. 2. She is more free also from the cares of the flesh. Nothing puts man farther from divine things than concupiscence; both she and her husband have no power over their bodies and cannot abstain from the flesh. The more the work of the body is done, the more desire increases, and God is put farther off. 3. She is free from the care of more small children, a great care and an impediment to spiritual perfection as daily experience shows. 4. She is freer of mind because she is not so tied to the government of a family as a wife is. The whole establishment is much simplified by the removal of the man. 5. She is more free from avarice and pride because by wearing black she has no temptation to excess and no need to dress according to position. Therefore she is not ashamed to go poorly clad. She has more money, thus, to give to the poor. 6. She is less exposed to temptations because she does not go to feasts and marriages, unsuitable to her state. 7. She finds her widowhood in general a check, preventing her from associating with men, from wandering in the streets, and from standing at windows, all things which the wife is freer to do because she is not suspected as the widow is.[42]

If these reasons do not appeal there are other considerations, not religious but philosophical or social, to give the widow pause before she plunges a second time into the sea of matrimony. In presenting these an Italian admirer of women rips open the whole question of woman's position in society and the wrongs done her as a human being in her bringing up and disposal in marriage, to argue against accepting such a bondage a second time. His statement of the case is long and traverses the ground we have been over in these three chapters on the training and vocation of women, and this is not the exact place for a summary, but the point of view is so astonishing to find in even a renaissance writer and the statement is so eloquent that I include it here to serve the double purpose of argument and summary. I have not used quotation marks though adding nothing of my own, because to save space I have had to omit a good deal and rearrange in part.

A woman's wrongs begin at birth when her father, bitterly disappointed not to receive a son, refuses her the joyful celebration prepared for a son and dampens the whole household by his downcast behavior. The mother too then neglects her baby and leaves her to servants, foster parents, or neighbors. The second wrong is that being deprived of her mother's milk and care she may drink corruption of body and soul from her nurse, and at best she enters childhood without any other preparation in infancy than conversing with nature with the aid of an untaught nurse. Then her father and mother must accept responsibility for her training or risk great evil. They train her for either marriage or religion, in knowledge of God and what is necessary to composure of mind, management of the house, and the special arts of women, cooking and sewing. So she reaches the end of childhood untried, except in obedience to father and mother, by whom she is guarded and sheltered from adverse chance and preserved in her virginity and simplicity like a little angel.

Now the father comes to a decision about her future. If he thinks her drawn to religion because of her attitude toward God, or if he cannot meet the expenses of marriage (perhaps swayed avariciously by the small dowry that satisfies the religious house where he intends to place her), he decides to make a nun of her. Concealing the great wrong done to her, he sets forth to her the great honor and profit he is providing for her, in that she, given as a virgin to God, will not only save herself from the corruption of the world and acquire a place in paradise among the angels, but also may by her prayers save all her family. So he takes her from her home and gives her to religion, and she goes from his control into the power of ecclesiastical superiors, and becoming the servant of God, is dead to the world. The timid girl is not able in that state to show any part of that prudence by which the woman ought to be able to reveal her chief excellence, because she has no occasion, freedom, will or knowledge. Giving the whole of her will to another in whose power she is, she can exhibit only the prudence allowed her of accepting willingly the fate and sacrifice which her father had made for her, and of subjecting herself to the yoke of religion. Well known is it how sweet and delightful is the celibate and monkish state, in which one does not serve a secular prince, but a heavenly; is not in the world but in heaven with the spirit, speaks to God, eats, drinks, wakes, and sleeps with him, far from all vanities, tribulations, and brutalities of the world; is happy, contented, rejoices and is grateful for such a perfect disposal, being in continual prayers, fasts, good thoughts, and the perfect discourses of the contemplative life, in order to escape sin and reach the sight of God in paradise. And still she preserves her virginity, simplicity, and holiness with complete satisfaction of mind, ignorant of the great wrong the world ascribes to her father in forcing her by threats to be enclosed between walls, imprisoned in a rule of iron, and under the obedience, correction, and punishment of superiors. And yet however wise womanly foresight shows itself, the world does not receive and admire it with a just eye, but interprets it in another way and holds it in little account, since in this article according to the world the greatest excellence of women does not consist.

It is all the same if the decision is matrimony. The father arranges everything without her knowledge, and often without consideration of her peace and happiness. Not all that he judges useful sons-in-law for himself are good husbands for his daughter. So this my simple little virgin just emerging from childhood must leave the house of her father and go to the house of a husband. In her father's house she has learned to show her prudence in doing the will of her father and mother, which many times she has known against her own mind and to her loss, without replying at all to whatever comes from their ordering. Through the great love and respect which she bears them and the obligation she owes them for having created and brought her up under their care, she cannot think of not doing their will. This same virtue is continued in the wife. Her principal ornament is the virginity preserved in the house of her father, because if she had in rare degree all the other virtues and lacked this, the rest are nothing. But the praise for preserving her virginity belongs to her father, mother, and governesses, not to her. Daily under parental correction, without free will in the matter, lacking occasion she has not shown entirely her own prudence. True, external actions often allow conjecture as to the state of the soul, and if in her father's house she has conducted herself with all the goodness enjoined upon her, everything will be the greatest argument of a good soul and the preservation of virginity by her own will, but the praise goes to her father since she has had no occasion to do otherwise.

The wife conducted to the house of her husband will dwell there like a simple, timid dove. On arrival with eyes that take in everything from head to foot, pleased or not with his bodily appearance, she notes his actions and the way he receives her, but retaining the whole in her mind alone she will show content if in any part at all it can be found, an act truly prudent and wise. Then having made him the gift of the sublime treasure of her virginity, in a few days she will discover what her fortune is. Finally then having considered well his quality, recalled the precepts of her dear parents, measured herself, she prudently begins to set before her eyes the care that religion lays upon her, with her marital chastity as queen of virtues attended by shame and sobriety, and with the chorus of all the others—modesty, continence, humility, frugality, diligence, industry and simplicity—and a mind so well composed and circumspect that the vices have no power to corrupt and contaminate it. Since the law makes one body of two, the husband the head, and the body less than the head, it is reasonable that the wife be governed by the husband. So she begins at once to submit herself to him and with sincere love to obey, caress, and serve him. Since his habits often differ from hers she sets herself prudently to the task of incorporating herself with him, and to guard perpetual peace she begins to show him by deeds that she loves, honors, and reverences him for no other reason than that he is her husband, rejoicing in his happiness and content, and comforting and aiding him in adversity. She will counterbalance his faults with her virtues, pride with humility, scorn with patience, wisely contenting herself with what cannot be changed. So there will be between them one form, one soul, one will perpetual and indissoluble. A result truly of great architecture, of supreme prudence, of great wisdom, that of two bodies unknown to each other, of diverse nations, habits and complexions through divine ordination and the wit of a woman is made so perfect and holy a composition from which the replenishing and greatness of the world results.

Next she will conduct the house with such order, dexterity, and beauty, according to her husband's will, which she holds for law imposed by God in legal matrimony, that his mind will grow continually more kindly disposed toward her. She will not care for external adornment of her body, knowing that the wise woman's greatest ornament is modesty, good habits, and chastity. Nor will she care for feasts, games, dances, and other such pleasures, but only to bear and bring up children, and as they begin to say "Tata, mamma" and other similar first words, she will put them often in her husband's arms so that he will become greatly softened with love not only for them but for her. If discord arises, she will remember that silence is one of the ornaments of women. She will not want all the gossip or report everything to her husband, but when he comes in from business she will make him comfortable and never show any jealousy that he loves and supports another woman, pretending not to know and closing her ears to all reports carried to her. So with true sweetness (which is the natural lord of our hearts) and with chastity, goodness, obedience, diligence, and other virtues of the mind she acquires the good will of her husband, which if indeed not equal to hers causes a perpetual peace, a most happy marriage, such as with the delightful spice of reciprocal satisfaction holds the happiness of the world. Not equal to hers must be said because always the woman as mother of love will more fervently love him, for not only does she honor him, respect him, hold him for father, lord, and her superior, but so great is her love that to be his perpetual companion is the chief end of her life, and to save him she is content to die. Many wives we see by ancient examples have died for love of their husbands, but few husbands for love of their wives.

It must be remembered, however, that chastity is the supreme virtue of a lady. Other virtues are ornaments added which gain splendor from it as the moon and stars light from the sun, but without it are obscured and worth nothing. Without chastity the woman is reputed of no value. What value to Lesbia the gifts of poetry, music, songs, if for so lasciviously loving Phaon she has been not a little blamed? Or to Sempronia the gift of Greek and Latin letters if she is notorious for licentiousness? Or to Semiramis having been empress and of great authority if before being empress she is called an unchaste woman? And so with many others who in arms and letters have shown high qualities of mind and strength, of what worth are their victories, their conquered kingdoms, their famous deeds if they are more known to the world for incontinence? Therefore the woman by the whiteness of chastity is held virtuous and famous. But the honor belongs to her husband. Clearly it must be said that not only when a virgin but when married, through being in the power of her husband she cannot show the perfection of herself.

The widow, on the contrary, by the death of her husband is made free of will. Then when she is free to sin or not can be seen the chastity of habits, continence of body, beauty and integrity of mind. As the lion, horse, and falcon freed from chains, reins, and cage show their true natures, so man's true nature can be known only when he rules himself and is chief among men, not held by laws. The woman then also freed from restraint shows her own character not only as it now is but as it has been. No part of virtue is achieved without labor, as Muzio says in his *Cavaliero*. When as a widow the lady is without protection from the malice of men, must work without aid, or counsel, then she shows her own perfection if she takes the good way, her own evil if she takes the bad.

This whole argument, the author, Horatio Fusco, says in his preface to Clelia Salamona Oliva, Contessa di Pian di Mileto, e Piagnano, was suggested by the condemnation of widowhood that he had heard in conversation in her house. He has wanted to show the great wrongs women of the age receive before they come to this state through forced submission to another's will. Though the death of a husband and the adverse circumstances that come from it should be prayed against, when it comes it ought to be considered an occasion to be able to ascend to great honor, ruling justly as the Countess herself has done in her widowhood. The woman who lives on after her husband may thank God greatly for the occasion he offers when her own wisdom and her own prudence, which before she has not been able to show the world for lack of opportunity, may be completely revealed to everyone. Christine de Pisan we can take as an eminent example of such a woman, comparable, it would seem, to the Countess. She admits that she would have preferred beyond all things to have lived on as a wife, but early deprived of her husband, whom she testifies she loved devotedly, she steadfastly pursued her way, supporting herself and her three children by her pen, until her fame spread everywhere.[43]

Womanly behavior in a widow followed the pattern set for the wife but with a sort of intensification that demands touching up some of the details. The wise woman, left a widow, who determined for one reason or another not to marry, had even more than the wife to deport herself without giving occasion for blame. Advice begins unanimously at the beginning with the mourning appropriate to the woman bereft of her husband. As a good woman she will know that the death of her husband is the greatest possible loss to her, for with him she loses not only half her own life, even herself, but also the ruler of her moments, guide of her actions, foundation of her life, captain and master of her will, and a heart of tender love. Floods of tears and bitter laments are allowable to her, even to be recommended; not to weep at all is sign of a hard heart and unchaste mind, says Vives. Then apparently conscious that some discrepancy might be found with previous concessions of his to the strength of some women's minds, he fortifies his sweeping generalization: "Notwithstanding, it may so chance that there be in women's minds such constancie and stedfastnes, that they may comfort themselves: and though they bee overcome and distressed, may by wisdome yet recover again. That would I greatly praise in a man, but in such a fraile kinde, it is no good token to have so passing great wisdome." Worse still, however, is it for a widow to be glad when her husband is gone because she is rid of her yoke and bondage and has recovered her liberty. A foolish opinion in Vives' estimation, for to lack a governor is not liberty but destitution, and like a ship without a master she is carried this way and that for want of discretion. Nor will he grant that she may be better off without a husband than to have such a man as she had. No good woman would ever say or think so, for if she loved him as herself, according to God's command, she would be as sorry as if she had died herself. "To a good woman, no husband can bee so ill, but shee had leaver have his life than his death." Setting aside wifely love that springs with marriage vows, it could be true that a widow might have cause to regret, even with tears, a harsh and unloving husband. In her unprotected state perhaps malicious persons will attempt to rob her and her children by lawsuits, so she, instead of staying in her own house, may be forced to frequent palaces and the houses of lawyers, whose rapacious hands may also despoil her of the necessities of life. Or she may be pursued by wicked men who assail her chastity and if unsuccessful in every other way blacken her with their tongues. Christine had to complain bitterly of the unjust lawsuits that plagued her on her husband's sudden death intestate, thankful to save even a small amount out of what should have been hers.

Let a widow therefore bewail her husband, if not for one reason then for another, but with due measure, not crying out or beating herself to display her grief to others. After the first burst of sorrow, grief giving way to reason, for the living images of him in her children, she should begin to read for consolation. Not the philosophers, warns Vives, since it is a Christian woman that he is instructing, but Christ's philosophy that all men are born to die to pay duty to nature, but souls are immortal, and leavng this life is to those living well here a departing into another life, blessied and eternal, into which those left behind will follow. As a final service she will give her husband honorable burial, but without excess or show, and she will scrupulously fulfill the will of her husband on bequests. Henceforth she will keep him alive by reverent remembrance and will live to please him.[44]

Now she must turn to the care of her household. Reorganization will have to be done with foresight and prudence comparable to a man's. If it is a big establishment with many men-servants Vives recommends putting an elderly, honest man in charge, to protect her from getting a bad name because of her servants. At least she should take an elderly woman of good sense to live with her for counsel and protection. She will shut her doors then to all men but her nearest relatives, and admit only honest women.

For herself she will institute a plain, abstemious regime. She will put off all jewels and rich dress for simple clothes, avoid delicate food, stay away from feasts, plays, sports, all public affairs except those offered by her relatives, and instead go to sermons, dispense charity, and as often as possible give herself to private devotions. In conversation she will leave off praising the deeds and sayings of princes, speaking of others and judging them, carrying news, scolding, and be content with sober talk with women of her own quality, and in due fashion with her ghostly advisers. For her children she will provide a tutor of mature age with whom she can familiarly discourse on her affairs without giving anyone cause for suspicion. Since she must supply the place of both father and mother, she must take unusual pains to guard a daughter from harm outside and within doors, by never permitting her out of the house unless she accompanies her herself as a restraint to lascivious young men, and never leaving her alone in the house without some responsible woman if she must be absent. When the girl is marriageable, she will seek advice from relatives and friends of wise repute, and either place her in the church or marry her. A son demands the greatest care and study for he is the column that supports the house and family. She will give over his bringing-up largely to the tutor, selected for his wisdom and seriousness, lest she should coddle and weaken him, though some women have done well at it themselves. Occasionally she will have some intelligent person examine him to see if the teacher is faithful and sufficient. As he reaches the age when her authority declines she will provide new reins—prayers, counsels, promises, examples of others, hope of honor, fear of punishment—warning him not in sharp and severe tones as many fathers do, and can do effectively, but with gentleness and sweetness.

Thus thinking continually on God in prayers, fasting, and chaste thoughts, governing her beloved children and instructing them in virtue, maintaining her chastity and preserving her reputation for it, without which she is of no value, loving her husband as alive and not dead, and by her abstemious life not only fortifying chastity but showing that she has buried all pleasure and delight with her husband, she will reveal to the world how much this state of widowhood is to be approved and taken for good by everyone through the grace of God, and especially she will show her own integrity. So runs advice to the mature woman left a widow.[45]

For the young widow, who has the greater need of advice and care, the virtues of women appropriate to widows are particularly rehearsed. Modesty, she is warned, becomes more important than ever because of her unprotected state and the general disposition of licentious young men to treat her as fair prey. Her dress will be black, by ancient prescription, as external evidence of the grief in her heart. Though in general black clothes are hated because of the occasion for wearing them, many widows find them sufficiently pleasing, for it is clear to a discerning eye that the vermilion and white of a beautiful woman's complexion shows far more to advantage against black than any other color; therefore the chaste and modest widow will flee all the vanities that lurk in black clothing and may invite lascivious looks. If nature has served her badly in various ways, an awkward walk or a loud laugh, she will try with increased industry to remedy defects, but in such a way as to conceal her care lest she set evil tongues to wagging. Although it seems difficult to believe that a laugh can issue from a disconsolate widow, yet it is so natural to laugh, and the circumstances that invite laughter are so varied, that this brief diversion cannot be denied to the sad mind and troubled face of a widow, if her laughter is silent and connected with something of honest gravity. It will even bring some praise, since not always should one complain and sigh. In her talk most of all she will heed with the greatest care all the sound advice heard from infancy as to when, how, and what to say or not say. She will choose only people reputed honest and good and free from suspicion to converse with, especially those who have power to increase her own goodness with learning, warnings, and healthful admonitions. In her own house when conversing with outsiders, she will always have some of her household present, especially if she is noble as well as young, and therefore has to listen and talk to many.[46]

The three eminently Christian virtues of humility, charity, and piety were particularly enjoined upon the widow, as more than ever appropriate and necessary to her. The specific analysis lacking in discussions addressed to the wife is to be found here, and I should like to take time to indicate the ground. Guilio Cesare Cabei put humility among the "Ornamenti della gentil donna vedova," naming it according to custom as necessary to all the other virtues if they are to be virtues at all, and enumerating twelve different ways in which it should be shown especially by the widow: 1. She will fix her eyes upon the ground and thereby curb the proud curiosity that urges one on to inordinate desire to look everywhere and see everything. 2. She will not be easily moved to laughter—presumably because laughter too implies a sense of superiority. 3. She will speak sparingly and without raising her voice, a means of subduing lightness of mind. 4. She will observe silence, except on being questioned, against the serious fault of boasting and vanity. 5. She will observe in all her affairs the rule common in such operations, and not try to be better than others. 6. She will believe and admit herself inferior to the rest, in order to escape arrogance. 7. She will confess herself unworthy and useless in everything, lest presumption make her think herself sufficient and more able for great things than she is. 8. She will confess her errors. 9. She will show obedience and patience in things sharp and disagreeable, in order to conquer unwillingness to accept the penalty for her sins. 10. She will submit to superiors, against the sin of serious rebellion. 11. She will not wish to study how to satisfy all her human desires, in order not to delight in always having her own way. 12. She will fear

God and remember all his precepts and instructions. A survey of this table of twelve commandments reveals clearly the reason for holding humility necessary for all virtues; it is a net set to catch all the other virtues by a special interpretation of their significance.

Charity, in our modern restricted sense, is the second Christian virtue specially assigned to the widow. Next to her duty to love God she should place her duty to aid men. She will give two kinds of aid, spiritual and material. The first needs some defining. She will be ready to teach others who do not know and who need instruction, to give faithful counsel to those in doubt, to offer suitable consolation to the oppressed, to correct and reprimand the erring with brotherly love when necessary, to forgive injuries received, to support with patience those who by illness or trouble are a burden, and to pray for others. Material aid, since she is free to dispense her goods as she wishes, she will furnish generously to those in need, and she will think only of heavenly rewards for her gifts to the poor who cannot return favors, and resist all temptation to seek profit by giving to those well placed to assist her.

To come at last to the first and greatest of all duties, love of God, the prudent widow, whose mind is set on heavenly things, will hold important and dear the great aids to piety, fasting, prayer, and reading of sacred lessons. She will use fasting chiefly as an aid to chastity. But fasting is much more than abstinence from meat and drink: the eyes will fast from curious looks, the ears from lying tales, rumors, and idle words, the tongue from detraction and murmuring, the hands from all idle signs and unjust deeds, the mind, above all, from vain thoughts and unjust desires and its own will. She will not only pray often and long, but she will strive to pray rightly, that is, humbly and for the right things. For light on sacred matters she will go first of all to the Holy Scriptures, which contain real wisdom for man. All human sciences are mere shadows. She will find the lives of holy men and women beneficial, and particularly the writings of the Holy Fathers.[47]

Such then are the virtues particularly appropriate and necessary for the widow. They are not different from the virtues belonging to all women, but they receive an added emphasis from her unprotected state, her greater freedom from worldly claims, and her opportunity for concentration on heavenly matters. Special instruction in modesty was naturally aimed primarily at young widows, more exposed to temptation and calumny than the older. The other virtues, humility, charity, and piety seem addressed more particularly to widows of maturity, since the exercise enjoined in their interpretation requires the judgment and knowledge that years of experience alone can give. One feels considerable anxiety in the minds of writers as to what use widows will make of their freedom from the rule of husbands. That concern seems at odds with the general advice not to remarry, but it is obvious that all the rules on behavior, interests, virtues, and aims in life are carefully framed to curb as much as possible their independence and freedom. Since the advice comes not only from churchmen but also from laymen, Protestant thinkers as well as Catholic, it is again evidence of the strong hold that the ascetic ideal had still upon renaissance men. Women who had sacrificed their virginity, but not their chastity, upon the altar of marriage at the death of their husbands should, if truly chaste and conti- nent, seize the opportunity to return as far as possible to their state before marriage. As has already been noted, desire to remarry was taken to indi- cate some taint of impurity. Always, it must be remembered, the supreme, first, and last test of women's worth was chastity. The generally preferred pattern for the widow rested on that conception.

Since St. Paul and the Holy Fathers, however, did not forbid remarriage, advice to widows included this alternative, with the great reservation that approval went only to the case of the young widow. The general picture is altered with her. She is in more temptation to sin because her passions are still strong and she is still attractive to men, who will give her little peace, and her opportunities to sin are greater. The young widow, if childless, may well be advised to remarry after a reasonable lapse of time. For the first time we meet with some serious advice on how a woman is to choose a hus- band circumspectly. A young Englishman undertook to instruct his wid- owed sister in the matter. Three types of men she should avoid, the ob- viously evil man (who is not likely to seek her), the crude, wealthy sort who tries to gain her by offering so much of this, so much of that, and the hand- some, well-enough-born, well-mannered man who commends himself and whose friends more plainly commend him to this effect: "Consider whether he be not a verie gentleman in his behaviour, and forgette not his qualities how commendable thei are, his activitie, his merie conceites, his pretie prac- tises: See how cleanlie and trimme he is in his apparell, how skilfull and neate he is about his horse, his Hawkes, his Houndes: His exercise also he useth, is gentleman like, abroad he useth his Bowe, within doores he syngs to his Lute, and so he hath wiped clean the outside of his Cuppe. As for learning he hath—enough for a gentleman." His faults and slips are to be excused as the toys of young men. The writer trusts his sister will not be deceived by all this. Let her look for a plain gentleman, well brought up, with more learning than lands, though he has a competent living, a manly face, a tongue that speaks sense. To know him she will have to make a keen analysis so as not to confuse wealth and wit, body and soul, life and living. All three things must be considered, his inward mind, his outward person, and his worldly state, but of these the most important is the first, for if he lacks virtue and godliness she herself may become debased.[48]

This picture of the wife become a widow allows one to see better the figure of the wife and lady, etched more sharply because it at last stands alone, out from under the immediate shadow of the husband. For purposes of generalization we must ignore such a concept of the widow as Fusco presented, that she should make her widowhood an opportunity to rule herself and in her freedom reveal her true self, an individual for the first time. This is the view that is the exception and not the rule. In the generally accepted ideal the woman has been completely submerged in the wife, and remains so by choice when she loses her husband. She becomes in fact even more than in her husband's lifetime the essential wife, in that though no longer under compulsion she continues absorbed in her housewifely and motherly duties more singlemindedly than before, and with her husband's image engraved on her heart she is still guided by constant reference to his known wishes and commands. The virtues so praised in the wife as the core of her character are emphasized as more necessary than ever to her, modesty and chastity flanked by humility and piety. The rest are implicit in the description above; obedience is still her law in living only for her husband, showing her love for him in her obedience and in burying with him all her joy, and exercising her discretion with all the greater caution and devotion to her children, the living images of her husband. Resignation, self-negation, submission to the will of another still control her being, are indeed the very habit of her mind and all her impulses.

In the perfect wife is then to be seen the perfect woman, the lady, as the renaissance largely still looked on her. The particular gifts of women, so laboriously found in her, more especially perhaps her particular lacks, proved conclusively the appropriateness of assigning to women of all ranks the vocation of the wife. The history of the first pair in the Garden of Eden brought this disposition within the intention and approval of God, thereby imposing unquestioning acceptance of her lot. More compelling than either of these grounds for this interpretation of woman's nature and work, though far less frequently admitted, was the necessity that fathers were under to ease their burden of supporting a family. There was no place in the upper levels of the social, economic scheme for any women except wives, active wives may they be called. Wives without husbands were something of an embarrassment one observes from the anxious discussion of their disposal.

To anyone in search of an ideal for the lady that by definition should set her off from all other women, most of the advice to ladies on the aims and conduct of their lives presents a monotonous, dull, and unrewarding portrait. It does not make any particular difference in the contents of these works whether the authors were churchmen, gentlemen, or scholars; Italian, French or English; early or late writers; or whether they wrote for ladies or for common women. There is, broadly speaking, one pattern for the wife whatever her rank, nationality (in Europe), or religion; the reason is of course that she is a Christian wife and the Church had settled her status and character long before the renaissance, in fact at the beginning of its history. The great authorities on marriage are still St. Paul and the early Church Fathers.

One may have the impression by now that there must be considerable difference between this perfect wife recommended to the lady as her complete model and the perfect woman described in chapter two by the defenders of her sex. It is enlightening to compare them on the point of the desirable virtues assigned to each. Here is the list that Della Chiesa gave for "holy women, valorous queens, and other great ladies:" devout, compassionate, religious, above all continent, obedient, temperate, law-abiding, patient, pitiful, firm in adversity, modest in fortune, just in rule, willing to die for family and country, charitable, and most resplendent of all, chaste. Add magnanimity and learning and the list adequately represents current thought on the essential perfection of women. Obviously any difference to be found does not lie in the qualities themselves, but must be sought in the attitude toward them, the point of reference for their significance, and the definitions and explanations offered for them. In truth even in these respects there is less difference than one might expect.[49]

The defenders of women, though they assigned chastity as the queen of virtues for women like any prescriber for wives, regarded it from a different point of view. They were more nearly framing a woman in her own right, in her own perfection, as an individual like a man. Thus they saw chaste women behaving in a variety of ways according to the peculiar nature of each woman. Lucretia, Susanna, Judith, and Saint Agnes were not to be blamed because they acted so differently when their chastity was threatened; they valued chastity equally but each according to her nature was driven to act by some other dominating desire; husbands furnished them no common denominator. In the praise of temperance and piety likewise the inner perfection of the individual is made the sole point of reference, not consideration of the needs or happiness of another, as in the case of a wife. Of the virtues which concern the perfect woman's relations with others, the most praised is her humanity, her devotion and service to others, seen in her as a part of her own nature, not as imposed upon her and exercised under pressure of a husband's demands and prescriptions. It is her natural kindness and sweetness that teach her to care only to please her husband and to count herself happy only as she is loved by him. The difference is important, though the result is the same, subjection and obedience to husbands. As for the great moral virtues most highly prized in men—liberality, courage, justice—there was not the argument one might have expected for their free exercise by women, but an acceptance of the limited sphere in which women might becomingly exhibit them. In the realm of studies alone renaissance men granted women the right to achieve greatness, exercising an intellectual virtue shared equally with men. Learning thus was made to share pre-eminence with chastity among the virtues for women, and that again is an important difference. But with this we have come to the end of comparison that can show the conception of womanly perfection any more free in the minds of eulogists of women than in minds bent on fitting all women to the Procrustean bed of husbands' specifications. There is in actuality little to choose.

We shall have to look elsewhere for any portrait of a woman that makes her indisputably into a lady.

CHAPTER SIX : *Love and Beauty*

Dino del Garbo uttered the right warning to anyone entering on the study of love when he postulated that the reader must be intelligent because the subject is philosophical, involving the natural, moral, and astrological sciences. One of the many flies attracted to the honey of Cavalcanti's *Canzone* on love, he struggled to interpret its meaning, only to be bogged down at times as he was free to confess. Garbo was more fortunate perhaps than he knew, for he came along in the fourteenth century, and the busy multiplication of commentaries upon commentaries by the long succession of medieval and renaissance oracles on love in all its aspects has not made the subject any easier for the modern student. The problem is simplified here, to be sure, by being centered upon the one aim of this book, a search for the renaissance ideal of the lady, but to understand what part the institution of love played even in that restricted area, it is necessary to skirt though not to wade deeply into its whole philosophy—natural, moral, and astrological.

Renaissance writers on the subject may be roughly divided into the philosophical and the practical. Some never descend from Plato's pure ethereal, some never ascend above Ovid's earthly level of how to get on with the art of making love. Many, however, perhaps most, start with abstractions and then slide comfortably into more understandable matters, the part of the subject which will occupy the larger share of this chapter. This division into two worlds presents difficulties because one must choose in effect between these two widely differing ideals. As Zoppio, a late sixteenth century writer, put it, "Ovid knows nothing of the Art of Love of Socrates, nor will Socrates ever put into practice the precepts of the Art of Ovid," and then he proceeded to argue at length against the Platonic love of the philosophers as not love at all, and even in its beginnings at the human level merely affection, well-wishing. Indeed it is hard to see how Castiglione's ladies and gentlemen ever could have got themselves, for the purposes of either sleep or love, out of the world of lofty speculation which he wove them into, though we are assured that they finally opened a window and let the morning air stream in. One must be highly suspicious that if that window was actually opened, the figments of the night vanished like cobwebs under the morning sun. Therefore since following the way of philosophy only would in the end take our lady quite out of human sight and comprehension, we do better to seek a middle path in our effort to learn what renaissance thought set up for the actual lady to aim at when she sought perfection in love.

Another source of difficulty arises in the fact that most of the books on love are written for men, and oddly enough almost all completely ignore the woman's part in what might be supposed to be necessarily a two-sided business. In these at best the woman is assigned a wholly passive role and the reader has to glean indirectly whatever applies to the lady. It is easier to see the lover than the beloved. But there are notable discussions of love addressed to the lady or represented as carried on by her, and even a few written by women for women. A case could even be made for accepting that all written on love applies to both and that lover is to be taken as a generic term, like man applied to the whole of the human race. Alessandro Piccolomini felt some need to explain how it was that for the most part when he had spoken of the lover and the beloved he had used lover of the man and beloved of the woman, although in a true union of lovers each is both lover and beloved. There was some reason for this, he said. He could write with more certainty of a man in love because he knew himself to have been in love but not necessarily to have been loved. Besides he had always been of the opinion that the man must be the first to turn to love, because the beauty that is the object of love more easily is reflected from the delicate and soft faces of women than from the robust and sterner faces of men. Finally, it seems that loving belongs principally to man since he is a more perfect animal than woman and loving, as he has already shown, is more perfect than being loved. But here, of course, he is venturing on more slippery ground.[1]

At first sight the very meaning of the subject under discussion may appear to deserve a place among these special difficulties. To renaissance, as well as medieval, minds definitions seem to have furnished sheer delight for their own sake. Tossed forth in strings with a sort of mental, or perhaps merely verbal, legerdemain they often serve rather to dazzle than illumine the reader's mind. And indeed there is bound to be confusion and contradiction when not only philosophers of every color were consulted but also orators, poets, theologians, and even physicians. We will not, however, deal in this treatise with the more abstruse and general definitions of love except to note that some writers felt a need to begin just there, and in the porch of their works sought a meaning that would include all meanings, with inevitably unsatisfactory results. Call love desire for what one lacks, and it lasts only until possession; call it a passion desirous of enjoying union with an object thought beautiful, and it is not true of God's love for us; or go wider afield and call it benevolence, or a desire for happiness or for what is pleasing or beautiful, and it is not then distinguishable from other desires, such as love of goods in the avaricious, of honors in the ambitious, of letters and knowledge in the learned. We shall not try to analyze, much less resolve, these and other similar perplexities, but follow the example of our predecessors. Domenichi, in his dialogue on love, with considerable patience quoted definitions from the ancients—Aristophanes, Lucretius, Cicero, Plato, and "other learned men"—and from the moderns who defined otherwise, he said, only to sweep them all aside as futile, and impractical. "Besides," he concluded, "all these philosophical subleties will hardly please the ladies" listening to him—or the reader, may we add, who is looking for a lady.

For progress in definition writers had to resort to classification, usually into three kinds, divine, human or rational, and animal or sensual. But, as Equicola said, the briefest classification is best, and a survey of definitions of the three kinds supports his division simply into two, divine and human. Divine love was assigned wholly to the realm of contemplation, and was concerned with earthly beauty only as the image of heavenly beauty and an incentive to seek to comprehend it. For an example we may take Romei's definition, in the words of his English translator. "The first and excellentest of all the rest, like unto the divine of-spring of that celestiall Venus, wherein the Seraphins immeasurable burning, do enflame with like affection all the rest of the Angelicall spirites, is called divine love. This was defined by Plato in his Phedro, to bee no other then a divine furie, which reduceth to memorie the forme of true beauty, in that farre from all brutish action, in the onely contemplation of his faire and deare beloved, he resteth satisfied; who beholding beauty as the Image of Divinitie, raiseth up by that meanes his minde to meditate on that beauty which is perfect and celestiall. This divine lover desireth that his deere affected should be set on fire, with so holy, chaste, & immaculate a love towards him. With such love, not onely yong men, but olde, religious, and men married may be inamored; and it is in the highest and most perfect degree of temperature." Pico della Mirandola might have found lingering here just a little too much of human attachment to the beloved. The human love that is our present concern, indeed might go up the ladder some way, but it kept the eye of the lover fixed on his beloved.

Human love was recognized as a mixture of the rational and animal elements in man and divided into two kinds according to which predominated. Romei defines the two in the following fashion. The human lover "without contaminating chaste thoughts, rejoyceth onely in beholding, discoursing, and conversing with his beloved, as also by her to be mutually affected. This [love] is discrepant from that in the divine lover, insomuch as admiring humane beauty, without lifting up the mind to that from whence she had her beginning, he meditateth on this beauty humane, not as the Image and representation of Divinitie, but as it were most true and essentiall beutie, and rejoyceth in this contentment: this is called chaste love, and is the second degree of temperance. It seemeth kissing unto this love is permitted for a reward; in that a kiss is rather the conjunction of soule then body, for by meane of a kisse, a most pleasing passage, of the liveliest spirits being procured from the one and others heart, the soules of lovers remaine so bound togither by the undivided knot of love, that of two ther is made one, which compounded after this manner, governeth two bodies, and therefore those chastely enamored, desire to attayne to a kisse, as being a true connexion of the soule. Wherfore the divine Philosopher in his *Convivio*, speaking of one inamored with chaste love saith, that kissing, the soule commeth into the lippes, from whence it flieth out, and is received."

The other kind of love, in which the senses play a prominent part, is defined by Romei in a limiting way of highly controversial nature, as love that "resolveth into desire of unition, with the thing beautifull, not onely in minde, but also corporally, yet by lawful and honest meane; and this love is that, which is the beginning of thrice sacred Matrimony, and in this, not onely an union of reciprocal love, but also a desire of eternitie is discovered: for by means, of this lascivious love, a man communicating his owne proper kinde, being fraile, maketh himselfe eternall." It is obvious that once the senses are given a central place in love, definitions will widely differ according to the ideal that writers accept for human behavior, or still more humanly according to their own experience. Some do not escape special pleading, as these two which view love from opposite extremes. Francesco de' Vieri makes love a fire in gentle hearts burning with great desire to possess the beauty of the beloved which has kindled the fire, and therefore it is the concern only of well-born persons of lofty minds, and is a noble, useful, and fortunate thing. While Jacques Ferrand, Doctor of Physic, viewing love as something to diagnose and prescribe for, agrees with Galen, he says, that it is a kind of dotage, proceeding from an irregular desire to enjoy a lovely object, and attended by fear and sadness.

But for a working definition, stripped of all particularities and generally accepted by renaissance writers, this brief statement will do: love is a passion desirous of enjoying union with an object esteemed beautiful. This leaves room for all the disagreements on every conceivable aspect, such as is love lasting, should the union be spiritual only or also bodily; is the end the enjoyment of beauty or the propagation of beauty; is love accident or substance; is it voluntary or destined; is it good or bad; is only beauty lovable, or ugliness too. Of all the possibilities, however, we shall be able to consider only a limited number.[2]

Beyond definition one of the favorite methods of exploring the nature of love was comparison with friendship. Goujon, whose little work on perfect friendship was published after his death by his son, thinks Aristotle's conception of friendship the best: "A love excellent and particular whereby two persons are so alike in manners, affections, and intentions that they are only one person." That sounds almost like a definition of love in marriage, but there is a wide difference. Goujon goes on to lay down three principal conditions necessary to perfect friendship—complete merging of wills, freedom of affection without any obligation, external occasion or cause, and community of interest in people and things. Friendship, to expand the terms further, is always honest and useful. It seeks virtue for the sake of the friend and is therefore more attached to the soul than the body, and can exist only between the good. It demands equality of age, condition, fortune, confidence. It must be reciprocal and known, or there is only benevolence, for one can be well disposed without direction toward a particular object, or without doing anything even when a particular object is in view. Most conspicuously it brings tranquility. Love, on the other hand, may be the opposite, dishonest and harmful, seeking only the enjoyment of beauty for its own sake, attached to body rather than soul, existing between evil persons, without equality of any sort, one-sided, and even unknown to its object, without measure distressful to the lover. This brand of love usually selected for comparison seems unfairly hand-picked for widest differences, as extreme at one end as the friendship described above is at the other. The question inevitably arose whether friendship is possible between men and women, between women, or only between men. The depreciators of women saw it of course as a noble affection suitable only to men, mature men, and found only between them. The frailty of women makes them unstable, and in their greenness young men also show the same fault, said Goujon. Others more generous, like Firenzuola, admitted women capable of it, but only with women. Firenzuola himself preferred love because it has, or can have, all the advantages of friendship, while friendship does not have all the advantages of love. Indeed Betussi called friendship love grown old, for people cannot become friends except by means of love, the beginning, middle, and end of all good works; and love to be perfect must, as friendship is said to do, have regard always for the useful, the delightful, and the good of both lover and beloved. As for whether one may have more than one friend, some claimed one advantage of friendship over love to be that friends can be multiplied. But others, like Montaigne, in accordance with the definition above, found perfection of friendship possible only with one human being, since perfect loyalty, helpfulness, and exchange of confidence would be impossible with more. For the most part love was taken to be an affair between men and women, and friendship strictly confined to men. Each had its advocates as the most perfect relation between human beings.[3]

Certain conditions and qualities were assigned to love with the usual disagreement. Some old philosophical disputes received honorable mention, if not lengthy discussion. For example, is love natural, that is, common to all things in nature and therefore shared by men and other animals?

Equicola, drawing all his material from the ancients, he says, explained the point this way: Love and nature are inseparably united, and neither can exist without the other. Love is first of all love of ourselves, a desire to live and to live in the best state, which is born in us and teaches us what to seek and what to avoid. All other affections rise from this love of ourselves, and only through it do we learn how to love others. Or to take another old dispute, is love a substance, essential, independent of variations, or is it an accident, something that can or can not be in the subject without changing its nature. Some poets called it a corporal substance, some theologians a spiritual substance, the Platonics a substance between body and soul; but most of the renaissance analysts called it an accident of either the body or mind, accompanied by other accidents—sadness, fear, pallor, blushes—arising from influences outside the body and fluctuating. For test, said Rosso, note that man is no less man whether in love or not. He may sink to the level of the beast, but he still has reason and free will to use. The boor can turn wise, but the bull can never be a man either wise or foolish. Is love then an ephemeral condition or is it to be known by its enduring quality? In any ideal conception of love permanency had to be assumed, for how can perfection exist with impermanency, and if love is to raise two human beings to new heights of excellence how can it be conceived as subject to decay. Experience, however, shows that love does come to an end. Loss of hope, or loss with the passage of years of what stirred love, beauty for instance, or absence are causes of failure in what at first may seem so fair and strong. The answer is that such failures belong only to sensual love. The true lover cannot wish to lose hope but seeks rather to prove himself more worthy; as beauty of the body fades, beauty of the mind increases and his love becomes ever more spiritual; in absence his thoughts are food for love, which grows best on such ethereal fare. Thus lovers that are virtuous cannot lose love.

Can love itself then be called a virtue as something which perfects human operations? The question was discussed at some length by Frachetta in his exposition of Cavalcanti's *Canzone*. Virtue taken in a large sense, he begins, covers any perfection or any power not only of man but of any object. Thus skill in sewing or spinning is called virtue in women; plants and stones have virtue also, because they have a particular power to do a particular thing. In a strict sense virtue means human perfection: of the body, strength, beauty, health; of the mind, knowledge, wisdom, prudence, and intelligence; of the "sensitive faculty," the moral virtues such as temperance, fortitude, and so forth. These are said to be of the sensitive faculty because they are moderated by the sensible passions, and moral because they are acquired by use and habit. Moral virtues thus come to signify no other than good habits acquired by use. These are more frequently and appropriately called virtues than the others because they make man simply good, where the others do not, but make him good with something added. We call a man good only when he is adorned with moral virtues. Love then, it is clear, is a virtue only in the larger sense as it is a power, and not in the strict sense. It is not a perfection of the body since it is in the mind, exists only as the mind comprehends it, and at the same time it is not one of the intellectual habits of the mind, such as those named above. It is not a moral virtue either, in that it does not make man simply good. It is, on the contrary, often found joined with vices. But if not strictly a virtue it cannot be called strictly a vice either because it is not necessarily opposed to virtue either of body or mind; only in a large sense can it be called a vice in that like all the passions it may be bad in its effects, inducing men to do evil and make bad judgments, by disturbing the control of reason over the sensual appetites. At worst it is to be considered only an impediment to virtue.

But if love itself is not a virtue except in the general sense as being a power, what qualities that may be called moral can be attached to it?

Bembo and others, said Rosso, call love sweet and gracious, but he, following Cavalcanti, calls it fierce and proud, so great and majestic compared to other similar accidents that it seems like a god and includes the true love of the *Symposium*, and the love of the creator for the created, and the love of a man who intends the good and the salvation of the beloved and not the contenting of his appetite. Strength, power, and violence are the attributes most often ascribed to it, because it is a passion so strong in itself that it produces effects that change the body more than any other passion can. It may even cause illness and death, not like a disease, said Garbo, which is inimical by its nature to health and life while love is not necessarily so, but only as it interferes with the natural operations of the body. Through its intemperance it can become cruel, and even turn to hate. Flood, fire, wind, tempest, endless were the metaphors and similes by which was attempted the description of the overwhelming power of love. Is love to be counted beneficent or malevolent then, this passion that we share with animals, that makes no lasting change in our essential selves, that yet under favorable conditions endures forever between two human beings, that can sweep all before it even to destruction? Either one or the other, said Equicola, according to its end, as it arouses good or bad thoughts. Both said Rosso, beneficent in that it exceeds all other passions, malevolent in that no other appetite sends men headlong more often than this. Again, as men had in mind the love of the senses merely, or the love controlled by reason, they were likely to label it one thing or the other. Here, as a part of ideal human properties and behavior, it is love in the good sense that we have to consider.[4]

Having learned something of the nature of love, a power and a condition at the same time, we proceed now to inquire with the renaissance how men

love the beautiful object. Grace is not a good synonym because it is usually employed to mean another attractive quality that may or may not accompany beauty, but is necessary to perfect beauty, and is more pleasing in itself without beauty than beauty is without it. Let these definitions stand, however, as containing the chief ideas associated in the renaissance mind with beauty as the cause of love.[6]

A great deal was said about the means by which this beauty of the body is known. Some argued that the mind is the only instrument for the recognition of true beauty since judgment is needed to determine what is harmony and proportion. But this refinement was skipped by most for the simple perception of beauty through the senses. Garbo might admit all the senses, except taste, but the sixteenth century, which could never quite leave off its Platonizing, almost to a man admitted only sight and hearing as means of perceiving the beauty of the body that arouses desire. Touch and smell are gross, belonging essentially to animals, touch the grossest and most material because it inflames the desire for physical union and thus leads to illicit embraces, and smell a powerful accessory, enervating the nerves of reason through odors and perfumes and holding it more easily asleep in amorous charms. Whereas sight and hearing are spiritual senses because they incite the mind to love beauty and to ascend from corporal to incorporal beauty and in some degree reveal the nobility of the mind itself. The palm, however, is given to sight, and some went so far as to maintain that beauty cannot be known at first except through the eyes. Men are said to have fallen in love by report, but in reality report has bred only good will, and friendship, which precede desire, and love comes after with sight. As for the blind, though they are said to fall in love, they do so imperfectly, only as far as they can perceive the beauty of the object by their imperfect means of perception. Ridolfi sets forth the claims of hearing and sight at some length, in a debate between two Italian gentlemen. The decision is left to their companion, a lady from France who has been praised for her writing, Varchi reported, by François de Billon, that doughty builder of the Impregnable Fort of Honor of the Feminine Sex. The lady thinks the argument for hearing ingenious but false. Beauty is found only in a body and can be known only by sight. Through the eyes beauty reaches the heart and then little by little sets the mind on fire. The eyes therefore are the noblest sense in man because of their powerful effects, most powerful on the lover.[7]

But if beauty is the single exciting cause of love, how is it that people love the ugly as well as the beautiful, asked the realists. There were various answers to that. Just as beauty is hardly to be found perfect, so ugliness will show some beauty, which when the lover sees it, will blind him to the defects. Also there is the other quality mentioned above called grace, perceived chiefly also by the eye, which shows in movements of the body, in speaking, and in other ways. And there are the virtues of the mind which make the body appear beautiful even when it is not. No one falls in love with ugliness; men love the beauty that they see. Nature has well taken care of this matter, said Nobili; relying on beauty to arouse desire for generation but unable to produce an entirely beautiful form, she gains her end by the beauty of parts, sufficient to excite the most fervent love, which then transforms the other parts—thinness becomes lightness, height and weight majesty, pallor chastity and modesty, redness brightness and liveliness. Mere opinion of beauty, therefore, works as well in exciting love as actual beauty, though perfect love must rest on actual beauty. From all this one can argue more confidently what has been said before, that when bodily beauty goes, love does not necessarily cease. Either the lover still finds beauty there, or beauty of mind which grows with age and even with sickness will have become the chief ground for love and love will last with it. So much for causes.[8]

Debate over the ends that lovers seek resolved itself almost altogether into the question of what was meant by union, or possession, or more specifically was bodily union necessary for perfect human love. Many writers are cloudy on the point, using veiled language that may be interpreted both ways. For example, Nobili says that love and possession, under the law and with temperance, between a young man and a young woman well brought up, is not a sin, and many are deceived who call copulation beastly. What does he mean by "under the law"? Apparently not "marriage," since the divine origin of marriage forbade raising the question whether copulation in marriage was a sin, though some, prescribing it only for purposes of engendering children, forbade pleasure in the act as sinful. A little later he says he has never known anyone to be content to love merely by seeing, hearing, and thinking of the beloved, all wish to touch; and if the much-talked-of spiritual union means union with the mind of the beloved, it is impossible in this world because we are attracted by means of corporal bodies and when we can see her purely, it will not be here but in the source of divine beauty. It is safe to infer that where there is vagueness the writer is advocating physical union.[9]

Writers often do give a beautiful picture of a union of minds only, that yet is meant to be human love. We will take Castiglione's for its explicitness, in Hoby's pleasant dress.

"Let him lay aside therefore the blinde judgement of the sense, and enjoy with his eyes the brightnesse, the comelinesse, the loving sparkels, laughters, gestures, and all the other pleasant furnitures of beautie: especially with hearing the sweetnesse of her voice, the tunablenesse of her wordes, the melody of her singing and playing on instruments (in case the woman beloved bee a musitian) and so shall he with most daintie foode feede the soule through the meanes of these two senses, which have little bodily substance in them, and be the ministers of reason, without entring farther towarde the bodie, with coveting unto any longing otherwise than honest.

"Afterwarde let him obey, please, and honour with all reverence his woman, and recken her more deare to him than his owne life, and preferre all her commodities and pleasures before his owne, and love no lesse in her the beautie of minde, than of the bodie.

"Therefore let him have a care not to suffer her to run into an errour, but with lessons and good exhortations seeke alwaies to frame her to modestie, to temperance, to true honestie, and so to worke that there may never take place in her other than pure thoughts, and farre wide from all filthinesse of vices. And thus in sowing of vertue in the garden of that minde, he shall also gather the fruites of most beautiful conditions, and savour them with a marvellous good relise.

"And this shal be the right engendring and imprinting of beautie in beautie, the which some holde opinion to be the ende of love."[10]

Physical union from this point of view is not a part of perfect love but rather stains true beauty. External beauty, though necessary to lead to true beauty, is only the shadow of it, and a man becomes more perfect therefore by union with the mind of the beloved, not with her body. This is the union that Piccolomini recommends to his young gentleman, in his *Della Institutione Morale* of 1560, after due apology for the opposite picture presented in his *Dialogo de la Bella Creanza de le Donne*, which, he says, he wrote at the age of twenty, but now for its errors repudiates what offends women because in these twenty-five years he has learned something.[11]

This Platonized kind of love did not satisfy many who were considering the human relationship between a man and a woman called love. Zoppio, as reported earlier, waxed eloquent at some length against it:

"Plato indeed, seems to be portraying love more for eunuchs than for men capable of progeny. Why should a lover, loving truly and completely, when opportunity offers, remain stupid, his gaze fixed, unless suspicion, or shame, or impotence, or the laws, or something else holds him back? Rather anyone free of everything that forbids amorous conjunction with his beloved should be counted capricious or insensate if he refuses it.

"It would be as if a young man, having made love to a woman and then left her for three years, should come to her as he could have done the second day, and she seeing him stand there all sighs, motionless, should ask him what troubled him that he sighed so from the heart. 'Only what you see, that you should wish me well,' he replies. 'I do.' 'And that you know I wish the same to you.' 'I know it.' 'And that you hold it dear.' 'I hold it dear. Do you wish anything else?' 'Only that you wish me well and know that I wish you the same.' Finally the virtuous lady says to him, 'Since you wish me well, and I wish the same to you, leave me to sleep by myself, as I will leave you to sleep by yourself. Good night,' and turns over on her side. Such an outcome would Platonic love have.

"I don't wish to subtilize, but when we set Platonic love against sensual desire, and exclude embraces from amorous practice, I do not know how or where this pure desire of beauty, Platonic love, appears, and how it can exist. Since in fact we are men we ought not to be like beasts, but we are not incorporeal substance and the delights of the senses have been given by nature for use. If man had nothing beyond sense no other love would come to him but the libidinous. If again man were pure intelligence and immaterial, there would not come to him other love than the divine, which loves divine beauty. But we are animals and rational beings too. It is not alien to man to be an animal, and accordingly it is not absurd, in the interest of the species, to desire copulation. It is appropriate to man also to be rational and to behave in a reasonable way. How is this amorous union to be made only by sight and not by touch if in touch is placed the height of sensual delight and the end that nature intends is to generate for the preservation of the species? Perhaps because love, being white and pure, ought not to admit any ugly or shameful action? That is as if someone were of such delicate taste that he did not wish to eat bread or drink wine because the grain grows in the fields fattened by dung. That copulation is delightful makes for love; that it has something of the impure is the blame of matter; that it is shameful is our decree because the consent of man has so ordained. Beauty and desire are the common objects of our rational human love, in which desire is referred to the sensual part, and beauty to the intellectual. If either part is lacking, love is not perfect rational love. Whoever loves then without presupposition of amorous conjunction does not love, but more appropriately may be said to wish well, to be affectionate, and such love is not truly love, but friendship and lovingkindness. Love then in my opinion should end in embraces, and most lovers will be found of the same opinion."[12]

Tasso agreed with Zoppio. Some speak of love, he said, as if they were only intellects, and seem to love only with the mind. They usually mention the eyes and mouth alone of the parts of the body. Man is composed of both mind and senses, and love therefore involves both and is the desire to embrace, though not all desire to embrace can be called love, as when it is a mere need of nature, or a desire of no one person more than another. The lover is one who desires to embrace because of the pleasure he has in one particular beauty. Pasquier put it more specifically; love in the heart cannot be separated from love in the body, and there is no lover that does not require it. No small pleasure comes through eyes, ears, and hand, "yet they are but dymme starres in respect of the other light, wherein I holde him altogither insensuate, who under anye other consideration pretendes to professe love to ladies." The particular end of love is the last pleasure, "lust of corporall conjunction." Only by this end does the lover come to content and absolute quiet. All knowledge begins with the senses, said Equicola, to quote one more instance. The soul must operate with natural instruments, each necessary to the other, soul to body, and body to soul. Abstinence and chastity are praiseworthy and most holy at every age, but too much abstinence breeds sadness and melancholy. Women are harmed if they are denied their desire, the senses are dimmed and the whole body corrupted. Nor is it any contradiction in terms to talk of temperance in the lover, these protagonists maintain. The discreet and prudent lover governs his affections not only with the desire of pleasure but with right opinion desirous of what is best, and when this law of living prevails temperance is added. Merely to desire embraces is not intemperance or incontinence. Furthermore, some writers, like Zoppio, argued, denial of this last act of love is denial of nature herself because her sole intention through beauty and love is generation for the preservation of the species. She has put in men and women for that purpose an ardent desire to bring forth their kind. Reproduction, therefore, may be regarded as another end that love seeks.

Grant that the natural and therefore desirable consummation of love is union of bodies, there were still doubts to be resolved and cautions to be imposed. One objection to physical possession was admitted to have some weight. Such possession often works change in men's feelings, and fear of loss of love sometimes persuades them to rest satisfied with sight and speech. Even this fear, however, was counted weak since for true lovers union of bodies, rather than diminishing, increases love. And if philosophy then raises its head to ask how possession can fail to kill love if by definition love is desire for what one lacks, the answer is that love is maintained in two wants, simple and perpetual union. The second arises after the first is satisfied. To be exact, love is really desire of perpetually enjoying the beloved. Also it must be admitted that desirable as this fruit of love is, if sought only for its own sake it cannot be accounted true love, or promise long continuance. To the true lover the beauty of mind of his beloved and the delights of communion between minds far outweigh the admitted joys of physical union. And reproduction of one's kind may preferably mean the generation of spiritual children in virtues, sciences, laws, poems, and orations through which, as Nobili put it, the living splendor of the individual seems to last forever, for in producing our intellectual likeness we share in divinity and eternity. Beauty then acts as a whetstone to refine our wit and excites this amorous desire of the intellect; the more quick and lively the wit, the greater the desire to produce science and valor. Though we do desire to enjoy beauty, the principal end of love is not that but to propagate children of our intellect and be immortalized.

One end of love, then, is possession of the beautiful object, according to the Platonists only through contemplation of her beauty and virtues, seeing the beloved all gracious, gentle, and loving, according to the others not only through contemplation but also by corporal union.[13]

Another end proposed for love was the transformation of the lover into the beloved, though it is so closely related to possession that it may seem only a part of that end. The desire to possess beauty was defined as a most ardent movement of all the senses to be united with this beauty in the most perfect way possible. The nature of love therefore is to join perfectly two lovers and make them into a single will, sharing the same thoughts and desires as if one. So the lover seeking perfect intimacy accommodates himself wholly to the nature, manners, and being of his beloved, until he is no longer himself but becomes transformed into her. At the same time by being thus engraved on his heart and memory through this long communication and subtle understanding, the beloved becomes transformed into the lover. The arithmetic of this process is more complicated than one might at first think, for not only are two made into one but two also become four, since each is both himself and the other. Or to put it more succinctly and mystifyingly, each is two, the two are one, and also four. This transformation is a spiritual change achieved through the spiritual senses of sight and hearing and the imagination, but the lover, out of his longing to become the same thing as the beloved even more than is possible, desires also bodily union, though he cannot thus achieve his end because bodies cannot penetrate each other. Consequently there can be no ending to this love because the lover is never satiated by bodily union and never wearied by spiritual union, which is nourished by incessant thinking. What has been thought is forgotten, to be thought again.[14]

This end of love, transformation, seemed to some to furnish a complete answer to one of those insoluble questions so dear to the renaissance heart, can a man love more than one woman at a time, or a woman entertain more than one lover. How can perfect love be divided, asked most writers. Transformation into two other people is impossible. Lovers penetrate each other and become one. How can there be motion in different directions at the same moment? How can the lover live and think in more than one beloved at once? How can he satisfy the moods and needs of two, if at the same hour one is glad and the other sorry, and both demand attention? Jealousy would be sure to arise, for no woman willingly sees her lover at the beck and call of another woman on the same terms as herself. She should not object, of course, if he shows due honor to others, men and women associates, for he must give his care to other matters that belong to human happiness, friends, children, country and the greater the part that he plays in public affairs the greater the honor that he brings to her. But perfect love will not brook two masters. In her case the question, as indicated above, takes a slightly different turn: if she is loved by two men must she content both. The answer is the same. To make love mutual she must become enamoured as her lover is, and therefore she can love only one just as he can. Otherwise she cheats her first lover of some part of the love that is due him, and is then ungrateful. One object in possession of the heart shuts out another.[15]

But is the beloved bound to make love mutual, that is the question that now faces her, again a much discussed question, heavily weighted in her lover's favor. Most writers thought she was bound and adduced a variety of reasons. She may be constrained to love by forces beyond her control: similar nativities according to astrologers, similar complexions which have led to similar upbringings and similarity in other things, say the moral and natural philosophers. Also the operation of love naturally brings love in return. Since loving is nothing else than transformation into the beloved, the lover then no longer belongs to himself but to the beloved, who therefore must love him as part of herself. In similar fashion since all lovers have the image of the beloved engraved on their hearts and mirrored in their minds, the beloved recognizes herself in her lover and is forced to love what she sees there, for naturally we love our likenesses. Naturally again we love those who love us for the pleasure and the testimony to our value that they give by loving us. But far more potent a reason for return of love is the moral obligation which the lady incurs by accepting the devotion and service of her lover. First of all, merely his election of her confers secret honor and commendation, showing in her the greatest perfection, such as forced him to love and serve her. Then he continues for months, years, ages to show his devotion in every possible way, chiefest of all in revealing to the world his true, rare qualities, not for his content but for her glory. How, in the name of courtesy, faith, loyalty, gratitude, the virtues that should adorn beauty and win love and reverence, should women who are loved not be bound to love in return? To refuse is to show pride, incompatible with womanly sweetness, cruelty—a most unnatural reward for the lover's sole desire to do good, and ingratitude—a brutish and shameful sin, the worst vice in a woman beloved, in whom nothing is more beautiful than a grateful mind and correspondingly nothing more ugly than an ungrateful. Well deserved is the blame and hatred thus engendered. Indeed men have a right to demand return of love. By nature and desire for good they must love, but love that feeds on love if denied its nourishment either dies or becomes a sterile kind of love. Again, if men are bound by nature to serve women, what merit is there in serving faithfully unless women are obligated to reward them? Women are not required to love as fervently as men—beauty, the moving cause of love, being less perfect in man than in woman, thus less potent in its effect, or to give the last greatest gift; but when love is known for honest love and the necessary resemblance is present, obligation rests upon the beloved to relieve her lover's pain, return his benefits, and open to him the heaven on earth that only possession of her heart offers.

Some writers, more realistic shall we say, found the question of reciprocity difficult to answer because women do scorn and flee lovers, and Varchi for one thought experience ought to bear more weight than all the authorities and reasonings together. He solved his difficulty by distinguishing two kinds of love. In love as commonly experienced, vulgar love he calls it, he would say return of love is unnecessary because always when reasons cease effects cease, and the many love for light and perishable reasons. Such a story as Dante's of Paolo and Francesca, which some used to support their argument that love must be returned, carried little weight, he thought, because Dante had put the words into a woman's mouth, and such a woman as can be believed merely excusing herself. In the other kind of love, heavenly love, necessarily the lover is loved in return because we naturally love those by whom we know ourselves beloved and from whom we receive benefits. By a short excursion we are thus led back to where we were. In the case of a second lover good reason for refusal of even this heavenly love lies in the point already argued, that a woman cannot accept him without being ungrateful to the first. Besides, she is almost sure to raise suspicions in the first, and so if prudent she cuts off at the first advance all hope for the second.[16]

Is there a difference, then, between the love of the man toward his beloved and the love of the woman toward her lover? Most writers assumed there is and carried on long arguments over whether perfection rests in loving or being loved. Perfection can be argued to belong to loving on the ground that action is more worthy than passivity. It is the lover who is active because he takes the initiative, makes the choice, pursues, wins, and holds the beloved. The beloved is passive, accepting, receiving. Zoppio draws out of Petrarch, the great lord of Italian lovers, an ingenious argument that love is more excellent in the lover than in the beloved. The very words of the poet show that love is found in the lover's heart in better fashion and with greater dignity: love *rules* in the lover, *dwells* in the beloved; *lives* in the lover, *sleeps* in the beloved; *nests* in the lover, *sports* in the beloved; *enters the heart* of the lover, *is in the eyes* of the beloved. The lover is filled with this divine fervor; the beloved is not, but must be implored to return love. If she remains obdurate she is counted ungrateful, and that is to argue that her value needs to be enhanced by loving in her turn. Thus to be loved is assumed to be a lesser thing than to love. Further, God himself both loves and is loved, but loves more than he is loved. It is not to be argued that his loving, of which he has the greater share, is less worthy than his being loved. Moreover, cause is greater than effect. Grant that beauty in the beloved is the cause of the lover's first movement toward her, yet he is still free to retreat or choose, and it is his choice that is the near, essential cause. Though both causes indicate virtue the second is greater than the first. Again, knowledge is greater than lack of it. The lover knows whether he loves and whom he loves and what sort of person he is loving and how he should treat her to win and hold. The beloved may not know any of this. And here is one ground for rejecting destiny, that is chance, as the cause of love, for if it were the lover would not know. Finally, it is he that boasts more of loving than anything else, not she; for examples, suggests Nobili, see Bembo's amorous letters.

On the other hand, arguments equally cogent may be mustered to show that being loved is nearer perfection. The lover lacking his great desire is an imperfect being, and therefore he seeks union to obtain perfection from his beloved, for abundance is in her perfection of being. Again, the end is more noble than the means. The lover making an idol of his beloved sets all happiness in her and most of all wants to be loved by her. She is the end in love and therefore more noble than he. Also there is greater virtue and excellence in the one who is honored than in the one who shows honor. The lover seeks constantly ways to honor and reverence his beloved; therefore she has the greater perfection. Nor is it true that to be loved signifies mere passivity. To be loved is most excellent action, because the beloved generates love in her lover, and turns him to her will. In this the lover is the recipient and therefore inferior to the beloved, the giver. Thus the old syllogism is overturned by denying the second premise, that the beloved is passive. The lover indeed can be shown to be passive himself, for words like loving, seeing, hearing, knowing, and so forth, used of the lover's responses to his beloved, represent him as receiving, and therefore do not really signify actions. All the work of the lover is spurred by the beloved. Or the major premise itself can be attacked. Some agents are less worthy than the objects they work upon, as fire in burning wood or cooking an animal.

As to Petrarch's authority in this matter, Zoppio with equal dexterity shows how he serves this side as well as he does the other. He calls love his lord and commander, but of his beloved he says that love sits with her in the shade of a laurel—"My lord and my goddess sit in the shade." Love and death dwell in her eyes, and love in nesting there finds pleasure and quiet shelter, but nesting in the lover's heart he gnaws and consumes it. Love shows respect to the beloved, but is a tyrant without respect to the lover, for if love had the same power over both and ruled in the heart of the beloved as in a city, he would rule her senses and make her come to her lover's will, humble, subject, and suppliant. But it is not so. Love rules in the heart of the beloved to dominate the lover. Love is in the lover as a subject; beauty is in the beloved moving love in the lover. In all this, love in the beloved is shown to have greater worth. Furthermore it is inappropriate to speak of the gratitude of the beloved when she returns love, as if she were placed in the position of an inferior receiving a favor from a superior. Instead, gratitude should be in the lover, a return of thanks for benefits received. Love of the beloved for the lover is not gratitude but grace, and a sign of the perfection in her. Her love is an acceptance of correspondency, which relieves, favors, and aids the lover in all the needs arising from this correspondency. This is grace, indeed great grace. When shown by the beloved in returning love, its essence lies in four things: conferring a benefit on one who has need of it, without having received a benefit from him, without hope of return, but wholly from a mind benevolently disposed. It is not a matter of chance but of intent. Since the lover confers no benefit but receives one, the beloved then is not and cannot be ungrateful.

If, however, it is assumed that loving is the same exercise in both men and women, and some writers say that they use the words lover, beloved, and enamored of both, then the question may appropriately arise, which is the more perfect lover, a man or a woman. Something of the feminist argument crops up here, but sides are not strongly taken. Most writers in fact present the arguments for both. Each can be shown to be more perfect, more ardent, more constant, and more suited for love. Men love more perfectly because they are more perfect beings. Having more knowledge and better judgment they are more constant and less suspicious. They love more fervently because they are stronger than women, and since the beauty of women far exceeds men's it must excite more ardent love in men, than men's beauty excites in them. Women, on the other hand, have tender and delicate hearts which are the proper subject and abode of love, and because they are naturally delicate and usually at leisure they continually nourish love with sweet and pleasing thoughts, where men are stern and for the most part engaged in serious meditations. They are more constant than men because man is warmer by nature and therefore less stable. They are more ardent because their sweet and sensitive nature is more easily inflamed, or, if you will, because their reason is not so strong and therefore less able to control passion. This controversy leaves in mid-air the dictum that the principal laws of love are equality of love and common sharing of all things.

Such questions as these were a favorite sport of renaissance casuists, as well as of their medieval predecessors. Chartier's *Delectable Demaundes* and Boccaccio's *Thirteene Most Pleasaunt and Delectable Questions* conveniently translated were still entertaining English readers late in the sixteenth century, and extensive collections under various titles, such as Landi's *Quaesiti Amorosi* and Tasso's *Cinquanta Conclusioni* with Zuccolo's observations on them continued to appear over into the seventeenth century. The list can be much extended by the treatises on love that are organized question-fashion. Most of the questions are trivial, calling only for brief answer, though Pasquier could stretch through sixteen pages a debate on which is the more agreeable, speech with the lady without sight of her, or sight without speech, or in other words which has the greater power, the eye or the word. But with all such displays of wire-drawn logic we shall scarcely advance our inquiry into the lofty role the lady should play in love, and may conclude with Zuccolo that these knots are of little importance, merely toys that ingenious minds loved to wind up.[17]

Far more lasting and important than any preceding consideration in its bearing upon the final assessment of the desirability of love is the question of the effects of the love here discussed, chaste, mild love, controlled by reason, learned by good education, founded on friendship, and far from any excess. The effects of such love are represented as wholly benevolent. Like the soldier the lover in the service of his lady scorns inertia, laziness, negligence; he keeps vigil, faces perils, fatigues, difficulties, and is magnanimous and free, and to his lady gentle and gracious. His law is the wish of his lady, which is unknown to him and hard to discover, and therefore a spur to exertion on the part of all his faculties. For love he cultivates all the virtues of social intercourse, becomes affable, discreet, courteous, painstaking, patient, familiar in company, pleasant at table, amiable in every way. Through his reverence for his lady and desire to serve and please her and to bring honor to her, his love becomes an inspiration and spur to noble deeds of learning and valor, in which all the mental and moral virtues are exercised and strengthened. Without love, some went so far as to say, no man can perfect himself in all the virtues and reach the achievement of which he is capable. Such love, pronounced Guazzo's debaters, is the chief producer of mercy, banisher of cruelty, breeder of friendship, guide in toil, the most perfect ornament of a man's life. In the light of all that can be said of love should not the wellborn seek, even with utmost pains, a lady with whom to fall in love? Can he afford to neglect, much less shun, such a compelling and renovating experience? For youth especially love is appropriate and even necessary, for on the threshold of life the passions are running strong and to restrain these first desires cripples the powers of youth and deforms age. But this love well used is always sweet and worthy of praise, bringing infinite benefits not only to youth but to maturity. Men are stupid and far from human that spend their lives without love, mere images and not men. Love belongs to man's happiness, argued Piccolomini, and it is a gross error to deny it, for love joined to virtue is our refuge from all our troubles. Therefore the lover is to be encouraged to go on loving, if the beloved is beautiful, noble, virtuous, worthy of every beautiful and worthy intellect, in hope that such a noble flame may bring forth continual fruits of virtue, glory, and honor.

More lightly Romei summed it up: "Love is a good and sweet thing: and more, whosoever findeth not himselfe inveigled with some of these loving snares, is but a sottish man, and of the common sort."

In all this discussion of the advantages if not the necessity of love clearly the gentleman and not the lady is the first object of solicitude. The effects of love upon her are not too clearly defined. As noted, some writers aver that lover and beloved are interchangeable terms, when the beloved is stirred to return love to her lover, but they toss the remark in like an afterthought and go on, as in the preceding paragraph, thinking about love and the man. To be sure Piccolomini in his early work on the perfecting of a lady argues, as in his later work he does for men, that her beauty, virtue, and good manners are of little value without love to adorn them and make every part perfect. Most happy are those that know the force of love before twenty, and wretched indeed are those who too late discover it and cannot have it. But since Raffaella uses this view as an argument to persuade the youthful Marguerita to break her marriage vows and take the lover in whose behalf the old woman has come, Piccolomini here may not be a convincing witness, even though later he says he includes both men and women when he talks about lovers. In general it is the woman as the object of a man's devotion, not the woman as a lover herself, that is analyzed. In her customary role of beloved she is indeed the cause of all the effects that are urged as baits to love; out of her perfection comes the ultimate perfection of her lover. Perhaps it would be a work of supererogation to try to show her perfection perfected by love.

How far writers were willing to go in ascribing the source of all good in the lover to her is well shown in Canoniero's defense of women. The excellence of women, he asserts, rests on eighteen reasons, the first seven of which, one observes, belong to her as the source of love. First, women make their lovers capable, and cause the simple and gross to acquire the virtue of prudence; and not only do they make the ignorant learned, but they make the learned more learned. For their prisoners of amorous passion study their own liberty to such good effect that their knowledge is quickened by their grief, and their sweet and well-composed words at times arouse the compassion of their jailers who set them free from their grief. The simple minded, ignorant by nature, when they begin to love, enter it with crudeness, but they find intellectual study so subtle that many times they achieve learning, the ladies having supplied what nature failed to give them. Second, women teach the virtue of justice so well that the torments of love, although they inflict pain beyond measure, become a comfort to lovers who recognize that they suffer justly. Third, women make men temperate in words and actions out of fear that they will not be endured or may fall into disgrace. Fourth, women give courage to the fearful and increase it in those who have it, making them strong to endure, zealous to perform, and patient to wait. Fifth, they create the virtue of hope in men's minds, so that those subject to the law of love suffer and hope, trusting in the faith and firmness and devotion of her who causes pain. Sixth, women make men contemplative, so much are they given to the contemplation of the beauty and grace of her whom they love, and of their own passion. Seventh, women make them tender so that when they are impassioned, with tears and sighs they demand the remedies from women. But the good effects on lovers here described in no way reveal corresponding good effects on the beloved. As a matter of fact she appears to teach these virtues by taking advantage of the high price her lover sets upon her favor to exercise a series of tyrannies upon him. It is her wisdom to be sure that dictates her behavior, looking to the good of both. For her, one may gather, loving is the begetter of wisdom and the preserver from ingratitude and the opportunity to study her perfection in the eyes of her lover and therefore better know herself.[18]

Granting, however, all that has been said in favor of love as a beneficent force, and of women as a necessary agent of this civilizing process, and setting aside moral considerations, certain serious charges brought directly against love and shadowed in the very arguments for it cannot be ignored in any comprehensive survey of renaissance thought on the subject. The gist of these charges is contained in a speech of Characlea's, the beloved in Pasquier's *Monophylo*. "I never sawe or knewe any one truely transfigured into the state of a perfite lover, on whome (notwithstanding he had possessed the actuall felicitie in love) did not attende inward perplexities, and outwarde disquietness, confused counsayles and careless execution, broken speeche and unsounde judgements, yea, such a generall negligence in all his actes and conversation of lyfe, that in a due consideration of the effectes of love in his example, it may be easily discerned that there is more gall than honye, less pleasure then payne, farre more care than commoditie, and more want of courage, than any true commendation of a noble minde."

Even the defenders of love admitted there was no denying the perturbation of mind brought about by uncertainty over the beloved's return of love, and by the griefs and sufferings derived, even at the best, from disappointments, delays, absence, and even merely by the inconveniences that the necessity of secrecy imposed, whereas tranquility of mind is one of the principal conditions of human happiness. Also such close dependence for happiness on another human being, and the duty to serve and return benefits involved loss of liberty, the prime condition for happiness to one of noble mind and lofty spirit. Furthermore, how conduct oneself according to the laws of reason, when the senses must inevitably be inflamed by desire? However much the lover may strive to control his senses by reason, he will not wholly succeed, and at the best struggle will be present with resultant clouding of the mind. Nor can age, dignity, or learning be trusted to save a man from behaving like a fool once he has yielded to the passion of love, Capaccio noted, and cited as a modern example the illustrious physician and philosopher Agostino Nifo da Sessa, who already beyond seventy became so besotted with love of a young girl that at the sound of a pipe he danced, forgetting the pain of his gouty feet. Again, the process of transformation works many changes, not all desirable, and because this alchemy of love can never be completely accomplished, greed, insatiability, and variableness are the lot of the lover, who cares nothing for what is not shared with his beloved, and finds everything in her good, even things that are doubtful in others. To a proud, free soul, transformation into the likeness of another, with resulting loss of individuality, must carry a certain humiliation. If there is added belief in the inferiority of the object into which one is transformed, the humiliation is increased, as it is by any service to an imperfect creature. Some critics went far in ridicule of the idea that real training in speech was obtained from conversation with women, and as for music and the dance that social affairs afforded, puritanically minded critics, though they admitted that music was good if used for personal pleasure and comfort, labeled it foolish if used for display and praise, and in connection with the dance enervating and even degrading. Dancing particularly was condemned as inimical to the life of reason and the occasion for immorality of all sorts.

One argument was occasionally especially pointed toward women, the risk to honor, so much greater than for men. She must hesitate long before she surrenders to a lover, however wise, the most precious possession she has, and of course she is far wiser never to yield it at all but to satisfy her lover in every other way so well that he will remain content with possession short of that. To both there is inescapable and serious danger in love fully realized.

These arguments against love were not unimportant, said Romei, but he and others immediately proceeded to refute them, or if not exactly to refute, at least to outweigh their importance by other considerations. The perturbations created by love are inherent in the scheme of things. Blame, if any, belongs to God and nature. Men have been created the combination of bodies and souls that they are. Senses, emotions, and desires are good and necessary to them, since they alone move men to action, by which life is preserved. All desires come from want and therefore involve some pain. At best therefore suffering must be accepted as necessarily an accompaniment of love because the lover is unhappy without possession, and he can never in the nature of things possess fully what is not wholly within himself. However he has his reward. In any case one moment of the lover's pleasure would be worth more than a thousand hours of unhappiness, but there is really far more joy than grief for the faithful lover, who has no regret for love, or desire to be cured, since he finds forgetfulness of his pains, his troubled days and nights, in the enjoyment of his beloved. Besides love is not the cause of all bitterness and distress, though many unhappy lovers seem bound to show that it is and trumpet their sorrows abroad. They find relief that way, Bembo admitted, but they create a false balance, for happy lovers do not have to ask all the world to share their joys. Mere freedom from the pain of love is bought too high with stupor in the heart and brutishness in the mind. Grant all the evils, greater evils are born of other ways of living. Not without high passions can a mind of high sentiment pass its youth, and the wise can avoid many of these evils and rule love with reason. Without love indeed man would be without virtue. Hear St. Augustine, said Romei: "To a Christian concupiscence and anger be necessary, to stirre up temperance, continence, tollerance, and fortitude." See also book fourteen of *The City of God*, where he says affections agree well with the beloved of God. Nor is love of man for woman, or woman for man love for something wholly outside, but for one's other self; neither one is complete without the other, for each has his own special work. Love makes pleasant the gifts of fortune—health, wealth, honor, position, power, and sweetens adversity. In the light of all these noble and necessary offices of love, love must be deemed good and essential to a good and pleasant life. In love there are joys exceeding all others in intensity, durability, and scope.

Or in a lighter vein some find excuse for excess in the young; lovers like poets must be allowed some exaggeration, and it is better even to risk some excess in youth. Young lovers indeed are allowed behavior that would be blamed in others—following their lady continually, always humbling themselves, spending the whole night sighing and weeping by her door, serving her in every way however low, praising her without being held a flatterer. Violent love though not to be sought is not to be wholly avoided by the young lover, on one condition. If he finds himself transfixed by the eyes of a lady, let him suspend pleasure until he learns whether she is worthy of love. If unworthy he should clip the wings of love before it can grow and think of some remedy in the beginning when he can still choose. He must take heed not to err because the blame will be his since he started it, and he must foresee all inconveniences that might follow. To provide for all contingencies, Torelli supposes that by chance, either through his merits, overpersuasive by their greatness, or through the frailty of the lady, an act less than honest takes place. The lover should then take more care than she that her honor in the world is preserved in the same state as at first, even giving his blood and life. Failure in this brings more blame actually to him than to the lady because through love or service he becomes committed and appears a conspirator. Marriage may be the best solution, and here shows the wisdom of choosing to love a free person, for he not only escapes the suspicion of adultery that inevitably arises from making love to a married woman, but can marry at need. Even inequality of rank is no bar to marriage, for if he chose her as his beloved and therefore his superior, he should not scorn to have her for his wife. If she is unworthy of this, much more she was unworthy in the first place to be mistress of all his thought.

Temperate and not inordinate love, however, it should be emphasized again, is the subject of all this argument by long excursions into many by-paths. High above the wretchedness and wickedness of the intemperate lover Pasquier, again, describes the state of the true and honest lover.

"Hee who by wisedome can avoyde the rage of passion, and applye him-selfe to the honest measures requisite to allure the heartes of Ladies, shall have a thousande advantages above the other overwhelmed with the bur-then of love: as first by his wisdome he shall not suffer himselfe to be over ruled with passions: his care shall not be turned into negligence, his courage into cowardnesse, his youth into age, his sweete speech into stammering, his libertie into thraldome, his pacience into murmour, his fayth into hypocrisie, his wealth into want, his devotion into devillishnesse, his sufferance into revenge, nor lastely, he shall be neyther blinde in himselfe, ignorant of God, nor unthankefull to the worlde: he shall bring no staine to his sex, as being a man to suffer himselfe to be conquered by the fragilitie of a woman, whome God hath not created, but as an inferior companion to the man, and much lesse shall runne into the babble of people, eyther for himselfe or his mistris, which the lover perplexed or envyroned with pas-sions, can not eschewe, although he thinke he walketh in the clowdes: as for example, so soone as he entreth into speeche of his mystris, howe easily maye we see the coales of affection kindle in his face, as both by chaunge of coulour, and also partialitie of speeche stryving alwaies to raise hir worthy-nesse, the same beyng one cause (I suppose) why the Poets figured love all naked, bicause he doth so easely discover himselfe to all."[19]

Inordinate love, given here again as a counterfoil to temperate love, was universally condemned, but it was taken seriously too as a state or disease that could not always be avoided and might afflict anyone. Methods of cure were therefore frequently discussed, and whole books written by medical men on systematic treatment for the afflicted young man. The first question was whether love is curable, or as Nobili put it, are we as able to free our-selves from love as to choose to love in the first place? Physician-like, Aubery started with the assumption that diagnosis is necessary. If the lover is ill of a kind of love that is nourished in a burning and melancholy humor—that is, a love become hard and inveterate by long use so that it is immoderate in the mind and the noble faculties as well as in the humors, and has become a delirium or mania in possession of the whole body; if his color is gray; if his mind is weak and extravagant; if he refuses aid, does not sleep night or day; if his pulse is feeble, slow, and uneven, his breathing irregular, heat excessive inside, and the outside cold—then he is incurable. Short of this extreme state, even if inordinate love is of some duration and settled character, most believed it could be cured with time, provided there was willingness on the part of the victim to make the effort required to apply specific remedies. If the disease is attacked at the beginning, then of course cure is assured, for reason and the exercise of moral virtues can stop the first sudden movements of love. Certainly in every case the prime requirement is that the lover must want to be cured.

Certain vigorous first measures for serious cases were recommended for all: complete withdrawal from the company of the beloved and all places that she frequents, banishing of all thought about her and everything in his room that reminds him of her and love, including lascivious books, especially *The Romance of the Rose* and erotic poets like Catullus, Ovid, Petrarch, Ariosto, Aretino, and also *Courtiers* and similar works. While still unable to banish throughts of her he may help his case by contemplating the disappointing and discouraging aspects of his case—doubts of success, dangers and anxieties involved, even the flaws in her beauty, and the imperfections of her sex. Above all he should shun idleness and engage in some worthy enterprise that fills the whole mind, like war, overseeing his estates, the loftier studies, and sports, like hunting and fishing, that absorb all one's capacities. Not often were religious exercises recommended, except by churchmen, but one physician said that he would have some divine stir up fear of death and hell and so send his patient to prayer and fasting—the only time to seek solitude—and the company of religious people. Physical hygiene was not neglected: temperance in eating and drinking with the diet restricted to simple, unexciting foods sauced with herbs, vinegar, oranges, and lemons, and such exciting foods as artichokes, truffles, oysters, peas, and beans avoided; plenty of physical exercise of the healthful sort, walking rather than horseback riding for instance; clothing that does not inflame to passion; chirurgical remedies such as bleeding, medicines for extreme leanness and wakefulness, various concoctions and powders for the bath; and for amusement, tranquilizing music, singing and playing, and pleasant discourse with joyous young men. Complete change of scene was highly recommended. Three remedies, a new love, many loves, and magic, occasionally recommended and obviously often resorted to, were considered in the more serious discussions as too desperate for use except in the most extreme cases, the last too dangerous to health and sanity ever to be used. A new love might drive out the old only to establish a new tyranny, and out of many one will only too likely surpass the others and merely repeat the pattern. Marriage as a cure was apparently seldom thought of, but the physician Ferrand does recommend it. As soon as the symptoms appear he would have the victim marry a young girl, as beautiful and captivating as his mistress, with the added charm of innocence. With her he may forget the other and form a stable and lasting devotion which has as its other basis that other aim of love, the reproducing of oneself.[20]

This consideration of what may be done to destroy infatuation has viewed the young man alone. The plight of the lady similarly enthralled seems hardly to have been glanced at. Partially the reason would have been that the object of infatuation was more likely to have been a professional, or one like-minded even if her status was that of an honest woman. Cure for such would be a gratuitous proposition. But the innocent, chaste, and conscientious girl or woman, whether married or unmarried, the object of so much solicitation, in so much danger from determined pursuit by the licentious youth of the day, whose wiles, deceits, and stratagems were the constant topic of warning to the girl in her father's house and the wife in her husband's, and almost the whole ground, it seems at times, for the training and subsequent treatment of women even of the highest rank— she must have needed quite as much cure for the hopeless entangling of her affections which such heartless pursuit created. As proof that the dangers were as great as the advice indicated, here is a passage from a letter of Pietro Lauro to a lady, Isabella Pia, on the subject of beauty in women. Merely the sight of a beautiful woman, says Lauro, is enough to set the hearts of most men of that degenerate age on fire, unless she is of the strictest decorum in manners and resolute in preserving chastity. Let a beautiful lady show herself desirous of being seen and she will be assailed by lascivious looks and burning sighs. Even the purely chaste lady cannot escape altogether such looks from those who without fear of God set themselves, by way of adventure, to reduce her to blame if not to worse. They can't imagine that many kindnesses and a long assault will not in the end soften any feminine heart, believing as they do that the woman is an animal desirous of embraces. And although many women do hold out against such designs, either through fear of shame or fear of God, or through pride which accompanies beauty, yet to endure such hammering is a sore thing.

In general, it seems, fathers and husbands would have liked to rely solely on force, practical imprisonment within the walls of the home and constant watch over every action, word, and almost thought, of their frail, female charge, with the hope that inaccessibility would preserve her from action damaging to the reputation of herself and her house. Failing that, incessant care to teach her that chastity was her paramount duty and only glory was urged the best, or some argued, the only way to prevent her from falling in love. Far less likely to be known was her predicament if she did fall hopelessly in love and wish to remain chaste or escape, than was the man's, and only one man, so far as I know, took seriously the need of cure for her as well as for him and wrote at some length on the matter. Vives starts his chapter on loving with the realistic admission that love, which he calls bad without reservations, is easy to fall into and hard to escape. Of course in the first place one should avoid the risk of falling in love by refusing to listen to lovers' flattery and complaints, but if in love already she must seek a remedy before irretrievable wrong is done. Cure is perfectly possible, though some say not. Love creeps in, it can creep out. First, he goes on to prescribe, the erring one must be sorry that she has knowingly thrown herself into that dungeon. Let her consider how many foolish things she has done without wit, brain, or reason through love, how much good time she has lost with unprofitable and foolish cares and how many occasions for good deeds she has missed, how she has burned and what misery she has suffered, and how she may benefit now from a purpose and will to come into a better mind. But she will have to keep her mind from wandering or else it will return to love. Let her set herself to some work and avoid sight and hearing of the person loved, turning from any thought of him either with reading, or praying, or some good conversation, or honest song, or study of some merry matter, clean and chaste. If the beloved has any fault she should remember that and not his virtues, and think how many times vices are hidden by fair seeming. Thus beauty makes people proud and disdainful, noble birth arrogant, riches intolerable, and strength cruel. She will be wise if she considers not what he has said that pleased her but what he has said, or done, that displeased—something peevish, foolish, foul, lewd, unthrifty, mad, or ungracious. From that she can conjecture what may lie hidden within, for people hide faults and show virtues to the utmost and therefore appear better than they are. We are deceived by mere pretenses of vices and virtues and unwisely after common opinion take for virtues what are not, calling liberal what is extravagant, bold what is foolhardy, eloquent what is babbling, witty what is fickle. Women are often deceived because they are unable to judge the truth from the outside, and lovers, especially, appear at their best. Then if delivered, let her thank God, for what virtuous Christian woman, or pagan either, of any wit or honesty ever loved any other man than her husband. She will neither love in this other way nor entice men to love; for both she will be damned.

So wrote Vives with understanding and sympathy, on what a girl or woman might do to cure herself of illicit love. He follows pretty much the same lines followed by advisers of men, with modifications for the women because of their limitation in freedom of movement and choice of companions. It may well be assumed that the others had in mind some such general adaptation of their advice to women. One writer much quoted above, Ferrand, does tacitly imply as much when he explicitly supplies one such modification. After suggesting that the lover may be helped by an attempt to persuade him that his mistress does not care for him as much as she pretends, he adds that with women the argument can be used of how common dissembling is in men, with the consequent danger to feminine honor. Perhaps the advice to husbands to guard their young wives from temptation by not neglecting their marital duty should be included here as one more instance of care, in this case, to prevent the rise of dishonest love. Far the most commonly expressed attitude, however, toward illicit love in women, usually by disappointed lovers, is the scorn and condemnation of them, as the despoilers of men, the sole cause of their degradation by excessive love.[21]

With pictures of love now, inevitably, somewhat mixed, we will proceed to examine at length renaissance attitudes toward the relation between love and marriage. Should the desired end of love be marriage, can love exist in marriage, should it, can a woman love both husband and lover, should a wife ever take a lover, how should her husband regard her doing so—these are the questions chiefly raised when marriage is injected into the subject of love. It seldom is, as a matter of fact, and in general one may assume that the elaborate system or cult of love which the renaissance delighted to construct (refining, with Plato's help, upon troubadour and medieval courtly schemes) existed in its own world, which either ignored the real world of marriage, children, and housekeeping, or reduced to ridiculous nonentity husbands always tyrannical and jealous. The renaissance world of love was commonly built on the assumption that love, being a passion, belongs to nature, and is governed by instincts far more powerful than civil laws. Love enters in a flash, uncontrolled by wish, and is therefore, above all the statutes of men and ungovernable by them. Love also is the worship of beauty, first physical then spiritual, and asks no return except love. Not for any material gain does the lover pursue his beloved, or the beloved with divine compassion yield to his suit and return to him all that she can in honor. To both of them nothing matters except the mutual satisfaction in their union. Their own pleasure is the sole aim.

Against all this, view the current beliefs about marriage in all Christian countries. Marriage is a social institution, existing for the welfare of the family and the state. Parents, most concerned for the future, are to choose a mate for son or daughter according to every other consideration than love—wealth, birth, age, reputation, parents, or profession. With the daughter must go a dowry in behalf of the stability of the new family, and for a sort of equality in contribution to that stability. After marriage the sole responsibility for support of the family falls upon the husband, and it is unfair for him to bear the whole load from the start, while his wife is left to her pleasure, without any care except what she voluntarily undertakes. As long as dowries are necessary, the choice of a mate must lie in the will of the parents. When all these requirements are satisfied or balanced, what room, was asked, is left for love? Even if parents accept love as desirable for the children's happiness, they cannot call it forth on demand, as a last consideration. Love rises freely or not at all, and compulsion is one of the chief conditions that kill any chance for love, even when two people are of such a compatible nature as to warrant an assumption that they are made to love each other, and indeed might, if let alone to allow mutual attraction to work naturally. The custom of dowries itself, it was frequently argued, corrupts marriage from the start, robbing it of mutual love not only by greatly restricting the choice but by turning it into a mercantile transaction out of which grows endless strife between husband and wife. What chance even can there be for the growth of love after marriage when each calculates with jealous eyes the sort of bargain that he has made?

As we have seen, writers on marriage had much to say about love, admonishing husband and, particularly, wife to cherish it. And the argument against a married woman's taking a lover would run as follows: the husband may be imperfect in many ways for the purposes of love, but the wife is to consider that it is her Christian duty to love him for no other reason than that God made him her husband, and she is therefore bound not to imagine a deeper perfection in beauty and generosity than his. But the subject for these writers is marriage as the vocation of woman and marital, not passionate, love, the love that is fundamentally friendship. Indeed, in general they considered passionate love not only incompatible with marriage, but undesirable. Husbands were warned to take care not to turn their wives into wantons by treating them like mistresses, but to use the marital act only for the procreation of children and never for pleasure. Also the wife was warned not to use her beauty and charm to rouse passion in her husband but by modesty and self-control to subdue his passion. The pleasures of physical union were not usually granted to the married pair. Therefore it followed that for the man marriage with a mistress long pursued in love should most of all be feared. The basis of their relationship had been passion, and as her lover he had been her professed servant with prompt readiness to obey her commands; the necessary change to authority would be hard to establish because of her former pre-eminence. Both would strive for mastery. And how would the husband escape the suspicion that she would meet other men as she had met him?

The woman too might well hesitate long before she married her lover. If choice were within her power, or if her parents refused her the lover long hoped for as a husband, she could comfort herself with the same considerations that made her hesitate: The matrimonial yoke is full of labor and pain, taken up only by necessity of law and custom; while the lover's knot is full of pleasure. If these are joined each loses its own special quality. Desire itself fails with too much indulgence, and is likely to be lost to the husband if he has been a lover before. A man marries for children, maintenance of the house, preservation of wealth, and all the other practical service a wife can render. If the mistress proves unsatisfactory in this role, and then his hopes as a lover are unrealized as a husband, he will be deeply disturbed, and dissension will arise. Marriage therefore should rest on simple friendship based on reason, for it must last, where love is only too likely to be wavering and changeable.

On the other hand, there were some to defend at length marriage as the true end of love, and love as the true base in marriage. What is the love of the young that aspires to marriage, asked Buoni, and defined it as follows: "It is the chief affection of all, chosen by the free mind of the lover, clothed with pleasure, generated by perfect beauty, which appears such to the external senses and from which as from its own nature arises the desire to follow and possess the beloved, with perfect union of the mind and body, and for the legitimate procreation of children." Thus the love that most writers on that subject considered in detachment from mundane, particularly domestic, affairs, and also from ordinary conceptions of morality, by one little phrase tacked on to the end of the definition, becomes the necessary condition preceding and supporting marriage. The noblest claims for love, the usual argument ran, are enhanced and made more enduring by marriage. All the parts of a lover, nobility, virtue, learning, and valor, appear more perfect and praiseworthy if found in marriage, a state more honored among men than the free state. Liberty is good, but it is particular, where marriage maintains the world and serves the common good. Though true lovers, under the conditions described, must be admitted happy and perfect, they may, if they marry, more confidently expect happiness to last through their lives. Marriage is vexing only when contrary minds are joined, a wrong that prudence can avoid. Therefore both young men and young women will conduct themselves with discretion, for dangers beset them. The young woman should love with such wisdom that if the desired end comes she cannot as a wife be reproached for any unchaste or even merely silly act. The youth will seek a girl or widow of high birth whom he can marry, and thus avoid the suspicion and blame that pursuit of another man's wife is almost certain to involve.[22]

Such a pair of lovers Alessandro Piccolomini postulated when he wrote the second version of his serious treatise on the bringing up of the young nobleman. He saw in the Platonized form of love a valuable aid to the complete development of youth, but more particularly he saw, or brought himself to see, this love as a part of nature's plan to effect the continuation of the human species. The copulative act, he reasons, is necessary to generation, but has something brutish about it since it is shared with animals. There is danger that man will abhor it, since he is born friend of chastity and nobility, with resulting damage to posterity. So wise nature has placed intense delight in the act to mend it, and put in man and woman this love which is a desire for beauty and is capable of lasting and refining effects. Thus disgust in producing children is sweetened, and matrimony, which is sometimes troublesome, is made bearable by love. He has written of love, he says, as it should be, chaste and modest, to demonstrate their error to those who love otherwise, and he has written of it as a prelude and later an accompaniment to marriage. By thus joining the two he intends to show love in its true form and to rebuke those who despise marriage.

Piccolomini, however, does not smooth out some inconsistencies. According to this revised version marriage adds union of bodies to union of minds, and he is eloquent enough on the physical pleasures of marriage: "Oh sweetest knot, Oh most delightful acts, Oh most holy laws that join two most virtuous minds in the marriage bed," and warns the husband not to deprive his chaste and loving wife of these caresses which he owes to her alone by human and divine laws. She will not stray if the pleasure and sweetness that she receives from her husband exceeds all other delights. But then he falls into the familiar strain that most writers on marriage adopt, and boldly asserts that man is a more noble creature than woman, though he does add in parentheses the concession that sometimes against the order of nature, women are born more prudent and wise than many men. Therefore he must conclude that the husband should have authority over the wife, not such complete authority as the father exercises over his children but such as the laws of marriage concede to him. Even Piccolomini warns the husband that he is headed for trouble if he does not see to it that he preserves in every act and every word a certain authority, to breed in his wife a certain respect and reverence which never ceases to bring the blush of shame to her cheek and prevents her from ever taking lightly his admonitions and exhortations. Such authority and seriousness should not harden into severity or rigidity, especially in the offices of love, but the husband must hold the reins over the whole house. Communion of minds is described only as sharing domestic problems, cares, and of course, joys. "The most incredible sweetness," concludes our author "is to be found in the company of a chaste consort, with whom, narrating occurrences, conferring on household affairs, sharing hopes for the children, he takes recreation and relief from a thousand labors for his family." And the wife to meet her husband's utmost needs becomes an echo of him, never beginning speech but answering promptly to his, mirroring in her face the joy or sadness in his.

But all this is far off from the communion of minds Piccolomini describes in his section on love. First of all it presupposed a certain equality as well as perfection of minds, like seeking like. There is no talk of inferiority in the beloved; if any difference is assumed, the odds are in her favor. One fear always with the lover is that the virtue of the beloved may excel his own, which results in his seeking to become more perfect and more worthy to possess her mind. As a true lover he desires for her every sort of prosperity, favor, greatness, honor above his own—there is no envy in him. Because of something divine in her he is filled with such reverence that in her presence he is, as it were, struck dumb with astonishment. Communion of minds between lovers means that they seek to know as perfectly as may be the virtuous thoughts of each other. The instruments are imperfect, but the eyes minutely regarding the beautiful parts of the beloved furnish the intellect with evidence of beauty of mind, and lovers gazing thus into each other's eyes learn more of the sweets of the heart than words can tell, with such intense delight, they say, that they cannot long endure to look so fixedly. Something of divinity harbors there in lovers' eyes. Only less, words are a means of possession which, sweet to the ear and true in sense, raise incredible delight. This amorous union makes perfect the love of the two and gives them a taste of happiness superior to all other mortal joys. A thousand years, finishes Piccolomini, would not be enough to declare its sweetness and perfection.

One feels that Piccolomini has done the best he could to end what became for him an undesirable, if not intolerable, division between a man's affections before marriage and after. He had changed his own opinions since he wrote his first book on human behavior in 1539, which he called *Dialogo de la Creanze de le Donne*, (or, we might translate it, *Dialogue on Higher Education of Woman*, or perhaps more exactly *Dialogue on a Finishing School for Ladies*) since he said in his preface to this earlier book that he wrote to correct some faults, not of very great importance in themselves, but liable to a harmful exaggeration because of the habit that the enemies of women have of making out of the smallest spots the greatest matter. Here he pictured the delights of love outside of marriage, and he did not escape blame for thus exalting illicit love. Though he did later retract anything in it said to the prejudice of women, avowing that he wrote in sport, parts of the book did seriously represent the author's beliefs, for in his *Institutione Morale* he refers to it for details on the duties of women to spare repeating them, and in the first version of the *Institutione*, published in 1542, he still maintained his attitude toward love as a thing apart from marriage. The central question of this book is how shall a man attain to the happiness for which he was made, and in the section on love he assumed that to the young nobleman and noblewoman who seek perfection, unquestionably the chaste love described by Plato in many of his dialogues, especially in his *Symposium*, and by Aristotle in the eighth and ninth books of his *Ethics* is eminently appropriate and essential. The only question is whether a young man should marry the beautiful and virtuous woman to whom he is bound in love, or whether he should choose another. When he came to the answer, in chapter two of the section on marriage, he said, contrary to what he assumed his readers will expect, that the two offices are incompatible and mistress and wife should not be one. Since the mistress is loved for other ends than the wife, neither should be jealous of the other.

In the revised version of this work, published in 1560, Piccolomini retained the chapter on love but added another longish chapter to explain his position. Here he abandoned his earlier stand and argued, as we have already noted, that the one relation, entirely delightful, together with the other, safeguarding generation, made the marital knot as comfortable and delightful as we see it to be. Then conscious that he was open to certain retorts of lack of realism, he tried to forestall them: If anyone objects to his making this love principally desire of the beauty of mind found in virtuous persons, because the greater part of those who are married lack such beauty, the answer is that the fault lies in the individual who rejects virtue and runs to vice. Anyway his business has been to draw the ideal, like those who treat of the Republic, Orator, Courtier, and so on, and not to report what is found in the imperfect actuality.

It is within man's choice, however, to combine the two loves, and though it can be done more easily in cities where those joined in marriage have seen each other and know in part their quality, even where this is not true, choice in some way may be made since love is in the free choice of man. Against the corruption of the age, he has written to show that love based on beauty is not to pass beyond the pleasure of hearing and seeing for the revealing of minds, for corporal union belongs to marital love alone for the benefit of succession. The young man is now to find in one woman first his beloved and then his wife. Thus Piccolomini has done what he could to purify love and beautify marriage. He seems unaware, however, of the inconsistency he ran into by refusing to marriage the equality he accepted for lovers, thus falling short of his aim to make marriage the true consummation of love.[23]

The problem of love in marriage up to this point has again been considered from the man's rather than the woman's point of view. Suppose, however, that the lover has, against all sage advice, chosen a married woman for his mistress, then the doubts and decisions become more particularly hers. Should she accept him, can she love both husband and lover, and what attitude might she reasonably ask her husband to take? The answers have been suggested in so far as they are the same for both. The more sophistical arguments, which are to be found set forth entertainingly in Piccolomini's dialogue between Raffaella and Marguerita, we will ignore here for the more solid assumptions already rehearsed, that love is necessary for the full development and happiness of both men and women, and that the obstacles to realizing love in marriage, particularly for the wife, are either inherent or practically insurmountable. The wife can identify her good with her husband's in material things, but the mind is a different matter. If her husband does not esteem things of the mind and prevents her from exercising with him the force of her mind, letting it rust away, then on honest opportunity she has a right to bestow her love, primarily if not wholly a communion of minds, on someone else who accepts it and holds it dear.

Conversation with men is indeed a necessity for a woman, Firenzuola holds, because she is so occupied in low exercises with little things that she "cannot as with bare feet walk through the flowering fields of philosophy" as men can. Through conversation she is helped to learn how to live well, and also is introduced to all the secrets of nature so delightful to know but inaccessible to her in any other way. It is perfectly honorable for a lady and a young man to discourse of virtue in order to acquire it for, touched by true love, even a youth of small worth and a crude woman are stirred to greater virtue. If the husband can give this too, then neither should seek love out of marriage, but because he often cannot or will not, and because the same laws of marriage as often mate a man of worth to a woman of lower mind, both men and women are seen loving elsewhere. Nor under the circumstances need people wonder why the members of such matches take a lover. We can imagine the circumstances more clearly in the picture painted by Heroët's "parfaicte amye." From common sense and a desire to raise the honor of the house a lady is given a master by her parents. He abuses her and plays the tyrant in every way possible. A long time after, long enough for her to know just what kind of husband she has and how hopeless it is to expect better of him, she is sought by a lover who undergoes suffering for her. The one she serves by evil chance, the other she commands by nature's own choice. Then which would she do wrong to, the one who accuses her if she loves, or the other if she does not? Surely she should be sorry only for her friend since a cruel law has known how to restrain her desire forever and to make her suffer for that which it has made her wish. If she is all his and he all hers, she ought to return to him all she can in honor. She should respect and reverence him for the complete loyalty he owes her.

It must be expected that husbands would not be pleased when their wives took lovers even if they married only for wealth and not for love. But also it must be expected that the renaissance would ask are they not unreasonable in this as in all the rest. As a matter of fact, said Renieri, neither should be forbidden to love others with good and honest love, not going beyond desire but leaping to contemplation of divine beauty. The husband should not be displeased that his wife should be loved, even if he greatly loves her, for the wife in love does not necessarily hate her husband, and besides love has another end than marriage, and does not at its best mean physical possession. Others indeed, as we know, went farther and argued that true love outside of marriage may go beyond desire to possession, and interpreted the law against adultery as aimed at promiscuous relationships rather than devotion to one mistress. Love so high is not variable, and is all the more necessary because the wound is incurable. As a final concession, both loves should be admitted really necessary, because they work diversely and to different ends, and work better separately, avoiding almost inevitable interference with each other.[24]

We have come now to the end of the more general aspects of love, which concern more especially the lover. The part of the lady in all this is not too clearly defined. Love is primarily a game at which men play, and women are involved because there have to be two to play it. Before going on to examine the treatises or parts of treatises that apply more specifically to women I should like to pull together some of the loose ends. One question that rises is what was held to be morality in love, this love that is above all man-made law, that is claimed to elevate lovers by teaching them to cultivate the great virtues which lead to perfection and ultimately to the contemplation of divine things. With reference to established law there were two answers. If union in such love is not to end in physical embraces, then morality is not in question. How can there be sin without evil act, or intention, or thought? Good, but what becomes of honor, that is, reputation, still objected the opponents of the system; how is the world to know that love is spiritual and not physical? In appearance the case seems to be the same for the lady who holds her lover to this higher plane and refuses full possession of herself, as for the lady who grants all: if her love is known she cannot escape prejudice. The obvious answer is that secrecy must be the first rule for both.

The way to love with honor, however, when union means full possession, needed special prescription, which is not lacking. First of all the right opinion must be held. Love is the natural, true law, and honor is merely a common opinion and therefore against reason, which despises common opinion and follows nature. The whole problem is then a purely practical matter of how to forestall suspicion and prevent discovery. Discreet behavior is the thing. With foresight the lady in love will build up a solid reputation for modesty, chastity, and holiness. She will, for example, show more devotion than her neighbors by going to mass earlier than they do, by showing modesty in all her actions in public, and by refraining from singling out her lover for attention. The good reputation acquired by these and other similar means will leave the way open to come to love subtly without suspicion, for no one more easily deceives than those that have not been accustomed to deceive. Honor thus lies only in proper management and conduct, in subtlety of artifice. The chastest woman in the world, it was pointed out, can be held the most lascivious if deportment is not well regulated, and the most lascivious the most continent providing her lover also knows how to act with discretion. Secrecy here again is the cardinal virtue in lovers, and it is important, therefore, for a lady to accept the service of a discreet man, who knows how to render his love not less evident to his beloved's eyes than unknown to the public, a man of fine wit, truth in words, and great courage. His discretion must be known before he is accepted as a lover, but, the lady is warned, he should be accepted before he is so blind with passion that he loses discretion and trumpets abroad her cruelty. Nothing then is impossible to two such who desire complete union.

Supposing, however, that by some bad chance love becomes known. What should the lady do? Heroët again lets us enter the lady's mind. She will not drop her lover for another, but concealing her knowledge from him she will exercise her prudence in finding consolation for the admittedly awkward position that she is in. Falling back on her firm belief in the law of love, she will reflect that the common and foolish multitude have no judgment, knowledge, or certainty, and therefore their blame is really praise. People of honor, on the other hand, both men and women, if they have been in the same straits and remember their experience, will pardon her since they believe with her that all honesty comes from loving. Even those who condemn her for not having strictly reserved the right of loving to her husband when they know her life and conduct, although they speak on his side, will excuse her by the law written within their hearts. That ought to be enough for her although in public they are enemies. If she were allowed to do anything to defend herself, she would destroy the barbaric right which men have established too much to their own advantage. Love is a virtue much more esteemed than not loving or not being loved. Or let it even be admitted that virtue (that is love) is vice, and banish all amorous service, and still if she loves, the worth of her lover excuses and absolves her.

With reference to public opinion then, based on the commonly held moral code, morality in love lies in the one case in not going beyond a certain point to actual physical consummation of love. That point might be physical contact that fell short only of the sexual act, it being counted a kind of supreme evidence of chastity if the lady allowed her lover to lie naked in her arms freely caressing her, but restrained him from full possession of her. More than one writer testified that he had known several instances of just this restraint in such freedom. In the second case, since perfect love is not realizable if limits are set to its expression, lovers in praiseworthy pursuit of the ideal are justified in opposing the edicts that impeded them and unjustly punish them, and morality therefore lies wholly in not being found out.

This conception of morality was obviously in the main built on a particular interpretation of honor. The renaissance tried hard to give to honor for men a loftier, more personal meaning than the customary reputation. Reputation depended on others and dwelt in others' minds, but honor, it was often said, dwelt within a man, independent of others' opinions, peculiarly his own, wholly in his own keeping. That was what was said, by way of description rather than definition. Definition, however, almost without exception limited honor to mere reputation as explicitly as this example from Tofte: "Honor, is the reputation and Credit, or the good name and Fame, of a Man, which the generous spirit priseth, at so high a rate, as before hee will have the same eclipst, hee will loose all his wealth, yea, and his dearest life to." And whenever it was employed to dictate behavior, honor cannot be distinguished from reputation. Dueling would have found scant moral support if it had not become a sort of bodyguard to honor, honor that could be stained by quite unjust charges of cowardice or disloyalty. Innocence, that is, a clear conscience could not save an upright man, famous for achievements on many a battlefield, from risking his life in single combat with a false accuser. For women, however, honor meant only one thing, good reputation without any refinements, and good reputation for only one thing, chastity. The truly chaste woman had nothing so much to fear as suspicion and malicious defamation of her character, and was hedged about with every sort of limitation to her freedom in order to protect her honor. It was little use to her to be chaste, she was cautioned incessantly, if men thought her otherwise. Hence the easy descent in this so-called Platonic system of love to a morality that feared only discovery and put a premium on secrecy and cleverness at circumvention.

Among various amorous doubts which Firenzuola sets a group of women to arguing, was raised first the question, why isn't it better for a woman to love another woman than risk her chastity with a man. By a somewhat devious way the proper conclusion is reached. The body is the instrument by which the soul performs all its operations on the earth, and therefore it is fair to believe that in a beautiful organ dwells a beautiful soul, and that the soul works much better if its instrument is beautiful and well constructed. Nature has made man and woman alike in virtue and power of mind and has given them beauty as a link to bind them together. But she has ordained that the beauty of woman should kindle greater desire in the breast of man than the beauty of another man inspires, and that that same beauty in man arouses more delight in women than in men. For proof observe the fact that no man, however much an enemy of women otherwise, can see a beautiful woman without feeling a natural desire to please her, and so it is with a woman at sight of a beautiful man. A woman then, having come to the knowledge of beauty of soul through that of the body, and having more knowledge of the beauty of a man and taking more pleasure in it than can come from the beauty of a woman, ought to command the love of a man rather than that of another woman. Dropping nearer to earth, lovers are advised that the blame they risk from those that regard them with unfriendly eyes is far less when love is between opposite sexes than the blame visited on the love of a man for a man, or a woman for a woman. The love of man for woman and woman for man has always been praiseworthy reason for a thousand services, and the biting tongue has no power to do much harm if conscience is pure and clean. This is one of the very rare instances, so far as my knowledge goes, when renaissance writers on love took note of the question that the Greeks assumed settled to the contrary without debate. Plato's *Symposium* was used as the great bible of love, but applied only to love between men and women, called the truest and purest love leading to comprehension of the divine.[25]

If the view of morality set forth in these pages seems of somewhat dubious quality to minds jaundiced, as lovers would have said, by ordinary opinions and rules of behavior, to lovers themselves within their special Garden of Eden, the snake of public opinion resolutely shut out, such morality took on all the hues of the highest idealism, as is most clearly shown in the qualities demanded of lover and beloved.

We have been held thus long to the general ideas on love and the part the lover plays, in spite of the small harvest for the lady's part, because without the system there is neither lover nor beloved, and without the lover there is no beloved. What has been contributed to the desired figure of the lady is a general framework. Human love governed by reason is the great elevating passion that all men and women of gentle birth should welcome, even seek to realize. The woman for her more perfect beauty incites such love in the man and works in him the transformation that bends him to her purifying service and sends him out to high accomplishment in her honor. She in turn by the union of minds, and bodies if she will, realizes her own perfections to a degree impossible without love, so that if she cannot find love in marriage she should accept a lover. Obligations and returns, so great, demand of her, as of him, devotion to a single love, out of which can grow permanent, increasing good. Though to her are ascribed the good effects of love on her lover, all the more important as they reach out to public welfare, the evil effects of love grown inordinate were seen as defects only in the lover, in his headstrong passion, bad judgment in choice of the object of his desire, and in his wandering, wavering will.

In the views so far presented the lady is the object of search, not the seeker, the wooed not the wooer, the granter not the petitioner, though some writers held the two parts interchangeable. In the few remaining works or parts of works the lady is given the center, made to stand on her own feet and take the initiative. We shall see now just how much of a womanly ideal is furnished by the books that set forth this system of love recommended to both men and women.

The choice of a lover always was supposed to be in the lady's hands, for though she was told that graciousness and gratitude dictated that she return love she was so bound only if he was worthy of her love, but now she is advised not only to take her time and consider all important points with care but, in defiance of all other advisers, to go where she can observe men, to the window or to church, until she sees what she wants, for first of all her eyes should be pleased. At closer range, she will weigh a great many things, some of great, some of lesser importance. Her own age and her lover's have a general bearing on the chances for success. She herself should be around twenty, not much later because at twenty-five she declines more than a man and will not have due time to share equally the fruits and gifts of love, and not much earlier because she is too tender from fourteen to eighteen to support patiently the flames of love. At twenty she will have some judgment. What about her lover, should he be young, mature, or older than that? There are arguments for all three, but youth has easily the preference, though not under twenty because before that the youth is unstable, timid, always longing for new love, inexpert, hasty, rash, suspicious, too disturbed by passions, always babbling his loves to an intimate, boasting beyond truth, and spreading tales. He lacks sufficient firmness of mind to be capable of true love. Middle youth is therefore best, between twenty-four and thirty. At twenty-four when judgment begins to rise, the lover learns to restrain vivacity of mind, is contented with having his beloved in his heart, finds a look or word from her enough, does not importune and dispute, but silently endures every trouble, and proceeds modestly to possess his beloved without disturbance. Firm, constant, not too green, and not too ripe, sums up Renieri. In a man is desired more power and proved age, in a woman less age and more beauty. A long life is now ahead, in which to experience love that grows more perfect and enduring, even lasting into old age. The chief objections to accepting an old lover—called old by some at fifty, some at sixty, or even forty—are that even at forty the lover cannot endure the fatigues of love as a young lover can; at fifty he has only two to four years to give enjoyment to his beloved, and after sixty he lacks natural heat, may even be incapable of "those sweet pastimes the ease of love requires," has infinite aches and little place for love. In any event the lady herself should be younger than her lover becaue if she is older she is much less apt in the service of love, and if equal then when he is in flower she is already past her prime.[26]

Another of the lesser considerations was rank. Certainly the lady should not choose for her lover a boor, peasant, or clown who is less ashamed to commit base acts, and errs more easily, and is only too apt to want to boast that he is favored by a lady. Indeed a lady of gentle birth who loves a low-born man shows unworthiness and baseness of mind, and merits blame and punishment. Come somewhat higher to artisans, tradesmen, and the like, the argument still runs against them, and all in favor of lovers of high rank. Great and powerful by family, riches, and virtues the nobly born are more likely to pay attention to matters that concern this passion, though busy too with affairs, where common men are likely to be given over to thought about the civil actions more necessary to life, this trade and that, and are far from such thoughts and care as belong to the lover. Also the noble and powerful lover can more easily find means to approach the beloved and join himself to her than the low born who lacks wealth and power. Men most often propose to love what they can easily obtain because what is not obtainable, or obtainable only with great difficulty, they do not ordinarily so much desire. Besides, in the noble lover reside in better form the more pleasing manners and virtues and deeds that arouse love, and so he will more easily move his lady to reciprocate than the lowborn man can, and his love will be made more perfect and enter more deeply into him because he knows that he is loved in return. Finally to all these advantages learning is added, so necessary for the full development of virtue which comes not so much of custom as of knowledge and learning. The good given by nature is increased and adorned by the exercise of letters, until the beauty of body that belongs with birth is matched by beauty of mind. The greater the nobility, the happier the beloved, agreed most, because it obliges the lover to do measurably worthy acts to increase his fame. But there were some who would have the lady look lower than the highest and choose a lover of equal or even a little lower rank. A lover of very high rank is loved and sought by everyone, and therefore likely to esteem less the love of the lady below him. He is only too likely to be proud and puffed up, doing things by violence rather than by favor, love, and friendship. His wealth enables him to buy, or think he can buy, love without exchange of good will. Wealth is indeed desirable, for it enables the lover to act more safely as well as more generously, but it should be moderate wealth, and though liberality is a great virtue and both lover and beloved should practice it, something like equality in this respect should be sought. Even if noble in every desirable way, the too fortunate are too much in the public eye, and always have a throng around, lessening opportunities to meet and increasing the danger of detection. Here the lover of lower rank has an advantage, for he will be less noticed when he comes to see her, and better still will be entirely unsuspected as not having any chance to win her.[27]

When the question comes up of what occupation is most to be desired in the lover we meet again the rivalry between the soldier and the scholar, an honorable debate of long standing. It was not, however, the old controversy, said Bargagli, of the supremacy of arms or letters, but of the fitness of the professor of either to be the lover who seeks perfection at every point. There is a case to be made for each, and he proceeds to set forth impartially both sides. In order to secure the mind and favor of the beloved, which is his desire, the lover must first of all give to her wholly his own will and mind. To make her certain of his good will, he should use terms that are clear and and not doubtful, strange and not common. What could be more obvious than that soldiers are to be preferred, for their beautiful and sound thoughts are directed like arrows at the destined mark, at love, and at the observation of a single lady. They cannot deceive as others can, but openly and loyally they show their ardent love in the exercise of their art, love acting as a spur to courage. Scholars, on the other hand, have only sonnets and madrigals by which to show their prowess, all of a kind, using the same words in praise of various ladies. The scholar also is retired and has no time for the lady if he is to achieve honor. Where the soldier can protect his lady and punish evil tongues by the law of arms, the scholar is unable to do so; and in fact, far from protecting his lady, he viciously attacks women, adept, as he is, at the use of words but not of the sword. Besides, ladies have always preferred soldiers, even at court, where the most noble scholars are found, and Venus herself, it should be remembered, loved Mars. The preference is well founded, because soldiers are more liberal, not so subtle, and more easily allured with the enchantments of women. They all succumb if a woman says they have a fair beard, well-proportioned legs, are comely on horseback, and good fighters.

The case for the scholar runs with equal persuasiveness. The scholar understands what love is, and shows his faith in the sweetest way by verse and prose that lasts and spreads her fame, not by arms and force which the beasts have. He has humanity gained from letters, and nobility. He can entertain endlessly by discourse on new and pleasing subjects, and by delightful stories, especially of love. The scholar also pleases in person; his handsome dress is appropriate to all in love. A certain gravity and majesty in repose, in action, and in dress, which belong to the scholar only, make him more authoritative than the soldier. If equal in estate, how is he behind the soldier in liberality, magnificence, and splendor? As for defense, ladies are gentle, quiet, and peaceful themselves and therefore have no need for defense by fierce and noisy arms. How much more suitable to them are gentle, peaceful letters! Contrary to the charge that the scholar has no time for the lady if he is to achieve honor, many scholars have been inspired to write first of all by love—Petrarch, Sannazzaro, Ronsard, and Bellay for example. It is foolish to argue that women at court favor only soldiers, said Bargagli in 1587, when at the court of Urbino not many years before such young scholars as Bembo, Castiglione, and Bibiena formed a noble academy and won fame by their writings.[28]

But all these considerations are of minor importance, even negligible, in comparison with the thing that really matters, the character of the lover, already partly sketched but needing more complete presentation. What sort of man should he be, adorned with what particular virtues? In Piccolomini's much questioned dialogue between Raffaella and Marguerita there is a full-length portrait of the ideal lover, which may well furnish a starting point for this description. It runs as follows.

Whoever is worthy the love of a gentlewoman should be of noble birth, which carries the greatest satisfaction; beautiful and gracious not only in face but in person and motions, because, though beauty is not in a man the principal thing sought in love, it is of very great importance and contributes great happiness when added to other parts; and well mannered and modest in all his words and actions without any affectation. Defender of the honor of women in general and in particular of his own lady, he will always profess veneration for all women, more or less according to their merits. In matters little and big he will keep the utmost secrecy in order to give no occasion for comment. He will have such great judgment that he will know how to court his lady at convenient times, but not too often, skillfully making it appear that he has some other compelling purpose in being where she is. He must always show himself a man of gentle condition, courteous and liberal with all generally, and especially with the ladies, and well garbed to give no sign of instability or little wit, but to indicate firmness of mind and self-control. He should not lack skill in the making of such toys as masks, costumes, and impresas, but should not be at it every day, and especially he should show such restraint and judgment that no one will know the chief purpose for making them. In short he should be known as a person of fine breeding, stability, virtue, and learning, a defender of women, magnanimous, skilled in seizing occasion when it offers, able to dissemble his thoughts, faithful to his lady, constant and ardent in loving her, and above all wise in knowing how to govern himself according to each day's circumstances, because no more particular rule can be given, but all must be left to his judgment.[29]

Here we have a picture of the gentleman in love, chiefly as the world will see him, comely in appearance, self-possessed, easy and gracious in manner, in a manly way devoted to ladies whom he seeks out in mixed society, expert in meeting all the demands of such intercourse, without revealing the secret center of all his thought and behavior. These are what may be called the external qualities of the perfect lover, the social virtues, which may exist without reference to the ideals belonging more intimately to the inner man, the moral virtues. What are they?

The list is pretty much the usual array, the inevitable four, prudence, justice, temperance, and courage, with most commonly the addition of constancy, modesty, and even chastity; and a variety of points more often named in connection with lovers than elsewhere, for example, tenderness, pity, hope, patience, and the already named secrecy. On sight of these familiar terms, however, it will not do to ride them off in all directions, or even in usual courses, for in the lover's world, as already indicated, virtues are likely to take on special, appropriate meanings, which are not always easily recognizable by moralists of other worlds. It would grow tedious to try to furnish an exhaustive lexicon here, but some of the more important or more specialized will serve to characterize, more exactly than the bare list can, the lover that should be sought by the lady of perfect character as well as fastidious taste, who will look to his inner worth far more than his external manners and behavior before the rest of the world.

Secrecy, so often insisted upon (the first lesson, Alberti called it), because essential against evil thinkers, was in reality a part of discretion or prudence. Perfect love should be lasting. Unless a lover is circumspect and discreet in all his words and actions his love will become known or suspected (and suspicion is as bad as knowledge here), and is likely to be short, bringing dishonor to himself and his lady. Among the questions that were so popular a sport with lovers, Chartier includes this: is it better for a lover to fail to enjoy his lady for fear of being seen, or to enjoy her and be seen. The answer is that it is better to fail, for he is no true lover if he brings dishonor to his beloved, although when he is with her he desires to accomplish his will. He ought to guard her honor above his own so that he may come another time the better to his pleasure. Secrecy, therefore, is of the utmost importance as a shield against the interference of public opinion. It is also necessary if the lover is to win the confidence of his lady, who must fear not only disgrace in the public eye but also serious trouble through the jealousy of husband and relatives, or to a lesser degree of other would-be lovers. Many women refuse to take a lover from these fears. If fortune favors the pair and discretion preserves the secret of their love, life and reputation will be safe, but the same dangers lurk for the lover in these jealousies and always he risks the unavoidable mischance that imperils everything. Then only his courage, a combination of robustness of body, moral virtue, and skill will preserve his lady and himself from ruin. This is the special courage that belongs to the lover.[30]

The other virtues more closely concern the personal relations of the lover and his beloved. First among these usually is named constancy, variously called loyalty, or fidelity. This means chiefly freedom from all aspiration toward other women. A true lover will not seek satisfaction elsewhere, even upon his lady's refusing him his desire though they are in a safe place. The fruit of love is to be desired, truly, but to love only for it is not true love or promising of long continuance. The perfect lover should be able to find dreams or thoughts of his lady sufficient without gathering the fruit that opportunity offers. Yet the question was raised whether after long absence a lover might, without too much blame, seek amorous intercourse with another than his beloved. Some conceded that it was no deep offense then, if nature alone was to blame, and no more affection was yielded than would serve the lover's turn. Some, more exacting, prescribed a lady who resembled the beloved. Friendship rests in the heart, argued Pasquier's lover on the point, and these small intemperances of nature, forced by instinct, do not violate love. Heroët's "parfaicte amye," however, went farther for herself though perhaps not recommending herself as a pattern to follow. Loving a god, she begins, one receives scarcely more pleasure from being loved than from seeing someone else drawn by his beauty to desire him also. So with her terrestrial god. If another more beautiful woman has a part of him, she praises her fortune and appearance, and approves because she holds her lover's pleasure as her own. She well knows that what comes from his heart belongs to her, for his heart is hers in exchange for her own. She therefore pardons a pleasure that touches his person only, a flame that will soon pass. Nor does she desire reciprocal liberty from him because she loves him too well to want any other friend. Can selflessness go farther?

But if a lover should wander thus, from long want of his lady because of absence or temporary fancy, or if he should do anything that might cause uneasiness in his beloved or doubt of his good faith, does the love of truth enjoined upon the true gentleman require confession to her? There was difference of opinion on the point. Garbo said that deceit in perfect love is impossible because pity is born of this passion, and the lover, desiring pity in return, cannot risk deceit for fear of losing pity. Another, however, decided that the lady should prefer a lover who is a deceiver but who conceals the fact and relieves her torments, to an unskillful lover who cannot make her believe in his loyalty though he sets his glory in it. As for the pity shown and desired by the lover, it was argued that no lover has real compassion for the ills of his beloved because adversity necessitates aid, which makes them equal and breeds friendship. Therefore the lover must even rejoice in the adversity of his beloved. The compassion of the beloved for her lover, on the other hand, is no sign of reciprocal love, but more often of the contrary. Constancy, by now, is assuming a wavering appearance, and we had therefore better pass on before it slips out of sight.[31]

Temperance was included among the virtues of the lover, though not so often recommended and not without some debate. For the lover who would rein desire within the limits of wholly rational love, temperance, without question, was required as the moderator of every word and action against excesses, through fear of offense to his beloved. All the more such a moderator was needed for the lover who risked his honor, and his lady's, by seeking ultimate satisfaction of sensual desire in embraces. How may temperance be understood for such? First of all, says Zoppio, one of the few who stop to reason on the point, it is unfair to draw comparisons between the prudent lover, whom we are being asked to envision, and those that are given over to the tyranny of unbridled desire for lack of discretion. Two ideas (to use the Platonic term, he adds) govern the affections—desire for pleasure and desire for what is best—and where reason rules in living, as with the prudent man, temperance necessarily is required. The lover does not cease to be a good and true lover through desire for embracing, and is not for that to be reputed intemperate, or incontinent either. It is true that he runs into danger of intemperance and incontinence and will not thus gain the habit of temperance and continence, but he can love and embrace without a trace of viciousness, seeking the natural enjoyment of physical union with the beloved under the conditions that reasonableness prescribes, with due regard for the honor of both and the secrecy necessary to maintain it. As for the lady, to whom prudence will dictate careful scrutiny on this point, she will do well, advises Casoni, to observe narrowly the eyes of her lover for by them she may see his nature. If the circle of his eyes is red and humid he loves women fervently; if his eyes are large and reddish and his face appears humid when he looks at her, there is excess of love; and if his eyes are not wholly open and his head is bent, his glance indicates libidinousness. All such she will be wise to avoid.[32]

Modesty and chastity are assigned also to the lover, but without much comment. Certainly they are not to be understood as operating to the same effect as in the woman. The question raised about chastity is not its importance but its possibility in the lover. Can a lover be said to have chastity, that is a lover who possesses his lady with physical union. Yes, his love makes him most chaste, if he is not moved by other women however beautiful, but desires only his beloved. Chastity for the lover, as for the wife, is to be viewed not in the general but only within the circuit of the personal relation between lover and beloved, as between wife and husband. Here, however, the duty is reciprocal to the same degree only for the lady in love, not for the husband. As for modesty, this virtue preserves the lover from saying, doing, or even desiring anything unworthy of himself and his condition. It is the best indication of good habits and the fear of infamy that every gentle spirit naturally possesses. What the soul is our speech shows; the modest lover therefore keeps from eyes and ears anything that offends, using veiled words, for example, when speaking of acts necessary but brutish to name directly. From modesty rises truth. Only the shameless and ambitious are liars either in praising themselves or disparaging others. Such modesty, however, does not work to suppress individuality or curb true liberty in the lover; rather it makes him more acceptable to society and especially to his beloved by removing what merely displeases and clouds his real worth.[33]

Among the other virtues especially applied to lovers, hope was counted essential, else love either dies stillborn, as when a man of lesser degree falls in love with a princess, or though enduring for a time, fed on self-deceit, finally fails. Strong desire at first is always accompanied by hope, but when desire is achieved content takes the place of hope, except as hope may be said to remain in that we hope to continue pleasure. Closely connected with hope, however, is fear, of which two kinds properly belong to the lover. First comes the fear of the lover that the merit of the beloved exceeds his own, and he will therefore not be able to achieve his end for lack of beauty, nobility, wealth, virtue, or the reputation of lacking these qualities. This fear spurs the lover to seek perfection in himself. Or the lover's fear may be reverence rising out of contemplation of the beloved's beauty and worth, an almost certain sign of true love. This is the fear most noble and appropriate to love, for by it the lover does honor to his lady. Industry was also enjoined upon the lover to enable him to serve his lady well. By taking his part in public affairs—and the higher his rank the greater is his responsibility to do so—he increases his own fame and thereby the honor of his lady. To converse fittingly with her he needs to know much of music, the arts, and the sciences, which furnish matter of interest, and to be well acquainted with the poets for stories with which to entertain her. On a lower level industry is commendable to save the lover, Alberti suggests, from making "an arte or occupation of his love, gadding abroad with frizled lockes, embroidered garments, and other open marks of their lightnesse."

But the list is endless. Let Buoni's array cover everything or suggest what has been omitted here: lovers of religion, humble, civil, faithful, grateful, generous in praises, human, temperate, full of decorum, secret, liberal, of habits suitable to their state, clean in body, constant, just, wise, active, diligent in suitable things, vigilant in public affairs, companions of the modest, listeners to old men, truthful, quick to remember, observant, reverent, patient, imitators of all true virtues. Obviously the vices that they will particularly shun are pride, discourtesy, infidelity, ingratitude, contempt, cruelty, and deceit. In short, as Sansovino sums it all up, the lover worthy of the lady should be of a quiet and calm nature with all the qualities belonging to a perfect man.[34]

Now, having chosen her desired lover in the light of this ideal with all the prudence at her command, the lady faces the question of what arts she should employ to gain his love. For this end she was conceded liberty to act beyond others of her sex. First, she must somehow convey to her beloved some hint of the state of her heart. Apparently those who had responsibility for the good behavior of maid or young wife were rightly warned so incessantly to keep her from the window, in Italy at least, for it was the window, according to some, that gave freest chance to attract the attention of the desired lover passing by; spitting or throwing little stones was specifically recommended by Gottifredi, and then sweet looks, courteous reverence to show him he has her favor. Seeing that he pleases, he will pass more often and finally must love. By signs, play of the eyes, and pantomime she can convince him of her love. The advantage of communication from the window is that she can hide herself away from others. If she does meet him on the street or at church she will if possible give him a glance, show her face, go with arms and neck bare, for every particle of body seen bare is a face to kindle love. She should not, of course, show too much or she will seem to lack chastity and modesty. Some advisers thought windows too dangerous because the lover by passing up and down, or singing to her at night, calls attention to himself and jeopardizes the safety and honor of both. Public places were thought safer by such advisers—at church many others are there for the same purpose, and eyes are free to seek out each other cautiously and converse by that most eloquent of all means. Feasts, plays, jousts, all present opportunities for first encounters and revelations, but with all due precautions against being observed. Once he knows that he is beloved, the lover can seek by every means to come to her. Though eyes are the best messengers and go straight to the heart, something more is needed to conduct love to its end. Conversation, the great need of lovers, is too seldom possible for men and women even in public, and too dangerous to attempt in asides, for eyes and tongue are almost sure to betray one. Furthermore, in a woman words must be never less than honest or far from the truth. To her lover she must show sincerity of heart by her speech, for the purity and beauty of soul thus revealed are not less powerful to kindle and preserve love than beauty of body is. She is therefore handicapped, as her lover is not, in making her love known by the double talk, or the open brief word that danger of being overheard makes almost the only speech advisable in public.

Other means of communication must be resorted to by both. Occasionally someone can be found to talk to both, whose integrity and discretion are unquestioned, but this is rare. Occasionally, too, opportunity may be found to send messages by favors made up of flowers and herbs, according to their significance and colors. But in the end letters, though most dangerous of all, are almost impossible to avoid. Indeed letters can hardly be neglected as a means of revealing the heart, for they carry a pledge of love and hold part of the fire of love. This fire a young woman can convey in writing with much less blushing, and even a young man tongue-tied with fear can become eloquent. Such a note well put is a very sweet thing to read, remarked Gottifredi, our guide in most of this practical advice, and he counseled his young Italian lady to study Boccaccio and Petrarch for models of prose, and verse too, so desirable if she only knows how to make it. Lovers demand poems as well as prose letters because poetry is more the friend of love, and the praises owed to love are more sweetly sung by poets. So the lady in love must study no less than her lover how to forward love, and please, and feed the fire which she has helped to kindle until she comes to the desired end. Above all, wrote Nobili, this eloquence just mentioned, which consists in words well ordered, affable, and gracious, and in amiability, has great power to move, for the more good qualities beauty has added to it, the more lovable and dear it is. No one ever loved the words or good manners of a woman for themselves, but they are loved as signs of internal beauty. For a practical guide in these matters, Nobili in 1567 was recommending Della Casa's *Galateo*, equally valued among the English and French beyond the turn of the century.

Nor is the lady without further resources to communicate her state. The kiss, potent to move love only less than the eye, though denied directly, can indirectly play its part. Let her kiss her lover's letters and favors in the presence of those bringing them, and when he is present to see, if she is holding a child, with eyes fixed on him let her kiss it vehemently with loving words. Tears Casoni recommends as one of the most effective artifices of love—"O miracle of love, which now hides the fire with tears, now builds a fire in hearts with a flood of tears, and now changing tears into the sweetest nectar brings it about that lovers do not envy the ambrosia which Venus serves at the great table of the gods." The toilet Gottifredi thought not very important beyond cleanliness, simplicity of head dress, and some variety in dress, but chiefly according to what pleases the lover. As for the use of magic, which women were charged with resorting to more than men because of their credulity, some writers gave recipes for love philters, but warned against their use.

When all is told, however, of artifice and conscious device, the art of kindling love is still to tell. Least of all by tears, sighs, herbs, and charms, said Alberti, can love be had; beauty itself is not enough unless adorned with humanity and grace; love in the end is to be won only by loving, and the slower its growth the surer its lasting. From the beloved if she is not less chaste than beautiful the gentle lover learns the art of loving her with chaste love, his amorous passion restrained by reason and shame and by reverence for her because she has some part of the divine gift of beauty. He in his turn, for neither remains passive once the spark is struck, strives to please her by seeking to resemble her in manners and in gentle civility, because likeness generates love, and by celebrating her chastity no less than her beauty, for with good reason the beloved and every gentle spirit is pleased with praise and honor. He sings nobly of love with significant words, thereby inciting the wish to love, and moves her to pity by recounting his faithful service and the great amorous passion which she has aroused.[35]

Now arises the crucial question each asks himself about the other, is love reciprocal. The lady, unwilling to give herself into her lover's power until his love and good faith have been made more than certain, and until she surely knows her own heart, will review in him the sure signs that she has been seeking. Recognizing her need to know how to read her lover aright, a few writers undertook to teach her.

The external signs of love were frequently rehearsed: loss of weight, pallor, sighs, tears, abstraction, desire for solitude, in extremity neglect of appearance, and even illness. Though of some value in judging the inclination of a professed lover, little reliance, the lady was warned, is to be put on such signs, because not necessarily sincere or indicative of lasting emotion, and not always present in one who truly loves. More significant is constant service, particularly in doing what is good for her, continual praise, liking and hating as she does to the point of imitating her actions and adopting her thoughts, which some considered the surest sign of devotion. Still surer to some was the lover's bold employment of all his powers, not for his own content, but only to achieve honor for his lady at no matter what cost in danger, toil, or even death. Likewise the beloved may judge surely the quality of her lover if he seeks to possess her beauty in proper ways, loving above the beauty of her body the true beauty of her pure mind. For beauty of body fades and love based on that fades with it and even changes to hate, where beauty of mind increases with age and love increases and endures. Yet how judge fairly, on this and other points, the lover made timid by his reverence for his beloved, so that, though bold enough in other affairs and filled with ardor even greater than that the bold lover displays, he does not dare to ask return for his suffering? Final proof of sincerity must meet the test of time. Pretense cannot last. Only true love can make a man endure long the troubles of loving. Added to courage, patience, and constancy, endurance of long suffering shows most clearly love worthy of response. Perseverance therefore is a true sign, involving determination in the lover to follow his own truest good in thus seeking the good of his beloved.[36]

One further sign, generally repudiated, will have to find a place here, though it will lead us on a long detour. Jealousy was a topic of great interest to the renaissance, the Italians particularly, as an accompaniment, or enemy, or result of love, and debate turned on its beneficent or maleficent character, and its significance as a sign of love.

The jealousy considered here, as Tasso stipulated, concerns only those worthy of love and therefore capable of using it to good rather than evil effect. Tasso defined jealousy as either grief that others have, or are, what one lacks, or fear that others too will love the beloved for her beauty. The second kind he repudiated as coming from a lover of ignoble mind who cannot bear to think of anyone else's having what he has, or what he wants to obtain, or even what he has been unable to obtain with all his pains. Enjoyment of what another covets, or fear of a sharer in what he wants alone, becomes a malady of the mind of the lover, totally degrading. The first kind Tasso found honorable and just. Held within reason it becomes a noble and even gracious virtue, by which the lover, anxious lest he lose the favor of his lady to a more worthy lover, fears to do things that will justly lose it, and therefore becomes temperate, liberal, and magnanimous. Jealousy then seems to become the cause of all the virtues and then love itself in disguise. Tasso, therefore, seemed to others to be somewhat carried away here, on the wings, no doubt, of his poet's imagination. More soberly he averred, in accord with common opinion, that there is no love without at least a little jealousy, which, kept well in hand, serves even to increase love. Varchi thought it against nature not to have a modicum, since even animals are jealous. What he would blame was not jealousy but excess. Nobili too accepted jealousy as an accompaniment to love, but only to weak and imperfect love, allowable at the beginning when a kind of doubt of being able to surpass rivals acts as a spur to praiseworthy deeds; grown desperate jealousy only debases. Romei took it as a sign of love that has been great, but is fading. The heart of one deeply in love is the proper subject for this most bitter passion called jealousy he said, but love is then weakening when jealousy appears, and when it kills hope by fear, love turns little by little to hate.[37]

Other writers, however, repudiated jealousy as in no way a necessary accompaniment to love, or a blessing; the truly noble mind is in fact incapable of it. Piccolomini attacked vigorously the admittedly widespread favorable idea of jealousy. Defining it, like Tasso, as a fear that the merits of another exceed our own, he condemned it by its effects. Allow the claim that jealousy sometimes stimulates the lover to become better and increases love; this is not an essential characteristic, but only accidental. On the contrary it is far more likely to destroy hope and become madness, so blind that it cannot see when a woman is doing a man harm, and consequently not knowing what is in her heart is led to suspect everything. It is true that jealousy cannot exist without love, but fallacious to argue that it is therefore a sign of love. Rather it corrupts love at the core, causes deep distress to both lover and beloved, and is indeed a sign of an evil mind toward her, for the jealous lover hates praise of her from others, desires instead vilification and deprivation of everything in order to make her dependent on him. Jealousy, therefore, Piccolomini concluded, is never found with true love, but destroys all the peace and pleasure of love.[38]

The causes of jealousy vary according to one's nature, breeding, or the custom of the country, said Varchi; and Tofte, in the notes which he furnished to his translation of Varchi's work on jealousy, named Italians as most subject to this vice and conjectured that those dwelling in hot regions showed excess of jealousy either because they were more given to love or because they considered inchastity of wife or mistress more of a blot than northerners did. It was even thought that love and jealousy were shown in different ways by men of different nationalities. The Greek lover, Equicola begins, always conceals his passion, if touched by jealousy blames himself, but driven to despair of ever recovering favor he falls to cursing his beloved. The German lover is liberal with presents at first, but if his jealousy is aroused he becomes avaricious and in the end wants his presents returned. The French lover is always gay and likes to give pleasure to his beloved, but when jealousy enters in he weeps and if reduced to despair changes to insults if possible. The Spaniard in love always appears wretched, he dies of jealousy, and once convinced he has lost his beloved he despises her. No need to speak of Italy he concluded because she shares the good in all the nations, found in the most illustrious middle among planets. Tasso, analyzing the sources of jealousy, thought it rises out of the belief of the lover that superior qualities of rivals are an impediment to love; or out of beauty itself as the cause of love in so far as beauty is loved or desired; or out of envy, grudging another's good. It may be increased by the mistress either carelessly or intentionally arousing suspicion, or by the rival boasting truthfully or falsely of his conquest, or by the lover himself if he irrationally turns everything into food for his jealousy. Cure is effected as occasions disappear, said Varchi, but Tofte objected that there is no cure if jealousy is deeply rooted, citing recent murders from jealousy by two Italians and one Englishman.

The inevitable question was raised of differences between men and women on this point. Varchi intended his book for women as well as men, he said, because they are no less given to love, and being generally less wise, more suspicious and timid, and loving with less restraint, they must therefore fall into this dangerous disease. They have a right to be more jealous than men, said one author, because men go about and see so many ladies that they can hardly help loving others whether they wish to or not. Also because women do not run about or speak their will or beg, as men do, their jealousy lasts longer.[39]

What weight the lady should assign to jealousy in her lover as indicative of true love, to bring this discussion back to the theme we are pursuing, received on the whole, in spite of some differences of opinion, a single verdict, none at all—unless perhaps a slight favor, in very early stages, and in young lovers. Boccaccio's answer to one of his famous *Thirteen Questions* may be taken to settle the point and warn the thoughtful lady to consider jealousy sufficient argument to reject a lover. The question was, which is greater, the grief of the unloved lover, or the jealous lover. The unloved lover may hope for a change in his beloved, came the answer, but the jealous one never, for, to quote the English translation, "The jealous hath his mind ful fraught of infinit cares, against the whych neither hope nor other delight can bring comfort, or ease the paine. For he standeth intentive to give a law to the wandring eies the which his possessor cannot give. Hee will and doth indevour himselfe to give a law to the feete, to the hands, and to every other act of his mistresse. He will be a circumspect knower both of hir thoghts, & of hir mirth, interpreting everie thing in evill part towards himself, beleeving that ech one desireth and loveth her whom he loveth. Likewise he imagineth everie word that she speaketh to be twaine, and full of deceit. And if he ever committed any detraction towardes hir, it is death to him to remember it, imagining to be by the like means deceved. He wil with conjectures shut up the waies of the aire, and of the earth. And breefly, the heavens, the earth, the birdes, beasts, and everie other creature that he thinkes dooth hinder his devises. And to remove him from this, hope hath no place, bycause in this doing if he find the woman faithfull, hee thinketh that shee espieth that which he dooth, and is therefore heedful therin: if he findeth that hee seeketh for, and that he would not finde, who is more dolorous than hee? if peradventure ye thinke that the embracing her in his armes be so great a delight to him as should mitigate

these pangs, your jugement is then fals, bicause such maner of colling
bringeth him in choller, in thinking that others aswell as hee hath imbraced
hir in the like sort: and if the woman peradventure do lovingly intertaine
him, he deemeth that shee dooth it to the end to remoove him from suche
his imaginations, & not for the tru love shee beareth him. If he finde hir
maliciously [*malinconio* in original] disposed, he thinketh that shee then
loveth an other, and is not content with him. And thus we can shew you
an infinit number of other suspicions & cares that are harboured in a
jealous person. What shall we then say of his life, but that it is farre more
greevous than that of any other living creature? Hee liveth beleeving and
not beleeving, and still alluring the woman."[40]

By consideration of all these things, the qualifications of her lover and
indications of return of love, the lady finally resolves her doubts about her
lover, and realizes at the same time that he must be seeking assurance of
her truth and constancy. The task is difficult for him also. Just as his freedom of action and common assumptions, which favor or at least condone
deceit in him where a woman is concerned, create difficulties for her in
coming at a true estimate of his character and purposes, so the conditions
of her life, her seclusion and lack of opportunity to show her mind, her
guarded actions accompanied by carefully inculcated fear and shame which
hide true nature, make it even more difficult for him to know her. All signs
must be held obscure in her. Finally, however, if every act, word, and gesture of hers, clearly grounded in virtue, indicates desire for union with him,
he may put some faith in her, and ask for a secret meeting, and when she
grants his request he may believe she loves him truly and firmly. She may,
therefore, find her own ways of resolving doubt in him. But she has still
to know her own heart as surely. Gottifredi presents her with signs by which
she may know when she is in love. When the inadvertent omission of what
she knows will please her lover causes unmeasured grief and unbelievable
pain; when missing the slightest opportunity to see him causes her to curse
her bad luck; when not seeing him for a day stretches the day to a year in
an inferno; when time spent with him is a minute, however long; when
leaving him means leaving her heart behind; when every moment night and
day her thoughts dwell only on him—then may she know herself in love. It
is a wise woman, says Heroët's "parfaicte amye," who takes counsel of her
love and further inquires of herself what strength and constancy are in her
love, and she suggests this supreme test. If her lover should do her injury
for a long time, would her heart be able to persevere, never desiring another
friend, refusing with excuses all other good coming from elsewhere, so
strongly moved that she feels both boldness and fear? If all this she knows
true of herself, she may with confidence pursue her love.

So at last the lady, recalling how her lover has steadily shown himself
loving with a chaste mind, desirous of her honor, keeping her reputation

safe by every means, never being bold and presumptuous in touching, is
reassured on the wisdom of her choice and makes up her mind to grant his
request to see her alone. In the name of modesty, however, she is advised
to hold him off for a time with excuses that at the same time do not deprive
him of hope. He will then persist and finally, casting off fear, she will happily
grant him an opportunity. To what end love will carry them depends, as
we have seen, on whether she is intent on maintaining it at the spiritual
level, or believes that love is not love without full physical expression.
In the latter case Gottifredi, practical to the end, suggests that on meeting
her lover under desired, favorable circumstances she still pretend at first
not to want what is most wanted, but he warns her not to prolong her
fencing if time is short. In the other case, question centered chiefly around
the kiss. Should it be allowed in chaste love that delights only in beholding
and conversing with the beloved without raising unchaste thoughts. It was
often granted, as belonging to a union of souls rather than bodies, for by
it came a most pleasing passage of spirits from the heart of each to the other,
as Romei said, binding their souls into one. On a somewhat lower, and
doubtless more practical plane, granting the kiss was advised as a little
gift of love which carries the greatest consolation, and thus allays the ardor
of desire and avoids several disadvantages which may arise from it. For
love is a subtle, varied thing and the kiss comes from its gentler side. The
lover, if refused, should not lose courage but persist, for however often the
lady refuses, she can be doing so only to prove his loyalty and care for her
honor. On her side, when she has found him loyal and secret she should have
pity on him and consent, on conditions which she will give as expedient,
counting honor in no way lessened by it.[41]

Love now reciprocal entails upon both lover and beloved equally the duty
of behaving in such fashion as to increase and preserve it. Food is necessary,
food furnished by hope joined to desire, and confidence of obtaining the
beloved. The duration of love even with lovers that realize the greatest
delight in each other remains a hope, mixed with fear because hope is not a
certainty. Not only the qualities of loyalty and secrecy, but all the others,
must continue to be sought and shown. Aid, comfort, and pleasure each
must bring to the other by every means possible. To the lover with his
freedom of action and speech special advice was given: that he seek friendship with men honest, noble, and worthy like himself, few, not many, or
he will be too well known to work secretly and may displease his lady, only
too easily persuaded that he has revealed her to his friends; that his talk
be modest, wise, without detraction of others, or praise of evil men or commerce with them, or scoffing at anyone, or quarreling or contending at law;
but that he act as reconciler, in his lady's presence if possible. Toward her
he should feel no pride, but serve her in all things, with all civility and
gentleness, showing her due honor, and giving no occasion to her by his

actions or words to change or be disturbed. The true lover, concludes Sansovino, never thinks of any but the beloved, lives only with her name, feeds only on the bitter sweetness of her beauty though he is accustomed to the whole earth, lives only in her as if transformed, has no care except to spend his powers and life for her, exalting her, being jealous for her, and defending her. Thus, thinking increases love. Special advice on the same topic was also offered the lady, at times in terms that dropped far below the ideal represented above. She should be secret, careful, and alone, avoiding close friends lest her lover prefer them. If she must have one, she should choose a plain friend who will not be dangerous but set off her beauty. She should avoid jealousy and never show it, never ask her lover where he has been or whom he was looking at, for she may be calling his attention to someone that he had not noticed but may prefer. She may allow herself to quarrel, but sweetly and not too often, or over mere trifles, or in such a way as to cause uneasiness and jealousy over herself; a quarrel is then a means of renewing love. So Gottifredi. But what is perfection for the lover is also perfection for the beloved, and Boccaccio held that if the lady is perfect in love she will teach her lover all the beautiful things that love generates, particularly free and lofty discussion.[42]

Now we come at last to the central purpose of this account of love, a synthesis, so far as it may be made, of the ideal qualities of the lady when she is viewed as the beloved of a gentleman worthy of her, and in her turn as the lover. To the minds of many renaissance theorists only in this role could either reach perfection, for without love the chief incentive to realize the best within oneself is lacking. More space has been spent thus far in setting forth the virtues of the lover than the beloved, because more advice was addressed directly to him, but what was said for one was claimed by some, the most thoughtful may we say, such as Piccolomini, Equicola, Tasso, to be said for the other. The beloved was to be taken as the counterpart of the lover. Secrecy, loyalty, patience, consideration, discretion, courage, temperance, hope, courtesy, liberality, and others are essential in her as well as in her lover. The lady, however, as has already been indicated, was expected to wear some of her virtues with a difference. Her less active, more secluded life prevented the full exercise of such virtues as courage and justice, and her extreme vulnerability to slander dictated concealment and caution beyond her lover's. Yet if her fear of discovery or of being deceived were excessive, she would lay herself peculiarly open to the charges of ungraciousness and ingratitude, the greatest of faults in a lady. For if she is to be loved, she must give love, and know how to love with art in order to satisfy her lover, and at the same time preserve the honor of both. Very small things, say those careful of perfection in the lady, belong to this art— graciousness in returning admiration, gaiety in reply, pleasantness in keeping holiday, courtesy in listening.

Courtesy is indeed a very necessary virtue for her, not only in order to be pleasing to her lover, but to protect herself from calumny. In public she must above all take pains not to give cause for blame. She will therefore be courteous to everyone and at the same time not single out any person by too particular attention. If occasion arises, as it may, to favor one suitor more than another, she will select one who is not her accepted lover, or more than one if possible. If ever she finds a suitor unworthy of her kindness, she will withdraw, but little by little to avoid his seeking revenge through scorn. Though many know her virtue and the cowardice of her suitor, and will not believe the lies that he tells about her, there are others who will believe and she will be wrongly defamed. She must remember that honor or blame do not rest principally in doing some one thing, or not doing it, but in being believed or not believed to do it, honor lying in nothing but the opinion of men. Therefore every art is necessary not only to do the right thing, but to give no occasion for tales of her affairs.

Again with reference to her lover, liberality is an important virtue for her, some even putting it first against cupidity, a vice killing to love. Since it is the lover's part to present his beloved with gifts even to the exhaustion of his resources, he runs grave risk of encouraging in her mere greed for his presents rather than love of himself for his own sake. Hence in her, liberality that usually has to be shown only in modest ways—if indeed she dares to give him anything at all—means especially absence of greed, even restraint of his generosity for his own sake. If on the other hand she is of greater rank and possessions than he, she in turn must guard against both avarice in withholding gifts and prodigality. She must use judgment, for moderate giving produces pleasure and gratitude, where too much delights less and usually produces scorn.

Discretion in the lady who would love obviously consists chiefly in selecting with great care the man who will have in his keeping not only her happiness but her honor and perhaps even her life. She must then match him in secrecy and caution in public not to reveal her preference, and in quickness of wit at dissimulation when awkward chance threatens discovery. At the same time, however, courage as well as discretion is needed, lest she be unreasonable in fear, and when only mild risk is involved unnecessarily deprive both herself and her lover of pleasure. She should not, for instance, be displeased if her lover, concealing the object of his love, risks showing her his devotion, because complete concealment of love greatly increases pain.

Constancy was worn by the beloved with no difference from the lover except as some argued her constancy of a steadier, purer ray than his. In temperament more hot and dry than woman, man finds constancy more difficult of achievement than she. The flame suddenly kindled in him by beauty creates such vehement desire, agitations, furors, and waverings between hope and fear that in his sharp and precipitate pursuit of his end he seems to love without reason, even lightly and uncertainly. Whereas woman, cold by nature, is moved with more difficulty, and having leisure while she is solicited to choose the lover suitable to her, is exempted by reason from the diverse agitations of these two contraries, hope and fear. Once attained, however, love endures longer in her. Or one may go even farther, and arguing her ethereal nature from her beauty, believe that her constancy draws from the spiritual character of her love. The soul being always one and immortal, of necessity her love is as immortal and always one, where the love of man, who is given up to the appetites of the flesh, follows the condition of flesh, corruptible, uncertain, and changeable.

In general the guide for the lady in love, Equicola advises, should be moderation in all things, if she wishes to be blameless. Vices imitate the virtues in appearance, and virtues turn into vices if overdone. Thus her humanity may be so great and common to all that it is to be called abjectness. Her greeting may be lively and merry, but her speech rude. Speaking sententiously in order to appear wise may degenerate into affected language. Standing mute like a marble statue in order to be believed unable to discourse because of purity of mind is a ridiculous pose. In conversation she can show chasity and modesty by speaking no word that offends these virtues, by showing disapproval of vices in herself and others and delight in virtuous and gentle deeds. Let her speak simply of things as they are, say nothing that can arouse suspicion, never too much, and never evil of anyone but good of the deserving, taking care not to make the difference too apparent. Excesses in the other direction are to be avoided, for example joking and jesting, which leads to talking like prostitutes, or assuming proud behavior through ignorance of what is suitable to preserve rank, or falling into superstition through desire to make public profession of religion.[43]

However, beyond all that may be said of the moral virtues requisite in the beloved no less than in the lover, there still remains one essential quality, belonging to both but placed pre-eminently in her, and that is physical beauty. Called by some the first good of the body and even the greatest gift of God to mankind, beauty by general consent is particularly the crown of woman, the most important condition of perfection in her. In order to have the whole picture of the lady in love it is necessary now, therefore, to consider at some length what has been postponed at more than one point because of its complexity, the parts of feminine beauty and various related questions that exercised renaissance pens.

For the description of ideal parts we will rely principally upon Agnolo Firenzuola, who wrote the most thorough and quotable renaissance treatise of feminine beauty. He announced at the beginning that he would speak mainly of the beauty of customarily uncovered members, and occasionally of the covered. Like most writers on the subject he was content to be less than complete in his catalogue "for modesty's sake." Some, however, debated freely the questions implied. Why should some members of a woman be called honest, like the head, face, hands, and be left uncovered, while others are held so dishonest that women will go to almost any lengths to conceal them, even after death? What is the relation of clothing to beauty; is a woman more beautiful naked than adorned with rich silks and gleaming jewels? If the majesty of beauty is more visible without these artificial aids, argued Luigini, another lover of women's beauty, waxing eloquent, then why should the poet, painter, or mere adorer stop short of revealing the charms of the place whence all of us come into the world and which of all the parts of woman gives the most pleasure to men to behold, "with such lifting of spirits as the sight of a little garden gives in spring, all sweet and white and vermilion." There are complete catalogues, therefore, for which some Aphrodite rising from the sea would have to be the model. The dilemma is not ours, shall we say fortunately, because even Firenzuola's catalogue is longer than seems wise or necessary to inflict on modern readers.

The preferred type of beauty is well known—long, fair, curling hair, dark eyes, arched black eyebrows, white skin faintly tinged with pink on throat, breasts, palms, or deepening into vermilion on the cheeks and lips, sweetly rounded flesh where flesh should furnish soft contours, the whole body delicate to sight and touch. Whatever may be the differences between the medieval ideal and the renaissance (which modern writers seem most interested in figuring), to a less penetrating, shall we say more roving, eye these features most commonly praised belong to a convention that reaches back to the Greeks. Whether they are tagged in neat threes to a round thirty—three longs for hair, hand and leg, three whites for teeth, throat, and hand, three reds for cheeks, lips, and nipples, or pursued downwards from crown to sole in more rational, elaborate fashion, a single pattern received at least lip service in treatise as well as story. That it was more than lip service may be strongly surmised from the concentration of renaissance beauty experts upon bleaching measures for hair and skin. One man, to be sure, says that he rejects common opinion which sets up rules for beauty and thus does wrong to a million rare beauties. But the writer is a Frenchman, that Alexander de Pont-Aymerie whose "paradox defensive" attempts to show how much more perfect in every way woman is than man.

Although it is not necessary for our purpose to run over the specifications for features that the renaissance loved to describe and praise, it may be well to set down an example to show what can be done when one sets his mind, perhaps heart too, on it. The description which follows comes from Firenzuola's second dialogue on the beauties of women. The words are strictly his but I have not used quotation marks because as usual I have taken some liberties with order and omissions. The mouth seems to have aroused Firenzuola's greatest enthusiasm; the fountain of all amorous delights he calls it. In general terms he describes the perfect mouth as leaning to the small rather than the large, revealing not more than five or at the most six upper teeth when it is opened without smiling or speaking. The lips should not be too thin, nor yet overly full, but full enough to show their vermilion against the surrounding flesh color. When closed they should meet evenly, the upper lip not extended beyond the lower, or the lower beyond the upper. Also the vermilion as it diminishes toward the corners should make an obtuse angle, and not an acute, nor should it be rounded like the chin. It is indeed true, he refines further, that when the underlip swells a little more in the middle than the upper with a kind of mark that seems to divide it into two parts, this little swelling adds great charm to the whole mouth, especially when it is open. Between the edge of the upper lip and what we call the end of the nose there should appear a certain space like a little furrow faintly tinted like flesh-colored roses. Sometimes closing the mouth on the right side with a pleasing motion and a certain grace, and opening it on the left as if secretly smiling, or sometimes biting the lower lip, not affectedly but as if inadvertently (so that it will not seem childish or lascivious) rarely, gently, sweetly with a little shy wantonness—such a play of the lips accompanied by certain movements of the eyes, which now gaze fixedly, now are cast down, is a gracious thing, an action which opens, or in truth sets wide open, the paradise of delights, and floods with an incomprehensible sweetness the heart of him who gazes with desire.

Thus, with details that often would take a painter's eye to recognize, the renaissance drew perfection for the outer form of the lady, a dream to fire the imagination of men, a pattern to measure their ladies by, a mirror for the ladies to estimate their powers and mend their defects. Whatever the moralists, or others writing on wives, could say against the sin or folly of trying to improve on God's design, in the lover's world beauty was of so high a price that failure to nourish, enhance, and preserve natural gifts and correct blemishes became the sin. If outward beauty harbors something of divinity, and is witness of perfection of mind and soul, in which we most resemble God, then reverence is due to it, and correspondingly, care. Rightly the beautiful woman tries even to increase her beauty, since nothing human is perfect, and the woman marred by some natural deformity or disfiguring illness does her utmost to simulate the beauty that alone on first encounter testifies to her virtue, and guards against some impression of deformity of soul. Thus, instances Liebault, if she should have red hair, a color indicating a person haughty and given to some great vice, she can bleach it. It is the natural condition of woman to be clean and beautiful to the eye; she therefore follows the law of her being when she devotes herself to business so little understood by those who condemn her. It is her right to show pride in her beauty and take great comfort in it. Her mirror is the good minister of love.

Yet comfortingly these seekers for beauty were assured that no one could ask that all the beauties be in one body. That were to be entirely unreasonable. Besides, without some lenience how could one find room for the fact that no matter how perfect a woman might be according to the generally accepted pattern, she did not command either the judgment or the love of all the men that knew her? Quite unaccountably it would seem the choice fell on a great variety of types of women reputed beautiful, and even on those who were by no means thought so except by their lovers. Some cared most for one feature, color, or shape, others for another, and even if the beauty were deceptive, the lady having had her hair curled, her face skinned for a new fine skin, her eyebrows plucked, and her teeth whitened to persuade her lover he had a paragon, it would have been wasted breath to tell him. Indeed the renaissance developed such passionate (or is dispassionate more exact) interest in the beauty of parts that lovers might have found good support for ignoring all the other less perfect features of their beloved to hang their adoration on the one beauty that enthralled them. Among other intensively cultivated fashions in verse and prose, more or less short-lived, the blazon ran its course. The Italians celebrated the particular beauties of their mistresses, but it was left for the French poets to explore fully the possibilities of eulogy applied to physical details, both in range and in elaboration, and to invent or appropriate a name for it. Sibillet said in his "Art Poetique Francois" that as painter and poet are cousins-german, it was not difficult for him to believe that the blazon of colors in arms was the origin in France of painting blazons in poetry. Brief and pointed was his prescription, but ingenuity challenged by the spirit of contest that rose among the blazoners of beauty and between them and their moralistic opponents spun out descriptions of the nose, eyebrows, teeth, tongue, and particularly more controversial details into *longueurs* that must have soon bored even their producers. The most famous of the blazons was Marot's *Blason du beau tetin*, which started the vogue, and the best, in his opinion, of these submitted in the contest he initiated was Maurice Sceve's on the eyebrow.[44]

But enough of this anatomizing of women's bodies, to which renaissance men devoted so much care, partly because, they said, it was impossible to find beauty perfect in any one woman and they must, therefore, consider parts, and like Praxiteles look to find one beauty here, one there. Wider considerations must now be given some notice, which will serve to round out this account of beauty as the first requirement of perfect womanhood. Behind the question of what constitutes beauty in the hair, the throat, the foot, lies the more fundamental question of the ultimate source of beauty. Does it lie in the relation of the parts to each other, proportion, or in coloring? Some thought in one, some in the other, and some in both or other things. Firenzuola, to let him speak in this as in so many other matters, placed beauty in proportion, a harmonious ordering of the different members, and thought Cicero's addition of sweetness of coloring superfluous, and he goes on at some length to dispose of color as a main consideration. Whenever the particular members of the body, with which will be produced the beauty of the whole, are in themselves beautiful—well put together, composed, and proportioned—they will necessarily shade the body with the delightful color essential to the harmonious beauty of the whole. This is so because in a body well tempered by the humors and composed of elements well mixed health is found, and health produces a lively color and shows outwardly its inward presence. Since the members of the body possess separately the color essential to the particular character, beauty, or essence of each—such as a shining whiteness like ivory in the cheeks and a flat whiteness like snow in the breast—they inevitably possess it in union, and thus they will necessarily diffuse through the body the sweetness of color which is needed, and which does not have to result from several colors compounded into one, or from one alone, but is different in different parts according to the variety and need of the diverse members.

Those who thought that color holds first place as the source of beauty could argue for their preference after the fashion of Canoniero who relies largely on Romei. The human body is called beautiful chiefly through its colors because they are a part of light, the greatest of all beauties perceived by the senses. The sun is itself the most beautiful of all objects, and as the source of light it is the means and chief cause of the revelation of all beauties. Light and colors differ only in that light is a clear color in a luminous body, and colors an opaque light in a colored body; that is, light is color without opacity, and color shaded light. Therefore since light is the greatest beauty in the world, and colors are parts of light and created by light, it follows that color has the first place in beauty. Again as concrete proof, lovers find colors most delightful to the sight, likening hair to the shining color of gold, cheeks to white privet and red roses, lips to rubies, and women therefore take the greatest care in this matter, esteeming the beauty of colors to be the most powerful incentive to love. As support for exalting color over proportion it was claimed that Petrarch praised only colors in Laura.

Others, more judiciously perhaps, placed beauty not in one thing alone. Liebault defined beauty of the body as resting in good proportion of parts, moderate plumpness, natural and vivid color. Aristotle had added height, they sometimes noted, but the renaissance seemed disposed to take their women as they came so far as size went.

Ultimately, however, something beyond cold perfection in shape, proportions, or color was described as necessary for perfect beauty. Light that same perfectly molded face with eyes that are lively in their modesty, full of love and joy and mirth, and with smiling lips from which issue sweet words and soft laughter—a most sweet messenger of tranquility and repose of heart Firenzuola calls it; add to the whole body of beautiful parts a bearing marked by modesty, gentleness, and control, the walk dignified, the motions chaste, the gestures seemly; and you have the I-know-not-what that captivates the heart when all the rest may leave it cold.[45]

We are now in danger of trespassing on territory that belongs to another quality closely allied to beauty, sometimes made a part of beauty but usually regarded as distinct, capable of existing independently of beauty though included as indispensable in the catalogue of perfection. There was much talk of grace, with some confusion between corporal grace and grace in the sense of favor, already referred to early in this chapter, gratuitously bestowed or with expectation of reward, or even spiritual grace divided by the theologians into many kinds—antecedent, concomitant, subsequent, and so on according to Canoniero's enumeration. All have in common the idea of pleasing, but only the first strictly belongs to this discussion of corporal perfection in women. We will ignore here, therefore, advice such as Canoniero's on how the lover is to put himself in the good graces of a mistress and stay there once he achieves his end, and ignore too Sardi's explanation that grace is a composition of beauty of body and mind and is shown in vivacity of intellect, calm emotions, chastity, gravity, modesty, affability, knowledge of causes and sciences, all of which are beautiful in themselves and in diverse ways make subjects lovable.

Grace as a pleasing quality belonging to the body—and Nobili called it corporal because it resides in the body and the eye perceives it—was rather described by its location and effects than defined. Attempts at definition reveal the difficulty: a beauty achieved in some hidden way by a certain particular union of some members, we cannot say how, was the best that Firenzuola could do. Consisting in order, shape, and proportion, it is shown principally, most said, in movements of the body and gestures, because in action due proportions show better than in respose. Also, some said, it is found in courteous manners, in lofty and lovable bearing, in fashion of speaking, even in the blush of shame and in pallor for want of love, though the blush can be rated more gracious than pallor because as signs of love in youth the one is delightful to see while the other belongs also to old age and can be besides the sign of ill health or an evil mind. Further, grace added to beauty is an enhancement of beauty, lending it wonder and reverence. Even of itself it most of all inflames a lover, arousing in the beholder such satisfaction of heart and content of mind that suddenly desire is aroused. Grace therefore, by common consent, is another thing than beauty, because it has more power to please. Also those who argued for the difference seem to have the stronger case because grace can be shown to exist without beauty. For instance a gift or favor of small worth graciously bestowed outweighs treasure given coldly or carelessly. Even a deformed old woman, when there is something well ordered in her movements, may be thought to be adorned with grace and therefore pleasing. Grace without beauty, how-

ever, is defective, as beauty is imperfect without grace. If one is to be preferred to the other, grace wins first place because it always pleases and
matched with intelligence may even make up for lack of beauty. Style is
the thing, and grace is style. With the Platonists, moreover, grace won
ascendancy because it belonged to both mind and body. One of them,
Francesco India, defined it thus: a certain external splendor of reason and a
certain becoming nimbleness in actions, which are born of the good disposition of the body and mind together, and which signifies perfect beauty.
Moreover, beauty belongs rather to the body, resting in the conditions of
matter, where grace, connected rather with form, through reason seizes the
mind more profoundly and with greater vehemence, working more secretly
with greater efficacy and force.

Such then in the eyes of renaissance men were the outward gifts of the
perfect woman. Not only must she have a well-proportioned body, shapely
members, delightfully formed and tinted features, but she must show in
every movement lively grace to add allurement, and in her aspect a noble
and virtuous air to raise reverence and admiration. When most impressive
Firenzuola gives her what he calls majesty: large, well composed, she carries herself in stately fashion, sits with a certain grandeur, speaks with
gravity, laughs with modesty, and breathes the odor of a queen. Such
beauty, seen in its perfection only in women, draws from its votaries dith-
yrambs in praise of its qualities and its effects. More delicate, more apparent than in men it draws the eyes of a man to itself, ravishes his mind,
pierces his heart. At sight of a beautiful face he forgets himself, his limbs
shake, his hair stands on end, and he sweats and shivers at the same time,
as one beholding a heavenly image is seized by a divine frenzy; then coming
to himself he bows his whole mind in adoration, as if acknowledging a god,
and offers himself a victim and a sacrifice upon the altar of a beautiful
woman's heart, so rhapsodizes Firenzuola for the benefit of the ladies of
Prato.[46]

The exaltation which was given women over men in this one respect of
beauty may account in part for the depreciation of beauty in men. There
was some difference of opinion as to whether the manly ideal should include
beauty and grace, and even in the acceptance of them strictures were made
on the kind that should be admitted. The comparison has some point here.
The Italians, enthralled and inspired by Greek art as they were above other
peoples of the renaissance, could not quite rid themselves of distrust of
human flesh, that legacy of the middle ages that still warps and clouds our
view of the nature of humanity. Chief evidence of this distrust is the general
neglect of beauty in the descriptions of the ideal man. Castiglione, to be
sure, gave beauty and grace to his courtier but he was more interested in
prescribing the sort appropriate to men. For the most part the subject was
ignored. As positive evidence we have such a protest as Pomponio Torelli's

against the scorn of many men for beauty in themselves and their misguided effort to put on a frightful and terrifying aspect in order to increase praise and reputation by thus appearing redoubtable. Whereas, he continued, as a sign of good disposition and finely tempered mind, a means of reconciling the minds of others, of attracting attention and winning favor at first sight, beauty is to be used well by one who aspires to perfection. Or more elaborately, India, a contemporary, argued that whatever can render a man more notable and illustrious should be cultivated in him. The great gifts of nature—health, which brings him to a well-conditioned old age; strength, not the strength that the good wrestler seeks but what is fitting for the gentle and complete cavalier to enable him to exercise the virtues of peace and war; vivacity and integrity of the senses, which increase pleasure and make a man more tractable to the dictates of prudence—all these good qualities of the body are made more illustrious to the eyes of the onlooker when adorned with beauty and grace as condiments. To a qualified gentleman and complete cavalier beauty and grace are as appropriate as for the sun to shine.

But if beauty is to be suitable for men, India finally rounds off, it ought not to be a soft and effeminate beauty, such as Romei exalts in his dialogues, perhaps to please the ladies and gentlemen of the court of Ferrara for which he wrote, but a beauty indicative of a noble mind, by which a man makes himself pleasing to others and apt for the actions of virtue. When beauty of features is praised in men, as by Boaistuau, it is for their wonderful construction for the functions assigned to them, not their shapeliness, or delightful color. The beard, so scorned as a rough blemish by the exalters of women's beauty, is particularly commended by Boaistuau as the ornament of virility and strength, "enriching the chin to reveal to us the maturity of the body and the difference of sex." Yet he can end by marveling that nature has made in so small a part as the face a beauty so great that sometimes we want to die for sheer pleasure in it, or stung to the point of madness by the beauty of some particular face, willingly would we sacrifice ourselves—and now he is speaking, he confides to a marginal note, of the beauty of both men and women, perhaps lest his extravagance bring misunderstanding. Castiglione can go so far as to commend a countenance not too delicate in proportions and features but manly and of a good grace, but he has only scorn for those courtiers who seek a womanish beauty by curling their hair, picking their eyebrows, and pampering themselves at every point like the most wanton woman in the world. He asks of his courtier only that he be of a good shape, well proportioned in his limbs, showing strength, lightness, and quickness for the exercises of war. Tennis he recommends as particularly good for training such qualities.

The grace that should accompany all actions was held in general to be unteachable and most happily possessed by such as have it naturally.

Castiglione, however, thought that it can be in good part achieved by diligence. First of all, whoever wants to have a good grace in bodily exercises must apply himself to mastering the principles of each exercise—riding, jousting, vaulting, wrestling, swimming, whatever is appropriate to the gentleman—from those most skillful in each. And as he progresses he will find occasion to observe various practicers and with the good judgment that must always be his guide pick out one good point here, another there to imitate. So also his grace he will steal from those that seem to him to have it, from each the part that deserves special praise, "even as the Bee in greene medowes fleeth alwaies about the grasse, choosing out flowers." And here Castiglione lays down the famous rule of Aristotle that he who would be most impressive in the exercise of his art must appear to use no art at all; for considering how grace comes, he says, he found this one rule the most general. Acquire great skill in the performance of difficult things and show great care in the doing of them, and you take away the grace of everything. It is a matter of knowing so well how to do perfectly whatever you do—ride, dance, sing, speak, dress—that you can do it with freedom and even as it seems carelessly. But even that freedom and carelessness is the product of art. In conclusion he applies his rule to women, who have such a great desire to be or appear to be beautiful that they go to endless trouble to supply what they think they lack and seem to think that all their care is kept very secret from men. Whereas in truth they betray by their painting, plucking of hairs, and such open measures their over-great desire to be beautiful and thereby deprive themselves of grace.

"Doe you not marke how much more grace is in a woman, that if she doth trimme her selfe, doth it so scarcely and so litle, that who so beholdeth her, standeth in doubt whether she bee trimmed or no: than in an other so bedawbed, that a man would wene she had a viser on her face, and dareth not laugh for making it chappe: nor at any time changeth her colour, but when she apparaileth her selfe in the morning, and all the rest of the day standeth like an image of woode without moving, shewing her selfe onely in torche light, as craftie marchantmen doe their clothes in their darke lights.

"How much more then doth a man delite in one, I meane not foule, that is manifestly seene she hath nothing upon her face, though shee bee not white nor so redde, but with her natural colour somewhat wan, sometime with blushing, or through other chaunce dyed with a pure rednesse, with her haire by happe out of order and ruffled, with her simple and naturall gestures, without shewing her selfe to bestow diligence or studie to make her faire?"

Artificial aids to beauty for men, it is clearly indicated, would receive scant attention. Torelli, viewing the whole duty of man, does with some patience sift out what little may be said for conscious care of appearance of the womanish sort. High color and curling hair can be viewed by a man only with disapprobation, but cannot be denied if born to him. Efforts to remedy defects of form may, however, properly be made if great care is taken to avoid affectation—hose or breeches can be designed to conceal a crooked leg, or hats worn longer or higher to correct inequalities of forehead or head. Neatness is necessary to show in the composition of a man's clothes a well-ordered internal disposition, but too much zeal in this obscures the candor and simplicity which can show the gentleman more beautiful in soul than in body. Even in cleanliness, though filth and ragged clothing are to be abhorred, measure is needed to avoid affectation—not every stain should be feared, especially dust from battle. Again the rule is no affectation, no calling attention to oneself by over-carefulness, but every part, action, and garment beautiful, appropriate and modest. Of the qualities bestowed upon the human form by beauty, dignity, authority, grandeur, and majesty belong more especially to men, and grace, charm, and cleanliness to women. Beauty must be adorned to show as much manliness in men as womanliness in women.

On one ground, however, beauty viewed simply as beauty would seem as important for men as for women. If beauty is the one essential cause of love, and women are held more perfect in beauty, on what is to be based the reciprocal love necessary for perfection? As a matter of fact little attention was paid to this knot. When discussed, it was likely to be solved either by assuming that the lady will yield her love to her lover out of gratitude, or grace if you like, or by arguing that love must always be more fervent in the lover because the greater beauty of the beloved stirs him more deeply than his can stir her. Yet the point was not entirely neglected that the lover should be beautiful just for this reason, that he may inspire in her a love reciprocal in every respect to what she inspires in him. It is altogether fitting, says Firenzuola, for woman to contemplate the beauty of man, and man the beauty of woman. Heroët's "parfaicte amye" has been following Firenzuola's advice, for she speaks of the beauty of her lover which for twelve years has been delighting her eye. At other rare points common ground in this matter between men and women is assumed. Carried over from the Greeks, general expositions of perfect proportions for the human body used the male frame as a model. Firenzuola, after drawing diagrams to show the general proportions of man and the method of measurement by the length of the head, coming back to his subject of the beauty of women, says that whatever is said of the man he always means of the woman too, both in this and in every other measurement, though there have been many learned and worthy writers who prescribe other measures for women. For proper proportions in women Sardi refers his readers to paintings and statues and the book of Pomponio Gaurico, *De symmetriis*, which one finds makes no specific mention of women.

These and any other small concessions aside, however, it must be clear
by now that beauty to the renaissance mind was one thing in women and
another in men. Beyond the more obvious differences already noted there
was one of deeper significance, again one would suppose in favor of women.
In every other case moral and practical considerations, extraneous in source
and even crippling in aim, seem to have controlled the making of an ideal
for women. But here is a realm where such considerations may not be
allowed to intrude for women, but do intrude for men. Women in so far as
they are the mistresses of their lovers' hearts were viewed almost always as
belonging to no other world, having no other duties to perform beyond the
affairs of love, and hence their concern to be beautiful looked only to the
need to delight their lovers. The standards of beauty by which they were
to be guided could be wholly aesthetic, limited only by what at the time
was pleasing in men's eyes. For men, on the contrary, it was rarely ignored
that they had a role to play in the world of public affairs; a fact that could
hardly be ignored since the very ideal of the lover, though it imposed such
absorption in serving and pleasing the beloved that there would seem to
have been no room for other duties, yet sent him out to win honor for her
by the performance of noble deeds. As Castiglione's analysis of beauty and
grace in the perfect courtier shows, the verdict rested on whether his features inspired beholders with confidence in his intelligence, strength of will,
and goodness, and whether his proportions and handling of his body im-
pressed them with his vigor, agility, muscular control, and aptness for
physical feats. Beauty as a quality different from morality and utility was
left entirely to women.[47]

As is already evident, however, this Platonizing renaissance could not
long talk about beauty of the body without joining to it, however perfunctorily, beauty of the mind. Beauty and goodness were said to be inseparable
companions, and physical beauty therefore was argued to be necessary to
perfection not only as an external sign of goodness but as a condition productive of goodness, the perfect body furnishing fewer impediments to the
working of the soul. Also it was argued that beauty of body comes from
beauty of soul. What must be thought, then, of the incontrovertible facts
that a beautiful body may house a mind bent on evil, and an ugly body be
illumined with the pure and shining rays of sheer goodness? In part at least
these paradoxes were explained as due to the hazards the soul meets in
being joined to an earthly body. The beauty of the soul, consisting in purity,
simplicity, and freedom from vices and perturbations, must at best be
marred by the imperfections and perturbations of the body, subject to
chance conditions of food, air, water, and place, to name the most obvious.
Only by exercise of the moral and supernatural virtues can even the clouded
beauty of the cabined soul be preserved, and such exercise of the virtues
depends on other variable conditions—temperament, descent, and educa-

tion. Small wonder if in the infinitely complex mixture of elements beauty of body should be matched with evil, and beauty of soul with ugliness. But as a rule, ugliness of body is to be taken as an index to ugliness of mind, just as beauty of body is witness to internal beauty. Hence came the oft repeated argument of woman's defenders, that she excels man in the goods of the mind as much as she excels him in beauty. True beauty, then, in the scale of perfection must be linked with goodness, cannot exist without goodness, and therefore in women it is to be supposed, says Domenichi somewhat cautiously, that the greater their beauty, the more complete their goodness. Once more we will find goodness practically identified with chastity, which is singled out as necessary to the full splendor of beauty, or even by some made the first condition of beauty—to the confusion of where one begins and the other ends.

Finally, Plato's ladder was in much requisition to give earthly beauty not only moral but spiritual sanctions. It was impossible, agreed lovers and philosophers, to see a beautiful woman and not be moved by love. Beauty itself is hardly beauty unless it is accompanied by love, for what is love but a desire for beauty. The first step upward therefore, to use Vieri's version, is love of the beauty of a particular body. The second step is the love of the beauty of all beautiful bodies, a move away from the too circumscribing particular to the liberating general. The third is the love of the beauty of noble minds through the gentle inclinations that proceed from a gentle and delicate temperament, a move toward the unseen by natural inclination. The fourth is the love of the beauty of noble minds acquired through the active virtues and the laws, in which the lover is drawn to love the invisible by the exercise of the moral powers of his own noble mind. The fifth is the love of whoever arrives at the beauties of the speculative sciences by the exercise of his intellect and emotions working together, a love acquired with the light of human reason aided by sight and hearing; this is a step concerned with invisible powers but still confined to the visible embodiment of those powers. The sixth step is the love of the ideal virtues of invisible creatures, whereby the lover leaves this earthly world, and then moves at last into the ultimate world of the ideal through love of celestial beauty, that is, God.

This or something like this seems to have been in the minds of those who said that the highest value should be placed on women's beauty because through it one might climb to God. How seriously these men held Platonic ideas about beauty is not our particular business to inquire here. The noble account put into Bembo's mouth at the end of Castiglione's *Courtier* of the working of beauty upon men's senses and through the senses upon their souls to bring them to right understanding and union with God convinces by its own reasonable procedure and fervor. But not so convincingly do others bring in something of the same ideas. Firenzuola has his chief expositor in his dialogues on beauty enlighten the ladies of Prato after this fashion. "All my talk, all my discourse, all my thoughts revolve about the beauty of you ladies. Let anyone blame me who will, I affirm not of myself but on the opinion of natural philosophers and theologians as well that your beauty is an earnest of heavenly things, an image of the joys of Paradise. How could man on earth ever bring his mind to believe that our future happiness, which has to consist chiefly in contemplating forever the omnipotent essence of God and rejoicing in his divine presence, can be lasting without fear of satiety, if he had not seen that contemplating the grace of a beautiful woman, enjoying her charm, drinking in with the eyes her lovely beauty is an incomprehensible delight, an inexpressible happiness, a sweetness which when it is over we wish to begin again, a content which takes us out of ourselves? And therefore, my dear friends of Prato, if at times I look a little too attentively at these your ladies, do not take it amiss. You know how Petrarch said to his lady, Laura, 'Were you less beautiful, I would be less ardent.' Do you think that when I look at them I intend to carry them away? Do not fear that I shall do them any harm. I do it only to prepare to enjoy the blessings of Paradise, where my behavior has not been such as to destroy my hope of going." Here the touch of something glib, condescending, even flippant might go far to convince one that Firenzuola, though he could study with infinite pains the elements of perfection in a beautiful woman's face, did not care a fig for the contemplation of unembodied beauty that would take him out of sight of his lady.

There was doubt in fact whether the beauty of women was a subject deserving of honor, and in general it seems to have been considered not quite appropriate to the pen of a serious and pious scholar. The question was included in Landi's amorous list, and was disposed of there with a brief, "Why not? The ancients made beauty a heavenly gift." And Firenzuola himself in his dedication to the noble and beautiful ladies of Prato tells us he has heard such charges and lightly tosses them off as unworthy of answer, regretting that that man of parts, Boccaccio, should have stooped to answer similar attacks. But Jean Pellet, Saintongeois, and medical student, when he published his translation into French of these dialogues of Firenzuola felt called upon to defend himself in his epistle to the beautiful and virtuous Damoiselles, Jane and Isabeau de Piarrebuffiere. He has been blamed, he says, for wasting time on this translation. He would have done much better to get up two hours before daylight and read until midnight Hippocrates, Galen, and the rest of the ancients, but instead he lets his youth run away on such things as this that will never advance him, mere trifles of those who have nothing else to do and find difficulty passing their time. No doubt his critics mean to look after his profit, but they ignore the fact that he does need sleep and his health suffers with too much study, which the doctors forbid. Besides, why can't they see that these books on beauty belong to medicine, treating, as they do, of color, a true witness to the entire state of the internal parts of the body.

What we have in such admissions of the lightness of studies of human beauty is in reality a part of that clash between two irreconcilable ideals, the Greek and the Christian, which the renaissance Italian particularly could not resist attempting to resolve. Plato seemed to show the way to glorify beauty and the love that it stirred by translating them to the ultimate source of all good. Pico della Mirandola went as far away from human considerations as he could get in his exposition of the canzone on love of his friend Benivieni, who he says deals there with celestial love, daring to call it by the holy name love, a masculine noun (in Italian), a symbol of perfection, while Cavalcanti in his much discussed canzone dwells only on earthly love, rightly denominating his love by Lady, because as the female is imperfect with respect to the male, so earthly love is imperfect with respect to celestial. But in the end Pico found himself out on a limb, because he came to feel that it was most inappropriate for him, a professor of the laws of Christ, to treat heavenly and divine love according to Plato instead of according to Christ. Both he and Benivieni agreed on the advisability of withholding his commentary from publication, until they could see whether by some revision what was Platonic could become Christian. Pico's early ensuing death prevented such revision, and Benivieni withdrew his objection on the importunities of others in whose prudence, goodness, and learning he had confidence. The dilemma was never solved. The farther the Greeks went in their worhsip of beauty, the more uncomfortable became the Christians; the nearer they came to Christian spirituality the more inappropriate appeared the adoption of Plato as authority instead of Christ.[48]

To return, however, to the immediate concern of this discussion, beauty as a part of the ideal of woman, it can be safely said that renaissance men preferred beauty in their wives and required it in their mistresses. And the model for the beauty of each part can be found adequately set forth by such treatises as Firenzuola's and Luigini's, the latter not so squeamish as to shirk the task he set himself of a complete inventory, unlike Marinelli, who refers his readers, after the briefest reference to hidden beauties, to his work on the diseases of women for answers to what they do not find in the present work on the *Ornaments of Women*.

It is time now to begin drawing to a close this survey of renaissance attitudes, speculations, beliefs concerning love. Three broad generalizations may be offered. First of all, it is clear that no real philosophy of love has been progressively set forth. There are overlappings and contradictions which it would be beside the point in this work to attempt eliminating, if indeed they could be eliminated in any work. The intention has been to present the most popular aspects of love that brought endless discussion, at times merely ingenious and finespun. Also should be clear the beneficent character of love in the ideal role it was assigned by renaissance thought. Acknowledging no law except its own, it worked to bring perfection to the individual, man or woman, and to lift into the realm of the ideal the relationship between men and women, debased at one end, in promiscuous and unstable unions, by gross sensuality, and at the other, in marriage, by concern for material well-being with the familiar pattern of domination in the husband and submission in the wife. In the end a portrait of the lady emerges different from the ideal that we have been exploring in the last three chapters. Here the question rises again, whether the lady is brought into focus any better than before or is she still an elusive figure. That is, does she yet in reality stand alone, complete, comprehensible without reference to another order of human beings, is her elevation into an infinitely desirable object actually exaltation—or shall we put it realization—of her worth, or is it depreciation in comparison with her lover?

If we take into consideration the whole body of this literature on love, the lady cannot be said to hold the center of attention. As was said at the beginning of the chapter, most of these books were written on men in love, not on women in love, or even on men and women in love. The pains and pleasures of the lover, the nobility or ignominy of the lover's fate as he was purified by true love or overwhelmed by the disorders and excesses to which mere physical love led, the duties imposed upon him to win and hold his lady's favor, the virtues necessary to adorn him and make him capable of his great role as lover—all these matters furnish the stuff of renaissance treatises on earthly love. The beloved, the object of his adoration, the true center of interest since without her all the rest would be meaningless, nonexistent in fact, remains most of the time a very shadowy figure. He stands out distinct and clear, she retreats as if behind veils. The general effect of this emphasis upon the lover to the obscuring of the beloved is to make the lady again dependent for significance and even existence on another creature of another sort. This is true in spite of some recognition of the fact that if the lover is to find satisfaction and completion in love, his beloved must return his love and thus become a lover while he becomes an object of love himself—each is at one and the same time both lover and beloved. Few writers remark on this, and then lightly, implying that there is no need to elaborate so obvious a point, or that it is not worth elaboration. For the most part it is left to poetry to present the lady at full length, but as the particular mistress through a particular lover's eyes. How far Petrarch and some other poets, but especially Petrarch, meant to go beyond their Lauras to the general case is difficult to say now, nor can it be settled by the undeniable practice of renaissance Italians of using Petrarch's poems to Laura as philosophical disquisitions and abstract portraits.

The importance of the lady as the object of love is lessened also by certain tones and attitudes that creep into these discussions of the serious, inspiring, and formative values of love. A lighter side cannot fail to strike the reader. The not altogether serious tone of the discussions, particularly when presented in dialogues that often do not lack elegance and urbanity, the inconclusiveness of the arguments, interrupted by pleasant diversions when the ladies were present, the agility displayed in setting forth both sides without decisions, the wire-drawn, far-fetched points employed, the general air of conducting pleasant intellectual sports—all tend to suggest discourse that is not to be taken too seriously as philosophy or earnest advice on one's conduct of life. The soldier may fight the better for having a lady, the scholar may strive for greater honors in his field, but there is no doubt that it was expected that all who loved should find their greatest compensation in hours of ease. One writer at least may be found to put love-making frankly among recreations suitable to gentlemen and ladies. Torelli advises that at all ages, love is to be sought as one of the two principal means of recreation; the other is music, and he will not say which is more important; both are honest. Love will lead the gentleman not only into contemplation of itself, but into action to be made more worthy of possessing it—gentle conversation, witty jests, and hardy deeds. The age set great store by conversation in mixed society which, Torelli remarked in 1596, had been introduced as recreation into all the great courts of France, Germany, Spain, and Italy. The lady is usually warned here again to remember the great golden rule for womanly behavior, silence, even as she lends herself to this courtly pastime, and to confine her speech within modest limits, not risking offense by display of learning which leads to contradiction, most unworthy in her, and not laying herself open to the charge of lightness of mind and looseness of morals by a licensed and running tongue sure to invite unseemly jests so ruinous to reputation. Some, however, allow her more even ground with men, so long as she remains a true woman. Guazzo rises to eloquence on the theme in his description of the perfect lady: "This lady in conversation is singular, and mervellous," to use Pettie's translation, "for of all the noble partes in her, you shall see her make a most delightfull harmony. For first, to the gravenesse of her wordes, agreeth the sweetnesse of her voyce, and the honestie of her meaning: so that the mindes of the hearers intangled in those three nets, feele themselves at one instant to bee both mooved with her amiablenesse, and bridled by her honesty. Next, her talke and discourses are so delightfull, that you wyll only then beginne to bee sory, when shee endeth to speake: and wishe that shee woulde bee no more weary to speake, then you are to heare. Yea, shee frameth her jestures so discretely, that in speakyng, shee seemeth to holde her peace, and in holding her peace, to speake."

With all these delights of social intercourse in mind Torelli concludes the gentleman may be said to be obligated to seek love because he will thus honor the ladies whom he is bound to serve, engage in conversation appropriate to him, and keep out jealousy, toil, and affliction of mind. This new whip will result in making love seem honest in itself, honored in him and useful to others.[49]

Thus outside of the treatises on women's beauty which must deal with the lady as such, it seems not at all to have been the aim of the renaissance, that is more especially of the sixteenth century, to show the effects of love upon women, or to exhibit the ideal woman through the medium of love, but rather to portray the softer, more amiable side of man in hours of ease when women become desirable and necessary companions. Hence the lady is made for the most part to play a minor role, as an object of worship easily shelved for more serious business, an adornment to the scene, and most of all an occasion to call forth in men pleasurable exertion of all their social powers, grace, eloquence, and skill.

Yet if we peer closely enough at her, make note of this and that little thing, and put together whatever writers did say on her, sometimes at considerable length, a kind of portrait takes shape of the lady in love, which presents differences from the other portraits of the preceding chapters. First of all she is seen taking the initiative in providing herself with a lover, and even if more generally she waits for a lover to present himself, the choice lies entirely in her own hands. She may be forced to accept a husband, whatever law and humanity may say, but she chooses her lover or refuses to take any lover at all. The lover thus of necessity becomes a petitioner and the lady is mistress of his fate. Not only does she make the initial decision, but since the bond accepted is free of external guarantees and lasts only as long as love lasts, she has the power to withdraw her consent. Her lover therefore must strive unceasingly to keep the favor he has won and increase it, and the question is debated which is more difficult to do. His chief virtue becomes the loyal, unquestioning service which he gives to his beloved. Her chief virtue is the graciousness with which she accepts it and the faithful love which she gives in exchange for his. But if a man is to worship and serve to the utmost of his powers, he must be provided with an object worthy of such devotion. Hence the claims for the absolute perfection of the beloved, which has already been sufficiently described. In all these points the lady may be said to have preference to her lover. The choice is hers, her word is law, she is the object of worship, worthy of adoration and absolute devotion as he is not—all in high contrast to the situation in marriage. In this reversal of roles may a sort of compensation be seen for the belittling of the woman in the wife?

Have we now come nearer to the goal of our quest, an ideal for the lady comparable to the ideal commonly held for the gentleman of the renaissance? However fair this particular view of woman is, it is only too clearly still incomplete and inadequate as a human ideal. The sole reference for the perfection of the lady as the beloved lies in the lover and her love. If she must leave the world of love, in which the two are sole inhabitants, in order to serve the demands of a husband, as a woman of perfected virtue she will perform well the duties that her vows impose upon her, but always with reservation of her true, inner self, which belongs to her lover in exchange for his which belongs to her. For both of them there is life only in each other, elsewhere only death. Though set on a pedestal for worship as a goddess in human form, she is seen only as a lover sees her, suited to his own peculiar specifications and needs. From the point of view of society as a whole she is not here seen in the round, and just so far as she is removed from the ordinary world by her position above it and her dedication to only one side of many-sided life she becomes a deficient and impracticable ideal. Love and beauty are not enough to make a renaissance lady comparable to a renaissance gentleman with all possible human perfections poured upon his head.

CHAPTER SEVEN : *The Lady at Court*

Consideration of the lady at court comes last for two reasons. Little was written on the subject—surprisingly little at first thought. At second thought perhaps not so surprisingly because the role was restricted to a small proportion of the women who might be called ladies, and at court women played a minor part except in what may be described as indoor amusements for leisure hours. Despite the paucity of material, however, this portrait of the lady promises the most disinterested view that we can hope to find in renaissance conceptions, disinterested in that she will have to play a special part of her own as a lady or no part at all. We shall have to take account of the lady as the wife of the ruler or as a ruler in her own right, but more particularly we are considering the lady of the palace, as Castiglione called her, who is the counterpart of the courtier, serving her Lady and her Lord, as the courtier does. This is the woman for whom the court is a profession. In Castiglione's view of her, she represents the perfection of womanhood as the courtier represents the perfection of manhood. We should come nearer than before, though only with caution and great reservations, to what may be called the renaissance ideal of the lady.

Something should be said first about the books from which this chapter has been drawn, to indicate their character and importance, since so much must be done on so little. The earliest, Barberino's *Del Reggimento e dei Costumi delle Donne*, which has already been described, comes too early to serve as a guide to renaissance thought—unless the contention of some that the renaissance began with Dante is accepted—but it is useful as a point of reference and it does what only one other writer thought of doing, that is, differentiate deliberately between the highborn and the lowborn.

The next important writer chronologically is this same exception, Christine de Pisan, who wrote *Le Tresor de la Cite des Dames*, also called *Le Livre des Trois Vertus*, in 1405. It was not published until 1497, but then again in 1503 and 1536. This fact and continued reference to her through the sixteenth century stretches her influence pretty well over the period this book has had to cover. Sympathetically, like Barberino, and realistically and authoritatively because as she says she knew women of all ranks and conditions, she offers advice to princesses, those dwelling in the courts of princesses, the wives of barons, knights, squires, and gentlemen, and then on to wives of rich merchants, clerks, small merchants, tradesmen, and laborers, and even out of her large-heartedness the women of evil life. She also has sections on widows, and virgins young and old. Of the writers on women in courts Christine is the most inclusive and specific at the same time. We shall have to draw largely on her.

For the full-length, idealized portrait of the lady at court, the third book of Castiglione's *Il Libro del Cortegiano* is beyond question the most interesting and most significant source. The fundamental pattern will come from him, and the others will be used to fill in details or perhaps to modify that pattern to something more generally representative of the time. The book was published in 1528, but circulated for some time before that in manuscript. In 1534 appeared another *Courtier*, a little book called *De Re Aulica* by Agostino Nifo, a professor of philosophy in several universities, who, like Castiglione, devoted a section to the lady at court. It was not translated into Italian apparently until 1560, under the title *Il Cortegiano del Sessa*, but was widely read and cited as a more practical work than Castiglione's. Castiglione obviously had no influence upon Nifo either in form or style, Nifo's chapters in general going in pairs—Pompeo Colonna's opinions on courtiers, followed by objections to these opinions—and his Latin barren of ornament. Castiglione's name does not appear but it is impossible not to believe that he was not one of "the writers of our time" whom Nifo opposes point by point, to produce a courtier the opposite in every way to the Courtier of Urbino. It would seem his readers took him so from the direct comparisons occasionally made, not by writers who accepted Castiglione's ideal but by those who took Nifo's and perhaps wished to justify their preference. Nifo will be useful by way of comparison.

One other writer of the same sort might be expected to be cited here, Lodovico Domenichi, whose thin little treatise called *La Donna di Corte*, appeared in 1564. But though the fact seems not to have been noted before, it is a fact that this is only a translation of the second book of Nifo's *De Re Aulica*. Domenichi made his own translation evidently, at least he did not follow the earlier one of 1560 in phrasing, and did his best to turn the original into a graceful tribute to his patron, unblushingly assuring him in Nifo's words that he had taken utmost pains: "While I was wholly intent on writing this little treatise of the lady at court and making it appear more pleasing and delightful I spared myself no work—what I could not find in myself I procured from those who know more with all modesty." Perhaps he did work hard; beyond translation he doubled the adjectives and added descriptive details here and there, and when he came to examples of courtly talk, all given by Nifo as taking place between himself and a blameless lady, Phausina, he assigned each to particular people by name, beautiful, witty ladies and gifted gentlemen of various cities and courts, whom, he says, he had known or heard tell of, and sketched in some little circumstances; but he would have worked harder if he had put together the whole out of his own head.

Two other books are important because they present sides of court life not included in the rest, and because they are of the practical sort. They were not composed by professional writers for publication but by loving parents for their daughters. Anne de Beaujeu, Duchess of Bourbon, daughter of Louis XI, wrote a little book for her daughter Suzanne around 1504. "The perfect, natural love which I have for you, my daughter," she begins, "and thoughts of the frailty of life and the innumerable great dangers of this world and sudden death that strikes at every hour, these give me courage and the desire, in spite of my poor, weak brain, to set down for you while I am still with you some little lessons, informing your ignorance and extreme youth, with the hope that at times you will remember them and be able to gain some little profit from them." She tells Suzanne how to take service in some great house if her mother dies before provision has been made for her, and then in view of the high estate that marriage is likely to give her how to conduct herself in a great court of which she is the lady—relation to her husband, treatment of all around her, particularly the humble, entertainment of strangers, management of her women, and care of her children. It was this little manuscript, so full of love and wisdom, that Anne's nephew, foster-son, and son-in-law, Charles de Monpensier, Duke of Bourbon, and Constable of France, from all his treasures chose to take with him when he fled stripped of all his honors and possessions. Suzanne had had it published after her marriage.

The other book was written by a father around 1586 for his very young daughter about to leave home for court. Guasco says he is thankful for her many gifts of fortune, good birth, health, beauty, and intelligence. He and her mother have taken great care with her training which she has rewarded by such accomplishment as already has brought her a spreading reputation. It is common opinion, he says, that if she, with all her acquirements, were to stay hidden in the house of her father there would be little use for them, and so he who loves her dearly has been persuaded to procure her a place at the court of Savoy, chosen for its worth and nearness. Hence this letter of advice as a parting present. Under eight heads he sets down the most needful things for her to know and remember—much must be a summary of what she has already been taught—and especially how to go on with her music and studies and shape herself to become, if worthy, a secretary of the Duchess. Lavinia evidently knew how to treasure her father's words, for somewhat fearful of his blame she explains in a preface to the book that she is having his letter published to save herself the long job of copying it for a friend. Here one sees most clearly the early framing of a lady at court.[1]

The subject becomes more complex as one goes into it. The puzzle is where to begin. Nifo, after the fashion of scholars, began his discussion of the court with the origin and history of courts, and out of the simple answer to the question why should there be courts at all, which he said was to give princes a home, he managed to draw his definition of a courtier as a person existing only to lighten the leisure hours of his lord. When he came to the lady he began with the question whether a woman could be a courtier at all, and answered no, because in the first place we never read of any such in history, and in the second according to such weighty authorities as Zenocrates, Galen, and Hermagoras, a woman never can be more than a child and therefore necessarily lacks the prudence and wit essential to the courtier.

Castiglione began with the courtier himself, taking in hand "to shape in wordes a good Courtier, specifying all such conditions and particular qualities, as of necessitie must bee in him that deserveth this name," and when he came to propose the shaping of a companion for his courtier he raised the question of the place of women in the court, important or negligible. Since he starts somewhat nearer to our purpose, let us begin at this point with Castiglione's answer to his question, here as everywhere in this book quoted from Hoby's translation.

"No Court, how great soever it be, can have any sightlinesse or brightnesse in it, or mirth without women, nor any Courtier can bee gracious, pleasant or hardie, nor at any time undertake any galant enterprise of Chivalrie, unlesse he be stirred with the conversation and with the love and contentation of women, even so in like case the Courtiers talke is most unperfect evermore, if the intercourse of women give them not a part of the grace wherwithall they make perfect and decke out their playing the Courtier."[2]

Castiglione does not make his gentlewoman of the palace, as Hoby likes to call her, resemble the courtier in all respects, reserving for her a special place, but he makes her equal to him in worth, and, as we shall see, in endowing her with perfection denies her no fundamental human quality essential to perfection in the courtier.

Since there is no meaning to the idea of a lady as a courtier except with reference to the gentleman as a courtier, just as there is no meaning to the idea of a courtier except with reference to a prince, some space will have to be given here to the courtier himself. Castiglione set out, he said, to form a perfect courtier, one who would know how to serve his prince in every reasonable way and thereby gain his favor. So he gave his courtier every desirable human quality, good birth, beauty, wit, grace, discretion, power to please his fellows, wisdom in counsel, aptness for arms and all physical exercises becoming to a gentleman—wrestling, swimming, vaulting, running, casting the stone, and tennis. He will be well versed in liberal studies, history, oratory, and poetry, sufficiently skilled himself in the arts of speaking, writing prose and verse in Latin, Greek, and the vernacular, drawing and painting, music, and dancing, in order to say well what he would, to be a good judge of the works of the masters, to fill his leisure when alone with pleasurable occupation, and to furnish his share of delightful pastimes in company. All his knowledge and skill he will carry with a grace and ease that cover up pains and lend the pleasure of spontaneity to his performance. The way of a gentleman is never the way of a professional. All the intellectual and moral virtues are necessary to the perfect courtier, but particularly courage, which Castiglione names among the virtues of the mind and describes thus: "Verie courage in deede commeth of a proper advisement and determined will so to doe, and to esteeme more a mans honestie and duetie, than all the perils in the world, and although he see none other way but death, yet to be of so quiet an hart and minde that his senses be not to seeke nor amazed, but doe their duetie in discoursing and bethinking, even as though they were most in quiet."

Among the courtier's accomplishments the art of conversation held such a high place that something should be said about it in particular. Story-telling, pat application of sententious sayings from philosophers and other wise men, invention of conversational sports and pastimes such as the discussions that form the body of Castiglione's book, and quick repartee were all expected of the courtier and brought praise and fame. Or as Castiglione summed up this requirement, the courtier should be "such a one that shall never want good communication and fitte for them hee talketh withall, and have a good understanding with a certaine sweetnesse to refresh the hearers minds, and with merry conceites and jestes to provoke them to solace and laughter, so that without being at any time lothsome or satiate, he may evermore delite." "Merry conceites and jestes" seem to have been favorite current coin to buy favor. Of the second book a good third is on this subject, chiefly commended examples. Whether there is any art in these or they are all the work of wit and nature was debated, and it was decided that something could be said on the subject because however good a wit men may have, conceits both good and bad will arise in his mind, and then judgment and art both polish and correct them and choose the good and refuse the bad with reference to the speaker, the company, and circumstance. The courtier will not try to make men laugh at all times, nor will he laugh at men in misery, or at wicked men who deserve severe censure, or at men in authority whose enmity might be gained thereby, and he will not offend women with taunts that touch their chastity or ribaldry that offends their ears. But in the nip lay the wit, which by exaggeration, pretence, turning of tables, play upon words and a hundred other tricks turned a man to ridicule, more or less pleasant to others and to himself.

The courtier thus accoutred with all the virtues and graces a man may show has yet one more care, to present himself as a well integrated whole, one part blending with another, all working in harmony. Here are Castiglione's words. "It behooveth our Courtier in all his doings to be charie and heedfull, and what so he saith or doth to accompany it with wisdom, and not onely to set his delite to have in him selfe partes and excellent qualities, but also to order the tenor of his life after such a trade, that the whole may be answerable unto these partes, and see the selfe same to bee alwaies and in every thing such, that it disagree not from it selfe, but make one bodie of these good qualities, so that every deede of his may bee compact and framed of all the vertues, as the Stoikes say the duetie of a wise man is: although notwithstanding alwaies one vertue is the principall, but all are so knit and linked one to another, that they tende to one end, and all may be applyed and serve to every purpose."

Last of all is raised the question of what is the end to which all this perfection works. For Castiglione the desired end was so to win the good will and favor of his prince that the courtier can speak the truth to him on every matter without fear or danger of displeasing him, and even when he sees him bent on some action unfitting for him, he may have courage to stand up to him and dissuade him from ill and set him to good. And by his own goodness accompanied by readiness of wit, pleasantness, wisdom, knowledge of letters and many other things the courtier will understand how to conduct himself in all circumstances in order to show his prince what honor and profit will come to him and his by justice, liberality, courage, meekness, and all the other virtues that belong to a good prince, and what slander and harm come of the vices opposed to them. "And therefore in mine opinion," concludes Castiglione, "as musicke, sportes, pastimes, and other pleasant fashions, are (as a man woulde say) the floure of Courtlinesse, even so is the training and helping forwarde of the Prince to goodnesse, and the fearing him from evil, the fruite of it. And because the prayses of well doing consisteth chiefly in two pointes, whereof the one is, in choosing out an end that our purpose is directed unto, that is good in deede, the other the knowledge to finde out apt and meete meanes to bring it to the appointed good ende: sure it is that the minde of him which thinketh to worke so, that his Prince shall not bee deceived, nor lead with flatterers, railers, and lyers, but shall know both the good and the bad, and beare love to the one, and hatred to the other, is directed to a verie good end."

This was the theory of courtiership that for a century seized the imaginations of fine, high-minded, mettlesome young blades in the courts of Europe. Nifo evidently tried to trim the proportions of his courtier more nearly to average size. Thinking perhaps of the books on counselors and ambassadors, and wishing to distinguish the courtier by service of a particular sort, he confined the term to those whose sole business is the amusement of princes by pleasant, witty discourse in their hours of leisure within the palace. To prescribe for such courtiers excellence in the activity which the prince takes delight in, music, letters, mathematics, or physical exercises in an endeavor to win his favor and thus secure benefits for themselves and profit to the prince in opportunities to draw him to whatever is honest is merely to form an obedient and obsequious servant, said Nifo, for he follows the will of another and not his own. Others in the court may serve such ends. Likewise to place in the courtier all the moral virtues is to make no difference between the good man and the good courtier. It often happens that many virtues shine in the same man, but the courtier is a courtier not by these other qualities which may make him a good man, but by a particular courtly virtue different from all the others. This virtue he identified as compounded of affability and urbanity but most especially urbanity. These two qualities are displayed in feasts, gatherings, and conversations. Affability arises out of sheer instinct to please, without thought of gain, and shows either love without wittiness, or love and wittiness together. Wit introduces something not quite true or sincere but pleasing in its exaggeration or distortion. For illustrations he relates little passages between himself and two ladies. When he once asked Phausina why she had at first shown him greater favor than she did now, though she knew him a much better servant than before, she said that in past days she had given him favors in order to attract and win him, but now that she had gained him she did not have to flatter him, but needed only to love him—true affability, comments Nifo, pleasing and graceful. Likewise when someone asked her whether she could love an old man, she replied, "I couldn't with lascivious love, but with pure love, yes, because I could wish every good thing to a child and an old man." The other sort came from Quintia, whom, he said, he was accustomed in every discussion to call "My Quintia" as a preface. One day he said, "Signora, I don't any longer wish to call you my Quintia, but dear Quintia, because at last you are not mine but your husband's, nor am I yours but my wife's. Yet you will always be dear to me as long as I live and after death too." She replied, "Would that I were always dear to you as now and always yours, for I would be the happiest of all lovers"— truly pleasing but what may be called false affability. Thus affability is appropriate to women. But urbanity is another thing. It shows in jests and practical jokes, not evil in themselves but useful to refresh man when he ceases from labor. Men who never say anything ridiculous are hard and rude, as if they are not to be softened by such pleasures, but those who jest or play with moderation, with some discretion as to fitness of matter, time, place and circumstances are urbane, for it is fitting to speak and to listen to those things which are appropriate to modest and upright men. The urbane man therefore will shun obscenity, distinguishing the scurrilous from the ridiculous. The jests that belong to him take astuteness and prudence, a store of knowledge and words for them, and looks and gestures suitable to each, all of which belong to a mature and serious age—the more serious the man the greater will urbanity show in him. Urbanity is clearly not for boys, except in a very limited way that does not go beyond the bounds of boyish manners. The office of the courtier is therefore to recreate the prince with pleasing and urbane things. If he has all the other goods, including high birth and beauty he will be a better citizen and serve the prince better in other things, but he will not be a better courtier.[3]

Thus having hung courtiership on one essential requirement, Nifo finds it easy to dispose of women at court. There must be women at court, for the princess too must have her attendants, but they cannot be called courtiers with any strictness of meaning, for urbanity is neither within the scope of women's powers nor suitable to her. As a woman may be said to be half a man, concedes Nifo genially, so she may be admitted half a courtier with the affability so appropriate to her chastity and purity. A reproach to her rather than praise is urbanity, where the line between decency and obscenity is so thin that Nifo can discuss the fine point of where scurrility becomes urbanity, which is not the question how far down toward obscenity can urbanity safely go, but how far up toward urbanity can obscenity be raised. It is sater not to try to define the point here. Even a Castiglione found, on second thought, some purification of his original manuscript desirable in this respect. Obviously we cannot follow Nifo's lead in the matter of women at court, or the ideal lady would be still farther to seek.

Since Castiglione too, however, is interested in differentiation, he searches for the special quality that belongs to a woman who lives at court, though in so doing he does not drop all the other excellent qualities that belong to perfection for her, any more than he drops them for the courtier. He has tied everything so neatly into a bundle that the passage may well be quoted.

"Leaving therefore a part the vertues of the minde that ought to be common to her with the Courtier, as wisedom, noblenesse of courage, staidnesse, and many more, and likewise the conditions that are meet for all women, as to be good and discreete, to have the understanding to order her husbands goodes and her house and children when she is married, and all those partes that belong to a good huswife: I say that for her that liveth in Court, me thinke there belongeth unto her above all other thinges, a certaine sweetenesse in language that may delite, wherby she may gently entertain all kinde of men with talke worthie the hearing and honest, and applyed to the time and place, and to the degree of the person she communeth withal. Accompanying with sober and quiet manners, and with the honestie that must alwaies be a stay to her deedes, a readie livelinesse of wit, whereby she may declare her selfe far wide from all dulnesse: but with such a kinde of goodnesse, that she may bee esteemed no less chaste, wise and courteous, than pleasant, feate conceited and sober: and therefore muste she keepe a certaine meane verie hard, and (in a manner) derived of contrary matters, and come just to certain limittes, but not to passe them."

It is in the role described here that Castiglione presents the ladies of the court of Urbino, both Duchess and ladies-in-waiting, the plan of his book allowing for no other views. According to definition the essence of courtiership in the woman could not be more fully revealed than in this mixed company of brilliant men and intelligent and witty women, who might be supposed to be able to discourse on most if not all the subjects with the same suavity and grace as the men if, as was sometimes done, they had been set to talking by themselves. The special quality assigned to the lady at court is the same affability described by Nifo. Castiglione's Italian, *una certa affabilità piacevole*, is well translated into Hoby's phrase, "a certaine sweetnesse in language that may delite." Castiglione goes on to set specifically the limits beyond which the lady may not pass if she is to delight. First of all, in her zeal to guard her purity she will not be so squeamish as to show her dislike of company and conversation that becomes a little lascivious by getting up instantly and going away, for it may easily be thought that she pretends to be so austere in order to hide what she fears others may discover in herself. Such rustic manners are always odious. Nor in walking this tightrope of courtliness should she, to show herself free and pleasant, speak unchaste words or adopt a certain loose and unbridled familiarity of manner to make men believe of her what is perhaps not true. But finding herself where such talk goes on, she should listen with a little blush and shamefacedness. Likewise she will not go seeking to hear evil reports of other women, as some do, who by repeating them with such delight in detail seem to have a sort of envy and in their smiles and certain other ways show that they take the greatest pleasure, until men, though they seem to listen willingly, most of the time come to hold a low opinion of them and to think they are being invited to go farther. And so women are drawn many times to go to such lengths that they deserve blame and at last fall so in esteem that they are despised and their company is no longer wanted, even though they may not be what they seem from dissolute laughter, babbling, scornfulness, and such evil ways. But the discreet lady will not willingly listen to those who speak evil of other women, but will be perturbed and show that she is incredulous and thinks an unchaste woman a sort of monstrosity.

And to conclude the whole matter, this woman of the palace will need discretion to understand the kind of man she is speaking to, knowledge of a great many things, and judgment to pick out what is suitable for a certain kind of person in order not to say what would offend him. She will guard against becoming a bore by praising herself indiscreetly or by being garrulous. She will not go mixing serious matters in light and laughing discourse, and still less jests and jibes in serious things. She will not foolishly pretend to know what she doesn't know, but with modesty seek to be honored for what she does know, avoiding affectation in everything. "In this manner shall she be indued with good conditions, and the exercises of the bodie comely for a woman shall she do with an exceeding good grace, and her talke shall bee plenteous and full of wisedom, honestie, and pleasantnesse: and so shall she be not only beloved but reverenced of all men, and perhaps worthy to be compared to this great Courtier, as well for the qualities of the minde as of the bodie."[4]

What subjects should ladies and gentlemen of the court discuss when they gather to pass the time? Chiefly love, it would seem, to judge from the endless dialogues on the subject given a court setting, but there was debate over whether a good prince should allow amorous discourses in his court. Nifo said that those who wrote on courts of the day put the greater part of courtliness in such discussions, arguing that since courtiers love ladies without lascivious desire, there can be discourse on love without desire, and therefore it should be fostered as the greatest opportunity to show and exercise affability. Nifo for his part is thoroughly skeptical on the whole matter. He cannot believe that it is possible for men and women to talk about love together without stirring desire, for such discourses seem always to have a mixture of some vice in them and to communicate it. Not even old men, experience shows, can safely be held immune. Least of all then is affability, which is truly a virtue, attainable through them. They should therefore be banished from the courts of good princes. But since the custom is approved at court Nifo decides it is his business to find some reason for permitting it and some way to make it a part of affability. Grant that courtiers can love without fleshly desire, also assume that amorous discourse is possible without desire and even that not always is desire to be condemned, any more than hunger or thirst, then whoever loves a maid in order to marry her, if he does not exceed measure or go beyond the laws, is not to be blamed for loving, and amorous discourses out of which come desire for marriage are not to be condemned if conducted with discretion. In the end, however, he seems to relent somewhat, for he introduces a discussion of love between himself and Phausina with this apology: "No one should wonder that in my little book on courtly matters I have included this question of love, because it belongs to women of the court to know also how to reason of this love."

And here is where Castiglione may take over, for he thought it requisite above any other thing for every honest gentlewoman at court to know what belongs to the communication of love, "for even as every honest gentleman for an instrument to obtaine the good will of women, practiseth those noble exercises, precise fashions and good manners which we have named, even so to this purpose applyeth he also his wordes, and not onely when he is stirred thereto by some passion, but oftentimes also to doe honor to the woman he talketh withal, seeming to him that to declare to love her, is a witnesse that she is worthie of it, and that her beawtie and worthinesse is such, that it enforceth everie man to serve her." How then in such a case is a woman to behave herself uprightly, how answer one that loves her in truth, how one that merely pretends to? His advice is specific. First of all she should avoid believing that whoever talks of love, loves her. If she is addressed in amorous terms that are disrespectful, she should answer in a way to show she is displeased. If the words are modest and covert, she should pretend not to understand and give his words another sense, seeking with discretion and wisdom to change the subject. If they are too plain to miss, let her take it all as a pleasant device to honor her rather than in earnest, depreciating her deserts, and acknowledging the praises as courtesy. So she will be counted discreet and be surer of not being deceived. A woman should always remember that men may declare themselves in love with a good deal less danger than women. If she is married and hatred of her husband or the vehement love of another bends her to love, she will grant her lover only her mind and never at any time give him any sure sign of love either in word or in gesture or in any way that can make him certain of it. If free to marry, she may show any sign of love except what may give hope to her lover of obtaining what she ought not to give. To the objection that if a woman takes hope quite away, a courtier would be wise never to love her, and thus she would suffer the imperfection of being without a lover, the answer is that such a woman of the palace would not take away hope of everything, but only of dishonest matters, and such a courtier as has been fashioned would not hope or indeed even desire them. "For if beautie, manners, wit, goodnesse, knowledge, sober moode, and so many other vertuous conditions which wee have given the woman, be the cause of the Courtiers love toward her, the end also of this love must needes be vertuous, and if noblenesse of birth, skilfulnesse in martiall feates, in letters, in musicke, gentlenesse, being both in speech and behaviour indowed with so many graces, be the meanes wherewithall the Courtier compasseth the womans love, the ende of that love must needes be of the same condition that the meanes are by the which hee commeth to it." This woman of the palace for her austerity and high excellence may have fewer lovers than others, but she will not lack a lover, because she will not be without those who are stirred by her deserts and who, confident in their own, know they are worthy to be loved by her.

Castiglione then has the talk veer from the problems of the lady in love to the problems of the courtier, how he may win the love of a lady and keep it in honor, and particularly whether it is fitting only to a young courtier to be in love, or may an old courtier love without slander or detriment to his high office. This is the occasion for Bembo's long and eloquent address on earthly beauty and love that leads to heavenly. And lest the lady should seem to have been left far behind in this reasoning, as the one whose physical beauty set the courtier to climbing the ladder but who was not set to climbing herself, the question proposed for the next evening's discourse was "whether women be not as meete for heavenlie love as men," to which already both answers had been given.

The lady at court, therefore, for purposes of dealing with her lovers and joining in discourse on high matters has need of skill in the subject of love, and amorous discussions are not only not to be condemned as courtly entertainment but to be fostered, on a high level of decency, wit, and purpose.[5]

Other arts practiced at courts—letters, music, drawing, painting, dancing, —are appropriate to her, and she will practice them with skill and in a becoming manner, not dancing violent steps, or singing or playing difficult music that shows more skill than sweetness, even shunning instruments that are unsuitable. "Imagin with your selfe," says Castiglione, "what an unsightly matter it were to see a woman play upon a tabour or drum, or blow in a flute or trumpet, or any like instrument: and this because the boistrousnesse of them doth both cover and take away that sweete mildnesse which setteth so forth everie deede that a woman doth. Therefore when she commeth to daunce, or to shew any kind of muiscke, she ought to be brought to it with suffring her selfe somewhat to be prayed, and with a certain bashfulnesse, that may declare the noble shamefastnesse that is contrarie to headinesse." As for other bodily exercises, feats of arms, riding, hunting, tennis, wrestling and the like, these are suitable to men but not to women for the same reasons. She will therefore not practice them, but she will have such knowledge of them as will enable her to praise gentlemen judiciously according to their deserts.

In dress she will avoid vanity and lightness, but since women are allowed and ought to have more care of beauty than men and their beauty is of different sorts, this lady of the court will have judgment as to what increases her grace and is appropriate to the exercise she intends at the moment. If she sees in herself a fair and smiling beauty, she ought to aid it with movements and words and clothing that indicate joyousness, just as another of a mild and grave nature ought to set it off with fashions of that sort, in order to increase what is the gift of nature. Also if she is a little fatter or thinner than is desirable, or paler or darker, she should help defects with her clothes, but conceal her purpose as much as possible, and keeping herself dainty and neat appear always to have taken no care or pains with herself.

"And thus," to summarize, "in conversation, in laughing, in sporting, in jesting, finally in everie thing she shal be had in great price, and shall entertaine accordingly both with jestes, and feate conceites meete for her, every person that commeth in her company. And albeit stayednesse, noblenesse of courage, temperance, strength of the minde, wisdom, and the other vertues, a man would thinke belonged not to entertaine, yet will I have her endowed with them all, not so much to entertaine (although notwithstanding they may serve thereto also) as to be vertuous: and these vertues to make her such a one, that she may deserve to bee esteemed, and all her doings framed by them."[6]

Thus has been answered the first question raised in this book on the woman of the palace, whether the rules for the courtier were not sufficient for her, and therefore it may be superfluous to try to paint a portrait of her. She is to have all the qualities of the courtier, but to wear them with a difference. To use Castiglione's words once more, "Principally in her fashions, manners, wordes, gestures and conversation the woman ought to be much unlike the man. For right as it is seemely for him to shew a certaine manlinesse full and steadie, so doth it well in a woman to have a tendernesse, soft and milde, with a kinde of womanlye sweetenesse in every gesture of hers, that in going, standing, and speaking what ever she lusteth, may alwaies make her appeare a woman without anye likenesse of man." The emphasis has fallen in the portrait of the woman at court upon her social value, decorative, recreative, inspirational, in the portrait of the courtier upon his relation to his prince as adviser, even instructor in the duties of the ruler. The lady, even so, is not left in the subordinate almost negligible position of Nifo's lady-in-waiting, for she matches the courtier in serious qualities and both together in the employments of leisure hours are lifted to an important role in court life. But in the course of a debate over whether the courtier as the instructor and guide of the prince has not been made superior to the prince, the claim is made that it is not unfit for the woman too to instruct her lady and serve with her the same end of courtliness which has been set for the prince. If Castiglione had set rules for her in this role, they would doubtless have been such as he laid down for the courtier. The repetition thus occasioned may well be taken for one reason why he chose to portray the other unequal side.[7]

Other writers throw some light on the relation between the women of the court and their mistress, whether a ruler herself or only the wife of a ruler. Guasco's letter to his daughter Lavinia on her going to the court of Savoy instructs her patiently and lovingly in what she may expect to find there, and how she must conduct herself to win and keep the favor of her lady, whose well-regulated house and care for liberal studies have persuaded him to entrust her further instruction and training to that court. The youth of Lavinia—she was only about twelve and going into service at an age less mature than usual, as her father remarks—draws explicit instruction, and allows us to see more distinctly what life at court meant to the attendants on the lady, much the same thing, one can assume, as to the courtiers attending the lord. The central fact of life at court is the will of the rulers. Lavinia is advised, in terms reminiscent of advice to the girl about to marry, to learn to subdue her will and her every wish to her lady's until she has no other. To serve and please she will have to do more than merely obey express commands. Her lady will expect her to do not only what she knows is wanted but what she can guess, and not only by external acts but with inward love and devotion. She will come then to think her lady's will her own and take the greatest delight in it, and her lady will increasingly love her. She will do all with modest cheerfulness, never showing a disturbed or sad face to her lady, who would then suspect dissatisfaction. She will take great pains never to allow her to think she has little love or reverence for her; even if her lady shows some disfavor or dislike of her she will never show displeasure or worry, but serve and love her more diligently than before, until finally her lady will be convinced and care for her more than ever. In like spirit she will never show displeasure or envy when someone else is more favored, but herself caress that person more than she does others, for besides the advantage that the favorite, seeing herself honored and loved, will use her power to procure favor for her with the patron, the most powerful way to make us love others is to see that they love not only us but also those that we love. She will do this sincerely, for she ought to think that the preference of such a discreet and just judge of her women as her lady is shows people to be superior. Therefore she will labor not only to equal but to surpass the favored in merit, which in the end will bring reward. She will be much happier if she intends to meet the humor of her lady and what pleases her in her attendants, learning from those more mature in age and longer in service.

Since our appearance and manners first strike people and win their approval, special care is needed, if at a loss, to observe how others behave to make themselves pleasing and to show the reverence she feels, acting with lightness and grace, naturally rather than ostentatiously with art. When in the presence of her lady and lord she should be composed, standing still, planted on her two feet firm as a statue, not moving agitatedly and twisting here and there, and, who knows, perhaps even yawning. Nothing is more prejudicial to one than to be seen serving in this careless way, appearing to show weariness of being found in such service and little reverence and love toward her lady, and an instability of mind indicated by such actions, things that bring servitors into scorn and perhaps into hate, not merely into discredit, with patrons. Her eyes should be held on linen and needle, or clavichord, or songbook, or whatever she is occupied with, or if she is doing nothing, on her lady with a modest aspect, not darting them here and there, which would be taken as a sign of incontinence. On receiving favors from her lady publicly she should take them modestly as given from her lady's generosity and not on her own merit, but not with such blankness in her face as to seem not to prize the gift. All favors should be accepted humbly, admitting herself of least merit and the others for their merit more in hope of favor than she, if she wishes to win love and approbation, and not envy, or even hate. If receiving favors is a ticklish business, asking them is more so. Rarely or never should she seek them for herself, and seldom even for others, reserving always such an advantage for greater need, and considering well for whom, for what, how and when the favor is to be asked. The person should be worthy, for the lady may from importunity or something else grant what she little cares to and the loss will be greater than the gain, or her denial may cause confusion and shame. Then she can ask no more favors, and her lady will wonder if she had been left dissatisfied and her love lessened. What is asked is important, something honest that can be pleasantly granted, and the time opportune, and her manner should leave no doubt of satisfaction even if the favor is denied. So she will serve her lady to the best of her ability, preferring her ease to her own, even supporting what is inconvenient for the sake of a little advantage to her, the first to offer service, not the last, if sure the order of the house is not against offering it at that time. She owes obedience to her lord and lady, but she should obey out of love and reverence, not from compulsion.[8]

On the more general subject of her relations with her companions and others at court Lavinia's father said he would have to write a whole book if he were to treat it fully. It is not his intention to consider all the infinite details of manners that belong to a civil way of life; others have done that and he will give her three books which will save him the labor. First of all *The Courtier* of Castiglione, newly reprinted, a work truly most noble and very necessary to whoever lives at court, and next to it *The Galateo* of Della Casa, a most fruitful book not less for the excellence of its style than for its diligence in giving minutely advice useful not only at court but in any situation whatsoever; and then the *Civil Conversation* of Guazzo, a book so useful that there is no one who makes profession of letters and manners who does not have it in his study—so much the more to be prized, adds Guasco, as being the work of "our courteous neighbor and my dear friend." These books he exhorts her strongly to read with all care because in them is taught in a short while what could not be learned from experience in many years, and besides without such reading, while one is acquiring by practice the way to behave toward others, many errors can be committed. From these books then and from the example of the many fine-mannered companions she will find in the court she will learn the greater part of what belongs to manners. But he will treat in general the things which occur to him.

What he picks out as needing emphasis reveals very largely the problems that a young girl going to court for the first time, in order to become a part of it, had to face and solve. Not only must she recognize and avoid the pitfalls which might, from ignorance and inadvertence, wreck her at the start, but she must carry herself in such a way as to win the good opinion of all who live at court. Pride and envy are the chief courtly vices. The newcomer must guard herself from the first in herself and from the second in others. To win favor she must show discretion, good will, courtesy, and wit, and toward her patrons, obedience and loyalty. The art of governing her tongue is what this solicitous father saw as most necessary for his daughter to learn, since, he said, there was more danger of committing errors by speech than by actions. Most of all she will follow the rule of talking little, always good since if one says enough he cannot avoid errors, but especially good in her novitiate, for besides her youth and her small experience in not having been outside her father's house, she is going to a court where she will find a great variety of nationalities and types of characters, and where the way of living is far different from what it was at home. Of course as she becomes acquainted with the business of the court and the nature of the people there, good sense will increase with age, and then she can be more assured in speaking. Her great care will be always to speak, not at random, but with due consideration of many things. Just as the value of some metals is known by the sound given to a touch, so she is to think her quality is known from her speech and the esteem then to be given her. Discreet speech will bring her love and esteem and foolish speech the opposite. Therefore, let her consider well what she has to say and to whom she says it. To observe decorum she will have to vary her speech according to the condition of those she meets, talking one way with superiors, another with equals, and another with inferiors, one way with men, another with women, still another with domestics, and so on, accommodating her thoughts to each, and never discoursing of things inappropriate to them, and especially things that she herself doesn't understand. Above all she will need to consider well how she talks with the men of the court that she is allowed to meet, to do it according to the custom of the court, because to women and, especially, girls care and modesty are more necessary than to men, men being generally praised for more understanding. Her models in these matters as well as in others should be the Spanish ladies with which that court is filled, for they surpass all others in the pleasing gravity, and grave pleasantness shown not only in their speech but in all their actions, so natural and suited to this nation.

Also in another matter they excel, the wit and readiness at jesting with which they carry on discussions. These she should seek to imitate. It is true that jesting is a gracious and noble thing and evidence of a fine wit, but there are few who do it well, because it takes readiness, wit, originality, and must be done without ulterior purpose, or disregard for the pleasure of others, or borrowing from some one else. All of this is more a matter of nature than art; art can only aid nature. But what is more important, and is up to neither nature nor art but to modesty alone, which is in her hands, is care not to offend anyone, either present or absent, in her jesting. Besides meeting all these other conditions her sayings will have to be such that they are courteous taunts rather than sharp rebukes, so given that they barely graze the skin and do not pierce to the heart of the person at whom they are aimed. Jesting must be done with great discretion, not too constantly for some may not like it, and she will have to learn to take as well as give pleasantly. But the father is at ease on these matters, having confidence in the goodness, discretion, and wit of his daughter. Who knows what she may not accomplish, whose sayings he has often enough related to his friends to their wonder.

In general in her conversing with her companions she will never praise herself, or dispraise as an occasion for praise; she will avoid faultfinding, a vice that makes conversation unpleasant, particularly when directed against what pleases another; she will never point out defects in others but praise the good in them; she will avoid carrying news that can sadden, for she then seems to lack feeling, but she will sympathize in adversity, and rejoice in prosperity; her own secrets and the secrets of her friends told in confidence she will be extremely cautious about revealing, especially cautious that they do not come to the ears of her patrons; and since mere intention may offend, she will guard against any indication of what might be taken for ill will. Finally, there should shine in all her words her truth and sincerity—what she says is what she thinks, for without this no praise is merited for any other virtue.

To avoid arousing the envy and hate so common in courts, certain particular precautions are pressed on the young Lavinia. Above all she must avoid quarreling with her companions, a shameful thing which spreads abroad in the court and perhaps coming to the ears of her patron could put her in disgrace with her and in discredit with the others, and she would then find herself shunned by all. The way not to come to such disorders is to study the nature of the people at court and the means of accommodating herself to them, together with avoiding occasions which could involve her in disputes. One of many such will be discussions on odious subjects. If by chance she falls into such talk with another, she ought suddenly to change the subject. Particularly she should keep from comparisons either of herself or her things with others, a most hateful subject, by which friendships are not increased but enemies are made. If others try it on her, she should refuse to talk. Tale-bearing, a common practice at court either with malice or without, must be completely avoided, for it is dangerous and cowardly, since the absent is unable to defend himself on the spot. Calumny is a serious sin even if he of whom it is spoken would never have to know it. The conscience alone is enough to accuse and punish the wrong-doer, besides the punishment that God prepares, in many times permitting the concealed to be made open. The very earth will tell when others are silent. It is best to believe that nothing is so secret that does not finally come to light, a belief that will aid her in all her actions. But offense is to be avoided not only in her own words but in consenting to what others tell. Not that she should come to blows with whoever speaks evil of another, but she should show at least by silence that she does not take pleasure in hearing it and that she cannot entertain any bad opinion of others, particularly her companions or other well-born gentlewomen. It will bring her in bad odor to show herself easily believing evil of others, which could perhaps argue that such had been her own judgment of them. She must remember also that silence at the wrong time can injure. Let her guard herself, then, against repeating anything that she has seen or heard to the prejudice of anyone if she would avoid cause for quarrels and hate. Her father assures her he does not believe her capable of this fault, or of lying, another great sin at court, which he mentions only to be complete. If she will show no care about being advanced in the goods of fortune or the body, but study with virtuous emulation not to fall off in goods of the mind and to surpass others in good manners and habits, she will disarm envy and endear herself to all.

Anne de Beaujeu touches on many of the same things in her advice to Suzanne in the event of her having to seek service in some court should her mother's death leave her unprovided for. Evil speaking, she says, is the fashion at court because it gains people an audience, but those who slander behind backs flatter to the face. It is not fitting either for a young woman at court to pry into or to busy herself about many things. Rather she ought to have eyes for everything but to look and see nothing, ears for everything but to know nothing, a tongue to reply but to say nothing which can be prejudicial to anyone. It is not good sense to seek to make a great stir, for fear always of the envy which is so great there. Against envy, after she has done all the service due her mistress, she should take pains to please each one according to his condition, doing him the honor which is his right, and especially the lords and ladies who have the greatest audiences and who are held wisest, though not otherwise than in accord with her conscience, honor, freedom, and loyalty. She should be humble, to small as well as great, sweet, courteous, pleasant, true in all things, and wise. If anything should be said through envy or hate that injures her honor, she should bear it patiently, feigning not to believe it, and be pleasant. For no anger or envy is so great that it cannot be softened by sweetness and humility. Let her mind her own business without inquiring or desiring to know what concerns others, and if she should happen to know something, take good care not to reveal it or show that she knows it, especially if it touches any one with too great prejudice, most of all the honor of her master and mistress.[9]

Lavinia's father, as has been indicated already, was deeply interested in her studies, and has a good deal to say on how she can manage at court to continue them. The subject weighs heavily on his heart, he says, because they have spent so much time and toil on them, and she has won so much and promises so much more, that it would be a great shame, even impiety, not to value them as she ought, and he goes over the reasons that should weigh with her. In these studies lies the way to achieve virtue, which in this world brings the greatest happiness. But if she does not wish to esteem virtue for itself, then she should do so for its shadow, the honor that it brings. She has had honor and praise in her childhood and great hopes are held for her future from this beginning, so that fear of blame if no other spur should excite her to go on, blame for not preserving and increasing in her youth what she had won in childhood with pain. He reminds her that more than three years before, he had had embroidered a piece of writing in her hand, which would perpetuate memory of her honor, that not yet nine years old she was so excellent in writing. If all this is not enough, at least the fact that her fame for excellence led to her being received into the service of such a great lady should move her to study, and also that all their hopes of her good fortune and recompense for the great burden on their house are founded on her worth. More than all these should weigh his love for her and her loving and filial fear of him, even though she is away from him under the command of another, and even when he is in his grave and only his memory remains, or failing all these the fact should weigh that he would be scorned if she neglected his gift. Last of all, love of God if all else is unavailing should urge her to the study of virtue, for He is jealous of the talent He gives.

She may think that she will not have time for this study, with new occupations, and without teachers and the care of her father and their servants, but she is old enough now by her own will to give attention to work. She will be busier, it is true, yet all the more will she show her virtue if she knows how to seize time for keeping what she has, and she will have the advantage that what she got with difficulty at home she will now use only to exercise it and improve it at court with pleasure. Only a little one day, a little more another is necessary, but it must be done well. Her lady, inclined to such studies, will arrange time for her, and may even appoint a teacher under whom she can make greater progress. Such a study as music which has to be carried on in company cannot be pursued every day, but by doing as well as she can when occasion offers, she will see how well she can perform and win praise. Her singing, if in no other way, will help in that it will keep her voice in breath, forcing her to sustain it, to try to go higher than is possible, to sing exactly, and to go from one voice to another with grace. With many songbooks in her room she can keep up her practice by singing now and then. She will also have her viola da gamba well tuned to aid in singing, and next best her clavichord. Surely there will be in such a company of ladies some able to vie with her in this and other accomplishments. Everything else she can do alone. On one point he is still more solicitous. He is very sorry, he says, that just as he had begun to teach her to write a letter moderately well and correctly enough, he cannot continue this duty. He will always provide her with some books suitable to this profession. If she reads and heeds what she finds in them, she will, little by little, upon the beginning he has made, acquire this knowledge which is necessary to the beauty of her writing, and which will be the greatest ornament to her. She will take the utmost care in this matter, both because of the nobility of the art and because of the great service that it can someday be to her lady. For great lords especially, this office of service with the pen includes more than correcting the language, and those who perform it are called secretaries, their duty being to be silent. Thus she has all these reasons for study, and besides, the advantage of having in her hand at all times some treatise to pass her time happily and avoid dangerous idleness.[10]

Guasco's fatherly interest extends also to matters of health, dress, and care of her belongings. Health is most important for her to preserve, he tells her, since she has so many enterprises in hand. She has a good start—a good constitution and never a taste of medicine. But she is going from a very simple regime at home where she is accustomed to food suited to children to the more varied and sumptuous fare at court. She must exercise some restraint and not let her appetite run away with her and cause some disorder as too much food of a rich sort and too little exercise will do. Outside of dinner and supper she should refrain from the heavier foods. For her growing age bread and an apple ought to be enough for lunch, as at home. If her companions do otherwise, she ought not to because she is unused to it and can do herself great harm in a short time. She should be sparing also of wine. Cleanliness is very important, in great part the point of difference between men and beasts, and for that all the more esteemed by a gentlewoman well born and a lady of such a palace as that of the Infanta's. It pertains to person and adornments. The hair, hand, and teeth are especially important, for here appears the beauty of a woman. It is not his business to teach her the care of these parts, others not lacking to do that, but he will say that she should not bleach her hair for that will damage her health. She should take a middle course in dressing it, between too artificial and too negligent an appearance, a good rule in all actions. Clear, fresh water is enough for her face, in which there is nothing to grieve her, as he puts it, not so willing apparently to praise her for external beauty as for internal. Her clothes she should keep clean, especially from spots which she is in danger of getting from service at the table. She is well enough provided with clothes and other things, but it has taxed him to do so, and therefore she must care for them well and preserve them. There are four ways of spoiling her things—breaking, staining what she uses, not caring for what she does not use, and leaving some to be stolen. Especially for the sake of her clothes, she should take care how she walks, stands, works, or does anything that may injure them. If any little break occurs in clothes and other things, it should be mended at once. Stains can be avoided by care in muddy and dangerous places—stains are more disgraceful than wear. Things not in use should be kept in order where she can find one thing without displacing a hundred, and well protected from moths, dust, and mice. Without showing distrust, it is well not to trust anyone. Much better to take care of our things than after we are robbed go searching and charg-

ing someone wrongly, losing both goods and friends. For servants it is best
to put in writing all that she gives them to do and especially any sums of
money. She will need to be sparing in spending because her father is not
rich and has her brothers to support, and it is a virtue in a woman to be
saving.

Then her father dwells at some length on the care she will need to bestow
on her room. Some friend has written him about the kind of room she will
be assigned in the palace. It will have a well and a stove and some little
lemon and orange trees which make a kind of garden, and be supplied with
an abundance of all the implements and furnishings that a noble and rich
citizen of a great city might require. And still more commendably, though
the room is so full of useful things, nothing on sight will seem to be there
except for ornament of the floor and walls. The father's heart has been so
lifted by the picture of such accommodations for his dear daughter that, as
he says, he has read and reread the letter until the words are inscribed in
his memory and he has quoted them here in order that she may understand
what industriousness can do. She will need to keep everything in order, including her musical instruments and strings and her pen. To persuade her to
the effort he continues, if a merchant busy with his trade can so well bring
order to so many objects, how much more she will be bound to keep order,
burdened with fewer things and much less busy than he, and as a woman,
even more inclined to such care than a man. Besides she will have a servant
to give orders to, which this good man cannot do, having no other help than
himself. But he does not intend by this that she should merely use her
tongue to issue commands to her servant, but that often she should do
things with her own hands, as much for escape from the idleness that can
never be enough blamed as for the exercise and health of her body. Also the
servant, seeing that her mistress knows how to do what she asks of her, will
be moved to do it without orders. In this way by accustoming herself in
her early years to care for her possessions as he has advised, she can be expected to be prudent and apt in the running of a house when that duty falls
upon her in the future, and although it is another thing to rule a family and
a whole house than a single room with the little held there, yet the spirit of
a person is to be learned in the little as well as in the big, as from a little
map of a great city with its towers, churches, bridges, and all the build-
ings that it contains can be designed another city. Now he thinks he has
said enough on this sixth head.[11]

Christine de Pisan too has a good deal to say on the woman of a court,
but since she writes evidently for somewhat older attendants I have not
tried to distribute her points among Guasco's. She does not try to cover all
the aspects of life at court as he does but lays down two general laws for the
woman who serves a princess, using a term commonly applied to all of high
rank. The first law is love of mistress whether good or bad (if too bad she

will leave her), which is shown by faith and loyalty at all points. For the
sake of her lady's soul she will exhort her to do good and will give no occasion for the contrary. She will not carry reports to her that can be turned
to the defiling of her soul, speaking ill of another or against honesty or honor,
or using evil words or replies that could trouble her mistress, and she will
do what she can to restrain others from such injurious practices. She will
not use flattery to gain favor as many servants do, especially to great lords.
To avoid misunderstanding Christine pauses here to distinguish between
flattery and the good service that some may call flattery. Good service
means guarding well the honor and profit of master and mistress, taking
care to give them pleasure and aid in all lawful and honest enterprises,
being sad as if for oneself when they are sad and likewise glad for their
prosperity, not just in front of them but behind their backs, excusing them
if evil reports come, and praising and honoring them. Quite rightly such
service is given not only in the interest of those served but to seek their
favor for one's own benefit because that too is the business of one who serves
at court. Such things done with a good heart are not flattery but true love
and pure loyalty borne by a good servant, and the true signs of it. Flattery
is this—when the mistress is known to have a vicious inclination against
soul, honor, and good morals to encourage her in this by counseling her
toward this sin and supporting her, speaking ill of others and in favor of
bad opinions or dishonesties which conscience disapproves, merely to please
the mistress.

For the good servant such a mistress raises a problem in the interpretation of loyalty. If the mistress wishes to take a lover, is the servant bound
by loyalty to help her carry out her wish and hide her deed, blaming it but
thinking she might protect her lady's honor better than another might do?
No, says Christine, she would do evil herself. If she thinks she is doing it to
guard her lady's honor, let her search her conscience and she will see that it
is something else—to have more favor and profit. Whatever the reason, she
does wrong and the blind will lead the blind into the ditch. If her mistress
has enough confidence in her to tell her her secret, this should be her reply:
"My lady, I thank you for your confidence in me in telling me what you
will wish concealed, and I promise you secrecy all my life. But truly it
weighs down my heart that you should wish to do such a thing, for peril
to soul and honor can come. There is nothing in my power that I would not
do to serve you even in this matter, but pardon me, I love better the salvation of my soul and conscience than your service. And I ought to prefer
your hate in order to do good rather than consent to wrong-doing. Better for
me to die. I know well that I am yours and ought to obey you, but in this
I would sin, which I am bound to do for nobody." But if she is wise and
true she will avoid leaving her mistress, as enough do, who to give themselves an air of sanctity go off telling how they were asked to do such and

such a thing but they well and good gave her a rebuff and would rather see her burn. This is not to say that even in such a case the good servant will not guard her mistress from all perils and defend her as she would her own child. Such a damoiselle once, when her lady was about to be surprised in the act, with inevitable loss of honor, set the place on fire so that all ran to her and her lady was saved. Another, who found her lady in despair and ready to kill herself because she was with child though unmarried, put heart in her and gave it to be understood that she herself was with child so that when the child came she could say it was her own. Such actions when the sin has been committed are good in order to guard another from despair and from taking an evil way out.

The second rule for women at court is that they ought to avoid too many friendships with men, though many think to the contrary. The first reason for this rule is that more than others these women of the court have to guard their own honor because it reflects on their mistress who will have praise or dispraise as they are good or bad. Women, whoever they are, if they delight in having several friends among men even though they intend no wrong but only want to laugh and amuse themselves, can with difficulty escape slander, not only by curious strangers who unceasingly try to hurt others, but certainly by their own companions. For women are not so blind as not to know that if men frequent their society long some will try to attract them if they can. When men see that several haunt the place where each would wish to be received alone, they malign and invent falsehoods and make a great deal of sport over the matter among themselves, whatever face they put on for the ladies, however gracious they appear. These jests and words are carried from mouth to mouth in towns, taverns, and elsewhere and each teller adds his own contribution. In such ways without having given any cause by sinning but only because of the simplicity of the women who don't think about it, women are blamed for wrong-doing even by those whom they entertain. If ladies and damoiselles of the court knew well what such "friends" say of them they would retreat and would prefer less diversion to so many words, and when men smile on them and promise body and service, they would with difficulty believe them. Some may ask, isn't it better, even for the sake of honor, to entertain several impartially than only one or two, when the rest can say this one is received in such a place, that one in another, some are in favor, others are not. The reply is that either case is bad when suspicion is aroused. Well, then can't women of the court dare to see friends or play without evil thought in a company where gentlemen are? The restriction is good, though displeasing, so far as it guards from what would be a greater inconvenience. But it is not her intent, Christine adds, to restrain women from entertaining men at an appropriate time and place, if they play properly in an honorable company, nor does she mean that if a prince or princess receives strangers or princes, or other valiant knights or squires it is not suitable for them to be feted and welcomed among ladies and damoiselles. It would be against honor to do otherwise. She has been talking only of those idle young men who have a habit of hanging around without anything else to do than to play in the halls where ladies and damoiselles gather, and her advice ought not to annoy anyone young and gay if she loves honor, any more than one who cares for his own health. What is more worthy, noble, and valuable should be cherished, and every woman of honor, good and wise, ought to be reputed a great treasure and a notable and singular object worthy of honor and reverence. Then since she is such and wishes to be held so, it is not fitting that men should hold her too cheap or be free of this great gift, her friendship. For the higher the esteem she places upon herself before all men, not through pride but through a greatness well becoming a woman, the greater the reverence in which they will hold her.

Like Guasco Christine discusses at some length the principal vices to which those who dwell at court are peculiarly open and how to avoid them. Envy is chief and most destructive. It comes purely of pride and comes to all, she says, who are not on their guard against pride by keeping before their eyes their poor, frail mortality, their coming from nothing, their wretchedness and sins, and who think they are worthy of great honors and material rewards even without deserving them. Since commonly every creature is thus deceived, each wants to excel his neighbor not in virtue but in greatness of state, honor, or substance. When he fails and sees others more advanced than he is or thinks he is, or fears that he will not come as high, then envy rises, and since at the courts of princes and princesses worldly honors and estates are distributed more generally than elsewhere, we may say, it is true that envy reigns there most of all because each wishes to have the greatest part of these honors. This envy a woman of the court will shun with all her might, for it destroys soul and heart and will. What measures can she take to prevent envy from rising in her? Detect it early. If she begins thinking that her mistress favors another more or more often calls her into counsel or seeks her company more, then she needs to take care that envy doesn't rise. Envy will make her say to herself, "Why does my lady prefer her to me? Am I not as noble or more so, as wise, and everything else? I have been here since childhood, she only recently came. I will prevent her from working her wiles to get more grace." But the wise lady will counter these doubts: "Foolish you are. God rewards you for doing your duty loyally, and you have as great worldly rewards as another. In God should be your hope. Why should you murmur if someone else has worldly goods? Do you wish to keep princes from doing their will? If your mistress prefers another she does no wrong. She gives her own substance. Perhaps you don't know your own faults and are too favorable to yourself, and your lady sees well that another is wiser, abler, better dispositioned, and more perfect than you, although you value yourself more. You can if you search your conscience find faults you have committed. You can't judge how this other appears to God, and therefore you should not want to meddle with the state of another, but think of your soul and govern yourself wisely, and do your duty and not concern yourself with who goes before or behind. Then those who see you so graciously support the pride and advancement of others without talking about it will love you the more." Such are the remedies the wise lady at court can well apply to the stings and pricks of envy. The other sins can give pleasure, but this alone gives nothing but sad thoughts, oppressed heart and spirit, downcast and altered face, only pain and torment.

The other great vice to which courts are given is slander, into which Christine goes at somewhat greater length than Guasco with only his very young daughter in mind. Slander arises out of hate, or mere opinion, or pure envy, and is directed against God's commands to do as you would be done by, and to love another as yourself. Hate comes commonly from injury by someone, or reputed injury. It is natural to hate a maligner, who may get one into the bad graces of mistress, lord, or friends, or even sent out of court without reason, causing the loss of service, advancement, estate, and even honor. It is natural in retaliation to speak ill of him in private, and in public if the slanderer is not too powerful, and some will say that it is right, but the wise lady at court will not do so, for four good reasons. First, God commands us to love our enemies. Second, she will act against her honor because a person of high birth never speaks ill of his enemy, knowing well that it can seem to people that he wishes revenge merely in words, the vengeance of people of little power and weak heart, which therefore wise people use little. Third, those who hear her will not believe her, for, they will say, whoever speaks in hate cannot be believed. Fourth, the person who may have injured her only a little will be so much the more angered at her for her evil-speaking that more injury may come. Better one injury than two.

Mere opinion is the second reason for slander. A person thinks that someone is bad or deficient in some one thing or all, or doesn't govern himself well in all cases or some, and without knowing the truth of the matter, which may be the opposite, misjudges and slanders freely with little consideration of the small good achieved. This is a common happening in court where many have the habit; no court is free.

Great evil is done by everyone who defames another, but especially when the defamed is the lord or lady who supports all. Yet some women of the court, if they see their mistress no more than speak low once or twice to someone, or show a private sign of friendship or a smile or pleasure, made perhaps by youth and ignorance and without thinking evil, or even if she is only extra fine in her clothes, a proper condition for many people, all too often will misjudge. But this is the least. They will do worse, for though they obey her, show her all reverence with knees on the ground, and flatter her, they will spread their opinions elsewhere. They take care that their mistress doesn't hear and think it enough to conceal their evil-speaking from her alone. Slander of a great lady is a greater sin than of others because the honor or dishonor of her is more spread through every country than of a simple woman, also because it is an act of treason against the vow to obey and to guard her honor and good, and because evil is returned for good and judgment given against the commandment of God. Even if she is what they say, they ought not to speak evil of her either among themselves or elsewhere, for words cannot be said so guardedly that they will not be reported, and her women are bound in every case to guard her honor, cover her shame, and if others speak evil to minimize the charges and excuse her. It is a great dishonor to do the contrary and inexcusable even if they are not well treated, because they can leave if not pleased, or if they need to serve because too great prejudice would result from leaving, then they can be silent and pretend that they see nothing since the remedy is beyond them. They can do loyally what belongs to them, not meddling with more, and pray God to better her, and try to mollify others who speak evil of her, often more out of spite that they aren't taken into her secret, or out of envy that other women know more, than for any other reason. And if the good lady of the court who wishes to act according to conscience and who loves the honor and good of her mistress sees her falling into peril and does not dare to speak in restraint of her, she will always go to the confessor of her mistress and tell him secretly and in confession what is said of her and the danger she is in, and beg him to let her know but never to accuse her.

To return to the general, for the women of the court to defame each other is unfitting and dangerous; the one who defames will be defamed in turn for retaliation. It is foolish in one who thinks herself blameless to speak boldly of the faults of another, for no one is really without fault. The honor of a court is hurt if everywhere people can say the women of the court slander each other. The court of a princess should be well-ordered, like an abbey, and backbiting should not be allowed. The third cause of slander, envy, is the least excusable—hate is natural for harm done, opinion can be founded on appearance, envy is pure evil.[12]

The qualities required of the lady-in-waiting—the Italians and French were happier in being able to turn their "courtier" into a feminine word— are now clear enough, the string surely need not be rehearsed here. What more should be added to make her into a princess? We shall have to rely on Christine de Pisan and Anne de Beaujeu for information on this point, both well acquainted with courts and desirous of aiding women who must bear on their shoulders a great weight of responsibility for the well-being of those about them and for the people of the whole realm. Christine attempted to give a complete picture of the good princess, as Anne did not, and therefore she will be the chief witness. And so movingly and persuasively does she write of the sweetness, kindness, generosity, courage, and wisdom of her good princess that I willingly follow her chapter by chapter. All these qualities shine through the words of this truly humane lady.

In the first place, even the virtues themselves take on a special color as they are seen controlling the behavior of a great lady. Christine begins, as the others do, with humility, seeing what temptations can come to one surrounded by riches, comforts, delights, ladies to kneel and satisfy every wish. Let her pray to be humble and remember what she is and who it is that gives her such things, and that He is greater. By her respectful behavior, low speaking, sweet carriage, kind face, and lowered eyes in saluting, she can guard against being puffed up with all the reverence she receives from men. There is no cause for pride in lordship, Anne, too, warned her daughter, with its dangers, responsibilities, and toils; the rudeness that comes from pride has often cost the nobles honors and estates. Next to humility she will want patience for the adversity that comes to all and for wrongs. With great constancy and courage she will take small account of envious darts, words spoken against her, pardoning the light offenses and even thinking little of the great. Charity above all she will have, that is love, pity, and liberality, for all the people of her realm, directed toward keeping peace for them and relieving them in their distresses. This point calls for expansion.

First on the keeping of peace. If the prince oppresses his people, they, feeling that their lady is full of goodness and love and pity, will come to her and beg her to intercede for them with the prince and make their peace. She then, accompanied by wise and good men to give her advice, will receive such petitioners kindly and hear them at her leisure and understand all they want to say. On advice she will find excuses for her lord and speak well of him, but if the people are not satisfied with this she will promise to do all in her power to make peace and to be their good friend in their petition and in every way that she can, and she will beg them to be loyal and obedient subjects of their lord and always to come to her as now with their needs. Thus the lady will reply so wisely to the ambassadors of the people that they will be content and lose any thought of rancor or rebellion that they had. Nor will she make them wait in vain hope, but will keep her promise without long delay, and will speak to her lord with the help of other wise people if it is desirable, and very humbly will she beg for the people. She will show the reasons for granting the petition, on which she will be very well informed, and how necessary it is if the prince wishes to reign long in peace and gloriously, loved by his subjects, and how kindness best befits a prince. Thus she will speak so as to win all or a part of her request, and then she will report him so wisely to his subjects that they will be well content with their prince and her, and very humbly thank her for the benefit.

Likewise charity will bid the wise princess to take pains to make peace between her lord and other lords and his barons and others if they are in discord. If some neighboring prince wishes to make war on her lord, or he wishes to make war on someone, the good lady will think of the great evils, infinite cruelties, losses of men, distraction of the country that come from war, and she will seek with all her power a way, guarding always the honor of her lord, to prevent this war. In this she will wish to work carefully, calling God to her aid and good counsel that the way of peace may be found. Or if it happens that some one of the princes of the realm, or barons, or knights, or other subjects who have power should do something wrong, even against the majesty of her lord, and she sees that to take him and punish him or move war against him would bring great evil to the land, as has often happened in France and elsewhere, then she will pity the people and wish to make peace. So she will admonish the people, her lord, and his counselors to give heed to this matter before they undertake anything, foreseeing the evil that will come. Every prince ought to avoid shedding blood as much as he can and especially that of his subjects, she will say to her lord; he should not without great consideration and deliberation undertake a new war, but may better find some more fitting way to make accord. She will not refrain from speaking or having someone else speak to those who have committed the wrong and reprove them for it, saying that the misdeed is very great and the prince angered with good cause and the sentence just, but that she who would always wish peace, in case they wish to repent or make amends, will willingly take pains to try to pacify him. By such words the good princess will use every means in her power to peace, as did the good Queen Blanche, mother of Saint Louis. Men are by nature more courageous and hot than women and their great desire for revenge will not let them think of the perils and evil which can follow. But the nature of women is more fearful and so they are of a sweeter disposition. Therefore if they are wise and willing they can be the best means to pacify men. Happy the country that has such a princess. And what happens to her? All the subjects that know her to be of such wisdom and goodness do not regard her as a mistress but she seems to them a goddess on the earth in whom they have sovereign hope and confidence, the preserver of peace in their country.

There is also charity that rises from devoutness known as almsgiving, a part of liberality. This also the good princess will have. The unequal distribution of goods, Christine begins, is not a charge against the justice of God, but made, as Basil says, in order that by giving to the poor the rich can deserve what God has given and the poor can by their suffering be crowned with the diadem of patience. The good princess will know that the goods which she has in abundance belong to the poor, not to her, and that she will be a thief if she does not give when she can. To accomplish her purpose she will commission some of her servants to inquire through the city or wherever she is where are to be found the honest poor—poor gentlemen or gentlewomen sick or defrauded of their estates, poor widows, housewives, sufferers, poor girls to be married, women in childbed, scholars, priests, or religious in poverty. These servants who are to be her deputies must be good, devout, charitable, and without greed, "for God knows," Christine exclaims, "how this affair goes by the ordering of some almoners of lords or prelates." Some say that princes can look to have only bad servants and bad counsel, but she believes the counselors of those whose will is all good do not dare to give bad counsel, for commonly the servant gives what his master wants, and the good lady will have servants like herself. To these good poor she will send secretly so that the poor do not know from whom the alms comes. She will not be ashamed, however, to visit at times the hospitals, and the poor on her estate, with a large company as is appropriate, and will speak to the poor and sick and comfort them sweetly. For the poor man is much more comforted by the visit of a great and powerful person than of another. The reason is that it means to him a rise in self-esteem. And it is true that everybody scorns him, and therefore it seems to him that when a powerful person deigns to visit and comfort him he recovers some honor, which is naturally what each one desires. So the princess herself acquires greater merit in such a case than a lesser person for three reasons. First, the greater the person and the more she humbles herself the greater her goodness. Second, as just said, she gives greater aid and comfort to the poor. Third, she sets a good example to those who see her do such things with such great humility, for nothing serves so well for an example to the people as what they see their lord or lady do. This is equally true of both good and bad deeds. Also she will visit the churches and holy places in her vicinity. This is not to say that she can give all to the poor. Her revenues, gathered legally and without extortion, are rightly hers, and she must retain enough for necessities, to keep her state, to pay her servants and her debts. It is a great merit in her, however, if she restrains superfluities, robes, and jewels that are not necessary, for what is saved can be used for the poor and good deeds—which is the real treasure.

These counsels, says Christine, are dictated by love and fear of God. The rest are moral teachings which worldly prudence will give to the princess. They do not conflict with those of God but follow and depend on them. It is impossible to displease God by living morally in this world. Of the good things that belong to the world the princess should love honor most, for as Saint Augustine says, to live well in the world two things are necessary, conscience and good reputation, which is honor and therefore to be loved. What belongs strictly to honor? Certainly not riches, at least if they serve according to the common way of the world. Always to keep within the law? This ought to be the least part which serves to perfect honor. What is most needful then? Good morals, for the rest may be lost and honor still had, and only for virtue renown spreads all over the world. Moral life rests for the princess on two things, on the moral rules which she wishes to hold and to practice, and on the manner and order of life which she wishes to adopt.

Then having evidently worked over with an eye to simplification the long array of moral virtues usually recommended to struggling human beings, Christine reduces them to two, sobriety and chastity, which any woman who wishes great honor must add to those mentioned above. Sobriety applies to everything that needs restraint from excess. It will make her content with such wines and foods as are given her. It will guard her against sleeping too much, for prudence says too much repose engenders vice and sin. Though every lady according to her state must be richly adorned, sobriety will tell the princess that she should not want finer clothes than her ancestors had, new fashions that invite affectation, or strange perfumes, in which ladies enough have been greatly interested; it will guard her from spending much money on delights of the body, money that might better be given to the poor. Sobriety also will keep her from speaking too much, a bad fault in a great lady; from lying, a worse fault, for truth in the mouths of prince and princess is more effective than in the mouths of other men, and necessary if people are to believe her; from maligning others, indeed any word of blame; from empty and dishonest words; from saying any unconsidered word especially in a place where it can be judged and spread abroad; from laughing too much and without cause; and from excess in all pastimes. Sobriety will teach her how to order her speech, a wise way, neither heavy nor too precise, but sweet, and calm, in a low voice with pleasing tones, without movements of the body or hands, or grimaces.

This virtue will also teach her many other things. It will make her not dangerous to serve, for she will not wish even in her high position more service than is reasonable. She will speak virtuous words among her women and girls, words which will make them say on hearing her that they show her very good, wise, and honest. She will speak graciously to them, teach them sweetly and if necessary reprove their faults, courteously warning them that they will be sent away if they do not mend, or punishing them, or finding some other way of correction, but always without rude speech, for that coming from the mouth of any woman turns people against her. She will make her commands reasonable in time and place and give them to those to whom they belong, each in her office. She will also willingly read instructive books of good morals and of devotion, and of worldly matters she will want to hear about valiant men, proved knights, and gentlemen, of their deeds and prowess, and about great scholars and their studies, and all learned men and women, their knowledge and good life. She will hate books of lubricity, which she will not want to have in her court, nor allow them to be shown to child, relative, or woman that she has. So much for sobriety, Christine concludes. Chastity will follow, for the princess that lives with sobriety lives so purely that in deed, word, seeming, action, face, bearing, state, and look there will be nothing to reproach.

Having covered by the word sobriety the principal moral virtues needed by the princess, Christine proceeds to the second part in which the life of good renown consists, the proper ordering of her days. Here it would be easy to condense her advice by indicating the steps that took the princess from her early rising, through prayers, almsgiving, attendance at council, dining, and so forth, to prayers again and bed. But that would be to lose the color and feeling of such a day. And so once more we will follow closely Christine's account. This princess of hers will rise early and first say her prayers. Queen Jeanne, wife of Charles V of France, rose before daylight and lit her candle to say her prayers, but she would not let her women lose their sleep. Then when ready she will go to hear mass, and will spend as much time at devotions as duties will allow. For it must be admitted that under some circumstances such a princess as is here envisaged will not have leisure for the long prayers that she would desire to make. Lords who see their wives good and wise not infrequently commit the government to them when they go away or are occupied elsewhere, giving them authority to rule and preside over the council of state. Such women then are more to be excused if they do not employ so much time at prayers as those with more leisure, nor do they have less merit for right and just attending to public matters in their control than they would have from longer time spent in prayers, providing that at heart they would prefer the contemplative life to the active. For the contemplative life can be lived well without the active, but the strictly good active life cannot be lived well without any part of the contemplative. This lady would then have things so well ordered than on issuing from her chapel she would find some poor awaiting her, to whom she herself with humility and devotion would give alms by her own hand. If any pitiful requests are to be made to her, benignly she will hear them and reply graciously, and those that she can grant in brief time she will not withhold long, and by so doing she will increase the alms and also her great renown. And if by chance she cannot listen to all the requests she will commission some wise men whom she will have with her for the purpose to hear them, and she will have instructed her deputies to be charitable and very expeditious.

Then, if a lady charged with government, on the days set for holding council she will go with such bearing and manners and countenance as when seated in her high seat she will indeed appear the lady and mistress of all, and each councilor will hold her in great reverence as their mistress of great authority. And so she will listen diligently to what is brought forward and to the opinions of all, and so well will she put her mind on matters that she will understand the principal points and the conclusions, and note well who speaks best and with most consideration, and who appears to her the wisest and of the most profound judgment, and also in the diversity of opinions she will take thought of what causes and reasons can move the speakers. Then when it comes her turn to speak or reply as the case may be, she will be so well advised of what she ought to do that she cannot be reputed simple or ignorant. And if she can be informed beforehand of what ought to be proposed and what are the weighty matters, and she can by wise counsel know what to reply, that would be good. For this purpose this lady will select certain prudent men of good judgment for her own counselors, whom she will know good, loyal, and not too covetous; for this is what has utterly shamed princes and princesses, that counselors have been filled with greed and turned their advice accordingly. Without fail those ruled by this vice cannot well or loyally, or to the profit of the soul or honor of the body give counsel. Thus the prudent lady ought to inquire carefully whether the men she chooses for counselors are of good life. Each day at a certain hour she will take advice from these as to what care she ought to take.

After this council of the morning, she will go to the table, which on solemn or feast days will be commonly in the hall, where will be seated in the order of their rank her ladies and girls and the persons appropriate to be there. All will be served according to their rank, and while the serving lasts, according to the good old custom of queens and princesses, she will have some appointed wise man tell of old deeds, good deaths, or moral examples. There will be no great noise. And after the tables are lifted and grace is said, if there are princes or lords, ladies or damoiselles, or other strangers to her, she, well taught in all matters, and well informed, will receive each in such honor as belongs to him so that all will be happy. With a cheerful face she will speak to them appropriately, to the old in a way more serious, to the young in another way more smiling. And if the company is entertained with some debate or amusing game she will know so well how to gratify all with her pleasing ways that they will say that she is a gracious lady who knows how to conduct herself under all circumstances. When it is time to withdraw, if the lady goes to her chamber she may rest a little there if she needs to, and then on a week-day if she has no greater occupation she will take up some handwork to avoid idleness. Around her will be assembled to work her women and girls, and there in private she will, if she wishes, encourage each to invent freely all sorts of honest amusements, and she will laugh with them, and thus, by putting everyone at ease she will be praised for her pleasant familiarity and kindness, and all will love her with their whole hearts. This will continue until the hour of vespers, which she will hear in her chapel, if a feast day or some important affair does not prevent her, or she will say them with her chaplain, and after that she will go to walk in a garden until suppertime. Then she will allow any who have business with her to enter and will hear them. Toward bedtime she will have prayers, and so will end the order of the common days of the prudent princess living in activity a good and holy life. As to other amusements in which ladies are accustomed to take pleasure, such as hunting, Christine says she will not put them into her order but leave them to the planning and wish of their husbands and themselves. In such things some license can well be given in time and place even to ladies who are very virtuous, without blame except that there should not be too much, and measure should be kept in the fashion.

A hundred, two hundred years later the hours of dining may have changed, the table no longer been taken up and put away, and the games and pleasant devices found other names and turns, but in the main the ordering of a day in the life of a serious and responsible princess, one may well believe, would include substantially the same activities.[13]

The rest of the advice that prudence has to give to princesses who love honor concerns such matters as her relation to her lord, the government of her children and her women, her behavior to her subjects of every rank, and the handling of her revenues. Of what Christine has to say on how a princess shall bear herself toward her lord in general and in particular, the general belongs to all women: love your husband and live in peace with him, or you will find the torments of hell and nothing but storms. We know those lessons well enough by now, but perhaps because it is a woman that is advising and because she never forgets that it is a princess she is addressing we had better see what she finds to say. She repeats them all here, she says, because though enough women of all estates do love their husbands dearly they do not through youth or for other reasons know all the rules. The noble princess desirous of honor, like any other women, will behave herself toward her lord, young or old, in all the ways that in such a case good faith and true love command—that is, be humble toward him, in deed reverence him and in word obey him without murmuring, and keep peace as far as in her power lies. She will show her love by being careful in all things that can pertain to the good of his person, soul and body: his soul by loving his confessor, because if she sees in her lord any touch of sin which if habitual can turn to his damnation and she does not dare to speak to him herself for fear of his displeasure and also as a thing not fitting for her to do, she will ask his confessor to tell him and admonish him well always to be a servant of God; for the maintenance of his health and preservation of life she will wish to speak often to his physicians to inquire how he is, and wise as she is she will wish to hear their opinions and will rule their meals according to his health. She will wish to know how he is served, and in this will not be ashamed to show great care herself. And since it is never the order of the royal state that the ladies are so commonly around their lords as other women are around their husbands, she will inquire often of the chamberlains and others around him about his condition and will be very glad of their advice. When with him she will say everything in her power to please him, and show him a happy face.

Christine foresees that someone perhaps will object here that she at every point prescribes that women ought to love their lords and show their love, but never says whether lords behave toward their wives as they ought, when everyone knows that there are husbands who behave anything but well toward their wives. Her answer is that the teaching in this book is addressed not to men, although they need it too, but to women for their profit, to teach them the remedies valuable to avoid dishonor, and to give good counsel. Suppose that the husband is of strange manners, perverse and rude, unloving toward his wife or in love with another woman. When she is assured of all this she ought to bear it and wisely dissemble, appearing not to see, considering what remedy she can find, for she will think like a wise woman—if you say rude things you will gain nothing, and if he does lead you an evil life and you strike back he may send you away, and then so much the more will people mock you and increase the shame and dishonor, and you will be worse off than before. A wife must live with her husband whatever he is. With all these things in mind, the wise lady will take pains by beauty and sweetness to draw him to her. And if she learns of infidelity and decides it would be best to speak to him of it, she will do so apart, sweetly and kindly. She will sometimes admonish by devotion, sometimes by the pity he ought to have for her, sometimes by smiling as if she were happy. She will have good men and his confessor speak to him. And also the noble lady, if she hears others speak evil of him, will find excuses for him and virtuously defend him, for she cannot endure to hear evil reports of him, and she will think that perhaps sadness will come of it and nothing will be gained from knowing. If she has tried everything and he will not amend, then her refuge is in God, and she will do all in her power to keep the peace and will not say anything more to him. And whoever acts in this way may be certain that no man can be found so perverse that at the end conscience and reason will not say to him, "You are very wrong and sin greatly against your good and honest wife," and he will amend and love her more, and so her cause will be gained by suffering well.

If it should happen that her lord should go on a long and dangerous voyage, or to war, she will pray to God devoutly, and will have processions and offerings made for him very carefully, and will increase her alms and keep herself in humble and simple state, manner, and dress. On his return with great joy and honor she will receive him and show a joyous face, and she will want to be informed of the best of his men, of the most proved and valiant, and will willingly hear the tale, and will receive them with great honor and give them beautiful gifts. Also she will wish to know how those who had the guarding of his body did their duty.

These are the ways that are held of great honor in ladies, which the princess who loves honor will wish always to have known to the world and never concealed. So she will learn of prudence that greater praise cannot be given to a lady or any woman than that she is true and loyal toward her lord and shows well that she loves him. For a woman who loves will not be false, and she shows her loyalty best by showing her love through the signs by which one commonly judges of the heart. For not otherwise can one judge of the intention than by works.

Further, if she loves her husband she will love his relatives and friends and show her love in the same way to them as to him. She will honor and serve them in every way, even better than her own relatives and friends, and if necessary procure the good will of her lord toward them and make peace between them. She will speak well of them and defend them and guard against any strife between them and her. If any one of them is dangerous and hard to handle, she will take pains to find out the best way according to his character, guarding always the honor that belongs to her. So she will love not only his relatives but also everyone that he loves. What if she knows some of them to be bad? She will still make no difference in her bearing, because she cannot make them good or change the love or hate of her husband, and if she should reveal her dislike she would only create disturbances and acquire that many more enemies. If she is certain, however, that any are vicious and at the same time wronging her husband, then providing she knows him inclined to believe her she will venture to tell him sweetly and calmly what she has to say. Thus she will love or treat lovingly all those that her husband loves so that it may be truthfully said of her that she loves only them. Her rewards will be the good grace of her lord and the good will of his relatives and friends, who can be of great value to her and keep her from many perils and obstacles. And this love will be a great sign of the love she bears her husband.[14]

If she has children, like every other mother the princess will diligently watch over them and their government, especially what concerns the teaching of morals and control of their bodies. How their lives are ordered, who have them in charge, and how such do their duty she will make her business to know, and she will not wait for the report of someone else but often visit her children in their rooms herself, see them go to bed and get up. Such things do the princess no dishonor. Rather it is great praise to be called careful, as a sign that she is wise and good, for children are of the greatest import to her and ought therefore to be very dear to her. She will see that they are well taught, first their letters and hours, and then she will take pains to gain the assent of their father to their learning Latin and the sciences, which are very suitable to the children of princes and lords. As they grow older and have understanding she will want them to be taught everything of the world that princes should know, particularly how to govern. She will see that all the lessons of the virtues are taught to them and the way to avoid vices. To these ends she will give great heed to the manners and morals of their tutor and his knowledge, as of the others around them, and if not good she will have them dismissed and find others. She will want her children often with her, and will observe carefully their manners, actions, and words, and she will strongly reprove them for misbehavior, if she wishes to instill fear into them, and reverence to her. She will reason with them to find out how well they understand and what they know, and she will wisely teach them.

It is to be assumed that most or all of the foregoing advice applies to all the children of a princess, both sons and daughters, since Christine does not limit it expressly, and such an upbringing in general is necessary to the sort of princess she envisages. She does now go on to prescribe more particularly for daughters. They will be governed by good and wise ladies, who are known to be of good reputation, devotion to God, worldly sense and honor, wisdom and prudence, in order to teach well what is fitting for the daughter of a prince to know. A lady who is given such a charge should be of sufficient age to be wiser than the child she governs and of more authority than other ladies of the court, for it is her business to keep from this daughter of a prince any girl or woman of bad character, of light or foolish or ugly manner so that the child may have no bad example. When the girl is old enough the princess will have her taught to read, first the hours and services, and then books of devotion and contemplation, or any that present good morals, but no vain, or foolish, or dissolute things because the lessons the child receives first are commonly followed through life. So the princess will take good care of the government and teaching of her daughters, and as they grow older she will take greater care and keep them for the most part around her and in fear of her, and will set them an example of wise behavior and discretion.[15]

But princesses might lack children and their lords might bestow little of their company upon them through absence or neglect or the customary order of court life so that marital and maternal duties might demand little of their time and care. More constant and inescapable was the daily companionship of their women and girls, and for them they bore complete responsibility. The ideal set up for these attendants of the princess has already been shown. What her duties were to them both Christine and Anne discuss at some length. The chief concern is moral character. Any lady that wishes to be chaste, says Christine, will want all her women so on pain of dismissal if they are not, and she boldly attacks the chief obstacle. It is the custom for knights and squires and all who associate with women, she says, to beg for love and win it if they can, a custom as prevalent in 1500 and 1600 as in 1400. The princess therefore will order her court in such a way that no one repairing there will be so bold as to dare to speak apart to any of her women, or even appear to attract them, and if he does or gives any sign of such intention, she will show such disapproval that he will not dare to persist. She will require of her women that they on their part conduct themselves toward said knights and squires and all men with due decorum, speak soberly and simply, disport and please themselves graciously and modestly in dances and honest amusements, such as give men no occasion to mock at them, and not be forward, or bold in words, faces, bearing, laugh, or carry their heads "like antlered deer." Such misbehavior is more blameworthy in women of the court than in others, for where there is most honor there should be the most perfect manners and morals. The opposite is believed, but, she modestly concludes, "We hope that this doctrine of ours will be carried in future in royal hands, and we say generally to all that it belongs to all ladies and girls at court to be wiser, more self-contained, better disciplined in everything, whether young or old, than others, as examples of all good and all honor to other women." How else shall they do honor to themselves or their mistresses? So in all things the princess will wish a corresponding honesty, in dress particularly, which although suitably rich and beautiful may be made in honest fashion and kept neat and clean. By her wise government she will arouse so much fear that no one will disobey or lift an eye with evil intent, and then no bad report will ever be made in foreign countries.

Unless she does hold them in fear and submission, insists Anne de Beaujeu to her daughter Suzanne, they will serve only their own pleasure and not their mistress's, a grave fault in them and a great dishonor to any woman in high place who allows it. For such laxity often leads to false opinions, principally of the mistress, such as the suspicion that if there had not been something in her that needed to be kept secret, her women would not dare to behave as they do. Such government though strict should not be harsh, but wise so that there may be no cause for rebellion or the least disobedience. If any do amiss the princess will show them their faults sweetly in few words, which are enough for the well-intentioned. The obstinate and perverse are not worth trying to correct but should be dismissed at once, and along with them all who are sharp-tongued, tale-bearing, quarrelsome and lying because of the harm that can come from them, for often all of this can turn to the prejudice of the master and mistress. But such dismissal must be graciously given or just so many enemies are sent abroad. Idleness, envy,

and mockery are the three sins that Anne particularly warns her daughter
to avoid in herself and also in her women, idleness because, as so often said,
it leads to all the vices, envy because it leads to slander and the destruction
of good friends and relatives, and mockery, evidently much in fashion at
court in all our centuries, because it is dishonest and a sign of poor understanding. Often those who are mocked, belittled, or turned to ridicule, are
better than those who mock, and the most perfect are those who ought most
to be on guard and to excuse the simplicity of the ignorant. If anyone says
that it is his nature to mock, he shows himself to be a fool by nature, and
if he does it by accustoming himself to it, he shows that he has associated
only with bad people. One may do it from youth and without thinking evil,
but it should be counted folly when it creates prejudice against another.

Like Christine Anne advised that pleasant pastimes be allowed to relieve
low spirits and divert youth and also to increase love between the mistress
and her women. For she will join them in their play, but without too much
familiarity, warns Anne, or too much private conversation. She foresees
danger in singling out any for special friendship because sometimes one will
tell something against himself, of which afterwards he will have reason to
repent. There is no friend so perfect in this world who, if you reveal your
secret to him, will not think afterward that you are bound to please him
more than before, and some will believe when you confide in them that you
will not dare to anger them or do anything without their advice. And if
friendship is broken, hate takes the place of love and the secret is told in
despite. The age is corrupt, Anne says, so that though the noble heart should
not be of such low condition, many of high birth, experience shows, are
capable of revealing the confidences of others, and take pleasure in doing
so, thinking that they even acquire reputation when it is the secret of
people of importance, and are held wise themselves for knowing the counsel
of great men. What then shall the poor lady do when her heart burns to relieve itself of the weight of a secret that touches her honor? Let her choose
some relative of her husband's or herself for a confidant for he will have
more cause than others to conceal it. When others do her the honor of con-
fiding some great matter to her, she should consider that no greater sign of
perfect love can be shown to her, and should therefore employ all her power
to comfort them and loyally counsel them, shielding and defending them
in this matter against all, for in her presence, if she is the highest in rank
of the company, she ought not to allow another to make charges, and if she
is the least, she ought to defend them and speak of some pleasant matter.
But such confidences are very dangerous, and one ought not to desire to
share the counsel of another, but ought to fear to know it.

To conclude, in all points the mistress must show herself mistress, not
only in bearing, manners, and appearance but in ornaments, robes, and
other appointments, which ought always to be better and richer than any

of her women wear. In nothing should they resemble her, and it would be indeed a fault to allow what would be overdressing in them, for in all things moderation is a virtue, which the princess herself will follow, holding to the custom of the country and her husband's pleasure.[16]

Christine, however, more than Anne, saw the duties of the princess reaching out beyond her family circle and the court to the subjects over whom she as well as the prince ruled, and especially to certain groups of her people with whom she would not ordinarily associate—men of religion, scholars as well as prelates, those who serve her lord as counselors, certain of the bourgoisie and even of the common people. If someone asks Christine why she speaks more explicitly of these here than of the barons and nobles, she will answer, because we assume that the princess associates with the barons and nobles commonly, as they do with her, and is therefore less in need of advice.

It is important to seek the favor of the first group because the good and devout pray to God for her and praise her in their sermons, and those words of praise can be a sword and shield against the murmurs and reports of her slandering enemies. Through them she will gain more love from her lord and also the common people, and she may win the support of the most powerful if need ever comes to her. So she will inform herself well on which of the scholars, both religious and other, are the most sufficient and of greater authority, and more worthy of confidence. These she will have come to her, now some, now others, and will speak to them very pleasantly, and ask their counsel, and use it; and she will invite them to dine at court in the company of her confessor and the people of her chapel, all honorable persons, and will show them great honor and wish them to be honored by her own, a most becoming thing, for those ennobled by learning ought to be honored. She has the power to do them good, give them colleges and convents. When she does so, the question arises whether she should give in secret or in public. We are told, says Christine, to give alms in secret to avoid pride, which is a mortal sin. But if she can give without pride in her heart, the wise princess will want her gifts known because she will thereby set a good example to others and thus her merit is doubled. Therefore if her gifts are notable, like rebuilding convents and churches, she will have them registered on tablets in the churches and other public places. If this seems to touch hypocrisy, she can call it just hypocrisy, in a way of speaking, for she intends good and escape from evil. She does not mean that under the shadow of this thing sin should be committed. This hypocrisy is necessary to princes and princesses who have to rule over others and to whom more reverence belongs than to others. Certainly she does no harm to anyone by desiring honor through doing good.

In similar fashion the princess will want to win the favor of other groups. She will wish to be good to her lord's counselors, whether prelates, chancellors, or others, and will have them come to her, receive them honorably, speak wisely to them, and as much as she can gain their love. This will be valuable to her in several ways. They will praise her good sense and government, which they will see for themselves is praiseworthy; they will not allow anything to her prejudice to pass in council, if someone out of envy wishes to harm her; they will correct for the prince any misinformation given by others; and if she wants something passed in council they will be more favorable toward it. Also it is important for her to have the good will of those employed in the common causes of the people, advocates in Parlement and others. She will appoint certain days to see them, especially those most prominent among them, and will be kind to them, in order to let them see her honorable way of living and her great wisdom. So she will wish all estates, the principal bourgeois of cities and towns, great merchants, and even the more honest of the artisans to have faith in her, and to that end she will take pains to be very sweet to them. Then if she should have occasion to seek financial aid, for example, she might count on the good will of these same merchants to help her. If she borrows, however, she will guard her honor at all points by paying back on time what she owes, so that her word may be good in all matters and confidence in her increased.

Now perhaps some will call all this bad advice, says Christine, never one to slide over objections, and will say that it is for a princess to command what pleases her, and for her subjects to obey and take pains to gain her love, never her part to gain theirs; otherwise they are not subjects and she is not mistress. These are wrong for two out of many reasons that might be given. First, although the prince is lord of his subjects, and wishes to be held for such, he would only too easily find, if they wished to harm him, that no one would hold him for lord. And for this reason and also because he would not be able all alone to subdue them if they were rebellious, and even if he had the power to destroy them, they would defend themselves, it is necessary that the prince hold them by love that comes from fear and not by force. Otherwise his lordship hangs in the balance. The proverb is true that he who is hated is never lord of his country. Therefore the prince who wishes to be called lord can show his good sense no better than to hold his subjects in love, for no fortress is so strong as the love and good will of true subjects. Secondly, assume that subjects have good will toward their prince and princess, they would never be bold enough to come familiarly to them unless they were sent for, nor would it be fitting for them to do so. So then the first advance must come from their rulers. And rightly subjects make a joyful to-do when they are shown honor, and their love and loyalty ought to be doubled in proportion to the sweetness they find at court. The princess will also have their wives visit her at times, and she will hold her great court to celebrate their lyings-in, and the marriages of their children, and will want them to be in the company of her ladies and maids. Thus they will be pleased and praise her wisdom, and she will gain great love among them.[17]

According to the way of the world, however, nobody is so just that all love him, and the most perfect would arouse envy. All prudent people will be well aware of this and look for a remedy. What should a princess know in order to conduct herself discreetly toward those who do not like her, or are enemies of her? This is a very different matter from previous considerations, writes Christine, for a woman follows her natural inclinations when she cares for her husband, children, and friends, but now it is a question of knowing how to vanquish and control her courage and will, a thing, as it were, against nature. So much the more then is this knowledge worthy of recommendation, and the person who knows how to use it is the more to be praised. For such self-control is a sign of very great strength and constancy in courage, which is among the cardinal virtues and without doubt always necessary to the wise lady and princess who loves the prize of honor, praise, and renown; otherwise her prudence cannot well be shown, or made known, or be perfect.

Therefore, if the princess sees that any of the powerful do not wish her well, but would hurt her if possible, estrange from her her lord, who might perhaps believe their blandishments and flatteries, or put her by false reports in bad repute with barons and subjects, she will pretend not to see anything of this, or to hold them as her enemies. But by turning a welcoming face toward them she will make them think that she holds them for friends. She will have the good sense and self-control not to overdo her part, for once her smile is perceived to be forced all would be ruined. Good sense keeps measure in this matter, and she will have to take thought beforehand how she will conduct herself, if she feigns that she wishes to be governed by them and their advice and calls them into her councils. She will speak of ordinary matters in great secrecy and confidence, contrary to her belief but in such a manner that they do not take her off guard and she remains mistress of her mouth. For if any word she says of them afterward is opposed to what they assumed, she would be in danger, since there is no great lord or lady to whom all their servants are loyal. But the heart that is great and full, with difficulty forever keeps silence about what displeases it, and in that lies her real danger. For if she betrays her true feeling her enemies will know that she knows they are not her friends and is merely pretending, and then they will think she is afraid and will esteem her less and only be more bold in harming her. If someone reports evil of her enemies to her and she thinks her reply will go back to them, she will blame the reporter and say that on the contrary she knows well that they wish her good fortune and honor, and are her good and loyal friends. If they do or say something to her prejudice that she can interpret as done or said for some other cause than evil, again she will act the part of the simple or ignorant that has not seen it and seems not to have been touched and not to have any suspicion against them. Yet she will seek to know all that she can about them and will be on her guard. So the wise lady will resort to this discreet dissimulation and prudent deceit, which is no vice but a great virtue when used in the cause of good and peace and to avoid harm without harming another. And here is the evil escaped and the good done by this feigning. If she acknowledges the evil done to her, she will have to oppose her enemies and take pains to avenge herself with resulting disorder, war, peril to her friends, and perhaps her lord will believe them rather than her. All a much greater evil than enduring and dissembling, which may even appease the anger of her enemies, at least disarm them, for they would not have the heart to hurt her as much as if she showed herself their enemy. Very disloyal and evil would anyone have to be to wish to harm one who thought him her friend. If their treason, moreover, becomes too great and therefore apparent to the world, then they would be so much the more dishonored and accomplish less, for everyone would blame them. There is no doubt that the lady gains more in such a case by holding herself as advised.[18]

Last of all the lessons of prudence for the wise princess, Christine handles the subject of how she will take care of her revenues, finances, and state at court. She will not be ashamed to wish to know the total of her revenues or pensions and to have the accounts of her receipts and expenditures brought to her on appointed days. She will want to know how her chief stewards govern their people and order their common life, and distribute food and offices of her court, and there will be nothing great or small of which she will not want to be informed, in order to know whether they are prudent, honest, and good men. If she finds they are not, she will dismiss them. She will know very well what expenses come to, what has been bought of merchants for her and in her name for others, and will order that they be paid at stated times, for she will not want their curses and hate and will prefer to live on less and spend more soberly than owe anybody. She will forbid taking anything from people against their will, and will pay what is just, and not make poor people of the towns and elsewhere come at great cost and trouble a hundred times and more, but appoint a place in her chamber where all can be paid. Nor will she want her treasurers or distributors of money to use the common fashion, that is to say be liars, leading the people on from term to term to think that they can pay them. Thus she will budget her finances into five parts: 1. Gifts to the poor. 2. The support of her house —she will know what it costs, to see whether it is as much as it ought to be considering her income, and that her lord does not administer it without her having a say about it. 3. Pay of her officials and women. 4. Gifts to strangers or others who will do her unusual service. 5. A fund left in the treasury on which she will draw at her pleasure what she wishes for jewels and clothing. Each part will be as large as she can make it proportionate to her revenue. By this rule she can keep order and not fail to have money for all these things.

On the fourth, a special aspect of liberality, Christine has some particular advice to give. The wise princess will guard herself from niggardly and also from foolish giving, and will exercise great discretion in making her gifts since this is one of the greatest things in the world that exalt lords and ladies, and is even necessary for them. There are special cases that should command attention. She will keep herself well informed about foreign gentlemen or others who have lost much by being imprisoned or ransomed, or who are in great need, and will aid them willingly according to her power, and graciously comfort them by encouraging them to hope for better fortune, which may mean more than her gift, for people value highly such words from a prince or princess. Further, if she sees any gentleman, whether knight or squire, of good courage and of good will to advance himself but with no great chance, and if she sees that he will be well employed, she will aid him for the honor of gentility. The receipt of presents also calls for liberality. If the presents are from great lords, she will reward the messengers so generously that they can praise her, and she will give more if they are foreigners than not, so that in their country they will tell their lords of her generosity, and she will want all to be done in good form. If the presents come from great ladies she will send them the like in her jewels, and even more beautiful things. But if a poor or simple person does her any service or presents her something unusual, out of her good will she will consider the means of the person, his rank, the greatness of the service, or its value, or goodness, or beauty, or strangeness, and she will reward him so well that he can take satisfaction from it, and with such a joyful aspect will she accept his gift that that will be half payment.[19]

To finish what belongs to a wise princess, Christine considers the excuses that will serve one who cannot, for any reason, put into effect the above rules. Suppose she has a husband of a peculiar sort, who holds her so restricted that she can speak with difficulty even to her servants and people of the household, and also so short of money that she hasn't a sou, as indeed enough of them do. To her prudence can give no advice except to be patient, do what good is in her power, and obey for the sake of peace. The man is too foolish of any estate, when he sees that he has a good and wise wife, not to give her authority to govern her affairs. However, there are too many so ill turned and so witless that they don't know how to see or recognize where goodness and sense are seated, and are set in their opinion that women do not have sense enough to govern, though we often see the contrary. These same women, however, held so short cannot be prevented by their husbands from being loved by their subjects if they are good, wise, and loving to them as much as is in their power, nor can they be prevented from being renowned for their good will, their acts, their discreet and good bearing.[20]

So far, as Christine says, she has been writing for women of authority, sense, and maturity, not the young who still are under the direction of other ladies, though, if they will study this teaching of hers and retain it, they will know how to govern themselves with prudence, and then when they reach an age of greater discretion, they may be given authority to do and govern as has been said, because their husbands and lords will see them of such wisdom. But she does have some particular advice for the young princess newly married. Such a princess should have in her train both men and women of a rank suitable to the rank of the prince, her lord. The gentlemen who serve her should not be too young, or talkative, or flattering, but wise and experienced. If they are married, so much the better, especially those who serve her at table and are most often around her and her women, and it is well for their wives also to live at court. Her confessor, the better to teach her what belongs to her soul, should be wise, learned in divinity, prudent in behavior, of good common sense, chaste, and upright. With regard to her women, it is all the more important on account of her youth that they should all, both old and young, be beyond reproach in character and life, because from the state and behavior of her companions is commonly judged her own character and if they are not good she will be supposed not to be good either, and also because a young mistress will take teaching and example from her women, good or bad as they are.

Because of her youth she ought to have one lady of sufficient age, wise, prudent, good, honest, and devout to whom is particularly entrusted her care, although perhaps there will be many of higher rank and relatives brought to court for her honor and company. This lady will have the difficult task of guiding amd maintaining her mistress in such wise conduct and good morals as cannot stain her honor, and of always keeping her favor and holding her by love. She must work with great discretion, prevent trouble before it happens, be on guard at all hours against any possible danger, and search often through the house, especially in the evening for fear some servant has carelessly left candle or wick or other thing that can cause harm. She will go about her ends not all at once, but will first take pains to seek to gain the love of her young mistress by her sweet and courteous manner, by giving her things that are pleasing to the young, and by showing herself loving. When they are by themselves she will order games and plays, and sometimes tell the tales and fables which are told to children to attract her mistress, only a child herself, in order that correction and instruction may be taken with better grace when they are necessary. For if this good lady pursues always a sober way without laughter or play, youth, which is inclined to joy and pleasure, will not endure it but will hold her in such great fear that dislike will follow and her corrections be taken in bad grace. When the lady sees her mistress pleased with her, then according to her age or the feeling she sees in her, in their chambers she will tell stories of ladies and damoiselles who are well behaved, how much they are honored, and on the contrary what evil befalls those who behave foolishly, and thus she will move the hearts of her mistress and all who gather around her and willingly listen. Sometimes it will be stories of saints of both sexes, and sometimes, to avoid boredom, stories that will make them laugh. And each will make up something in her turn. Because youth appropriately laughs and plays, she will give her mistress enough time at certain hours with her young companions. She will teach her some good and brief prayers and exhort her to say them on rising, telling her she has heard that anyone who addresses her first words to God will have no ill adventure that day. She will have her mistress dressed becomingly without being too long about it as many ladies are, with great waste, and she will teach her all the things of behavior, speech, countenance, and clothes that belong to a high princess, so that people will say that for her youth they have never seen a lady so well behaved. This is all on the assumption that she is of a good disposition and wishes to be such. For some are not. Correction for some fault of youth will have to take the difference into account. If the princess is sweet and good and loves the lady, she will be afraid of losing her and will be corrected with little threatening; but if she is perverse, the lady will take her apart and tell her sharply that she will go to her relatives and friends, or her lord.

The wise lady in charge of this young princess will also teach her what she owes her lord. If he is young and the lady sees between them the love that young married people commonly have for each other, she will do all in her power to nourish that love and exhort them to say sweet and loving words to each other and to enjoy all the pleasures of love. She herself will take great care to carry between them gracious messages and gifts and commendations and salutations to keep them always in peace and love, and she will work to keep out all contrary things. And when her lord is not there and her mistress is in bed, she will please her by telling her the good words she has often heard him say of his love for her, and how good he is and handsome and gracious and the like.

Since even the young princess cannot live a completely secluded life, the problems of mixed company and public assemblies will have to be met by this wise lady. She will have to teach her young charge how to meet and talk to the lords, knights, esquires, strangers, and others that custom allows to come sometimes to princesses and ladies and that their lords and relatives bring to them, and how to behave at feasts and dances. At such assemblies it sometimes happens that men are taken with love of ladies, or wish to pretend that they are. The lady, who will always be near her mistress on these occasions, will be quick to perceive what some young may be thinking, but she will say nothing to anyone. When they return home and are alone her mistress may say that so-and-so was very gracious, and then the wise lady will reply, "I don't know that he is, but I have never seen anyone so pleasant, handsome, gracious as my lord." If the lord is old, she will say, "Certainly I looked at nobody but my lord. Among the others he seemed indeed the lord and prince, and how well he spoke." Of what she thinks she will say nothing but watch to see whether any seek the company of her mistress, trying to make her acquaintance through relatives or friends, or whether they or any of their men try to make the acquaintance of any of her women. If not, she can rest in peace, but if so, then she will take great care and thought to find a remedy and do her duty, working very wisely and secretly. If the young man is bold, she will greet him so pleasantly that he will be persuaded she is worth most to him since she is nearest the princess, and she will have all his offers, and then well provided with an answer she will say:

"Sir, I knew well that you had in your heart what you have said to me and therefore I wished that such words would come from you, and desired your acquaintance so that I rather than another might know. And without a long sermon or too many words I wish to say once for all that so long as I am alive and in her company, this young lady, who by the confidence of her friends and her lord has been put in my charge, shall do no evil, nothing from which reproaches come, or hear words other than are fitting for a lady such as she is. For with the aid of God I trust well to defend her. Not that she is not easy to guard. I know well all her love is in her lord as it ought to be and she is all good and well conditioned and never thinks of such loves. And so I know that if you or any other had said this to her she would hate above all things one who had her trust and yet thought such a thing toward her. So I beg you, Sir, as earnestly as I can that you no longer desire to do or even think of this, for I swear that you will lose your pains. And in order that you may have no hope I swear to you upon my soul that even if she wished it (which I know well she never would) I would put up such bars she could not."

The lady will show no change in her face when she leaves him, but keep a calm look and assured manner as if they had talked of other matters, in order that no one else may know. Of course she will not be able to prevent his coming and going by some concealed way that he finds through some acquaintance, for if she spoke too great harm would result. Then she will put up with it and guard her lady closely. But if, in spite of her close guarding, she cannot prevent her mistress from learning his intention by covert words, still she will not be alarmed because she knows that many ladies and damoiselles have love made to them by someone who may be a little inflamed but yet never loves them. She will, however, take great care to find out whether her lady feels any more pleasure in speaking of him than of another, or is particularly happy when she sees him. Thus when they are quite alone, with great pains by sweet words she will draw from her what is in her heart concerning this man, and whether he has touched or spoken to her, and reply accordingly. If the princess says that he troubles her, and she clearly has no such thought as his, the lady will be joyful and exhort her to hold to her good purpose. She will tell examples of evil that can come, dishonor, reproaches, deceptions in men, and she will tell her how to reply wisely when he speaks to her of love, and how, showing no signs of being moved or displeased by such words, she will hold him off the best she can and guard well her words, smiles, anything in her face by which she can attract or give him any hope. When he asks for her, she will have him told she is resting, or busy and cannot see him this time. Then at last he will see that he loses his pains. And the lady will warn her mistress not to say anything of this to man or woman for evil can come of it, and it is good sense to be silent, nor is it any point of honor in a woman to boast of such a thing. Also her silence will be a protection to her, for she might choose a confidant who would not give her good counsel but encourage her in folly.

What if the princess shows herself by certain signs bent on folly and unwilling to follow wise counsel, though she denies it? The lady will grieve, but she must do her duty and admonish her charge of her danger without dissembling or concealment in sweet or threatening words, and turn her if she can from her thought. But if nothing avails and she sees her conversing on the side with some of the other women, taking messages from the outside, avoiding her in everything, and of such a haughty spirit that she obviously no longer wishes to accept her guidance but replies proudly, and mocks at her with her women—"What the devil shall we do with this old thing? She does nothing but scold. The fires of hell take her;" and another says, "You have only to order pitch to be smeared on the steps to break her neck"—obviously there is no remedy to be had. It is impossible to guard one who will not guard herself. Then this lady will have to weigh the good of remaining at court. If she stays, the affair would not die but would ultimately come to the knowledge either of the relatives or husband of her princess, who would then blame her and ask why she did not tell them so that they could have found a remedy. She might do that, but what of the dangers and evils that could follow? Well may one hesitate to report such things to husband, or relatives, or anyone. To stay longer would not be without great peril from the hate of mistress or lover since they would fear and doubt her, and think she would thwart them. If wise she will use her great wisdom and art in taking action. She will keep everything to herself, speak no more of good or evil to her mistress, and appear to have no displeasure in her heart. She will leave the court but in order to conceal

her real reason for going she will give some other—sickness, age, or un-
fitness to be around her lady because of some weakness that needs to be
cured. This same mistress perhaps will not actually want her to go because
she will think herself freer to do as she wishes while she has her, people not
being disposed to talk so much when she is in the company of such a lady,
and so she will flatter her and make her inducements to stay. But the good
lady will know how to excuse herself by saying that she is indeed ill now
but will return when cured; and not for any tenderness toward her mistress
will she consider staying because of such blandishments, if she is wise, for
afterward she would repent. If her lady is glad of her departure and makes
no protest, when she comes to go she will speak to her on her knees, humbly
thanking her for all her kindness and honors, and begging her pardon for
any displeasure she has caused out of only her own love and jealousy, and
she will end that she is sad to leave her but is old and weak and unfit to
serve longer, and never will her lady have one who will serve her more
loyally or honor her more. Then the princess may reply kindly since she is
glad of her departure, and say that she knows nothing against her except
the accusations the lady has made. The lady will know enough not to
argue, and will answer merely that her suspicions grew out of her great
fear for her charge, and will beg her to pardon her, and promise never to
reveal her suspicions to anyone, and then she will depart. Christine here
recommends for study The Epistles she wrote in *The Duke of True Lovers*
which Sabille sent the duchess in similar circumstances.[21]

To princesses both young and mature Christine has something to say
in the event of widowhood. As far as she follows the line addressed to
widows in general—their mourning, their devotion to their husband's
memory, their carrying out of his wishes—we will not need to repeat, but
we will touch on the points arising specially out of the rank of these widows.
The older princess who has children of age will take great care, if the father
has not, to divide the lands between them with great circumspection and
on the advice of the barons and wise men of the council, and she will work
with all her power to hold them together in love and peace. If it happens
that her sons are still under age, and war or contest arises among the barons
over the government, she will employ all her prudence and wisdom to put
and hold them at peace. No foreign war could be so ruinous as this. If it
happens that some lands rebel, or the country is attacked by enemies, as
often does happen when the heir is under age, she will have need of great
prudence to guard the possessions of her children. She must work to hold by
sweet words the love of the barons and lords in order to keep them loyal
and get good counsel from them, and also of the knights, esquires, and
gentlemen that they may fight boldly at need, and of the people that they
may support such a war for their young lord. If she has no children she will
take due account of what belongs to her, and if anyone wishes to deprive

her of her right, as often is done to widows great and small, she will seek
good counsel and use it in guarding her right boldly by law and reason,
without heated words to anyone, but reasonably and courteously. But she
will guard her right. The young widow without children will go back to
live in her own land for more ease. Then she will look to the good of her
people in the same ways advised to the mature princess above, only perhaps on a smaller scale, sending for the principal men, the bailiffs of her
castles, to learn how they have governed, keeping the good, replacing the
bad, courteously entertaining her officials and their wives, and the ladies
of the country, also the bourgoisie, and the little women of the villages of
whom she will make much, with praise for their little gifts and talk about
their food and housekeeping and visits in childbirth to both rich and poor,
in general making gifts to the poor, honoring the rich, and holding their
children as hers. Such were the ways, says Christine, that very noble queens
and princesses of France held in their widowhood, Queen Jeanne, Queen
Blanche, the Duchess of Orleans. So the young widow will live simply and
chastely as before, only still more circumspectly. Specially she will avoid
all talk of marriage with anyone apart, concealed or without the knowledge
of her friends, for this will never be to her honor and she can be much deceived. In everything she ought to consult her friends and do nothing
without them, for to marry at her will without their consent would incur
great blame, and indeed she ought to think that they know better than
she what is good for her. The very young widow of course will go back to
her parents and be under their government again, obedient as before in
all things.[22]

Up to this point Christine has been considering, she explains, powerful
ladies, queens, duchesses called princes by common usage of the place as in
Italy and elsewhere, and countesses, not all of them called princesses in all
countries, but all covered here by the term princess. Other ladies who dwell
in castles or other manors on their lands, or in closed towns are somewhat
different in power and state and it is therefore fitting to speak of some
things belonging specially to them. She takes up first the baronesses of
France, Brittany, and other parts who surpass in honor and power many
countesses although the name of baron is not so high as that of count. The
power of some barons is very great because of their lands, through which
their wives hold very great estate. No doubt it belongs to a baron who
wishes to be honored in his rank to spend the least time at home, for to
follow arms, attend the court of his lord, or travel is his office. His lady
stays at home to represent him, and, although there are enough officials,
to be sovereign over all. She should rule with such wisdom that she is
feared and loved, and next to her lord is a refuge to his men. She must know
the laws and customs of the place in case of need to defend herself against
those that would harm her. She should be sweet, humble, and charitable

to the obedient, and work with the counselors of her lord, listening to the opinions of the wise old men to avert blame from herself and specially the charge that she wishes to act out of her own head. She must in truth, however, have the heart of a man: that is, know the laws of arms and everything that belongs to them so that she is ready to command her men if necessary in attack and defense; see that her fortresses are well provisioned if she is in any doubt or of a mind to undertake anything; test her men to know their courage and will lest she trust them too much; look to what power she has in men and what help outside she can call on so that she is certain not to wait in vain on foolish promises; take care how she will be able to provide when her lord comes—what money she has and can have to do this; guard herself the best she can from too heavily taxing her subjects for from that one gets too much their hate; speak boldly and firmly to them of what will be deliberated in council, not giving one reason today, another tomorrow; and by her brave and high words give courage to her men-at-arms and spur them to be good and loyal. So should the wise baroness do whose husband has given her charge in his absence. What has been said of the widows of princes is expedient for her also if she is widowed.

The wives of knights, squires, and other gentlemen who travel or follow the wars must be wise in government also because for the most part they live at home without their husbands. It is fitting that they have the government of their estates, and particularly that they know well the revenues and, as much as they can, persuade their lords to live within their income and not so much above that at the end of the year they find themselves in debt to their people and other creditors. It is no shame to live according to income however small, but a great shame if their creditors are always raising a clamor at their doors, or if by necessity they tax their people extortionately. Such a lady must know what taxes are due her that she may not be deceived, as many are ready to deceive her, but she should be pitiful rather than rigorous to the poor. She must be a good manager, know all the business of her farms: the seasons to sow crops, the best ways of cultivating the land in a dry or wet country, the depth of the soil, the crops best suited to the soil, and the same for vines. She must see that she has good laborers and overseers in each office, not too old for then they are weak and lazy, not too young for then they are too ready for play. To make sure that they rise early she will rise early, and throwing on a robe go to her window to see that they start out. She will go to the fields herself to see how they work, for they know very well how to sleep in the fields under a tree, leaving their work-horses or cattle to graze in a pasture and not heating them except enough to say in the evening that they have done their day's work. And she will early take measures for the disposal of her harvests and when the time comes to sell take precautions that her agents play no tricks to defraud her. Rising early is necessary for overseeing, for there are also her shepherds to watch, to learn how they care for their animals, not neglectful but guarding them from too hot a sun and from rain. If she goes often with one of her women to see how they work, the shepherds will be more careful of the lambs, which often die for lack of care. She will be present at the shearing. If she has great fields and pastures she will have many cattle and raise calves, which will bring her money when they are big. In winter she will keep her men well employed cutting wood for the fires, and making things which can be sold. Likewise she will look after her women and chambermaids, to keep them busy. She and her daughters and girls will employ themselves making cloth for every sort of purpose, too many to tell.

Christine has a special word also for the daughters of gentlemen who find themselves married to rich men of the cities and towns, bourgeois, or big merchants. They are not the worse married, she says, if they take it rightly. Some from want of sense, or from pride, are discontent because they think their husbands lowborn in comparison to themselves. A great folly. No one is a lowborn boor unless he acts it, no one a gentleman unless he is virtuous. They should show themselves gentlewomen by their good morals and deeds. They should humble themselves before their husbands in obedience and reverence, as the law of marriage requires, for thus they increase their honor; in the company of other women they should be found courteous, humble, humane; to their servants they should not be too bold or demanding of service; to all people it is their duty to be amiable and kind, of themselves honorable in bearing, manners, and clothing.

Up to this point Christine has been addressing only women of some authority. When she proceeds to consider those below, wives of clerks and of people in the council of kings or princes or justices or clergy, also of the bourgeois and merchants of ancient lineage, she directs them to what has already been said, for each, if she looks, will find something appropriate to her, unlike some foolish people who are too pleased to listen to the preacher as long as he speaks about the duties of another rank than theirs and say he is right and preaches well, but who when he comes to their own duties lower their heads and shut their ears as if he were doing great wrong to speak of them. The wise preacher speaks to all so that one set cannot murmur and mock at the other. The advice that she proceeds to direct to these wives who have no authority outside of their houses but who have substance follows the line of all advice to wives as just wives, assuming for them closer personal relations with their husbands and more intimate care of everything including the clothing of their husbands, the overseeing of all household activities, particularly meals and entertainment of guests of honor, than for the others.[23]

Beyond these even, Christine has much more to say to women, to the "little" women to whom she has exhorted great ladies to be kind, and to ladies themselves on matters already discussed in other chapters. Two more pieces of advice may be added here because they are addressed to women of all ranks, and because they will not be found elsewhere in the same detail. Discontent with one's station expressed by restless striving to seem to be someone else, with its necessary accompaniment of extravagant spending, seems to Christine a prevailing, serious fault of the times. In the upper ranks each tries to dress like that above, duchesses like queens, countesses like duchesses, simple ladies like countesses, damoiselles like ladies. No rule is held. If anyone puts on extreme dress, the rest follow. Fashions change constantly, in France more than elsewhere. The results are lamentable. Pride comes from all this false emulation and display, and envy. Friendships are broken. Poverty follows too much expenditure for such things, and it is a great shame to be in debt to dressmakers and all the rest employed to satisfy this pride. Yet husbands even encourage their wives in their folly and are angry if they do not keep up with the rest, thinking, "I am more a gentleman than he, so my wife should go before his, and the other will think I am richer or in higher office." Even the churches are invaded with this ostentation, especially in Paris, Picardy, and Brittany, Christine says. Priests and bishops should refuse church offices to women so unfittingly garbed for them. The same senseless struggle goes on at every level. The ordinary laborer's wife wants to dress like an artisan's wife, the artisan's wife like her better, the merchant's like those above as far up as his wealth will carry her. Such disorder is not fitting, particularly in France, which is the most noble realm in the world, says this adopted daughter, and where all things ought to be best ordered. Because of their wealth the wives of merchants have become the greatest sinners in this respect. The merchants of France are not like those of Italy, Venice, or Genoa for example, who go beyond the sea and have agents in all countries, buy wholesale at great cost and then send their merchandise to all countries in great consignments and so gain great riches, and are called noble merchants. But those of France buy wholesale and sell retail for four sous or more or less, though they may become rich. Then it is a sight to see what establishments they set up.

One such so surpassed others that it was worth putting into a book, said Christine. The world was invited to celebrate the lying-in of this merchant's wife. To reach her chamber you had to pass through two other very beautiful chambers, in each of which was a big bed, well and richly curtained, and in the second a great open cupboard covered like an altar with silver vessels. From this you entered the room of the wife all curtained with tapestry made to her design worked very richly with fine gold, furnished with a handsome bed likewise curtained with a most beautiful gold-embroidered fabric, and rugs all like gold on the floor around the bed to walk on. The great sheets of rich material showed under a covering of such fine linen of Rheims that it was valued at three hundred francs, and over this covering which was worked with gold was spread another wide sheet of linen soft as silk, made all in one piece without a seam, by a method newly discovered and of great cost estimated at two hundred francs and more. This was so large that it covered the whole bed and hung down on all sides. And in this chamber was a great ornamented cupboard covered with gold vessels. In the bed was the wife of the merchant dressed like a damoiselle in crimson silk and huge pearl buttons against big pillows covered with the same silk. And God knows all the other superfluous expenditure for feasts, baths, and various gatherings, according to the custom of Paris at lyings-in. A report of this affair reached the chamber of the Queen, where some said the merchants of Paris had too much blood, at times a cause of various diseases—that is to say that great wealth can well lead people astray—and therefore it would be better that the king tax them so that their wives might not vie with the Queen of France, who scarcely had more. Pride and not sense lies in such goings-on was Christine's comment, and those who affect them do not acquire esteem but scorn, for although they assume the state of high ladies or princesses they are not such, nor are they called such. They do not lose the name of merchants, or wives of merchants, or rather vendors and not merchants since they sell retail. It is great folly to clothe oneself in the habit of another, when everyone knows well what he is. If those who commit such excesses would leave their merchandising and take on altogether the state of lords it would make sense, but it is too foolish not to be ashamed to sell their goods and yet to be ashamed of the costume that goes with the work, which is very beautiful, honest, and maintained by law, and the state of merchant is good and honorable in France and in every country. So their wives should keep from superfluities which are not good for the body or soul and can be the cause that their husbands are charged with some new tax. If they are rich, let them use their wealth for the poor.[24]

The other passage, abandoning distinctions between the classes, considers the proper behavior of women to women, of old women to young and the young to the old, between whom commonly, observes Christine, is debate and discord. And first the old, who, having more perfect understanding and more experience, are wiser than the young, and should show that wisdom in every way, in act, in dress, in face, in word, and avoid what can be taken as folly—dancing, playing, laughing foolishly. If joyous they should take their joys not like the young, but more calmly. Foolish old people are the worst. The old need to guard against the passions of age, anger, stinginess, and bad humor. "Who are you?" let the old woman say to herself. "You can't cure everything that displeases. Be more peaceable, don't speak ungraciously—look at your face when you do. Be more

sociable and pleasant to your people, and when you must reprove them
do it more courteously. Have patience, beware of anger. Speak discreetly,
foolish words from the old cause ridicule." And as to contention with the
young, when she is moved in thought and word against young people
because of their youth, she should say to herself, "You were young once,
you did these things in your time. Would you have wanted old people to
speak so to you? Think how great are the tempests of youth and have
pity, for you have passed this way." One ought to reprove youth for follies
but never to hate or defame. Age has enough faults of its own. Then to
the young Christine lays down five rules for their behavior to the old: 1.
Show them reverence, don't mock, or displease, or argue with them. 2.
Obey them because they are wiser, and listen to their counsels. 3. Fear
them as your father and mother. 4. Aid and comfort them—there is no
greater infirmity than old age. 5. Consider the good you have received
from them, sciences, laws, and so forth.[25]

We have followed Christine closely a long way, even beyond the court,
because she alone has written at such length on women at court, and she
has differentiated between ladies and women of lower birth, where differentiation has point. As has been said earlier, one of the striking characteristics of writers on ideal behavior for the lady, the woman of the privileged classes, is the lack of accommodation of their advice to the position
she held in society. The lady in their minds evidently was first of all a
wife, first and last a wife we may say, for most of them never got beyond
that fact. The result is that the books addressed to the lady might as
well have been addressed to women of the lower classes, and therefore
fail to depict in more than the vaguest way the lady as such, whereas
the books addressed to the gentleman are cut to fit him at every point.
The Christian Woman of Vives is an excellent illustration of the type.
Though he dedicated his book to Queen Catherine, and told her that
in it he had presented her image, to be a model to her daughter, the
Princess Mary, as the title warns, he then completely ignores the queen
and the princess and presents an image of any woman, every woman. He
of course intended a book which could go into the hands of every woman,
and it may be that in the Queen he saw only the woman, but the problems
of a queen, terrible problems for that Queen, are left untouched, nor could
Mary have learned there the lessons she needed for the court roles that
she must play. The Queen was noted for her learning, and her wit in the
disputes she loved to institute with the learned and witty men she gathered
at court. Vives' image of her omits all that side. Henry found her no mean
antagonist when the final struggle came between them. In Christine de
Pisan's counsel for princesses Catherine would have found much to support
if not instruct her. It is probably true to say that Vives expected his princesses to extend his directions to fit their needs, but Christine began at

the top with the extensions and when she came lower, advised humbler women to take what belonged to them from the advice already given, and then noted the necessary additions. Thus she showed the place of all in the social scheme, and though she illustrated the common lot of all women she did not level all distinctions, as almost all other writers in effect did.

In this chapter, obviously, we come the nearest to a conception of the woman of the privileged classes, the lady, as an embodiment of human perfection from the same point of view and in the same terms that the man of the privileged classes, the gentleman, was considered; that is, as an individual set off from others less fortunate by birth, training, wealth, position, enabled therefore to develop all his powers to their height, and given authority and responsibility for the welfare of the state. The fundamental pattern for women is kept here, modesty, chastity, sweetness, gentleness, piety, unselfishness, devotion to husband and children, and the capacity to run a household well. But this is not the whole woman as it is in other views, and these very virtues are modified and enlarged to fit the loftier role of the lady. If modesty is prescribed, it is with a warning against excess that leads to foolishness. Food and drink are to be regulated by considerations of health, not the avoidance of drunkenness and lasciviousness. Dress is to be suited to station, occasion, and physical type, and not governed solely by desire to avoid arousing the concupiscence of susceptible men. If chastity is prescribed, it is not made the sole aim and test of all the other virtues, but it is rather assumed to follow naturally the exercise of the other virtues. If talking little is recommended, it is to the very young for their lack of experience, or on special occasions. Silence can injure as much as speech, Guasco warned his daughter. On the contrary the great art most essential to the lady is shown to be the art of speech: discourse with every sort of people, men and women, courtiers, churchmen, and merchants, fine ladies and bakers' wives, foreigners; on every sort of subject, the great sports of riding, hunting, feats of arms, government, love, domestic matters; on every sort of occasion, leisure hours in mixed company where talk of love and witty jesting were most appropriate, conferences with the wise men of the state, visits to the poor and the sick. If liberality is exhorted, it is not merely the giving of alms to the poor but the bestowing of great benefits, building of churches, support of ambitious youth, to the enhancing of princely or lesser reputations. If we look at these views of the woman at court as courtier, or as princess, and the woman of lesser rank in her castle and of still lower degree in her manor, presented in these few books, the picture emerges of a woman taken seriously, taken for granted, trained like a man to rule her realm great or small with wisdom, justice, and humanity, and, as a woman, with sweetness too. Intelligence, truth, sincerity, and sheer goodness are assumed at every point. It is where consideration of actual circumstances enters that the lady comes clearest. Wives of lords had to bear responsibility for the ordering of things within doors and, in the absence of their lords, without doors also, even to the command of their armed men when castles and lands were involved, and of the laborers in the fields when the farming of estates was the chief concern. For gentlemen and lords went away in the service of their rulers or on business and seem more likely to have been away most of their time than at home. Most unrealistic then were the books on ladies that in pretending to portray the ideal reduced them to the level of the most humble housewife.

But these same reductions to mediocrity and nonentity usurp the scene. To hundreds of such books can be opposed only a handful of these books on the lady of the palace, castle, and manor. It is impossible to frame the prevailing theory of the lady from these that come the nearest to presenting anything that may claim to be a theory of the lady. What men thought the ideal should be must be taken from the mass of witnesses, and they show not a lady but a woman, and a woman who is a wife.

CHAPTER EIGHT : *Conclusion*

Such, then, were the ideas on ladies current in the renaissance, as faithfully presented as possible. The warning of the introduction is clearly justified: these chapters do not add up to a single, commanding figure as the chapters on the gentleman did. In place of the stately definition of the dignity of highborn men, the position of highborn women with reference to men must be sought in the vilifications and exaggerations of attacks on the fundamental nature of women and defenses often as humiliating and exaggerated. From such arguments a portrait of an ideal woman does emerge. Theories on the proper upbringing and education of women are restricted to preparation for the one vocation recommended to all but a chosen few, and the ideal that emerges here is purely and simply the wife, wholly built on requirements of a husband and therefore different in some respects and particularly in tone from the first portrait. Into another world entirely is the lady removed when love and beauty become the end-all and be-all of her existence. Some of the words are the same, but they mean other things. Little in all these views belongs to the lady at court, where she comes nearest being considered in her own right, but her peculiar offices or her powers set her off from ordinary ladies, and hence the few books that look at her with unprejudiced eye, even setting aside their fewness, do not paint a general ideal of the essential lady, as the books addressed to gentlemen do present the essential gentleman, who came before the nobleman. For a conclusion, it is clear, a summary or synthesis is impossible. Each chapter has had to have its own conclusion. To bring this study of the renaissance lady to a close, therefore, I should like to touch on aspects that might have been discussed but were not, partly to fill in cracks, partly to suggest further studies, though in doing so I may seem to be riding off in all directions rather than drawing in.

Following the full tide of the renaissance from Italy to England has taken us over a good two hundred years, roughly from 1400 to 1600, with glances behind and ahead. The slowness with which Italian ideas and patterns moved northward into France and England accounts for the spread. It was Italy of course that defined and ruled, one might say invented, the renaissance. On the subject of women particularly there is an underlying, long-drawn-out continuity in time and space, from Barberino even of the beginning of the fourteenth century to Du Bosc and Braithwait well over the edge of the seventeenth century, or if it pleases more to find unity in dissection for dispraise, from Boccaccio's *Laberinto* to Olivier's *Alphabet*. The differences are far less significant than the resemblances, and lie rather in external conditions than in expressed ideas. Writers themselves seem to have been little interested in national differences, chiefly, it may be presumed, because they all draw their ideas from common sources, Aristotle, Plato, Cicero, Jerome, Paul, and because nationalism was only beginning to rise in the sixteenth century. The same lack of national consciousness appears elsewhere, in writers on statecraft for example, who seldom trouble to fit generalizations to their particular courts or even to illustrate them from national and contemporary sources. To suggest what sort of modifications may be looked for here I will note the few comments and comparisons that turned up.

There seems to have been general belief that the women of France were freer than elsewhere. More than one Frenchman claims it, and others support the claim. Billon, writing in 1550, said that in France women were more free and better treated than in Germany where they were forced to carry baggage after an army, and were reduced to the basest kind of work as servants, and also than in Italy where if they were honest and good they were jealously shut indoors so that sometimes even brothers dared not approach—only strumpets were free. And by that token he held the greatness of France proved since in all the nations of Europe where women were held more subject the men were too.[1] Guazzo seems to agree for he remarked that in France, in particular, måids were free to refuse or accept husbands, and men had free access to houses where maids were and might entertain them with easy familiarity.[2] It was in Italy and England, said Erasmus, that very young girls would be found married to old men, really old men of seventy.[3] The English, however, came off not too badly in comparison with the French, for their ladies were famous, or notorious according to the point of view, on the Continent for their freedom. Sir Thomas Smith may be taken as giving a judicious statement of the case when he said in his *De Republica Anglorum* that English wives had more liberty than Italian or Spanish, almost as much as French, and for the most part had the management of the household.[4] The English on other points seem to have had a more liberal attitude. For instance Elyot, as we have seen, argued in favor of later marriage for the sake of better training of the girl, where the Italians urged early marriage to increase the chance of preserving virginity until marriage,[5] and Cleaver could even advise young people to see each other frequently and under all conditions so as to judge each other well.[6] Mulcaster sent girls to the elementary school with boys, and preferred men as tutors to girls for the sake of more solid education.[7] In one respect Italian women seem freer, for large numbers studied and wrote books as a matter of course, where French and English women writers are distinctly apologetical, Christine to begin with, though writing became her profession, Louise Labé, Madeleine Des Roches, Dorothy Leigh, and Margaret Tyler, for examples.

Differences in national characteristics did occasionally employ the pens of writers, most often in the books on travel, where the manners to be looked for dictated advice on behavior, but men of course are the subject. One defender of women touched off the excellencies peculiar to each nation. German women, said Maggio, are remarkable for their chastity and sobriety; French for their sufficiency and humanity; Spanish for their fine breeding and faith; English for their hospitality and sincerity, and Italian for their judgment.[8] There seems to have been a little more interest in differentiating national types of lovers. Though it may little aid our immediate purpose, I will quote here a rather thorough exposition of Italian, Spanish, French, and German fashions in love. It is a rare list that includes the English for any purpose.

"It is observed," says the physician Ferrand, in the words of his English translator, "that Easterne People pursue their desires, without either moderation, or Discretion; yet in a kinde of base servile way. Those that inhabit the more Southerne parts, love with Impatience, Rage, and Fury: those that inhabit the Westerne Countries are very industrious in their Love: and the Northern are very slowly moved or touched with Love.

"The wily Italian in courting his Mistresse, cunningly dissembles his Love, and insinuates himselfe into her Favour by Pleasant Discourses, Sonnets, and Verses, composed in her praise: and if hee be so happy as to enjoy her, he is presently jealous of her, and like a Prisoner, keeps her up under Lock and Key: but if he faile in his suit, hee then begins to hate her, as much, as before he loved her; and will not stick to doe her any mischiefe that lies in his power.

"The eager and Impatient Spaniard, being once enflamed with these Desires, runnes headlong on in his Love, & without Intermission followes his suit; and with most pitifull Lamentations Complaining of the Fire that consumes him, Invocates and Adores his Mistresse. But when at length by any the most unlawfull meanes he hath encompassed his Desires; he either grows jealous of her, and so perhaps cuts her throat; or else basely prostitutes her for money: But if hee cannot effect his purpose, he is then ready to run mad, or kill himselfe.

"The effeminate Frenchman endeavors to win his Mistresses affection by faire honest meanes; entertaining her with Songs, and Pleasant Discourses. If hee chance to be jealous of her, hee tortures himselfe extremely, and weeps and laments his own unhappinesse; But if shee chance to put a trick upon him, and deceave him at last; he then begins to brave it, and casts opprobrious and injurious termes upon her, and sometimes too falls to downe-right violence. And if he have once compassed his Desires, and enjoyed her, he presently neglects her, and begins to look after a new one.

"The German is of a Disposition quite contrary to that of the Spaniard: for hee comes on in his Love by degrees, & takes fire by litle and litle: And when hee is once Inflamed, he proceeds with Art and Judgement, and endeavours to winne his Mistresses favour by Gifts. If hee be once jealous of her, he with-drawes his Liberality: if she deceave him, he makes little stirre about it: and if he speeds in his suit, his love growes as soone cold againe.

"The French is given to flatter, and counterfeit Love: the German hides it: the Spaniard is apt to persuade himselfe that his Mistresse loves him: and the Italian is continually tormented with Jealousie.

"The French affects one that is witty and pleasant, though she be not very faire: The Spaniard cares not how dull or heavy she is, so she be faire: the Italian would have her Modest and Fearefull: and the German, likes one that is somewhat hardy.

"So likewise in the pursuit of their Loves, the Frenchman, if a Wise-man, becomes a Foole: the German, after his slow onset, having been held long in suspence, of a Foole, becomes a Wise-man: the Spaniard hazards all for the enjoying of his Desires: and the Italian despises all danger whatsoever."

Later in considering the efficacy of dwelling upon the imperfections of the beloved as a cure for love, Ferrand adds this observation on differing ideals of beauty: "The Italian desires to have her thick, well set, and plumpe: the German preferres one that is strong: the Spaniard loves a wench that is leane: and the French, one that is soft, delicate, and tender." All these differences are evidently to be taken into consideration in diagnosis and prescription. Whether they may be found helpful in distinguishing the French ideal mistress from the Italian, I leave to others to explore.[9]

In general these glimpses suggest that one may expect to find some differences in emphasis upon the ingredients of the prevailing ideal for women's character and behavior, as architecture, customs, fashions, manners, and temperaments vary from country to country, city to city. The Italian may have had to fear more than the French or English the dangers to chastity that windows presented, and his warm and jealous disposition may have dictated more complete seclusion of both maid and wife. In theorizing, however, on the place love should take in the life of the well-born man and woman, nationality will probably be found to have made no difference. Where it might have been expected to show most, in England, the English habit of borrowing philosophy from abroad satisfied what little appetite they had, with the treatises the Italians and French produced for home consumption. In the one book most likely to contain native ideas, Lyly's *Euphues*, not only is ideal love omitted but the little said on love is in dispraise of it. To be sure, sonnets, after the French pattern particularly, were poured forth in a flood for half a century, but sonnets were a very practical means of soliciting favor from a flesh-and-blood lady, the more highfalutin the better. One idea writers of all nationalities seem to have had in common since their prescriptions are fundamentally the same— they felt happier if their women were little seen and little experienced in common conversation with men. And though the English wife seems to have been somewhat envied by continental wives for her freedom, obedience was the rule set down for her, and a foreign observer recorded that wives in England, though very free and much honored, were entirely in the power of their husbands, even giving up their names except that duchesses, countesses, and baronesses when they married gentlemen of inferior rank retained their name and title, "which for the ambition of the said ladies, is rather allowed than commended."[10]

Differences may also be sought in Catholic and non-Catholic views of marriage. There were still rumblings in the sixteenth century against celibacy of clergy as essentially a derogation of marriage. An anonymous Frenchman published a little treatise on the utility and honesty of marriage against the general scorn of marriage. He charged those who denied marriage to ecclesiastics with a preference for fornication and defended the legality of marriage for priests. It was a kind of lèse-majesté, he said, to spread such false opinions for they destroy prince and people.[11] Thomas Becon, with the same motives, published his *Golden Booke of Christen Matrimonye* in 1542 to exalt with all the eloquence at his command the state of man originally ordained by God, against those who put virginity and asceticism first.

"Let other praise Chastitie so muche as they liste, which they saye (wold God it were so) filleth heaven, yet wil I commend matrimony, which replenyseth bothe heaven and earth. Let other set forth simple living with so many prayses, as they can accumulate and tomble one in anothers necke, for as much as it is voyde of all care, trouble and disquietness, yet wyll I for ever more commend the state of honorable wedlocke which refuseth no kynde of payne and trouble, so that it may bryng any profit at all to the publique weale of Christendome. Let other approve solitarye lyvinge, whych is pertaker of none of all those burdens, that the common sorte of men doo sustaine, yet wyl I preferre that state of living, which accordinge to the order of charitie, is redy at all times to beare the burdens of other, and to seke the quietnes of other no lesse than of it selfe. Let other praise that kinde of life, wherby mankynde decayeth and in processe of time should bee utterly destroyed, yet wyl I commend that manner of life, which begetteth and bringeth forth to us excellent Kinges, noble Princes, Prince-like Dukes, Puyssaunt Lordes, valeaunt Knightes, conninge artificers for the maintenaunce of the common weale, learned wittes, etc. Let other avaunce that life, wherby Monarchies, Empyres, and Kyngdomes bee made desolate, barren and unfruitfull, yet wyl I most of all prayse that life which maketh Realmes to florishe with innumerable thousandes of people, wherby the publique weale is preserved in safe estate. Let other praise such as may justly seeme to bee monstures of nature for theyr sterilite and barrennes, yet will I commend them, which according to theyr fyrst creation and the natural disposicion, that God from the beginning angraffed in them, are fruteful as a plenteous vyne. Let other—."

But Becon grows opprobrious, not to say scurrilous, in his zeal and we do not need to follow him further. He scores the times for licentiousness, partly shown in general disdain for marriage both by the married and unmarried, and sees as one cause of this disdain the greed of noblemen who marry their children very young without regard for their future happiness.[12]

Another Englishman, William Gouge, who published his *Domesticall Duties* in 1622, seems no longer to be worried by celibacy among the Catholics, but he thought them wrong in holding only the single life chaste. He opposed them also on their attitude toward the marriage rite. Defect and abuse he said are equally bad. Conception is not the only end of this duty, which is to be rendered to the barren also as a seal of mutual love. Living separately is allowable to the married only for weighty affairs—war, embassy, trade, law, court—but not, as Catholics teach, for certain reasons for a certain or uncertain time, as by consent to attain a more perfect state (no state more perfect than marriage), or because of demerit (adultery a good cause for divorce, and crime a cause perhaps for temporary restraint but not permanent). Unnecessary separation is against marital duty, and so are separate rooms and beds.[13]

I found no Catholic argument on the subject, but what they had to say against these charges may be inferred from the way they handled virginity, chastity, and marriage in the books so often quoted in earlier chapters. They did exalt virginity, claiming it a more lofty state than marriage, but then they passed on to praise of marriage as a holy state too. The monk Savonarola was reluctant to recommend the monastic life even for widows, seeing very few suited to sustain its rigors. But virginity might be praised not as a permanent state but as necessary for the girl to preserve until marriage. So Vives praises it in superlative terms to impress the maid with the importance of her chief claim to honor, not to persuade her to choose the church for her vocation rather than marriage. The chapter he devotes to the subject is too long to quote entire, but I will select a few parts to show how such an argument ran.

"Nowe will I talke altogether with the maid her selfe, which hath within her a treasure without comparison, that is the purenes both of body & mind. Now so many thinges come unto my remembrance to say, that I wot not where is best to begin: whether it were better to begin where as saint Augustine doth, when he will intreate of holy virginitie. All the holy

Church is a virgin, married unto one husband Christ, as Saint Paul writeth unto the Corinths. Then what honour bee they worthy to have, that bee the members of it which keepe the same office in flesh, that the holy Church keepeth in faith, which foloweth the mother of her husband and Lord: for the Church is also a mother & a virgin? Nor there is nothing that our Lord delighteth more in, than virgins, nor wherein Angels more gladly abide, and play with. For they bee virgins also themselves, & their Lorde, which would have a virgin unto his mother, and a virgin to his deare disciple, and the Church his spouse a virgin. And also he marrieth unto himselfe other Virgins, and goeth unto marriages with virgins. And whither soever hee goeth, that lambe without spot, which made us cleane with his bloud, an hundred & forty thousand virgins follow him. . . . Be not proud maide, that thou art holy of body, if thou be drunken in minde, nor because no man hath touched thy body, if many men have pierced thy minde. What availeth it, thy body being cleane, when thou bearest thy mind & thy thoght infected with a foule & horrible blot? O thou mayde, thy minde is withered by burning with mans heate: nor thou frettest not with holy love, but hast dryed up all the good fatnes of the pleasures of paradise. . . . I pray thee, understand thine owne goodnesse maide, thy price cannot bee esteemed, if thou joyne a chast mind unto a chast body, if thou shutte up both body and mind, & seale them with those seales that none can open, but hee that hath the keye of David, that is thy spouse, which resteth so in thee, as in a temple most cleane and goodly. Thinkest thou this any small thing, that thou maiest receive onely by pureness that thing, which cannot be comprehended in this whole worlde? How glad is a woman, if she beare in her womb a child which shal be a king? But thou bearest a king already not only in thy wombe, but also in thy mind, which is more goodly: yea & such a king, in whose garment this title of virginitie is written: King of all kinges, and Lord of all Lords. . . . The holy Virgin Mary conceived first in her mind our Lord Christ, and after in her body. And it was a more honorable, noble, and excellent thing to conceive in minde, than in bodie. Wherefore thou art partner of the more excellent conception. O happy art thou, that art marvellously mother to an excellent and marvellous child. . . . O thou mayd, thinkest thou this but a small thing, but thou art both mother, spouse and daughter to that God, in whome nothing can bee, but it must be thine, and thou maiest with good right challenge for thine? . . . Now think with what diligence this pearle ought to be kepte, that maketh thee like unto the Church, like unto the virgin Mary, sister unto Angels, mother unto God, and the spouse of Christ, beside worldly honours, which ought to have no place, or very little place in a Christian bodies heart? but yet also they as it were fasten their eyes upon a virgin. How pleasaunt and deare unto every body is a virgin? Howe reverent a thing, even unto them that bee ill and vicious themselves."[14]

Erasmus has these judicious words to say on the relative merits of the three states. He will not attempt, he says, to put into words what great praise of perpetual virginity there is among Christians. Nor will he compare virginity, widowhood, and matrimony, which argument he sees very contentiously treated by zealots. It is an invidious kind of praise to depress virginity in order to exalt matrimony, or to admire widowhood in order to deprecate second marriages. Each has its own praises in Holy Scriptures. First the dignity of virginity is praised, if voluntary and if accompanied by other virtues, next widowhood, third marriage. But scorn has no place. Virginity is not preferred to marriage as gold is to brass, but as a gem to gold.[15]

Virginity so prized in the maid was held by all writers on marriage as the greatest gift she could bring to her husband, and chastity, synonymous with virginity in the maid, was obviously not conceived by Catholics as ending with virginity on marriage, but as we have seen was counted still the greatest virtue of the wife in her fidelity to her husband. Chastity of a more absolute kind might be found in virginity, but it was still chastity, purity, in marriage. And marriage itself, though set below virginity as an ideal, was honored by Catholics only next to virginity. More light on the subject may be had by those interested, beginning, if it can be found, with a book listed by Du Verdier. The entry reads, Emond Auger, Jesuit, *Discours du Sainct Sacrament de Mariage en 2 livres per Chapitres contre les Heresies & Medisances de Calvinistes, Bezeans, Occhinistes & Melanthonistes*, 1572. I have not thought plunging into such a sea likely to be rewarding enough to warrant prolongation of an already too protracted study. The few comments offered by the numerous writers on marriage that furnish the portrait of the wife in these pages are rather theological than moral in character and further research seemed unlikely to affect general conclusions.

The real obstacle to framing a consistent, complete ideal portrait of the lady of the renaissance lies not in whatever differences may be found in time, or place, or religion, but, as has already been pointed out, in the failure of renaissance theorists to see the lady for the most part as other than a woman. It is on the rock of marriage that renaissance theory foundered. Almost all writers on women saw them as wives and could not view them in other roles, though they had no difficulty at all in viewing the gentleman without reference to his domestic role. It may be profitable to recognize two ideals, the one commonly written about which practically leaves the lady, even the queen, like any other woman a wife, and the other, rarely acknowledged and more rarely presented at length, which sets her off from women of lower birth. The inadequate character of both of these pictures has been sufficiently noted from time to time. Actually the model for the commonly accepted portrait of the renaissance lady need not be a lady at all. Neither St. Paul nor the Church Fathers, whose pattern formed the basis of renaissance thought, wrote to emphasize class distinctions. Jerome advised the noblewomen who were his friends to spin in order to avoid the sin of idleness. It was the ordinary woman in her house, cooking, cleaning, spinning, sewing, waiting on her husband, tending her children, who was the model generally proposed.

There is some inclination today to view the Virgin Mary as the archetype for medieval and renaissance ladies, herself the lady par excellence. The subject will bear further examination in the light of this study. I am highly skeptical of the proposition chiefly because I found very few references to the Virgin by these writers on secular ideals. The most notable reference perhaps, is Boccaccio's at the end of his long diatribe against women in the *Laberinto*, for which he was so often blamed. As proof of their vanity he offers their presumptuous glorification of themselves through the Virgin— it was a customary argument against the usual saddling of women with blame for the loss of Paradise through Eve, that the Virgin more than redressed the balance by bringing the Savior into the world. There is no resemblance at all, except in the one fact of sex, argues Boccaccio, because this one spouse of the Holy Spirit was a thing so pure, so virtuous, so full of grace, so rémoved from all bodily and spiritual taint that in respect to other women she was formed, as it were, not of the same elements but of a quintessence fit to be the habitation of the son of God. God, wishing to become incarnate for our salvation, in order not to come to dwell in the "pigsty" of modern women, prepared her from eternity as a chamber for so great a king. So all her ways were different from theirs. And likewise her beauty, which, without artifice or paint, is so great that it draws the attention of the angels, and to the blessed spirits, if one may say so, adds glory and unspeakable delight. Where women in their vanity, painting themselves to deceive, the more arouse evil appetites, the beauty of the Queen of Heaven suppresses every low thought and unchaste desire in those who gaze on her and fires them wonderfully with ardor to do good. For this no vainglory or pride comes to her, but only an increase in humility. Here is a pattern for women, he ends, if they would only follow it.[16]

But the lady, the wife, is far more often told to follow the example of St. Augustine's mother, Monica, rather than the Virgin, who was perhaps not a lowly enough figure. Though knowledge of all womanly arts and humility, in more perfect quality than can be even in God, were given to the Virgin, as the mother of God and Queen of Heaven she could not have been seen in subjection to a husband. In all the virtues, gifts, and powers of the human being she was made to excel in every way, not only in the rest of the Christian virtues so prized in all women—peace, patience, goodness, sweetness, kindness, faith, modesty, continence, chastity, piety (I am following Albert the Great's list), but in the cardinal four—justice, prudence, fortitude, temperance; not only in knowledge of domestic affairs but in knowledge of all mechanical arts and all the liberal arts—grammar, rhetoric, the Holy Scriptures, physic, medicine, music, astronomy, arithmetic, geometry, metaphysics. Every kind of wisdom was in her to perfection. But Albert the Great, Bishop of Ratisbon, was not intending by such praises to turn the Virgin into a great secular lady, for he defined all these gifts in religious terms suitable to a being without sin and incorruptible. For example, if temperance means firm restraint of illicit desires then the Virgin did not have it, for she had no illicit desires; but if it is unchanging and complete love of God which directed all her impulses to good, then she did. Or she transcended all in wisdom because she was the most humble of all human and angelic creatures, and where humility is found, there is wisdom, the more humility the more wisdom. No knowledge was hidden from her, and all her knowledge came from the Holy Scriptures.

Bodily beauty was always a part of the perfection of the Virgin, and could be described in terms as fervent as the beauty of an Italian lady of the renaissance, but with a difference. Albert the Great carefully picked for her the features that were taken to indicate inner perfection. Since the color of hair indicates the prevailing humor, he gives her black hair in preference to red as showing a firmer mind, and more beautiful in contrast to the red and white of her complexion, of the proper mixture to indicate equality within. For the same reason her eyes would have been black. In height, flesh, and proportions she would have had what is most commanding and elegant in women in order to produce perfection in her son, since naturally and as a rule like begets like.[17] Nicolò Franco in his work on beauty of body and mind praises the Virgin as the embodiment of all the excellencies of both body and mind, and while specifically describing her physical beauty throws the emphasis on her virtues by a rhetorical device. She was exalted, he said, not by the gold, purple, jewels, and garlands that adorned her beauty, but by the majesty of her chaste mind. It was not the whiteness of her limbs, rivaling alabaster, that made her body shine, but the purity within. It was not the weaving of her golden hair with bands that made her hair beautiful, but the clear virtues which firmly bound her mind and showed her worthy of veneration, that pure, holy, spotless, and devout simplicity which was the ornament of her body and minister of her will. It was not the veils shot with gold which proudly embellished her head, but the highest continence, most powerful despiser of all the vanities. Nor was its shining clearness the quality that made her forehead admired, but the honesty and shame which as the mirror of her mind showed her invincible against human desires. It was not the ivory whiteness or the jeweled rings that made the hands of the Virgin gracious, but the fidelity visibly shown in the beauty, dignity, and devotion with which they ruled, restrained, supported, and tended the true son of the high God, creator of all that is beautiful, and there was sufficient adornment to those hands in the invisible scepter of that heavenly kingdom to which she was to ascend, supreme queen without end. The jewels in the Virgin's mouth were not the pearls and rubies there, but the high ministers of sense and modesty which issued from it in words never unaccompanied with humble vigilance, nor did the beautiful mouth open or close that it was not like the opening and closing on the sweetest melody of the choirs of Paradise.[18]

If these passages, including Boccaccio's, are typical, they may suggest why the Virgin can probably only with the greatest caution be held a model for earthly ladies, in her goodness and wisdom too holy and perfect, and in her glory and power too exalted.

A little more can be said here about what has been called the second, specialized view of the lady found so rarely in renaissance writers on human ideals. The incongruity of assigning to women born to prominence merely the virtues and capacities appropriate to the ordinary run of women did draw occasional comment. Du Bosc roundly said in 1632, "It should not be thought that in speaking of this accomplished woman whose portrait we are drawing we intend to paint a mother of a family who knows well how to give orders to her servants and has the duty of taking care of her children. Music, history, philosophy, and other such exercises are more appropriate to our picture than those of a good housewife."[19] I found only two writers, however, attempting analysis of any length, Torquato Tasso and Agostino Nifo. The question of the differences between the virtues suitable to men and those suitable to women was raised as well as the question of the virtues appropriate to highborn women to distinguish them from lowborn. Tasso pondered the matter and came to the conclusion society in general accepted. He wrote his *Discorso della Virtù Femminile e Donnesca* in 1582 for the Duchess of Mantua, a fact which should be given due consideration. After a study of Plato's and Aristotle's views he decided that man is disgraced by cowardice, woman by inchastity. Courage is a virtue of women too but not absolutely, only relatively to men. Of the intellectual virtues, prudence, justice, clemency, women likewise have less than men, but temperance, a part of which is chastity, belongs so particularly to them that many actions would be called intemperate in them that could not in any way be deemed intemperate in men. Having followed Plato and Aristotle thus far he suddenly reminded himself that he was writing to a woman of royal and heroic blood who with her own virtues equals the manly virtues of all her glorious ancestors, and therefore his theme is not the virtue of mere women but the virtue of ladies, as great as that of lords. Considering then this virtue of the highborn, just as there are some men who excel ordinary humanity and are called heroic, so among women many are born of heroic mind and virtue, and many born of royal blood though not exactly heroic are like heroic women, in that neither to heroic nor to royal women belongs the government of a family, or if it does, it is with a difference. If the governing of a royal family belongs in some way to a queen, it is not the essential virtue of the queen as it is of the mother of a family whose particular virtue is frugality, where the queen's is beauty and delicacy—the one has for her object the useful, the other the ornamental. The heroic woman transcends in virtue not only all women but all human beings, delights only in prudent and brave operations, and her virtue is not the imperfect but the perfect virtue, not the mean virtue but the whole virtue.

Then feminine modesty and chastity are no more becoming to her than to the cavalier, because these virtues belong to one whom the other greater virtues cannot belong to. Nor can she be called infamous if she commits some unchaste act, because she does not sin against her own virtue, and infamous is appropriate only to that man and that woman who sin against their own virtues. Though it cannot be denied that Semiramis and Cleopatra would deserve more praise if they had been chaste, and Zenobia and Artemisia are to be preferred to them for their temperance, yet if the heroic woman has not sought love out of unbridled desire, she should not be blamed but rather praised, like the Queen of the Amazons who came to Alexander, or Sheba to Solomon. Infamy and dishonor follow vice, but where there is no vice, that is confirmed habit, there is no dishonor. Who can think Dido dishonored? There is carnal love, and benevolent love, and a mixture of the two which has something divine about it. That is heroic virtue in heroic women which matches the heroic virtue of men, and to the women gifted with this virtue chastity belongs no more than courage or prudence, nor is any distinction to be found between the works and offices of heroic women and of heroic men, unless perhaps only those belonging to generation and the perpetuation of the species, which however are in part neglected and passed over by heroic women. For modern examples, ended Tasso, take Mary, sister of Charles V and Ferdinand (the Duchess's father); Marguerite of Austria, Duchess of Parma; the present Queen of England "who ought not to be omitted because if indeed our bad fortune has willed that she be separated from the Church, yet the heroic virtue of her mind and the loftiness of her remarkable genius rouses the greatest good will in every gentle and valorous soul," and also Catherine de Medici, Renata of Ferrara, Marguerite of Savoy, and of course the Duchess of Mantua herself with her sister Barbara.

Here in the top ranks of women equality with man is postulated unreservedly, and on a side I have not noted elsewhere. A single standard of virtue and action is assumed for men and women. If heroic men are not made infamous by inchastity, then women of heroic mold are not either, not that chastity is denied to be a virtue, but that other virtues have far more importance in human beings of surpassing gifts, and sex is then of no significance. This view was strictly limited for Tasso to women of the highest ranks.

Nifo's discussion of the subject appears in the last chapter of his little book on the ideal prince. It had always seemed to him, he said, important and yet difficult to say what virtues, affections, and actions are to be desired in noblewomen and princesses. If you read the ancients carefully you will find that they neither fully considered nor wholly left out the subject. They praised such women for fortitude, for chastity, for constancy, for making peace, for learning, eloquence, and poetry, for prudence, for liberality, for conjugal love and faith, and for industry. It is not easy, however, to see in such a list what specially belongs to women who are nobles or princes. Aristotle, in his *Rhetoric*, assigned to men and women in common such virtues as fortitude, justice, and others, but temperance, which is accompanied by moderation, modesty, shame, chastity, continence, abstinence, sobriety, and silence, he gave specially to women. Cicero in Book I of his *Offices* said that cleanliness and neatness are not unsuitable or unrequired in highborn women, but sweat and labor are more fitting for men, and he thought other virtues such as justice, fortitude, and the like, of no value in women as women, even unsuitable in them unless as aids to the virtues and necessities of men. Here Aristotle was of a different opinion for he said that the actions of princesses and noblewomen ought not to be illiberal or mercenary, but such as bring peace and serve magnificence. But then the quality particularly praised in highborn women by the philosophers was patience under the adversities of their husbands. Alcestis and Penelope would not have won such glory if they had not possessed it. In all women conjugal love was the affection most praised, but not unaccompanied by shame and modesty. Again, commiseration and pity were praised, also sweetness—as wrath is the most shameful in noblewomen so sweetness is the most beautiful. Constancy too is divine and admirable, consisting in not fearing dangers. Then Nifo without trying to discriminate where the ancients had left some confusion concludes with the general recommendation that these virtues, actions, and affections when joined with beauty and height make the noblewoman lovable, renowned, blameless, and blessed.

A look back over Nifo's chapters devoted to the qualities that princes should cultivate may help in interpretation of the prescription for princesses. Prudence and justice come first as necessary, and justice most becoming. Then he says modesty is especially well seen in a prince, first of all to moderate pride, that is, lust for honors; for seeking to be adored by his subjects and to hear prayers on bended knees leads to ambition and not justice. Rulers and conquerors who graciously grant relief from heavy taxes, restrict expenditures, refuse triumphs, and return to living as before after victories, are modest, remembering their mortality. Modesty also pertains to probity of manners, such probity as Alexander showed when he treated his enemies with kindness and liberality, and bore rudeness and license of speech toward himself with good humor. Neither should princes lack mildness, for they ought not to be formidable on account of their power, but rather to seem lovable by the greatness of their liberality, and thus to be loved rather than feared, love bringing reverence and obedience, and fear hate. Two companions of justice are also most appropriate to princes, innocence, that is, absence of desire to harm anyone, and mercy, no less suitable than fortitude and a bringer of love. Piety and religion, knowledge of God and obedience to the divine will, shine especially in princes. And then he adds humanity, shown in aid and protection of men, approachability, that is, an ear for the quarrels and injuries of men in order to conciliate and remedy them, and last honesty, by which with firm election the mind decides to do all that accords with virtue, particularly fitting for the prince, therefore, who, knowing himself and leaving all that is alien to him, chooses a way of life free from vice and shame. Most of the virtues named here are the very ones so often urged on women as if peculiarly theirs rather than men's—modesty, innocence, mercy, humanity, readiness to promote peace and relieve distress, and honesty, always something more than chastity. The definitions and applications that accompany them here, freed from the limitations and special meanings assigned by a preconceived view of the role and character of women, may be taken as fundamental conceptions, philosophical and objective, of human qualities belonging to perfection. With all this in his mind, when Nifo turns at last to consider the qualities desirable in women of the same high rank and power, it is reasonable to assume that he did not empty words of the meanings just assigned but the more readily gave up the effort to find a special set of virtues or definitions of them tailored to women's size and shape.[20]

In all candor I think that too much may be made of the differences indicated or even explicit and stressed between the qualities assigned to men and to women by renaissance writers. In the first place, when one is writing on the subject of women he is not writing on men, and if he recommends certain qualities in her he is not necessarily denying them to men. A look at similar treatises addressed to men, as in the case just cited, will show the same qualities assigned to men, such as modesty, and even silence. The Stoics of course made a great virtue out of silence, a sign of wisdom and strength in men. In the second place, though there are differences, the differences lie more in emphasis than in meaning, and in the external circumstances under which they were exercised. It is observable in the books on the princess or lady at court how much nearer the ideal for woman draws to that for men under the pressure of similar circumstances. Further, the complaints that men made against women so voluminously and vociferously, particularly through the sixteenth century, all arise, paradoxically,

ironically, comically enough, out of resentment that women are not behaving according to the very human pattern prescribed for men, fidelity,
truth, common sense, courage, generosity, and even the fortitude, prudence,
and intelligence that only studies can perfectly develop.

This is not to deny that the resulting ideal for the lady so generally held
is not a very different picture from that held for the gentleman, but only
to suggest that the result represents a certain amount of confusion in
thinking and a most unrealistic separation of theory from fact. So far as
this wifely ideal is thought of as fitting the circumstances of the humbler
sort of women, there is something to be said for it as a working hypothesis,
though so much would not have been said about submission and obedience
and the inborn superiority of all men to all women if wives in general were
not asserting themselves, not to say usurping the role of Adam like very
Eves. But when it is made, as almost unanimously it was made, to represent the ideal that the lady, from simple gentlewoman to queen, should aim
at, then it ignores almost preposterously, may one say, facts, circumstances,
and reality even in the ideal realm. It was originally my purpose to conclude
this study of the lady drawn from theoretical treatises with a picture drawn
from history and fiction of the ideal that ladies actually followed. Time is
running out, however, and to do justice to such a picture would require
another book. I will merely suggest the pattern that history would afford
by quoting one of the less well-known tributes by contemporaries to Queen
Elizabeth. It appears in a list of learned women which D'Aubigné drew from
his own recollection for the pleasure of his daughters around 1598. "We
have this torch of eternal fame which has shown in England, the Queen
Elizabeth, of whom one act alone will prove to what height of knowledge
God had raised that mind. That is that she replied in one day to eight ambassadors in the languages appropriate to them. But the most praiseworthy
part of this soul blessed of God has been the practice of her theory, for she
has so well put to use her Ethics and Politics that she has held the ship of
her kingdom steady for forty years in the midst of a very troubled sea and
in a tempestuous age. Her name and memory will be blessed forever." The
whole list is interesting, beginning with Marguerite of Navarre and Louise
Labé of Lyon, "the Sappho of her time," and ending with Louise Sarrasin
of Geneva, the dearest to him because without her he would never have
learned Greek, and Catherine de l'Estang his mother, whom he had never
seen but whose books he had studied. Two other names familiar to this
study appear, the Des Roches of Poitiers, mother and daughter, and Marie
de Gournay "celebrated by Michel de Montaigne." Here is a store of real
ladies to start out with.[21]

Finally, there remains the challenge of comparison between these
thoughts of men of another age and our own, which I constantly felt but
with restraint praiseworthy or not have not taken up. That too calls for

another book. The story of women's freedom since the renaissance has been a series of advances and retrogressions with the balance surely on the side of gains. Today, however, we are at best little ahead of the most enlightened opinion of the renaissance, and if one is inclined to smile in superior fashion at some of the opinions of even the wisest of renaissance men, the smile is likely to disappear the next moment at sight of words from some of our wisest that are no wiser than their predecessors on the matter of women's nature. For example may I quote a passage from R. F. Harrod's recent *Life of John Maynard Keynes*. He is accounting for the phenomenon of two women, Virginia Woolf and Vanessa Bell, daughters of Leslie Stephen, belonging without question to the core of the Bloomsbury group, accepted, that is, on equal terms with such men as Lytton Strachey, Duncan Grant, Keynes, and of course their husbands, Clive Bell and Leonard Woolf.

"In their persons they were beautiful and clever and had also a sense of fun and liveliness. They were very individual people, with complex characters which it was a pleasure to their clever men friends to unravel. Furthermore they had a peculiar quality which differentiated them from the majority of their sex, and was essential for the purpose in hand—intellectual coolness. (One need not imply that in most women the absence of this trait is a deficiency; this turns on the function they are destined to perform.) With Virginia and Vanessa all the subjects under the sun could be equally discussed, all opinions, however outrageous, quietly assessed. The men who frequented their society knew that they were in no danger of hearing those rising, strident tones of emotion which must destroy good talk. They had no tendency, as an argument took this turn or that, to read into its bearing an affront to their class, their set, their sex, or themselves."[22]

Vives and Harrod would find themselves in perfect agreement on the essential nature and function and place of women. Should we end where we began with Christine de Pisan's observation that the wisest of writers generally, somewhere along the way, find occasion to belittle women, and if they do not now agree, as she adds, in assuming that the nature of women is inclined wholly to evil, they still agree, these moderns and their predecessors, that women are by nature inferior to men, though nature can by some inexplicable whim produce a woman, two women, entirely comparable to men in intellectual gifts. There is still in theory not one human race but two, as Marie de Gournay lamented three hundred years ago.

Notes

CHAPTER II

1. Christine de Pisan, Le livre de la cite des dames, composed 1404, unpub., Eng. trans. by Bryan Ansley, Citye of ladyes, 1521, cap. 1–2.
2. Lombardelli, De gli ufizzii et costumi de' giovanni, 1579, cap. XVI, p. 124.
3. Heale, Apologie for women, 1609, pp. 1–3.

MOTIVES FOR BLAME

4. Matheolus, Le livre de Matheolus, Fr. trans. by Le Fevre, 1492, rep. 1846, p. 150.
   Boccaccio, Laberinto d'amore, 1558, ff. 19–26.
5. Olivier, Alphabet, 1617, Advis de l'autheur; Responce, 1617, Epistre au lecteur, pp. 46–47, 101.
   Antoninus, Saint, Tractatus de sponsalibus, 1511, Prohemium.
6. Marinella, La nobilta, 1600, f. 41.
7. Bruni, Difesa della donna, 1559, lib. I, f. 5.
8. Christine de Pisan, bk. I, cap. VIII.
   Jane Anger, Her protection for women, 1589, p. 2.
   Meynier, La perfection des femmes, 1625, pp. 12–13.

MOTIVES FOR PRAISE

9. Maggio, Un breve trattato, 1545, ff. 5a–6a.
10. La defensione delle donne, 15th cent. MS., pub. 1876.
    Garzoni, Le vite delle donne illustri, 1588, pp. 161–164.
    Crenne, Epistres familieres, 1538, Epist. III.
    Lavocat des dames de Paris, c. 1532.
    Speroni, Dialogo delle lodi delle donne [di Ferrara], 1542.
    Manfredi, Per donne romane, 1575; In lode di donne di Ravenna, 1602.
    Le Delphyen, Deffense en faveur des dames de Lyon, 1596.
    Domenichi, La nobilta delle donne, 1558, f. 2.
11. Garzoni, ded.

ATTITUDE OF WOMEN TOWARD THE DEBATE

12. Tasso, T., Of marriage and wiving, 1599, f. Ha.
13. Terracina, Discorso sopra tutti li primi canti d'Orlando Furioso, 1550, f. 11.
14. Christine de Pisan, L'epistre au dieu d'amours, 1399, Oeuvres poétiques, 1886, vol. II, pp. 13–14.
15. Gournay, Marie de, L'egalité des hommes et des femmes, 1604, rep. in Les advis, 1634, pp. 278–279; Le grief des dames, rep. in Les advis, pp. 356–357.
16. Billon, Le fort inexpugnable, 1555, f. 17a.
17. Bronzini, Della dignita, 1624, pp. 31–32.
    Manfredi, Cento sonnetti, 1602.

A NECESSARY EVIL: FIRST VIEW

18. Matheolus, lib. III.
    Guazzo, La civil conversatione, 1574, Eng. trans., 1581, rep. Tudor trans., 1925, Vol. I, p. 232, bk. II.

Castiglione, lib. III. (The most urbane running over of charges against women, with the answers.)
Bronzini, p. 100.
Boccaccio, La laberinto, 1558, f. 27.
Chasseneux, Catalogus gloria mundi, 1546, pt. II, ff. 46a–48.
Barbo, L'oracolo, 1616, pt. II.
19. Le Fevre, ff. D4–D4a.
La defensione delle donne, lib. I. pp. 62–88.
Brinon, pp. 13–14.
Taillemont, Le discours, 1557, Disc. II, Aux lecteurs, p. 190.
Passi, I donneschi diffetti, 1602.
Discorso interno alla maggioranza dell' huomo, 1589.
Biondo, Angoscia, 1540.

WOMEN INFERIOR, BUT COMPARABLE TO MEN IN THEIR OWN SPECIAL ROLE: SECOND VIEW

GENERAL

20. Domenichi, La nobilta delle donne, 1549, lib. II, ff. 81a–82.
21. Heale, pp. 37–41.
La defensione delle donne, pp. 56–62.
Christine de Pisan, Citye of ladyes, bk. I, cap. X.
Capella, ff. 6–8.
Lesnauderie, La louange de mariage, 1523, ch. I.
22. Bruni, lib. III.

CREATION

23. Brinon, ch. 1.
Taillemont, pp. 83–88.
Camerata, Trattato dell' honor vero, 1567, f. 20.
Agrippa, De nobilitate, 1532, ff. A6–A7.

THE FALL

24. G., I., An apologie for woman-kinde, 1605, f. B3.
Dialogue apologetique, ch. I.
Billon, f. 149a.
Marinella, ff. 44–45a.
Coccio, Della nobilta, 1544, f. 15.
Postel, Les tres-merveilleuses victoires des femmes, 1553, ch. III, p. 7 (St. Gregory).

TEMPERAMENT, PHYSIQUE

25. Maggio, ff. 8–15a.
Domenichi, La nobilta, 1558, lib. II, ff. 58–62a.
La defensione delle donne, pp. 36–37.
Billon, ch. III, f. 6a.

ESSENTIAL PURPOSE

26. Gournay, L'egalité, p. 282.
Breton, Praise of virtuous ladies, 1606, pp. 8, 24–27.
Billon, ch. II.
Domenichi, La nobilta, 1549, ff. 15–17.
La defensione delle donne, pp. 19–30, 40, 43 (accomplishment of women in the domestic realm).

INFERIORITY

27. Vives, De officio mariti, Eng. trans. by Thomas Paynell, The office and duetie of an husband, 1553?, ff. U2, Q8.
    Jane Anger, p. 4.
    Bronzini, p. 41.
    Serdonati, Libro di M. Giovanni Boccaccio delle donne illustri, 1596, Intro. to his additions, pp. 481–482.
    Billon, ch. X, ff. 159a–162.

WOMAN THE EQUAL OF MAN: THIRD VIEW

PROTEST AGAINST SUBJECTION

28. Oratione dell' humile invaghito, 1571, ff. D–D2a.
29. Billon, ff. 7a–10a.
    Christine de Pisan, Citye of ladyes, bk. II, cap. VII.
    Canoniero, Della eccelenza delle donne, 1606, p. 25.
    Domenichi, f. 19.

EQUALITY

30. Firenzuola, Dialogo delle bellezze, 1548, rep. 1802, pp. 33–35.
    Dardano, f. 2.
    Bruni, lib. IV, f. 73a.
    Gournay, L'egalité, p. 278.
    Tofte, Blazon of jealousie, 1615, p. 35, note q.
    Taillemont, Disc. I, pp. 93–96.
    Zinano, L'amata, overo virtù heroica, 1591, p. 8.

SUPERIORITY ARGUED BY EXTREMISTS: FOURTH VIEW

31. Filogenio, Della perfettione delle donne, 1561.
    Maggio, Un breve trattato, 1545.
    Marinella, La nobilta e eccelenza delle donne: e i diffetti e mancamenti de gli huomini, 1600.
    Chiesa, Theatro delle donne letterate con un breve discorso della preminenza, e perfettione del sesso donesco, 1620.
    Agrippa, De nobilitate & praecellentia foeminei sexus, 1529.
    Pont-Aymerie, Paradoxe apologetique, 1596, Eng. trans. by Anthony Gibson, A Woman's Worth, 1599, p. 21.
32. Camerata, Trattato dell' honor vero, 1567, ff. 1–24.

PERFECTION IN WOMAN

GENERAL LISTS

33. Christine de Pisan, L'epistre au dieu d'amours, Oeuvres poétiques, 1886, vol. II, p. 1.
    Moderata Fonte, Il merito delle donne, 1600.
    Bouton, Le miroir des dames, c. 1477, pub. 1748, pp. 199, 202, 145.
    Chiesa, pp. 36–37.
    Newstead, An apology for women, 1620.

CHASTITY

34. Guazzo, Dialoghi piecevoli, 1586, Dial. X, pp. 129–130, 134.
    Dolce, Dialogo della institutione delle donne, 1547, f. 23a.
    Bouton, p. 202.
35. Brinon, ch. V, X.
    Nannius, Dialogismi heroinarum, 1541.
    Bouton, p. 145.

MODESTY, HUMILITY, CONSTANCY, TEMPERANCE, PIETY

36. La defensione delle donne, pp. 51–54.
    Pont-Aymerie, pp. 24, 87, 68–77 (temperance).
    Capella, f. 6.
    Domenichi, ff. 11–12a (piety).

HUMANITY

37. Vigoureux, La defense, 1617, pp. 92–93.
    Christine de Pisan, Citye of ladyes, bk. I, cap. X.
    Puttenham, The arte of English poesie, 1589, bk. III, ch. XXIIII, p. 243.
    Billon, ch. II, p. 22.

LIBERALITY

38. Piccolomini, Della institutione morale, 1560, lib. VI, cap. VII, VIII, pp. 257–263.
    Capella, f. 7a.
    Christine de Pisan, bk. II, cap. LXV.
    Maggio, f. 19.

COURTESY

39. Spenser, Fairie Queene, bk. VI, canto II, stanzas 1, 2.

COURAGE

40. Capella, ff. 17–19.
    Christine de Pisan, bk. I, cap. XIV.
    Brinon, ch. VI, pp. 173–174.
    Maggio, ff. 17–19.
    Chasseneux, f. 46a.
    Bacon, Discourse in praise of the Queen, Letters and life of Francis Bacon,
        Spedding, 1858, vol. I, p. 126.

JUSTICE

41. Elyot, The governour, 1531, Everyman Lib., bk. III, ch. I, p. 195.
    Capella, f. 7a.
    Mori, Ragionamento in lode delle donne, 1580, f. 5a.

PRUDENCE

42. Christine de Pisan, bk. I, cap. XLIII.
    Capella, ff. 9–11.
    Mori, ff. 5a–6.

LEARNING

43. Capella, f. 16a.
    Oratione dell' humile invaghito, 1571, f. B4a.
    Christine de Pisan, bk. I, cap. XXVII.
    Firenzuola, Epistola . . . in lode delle donne, 1548, p. 10.
    Garzoni, p. 171.
    La defensione, lib. II, pp. 37, 93–111.
    Postel, ch. V.
    Crenne, Epistre III.
    Dialogue apologetique, ch. VIII.
    Maggio, ff. 27–28.

SUMMARY

44. Tasso, T., Del maritarsi discorso, p. 192.
    Billon, f. 152a.
    Piccolomini, lib. III, cap. II.

NOBILITY

45. Marinella, lib. II, f. 33a.
   Bruni, f. 19.
   Bronzini, Della dignita, 1625, Giornata quarta, pp. 16–19.
46. Institucion of a gentleman, 1555, f. 8a.
47. Tiraqueau, De nobilitate, 1573, cap. 18, 20.
   Bonus de Curtili, Tractatus nobilitatis, pt. IV, Tractatuum ex variis juris inter-
      pretibus, 1549, vol. XII, pp. 3–21.
   Smith, De republica, 1583, bk. I, ch. 16.
48. Glover, The catalogue of honor, 1610, pp. 12–14; Charters granting titles to Burgh-
      ley, etc.
   India, Discorsi della bellezza et della gratia, 1597, f. A4.

CHAPTER III

SCARCITY OF MATERIAL

1. Vives, De institutione feminae christianae, 1538, Eng. trans. by Richard Hyrde,
      Instruction of a Christian woman, 1592, ded.
   Dolce, Dialogo della institution delle donne, 1547, ff. 5–5a.
   Guazzo, Dialoghi piacevole, 1586, Dial. X, ff. 135a–137.
   Antoniano, Dell' educatione cristiana de i figlivoli, 1584, f. 90.
   Beaulieu, L'espinglier des filles, 1550, ch. 2.

CHILDHOOD

2. Giussano, Instruttione a' padri, 1603, cap. 18.
   Vives, bk. I, ch. I–III.
   Jones, The arte and science of preserving bodie and soule, 1579, pp. 4–5.
   Bruto, La institutione di una fanciulla nata nobilmente, 1555, ff. 12–18a.
   Dolce, f. 9a.
   Antoniano, ff. 20–28, 164–164a.
   Ascham, The scholemaister, 1570, rep. 1863, pp. 33–35.
   Erasmus, Christiani matrimonii institutio, 1526, ff. B6–C2.

VIRTUES TO BE INCULCATED

GOODNESS

3. Bruto, ff. 10a–14a.
   Vives, bk. I, ch. II.
   Dolce, f. 9a.
   Salter, A mirrhor mete for all mothers, 1579, ff. B2a–B3.
   (Eng. trans. of Bruto above used throughout for direct quotation); Bruto, ff.
      12–14.

CHASTITY

4. Leigh, The mother's blessing, 1621, 7th ed., pp. 30–33.
5. Rich, The excellencie of good women, 1613, p. 22.
6. Bruto, f. 44a; Salter, ff. D3a–D4a.
7. Vives, bk. I, ch. XI, ff. HIIa–HIII.
   Capaccio, Il principe, 1620, Avvertimenti 23, 65, 619.

OBEDIENCE

8. Beaulieu, ch. 3.
   Vives, bk. I, ch. XVI, ff. Ma–M3.

PIETY

9. Bruto, f. 32; Salter, ff. CIVa–CV.
   Dolce, f. 10a.

HOUSEHOLD ARTS

10. Vives, bk. I, cap. III, ff. B4–B5; B7a–B8.
    Jones, pp. 20–21.
    A booke of curious and strange inventions, 1596.
    A booke of cookerie, 1597.
    Dolce, f. 12.
    Bouchet, Epistres morales & familieres, 1545, Epist. 10.
    Bruto, ff. 40–40a.

HYGIENE: FOOD, DRINK, CLOTHES, PAINTING

11. Vives, bk. I, cap. VIII, IX.
    Dolce, f. 24a.
    Antoniano, f. 91a.
    Salter, f. CIVa.
    Bouchet, Epist. 10.
    Beaulieu, ch. 4, 5.

MANNERS

12. Vives, bk. I, cap. XII.
13. Decor puellarum, 1461, lib. III, IV. (In Italian.)
    Barberino (1264–1348), Del regimento e dei costumi delle donne, rep. 1842, pt. I,
       p. 40. (First printed 1815.)
    Le doctrinal des filles, 1490?
14. Becon, A new catechisme, Worckes, 1564, p. 532.
15. Decor puellarum, lib. IV (Italian); Bouchet, Epist. 10, f. 28a (French); Tofte,
       Blazon of jealousie, 1615, note Z, p. 27 (English).
16. Pius II, De amoris remedio, f. 9.
    Artus, Discours contre le mesdisance, 1600, f. 18a.
17. Bouchet, Epistre X.
    Vives, bk. I, cap. XII, f. I VIa.

AMUSEMENTS

18. Beaulieu, ch. 6, 7, 12.
    Vives, bk. I, cap. X, XIII.
    Bouchet, Epist. 10.
    Jones, pp. 22–23.
    Bruto, ff. 37–38a.

ON REACHING MARRIAGEABLE AGE

19. Salter, f. B3a.
    Antoniano, f. 164a.
    Stiblinus, Coropaedia, 1555.
20. Vives, bk. I, ch. XVI.

CONCLUSION

21. Barberino, pt. 2–4, pp. 56–96.
22. Guazzo, Dial. X, ff. 129–130a.
    Luigino, Libro della bella donna, 1554, lib. III, p. 288.

CHAPTER IV

INTRODUCTION

1. Vergerius, De ingenuis moribus, trans. by W. H. Woodward, Vittorino da Feltre, and other humanist educators, Cambridge University Press, 1905.
2. Batty, The Christian man's closet, Eng. trans. by Lowth, 1581, f. 55a.

AGAINST LEARNING FOR WOMEN

3. Bruto, La institutione di una fanciulla nata nobilmente, 1555, ff. 26a–28a; Eng. trans. by Salter, A mirrhor mete for all mothers, matrones, and maidens, 1579, ff. C1–C2.
    Antoniano, Dell' educatione christiana de i figlivoli, 1584, ff. 153a–154.
4. Leigh, The mother's blessing, 1621 (7th ed.), pp. 4–17.
    Des Roches, Madeleine, Oeuvres, 1579, Epistre aux dames, Ode 3.
    Tyler, The mirror of princely deeds and knighthood, 1583–1599–1601, pt. I.

FOR LEARNING

5. More, Correspondence, ed. Eliz. F. Rogers, 1947, no. 63, 1518? Trans. taken from Hints on education, 1821, appendix.
6. Vives, De institutione feminae Christianae, 1538, Eng. trans. by Hyrde, Instruction of a Christian woman, 1592, bk. I, ch. IV, ff. C–C5; De officio mariti, Eng. trans. by Paynell, Office of a husband, 1553, ff. O7a–P5.
7. Hyrde, A devout treatise upon the Pater noster, trans. by Margaret More, 1524, preface; Vives, Instruction, 1540, ded. to Queen Catherine, f. A2a.
8. Brachart, Harengne, 1604.
9. Des Roches, Secondes oeuvres, 1583, Dialogue de Placide et Severe.
10. Elyot, Defence of good women, 1545, ff. DII–DbI.
11. Mulcaster, Positions, 1581, rep. 1887, ch. 38, pp. 176, 179.

DIFFERENCES IMPOSED BY SEX AND RANK

12. Mulcaster, ch. 36, p. 133; ch. 39, p. 183; ch. 38, pp. 167, 174–176.
    Bouchet, Le panegyric, 1527, f. MIa-MII.
    Antoniano, f. 153a.
    Aubigné, "A mes filles touchant des femmes doctes de notre siecle," c. 1598, Oeuvres complètes, 1873–1892, vol. I, pp. 445–450.
    Artus, Discours . . . qu'il est bien seant que les filles soyent scavantes, 1600.

STUDIES

13. Bruto, ff. 20–30a.
    Bouchet, Le judgment, 1538, f. bbII; Les triumphs, 1532, Epistre de lacteur a tous des devotz viateurs cristifers.
    Stiblinus, Coropaedia, 1555, p. 3.
14. Bruni, Leonardo, De studiis et literis, ed. 1880 from Leipzig ed., 1496, compared with 1642, 1645.

15. Dolce, Dialogo della institution delle donne, 1547, f. 23a.
16. Hyrde, Instruction, 1540, ded.
17. Vives, Instruction, bk. I, ch. IV, ff. C3–C4; Office, ff. P7–Q3; De ingenuorum adolescentium ac puellarum institutione.
    Artus, ff. 17–17a.
18. Mulcaster, ch. 38, p. 181.
19. Erondelle, The French garden, 1605.
    Puttenham, The Arte of English poesie, 1589, bk. III, ch. X, p. 132.
20. Mulcaster, pp. 181–182.

CONCLUSION

21. Filogenio, Ragionamento delle perfettione delle donne, 1561.
    Vives, Instruction, bk. I, ch. IV, f. C7.

CHAPTER V

GENTLEMAN: ARGUMENTS FOR AND AGAINST MARRIAGE

1. Erasmus, Opus de conscribendis epistolis, 1546, Laus et vituperatio matrimonii, pp. 185–189.
   Lauro, Letters, 1553, pp. 192–195, to Sigismundo Ehem.
   Les tenebres de mariage, c. 1600.
   Tasso, E. (and T. Tasso), Dello ammogliarsi piecevoli contese, 1595, Eng. trans. Of mariage and wiving, 1599, f. B.
   Le purgatoire des mauvais marys, 1480?
   Barbaro, De re uxoria, 1513, lib. I, cap. I.
   Bouchet, Epistres morales & familieres, 1545, Epist. VII.
   Lesnauderie, La louange du mariage, c. 1523, ch. 1.
   Alberti, Della famiglia, lib. II, Opere volgari, 1844, vol. II, pp. 137–157.
   Agrippa, Declamatio, 1532, ff. dVa–EIIIIa.
   Becon, The golden booke of matrimonye, Worckes, 1564, ff. 559–673a.
   Rouspeau, Quatrains spirituels, 1593.
   Tillier, Le livre du philogamie, 1578, liv. I, ch. 3. (Arguments for and against.)
   Trotto, Dialoghi del matrimonio, 1578, Dial. I. (Arguments for and against.)

CHOICE OF WIFE

BIRTH

2. Tillier, liv. I, ch. 4.
   Romei, Discorsi, 1586, Eng. trans. by Kepers, The courtiers academia, 1598, Disc. III, ch. IV, pp. 229–233.
   Bonus de Curtili, Tractatus nobilitatis, pt. IV, Tractatuum ex variis juris interpretibus, 1549, vol. XII, pp. 23–31.
   Piccolomini, Della institutione morale, 1560, lib. XI, cap. III, p. 493.
   Vauquelin de la Fresnaye, Satyres, 1612, pp. 353–354.
   Alberti, lib. II, pp. 161–163.

WEALTH

3. Taillemont, Le discours, 1557, Disc. I, p. 124.
   Lauro, pp. 192–195, to Sigismundo Ehem.
   Barbaro, lib. I, cap. VI.
   Tiraqueau, De legibus connubialibus, 1566, **Lex. I.**

AGE

4. Barbaro, lib. I, cap. III.
  Piccolomini, lib. XI, cap. III.
  Tillier, liv. I, ch. 3.
  Marconville, De L'heur, 1569, ch. 7.
  Lauro, pp. 99–103, to Isabetta Navagiera.

BEAUTY

5. Tillier, liv. I, ch. 5.
  Spifame, Les premiers oeuvres, 1583, La louange du mariage contre Des-portes.
  Barbaro, lib. I, cap. V, f. BII.
  Guazzo, La civil conversatione, 1574, Eng. trans. by Pettie, 1581, rep. Tudor trans., 1925, bk. III, vol. II, pp. 8–11.
  Cholieres, Les neuf matinees, 1585, Mat. V.
  Trotto, Dial. II, pp. 159–160.
  Alberti, lib. II, pp. 159–161.
  Vauquelin de la Fresnaye, pp. 354–356.

COMPARATIVE VALUES

6. Barbaro, lib. I, cap. VII, f. B6a.

DUTIES OF HUSBAND

AUTHORITY

7. Fenton, A forme of Christian pollicie, 1574, bk. VI, pp. 247–248.
  Giussano, Instruttione a' padri, 1603, cap. 7, 8, 10.
  Brinon, Le triomphe des dames, 1599, ch. 4, p. 88.
  Trotto, Dial. II, pp. 154–155.
  Gouge, Of domesticall duties, 1622, Treat. 4, pp. 349–420.
  Bouchet, Le jugement poetique, 1538, f. AII.
  Batty, The Christian man's closet, 1581, Eng. trans. by Lowth, bk. I, p. 5.

INSTRUCTION

8. Fenton, bk. VI, p. 260.
  Piccolomini, lib. XI, cap. VI.
  Alberti, lib. III.
  Marconville, ch. 10.
  Vives, Office, f. P7.
  Markham, Country contentments, 1615, pt. 2, p. 1.
  Lombardelli, Del' uffizio, 1583, pp. 50–52.
  Erasmus, Christiani matrimonii institutio, 1526, ff. T4a–T7.

CORRECTION

9. Vives, Office, ff. Z2–Z6a.
  Bouchet, Epist. VII, f. 22.
  Benvenuto Italiano, The passenger, 1612, pt. I, Dial. I, p. 51.
  Heale, An apologie for women, 1609. (In support of his argument Heale cites Sidney's Arcadia, bk. 2 and 3, Vives' Office of a husband, and Aristotle's Econ. I, c. 3 and 4.)
10. Tiraqueau, Law III.
  Trotto, Dial. II, p. 171.
  Piccolomini, lib. XI, cap. VI.
  Cherubino da Siena, Vite matrimonialis regula, 1482, pt. 1.
  Vives, Office, f. Aa4.

GENERAL BEHAVIOR TO WIFE

11. Trotto, Dial. II, pp. 172–181.
    Batty, The Christian man's closet, 1581, Eng. trans. by Lowth, bk. I, f. 5.
    Christine de Pisan, Citye of ladyes, bk. II, cap. 25.
    Vauquelin de la Fresnaye, pp. 360–362.
    Tiraqueau, Lex. VI.
    Canoniero, Quistioni, 1606, pp. 49–51.

CONJUGAL LOVE AND JEALOUSY

12. Tasso, T., ff. 10a, 12.
    Tillier, liv. II, ch. 2.
    Vives, Office, ff. R2–R8a.
    Bouchet, Epist. VII. f. 23.
    Gouge, Treat. 2, p. 224.
    Lesnauderie, ch. 1.
13. Fausto da Longiano, Delle nozze, 1554, p. 41.
    Vauquelin de la Fresnaye, pp. 361–364.
    Bernardus, Sylvester, De cura rei familiaris, Eng. trans., Governance of a household, 1553, E.E.T.S., 1870.
14. Modio, Il Convito, 1558, pp. 349–351.
    Tofte, Blazon of jealousie, 1615, note C, p. 29. (See also Dolce, Dialogo piecevole . . . nelquale Messer Pietro Aretino parla in difesa d' i male aventurati mariti, 1542.)

SUMMARY

15. Trotto, Dial. II, p. 197.
    Sandys, Sermons, Parker Soc. 1841, vol. 46, Serm. 11, 16, pp. 202, 313–330.

LADY: WHETHER TO MARRY AND WHOM

16. Erasmus, Christiani matrimonii institutio, 1526, f. S5.
    Muzio, Operette, 1550, Trattato di matrimonio, alla Signora Tullia D'Aragona.
17. Fusco, La vedova, 1570, ff. 10–13.
    Taillemont, pp. 111–119.
    Erasmus, ff. N6a–N8a.

SUBJECTION

18. Gouge, preface; Treat. 1, p. 26; Treat. 3, pp. 267–284.
    Erasmus, Institutio, ff. S5–S7a.
    Champier, La nef des dames, 1515, pt. IV, ch. VIII.
    B. Ste., Counsel to the husband: to the wife instruction, 1608.
    Fausto da Longiano, p. 38.
19. Tiraqueau, De legibus connubialibus, the central idea.
    Bouchard, τῆς γυναικείας φύτλας, 1522, ff. 37a–39.

VIRTUES

OBEDIENCE

20. Lombardelli, Uffizio della donna maritata, 1583, ded. letter to Delia, pp. 6–7.
    Vives, Instruction, bk. II, ch. IV; Office, f. F2.
    Trotto, Dial. I, pp. 85–88.
    Tasso, T., Of mariage and wiving, 1599, ff. 10–10a.
    Erasmus, Institutio, ff. S8–S8a.
    Fausto da Longiano, p. 42.

Barbaro, lib. II, f. CIa.
Becon, A new catechisme, Worckes, 1564, f. 513.
Hannay, ff. C–C2.

CHASTITY

21. Vives, Instruction, bk. II, ch. III.
    Trotto, Dial. I, pp. 90–97.
    Belmonte, Institutione della sposa, 1587, pp. 26–36, 83–85.
    Moderata Fonte, Il merito delle donne, 1600, p. 28.
22. Lanteri, Della economica, 1560, p. 262.
    Benvenuto Italiano, pt. II, Dial. II, pp. 607–611.
    Spontone, f. 84a.

SILENCE

23. Trotto, Dial. I, pp. 102–103.
    Vives, Instruction, bk. I, ch. VII, f. C5a.
    Barbaro, lib. II, cap. III, ff. C6a–C7a.
    Trissino, I ritratti, 1524, f. BIII.
    Braithwait, The English gentlewoman, 1641, pp. 89–90.
    Guazzo, bk. II, vol. I, p. 169.
    Tillier, liv. II, ch. 4.

PRUDENCE

24. Lombardelli, pp. 11, 25.
    Vives, Instruction, bk. II, cap. IV, f. P5a; cap. VI.
    Trotto, Dial. I, pp. 113–116.
25. Vives, Instruction, bk. II, cap. VII; Office, f. S8.
26. Erasmus, Institutio, ff. O7–P5a.
    Baldwin, A treatyse of moral philosophy, 1564, bk. V, cap. IX, f. 132.
    Valerio, Instruttione delle donne maritate, 1575, rep. 1744, cap. 3, 4, 5.

LOVE

27. Barbaro, lib. II, cap. I.
    Fausto da Longiano, p. 38.
    Cherubino da Siena, pt. 3.

MODESTY: BEHAVIOR IN PRIVATE AND PUBLIC

28. Barbaro, lib. II, cap. II.
    Cabei, Ornamenti della vedova, 1574, cap. 6, p. 41.
    Belmonte, pp. 34–35.
    Spontone, p. 186.
    Fausto da Longiano, p. 38.
    Tillier, liv. II, ch. 3.
    Vives, Instruction, bk. II, ch. IX.
    Lombardelli, p. 18.
    The Ancren riwle, E.E.T.S., 1944, no. 216, p. 121.

DRESS, PAINTING

29. Vives, Office, ff. X4–Y8; Instruction, bk. II, ch. VIII, Of raiments; bk. I, ch. IX,
    Of the raiments; bk. II, ch. VI, Howe shee should live betweene her husband
    and her selfe privatly.
    Vincenzo da Bologna, Preclara operetta dello ornato delle donne, 1530?, ff. AIIIa–
    bIV.
    Markham, The English huswife, 1615, pp. 1–3.
    Lombardelli, pp. 28–35.
    Barbaro, lib. II, cap. IV.

Tillier, liv. II, ch. 5.
Giussano, cap. 12–14, pp. 63–80.

HUMILITY, PIETY, PLEASANTNESS

30. Trotto, lib. I, p. 87.
Lombardelli, pp. 10, 44–45.
Belmonte, pp. 3–6.
Vives, Instruction, bk. II, cap. 6, ff. S3a–S4.

FAULTS

31. Capaccio, Il principe, 1620, Avvertimento 65.
Vives, Instruction, bk. II, ch. IX, ff. N6a–X2; Office, ff. E6–E8.
Lombardelli, p. 41.

HOUSEHOLD MANAGEMENT

DIVISION OF AUTHORITY

32. Tillier, liv. II, ch. 7.
Tiraqueau, Lex IV, f. 98.
Trotto, Dial. II, pp. 182–183.
Piccolomini, lib. XI, cap. IIII, p. 495.
Hannay, A happy husband, 1618, f. C3a.
Gouge, ded.

ARTS

33. Alberti, pp. 335–345.
Vives, Instruction, bk. II, ch. X.
Belmonte, pp. 37–41.
Guazzo, Dialoghi piecevoli, 1586, Dial. X, ff. 132–133.
34. Tasso, T., ff. 18a–21a.
Valerio, cap. 13.
Barbaro, lib. II, cap. VII.
Jones, The arte and science of preserving bodie and soule, 1579, p. 20.
35. Trotto, Dial. I, pp. 76–82.
Markham, ch. II, pp. 36–39; pp. 4–5.
Vives, Instruction, bk. II, ch. X, ff. X8–X9.

SERVANTS

36. Bouchet, Epist. XI, XII.
Cousin, De officio famulorum, 1535, Eng. trans. by Chaloner, Of the office of servauntes, 1543.
Alberti, lib. III, pp. 329–333.
Tasso, T., ff. 14–17a.
Lanteri, pp. 41–56.
Trotto, pp. 104–107.

HOSPITALITY

37. Belmonte, pp. 56–59.
Trotto, Dial. I, pp. 91–92.
Rich, The excellencie of good women, 1613, p. 24.

CARE OF CHILDREN

38. Lombardelli, pp. 54–57.
Bouchet, Epistre VIII.
Vives, Instruction, bk. II, cap. XI, ff. Y2–Y4.

39. Sainte-Marthe, Paedotrophia, 1587.
   Jones, p. 5.
   Vives, bk. I, cap. I; bk. II, cap. XI, f. Y5a.
   Barbaro, lib. I, cap. VIII.
   Tillier, liv. II, ch. 8.
   Batty, f. 52a–60.
40. Vives, bk. II, cap. XI, f. Y6a–Z5a.
   Trotto, Dial. I, pp. 107–109.

SUMMARY

41. Markham, pt. II, p. 4.
   Trotto, Dial. I, p. 83.
   Lombardelli, letter at end.
   Vives, Office, f. CC7; Instruction, bk. II, ch. XV.
   Luigini, Il libro della bella donna, 1554, cap. 1, 2, 3.

WIDOW

REMARRIAGE

42. Savonarola, Della vita viduale, 1495? liv. I, cap. 1, 2, 3.
   Cabei, Ornamenti della gentil donna vedova, 1574, cap. 3.
   Tillier, liv. I, ch. 3.
   Erasmus, Vidua Christiana, 1529, ff. 49–58.
43. Fusco, La vedova, 1570, ff. 2–32.
   Trotto, Dialoghi del matrimonio, 1578, Dial. I, pp. 13–58.
   Christine de Pisan, Chemin de long estude, 1549, ch. 1.

PROPER BEHAVIOR OF MATURE WOMAN ON DEATH OF HUSBAND

44. Vives, Instruction, bk. III, cap. I, II, III.
   Cabei, cap. 1, 2.

RULE OF HOUSEHOLD

45. Vives, bk. III, cap. V.
   Cabei, cap. 14, 15.
   Fusco, pp. 37–47.

THE YOUNG WIDOW

46. Cabei, cap. 4–8.
   Trissino, Epistola . . . vedova, 1524.

SPECIAL VIRTUES

47. Cabei, cap. 9–13.

CHOOSING A SECOND HUSBAND

48. Kingsmill, A godlie advise touchyng mariage, 1580, ff. I II–KII.

CONCLUSION

49. Carroli, Il giovane ben creato, 1583, lib. II.
   Della Chiesa, Theatro delle donne letterate, 1620, pp. 36–37.

CHAPTER VI

DIFFICULTIES

1. Garbo, Guidonis de Cavalcantibus . . . cantio, 1498, Ital. trans. pub. 1813.
   Zoppio, Psafone, 1617, p. 101.
   Piccolomini, Della institutione morale, 1560, lib. X, cap. XIII, p. 475.

DEFINITIONS

2. Domenichi, Dialoghi, 1562, Dial. d'amore, pp. 29–33. (See also Manso, I paradossi, 1608, ff. 91–116.)
   Equicola, Di natura d'amore, 1531, lib. II, ff. 39, 70–74a.
   Romei, Discorsi, 1585, Eng. trans. by Kepers, The courtiers academie, 1598, Disc. I, pp. 39–41.
   Vieri, Discorsi, 1586, Il secondo ragionamento d'amore, p. 104.
   Ferrand, Erotomania, 1610, Eng. trans. 1640, p. 31.

FRIENDSHIP

3. Goujon, Le tresor de lamitie parfaicte, 1626, pp. 1–24.
   Firenzuola, De' ragionamenti, 1548, rep. 1802, vol. II, pp. 60–63.
   Betussi, Il Raverta, 1544, rep. 1912, p. 27.
   Montaigne, Les essais, 1588, Eng. trans. by Cotton, revised by Hazlitt, bk. I, ch. XXVII.
   Domenichi, Dial. de' rimedi d'amore, pp. 91–92.
   Buoni, Lettioni, 1605, Let. 9, ff. 68–71.
   Piccolomini, lib. IX, X, cap. II.

QUALITIES OF LOVE

4. Equicola, lib. II, ff. 40a–41, lib. 3, ff. 83–88.
   Manso, I paradossi, 1608, f. b3a.
   Rosso, Comento sopra la canzone di Guido Cavalcanti, 1568, pp. 22–24.
   Frachetta, Spositione, 1585, pp. 47–59.
   Piccolomini, lib. X, cap. VI.
   Garbo, p. 94.
   Zoppio, pp. 50–57.

CAUSES OF LOVE

5. Sansovino, Ragionamento, 1545, rep. 1912, pp. 162–163.
   Canoniero, Quistiori, 1606, pp. 63–68.
   Boccaccio, Regole bellissime d'amore, 1561, ff. 5a–6.
   Romei, Disc. II, pp. 34–36, 47.
   Nobili, Trattato dell'amor humano, 1580, ff. 32a–33a.
   Tasso, T., Il cavaliere amante, 1578, pp. 19–20.
   Aubery, L' antidote d' amour, 1599, ff. 67–92.
   Equicola, lib. IV, ff. 118a–125.

BEAUTY THE FIRST CAUSE

6. Baldini, Volgari discorsi, 1585, Disc. I, pp. 22–23.
   Bembo, Gli Asolani, lib. III, p. 114.
   Romei, Disc. I, p. 6.
   Betussi, p. 11.
   Liebault, De l'embellissement, 1582, pp. 1–4.

MEANS OF KNOWING BEAUTY

7. Frachetta, p. 31.
   Garbo, pp. 85–86.
   Aubery, ff. 13–15a.
   Franco, Dialogo . . . delle bellezze, 1542, f. 16a.
   Piccolomini, lib. X, cap. III.
   Betussi, Il Raverta, p. 15; La Leonora, 1557, rep. 1912, p. 336.
   Zuccolo, Discorso, 1588, Conclusioni 28, 29, f. 65a.
   Equicola, lib. IV, ff. 115–116a.
   Ridolfi, Artefilio, 1560.

UGLINESS AND LOVE

8. Canoniero, p. 59.
   Nobili, ff. 7–8.
   Firenzuola, Ragionamenti, 1525, Quest. 3.

END OF LOVE: UNION OF MINDS OR PHYSICAL UNION

9. Nobili, ff. 8a–13a.
10. Castiglione, Il libro del cortegiano, 1528, Eng. trans. by Hoby, 1561, Everyman
    Lib., pp. 313–314.
11. Piccolomini, lib. X, cap. VIII, p. 455.
12. Zoppio, pp. 113–114.
13. Tasso, T., pp. 24–25.
    Pasquier, Le monophile, 1555, Eng. trans. by Fenton, 1572, bk. I, ff. 31a–32. (See
    also Recueil, 1555, Dial. I, ff. 50a–56a.)
    Equicola, lib. IV, f. 117; lib. II, f. 39.
    Romei, Disc. II, p. 50.

TRANSFORMATION OF LOVER INTO THE BELOVED

14. Casoni, Della magia d' amore, 1591, f. 14.
    Equicola, lib. IV, ff. 132a–133.
    Renieri, Vero sogetto d' amore, 1566, ff. B4–B5.
    Tullia d' Aragona, Dialogo, 1547, rep. 1913, pp. 222–223.
    Zuccolo, Conclusione 36, f. 69.
    Romei, Disc. II, p. 67.
    Baldini, Disc. II, pp. 50–53.

ONE LOVE OR MORE

15. Piccolomini, lib. X, cap. VIII.
    Romei, Disc. II, pp. 69–71.
    Varchi, La seconda parte delle lezzioni, 1561, ff. 50–54.

RECIPROCITY

16. Varchi, ff. 43–44.
    Romei, Disc. II, pp. 57–60.
    Pusterla, Oratione, 1568.
    Renieri, ded., ff. B4–14.
    Betussi, Il Raverta, pp. 24–25.
    Nobili, ff. 35–38.
    Zuccolo, Conclusione 23.

DIFFERENCES BETWEEN LOVER AND BELOVED

17. Zoppio, pp. 64–67.
    Piccolomini, lib. X, cap. XII.
    Romei, Disc. II, pp. 60–62, 37.
    Nobili, ff. 51–53.
    Zuccolo, Conclusioni 22, 24, 25, ff. 53–56, 58–64a.
    Betussi, pp. 69–75.
    Landi, Quaesiti amorosi, 1551, p. 42.
    Ferrand, pp. 213–214.

EFFECTS OF LOVE

18. Equicola, lib. III, ff. 90–91.
    Baldini, Disc. II, pp. 54–60.
    Frachetta, pp. 47–48.

Guazzo, La civil conversatione, 1574, Eng. trans. by Pettie, 1581, rep. Tudor
trans., 1925, bk. II, vol. I, p. 234.
Piccolomini, lib. X, cap. XIII.
Domenichi, p. 96.
Romei, Disc. II, p. 56.
Canoniero, p. 19.

REFUTATION OF CHARGES AGAINST LOVE

19. Pasquier, bk. II, ff. 4a, 21.
    Capaccio, Il principe, 1619, p. 217.
    Tahureau, Les dialogues, 1565, pp. 44-52, 27-34.
    Romei, pp. 53-58.
    Bembo, lib. I, pp. 28-31, lib. II, pp. 63-68. (The whole book is an argument over
    whether love is good or evil.)
    Torelli, Trattato del debito cavalliere, 1596, ff. 173-174a.
    Heroët, La parfaicte amye, 1547, liv. III.
    Nobili, ff. 44a-48.

CURES FOR INORDINATE LOVE

20. Nobili, ff. 39-44.
    Aubery, ff. 110-138.
    Varchi, La seconda parte, 1561, Cinque questioni d'amore, no. 5, ff. 54-55a (cor-
    rected paging).
    Pasquier, ff. 16a-24.
    Domenichi, pp. 90-146.
    Pius II, De amoris remedio, 1473?
    Sacchi, Dialogus contra amores, 1510, ff. A5, B4a-C3.
    Ferrand, pp. 217-363.
21. Lauro, Lettere, 1553, pp. 87-89, to Isabella Pia.
    Vives, Instruction, bk. I, cap. XIV.
    Croce, Dialogue galante fra una madre compassionevolo, & una figlia inferme per
    amor, 1623.

LOVE AND MARRIAGE

22. Pasquier, bk. I, ff. 10-26.
    Gottifredi, Specchio d'amore, 1547, pp. 289-291.
    Buoni, Lettione 9, f. 43.
    Renieri, ff. 37-40.
23. Piccolomini, Della institutione morale, 1560, lib. X, cap. XIV (mistress and wife
    one); lib. XI, cap. VI (limitations on wife); lib. X, cap. IV, VII (communion of
    minds between lover and beloved). Della institutione, 1542, lib. IX, cap. I,
    lib. X, cap. II (mistress and wife two).
24. Firenzuola, Ragionamenti, 1548, Opere, 1802, vol. II, pp. 53-55.
    Heroët, liv. I, pp. 16-17.
    Renieri, ff. 40-41.

MORALITY IN LOVE

25. Exhortation aux dames, 1597.
    Heroët, liv. I, pp. 14-16.
    Tofte, Blazon of jealousie, 1615, note o.
    Firenzuola, pp. 48-52.

CHOICE OF LOVER

AGE

26. Gottifredi, pp. 254-265.
    Betussi, Il Raverta, pp. 107-111.

Piccolomini, De la bella creanza de le donne, 1562, pp. 45–50.
Sansovino, pp. 154–156.
Boccaccio, Regole, ff. 8–10.
Renieri, f. 35.
Alberti, Hecatonphila, 1471, Eng. trans. 1598, ff. 5a–7, 9a–12.

RANK

27. Domenichi, Dial. d'amore, pp. 39–40.
Garbo, pp. 103–104.

OCCUPATION

28. Pasquier, ff. 14a–15.
Bargagli, Trattatenimenti, 1587, pp. 41–59.
Chartier, Les demandes damours, 1400?, Eng. trans. Delectable demaundes, 1566.

QUALITIES OF LOVER

SECRECY

29. Piccolomini, De la bella creanza, pp. 50–52.
30. Alberti, ff. 3a, 12.
Chartier, f. A4a.

CONSTANCY

31. Pasquier, bk. I, ff. 26a–27.
Landi, Varii componimenti, 1552, Quaesiti amorosi, p. 65.
Heroët, pp. 10–12, 20.
Garbo, pp. 113–114.
Zuccolo, Conclusione 43, f. 88.

TEMPERANCE

32. Zoppio, pp. 119–120.
Casoni, f. 49.

CHASTITY, MODESTY

33. Boccaccio, Regole, ff. 25a–26.
Equicola, lib. V, ff. 155–158.

HOPE, FEAR, INDUSTRY

34. Alberti, f. 10.
Buoni, Lettione 9, ff. 50a–60.
Sansovino, pp. 164, 176.
Zampeschi, L'innamorato, 1565, Dial. 3.

ART OF WINNING LOVE

35. Gottifredi, pp. 260–263, 268–279.
Sansovino, pp. 170–171.
Nobili, f. 50.
Betussi, Il Raverta, pp. 103–107.
Canoniero, p. 33.
Casoni, f. 49a.
Grevin, Cinq livres de l' imposture, 1567, liv. II, ch. 52, 53.
Alberti, ff. 13a–17.
Vieri, pp. 107–114.

SIGNS OF LOVE

36. Domenichi, Dial. d' amore, pp. 34–36.
Renieri, ff. 17a–21.

Moderata Fonte, Il merito delle donne, 1600, pp. 37–38.
Betussi, Il Raverta, pp. 78–79.

JEALOUSY: VIRTUE OR VICE; SIGN OF LOVE

37. Tasso, T., Il forestiero napoletano, 1586, pp. 36–40.
Viti, Lezioni della gelosia, 1585, p. 13.
Varchi, La seconda parte della lezzioni, 1561, Lezzione sopra un sonetto del M.
   Giovanni della Casa, Eng. trans. by Tofte, 1615, pp. 12–16, 55–58.
Canoniero, pp. 84–105.
Nobili, ff. 29–31a.
Romei, Disc. II, p. 49.
38. Betussi, Il Raverta, pp. 100–101.
Speroni, Dial. d' amore, pp. 1–10.
Piccolomini, Della institutione morale, 1560, lib. X, cap. VII.
39. Varchi, pp. 21–22, 33, 35, 58; Tofte, notes p, q, s.
Equicola, lib. IV, ff. 145a–146.
Tasso, Della gelosia, 1585.
40. Boccaccio, Filocopo, 1564, ff. 221a–222, Eng. trans. 1587, Quest. 5.

TESTS BY WHICH THE LADY MAY KNOW HERSELF IN LOVE

41. Nobili, f. 50.
Gottifredi, pp. 266, 279–283.
Heroët, liv. III, p. 67.
Romei, Disc. II, p. 40.
Castiglione, p. 315.

PRESERVATION OF LOVE

42. Sansovino, pp. 172–178.
Vieri, pp. 111–114.
Gottifredi, pp. 292–297.
Boccaccio, Regole, ff. 23, 25a–27.
Alberti, ff. 33a–34a.

MORAL QUALITIES OF LADY

43. Piccolomini, De la creanza, pp. 39–43.
Equicola, lib. V, ff. 166–168.
Tasso, T., Il cavaliere amante, p. 24.
Brinon, Le triomphe, 1599, pp. 290–298.

BEAUTY CHIEF REQUIREMENT

44. Firenzuola, Dialogo della bellezza, 1548, Disc. I, ff. 62a, 64a; 99–100 (the mouth).
Luigini, Il libro della donna, 1554, lib. II, pp. 50–54; lib. III, pp. 78–95.
Eloghe pastoral, 1536.
Bretin, Poesies amoureuses, 1576, f. 40a.
Pont-Aymerie, Paradoxe apologetique, 1596, pp. 134–140.
Liebault, De l' embellissement, 1582, Epistre.
Marinelli, Gli ornamenti, 1562, ded.
Casoni, ff. 47–47a.
Sibillet, Art poetique françois, 1573, ch. X, pp. 126–127.
Les blasons anatomiques, 1550, rep. 1866.

PROPORTION OR COLOR

45. Firenzuola, ff. 65–67.
Zoppio, ff. 234–239.
Canoniero, pp. 24–26.

Romei, Disc. I, pp. 18, 28.
Liebault, p. 4.
Franco, ff. 23–24a.
Nobili, ff. 3–3a.

GRACE, MAJESTY

46. Canoniero, pp. 25, 48–49, 53–55.
    Sardi, Discorsi, 1586, Della bellezza, p. 14.
    Nobili, ff. 6a–7.
    Firenzuola, Disc. I, ff. 84–88; 68, 62a (majesty).
    Vieri, Discorso delle bellezze, 1580, p. 11.
    Landi, p. 30.
    Garzoni, Le vite, 1588, p. 168.
    India, Discorsi, 1597, Della bellezza, pp. 34–36.
    Zuccolo, f. 58a.

BEAUTY IN MEN

47. Torelli, ff. 91a–93a.
    India, ded., ff. 1–4, 24.
    Boaistuau, Bref discours, ff. 108–110.
    Castiglione, pp. 33, 38–49, 65–67.
    Liebault, Au lecteur, ff. aII, pp. 5–7.
    Franco, f. 90.
    Firenzuola, Disc. I, ff. 71, 74, 75–75a.
    Heroët, p. 5.
    Sardi, p. 11.
    Gaurico, De symmetriis, 1603. (Ded. dated 1542.)

BEAUTY AND GOODNESS

48. Sardi, pp. 7–9.
    Gozzi, Dialogo della bellezza, 1581, ff. 5–6.
    Luigini, pp. 283–286.
    Domenichi, Dial. d' amore, pp. 11–18.
    Vieri, pp. 19–20.
    Castiglione, bk. IV, pp. 319–320.
    Firenzuola, Disc. I, ff. 70a–71.
    Landi, p. 30.
    Pellet, Discours de la beauté des dames, 1578.
    Pico della Mirandola, Commento (on Benivieni's Canzone del amor celeste &
        divino), lib. III, cap. I–II, in Opere di Girolamo Benivieni, 1519. (See also
        Benivieni's Ad lectorem.)
    Canoniero, pp. 23–24.
    Franco, f. 48.
    Trissino, I ritratti, 1524, ff. CIa–DIIIa.

CONCLUSION

49. Torelli, ff. 171–180.
    Guazzo, bk. II, p. 241.

CHAPTER VII

SOURCES OF CHAPTER

1. Barberino, Del reggimento e dei costumi delle donne, begun c. 1290, not printed
    until 1815, rep. 1842, pp. 27–31, Introduzione.

Christine de Pisan, Le tresor, 1536, written 1405.
Castiglione, Il libro del cortegiano, 1528, Eng. trans. by Hoby, 1561, Everyman Lib. III.
Nifo, De re aulica, 1534, cap. X, end.
Domenichi, La donna di corte, 1564, f. 19.
Anne de Beaujeu, Les enseignements, written in 1504 or 1505, pub. before 1521, f. AII.
Orliac, Jehanne, Anne de Beaujeu, Roi de France, 1926, p. 171.
Guasco, Ragionamento, 1596, ff. 4–8.

POSITION OF WOMEN OF THE COURT

2. Nifo, lib. I, cap. IX; lib. II, cap. IV.
Castiglione, bk. I, p. 29, bk. III, p. 188.

CHARACTER AND FUNCTION OF THE COURTIER

3. Castiglione, bk. I, pp. 31–85; bk. II, pp. 93–133; bk. III, p. 202 (courage); bk. II, pp. 133, 135 (conversation); bk. II, p. 94 (harmonious whole); bk. IV, pp. 261–262 (purpose).
Nifo, lib. I, cap. IX, XII, LII (purpose); lib. I, cap. XLV–XLVII (qualities not required); lib. I, cap. XIII–XVII, XXXV, XLIV, XLVIII–XLIX, L–LIV (necessary qualities); lib. II, cap. V (illustrations of affability).

QUALITIES AND FUNCTION OF THE WOMAN OF THE COURT

4. Nifo, lib. II, cap. IV.
Castiglione, bk. III, pp. 190–192.
Anne de Beaujeu, ff. A6–B6.

LOVE AS SUBJECT OF CONVERSATION AT COURT

5. Nifo, lib. I, cap. XXX–XXXIII; lib. II, cap. VI, VII.
Castiglione, bk. III, pp. 236–243.

ACCOMPLISHMENTS

6. Castiglione, bk. III, pp. 193–195.

DIFFERENCE BETWEEN MEN AND WOMEN OF THE COURT

7. Castiglione, bk. III, p. 189; bk. IV, p. 297 (point of resemblance).

RELATION TO MISTRESS

8. Guasco, ff. 12a–15.
Barberino, pt. XI, pp. 218–220.

RELATION TO COMPANIONS

9. Guasco, ff. 25a–26 (books recommended); ff. 26–27a (speech); ff. 27a–32a (avoidance of envy).
Anne de Beaujeu, ff. A9–A10.

STUDIES

10. Guasco, ff. 15a–21.

HEALTH, DRESS, CARE OF BELONGINGS

11. Guasco, ff. 21–23a; 24–25a (care of belongings).
Anne de Beaujeu, ff. A10a–A11.

ADVICE TO THE MORE MATURE WOMAN OF THE COURT

12. Christine de Pisan, pt. II, ch. II–VIII, ff. 68–74 (rules for relation to lady); ff. 74a–85 (vices to shun).

QUALITIES OF THE PRINCESS

13. Christine de Pisan, pt. I, ch. III, VII (Christian virtues); ch. VIII, IX (making peace); ch. X (sharing her wealth); ch. XI (moral virtues); ch. XII (ordering of the day).
Anne de Beaujeu, ff. A5a, B6a–B11, C4a–C5a.

RELATION OF PRINCESS TO HER LORD, HIS RELATIVES, AND FRIENDS

14. Christine de Pisan, pt. I, ch. XIII, XIV.
Anne de Beaujeu, ff. C6–C7.
Barberino, pt. 5, pp. 129–130, 142–147.
Roseo da Fabriano, Institutione del principe Christiano, 1543, trans. from the Spanish, cap. 4–15.

CARE OF CHILDREN

15. Christine de Pisan, pt. I, ch. XV.
Anne de Beaujeu, ff. D3a–D7.

RULE OF HER WOMEN

16. Christine de Pisan, pt. I, ff. 38–39. (Chaps. irregularly numbered from here on.)
Anne de Beaujeu, ff. C7a–D2.
Barberino, pt. 5, pp. 127–128, 137–140.

WINNING FAVOR OF SUBJECTS

17. Christine de Pisan, pt. I, ff. 34a–37a.
Anne de Beaujeu, ff. B11–C4, D2a–D3.

TREATMENT OF ENEMIES

18. Christine de Pisan, pt. I, ch. XVI.

HANDLING OF REVENUES

19. Christine de Pisan, pt. I, ff. 39–42.

PRINCESSES UNABLE TO FOLLOW THIS ADVICE

20. Christine de Pisan, pt. I, ff. 42a–43a.

THE YOUNG PRINCESS NEWLY MARRIED

21. Christine de Pisan, pt. I, ff. 48–51a (general); 52a–60 (behavior in mixed assemblies, lovers).

WIDOWHOOD OF PRINCESSES

22. Christine de Pisan, pt. I, ff. 44–48.
Anne de Beaujeu, ff. D8–D8a.
Barberino, pt. 6, pp. 175–176.

LADIES OF LOWER RANK WITH AUTHORITY AND WITHOUT

23. Christine de Pisan, pt. II, ch. IX, ff. 85a–87a (baronesses); ff. 88–90 (wives of knights, squires, and gentlemen); ff. 93a–95 (daughters of gentlemen married to rich bourgeois, merchants); pt. III, ff. 98a–106 (wives of clerks, divines, etc.).

DISCONTENT WITH STATION

24. Christine de Pisan, pt. II, ch. XI, XII, ff. 90a–93; pt. III, ff. 107–108a (extravagance of a merchant's wife).

BEHAVIOR OF WOMEN TO WOMEN

25. Christine de Pisan, pt. III, ch. VI, ff. 114a–118 (old to young, young to old). Anne de Beaujeu, ff. D5–D6a (dress and behavior of older women compared to young).

CHAPTER VIII

1. Le Fort Inexpugnable, 1550, p. 180.
2. Civil Conversation, Tudor trans., bk. III, vol. I, p. 5.
3. Christiani Matrimonii Institutio, 1526, f. N4a.
4. Bk. III, ch. 6.
5. The Defence of Good Women, 1545, ff. DII–DbI.
6. A Godly Forme of Household Government, 1630 (1588), f. G4a.
7. Positions, 1581, rep. 1888, ch. 38, p. 182.
8. Un Breve Trattato, 1545, f. 38a.
9. Erotomania, 1610, trans. 1640, pp. 89–92.
10. Rye, W. B., England as Seen by Foreigners, 1865, p. 10, from Emanuel Van Meteren.
11. Le Traicte de Lutilite et Honneste de Mariage, 1527.
12. Ff. 559–564.
13. Treatise 2.
14. Instruction, 1592, bk. I, cap. 6, ff. D4a–D8a.
15. Vidua Christiana, 1529, ff. 52–53.
16. Laberinto, 1558, ff. 24a–25a.
17. Opus in Evangelium Missus est Gabriel Angelus, c. 1473.
18. Le Bellezze, 1542, pt. II, ff. 94–98. See also for another example Auvergne, Devotes Louanges a la Vierge Marie, 1509.
19. L'Honneste Femme, p. 177.
20. Libellus de his quae ab Optimis Principibus Agenda Sunt, 1521.
21. Oeuvres Completes, 1873–1892, vol. I, pp. 445–450.
22. Harrod, *Life of John Maynard Keynes*, Harcourt, Brace and Company, 1951, p. 175.

Preface to the Bibliography

By way of introduction to the Bibliography, or appendix as one chooses, I have included a survey of the whole field under the title "The Literature of Gentility." The variety of books has seemed to be a surprise to many— "What can you find on such a subject?"—and it has seemed advantageous to show the range for both the gentleman and the lady. Also some explanation seems due of why the limits have been extended at times beyond reasonable expectation.

This bibliography for the lady, like that for the gentleman, has been planned beyond my own uses only as a suggestive list for students on the hunt. The variety of material, sketched in the appended essay, may make it useful for many, even unrelated, proposals. In search myself for generally held conceptions of the renaissance I have been interested in printed books as presumably more widely distributed than manuscripts might be, and have paid, with a few exceptions, only incidental attention to the collections of manuscripts published in modern times.

As far as practicable I have drawn the titles from the originals, indicating when they have been taken from reprints (time always pressed too hard, particularly abroad, to allow much going over of originals of what had been read in reprints). Titles of books unseen are marked with a double dagger. They are given as found in various sources unidentified except where taken from Du Verdier. The edition that appears is either the only one available at the time or the one I chose, though not the earliest, for its better editing (so claimed) and its completeness through additions (also claimed), or in the case of an old book I have taken a later edition as more nearly contemporary particularly in dedicatory letters, or perhaps only because the print was easier to read. In general the same edition of course appears in the notes. The exceptions are explainable by the fact that when it came to final checking I had to use the edition that happened to be available.

Complete titles have been my aim, with the one exception of complimentary phrases which I left out at the beginning. If I were doing it over again I should put them all in as in some cases having biographical value, or who can tell what value to another student? The omissions are indicated.

Spelling and punctuation follow the originals even to what may be printer's errors, except that in English and Latin titles I have modernized the use of "i" and "j," and "u" and "v," dropped ligatures, and expanded conventional Latin contractions. Capitalization furnished a problem since some titles were all in capitals, of interest only in true bibliographies. I have adopted modern English usage, dropping all capitals except for initial capitals to proper names and adjectives, and of course the beginning of sentences or phrases punctuated as sentences. I have, however, in no instance supplied capitals where lower case was used for proper names and adjectives and the first word after a period.

Printing data, place, printer, and date, have been given with the title where obtainable either from title page, colophon, or elsewhere without indicating source. Absence of such data means they are not known to me. Further data within parentheses have been drawn in general from the Catalogues of the British Museum Library and the Bibliothèque Nationale of Paris, and consist chiefly of the dates of other editions, earlier and later (carried through the eighteenth century) and of translations, some indication of character if the title is obscure, and references to sections related to the subject if only part of a larger work. For brevity no indication is given of reimpressions within the same year, or of undated editions, and no attempt has been made to distinguish between reimpressions and new editions. A few call numbers of the Bibliothèque Nationale have been given because I was able to find them only through the kindness of Madame de la Fontinelle. I should emphasize that I have been interested in noting other editions than the one I used only for what indication they may give of the popularity of the book and thus something of its representative value. I had neither time nor skill to rise to bibliographical thoroughness and exactness.

The form of the names in the alphabetical list is in general what appears in the catalogues of the British Museum Library and the Bibliothèque Nationale, or in biographical dictionaries. Spelling in the titles is inconsistent in all languages.

A word should be said here about the supplementary list for the gentleman which has been appended to this work in order to make available what further titles have turned up during the search for material on the lady. I have looked at some of these books but so few, in proportion to the whole number, that I have not distinguished them from the rest. The same form has been followed as for the lady, which in general follows the pattern of the original list for the gentleman.

The Literature of Gentility

Bibliographies are deceptive things, I realize after having put together two such lists: that published some years ago for my *Doctrine of the English Gentleman in the Sixteenth Century*, and now this second for the lady. So much lies beneath the dull surface of rows of names, titles, places, printers, and dates that I want to take this opportunity to survey briefly this literature of gentility—its scope, its character, its general significance.

Though at first my main business was with the English renaissance I set no geographical limitations, since boundaries are too difficult to draw in renaissance studies, and I have swept up all I could find from earliest medieval times, simply for lack of any nearer good starting point. Types and originals of types flourished in the middle ages and continued green, or only slightly yellowing, to the end of the renaissance, and beyond, for which reason I set a late date as the formal end of my period, 1625, the death of James I. After him the general atmosphere entirely changed, as later treatises show, and with the passing of Sir Francis Bacon the next year the last lingering sparks of the English high renaissance may be felt to have gone out too. As for territory, whatever subsiding land and inrushing waters may have done ages back to isolate the British Isles from the continent, one may, so to speak, pass dry-shod from Italy, France, and Spain to England and back again, by way of the mind, through all the renaissance as well as through the middle ages, as everybody knows. By importation, translation, and imitation the English made themselves one with Europe in this field as in all others. And in truth, because Italian and French presses particularly were more busy, or at least more numerous, than English, it is only by a study of continental work that the true shape of English thought can be clearly seen. And, as the title of this book shows, when it came to seeking a completion of the English conception of gentility in the ideal set up in theory for the lady the picture had to be found almost entirely in continental treatises. Against this spread in time and place I have appended to both bibliographies indexes of subjects by nations.

By the term "literature of gentility" I mean to indicate that my field has been narrowed to treatises on the theory of what ladies and gentlemen ought to be, as distinct from concrete representations of them in history and biography, and in fiction. Even so, as may be seen, it is a large field to plough, and though the limitation imposed has its disadvantages, particularly in the case of the lady, in my judgment the effort to survey only theory has brought results sufficient to justify it. In practice, however, it is not so simple a matter as it may seem at first thought to decide where theory ends and concrete portrait begins, or even, for that matter, where gentility ends and common humanity begins. Many of the books in these lists will seem of doubtful claim to inclusion, but I have decided to err rather on the side of too wide and too much than too narrow and too little; and I have even, as a sort of guide to the direction in which the various types of books tended to go, included some that represent the farthest extreme, and that, considered simply in themselves, would have no claim to a place here. This has seemed wise particularly for the lady.

For example, love belongs clearly and specially to the proper equipment of lady and gentleman, and treatises such as Equicola's consider the specific ways by which either may attract the other, and after obtaining, hold and increase love. But Equicola's treatise looks both ways, higher and lower. If his love, founded on the senses and seeking the ultimate satisfaction of the senses, and his directions for accomplishing such an end are presented in a more explicit way, stripped of all reference or pretense to philosophical definitions, you have Piccolomini's dialogue called *Della Bella Creanza delle Donne*, where the old dame Raffaella, by describing the delights of love to the innocent and ignorant, neglected young wife Margherita, persuades her to take a lover. If Piccolomini's intention was satiric, as some defenders claim, it might as well not have been, both in consideration of the typical character of its matter and of its later acceptance as a portrait of the ideal. Then change Raffaella into Nanna talking to her daughter Pippa in plainer terms still for a widened sphere of action, and with the end not love but riches, and you have Aretino's dialogues on the arts and deceits of courtesans. Piccolomini's dialogue still maintains the fiction of gentility, but in fact it serves the same purpose as Aretino's. For this reason though Aretino's *Ragionamenti*, do not, on the basis of ideality, belong among these treatises for ladies and gentlemen, I have included them. Or may one even argue that they do belong, since Aretino assures the reader in one title that he thus exposes these harpies in order to warn young men away? I have said that Equicola looks higher as well as lower. Particularly in defining the different kinds of love he approaches love in the abstract. That strain followed far enough leads to treatises like Ficino's, and Pico della Mirandola's, so highly philosophical that this human love between men and women sinks wholly out of sight. Or the turn may be religious instead of philosophical, as with Godofredus. I have represented these extremes with a few entries, though strictly speaking they lie beyond the confines of my subject.

Likewise with the subject of marriage, some authors wrote for entirely other ends than to teach husbands and wives, noble or ignoble, their duties to each other. The controversy over celibacy for the priesthood must have produced many more defenses of marriage than have come to my notice, but in order to suggest the stretch of that subject. I have included a few that did, such as Poynet's praise of marriage as an attack on celibacy, and Martin's refutation of Poynet. Over into the religious realm goes also another type of treatise, those presenting a picture of womanly virtues. When the model becomes Solomon's wise woman, or Santa Monica, or even the Virgin Mary, the picture is far off from the secular ideal of the lady. But I have included a few examples of this type, such as Le Roy's *Livre de la Femme Forte*, and Auvergne's *Devotes Louanges a la Vierge Marie*, not only because the secular ideal often imperceptibly merges into it, but also because it sharpens the outlines of the secular ideal.

Another problem in selection is presented by form. Indubitably the field cannot be assumed to be covered if one stops with prose treatises. The renaissance made no such discrimination; nor can we. Equicola in an extended discussion of authorities on the nature of love, at the beginning of his book on the subject first rules out the mere versifiers of his time who, in dreams and complaints *ad nauseam*, recount their hopes, fears, jealousies, cares, torments, griefs, reconciliations, accusations against fortune, the gods, and nature, or who, if they praise their mistress exhaust heaven and earth for similes to express her perfections. For their emptiness, exaggerations, tastelessness, he says, they are beneath his notice. But he will name among those dedicated to love and the muses, for their grace, elegance, and learning, Guitton di Arezzo, Guido Cavalcanti, Dante, Petrarch, Barberino, and Jean de Meung, in whose *Romance of the Rose* the whole art of loving is enclosed, and will put them side by side with prose writers, Boccaccio, Ficino, Pico della Mirandola, Alberti, Bembo. Some poems on love are as much essays as are the prose works and offer no real problem. I have used this consideration as a general principle of selection, including all poems that sound general, explanatory, and philosophic in intention, and omitting those that seem personal, descriptive, wholly emotional in their appeal.

In prose works it is relatively easy to draw the line between abstract theory concerning the ideal and its concrete embodiment in fiction and history. But one becomes well aware that much theory is directly expressed in both fiction and historical documents, particularly letters. I have not pretended to explore these sources, but I have not ignored what came my way, especially through contemporary comment, Bronzini's for example. Hence I have again stepped over the line in including some collections of letters—whether real or fictitious is of no matter for this purpose—and also collections of those examples and lives of women from Eve to the daughters of Sir Thomas More which these ages were so fond of citing, and a few stories or histories such as Lyly's *Euphues* and Bouchet's account of St. Radegone, queen of Clotaire I, who is a model in her behavior as maid, wife, queen, and nun.

So much for these more general considerations that have guided the compiling of the bibliographies. And now as to the subjects of the books which are covered by the terms "literature of gentility." The range is wider than one might at first expect, but far wider for the gentleman than for the lady, as a glance at the classified indexes will show. In testimony to the many-sidedness of the ideal for the renaissance gentleman there are handbooks for him as prince, courtier, ambassador, counselor, magistrate, and plain gentleman living upon his country estate. There are complete schemes for his education, from birth to manhood, and textbooks on all the matters of most moment to him, from ethics to agriculture, not excluding heraldry and letter writing. There are "perfect methods" for training hawks and horses, fighting duels, drawing the long bow. There are instructions in the fine arts of music, painting, and dancing, and philosophical and other discourses on their companions, love and beauty. There are guide books, for touring Europe was the last stage in his education. The most important of the books in this list are those belonging to the first group, which try to define the gentleman, and set forth his special ingredients, his special place in the scheme of things, such as the anonymous *Institution of a Gentleman* and the earlier *Governor* of Sir Thomas Elyot among English treatises, and Castiglione's *Courtier*, of course, among Italian. Such books have an ancient and honorable history. In the middle ages the civilians and canonists seem to have been very busy defining in their *De Nobilitate's* and *De Principe's* the characteristics, rights, and powers of rulers, both kings and nobles. The issue was joined between church and state, and in such a controversy the delimiting of power and character became important. A large number of these treatises appeared from Dante's time to the end of the fifteenth century. The *De Nobilitate's* usually take the form of compilations of all available answers to moot points. These old treatises were still considered important enough in the sixteenth century to be collected and reprinted, along with a mass of other legalistic medieval matter, in two series of twelve great folios each, one at Lyons in 1549, and the other at Venice in 1584. In 1558 André Tiraqueau, a French lawyer of prodigious learning, published a heavy folio, *De Nobilitate*, a compendium in which any inquisitive modern may conveniently find all the points apparently ever made on this intricate subject, including a complete survey from this point of view of all professions and trades, even down to midwifery. Tiraqueau's list of authorities cited in his work covers more than three pages in triple columns.

Interest in the subject was also still great enough in the sixteenth century to produce fresh attempts at definition, which, however, usually covered the same ground, though in less exhaustive fashion. Perhaps the most complete Italian treatise is Muzio's *Il Gentilhuomo*, published in 1571, which, he admitted, is at best a confused discourse. On the much debated point of whether arms or learning confers more nobility he of course gave the palm to learning, being himself a scholar, and thereby sufficiently roused the ire of a soldier, Domenico Mora, to provoke in answer *Il Cavaliere*, where Mora had no difficulty, he thought, making out a better case for arms. There was a considerable body of treatises concerning the source of nobility, and the point appeared as a part of many treatises on the general subject. In 1577 L'Alouette redefined nobility in the hope of reforming the nobles of France, and Thierrat as late as 1602 attempted to sum up the matter for Prince Henry. The most polished treatise of this kind was written by the Portuguese bishop, Osorio, in 1542, reprinted six times during the century, translated into English in 1576, and included by Gabriel Harvey in his list of popular works by foreign writers. Osorio was often quoted by clergymen, soldiers, and heralds, and Roger Ascham, though he found him too Ciceronian, accorded him admiration and friendship. Such treatises of native growth are far to seek in England, though the matter is often touched on in works on other subjects—war, dueling, and particularly heraldry. The heralds, those other curious preservers of relics, were still publishing the old lists of privileges, not without consciousness of their probable offense to the "churl's brood," who by this time were finding ready means to force their way in among their betters. "I would have them all understand," Sir John Ferne warned this "churl's brood" in his dedicatory epistle to *The Blazon of Gentrie*, "how gently I have delt with them, in that I have not opened unto our Gentry and Nobles, the one halfe of those severe lawes and constitutions, both provinciall and imperiall, justly layd upon that base and obscure state of the ungentle, because I would not have them altogether troden under foote, in this our common wealth, since that by the customes of our nation, and lenitie of our soveraigns, they are suffered to enjoy a greater freedome of life, then in any other nation." As a matter of fact, in the sixteenth century these long lists of privileges and exemptions, boiled down to fit the truth, would amount to one little paragraph.

The other group of old treatises which were precursors to the "Courtiers" and "Gentlemen" of the renaissance set forth the prince. These works usually emphasized the office rather than the man, debating the supremacy of royal or sacerdotal power, and the excellence of a kingdom over every other form of government. The good king was set over against the tyrant, and his bringing up, virtues, and duties, as a man, the head of his household, and the ruler of his people, were described, sometimes only briefly, sometimes at length, as in Egidio Colonna's *De Regimine Principum*, written around 1280 for Philip the Fair. Colonna, following his master St. Thomas Aquinas, chiefly summarized Aristotle's *Ethics* and *Politics* with small reference to Christian teachings. He set the pattern for all subsequent writers on the science of government, and survived in his own form until the seventeenth century, his book being reprinted eleven times between 1473 and 1617.

The sixteenth century, as a matter of fact, was very busy turning out new "Institutions of Princes," "Offices of a King," and "Politic Discourses" cast in the same mold. Italy led in numbers as usual, but all countries made their contributions. Continental writers were well known in the original in England—Machiavelli, Patrizi, Lipsius, Budé, Bodin, Omphalius, and Foxius Morzillus. Several others were translated—Erasmus, Guevara, Coignet, Hurault. Few of these writers took contemporary conditions into account, notable exceptions being Machiavelli and Coignet, ambassador and counselor. Coignet wrote in an endeavor to drag France out of that abyss into which corruption at court and religious dissension had plunged her, and from which Montaigne despaired of escape. He mingled modern examples with ancient and analyzed some of the existing causes of disorder, such as dueling. James I, before he became king of England, wrote for his son, Prince Henry, the most realistic of treatises in English, analyzing the faults of his people—clergy, nobility, merchant and artisan classes—and advising remedies. It was safer, however, to stick to Plato, Aristotle, Cicero, and Seneca. Even James had to defend himself from the hornets he stirred up by his advice about how to handle Puritans and preachers who rashly tried to meddle in affairs of state. So an endless number of books poured forth the praises of monarchy, precepts for the upbringing of princes, rules for the management of kingdoms. Though addressed to the supreme ruler, they were intended also and often expressly recommended for gentlemen, the lesser rulers, and occasionally even for common men that they might judge their own duty better by knowing what belonged to those set over them. Outside of special matters like appointing ambassadors and imposing taxes, the "institution" of a prince was the "institution of a gentleman." Not only was the prince himself a gentleman, but there was only one source for all schemes of education, the ancients. Upon the advice of Plato, Aristotle, Cicero, Quintilian, and the rest were modeled the infancy, childhood, youth, and maturity of all born above the common lot.

I have dwelt thus long on these old treatises and their direct descendants in the renaissance because the treatise on nobility married to the treatise on kingship produced the handbooks for gentlemen, whether courtiers, ambassadors, counselors, governors, or plain gentlemen. For though it was recognized that much of the advice for the king, as I have said, applied to the gentleman, there were differences that needed to be expressed, points that needed expansion for particular uses. Economic and political changes made re-definition of the gentleman's status and function an obvious necessity. There were books enough on the prince's training, said Lawrence Humphrey, but few on the gentleman's.[1] Ludovick Bryskett, Spenser's and Sidney's friend, announced in his preface that his *Discourse of Civil Life* was aimed at the children, not of princes, but "onely of such gentlemen of meaner qualitie as may be fit instruments for the service of their commonwealth." From Castiglione's time onward a stream of these books issued

[1] *The Nobles*, 1563, ded. to the Inner Temple.

forth in all countries, defining the gentleman and prescribing his qualities, in an effort to hold up an ideal that seemed to be fading for the possessors of old names and was not yet realized by the new claimants to titles.

Castiglione's *Courtier* stands out as the example par excellence of all the renaissance attempts to portray the perfect man. No one before or after him clothed so urbanely, vividly, and convincingly the dry bones of an abstraction with the color and shape of life. He wrote like the true artist with his eye on the object—the Italian gentleman, as he came and went in the cultivated circle of Urbino, also like the artist idealizing what he saw. For the renaissance in all Europe Castiglione moved among the immortals, Plato and Xenophon and Cicero, who had painted the ultimate ideal. In England he became, in Hoby's translation, a sort of gentlemen's bible for Elizabethan courtiers, and was heartily recommended even by Ascham, that arch opponent of "Englishmen Italianated." But he had not written for Englishmen, and hence did not suit so well the homespun gentleman who did not go to court. No native treatise can rival *The Courtier* as literature, but the three outstanding attempts to define and train English gentlemen are not without some literary merit and bear the authentic native stamp. The three authors belong to three different groups of this elastic class, and present as many different points of view. The earliest is Sir Thomas Elyot, a lawyer of Sir Thomas More's circle. Interested himself in administrative problems, he conceived the gentleman ideally as a lawyer trained to govern England well, and wrote his *Governor* accordingly. It is rather a discourse on education and morals than a portrait, and as thoroughly English in this emphasis as *The Courtier* is Italian in its emphasis on personal perfection. Published first in 1531, it was reprinted many times during the century, and still quoted well on into the next. This popularity was deserved, for though not graceful and well proportioned like *The Courtier*, the book is occasionally enlivened with racy comment and personal experience, and sweetened with the obvious kindliness and sincerity of the writer, who is anxious lest his gentle readers, unused to serious discourses, should grow "fatigate." On the other hand the anonymous author of *The Institution of the Gentleman*, which appeared in 1555, obviously belonged to the landed gentry, and saw the gentleman as worthily performing his duty if he merely stayed at home, capably administering his own estates, and serving the whole community as a justice of the peace. There is amenity to this book, as to *The Governor*, in the style and in the spirit that inspired it—pride and faith in the beauty and worth of the gentleman's calling. The third writer, Lawrence Humphrey, was a clergyman, successively President of Magdalen College and Dean of Gloucester and of Winchester. To him the important function of the gentle class was the protection of true religion from destruction by ignorance or malice. His book, *The Nobles*, published in English in 1563 (it had previously appeared in Latin), shows this bias in its emphasis on the Christian duty of the gentleman, but Humphrey does not, like seventeenth century admonishers of the gentleman, (Clement Ellis, for instance, in his *Gentile Sinner*) christianize his whole point of view. And yet, though the emphasis is different in each of the three books, the qualities prescribed are the same, and in viewing the gentleman primarily in relation to his duty and importance to the state Elyot set the pattern for the century.

A more highly specialized group of treatises than these that set forth the general ideal is that of the handbooks for courtiers, ambassadors, counselors, secretaries. They cover much the same ground but with specific attention to the specific problems of the man who would serve his prince in a special capacity. The Italians differentiated between the courtier who belonged to the prince's household and served his person, and his advisers and representatives who served both him and the state in an official way. The main recommendation of the courtier was his power to please in hours of recreation; of the others, wisdom and experience in public affairs. Agostino Nifo, a contemporary of Castiglione, drawing this distinction, criticized most of the treatises on the courtier for making him either a mere flatterer or buffoon in his effort to entertain, or such a paragon of virtue and learning that he rivaled his prince and was sure to weary him. In both cases certain nice questions arose which furnished the chief subject matter. How far may an honest courtier follow his prince in questionable and even vicious amusements, or an honest counselor yield to an obdurate prince bent on rash or evil designs, or an honest ambassador serve faithfully both the master by whom he is sent and the master to whom he is sent? Or in other words, are a good courtier, a good counselor, a good ambassador one and the same thing as a good man? The answers varied: choose an honest prince to serve, said some; be as honest as possible without losing favor and influence, said others; never compromise, said a few. It will be remembered that More discussed some of these matters with Hythloday in his friend's garden in Antwerp. There is a curious sameness in these handbooks, especially in those for counselors and ambassadors. If composed in Latin they might as well have been written by Frenchmen as Italians, by Germans as Spaniards. They are dateless and characterless, each chewing the cud of its predecessors, adding nothing in the process, and subtracting nothing either.

Next in general importance to all these treatises that construct the framework for the gentleman is the group that considers his formal education. At many points the two sets overlap, but the educational treatise is chiefly interested in prescribing the subjects, books, methods, and exercises suitable to the proper development of his mind and body. Again it is not possible to draw a clear line between treatises intended specially for the gentleman and others of a more general purpose. Such men as Erasmus, Sturm, and Vives, who were exceedingly influential in England, wrote with the general cause of education at heart and the production of scholars rather than gentlemen. Even Ascham, probably the best known of English pedagogues, had a professional aim in view, writing for the gentleman who must turn his wits to making a living—the younger son without patrimonial acres. Mulcaster is more general in his treatment of education for the upper classes, and coming toward the end of the century, shows a disposition to make a fresh approach to English problems and rely less on ancient theorists. He says in the preface to his *Positions*, "In this kind of argument wherin I presently deale, it is no proofe, bycause Plato praiseth it, bycause Aristotle alloweth it, bycause Cicero recommends it, bycause Quintilian is acquainted with it, or any others else, in any argument else, that therefore it is for us to use." The outer reaches of this general group include special appeals for particular subjects and ultimately textbooks on all the matters thought proper for gentlemen to know. History was, all told, the most prized because of its practical value in teaching men to govern well. How to suck out its "sap and sweet marrow" busied many a learned head—Patrizi, Foxius Morzillus, Bodin, to name a few. Others culled examples and classified them under politic headings for ready reference, as Erasmus thought it not beneath himself to do. His *Apophthegms* and *Adages* were known everywhere throughout the sixteenth century. The popularity of travel abroad, especially in France and Italy, brought out numerous "perfect methods" for learning foreign languages. John Florio's *First* and *Second Fruits* present lively pictures of London life by way of luring the gentleman on to a working knowledge of Italian. But most of the textbooks which I have included are of interest to the theorist only in their prefaces and dedicatory letters, perhaps only in their titles, where the general or specific advantage to the gentleman of mastering the text is pointed out as persuasively as possible. And it must be said that according to these prefatory claims there was very little that the gentleman could not find of great importance to himself in one capacity or another.

The gentleman was viewed, however, not only as a prospective governor, lawyer, or scholar to be trained in the science and art of these callings, but also, and more anciently, as a defender of his country. For his education on this side numerous books appeared, some persuading him that he ought to become a soldier, and others teaching him what a soldier, that is a commander, should know. The existence of the first type shows that war could no longer be assumed to be of immediate interest to the English gentleman, as it had been to the knight. It is significant, I think, that while Castiglione equips his courtier to excel at fighting, no English treatise of the sort does. The argument for war is left pretty much to old soldiers like Thomas Churchyard, Geoffrey Gates, and Barnaby Rich, who, retired from the field, took up their goose-quills and contended for the honor of their profession. Quaint bits slip out. Stephen Gosson argued that all Spanish wars were unjust, all English wars just because they were fought in defense of "an innocent maiden queen."[2] Gates contended that peace is a preparation for punishment: "When the Lord meaneth to plague a wicked natione for sinne and to translate them to the power and scepter of another nation: then he filleth them with the fatnesse of the earth, and giveth them peace that they may wax rotten in idlenesse, and become of dulle wittes, slowe of courage, weake handed, and feeble kneede: that when the spoiler commeth, they may in al pointe be unfurnished of warlike prowesse, and not able to resist."[3] The second set on the art of war leans heavily as usual on old authorities, particularly Vegetius, covering such topics as the equipment of the soldier, the number and proportioning of men among gunners, pikemen, and horsemen, the defense or attack of a fort, the order of battle, and the like. Another topic usually included was the qualities which the soldier should have, particularly the walk of life that he should come from. Barnaby Rich rejected husbandmen because, though used to coarse fare, they must have their fill or their courage fails, and they also lack nimbleness and readiness, and, as he put it, "are utterly voyde of one of the greatest graces that to a soldier doth pertayne, which is to be delightsome in the wearing of his apparell, and in the keeping of his furniture."[4] The qualities of the commander were usually prescribed too, in much the same terms as those of the prince, courtier, or plain gentleman.

One special problem exercised the militant English mind, the relative merits of the old English weapon, the long bow, and firearms. There were stout defenders of the bow up to the end of the sixteenth century. One of the most doughty, Sir John Smith, found the chief cause of the evil days into which the military art had fallen in the abandonment of old weapons for new—not only bows for guns, but short swords for rapiers a yard and a half long, old armor for none at all (witness Sidney), and even old words for foreign terms, legar for camp, beleaguered for besieged, colours for ensigns. Churchyard's protest against the new arms reminds one of modern arguments against new implements for killing.

> In elders daies when manhood shone, as bright as blasing starre,
> And Christian hart and noble mind disdained this turkish warre,
> The Bow was used as force of man, & strength of arms might draw
> To glad the friend and daunt the foe, and hold the world in awe.
> But when that strength and courage fail'd, and cunning crept in place
> The Shot and roring Canon came, stout people to deface.[5]

---

[2] *The Trumpet of Warre*, 1598, pt. IV, ff. E6–E7a.
[3] *The Defence of Militarie Profession*, 1579, p. 20.
[4] *A right exelent dialogue*, 1574, ff. G VIII–G VIIIa.
[5] Published along with other prefatory pieces in Rich. Robinson's *The Auncient Order . . . of Prince Arthur*, 1583.

But if the gentleman needed spurring to his duty as defender of his country he was quick enough at defense of himself and needed the curb instead. Treatises on dueling, the circumstances and laws of it and the handling of weapons made up a formidable part of this gentleman's library. Some writers devoted themselves to an attack on dueling as against the laws of God and man; others defended it as the only method suitable to the gentleman of sustaining his honor against attack. Many, deploring it as wholly evil, saw no way to root it out, and bent their energies to reducing it to some order, whereby might be lessened its greatest evils, such as invoking it on trivial occasions, unfairly acquiring the position of the challenged, a great advantage in the fight, and employing tricks to insure victory. One of these was Girolamo Muzio, whose book was widely known and translated into English by Saviolo, a famous Italian fencing master of Elizabeth's time. Having settled the etiquette of the duel Muzio went on to teach the practice with rapier and dagger, the new weapons of the Italian system. Churchyard was not the only objector to these new weapons which were threatening to supplant the old sword and buckler. George Silver, an English rival of Saviolo, sprang to the support of the old as late as 1599 with his *Paradoxes of Defence*. But Silver, like the defenders of the bow, was speaking for a lost cause. Wars were to be waged by more destructive weapons and finesse was to rule the private art of defense.

Companions of these treatises on dueling are a group on honor. Once challenged, however reluctant to try his cause that way, the gentleman could not refuse to fight because his honor was at stake. Just what this honor was no renaissance gentleman could really tell, but many attempted to define it, partly as a characteristic belonging only to the gentleman, never to a man of the lower classes, partly as the sole significance and necessity of the duel. Foxius Morzillus gave it the most extended and idealistic treatment that I have found.

Another set of treatises was devoted to heraldry and devices or emblems. Heraldry was a very important subject, the heralds said, for gentlemen to master, if they were going to be intelligent about their own insignia, and able to distinguish real from upstart gentlemen. Indeed it could be shown to be a liberal education besides in astronomy, botany, zoology, geometry—from what realm does the herald not draw his figures, and in moral philosophy—what virtues does he not hold up to the admiration and emulation of men. "Albeit," Ferne warned, "I would not wish gentlemen too curious in the signes of their coate-armour: for if any man should communicate in his life or conversation, but halfe the partes or quallities of that beast which he beareth in his coate of armes, on my credit, it were more fit for him to be stabled amongst brute breasts, then chambred with the noble."[6] Curious hodgepodges these books are with their pseudo-history of heraldry, exhaus-

[6] *The Blazon of Gentrie*, 1586, p. 237.

tive differentiations between gentlemen, and minute analyses of the meanings of heraldic symbols. Heraldry like the military art had fallen into disrepute for one reason or another, as suggested by its urgent recommendation to gentlemen as an important part of their mental equipment, but a sort of lesser branch of it was very popular among the elegant pastimes of the age. The making of emblems and devices or *impresas* originated in Italy, and occasioned many books of examples, reducing their construction to strict rules, and differentiating between them in the handling of the allegorical figures and verses which they both contained. Scholars, wits, and cavaliers tried their hand at the intriguing toys, the English as usual more given to translating than inventing.

On the general subject of etiquette the English wrote little, and that chiefly for children. The adult in England found his guide to refinement of manners in foreign works, two Italian books particularly translated into English, Guazzo's *Civil Conversation* and Della Casa's *Galateo*. Both were on everybody's lips, and "Galateo" became a synonym for etiquette book, or etiquette itself of an exaggerated, affected sort. But neither to Della Casa nor to Guazzo can be ascribed wholly the plague of affectations that swept England. Far more potent must have been the behavior of returned travelers, young blades that went abroad with little in their heads and came back with external embellishments only, though it may be supposed that for lack of the corrective which English books on English manners would have supplied, the influence of these Italian books to some extent intensified this injudicious imitation of foreign manners, unsuitable for the downright Englishman who had not enough of the native grace of the Italian or Frenchman or Spaniard to make ceremony pleasing. James Cleland apparently did well to prefer to all the elaborate bowing and sweeping flourishing of hats "the good olde Scottish shaking of the two right hands togither at meeting with an uncovered head."[7]

The need, however, of engrafting something of foreign refinement upon the young gentleman, as a rounding off of his education, was one of the solid beliefs of the times. As one writer put it, less poetically than Shakespeare, "Certainly, upon his dunghill, the English Gentleman is somewhat stubborn and churlish. Travel will sweeten him very much, and imbreed in him Courtesy, Affability, Respect and Reservation."[8] Several books of advice for travelers made their appearance, chiefly concerned with listing the kinds of information they should seek, and sometimes throwing in, usually by way of satire, advice as to behavior in different countries, in the style of this passage from Florio's *Second Fruits*. Keep company with the best, he said, "but remember that the Donnes of Spaine, the Earles of Germany, the Monsieurs of Fraunce, the Bishops of Italy, the Knights of

---

[7] *The Institution of a Young Nobleman*, 1607, bk. V, ch. 5, p. 177.
[8] William Higford, *Institutions or advice to his grandson*, 1658, pt. III, p. 84.

Naples, the Lords of Scotland, the Hedalgoes of Partingale, the younger brethren of England, and the Noblemen of ungherie, doe make a very poor company. And take heede you never give credite unto the Faremos of Rome, unto the addesso of Italie, to the magnana of Spain, to the by and by of England, unto the warrant you of Scotland, nor unto the tantosts of France, for they are words of small importance."[9]

One further group of treatises for the gentleman is worth distinguishing, those on his outdoor recreations—riding, hunting, hawking, fishing, and shooting the long bow. Ascham's *Toxophilus* was the standard treatise on the last topic, an entertaining work for its many sidelights on the times, and its direct, vigorous style. Books on the kindred sports of hunting and hawking would fill a good-sized library. Every part from the management of the great horse to the feeding of dogs and curing of hawks' diseases seems to have been the gentleman's business to know. Turberville's works on falconry and hunting are illustrated with woodcuts showing Queen Elizabeth at the kill, or picnicking in the woods in the midst of her courtiers, illustra· tions which served equally well for editions published after the accession of James by a judicious change of the central figure into doublet and hose. There was not lacking for all these activities the argument for their further solid value in hardening the body to endure the toils of war, and sharpening the wits to solve the problems of statecraft by pitting them against wily beasts.

So far I have been taking up the books addressed explicitly to the gentleman, with little or no reference to the domestic side of life, in which the lady inevitably figures. Now I should like to turn to the other bibliography devoted to the subject of the theory of gentility as it applied to women. There is no hard and fast line that can be drawn between the two, as is illustrated by the inclusion of the subjects of love and beauty in both. And since the lady is considered practically only in relation to the gentleman, there is not much that concerns her that does not concern him too. I will take up first the books that belong to both, and then those that treat the lady only.

By far the largest group deals with the war between the sexes, an ancient war—in literature. It is to be remarked that, contrary to expectation perhaps, the defenders of women far outnumber their detractors. Some fight equally well on both sides, and chiefly the subject would seem to have furnished a handy opportunity for the sharpening of wits from the middle ages to well into the eighteenth century. The titles to these books usually indicate clearly their tenor—*Invectives, Alphabets of Vices* on the one side, *Apologies, Blasons, Triumphs, Garlands, Champions* on the other, but occasionally an intended insult is deepened with a title promising praise, such as *La Grand Loyaulte des Femmes*. Not only are the sexes involved in this

[9] 1591, ch. 6, p. 95.

controversy, but also the institution that combines them, marriage, is often made to stand or fall at the same time.

The books on marriage vary greatly in character. Some present the legal aspect of both betrothal and marriage, throwing in by the way advice as to behavior. Some are complaints of the great disadvantages of marriage, usually to the man, sometimes to the woman, and these, as noted before, run over into the controversy about celibacy for the priesthood. The answering defense of marriage is woven somewhere into most of the treatises. The chief topic, however, is advice to men and women on the married state. Some of these books are addressed to men on the proper choice of a wife, duties and proper behavior to her, or on such questions as whether a scholar should take a wife, or whether a man is really disgraced by a graceless wife. A great number of the *Institutions, Commendations, Precepts,* and *Doctrinals of Marriage* are addressed to women, and portray the perfect wife, whatever the husband may be. The contents vary but little: the chief business of the wife—care of the household, bearing and upbringing of children, behavior toward husband, personal adornment, and conduct indoors and out. Occasionally advice on the choice of a husband is included but far less often than advice to men on the choice of a wife. Much dwelt on are the sins in matrimony, deadly and venial. The problems of widowhood and second marriage are often included in these general treatises, and sometimes they form the topics of whole books. Another subject often touched on is the alternative vocation to marriage, that is the religious life, which with its accompanying state of virginity was admittedly the more ideal vocation but was not recommended to all women. Praise of virginity alone furnishes the topic of many discourses and letters.

The second largest group of treatises concerns love in all the ramifications of that complicated activity, viewed either as occupation or recreation. Definitions of love, kinds of love, causes, powers and effects of love, torments of the lover, diatribes against love, cures for love, rules for wooing, advice on choice of lover or mistress, furnish the substance of these books. Discussions of beauty as the prime cause of love, and jealousy as a frequent if not necessary concomitant of love stretch into books devoted to one of these topics alone. The level ranges from philosophical, religious, or highly moral to satiric and elegantly bawdy, as the writer is a son, or daughter, of Plato, or of a Church Father, or of Ovid. I have already indicated the extremes. On the practical side there are handbooks on the use of mottoes, flowers, and other signs for conveying secret messages, besides those on the making of *impresas*, and collections of recipes for the enhancement of natural beauty and the repair of defects. Most of the books on love are addressed to men as the more active agents and sharers in this pastime for two. The art of love was an accomplishment necessary to the gentleman for the complete realization of himself, and for recreation in lighter hours. It was the most elegant topic for after-dinner conversation and as an aid to ex-celling at that there were books of proper phrases, and the ever popular lists of questions for debate, as for example, which is worse off, the lover who has had his love and lost her, or the one who sees his love daily but can never enjoy her. Boccaccio's famous list from *Il Filocopo* was frequently lifted and translated. The elaborate dialogues between ladies and gentlemen after the fashion of Castiglione were models for such conversations. Though usually addressed to men these books applied in part to women also, of course, and some in the group were addressed particularly to women. As they touch women they may be said to present another vocation to her, that of mistress, whether she is maid or already wife.

The Italians were by far the most interested in this subject, producing more than half the books listed. How should they not be thus absorbed since they possessed the great exemplars and authorities, Dante and Petrarch, whose sonnets they loved to subject to minute dissection and exposition? Others such as Cavalcanti and Della Casa furnished like exercise of wit. The English were little interested in these abstractions, and in general viewed love and beauty as either unimportant elements in life, or the siren snares set by women, a feverish infection well left behind in youth. No Englishman makes love a part of gentlemanly perfection. What interest was felt in the subject expended itself in translations from the Italians, French, and Spanish.

The remaining important books addressed to women in particular are on their bringing up, education, and appropriate accomplishments, but these books make a very small section of this library for gentlefolk that we are exploring. Few were in any way comparable to the "Gentlemen," "Nobles," "Courtiers" that embody the general ideal for men. Most notable are two by women themselves, Christine de Pisan's *Le Tresor de la Cite des Dames*, written in 1405, and Anne de Beaujeu's advice to her daughter Suzanne, written a century later. Other writers, like Tasso, view various aspects of the lady at court, and still others present the ideal in terms of the rather limited set of virtues that the lady was assigned; but these are only partial views, as are the discussions introduced into books on the courtier, like Cas-tiglione's and Nifo's. On the formal education of women, a much discussed subject for the gentleman, there are no complete treatises at all. What is said on the matter comes in casually in connection with other things, marriage chiefly and early bringing up as preparation for marriage. A chap-ter in Mulcaster's *Positions* on the education of girls, and the second book of Vives' *De Ingenuorum Adolescentium ac Puellarum Institutione* are the most extended of such treatments. In the main the books on the upbringing of highborn girls are distinctly religious in tone and take a narrow view of the aim of that upbringing, that is, the production of a Christian woman and wife. To fill in vacant hours and avoid the temptations of idleness, sewing, embroidery, and the like were almost invariably recommended. The minds of English ladies seem to have run rather to the other feminine accomplishment, cooking, particularly in its more refined forms of preserving, candying, and brewing medicinal draughts. The English at any rate published cook books, where the Italians furnished designs for embroidery

Such then in the main are the subjects that busied the pens of renaissance writers who thought to foster gentility with principles, precepts, and other aids to proper appearance and behavior. The theme attracted the best minds of the time, and all ranks and professions—popes, bishops, monks, kings, statesmen, lawyers, soldiers, scholars, physicians, poets. Pius II warns against the wiles of women, Savonarola describes the widow's proper behavior, Gerson attacks the *Romance of the Rose* as derogatory to women and debasing of morals, Burghley sets down precepts for his son on personal and domestic matters including the choice of a wife, Bodin lays out a scheme for the study of history, Erasmus and Vives compose books of advice on marriage, Tasso discourses in prose on love, jealousy, the special virtues of a woman of high rank, and marriage. The greater part of these works are written by those who could or did simply set themselves down as gentlemen. Women are not unrepresented but are negligible in numbers, most of all on themes of special importance to the other sex. The shadowy Juliana Berners can lay too slight a claim to the treatises on manly sports which go catalogued under her name to be included here. Christine de Pisan is solid enough in the flesh, and contributes, besides a translation or adaptation of Vegetius, various books of commonplaces on political matters, but she writes more originally and importantly on her own sex.

The particular purpose behind all these treatises varies with circumstances. Some authors, such as husbands, or fathers of sons or daughters, would seem to have begun from purely domestic reasons. Many had an ax to grind, seeking the favor of royal or noble patrons, and disclose their aim either in laudatory dedications or in the body of the work itself. Foxius Morzillus turns his institution of a kingdom into a eulogy of Philip II; Budé writes on the same subject primarily to recommend scholars to royal support, for he sandwiches between the customary precepts for the prince long chapters on the advantages of learning, the high reputation of scholars and their honors as recorded in Roman and French history, and the honor and glory that come to kings from letters. Englishmen wrote on the advantages of a kingdom in order to extol England and Elizabeth, to maintain her independence of any power abroad, or to justify her policy in Ireland. For examples see Merbury's *Brief Discourse of Royal Monarchy* and Beacon's *Solon his Folly*. However particular the motive behind the book, it does not of course necessarily invalidate the ideas, or convict the author of insincerity. But in assessing significance and representative quality, not only this particularity, but further purposes, such as the satiric, or rhetorical, disturb the modern reader, and necessarily set him on his guard. Style for its own sake was highly valued, and gentlemen as well as scholars sought themes for exercise of their wits and pens in eloquence. Such an exercise was Osorio's *De Nobilitate*, so avowed in the preface. For what other purpose would Alberti have written both for and against women, as others did? Pazzi and Tasso match each other's verses, word for word, on opposite sides of the same theme. Petrarch in his remedies of fortune takes both sides of every case with equal persuasiveness. At this distance it is difficult to detect lurking satire, and of course a satiric tone can be used to cover serious belief. One's chief protection lies in generality. What all men were saying must indicate the mental climate of the times, whatever the tone or occasion taken by individuals.

But it is another matter again to estimate how influential any particular writer or book was. Some gauge for popularity, that is representative value, doubtless can be found in the reprintings, new editions, and translations, and for this reason chiefly I have noted all that I have found. Direct reference to other contemporary writers is comparatively infrequent, and direct quotation still less frequent. Direct use without indication of borrowing is difficult to determine, because the bulk of all that these treatises contain is made up of commonplaces, culled mostly from the ancients, whose names besprinkle the pages of all writers. But there is plenty of evidence that these same commonplaces were not of mere academic interest, for the letters, speeches, and fiction of the time are full of the same ideas and rules for conduct.

Because of the commonplace nature of the contents these treatises are on the whole very dry, even boresome reading. Their abstract character is generally relieved only by concrete examples drawn from antiquity, which soon lose their novelty, and which do not illustrate for us the sixteenth century, however clearly they may have suggested contemporary parallels to those for whom they were originally given. The age even seems to have voiced some protest against these abstractions, if one may judge by frequently proffered claims that experience and example had furnished the model to the writer, not Plato's *Republic*, or Xenophon's *Cyrus*, or Horace's *Poet*, or Castiglione's *Courtier*, or Sir Thomas More's *Utopia*. But for a modern eye at least the difference between the avowedly theoretical and the avowedly practical treatise is usually too small to be seen. To this endless repetition of ideas and examples are added two even worse faults, prolixity of style and formlessness of structure. Rare indeed is the author who can organize his accumulations from the ancients into a composition and express himself with economy. Besides its delight in these ant-heaps of learning the age also loved the opposite form of borrowing, epitomes, the dry bones of an author, or authors, set forth without any enlivening or even relating of the parts. Nash, in a prefatory letter to Greene's *Menaphon*, addressed "To the Gentlemen Students of both Universities," had a hard word to say on the matter: "Those yeares, which shoulde bee employed in Aristotle, are expired in Epitomes . . . And hence could I enter into a large fielde of invective against our abject abbreviations of the Artes." And others could be quoted to the same tune.

And yet, dull in the reading as these books on the whole are, they possess two elements of intrinsic interest for the student of literature—aside from their main contents, their language and the occasional sidelights they furnish on contemporary men and manners. I shall here confine myself to commenting on the English section, though the same sort of comment might be made on all. These didactic composers and compilers were, along with Shakespeare and Bacon, the begetters of our English prose, many of them conscious of their role. From Elyot to Mulcaster they labored valiantly to establish the right to use their mother tongue for learned purposes, whether of translation or composition, against those who thought it too barbarous and who would admit only Latin; and to make English more adequate for such use by refining and enlarging, against those who jealously resisted any implication that improvement was needed. "Ink-horn terms skummed from the Latin" excited the ire of these early one hundred per-centers.[10] Elyot, one of the first to interest himself in supplying the English gentleman with the new learning, found his native tongue inadequate for his *Governor*, and deliberately borrowed from Greek, Latin, and French. He defends and explains his practice in the preface to a book that he published two years later than the *Governor*, called *Of the Knowledge that Maketh a Wise Man*. The progress of the expansionists against the isolationists, shall we call them, is recorded and illustrated in these treatises. Toward the end of the century Bryskett could announce that he found English, for purposes of translation, less copious and sweet than Greek and Latin but adequate.[11] By 1622 Francis Markham could write of "our language which questionlesse is now as perfect, as significant, and as glorious as any other."[12]

As for the sidelights, they are tucked away in unexpected corners, little pictures of contemporary life that occasionally relieve the monotony. Particularly in prefaces and dedicatory epistles the student of manners would do well to search, however forbidding the title. Here is one sample, an invective against "these rude youthes, & skillesse minions of the court, great companions and wooers of the Citie, Counterfaite Courtiers which simper it in outward shewe, making pretie mouthes, & marching it with a stalking pace like Cranes, spetting over their own shoulder, speaking lispingly, & answering singingly, with perfumed gloves under their girdels their

[10] Fulwood, Wm., *The Enemy of Idleness*, 1568, f. BIIIIa.
[11] *A Discourse of Civill Life*, 1606, Preface, written fully twenty years before it was published.
[12] *Five Decades of Epistles of Warre*, 1622, Preface.

buskins pinkt & cut, their short clokes, their little cappes, their hair curled after the manner of Cesarea, sometimes a little long locke turned up like a pigs tayle betweene their temples & the ear: And in this attire, with a word or two of Frenche, Italian, or Spanish, which they cary in their budgettes, they dare devise with any noble person of the affayres of the realme, & pronouncing with a majesty, how the king hath shewed greate favour to such a gentleman."[13] At times a historic figure enters, and one sees the great Burghley at his dinner table, so considerate of the meanest gentleman there "that he left not one at his table, whom he did not reason with, and heare speake at their turnes," as the Frenchman, Hotman, reports in one of those very rare references to living men.[14] Or one gets a glimpse into literary circles from George Gascoigne's scornful exposure of those blockhead readers and critics of his age who thought that a contention in verse between Churchyard and Camel was a quarrel between two neighbors, one of whom objected to the other's camel trespassing in his churchyard. "Laugh not at this lustie yonkers," he continues, "since the pleasant dittie of the noble Erle of Surrie beginning thus, In winters nist returne: was also construed to be made in deede by a Shepheerd. What should I stand much in rehearsal how the L. Vaux his ditty beginning thus, I loath that I did love, was thought by some to be made upon his deathbed, & that the soulkind of M. Edwards was also written in extremitie of sicknes. Of a truth my good gallants, there are such as having onlie learned to read English, interpret latin, greke, french, and italian phrases or metaphors, even according to their motherlie conception & childish skill."[15]

One last question may be raised: how did the gentleman for whom these many tomes were produced regard them. On the whole with serious attention apparently, in the reading at least. The letters of the age, as must have been the conversation, are strewn thick with the "moral maxims, quick sentences, and lively examples" so laboriously collected by the motley crowd that have been passing before us in review. Gabriel Harvey has left us, by way of raillery, a pretty survey of these latest fashions in books among university wits, which may well serve to round off this brief survey.

"Schollars in ower age ar rather nowe Aristippi then Diogenes: and rather active then contemplative philosophers: coveting above alle thinges under heaven to appear sumwhat more then schollars if themselves wiste how; and of all thinges in the worlde most detestinge that spitefull malicious proverbe, of greatest Clarkes, and not wisest men. The date whereof they defende was exspired when Dunse and Thomas of Aquine with the whole rablement of schoolemen were abandonid ower schooles and expellid the Universitye. And nowe of late forsoothe to helpe countenaunce owte

---

[13] *The Philosopher of the Court written by Philbert of Vienne* . . . Englished by George North, 1575, "The definition of this new philosophie," p. 16.

[14] *The Ambassador*, 1603, f. D8a.

[15] *The Steele glas*, 1576, Epistle to the young Gentlemen.

the matter they have gotten Philbertes Philosopher of the Courte, the Italian Arch bysshoppies brave Galateo, Castiglioes fine Cortegiano, Bengalassoes Civil Instructions to his Nephewe Seignor Princisca Ganzar: Guatzoes newe Discourse of Curteous behaviour, Jovios and Rassellis Emblemes in Italian, Paradines in French, Plutarche in Frenche, Frontines Stratagemes, Polyenes Stratagemes, Polonica, Apodemica, Guigiandine, Philipp de Comines, and I knowe not howe many owtlandische braveryes besides of the same stampe. Shall I hazarde a litle farther: and make you privy to all our privityes indeede . . . Aristotles Organon is nighhand as little redd as Dunses Quodlibet. His oeconomicks and politiques every on hath by rote. You can not stepp into a schollars studye but (ten to on) you shall litely finde open either Bodin de Republica, or Le Royes Exposition uppon Aristotles Politique or sum other like Frenche or Italian Politique Discourses.

"And I warrant you sum good fellowes amongst us begin nowe to be prettely well acquaynted with a certayne parlous booke callid, as I remember me, Il Principe di Nicolo Macchiavelli, and can peradventure name you an odd crewe or tooe that ar as cunninge in his Discorsi sopra la prima deca di Livio, in his Historia Fiorentina, and his Dialogues della Arte della Guerra Tooe, and certayne gallant Turkishe Discourses tooe as University men were wont to be in their parva Logicalia and Magna Moralia and Physicalia of both sortes."

But for all his apparent scorn of the moderns we find Harvey defending himself against the charge of holding heterodox opinions, with this argument: "I never yit tooke uppon me the defence of ani quaestion which I culd not shew with a wet fingar out of sum excellent late writer or other; and especially out of Menlancthon, Ramus, Valerius and Foxius."[16]

---

[16] *Letter-book*, pub. 1884, "A pleasaunt and merry-conceited letter to himself just before his master's commencement;" Letter to John Young.

Bibliography

SPECIAL BIBLIOGRAPHICAL SOURCES

BRONZINI, CHRISTOFORO. Della dignita, & nobilta delle donne . . . Firenze, 1624, etc. (See nos. 135, 136, 137. Frequent references to contemporaries.)

DU VERDIER, ANTOINE. La bibliothèque d'Antoine Du Verdier, . . . contenant le catalogue de tous ceux qui ont escrit ou traduict en françois et autre dialects de ce royaume. Lyon, 1585. (Also 1772 with a list by F. Grude La Croix-Dumaine.)

EQUICOLA, MARIO. Libri di natura d'amore . . . Vinegia, 1531. (See no. 281. Bk. I gives a survey of authorities on love.)

FONTANINI, GUISTO. Della eloquenza Italiana . . . Venezia, 1737. (See Bk. III, classe V, capo. VI, Canzonieri di donne, e per donne illustre.)

GAY, JULES. Bibliographie des ouvrages relatifs au mariage, aux femmes et à l'amour. Paris, 1856.

GESNER, CONRAD. Pandectarum sive partitionum universalium . . . libri XXI, Tiguri, 1548. (Arranged under subjects.)

HENTSCH, A. A. De la littérature didactique du moyen âge s'adressant spécialement aux femmes. Cahors, 1903.

LORENZETTI, PAOLO. La bellezza e l'amore nei trattati del cinquecento. Pisa, 1917. (See pp. 165–175.)

MAULDE-LA-CLAVIÈRE, RÉNÉ DE. Les femmes de la renaissance. Paris, 1898.

MELZI, GAETANO. Dizionario di opere anonime e pseudonime di scrittori italiani. . . . Milano, 1848.

PALLISER, MRS. BURY. History of lace by Mrs. Bury Palliser entirely revised, rewritten, and enlarged under the editorship of M. Jourdain and Alice Dryden. London, 1902. (Bibliography appended.)

PASSANO, G. B. Dizionario di opere anonime e pseudonime in supplemento a quello di G. Melzi. Ancona, 1887.

RODOCANACHI, E. La femme italienne avant, pendant et après la renaissance. Paris, 1922.

URBANI DE GHELTOF, G. M. I merletti a Venezia. Venezia, 1876. (Chiefly taken from Palliser.)

BIBLIOGRAPHICAL LIST FOR THE LADY

ABRAVANEL, JUDAH. *See* Leone Ebreo.

ACIDALIUS, VALENS. See *Disputatio.*

1. ACTEFELD, CONRAD VON. Libellus haud inconcinne de fallaci et lubrico muliercularum statu conpositus, à Pasquillo Mero Germano, apostolico poëta, & in usum, commodumque adolescentum, & juniorum hominum nondum sub jugo, & temone matrimonii ligatorum accommodatus, & in quatuor tomos digestus. 1562.

2. ACOSTA, CHRISTÓVAL. Tratado en loor de las mugeres, y dela castidad, onestidad, constancia, silencio, y justicia: con otras muchas particularidades, y varias historias. Dirigido ala Serenissima Sennora Infanta Donna Catalina Daustria. Por Christoval Acosta Affricano. Venetia, Giacomo Cornetti, 1592.

3. ‡————Libro del amor divino, y del natural, y humano.

4. ‡Advertissemens & meditations necessaires à une dame Chrestienne mariee, pour vivre sainctement en son estat, distribués par ordre sur chaque jour de la sepmaine: & une priere à ce propos. Tholose, I. Colonniés, 1572. (Du Verdier.)

5. Ladvocat des dames de Paris. Touchant le Pardon sainct trotet. (Biblio. Nat. Y.² 2715.)

6. AGNELLI, COSIMO. Amorevole aviso alle donne, circa alcuni loro abusi. Di Cosmo Agnelli. Ferrara, Benedetto Mammarello, 1592. (Also 1582.)

7. ‡AGOULT, GUILHEM D'. La maniera d'amar dal temps passat. (12th cent. Du Verdier.)

8. AGRIPPA, HENRICUS CORNELIUS. (I) Henrici cornelii Agrippae de nobilitate & praecellentia foeminei sexus, ad Margareta[m] Augustam Austriaco[rum] & Burgundionum Principem. . . . (II) De sacramento matrimonii declamatio ad Margaretam Alenconiae Ducem. . . . Antverpiae, apud Michaelem Hillenium, 1529. (Also 1532; 1567. Eng. trans. see below. French trans. 1530; 1578; 1686; 1713; 1726. Germ. trans. 1540?; 1566; 1650; 1736. Rep. 1852. Ital. trans. 1544; 1545; 1776. Polish trans. 1575.)

9. ————(Eng. trans. of I). A treatise of the nobilitie and excellencye of woman kynde, translated out of Latine into englysshe by David Clapam. London, Thomas Berthelet, 1542. (Other trans. 1652; 1670; 1683?)

10. ————(Eng. trans. of II). The commendation of matrimony, made by Cornelius Agrippa, & translated into englishe by David Clapam. Londini, in aedibus Thomae Bertheleti, 1545.

11. ALBERTI, LEONE BATTISTA. Avvertimenti matrimoniali. First pub. in *Opere volgari*, Firenze, 1844, vol. I, pp. 192–210. (Complaints against bad wives.)

12. ————Baptistae de Albertis poetae laureati de amore liber optimus feliciter incipit. Firenza, 1471. (In Italian. Also 1491; 1524; 1525; 1528; 1534; 1545; 1568, title *Opuscoli morali*; 1572. French trans. 1534; 1536; 1537; 1539; 1540; 1584; 1597. Eng. trans. see below.)

13. ————(Eng. trans.). Hecatonphila. The arte of love. Or, love discovered in an hundred severall kindes. London, by P. S[hort], for William Leake, 1598.

14. ————Leonis Baptistae Alberti Deiphira, sive opus in amoris remedio. Mediolani, per A. Zarotum, 1471. (Also 1491; 1528; 1534; 1545; 1547; 1568; 1572; 1574. Ital. and French, 1555. French trans. 1547; 1574.)

15. ————Della famiglia (or La famiglia). First pub. 1845. (Another ed. 1908. Bk. III pub. separately twice: (1) in 1734 with title *Il governo della famiglia*—a book attributed to Pandolfini but actually Alberti's own condensation of Bk. III; see Bonucci's ed. *Opere volgari*, 1844, vol. II, pp. XXV–XLVI; (2) in 1843, 1871, with title *Il padre di famiglia*.

16. ————Intorno al to donna. First pub. *Opere volgari*, Firenze, 1844, vol. I, pp. 215–224. (Detraction of women.)

17. ————Sofrona, dialogo ove si ragiona della difesa delle donne. First pub. *Opere volgari*, Firenze, 1844, vol. I, pp. 229–236. (Sofrona attacks Alberti for his detraction of women.)

18. ALBERTUS MAGNUS. I. Alberti Magni opus in evangelium Missus est Gabriel angelus. II. Alberti Magni de laudibus beatae Mariae Virginis. Argentorati, per J. Mentelin, c. 1474. (Also 1488; 1509.)

19. ———— Liber de muliere forti venerabilis domini Alberti magni ordinis fratrum predicatorum. quondam episcopi Ratisponensis. materias pertinens frugi feras. variis sacre scripture documentis fulcitas. predicatoribus verbi dei ac sancte contemplationis arcem diligentibus maxime proficuas. Coloniae, H. Quentell, 1499.

20. ‡ALBIN DES AVEUELLES (Canon of Soisson). Opuscules en ryme Françoise assavoir, La clef d'amour, les sept arts liberaux d'amour. Declaration morale de l'amant, renonçant à folle amour. Paris, 1548. (Du Verdier.)

21. ALEXIS, GUILLAUME. Le debat de lhomme & de la femme fait & compose par frere Guillaume Alexis religieux de lyre et prieur de bussi. Paris, Guillaume Nyverd, 1520? Eng. trans. see below. ("Lhomme" argues the evil character of women, and "La femme" their good character. Verse.)

22. ———— (Eng. trans.). Here begynneth an interlocucyon/with an argument/betwyxt man and woman/& which of them could prove to be most excellent. London, Wynkyn de Worde, 1525.

23. ———— Le grant blason de faulses amours fait par frere Guillaume Alexis Religieux de Lyre et prieur de Bussy En chevauchant avec ung gentil homme entre Rouen & Verneul au Perche. (Also 1486; 1501; 1512; 1532; 1533; 1538; 1614; 1726; 1734. Brunet notes that there were seven or eight editions before 1500, nine or ten between 1501 and 1530. See *Le contreblason de faulces amours*.)

24. ‡Alonso de Cordoba, Martin. Alabanzas de la virginidad y Vergel de nobles doncellas.

25. Lamant rendu cordelier a lobservance damours. (Du Verdier gives 1473. Belongs to type of *The Romance of the Rose*. Verse.)

26. Amboise, François d'. Dialogues et devis des damoiselles, pour les rendre vertueuses & bien-heureuses en la vraye et parfaicte amitié. Contenans plusieurs bon enseignemens, tres-utiles & profitables à toutes personnes: enrichis de quelques histoires facetieuses, & discours de la nature d'amour, pour bien & honnestement se gouverner en toutes compagnies. Paris, Robert le Mangnier, 1583. (Also 1581. Note in B. M. Catalogue: "Imitated from A. Piccolomini, *Dialogo, nel quale si ragiona della bella creanza delle donne.*")
Ambrogini, Angelo. *See* Poliziano.

27. Amman, Jobst. Gynaeceum, sive theatrum mulierum, in quo praecipuarum omnium per Europam in primis, nationum, gentium, populorumque, cuiusque dignitatis, ordinis, status, conditionis, professionis, aetatis, foemineos habitus videri est, artificiosissimis nunc primum figuris, neque usquam antehac pari elegantia editis, expressos à Jodoco Amano. Additis ad singulas figuras singulis octostichis Francisci Modii Brug. Opus cum ad foeminei sexus commendationem, tum in illorum maxime gratiam adornatum: qui à longinquis peregrinationibus institutae vitae ratione, aut certis aliis de causis exclusi, domi interim variorum populorum habitu, qui est morum indicium tacitum, delectantur. Francoforti, impensis Sigismundi Feyrabendii, 1586. (Germ. ed. 1586, by the same printer.)

28. The ancren riwle. c. 1250. (Pub. 1853 for Camden Soc., vol. 57; also a modernized ed., 1924. Rules for nuns.)

29. Andreas Capellanus. Erotica. Seu, amatoria Andreae capellani regii, vetustissimi scriptoris, ad venerandum suum amicum Gwalterum scripta. Numquam ante hac edita, sed saepius a multis desiderata. Nunc tandem fide diversorum mss. codicum in publicum emissa Dethmaro Mulhero. Dorpmundae, typis Westhovianis, 1610. (Also two earlier ed. undated; 1614. Written c. 1250.)

30. ‡Anger, Emond (Jesuit). Discours du sainct sacrement de mariage en 2 livres par chapitres contre les heresies & medisances des Calvinistes, Bezeans, Occhinistes & Melanthonistes. Paris, Gabriel Buon, 1572. (Du Verdier.)

31. Anger, Jane. Jane Anger her protection for women. To defend them against the scandalous reportes of a late surfeiting lover, and all other like Venerians that complaine so to be overcloyed with womens kindnesse. Written by Ja: A. Gent. London, Richard Jones, 1589.

32. Angier, Paul. L'experience de M. Angier Carentennois, contenant une brefue defence en la personne de l'honneste Amant pour l'Amye

de Court contre la contr' amye. In *Opuscules d'amour*, par Heroet, La borderie, et autres divins poëtes. Lyon, Jean de Tournes, 1547, pp. 201–236. (Also 1545 Du Verdier; 1556; 1544, in Guevara, *Le mepris de la court.*)

33. ANNE DE BEAUJEU. A la requeste de treshaulte et puissante princesse ma dame Susanne de Bourbon/femme de tresillustre & puissant prince: monseigneur Charles duc de Bourbon/et Dauvergne/et de Chastellerault: Connestable/Per/ & Chambrier de France: & fille de treshaulte et tresexcellente dame madame Anne de France/duchesse desdictes du chez: fille et seur des royes Louys. VI. [XI] & Charles. VIII. Lyon. (Written in 1504 or 1505 and pub. before 1521. Also, according to Du Verdier, 1535, with title *Doctrinal ou instruction des filles, fait à la requeste de Madame Susanne duchesse de Bourbon*, Tholose, and later by N. Rigaud, Lyon, anonymously. One of the few treatises that consider the special requirements of a lady of high rank.)

34. ‡ANTI-DRUSAC ou Libert fait à l'honneur des femmes nobles, bonnes et honnêtes par maniere de dialogues. Toulouse, 1564.

35. ANTONIANO, SILVIO. Tre libri dell' educatione cristiana de i figlivoli, scritta da M. Silvio Antoniano ad instanza di Monsig. Illustriss. Cardianale di S. Prassede, Arcirescono di Milano. Verona, Sebastian dalle Donne & Girolamo Stringari, 1584. (Discusses matrimony and the education of both boys and girls.)

36. ANTONINUS, SAINT (Archbishop of Florence). Tractatus notabilis de excommunicationibus, suspensionibus interdictis, irregularitatibus et penis, fratris Antonini. Ejusdem tractatus de sponsalibus et matrimonio extractus de Summa theologica. Venetiis, J. de Colonia, & Johannis Matheu de Gherretzem, 1474. (Also 1476; 1480; 1511).

37. Apologia mulierum. Pub. Paul Heyse, *Romanische inedita auf italiänischen Bibliotheken*, Berlin, 1856, pp. 79–121.

38. ARAGONA, TULLIA D.' Dialogo della signora Tullia d'Aragona della infinità d'amore. Venezia, Gabriel Giolito, 1547. (Also 1552.)

39. ARDENNE, REMACLE D'. Remacli Arduenne, florenatis amorum libri. Parisiis, in aedibus Johannis parvi: & Jodici Badii Ascensii, 1513. ARETINO. *See* Pietro.

40. ‡ARMIGIO, BARTOLOMMEO. Dialogo della medicina d'amore, nel quale s'insegnano i modi, di slegarsi à chi vien preso indegnamente d'amor di donna. Brescia, F. & P. Maria Marchetti, 1566.

41. ARRIVABENE GIOVANFRANCESCO. Delle lettere di diversi autori, raccolte per Venturin Ruffinelli, con una oratione a gli amanti: per M. Gioanfrancesco Arrivabene. Mantova, Venturin Ruffinelli, 1547. (See *Oratione di M. Gioanfran. Arrivabene a gli amanti, nella quale mostra di richiamargli da tutti gli amori al solo Platonico*, ff. LXIII–LXXXI.)

42. ‡———— Dialogo amorosa. Venetia, 1543.

43. Artus, Thomas, Sieur d'Embry. Discours contre la medisance.—Si l'on peut dire que la vertu est plus rigoureusement punie que le vice dialogue.—Qu'il est bien seant que les filles soyent scavantes, discours. Paris, Lucas Breyel, 1600.

44. ‡Asylum Veneris, or a sanctuary for ladies, etc. London, 1616.

45. Aubery, Jean. L'antidote d'amour. Avec un ample discours, contenant la nature et les causes d'iceluy, ensemble les remedes les plus singuliers pour se preserver et guerir des passions amoureuses. Par Jean Aubery Docteur en Medicine. Paris, Claude Chappelet, 1599. (Also 1663.)

46. Aubigné, Théodore Agrippa d' (1552–1630). Oeuvres complètes, ed. Eug. Réaume et F. de Caussade, 6 vols., Paris, 1873–1892. (See letter, "A mes filles touchant les femmes doctes de nostre siecle," vol. I, pp. 445–450.)

47. ‡Aureolus liber de nuptiis.

48. Auriol, Blaise d'. La chasse et le depart damours faict et compose par reverend pere en dieu messire Octovien de sainct gelaiz, evesque dangoulesme et par noble homme blaise dauriol. Paris, Antoine Verard, 1509. (Praise of women, complaint of wrong done by Matheolus. Verse.)

49. Austin, William. Haec homo, wherein the excellency of the creation of woman is described by way of an essaie. London, R. Olton for R. Mabb, 1637. (Also 1638; 1639. See *Haec-vir* and *Hic mulier*.)

50. Auvergne, Martial d'. Le cinquante deuxiesme arrest d'amours, avecques ses ordonnances sur le fait des masques. Cum privilegio amoris amplissimo. 1528. (Also 1538; 1544; 1546; 1555; 1566; 1579; 1585; 1587; 1597; 1731.)

51. ———— Devotes louanges a la Vierge Marie. Paris, 1509.

52. ‡Averell, William. A dyall for dainty darlings, rockt in the cradle of securitie. A glasse for all disobedient sonnes to look in. A myrrour for vertuous maydes. London, 1584.

53. Avity, Pierre d', Seigneur de Montmartin. Bannissement des folles amours, par le Sr. D'Avity Gentil-homme ordinaire de la chambre du Roy. Ou sont adjoustes quatre beaux & excellents traictés, tres curieux & memorable, enrichis d'excellentes annotations & beaux commentaires comme il se void en la page suivante. [Not added.] Lyon, Barthelemy Vincent, 1618.

54. Aylmer, John (Bishop of London). An harborowe for faithfull and trewe subjectes, agaynst the late blowne blaste, concerning the government of wemen. Wherin be confuted all such reasons as a straunger of late made in that behalfe, with a breife exhortation to obedience. Strasborowe, 1559. (See Knox, and Leslie.)

55. B., Ste. Counsel to the husband: to the wife instruction. A short and

pithy treatise of severall and joint duties, belonging unto man and wife, as counsels to the one, and instructions to the other; for their more perfect happinesse in this present life, and their eternall glorie in the life to come. London, Felix Kyngston, for Richard Boyle, 1608.

56. BADUEL, CLAUDE. Claudius Baduellus. De ratione vitae studiosae, ac literatae in matrimonio collocandae, et degendae. Lugduni, apud Seb. Gryphium, 1544. (Also 1577; 1581; 1717. French trans. see below.)

57. ————(French trans.). Traicté tres utile et fructueux de la dignite de mariage et de l'honneste conversation des gens doctes, et lettrez. Nagueres doctement composé en langue Latine. Par maistre Claude Baduel, et depuis traduict en langue Francoyse. Par maistre Guy de la Garde, . . . Paris, Arnoul L'Angelier, 1548.

58. BAEZA, MIGUEL DE. Los quatro libros del arte de la confiteria, compuestos por Miguel de Baeza, . . . Alcala de Henares, J. Gracian, 1592.

59. BALDACHINO, FILIPPO. Predica damore. 1510? (Also 1556. Power and effects of love. Verse.)

60. BALDINI, VITTORIO. Tre discorsi volgari. L'uno di quel ch' è col mezo d'amore. L'altro dell' amore del Petrarca, ch' è l'amore propriamente detto. Il terzo della compassione. Havuti nell' Academia Ferrarese. Ferrara, Vittorio Baldini, 1585.

61. BALDWIN, WILLIAM. A treatyse of moral philosophy containing the sayinges of the wise. Wherin you maye see the worthye and pithye sayinges of the philosophers, emperors, kinges, and oratours, of their lives, their aunswers, of what lignage they come of, and of what countrey they were, whose worthy and notable preseptes, counsailes parables and semblables doth hereafter folow: first gathered and englished by William Baldwin, after that twise augmented by Thomas Paulfreyman, one of the gentle men of the Queenes majesties chaple, & now once againe enlarged by the first aucthor. London, Richard Tottill, 1564. (Also 1547, 1st ed.; 1550? exactly like the 1st; 1555 and thereafter augmented; 1557; 1567; 1575; 1584; 1591; 1620?; 1651. See bk. V, cap. IX, Of woman.)

62. BANDARINI, MARCO. Le due giornate del Poeta Bandarino, dove si trattano de tutti i costume, ch' in le città de Italia à loco per loco usar si sogliono. 1556. (See D₃-H₄, what sort of qualities the men of the different cities admire in women, how they make love, defense of women.)

63. BANSLEY, CHARLES. A treatyse shewing and declaring the pryde and abuse of women now a dayes by Charles Bansley. London, Thomas Raynalde, 1550? (Verse.)

64. BARBA, POMPEO DALLA. Espositione d'un sonetto platonico, fatto sopra il primo effecto d'amore che e il separare l'anima dal corpo de l'amante, dove si tratta de la immortalita de l'anima secondo Aristo-

tile, e secondo Platone. Letta nel mese d' Aprile nel 1548. Fiorenza, 1549. (Also 1554.)

65. BARBARO, FRANCESCO (1398–1454). Francisci Barbari patricii Veneti oratorisque clarissimi de re uxoria libelli duo. Paris, in aedibus Ascensianis, 1513. (Also 1553; 1612; 1639. Ital. trans. 1548; 1778; 1785. French trans. 1667. Eng. trans. see below.)

66. ————— (Eng. trans.). Directions for love and marriage. In two books. Written originally by Franciscus Barbarus a Venetian Senator. And now translated into English by a person of quality. London, for John Leigh, 1677.

67. BARBATIUS, JOANNES. Barbae majestas, hoc est, de barbis elegans, brevis et accurata descriptio, in qua significatur, qualis barba virum deceat, quantumque decus, authoritatem, commoditatemque illi afferat, an abradenda sit necne, an veteres illud in more habuerint, quisve primus tonsores Romam adduxerit, barbamque radi curaverit. Ultimò quaeritur: an sacerdotibus barbam gestare conveniat. Omnia pulchris et jucundis argumentis, rationibusque ex S. Scriptura, utroque jure, aliisque probatis authoribus desumptis, pertractata & collecta per M. Joannem Barbatium barbarum amatorem. Francofurti, in officina Michaelis Fabri, 1611.

68. BARBERINO, FRANCESCA DA (1264–1348). Del reggimento e dei costumi delle donne. Rep. 1842. (First printed 1815, then 1842; 1871; 1875.)

69. ————— I documenti d'amore. Rep. 1905, vol. I; 1917, vol. II. (First printed 1640. Rep. 1898; 1901; 1910; 1905–1927.)

70. ————— Tractatus amoris et operum eius qui non est de libro sed facit ad glosas prohemii libri precedentis. Rep. 1898 with title *Tratatto d'amore*. (Also 1901 under title *Il trionfo d'amore*. Curious combination of pictures, verses, and commentary, celebrating a love subject to reason and divine control.)

71. BARBO, GIOVANNI BATTISTA. L'Oracolo, overo invettiva contra le donne, opera dell' eccellente M. Gio. Battista Barbo, Academico Fecondo. All Illustre Sig. Pasquino Romano. Vicenza, per G. D. Rizzardi, 1616. (Verse.)

72. BARGAGLI, SCIPIONE. I trattenimenti di Scipion Bargagli; dove da vaghe donne, e da giovani huomini rappresentati sono honesti, e dilettevoli giuochi: narrate novelle; e cantate alcune amorose canzonette. Venetia, Bernardo Giunti, 1587. (Also 1591; 1592.)

73. BARRONSO, CHRISTOPHLE DE. Le jardin amoureux contenant toutes les reigles damours: aveques plusieurs lettres missives tant de lamant comme de lamye: faict & compose par maistre Christofle de barronso. Lyon, 1501. (Verse. Letters in prose.)

74. BATTUS, BARTHOLOMAEUS. De oeconomia christiana. (Eng. trans. see below.)

75. ——————— (Eng. trans.). The Christian mans closet. Wherein is conteined a large discourse of the godly training up of children: as also of those duties that children owe unto their parents, made dialogue wise, very pleasant to reade, and most profitable to practise, collected in Latin by Bartholomew Batty of Alostensis, And nowe Englished by William Lowth. London, Thomas Dawson and Gregorie Seton, 1581.

76. BEAULIEU, EUSTORG OR HECTOR DE. Les divers rapportz. Contenant plusieurs rondeaulx, dixains, & ballades sur divers propos, chansons, epistres, ensemble une du coq a lasne, et une aultre de lasne au coq, sept blasons anatomiques du corps feminin, lexcuse du corps pudique contre le blason des blasonneurs des membres feminins, la responce du blasonneur du cul a laucteur de lapologie contre luy, noms & surnoms tournez, gestes, Pater & Ave des solliciteurs de proces, aultre Pater de la ville & cite de Lectore en Armaignac, le In manibus du peuple sur le deluge quel craignoit ladis avenir, et aussi ung aultre In manibus sur la grande famine qui regna lan mille cinq cens vingt & neuf (mesmement au pays de Guyenne) oraisons a Jesuchrist, epitaphes, une deploration, et aulcuns dictz des trespassez incitatifz a penser a la mort, le tout compose par M. Eustorg, de Beaulieu, natif di la ville de Beaulieu, au bas pays de Lymosin. Lyon, Pierre de saincte Lucie (dict le Prince), 1537. (Also 1544.)

77. ——————— L'espinglier des filles, compose par Eustorg, aultrement dict: Hector de Beaulieu, ministre evangelique . . . Reveu et augmente par luy mesme (depuis sa premiere impression) comme on verra. Basle, 1550. (Also 1565 with title *La doctrine et instruction des filles christiennes*, etc.)

78. ‡BEAUNAY, JEAN DE. Le doctrinal des prudefemmes aveq des gloses en prose entremeslees parmy les rimes. Lyon, Olivier Arnoullet. (Du Verdier.)

79. BECON, THOMAS. The golden boke of christen matrimonye. By T. Basille. London, J. Mayler f. J. Gough, 1542. (Also 1543; 1564 in *The worckes of Thomas Becon*, rep. 1843.)

80. ——————— A new catechisme sette forthe dialoge wise in familiare talke betwene the father and the son, lately made and now fyrst of all published by Thomas Becon. *The worckes*, 1564, pt. I, f. CCLXXXV. (See f. CCCCCIX, Of the duetye of husbandes toward theyr wyves, and f. CCCCCXIII, Of the dutey of wives toward their husbandes.)

81. BELMONTE, PIETRO. Institutione della sposa del Cavalier Pietro Belmonte Ariminese, fatta principalmente per Madonna Laudomia sua figlivola nelle sue nuove nozze. Roma, per gl' heredi di Giovanni Osmarino Gigliotto, 1587.

82. BEMBO, PIETRO. Gli Asolani di Messer Pietro Bembo. Venetia, case

d'Aldo Romano, 1505. (Also 1515; 1517; 1522; 1530; 1540; 1544; 1546; 1553; 1556; 1558; 1560; 1572; 1575; 1584; 1586; 1743. French trans. 1545; 1551; 1553; 1576. Discourse on love.)

83. BENOIST, RENE. Catechese et instruction touchant les ornemens, vestemens, & parures des femmes Chrestiennes, avec un autre catechese de la penitence, un advertisement de S. Augustin de la maniere de faire penitence: & une exhortation de S. Ambrose à vraye penitence. Plus, une instruction de la femme mariée. Par M. Rene Benoist. Docteur regent en la faculté de Theologie, à Paris. Paris, Nicolas Chesneau, 1573. (Privilege dated 1563.)

84. ‡————— Exortation catechistique du mariage en laquelle est enseigné ce qu'il faut faire pour se marier hereusement avec la grace de Dieu. Paris, Jean Postel. (Du Verdier.)

85. BENTLEY, THOMAS. The monument of matrones: conteining seven severall lamps of virginitie, or distinct treatises; whereof the first five concerne praier and meditation; the other two last, precepts and examples, as the woorthie works partlie of men, partlie of women; compiled for the necessarie use of both sexes out of the sacred scriptures, and other approoved authors, by Thomas Bentley of Graies Inne Student. London, H. Denham, 1582. (Contains Lamps 1–4. Compiled from writings of Francis Abergavenny, Anne Askew, Theodore de Beze, Lady Jane Dudley, Catherine Parr, Elizabeth Tyrwhitt, and others.)

86. ‡————— The fift lampe of virginitie: conteining sundrie forms of christian praiers and meditations, to bee used onlie of and for all sorts and degrees of women, in their severall ages and callings; . . . now newlie compiled to the glorie of God, & comfort of al godlie women, by the said T. B. Gentleman. London, William Seres, 1582.

87. ‡————— The sixt lampe of virginitie; conteining a mirrour for maidens and matrons: or, the severall duties and office of all sorts of women in their vocation out of Gods word, with their due praise and dispraise by the same: togither with the names, lives, and stories of all women mentioned in holie Scriptures, either good or bad: . . . newlie collected and compiled to the glorie of God, by T. B. Gentleman. London, Thomas Dawson for the assignes of William Seres, 1582.

88. ‡————— The seventh lamp of virginitie, conteining the acts & histories, lives, & deaths of all maner of women, good and bad, mentioned in holy Scripture, . . . Newely collected, and compiled to the glorie of God, and benefite of his Church, by the saide T. B. G. London, 1582.

89. BENVENUTO ITALIANO. The passenger: of Benvenuto Italian, professour of his native tongue, for these nine yeeres in London. Divided into two parts, containing seaven exquisite dialogues in Italian and English:

The contents whereof you shall finde in the end of the booke. To the Illustrious and renowmed Prince Henry, Heyre apparant to the Kings most excellent Majestie of Great Britaine, etc. . . London, printed by T. S. for Richard Redmer, 1612.

90. BERCHER, WILLIAM. A dyssputacion off the nobylytye off wymen/betwene dyvers ladis/and gentlemen off ytalye at a place called Petriolo/one of the bayns of Siena the noble cyttye of Toscane. First printed by Roxburghe Club, London, 1904. (Ed. R. Warwick Bond, who shows in his notes that Bercher borrowed wholesale from Domenichi, who had Agrippa and Capella as models. See the three.)

BERGOMENSIS, JACOPUS PHILIPPUS. *See* Foresti, J. P.

91. BERNARDUS, SYLVESTRE. Epistola Bernardi Sylvestris, viri quidem eruditissimi de cura regimine rei familiaris ideo in hoc apposita volumine quod nonnulli eam a sancto Bernardo putant esse compositam. (Eng. trans. see below.)

92. ———— (Eng. trans.). Here begynneth a shorte monycyon, or counsayle of the cure & governaunce of a housholde/accordynge unto policy: taken out of a pystle of a great lerned man, called Bernarde sylvestre. London, Robt. Wyer, c. 1535.

93. ‡BERNIER, S. Apologie contre le livre intitule: Alphabet de la mechancete des femmes, par le S. Bernier.

94. BERRUTO, AMADEO. Dialogus quem composuit R. P. D. Dominus Amadeus Berrutus Episcopus Augustinensis Gubernator Rome dum esset in minoribus tempore Julii II in quo precipue tractat: An amico sepe ad scribendum provocato: ut scribat: non respondenti sit amplius scribendum et hinc incidenter multa pulchra. De amicitia vera. De amore honesto. De amicis veris. De Epitetis curie Romane & aliorum principum. De curialibus non minus vere quibus facere scribit. Et plura novoque stilo addit hisque Pius II in de miseris curialium scripsit. postea vero gubernator factus a Leone. p̂p. x. multa pulchra accomodate addidit: quibus docet quales esse debeant qui magistratibus publicis preponuntur. Et in eo quatuor colloquutores seu collectatores introducuntur videlicet. Amadeus. Austeritas. Amicitia. & Amor. Romae, per Gabrielem Bononiensem, 1517.

95. BERTHAULT DE LA GRISE, RENE. La penitence damour. Lyon, 1537. (Story trans. from Ital. Second title page: La penitence damour en la quelle sont plusieurs persuasions & responces tresutiles & prouffitables, pour la recreation des esperitz qui veullent tascher a honneste conversation avec les dames, et les occasions que les dames doibuent fuyr de complaire par trop aux pourchatz des hommes, & importunitez qui leur sont faictes soubz couleur de service, dont elles se trouvent ou trompees, ou infames de leur honneur.)

96. BETUSSI, GIUSEPPE. Addizione di M. Giuseppe Betussi fatta al libro delle donne illustri tempo del Boccacio fino a' giorni nostri, con alcune altre state per innanzi. Fiorenza, Filippo Giunti, 1595. (Pub. 1596 with Betussi's Ital. trans. of Boccaccio's *De mulieribus claris* and another addition by F. Serdonati, each with a separate title page. See Boccaccio.)

97. ———————— Dialogo amoroso di messer Giuseppe Betussi. Venetia, A. Arrivabene?, 1543.

98. ———————— La Leonora, ragionamento sopra la vera bellezza di messer Giuseppe Betussi. Lucca, Vincenzo Busdrago, 1557.

99. ———————— Il Raverta, dialogo di messer Giuseppe Betussi, nel quale si ragiona d' amore et degli effetti suoi. Vinetia, Gabriel Giolito, 1544. (Also 1545; 1549; 1550; 1562.)

100. BILLON, FRANÇOIS DE. Le fort inexpugnable de l'honneur du sexe femenin, construit par Françoys de Billon, Secretaire. Paris, Jan d'Allyer, 1555. (Also 1564, with title, La defense & forteresse invincible de l'honneur & vertu des dames, divisé en quatre bastions. Le premier desquelz contient la force & vertu, dont elles sont meublées: addressé à tresillustre & magnanime Dame, ma dame Catherine de Medicis, Royne, mere du Roy. Le second est de chasteté & honnesteté, à ma Dame la duchesse de Savoye. Le tiers embrasse leur clemence & liberalité, à ma Dame la duchesse de Nevers. Le quart leur devotion & pieté, à dame Anne de Ferrare, Duchesse douairiere de Guise. Par Francois de Billon, Secretaire.)

101. BIONDO, MICHELANGELO. Angitia cortigiana, de, natura, del, cortigiano. Roma, Antionio Blado, 1540. (Attack on courts and men and women at court.)

102. ———————— Angoscia, Doglia e Pena, le tre furie del mondo. Vinezia, Comino da Trino, 1546. (Also 1542, the first two parts issued separately. Diatribe against women.)

103. BLANCHON, JOACHIM. Les premieres oeuvres poetiques de Joachim Blanchon. Au treschrestien Henry III. Roy de France et de Pologne. Paris, pour Thomas Perier, 1583. (See troisieme livre, *Meslanges*: pp. 225–244, *Le trophee des dames a la Royne mere*, a catalogue of famous women; pp. 245–251, *Stances du mariage par antithese a celles de Ph. Des. P.* See Desportes.)

104. (BLASON). Le blason des basquines & vertugalles. Avec la belle remonstrance qu' ont faict quelques dames quand on leur a remonstré qu'il n'en falloit plus porter. Lyon, Benoist Rigaud, 1563. Rep. 1833.

105. ———————— S'ensuivent les blasons anatomiques du corps féminin ensemble les contre-blasons, de nouveaux composez et aditionnez, avec les figures, le tout mis par ordre; composez par plusieurs poetes con-

temporains; avec la table des dictz blasons et contre-blasons imprimez en ceste année. Paris, Charles L'Angelier, 1550. Rep. 1866. (Also 1543; 1554. Du Verdier gives *Blasons anatomiques*, Lyon, 1536.)

106. ———— Blasons, poésies anciennes des XV et XVImes siècles, extraictes de différens auteurs imprimés et manuscripts, par M. D. M. M[éon]. Nouvelle édition augmentée d'un glossaire des mots hors d'usage. Paris, 1809.

107. ———— Blasons supprimés dans le recueil de Méon publié à Paris, en 1809. Paris, 1881.

108. BOAISTUAU, PIERRE (called Launay). Bref discours de l'excellence et dignite de l'homme. Faict en Latin par Pierre Bouaystuau surnommé Launay, natif de Bretaigne, puis traduit par luy mesme en Francois. Dedie a Messieurs Jacques & Alexandre de Betoun, Gentilzhommes Escossois freres. Paris, Vincent Sertenas, 1558. (Also 1559; 1560. Eng. trans. see below. Germ. trans. 1609. Welsh trans. 1615, *Theater du mond sef ivv Gorsedd y byd*. Beauty of men and women, examples.)

109. ———— I. Theatrum mundi. The theatre or rule of the world, wherin may be seene the running race & course of every mans life, as touching miserie and felicitie, wherein be contained wonderfull examples and learned devises, to the overthrow of vice and exalting of vertue. II. Whereunto is added a learned and pithie worke of the excellency of man, written in the French and Latine tongues by Peter Boaistuau, Englished by John Alday, & by him perused, corrected and amended, the olde translation being corrupted. London, Thomas East, 1581. (See II, pp. 218–272, Beauty of men and women.)

110. BOCCACCIO, GIOVANNI. De casibus virorum et foeminarum illustrium. 1544. (Also 1475?; 1520? Eng. trans. see below. French trans. 1476; 1483; 1506?; 1515; 1538; 1578. Germ. trans. 1545. Ital. trans. 1598. Span. trans. 1511; 1552.)

111. ———— (Eng. trans.). Here begynneth the boke of Johan Bochas /discryving the fall of princes/princesses/and other nobles: translated into Englysshe by John Lydgate monke of Bury/begynnyng at Adam and Eve/and endyng with kyng Johan of Fraunce/taken prisoner at Poyters by prince Edwarde. London, Richarde Pynson, 1527. (Also 1494; 1554; 1555?; 1558.)

112. ———— De mulieribus claris. 1473. (Also 1475; 1487; 1531; 1539. Eng. trans. 1789. French trans. 1476; 1483; 1493; 1515; 1538; 1551; 1578. Germ. trans. 1473; 1479; 1488; 1541; 1543; 1545; 1566. Ital. trans. see below. Span. trans. 1511; 1528; 1552.)

113. ———— (Ital trans.). Libro di M. Giovanni Bocaccio delle donne illustri. Tradotto di Latino in volgare per M. Giuseppe Betussi, con una giunta fatta dal medesimo, d'altre donne famose. E un' altra nuova giunta fatta per M. Francesco Serdonati, d'altre donne illustri.

Antiche e moderne. Con due tavole una de nomi, e l'altra delle cose piu notabili. Fiorenza, Filippo Giunti, 1596. (Also 1506; 1545; 1547; 1558.)

114. ———— Il Filocopo di M. Giovanni Boccaccio. Di nuovo riveduto, corretto, & alla sua vera lettione ridotto da M. Francesco Sansovino. Con la tavola di tutte le materie che nell' opera si contengono. Venetia, Francesco Lorenzini, 1564. (Also 1472; 1476; 1478; 1481; 1488; 1497; 1503; 1520; 1527; 1530; 1538; 1551; 1554; 1566; 1575; 1588; 1594; 1612. Eng. trans. see below. French trans. 1542; 1555; 1575. See lib. V, f. 202–248, for the thirteen questions on love.)

115. ———— (Eng. trans.). Thirteene most pleasaunt and delectable questions, entituled, a disport of diverse noble personages, written in Italian by M. John Bocace Florentine and poet Laureat, in his booke named Philocopo: Englished by H. G. London, A. Jeffes, 1587. (Also 1566–1567; 1571. The fifth part of Filocopo. French trans. of this part alone, 1530; 1541. Span. trans. 1545; 1553.)

116. ———— Laberinto d'amore di M. Giovanni Boccaccio. Di nuovo corretto, et aggiunte le postille, con la tavola delle cose degne di memoria. Vinegia, Gabriel Giolito, 1558. (Inside title: *Invettiva di M. Giovanni Boccaccio, contra una malvagia donna, detto laberinto d'amore, et altrimenti il Corbaccio.* Also 1487; 1515; 1516; 1520; 1522; 1525; 1529; 1532; 1536; 1545; 1551; 1563; 1564; 1569; 1575; 1583; 1584; 1592; 1594; 1597; 1616. French trans. 1571 according to Du Verdier; 1787, *Voyage imaginaires, songes,* etc., vol. 303, f. 17.)

117. ———— Regole bellissime d'amore in modo di dialogo di M. Giovanni Boccaccio. Interlocutori. Il Signor Alcibiade, & Filaterio giovane. Tradotte di latino in volgare, da M. Angelo Ambrosini. Opera degna, e bella. Dove s'insegna che cosa sia amore. Qual siano i nobili effetti, & saporiti frutti di quello. Qual siano le persone che non sono buone all'amore. In che modo s'acquisti. Come s'accresca. Come si possi mantenere. Come mancha. Con altre bellissime regole d'amore. Venetia, 1561. (Also 1574; 1586; 1597; 1621; 1624; 1792. See Boccaccio, supposititious works, *Dialogo d'amore.*)

118. ‡BOMBINI, BERNADINO. Discorsi di Bernadino Bombino intorno al governo della guerra, governo domestico, reggimento regio, il tiranno, e' eccellenza dell' uman genere. Napoli, l'Amato, 1566.

119. BONSI, LELIO. Cinque lezzioni di M. Lelio Bonsi lette da lui publicamente nella Accademia Fiorentina Aggiuntovi un breve trattato della cometa e nella fine un sermone sopra l'Eucarestia da doversi recitare il giovedi Santo del medesimo autore. Fiorenza, I Giunti, 1560. (Bonsi's ded. letter dated 1549. On two of Petrarch's sonnets, "L'aspettata virtu, che'un voi fioriva," and "Pommi ove 'l sole occide i fiori, e l'herba.")

120. Bonus de Curtili. Tractatus nobilitatis fertilis & perutilis. Boni de curtili Brixensis. J. U. doctoris. In Tractatuum volumen duodecimum è variis juris interpretibus collectum. Lugduni, 1549, pt. 3, sections 184–198, pt. 4, sections 23–31.

121. (Book).‡ This is the boke of cokery. London, R. Pynson, 1500.

122. ———— A booke of cookerie and the order of meetes to bee served to the table, both for flesh and fish dayes. With many excellent wayes for the dressing of all usuall sortes of meates, both bak't, boyled or rosted, of flesh, fish, fowle, or others, with their proper sawces. As also many rare inventions in cookery for made dishes: with most notable preserves of sundry sorts of fruits. Likewise for making many precious waters, with divers approved medicines for grievous diseases. With certaine points of husbandry how to order oxen, horses, sheepe, hogges, etc. with many other necessary points for husbandmen to know. London, Edw. Allde, 1620. (Also 1629; 1634; 1650.)

123. ———— A booke of cookerie, otherwise called: The good huswives handmaid for the kitchen. Wherin is shewed the order how to dresse meates after sundry the best fashions used in England & other countries: with their apt and proper sauces both for flesh and fish: as also the orderly serving the same to the table. Wherunto are annexed sundry necessary conceites for the preservation of health. London, E. Allde, 1597. (Also 1594.)

124. ———— A booke of curious and strange inventions, called the first part of needleworkes, containing many singuler and fine sortes of cut-workes, raisde-workes, stiches, and open cutworke, verie easie to be learned by the dilligent practisers, that shall follow the direction herein contained. Newlie augmented. First imprinted in Venice, and now againe newly printed in more exquisite sort for the profit and delight of the gentlewomen of England. William Barley, 1596. (Plates.)

125. ———— Book of cookery. London, R. Jones, 1594. (Also 1597.)

126. ———— A book of cookrye, gathered by A. W. and now newlye enlarged. E. Allde, 1584. (Also 1587; 1591; 1594. See W., A., in B. M. Catalogue, last ed.)

127. ———— A noble book off cookry ffor a prynce houssolde or eny other estately houssolde. Reprinted verbatim from a rare MS. in the Holkam Collection. Edited by Mrs. Alexander Napier. London, 1882. (Written after Neville's feast, 1467; begins, "The ffeste off kynge henry the IIIIth to the herawldes and ffrenche men when they had justed in Smytheffelde.")

128. ———— A proper new booke of cookery. Declaring what maner of meates be best in season for al times of the yeere, and how they ought to be dressed, & served at the table, both for fleshe dayes and

fish daies. With a new addition, very necessary for al them that delight in cookery. London, William How, 1575. (Also 1557–1558; 1576.)

129. BORCHOLTEN, JOHANNES. De gradibus tractatus, in quo, simul ad ostendendam uberiorem graduum utilitatem, de matrimonio et successionibus ab intestato agitur, autore Johanne Borcholten, . . . Helmstadii, J. Lucius, 1589. (Also third ed. 1598.)

130. BOSCHEUS, JOANNES, NEUSTRIUS. Tractatus δικαιογαμίας, sive de justis, ac legitimis nuptiis libris septeem distinctus, authore Joanne Boscheo Neustrio Jure consulto clarissimo. Lugduni, 1549. Sextum volumen tractatuum e variis juris interpretibus collectorum.

131. BOUCHARD, AMAURY. Almarici Bouchardi Angeliaci Sanctorum Praesidis—τῆς γυναικείας φύτλας: adversus Andream Tiraquellum Fontiniensem. Parisiis, in chalcographia Jo. Badii Ascensii, 1522. (See Tiraqueau. Defence of women.)

132. BOUCHET, JEAN. L'amoureux transy sans espoir. Paris, A. Verard, 1503? (Verse.)

133. ———— Les angoysses & remedes damours. Du Traverseur/en son adolescence. Poictiers, Jehan & Enguilbert de Marnef, 1536. (Verse.)

134. ———— Epistres morales & familieres du traverseur. Poictiers, Jacques Bouchet, 1545. (See pt. I, 4, on nuns, and 6–12, on duties of husbands and wives, praise of marriage, duties of parents to children and of children to parents, advice to young girls who wish to marry, duties of servants, masters, and mistresses. Verse.)

135. ‡———— La fontaine des amoureux.

136. ———— L'histoire et cronicque de Clotaire Premier de ce nom. VII roy des Francoys. et monarque des gaules. Et de sa tresillustre espouse: madame saincte Radegonde extraicte au vray de plusieurs cronicques antiques & modernes. Poictiers, Enguilbert de Marnef, 1517. (The queen is a model in her behavior as maid, wife, queen, and nun.)

137. ———— Le jugement poetic de l'honneur femenin & sejour des illustres claires & honnestes dames par le Traverseur. Poictiers, Jehan & Enguilbert de Marnef, 1538. (Also 1536, Du Verdier. Mentions Christine de Pisan.)

138. ———— Le panegyric du Chevallier sans reproche. Poictiers, Jacques Bouchet, 1527.

139. ———— Sensuit le Temple de Bonne Renommee: et Repos des Hommes et Femmes illustres, trouve par le traverseur de voyes perilleuses en plorant le tresregrette deces de feu prince de Thalemont unicque filz du Chevalier et prince sans reproche. Paris, 1516? (Verse.)

140. ———— Les triumphes de la noble & amoureuse dame e lart de honnestement aymer. Composé par le Traverseur des voyes perilleuses.

Nouvellement imprimé à Paris. Poictiers, Jehan & Enguilbert de Marnef, 1532. (Also 1535; 1536; 1537; 1539; 1541; 1545; 1555; 1563. Verse.)

141. BOUTON, PHILLIPPE. Le miroir des dames. (15th cent. Pub. 1748, incomplete, by Lambert Douxfils, *La danse aux aveugles et autres poésies du XVe siècle*, pp. 187–205; also 1882, by M. E. Beauvois, *Un agent politique de Charles-Quint*, and erroneously attributed there to Claude, the son of Philippe. A list of good women beginning with Eve and ending with contemporaries, 1477–1482.)

142. ‡BRACCIOLINI, POGGIO. Poggii Bracciolini, florentini, Dialogus, an seni sit uxor ducenda circa an. 1435 conscriptus, nunc primum typis mandatus et publici juris factus, edente Gulielmo Shepherd. Liverpooliae, typ. F. Harris, 1807. (Also 1823. French trans. 1877.)

143. BRACHART, CHARLOTTE DE. Harengue faicte par damoiselle Charlotte de Brachart surnommee Aretuze qui s'adrese aux hommes qui veuillent deffendre le science aux femmes: avec quelques poësies faictes par la dite damoiselle, sur la blessure, mort, & tombeau du Baron de Chautal. Ensemble une elegie sur la mort de madamoiselle de Montaignerat. Chalon sur Saone, Jean des Preyz, 1604. (Poems missing in this Bib. Nat. copy.)

144. BRAMOSO, ACADEMICO pseud. (Cipriano Giambelli). Discorso intorno alla maggioranza dell' huomo, e della donna fatto dall' Accademico Bramoso dell' Accademia de' solleciti di Trevigi. Trevigi, Angelo Mazzolini, 1589.

145. BRASAVOLA, ANTONIO MUSA. Antonii Musae Brasavoli Ferrariensis. Ad Magnificam & Illustrem Dianam Estensem contrariam, De hominum aequalitate, & quare alter alterum excellat. Venetiis, in officina S. Bernardini, 1537.

146. BRATHWAIT, RICHARD. Ar't asleepe husband? A boulster lecture; stored with all variety of witty jeasts, merry tales, and other pleasant passages; extracted, from the choicest flowers of philosophy, poesy, antient and moderne history. Illustrated with examples of incomparable constancy, in the excellent history of Philocles and Doriclea. By Philogenes Panedonius. London, R. Bishop for R. B., 1640. (Virtues of women, illustrated with stories.)

147. ————— The description of a good wife; or a rare one amongst women. London, for Richard Redmer, 1619. (Also 1618, see Hannay. Verse.)

148. ————— The English gentleman and English gentlewoman, both in one volume couched, the 3rd edition, revised, corrected & enlarged; with A ladies love lecture, and a supplement lately annexed, and entitled The turtle's triumph. By Rich. Brathwait. London, John Dawson, 1641. (Also 1631; 1633. Title page to second part: The Eng-

lish gentlewoman, drawne onto the full body: expressing what habilliments doe best attire her, what ornaments doe best adorne her, what complements doe best accomplish her. The third edition revised, corrected, and enlarged. By Richard Brathwait. London, J. Dawson, 1641. Second part alone, 1631.)

149. BRETIN, FILBERT (Doctor of medicine). Poesies amoureuses reduites en forme d'un discours de la nature d'amour. Par Filber Bretin, . . . Plus les Meslanges du mesme auteur . . . Lyon, Benoist Rigaud, 1576.

150. BRETON, NICHOLAS. The praise of virtuous ladies: an invective against the discourteous discourses of certain malicious persons, written against women, whom nature, wit, and wisdom, (well considered) would us rather honour then disgrace. For proof whereof, read what follows: written by the said author, N. Breton, Gentleman. London, Thomas Creede, 1606. (Also 1582?; 1597; 1599.)

151. BRINON, PIERRE DE. Le trionph des dames, a trez-haute, trez-puissant, & trez-illustre Princesse Madame Catherine Henriette de Joyeuse, Duchess de Monpensier. Rouen, Jean Osmont, 1599. (Bib. Nat. R. 24057, ch. VIII, *Des femmes doctes*, missing.)

152. BRONZINI, CHRISTOFORO. L'advocat des femmes, ou de leur fidelité et constance. Dialogue du sieur Christofle Bronzini d'Ancone. Contre les medisans de ce temps. Traduit d'Italien en François. Par S. D. L. Paris, Toussainct Du Bray, 1622.

153. ———— Della dignita, & nobilta delle donne. Dialogo di Cristofano Bronzini d'Ancona. Diviso in quattro settimane; e ciascheduna di esse in sei giornate. Alla Serenissima Arciduchessa d'Austria Maria Maddalena Gran Duchessa di Toscana. Settimana prima, e giornata prima. Di nuovo ristampata, e corretta dall' autore. Firenze, Zanobi Pignoni, 1624. (Ded. letter dated 1622. Includes also *Giornata seconda*, and *Giornata terza*, with separate paging.)

154. ———— Della dignita, & nobilta delle donne. Dialogo di Cristofano Bronzini d'Ancona. Divisio in quattro settimane; e ciascheduna di esse in sei giornate. Alla Serenissima Archiduchessa d'Austria Maria Maddalena Gran Duchessa di Toscana. Settimana prima, e giornata quarta. Firenze, Zanobi Pignoni, 1625.

155. ———— Della dignità, & nobiltà delle donne. Dialogo di Christofano Bronzini à Ancona. Settimana seconda, e giornata ottava. Firenze, Simone Ciotti, 1628.

156. BRUNELLUS, JOANNES. Tractatus de sponsalibus et matrimoniis, in quo etiam de spiritali matrimonio obiter agitur, editus ab Joanne Brunello eruditissimo ac disertissimo utriusque juris doctore, & sacrorum canonum interprete, ad Illustrissimum virum, ac Reverendissimum in Christo Patrem Joannem Aurelianensem. . . . Parrhisiis, impensis honesti viri Jacobi Hoys, 1521.

157. BRUNI, DOMENICO. Opera di M. Domenico Bruni da Pistoia intitolata difese delle donne, nella quale si contengano le difese loro, dalle calumnie dategli per gli scrittori, & insieme le lodi di quelle. Nuovamenta posta in luce. Firenze, i Giunti, 1552. (Also 1559.)

158. BRUNI, LIONARDI D'AREZZO. Leonhardi Aretini de studiis et litteris ad illustrem dominam baptistam de Malatesta tractalus. Liptzk, per Martinum Lantzberg, 1501. (Also 1472?; 1477?; 1478?; 1483; 1496; 1536; 1642; 1645.)

159. ‡BRUSONIO, LUCIO DOMITIO. Mulierum mores & ingenia, Bruson. 4.1.

160. ———— L. Domitii Brusonii Contursini Lucani facetiarum exemplorumque libri VII. Romae, per Jacobum Mazochium, 1518. (Also 1559?; 1560. Alphabetically arranged. Some women included.)

161. BRUTO, GIOVANNI MICHELE. La institutione di una fanciulla nata nobilmente. Anvers, Jehan Bellere, C. Plantain pr., 1555. (Italian and French. Eng. trans. see below.)

162. ———— (Eng. trans. I). A mirrhor mete for all mothers, matrones, and maidens, intituled the Mirrhor of modestie, no less profitable and pleasant, then necessarie to bee read and practised. London, f. Edward White, 1579. (By Thomas Salter without acknowledgment though a close translation after the opening pages.)

163. ———— (Eng. trans. II). The necessarie, fit, and convenient education of a yong gentlewoman. Written both in French and Italian and translated into English by W. P. And now printed with the three languages togither in one volume, for the better instruction of such as are desirous to studie those tongues. London, Adam Islip, 1598. (A new translation.)

164. BULLINGER, HEINRICH. The christen state of matrimonye/wherin housbandes and wyfes maye lerne to kepe house together with love. The origenall of holy wedlok: whan/where/how/and of whom it was instituted & ordeyned: what it is: how it ought to proceade: what be the occasions/frute and commodities therof. Contrary wyse/how shamefull and horrible a thinge whordome and advoutry is: How one ought also to chose hym a mete and convenient spouse to kepe and increace the mutuall love/trouth and bewtye and wedloke: and how maryed folkes shuld bring up their chyldren in the feare of God. London, J. Mailer f. J. Gough, 1543. (Also 1541; 1546; 1552; 1575. Trans. by Miles Coverdale. Preface by Becon.)

165. ‡———— Sermonum decades quinque, de potissimis Christianae religionis capitibus, etc. Tiguri, in officina C. Froschoveri, 1557. (Also 1577; 1587. Eng. trans. see below. French trans. 1564. Germ. trans. 1582.)

166. ———— Fiftie godlie and learned sermons, divided into five dec-

ades, conteyning the chiefe and principall pointes of Christian religion . . . Translated out of Latine into English, by H. L. Student in divinitie. London, Ralphe Newberrie, 1577. (Also 1584; 1587. Rep. Parker Soc., 1848, vol. 7, Decade II, Sermon X, pp. 393–408.) BUONAGENTE, ANNIBALE. *See* Pigro Olimpico.

167. BUONI, TOMMASO. Academiche lettioni di tutte le specie de gli amori humani, di Tomaso Buoni. . . . In cui con stile grave si tratta dell' amor naturale, sociabile, humano, dell' amor de' giovani, de' maritati, de' progenitori, de' figlivoli, di se medesimo, de gli amici, della sapienza, della patria, dell' oro, dell' intemperato, & del divino. Venetia, Gio. Bat. Colosini, 1605.

168. ————— I problemi della bellezza, di tutti gli affetti humani. Di Tomaso Buoni. . . Con un discorso della bellezza del medesimo autore. Venetia, Gio. Bat. Ciotti, 1605. (Eng. trans. see below.)

169. ————— (Eng. trans.). Problemes of beautie and all humane affections. Written in Italian by Tho: Buoni, cittizen of Lucca. With a discourse of beauty, by the same author. Translated into English, by S. L[ennard]. Gent. London, Edward Blount & William Aspley, 1606.

170. ‡BURSATI DA CREMA, LUCREZIO. La vittoria delle donne. 1621.

171. ‡C., M. The second part of the history called the nature of a woman, 1596.

172. ‡C. DE C., SIEUR DU F. Discours sur le mariage avec quelques sonets, chansons, épitaphes, le tout en vers franç., par C. de C., sieur du F. Paris, Linocier, 1587.

173. CABEI, GIULIO CESARE. Ornamenti della gentil donna vedova, opera del signor Giulio Cesare Cabei. Nella quale ordinatamente si tratta di tutte le cose necessarie allo state vedovile; onde potrà farsi adorno d'ogni habito virtuoso, e honorato. All' Illustriss. Signora Ginevra Salviati de' Baglioni. Venetia, Christoforo Zanetti, 1574.

174. CAGGIO, PAOLO. Iconomica del signor Paolo Caggio gentilhuomo di Palermo, nelle quale s'insegna brevemente per modo di dialogo il governo famigliare, come di se stesso, della moglie, de' figlivoli, de' servi, delle case, delle robbe, & d'ogni altra cosa à quella appartemente. Vinegia, al segno del Pozzo, 1552.

175. CALVI, MAXIMILIANO. Del tractado de la hermosura y del amor, compuesto por Maximiliano Calvi. Libro primero. El qual tracta de la hermosura, dirigido a la S. C. R. Magestad de la Reyna Donna Ana nuestra Sennora. Milan, Gotardo Poncio, 1576. (Three parts with separate title pages—*Libro segundo. El qual tracta del amor*, ded. to Philip II; *Libro tercero. El tracta contra Cupido*, ded. to Don Juan de Austria.)

176. CAMERATA, GIROLAMO. Trattato dell' honor vero, et del vero dishonore.

Con tre questioni qual meriti piu honore, ò la donna, ò l'huomo. ò il soldato, ò il letterato. ò l'artista, ò il legista. Di M. Girolamo Camerata . . . Bologna, Alessandro Benacci, 1567.

177. CAMPANI, FABRIZIO. Della vita civile, overo del senno libri dieci. Del Capitano Fabritio Campani D'osimo. Nelli quali con somma chiarezza, e facilità non solo si trattano le più curiose materie theologiche, naturali, politiche, ethiche, & economiche; ma etiando si discorre di tutto quello, che nella vita, e conversatione commune si debbia ò sequire, ò schifare. Opera utilissima ad ogni persona, che desidera con molto diletto, e poco fatica acquistare la cognitione di molte cose. Nuovamente data in luce. Venetia, Francesco Bolzetta, 1607. (Unorganized medley of scraps.)

178. CAMUZIO, ANDREA. Andreae Camutii Serenissimae imperatricis physici, de amore atque felicitate libri novem. Hactenus in lucem nusquam aediti. Viennae Austriae, Stephanus Kreuzer, 1574. (Highly philosophical.)

179. CANONIERO, PIETRO ANDREA. Della eccellenza delle donne di Pietro Andrea Canonhiero. Dottore di Filosofia Medicina & Teologia. All' Illustriss. Sig. Cavaliere Belisario Vinta. Primo Secretario e consigliero di Stato del Sereniss. Gran Duca di Toscana. Firenze, Francesco Tosi, Fabeni, 1606.

180. ———— La prima parte delle quistioni discorse nell' Accademia de gli Spensierati da Pietro Andrea Canonhiero, detto L'Errante, Dottore di Filosophia, Medicina, e Theologia, nel Principato del molto Illustre Sig. Cavaliere Vincentio Panciatichi. Al Serenissimo Sig. Don Ferdinando Medici, Gran Duca di Toscana. Firenze, Volcmar Timan Germano, 1606. (Della bellezza; Della grazia; Dell' innamoramento; Dello sdegno, e dell' odio; Della gelosia.)

181. CAPACCIO, GIULIO CESARE. Illustrium mulierum, et illustrium literis virorum elogia, a Giulio Cesare Capacio . . . Neapoli, apud Jo. Jacobum Carlinum & Constantinum Vitalem, 1608.

182. ———— Il principe del Signor Giulio Cesare Capaccio Gentil'huomo del Serenissimo Signor Duca d'Urbino; tratto da gli emblemi dell' Alciato, con ducento, e più avvertimenti politici, e morali. Utilissimi à qualunque signore per l'ottima eruditione di costume, economia, e governo di stati. Con due copiose tavole, l'una de gli emblemi, & l'altra delle cose più notabili. Al serenissimo Federico II di Montefeltro della Rovere Principe d'Urbino. Venetia, Barezzo Barezzi, 1620. (Opposed to women in goverment, *Avertimenti* XXII, XXIV, LXV—Elizabeth of England a horrible example. On love, *Avertimenti* CVI–CXIV. On marriage, *Avertimenti* CLXXXII–CLXXXIX.)

183. CAPELLA, GALEAZZO FLAVIO. Galeazzo Flavio Capella Milanese della eccellenza et dignità delle donne. Vinegia, Gregorio de Gregorii, 1526. (Also 1525. See Bercher and Domenichi.)

184. CAPILUPI, LEGLIO. Laelii Capilupi Mantuani cento Virgilianus in foeminas. Lugduni-Batavorum, apud Franciscos Hegerum & Hackium, 1638. (In *Dominici Baudii amores*, pp. 141–157. Also 1550; 1565.)

185. Le caquet des bonnes chambrieres/declarant aucunes finesses dont elles usent vers leurs maistres & maistresses. Imprime par le commandement de leur secretaire maistre Pierre Babillet. Item une pronostication sur les maries & femmes veufues. Avec la maniere pour congnoistre de quel boys se chaulfe amour. Lyon, Barnabe Chaussard. (Bib. Nat. Ye. 2946.)

186. CAROSO, FABRITIO. Nobiltà di dame, del Sr. Fabritio Caroso da Sermoneta, libro altra volta, chiamato Il ballarino. Nuovamente dal proprio auttore corretto, ampliato di nuovi balli, di belle regole, & alla perfetta theorica ridotto: con le creanza necessarie à cavalieri, e dame. Aggiontovi il basso, & il soprano della musica: & con l'intavolatura del liuto à ciascun ballo. Ornato di vaghe & bellissime figure in rame. Venetia, presso il Muschio, 1600. (Also 1581; 1630.)

187. CARROLI, BERNADINO. Il giovane ben creato di Bernadino Carroli da Ravenna; diviso in tre libri. Nel primo de quali si contiene come si deve vivere christianamente. Nel secondo, come si deve governar la famiglia, & che buoni costumi debba tenere, & osservare. Nel terzo, s'impara a tutto quello, che s'appartiene all'arte dell'agricoltura. Libro utile, & necessario ad ogni persona. Ravenna, Cesare Cavazza, 1583.

188. CASA, GIOVANNI DELLA. Il Galateo. In rime et prose. Vinezia, Nicolo Bevilacqua, 1558. (Frequently reprinted, trans. into Eng., French, German, Spanish. Very few references to women but included here because Guasco recommended it to his daughter for constant study along with Guazzo and Castiglione.)

189. CASONI, GUIDO. Della magia d'amore, composta dal Signor Guido Casoni da Serravalle, nella quale si dimostra come amore sia metafisico, fisico, astrologo, musico, geometra, aritmetico, grammatico, dialetico, rettore, poeta, historiografo, jurisconsulto, politico, ethico, economico, medico, capitano, nocchiero, agricultore, lanifico, cacciatore, architetto, pittore, scultore, fabro, vitreario, mago naturale, negromante, geomante, hidromante, aeromante, piromante, chiromante, fisionomo, augure, aurispice, ariolo, salitore, e genetliaco. Dialogo primo. Con una copiosissima tavola di tutte le cose notabili. Venetia, Jabio & Agostin Zoppini, 1591. (Also 1592; 1596. Goes only to "l'amore aritmetico.")

190. CASTIGLIONE, BALDESSARE. Il libro del cortegiano. Venezia, Aldo, 1528. (Editions too numerous to cite here. Eng. trans. see Hoby, Sir Thomas.)

191. ‡Castigos y doctrinas que un sabio dava a sus hijas. (Pub. 1878. *Dos obras didacticas*, etc., Soc. de Bibl., Madrid. 15th cent. Marriage.)

192. CASTILLEJO, CHRISTOBAL DE. Las obras de Christoval de Castellejo. Corregidas, y emendadas, por mandado del Consejo de la Santa, y General Inquisicion. Anvers, Martin Nutio, 1598. (*Libro primero: contra el amor*, l. 77; *capitulo del amor*, ll. 83–108. *Libro segundo, Dialogo de las condiciones de las mugeres*, ll. 161–208. Interlocutores, Aletho, y Fileno.)

193. —————— Sermo de amores del maestro buen talante llamado fray Nidel dela orden dl fristel. Agora nuevamente corregido y enmendado. 1542. (Also 1544 with title *Dialogo de mugeres*. Interlocutores, Alethio, Fileno; 1553, see Ulloa; 1598, see Obras.)

194. CATANEA PARASOLE, ELISABETTA. Teatro delle nobili e virtuose donne, dove si reppresentano varii disegni di lavori novamente inventati e disegnati di Elisabetta Catanea Parasole . . . Roma, 1616.

195. CATANEA PARASOLE, ISABELLA. Pretiosa gemma delle virtuose donne, Dove si vedono bellissimi lavori in aria, reticella, di maglia e piombini, disegnati da I. C. Parasole. E di nuovo dati in luce da Luchino Gargano, Venetia, 1600. Secondo libro della Pretiosa gemma dove con nuova inventione si vedono bellissimi lavori di varie sorti di merli grandi e piccioli, punti in aria, parti tagliati etc. Ibid. Luchino Gargano 1601 di 42 tavole. Facsimile Venezia, 1878.

196. CATTANI DA DIACETO, FRANCESCO. I tre libri d'amore di M. Francesco Cattani da Diacetto. Con un Panegerico all' amore; et con la vita del detto autore, fatta da M. Benedetto Varchi. Vinegia, Gabriel Giolito, 1561. (Also the *Panegirico*, 1526. Wholly philosophical.)

CAVALCANTI, GUIDO. (For interpretations of his canzone "Donna mi prega" see Egidio Romano, Paolo del Rosso, Girolamo Frachetta, Dino del Garbo, Pico della Mirandola in *Commento sopra una canzone d'amore di Girolamo Benivieni*, lib. III, cap. I–III. Others, either not published or unseen, by Plinio Tomacelli, Ugo dal Corno, Francesco de' Vieri, Jacopo Mini. On these commentators see *Rime di Guido Cavalcanti*, Firenze, 1813, pp. XXVII–XXIX.)

197. ‡CAVE, FILOLAO. Dialogo amoroso. 1523.

198. CAVRETTO, PIETRO (Haedus, Petrus). Anterotica, seu de amoris generibus, auctore Petro Haedo, id est Cavretto. Tarvisii, per Gerardum de Flandria, 1492. (Also 1503; 1608.)

199. CECIL, WILLIAM (Lord Burghley). Certaine precepts, or directions, for the well ordering and carriage of a mans life: as also oeconomicall discipline for the goverment of his house: with a platforme to a good

foundation thereof, in the advised choice of a wife: left by a father to his son at his death, who was sometimes of eminent note and place in this kingdome. And published from a more perfect copy, then ordinary those pocket manuscripts goe warranted by. With some other precepts and sentences of the same nature added taken from a person of like place, and qualitie. London, by T. C. and B. A., 1617. (Also 1618; 1636.)

200. Cerratus, Paulus. Pauli Cerrati Albensis Pompeiani de virginitate libri III. Parisiis, apud Simonem Colinaeum, 1528.

201. Certosino, Dionisio (Leuwis, Dionysius de). Trattato del D. Dionisio Certosino della lodevol vita delle vergini. Venezia, Giovanni Giolito, 1584. (Prefacing letter by Giolito—urged to publish this little book as more easily grasped by simple virgins.)

202. ‡Cesena, Benedetto da. De honore mulierum. Venise, 1500.

203. Champier, Symphorien. La nef des dames vertueuses composee par maistre simphorien Champier docteur en medicine contenant quatre livres. Le premier est intitule la fleur des dames. Le second est du regime de mariage. Le tiers est des propheties des sibilles. Et le quart est le livre de vraye amour nouvellement imprimiez a Paris pour Jehan delagarde libraire. Paris, Jehan delagarde, 1515. (Also 1503; 1531.)

204. ——————— La nef des princes et des batailles de noblesse avec aultres enseignemens utilz & profitables a toutes manieres de gens pour congnoistre a bien vivre & mourir dediques et envoyes a divers prelas & seigneurs ainsi quon pourra trouver cy apres composes par noble & puissant seigneur Robert de Balsat conseiller & chambrelan du roy nostre sire & son seneschal au pays dagenes: Item plus le regime dung jeune prince & les proverbes des princes & aultres petis livres tres utilz & profitables les quelz ont este composes par maistre simphorien Champier docteur en theologie & medecine jadis natif de lionnoys. Lyon, Guillaume Balsarin, 1502. (Also 1525. At the end with the colophon in what amounts to a table of contents are the following items: "fo. XLII. sont contenus plusieurs notable dicts des philosophes a lobprobre des femmes vicieuses & Honneur des bonnes;" "fo XLVa. Cy commence ung petit livre intitule la malice des femmes: le quel a este recueilly de matheolus & aultres qui ont prins plaisir a en mesdire par affection desordonnee lequel est cy couche non pour mesdire: mais par doctrine pour eviter aux inconveniens qui peuvent advenir par femmes: par quoy sil ya aulcuns motz qui sovent desplaisans & mordans soyent attribues au bigame Matheolus.")

205. Chartier, Alain. Les oeuvres de Maistre Alain Chartier. Paris, Samuel Thiboust, 1617. (Also 1529. Contents vary. See *La belle Dame sans Mercy*, p. 502; *Copie de la requeste baillee aux Dames contre*

Maistre Alain, p. 523; *Copie des lettres envoyees par les Dames à Maistre Alain, Excusation de Maistre Alain, contre ceux qui dient qu'il a parlé contre les Dames en son Livre nommé, La belle Dame sans mercy*, p. 525; "*Doulceur, courtoisie, amitié/Sont les vertus de noble femme*," p. 527; *Le debat des deux fortunes d'amours*, p. 549; *Le livre des quatres dames, compilé par Maistre Alain Chartier*, pp. 594–684; *Complainte d'amour, et response*, p. 684; *Le parlement d'amour, nouvellement mis en lumiere*, p. 695.)

206. ———— Les demandes damours avec les responces. Paris, J. Bonfons, 1550? (Also 1529 in *Les oeuvres*. Eng. trans. see below.)

207. ———— (Eng. trans.). Delectable demaundes, and pleasant questions, with their severall aunswers, in matters of love, naturall causes, with morall and political devises. Newly translated out of Frenche into Englishe, this present yere of our Lorde God. 1566. London, John Cawood, 1566. (Also 1596.)

208. CHASSENEUX, BARTHÉLEMY DE. Catalogus gloriae mundi, laudes, honores, excellentias, ac praeeminentias omnium ferè statuum, plurimarumque rerum illius continens: à spectabili viro Bartholomeo à Chasseneo, . . . editus. Cum indice illustratus. Lugduni, per Georgium Regnault, 1546. (Also 1529; 1576; 1579; 1586; 1612; 1617; 1649. See *Secunda pars: Dignitates, laudes, & excellentias hominis, praecipuè mulierum, complectens*, ff. 43–63.)

209. ‡Le chasteau de virginité. Paris, Jean Treperel, 1506. (Du Verdier.)

210. CHELIDONIUS, TIGURINUS. A most excellent hystorie, of the institution and first beginning of Christian princes, and the originall of kingdomes: whereunto is annexed a treatise of peace and warre, and another of the dignitie of mariage. Very necessarie to be red, not only of all nobilitie and gentlemen, but also of every publike persone. First written in Latin by Chelidonius Tigurinus, after translated into French by Peter Bouaisteau of Naunts in Brittaine, and now englished by James Chillester, Londoner. London, H. Bynneman, 1571. (French trans. 1559; 1567.)

211. CHERUBINO DA SIENA. Vite matrimonialis regula brevis. Florentie, per Nicholanum Alamanum, 1482. (The subtitle of the second work in a book with no title page. Also 1490.)

212. CHEVALIER. Cy est le chevalier aux dames/De grant leaultes et prudence,/Qui pour les garder de tous blasmes/Fait grant prouesse et grant vaillance. Mets, Gaspart Hochfeder, 1516. (Verse.)

213. ———— Pour par chevalier[s] et escuiers entreteni[r] dames et damoiselles en gracieuses demandes et responses et pour joyeusement deviser et passer le temps ensemble affin aussi deviter oyseuse mere et nourrice de tous vices: jay tissu un petit livret ou quel jay en-

trechangie plusieurs honnestes demandes et responses que fist nagaires
une damoiselle a un gentil chevalier sage et courtois touchant le fait
et mestier damours. (Bib. Nat. Rés. Ye. 93.)

214. CHIESA, FRANCESCO AGOSTINO DELLA. Theatro delle donne letterate
con un breve discorso della preminenza, e perfettione del sesso donnesco. Del sig. Francesco Agostino della Chiesa, dottor di leggi di
Saluzzo. Mondovi, Giovanni Gislandi, e Gio. Tomaso Rossi, 1620.

215. CHOLIERES, NICOLAS DE. Les apresdisnees du seigneur de Cholieres.
Paris, Jean Richer, 1587. Rep. Oeuvres, Paris, 1879. (II. Du marriage.
S'il vaut mieux n'estre marié que de l'estre. III. De la puissance maritale. A sçavoir si le mary peut battre et chastier sa femme? V. Du babil et
caquet des femmes.)

216. ——————— La forest nuptiale où est représentée une variété bizarre,
non moins esmerveillable que plaisante, de divers mariages, selon
qu'ils sont observez et pratiquez, par plusieurs peuple[s] et nations
estranges, avec le manière de policer, regir, gouverner et administrer
leur famille. Paris, Pierre Bertault, 1600. (See the preface for comment
on marriage.)

217. ——————— La guerre des masles contre les femelles: representant en
trois dialogues les prerogatives & dignitez tant de l'un que de l'autre
sexe. Avec les meslanges poëtiques du Sieur de Cholieres. Paris, Pierre
Cheuillot, 1588.

218. ——————— Les neuf matinees du seigneur de Cholières. Dediees à
Monseigneur de Vendosme. Paris, Jean Richer, 1585. Rep. Oeuvres,
Paris, 1879. (Mat. II. Des lois et de la medicine. A sçavoir si la juris-
prudence est à preferer à la medicine. Mat. V. Des laides et belles femmes.
S'il vaut mieux prendre à femme une laide qu' une belle. Mat. VI. De
la jalousie du mary et de la femme. Mat. VII. De l'inegalité de l'aage
des mariez. Si un vieillard doit prendre une jeune fille, ou une vieille
rechercher un jeune homme. Mat. VIII. Des lettrez et querriers. Si une
fille doit plus desirer d'estre accouplée par mariage à un homme d'estude
qu'à un guerrier. Mat. IX. De la trefve conjugale. En quel temp n'est
loisible au mary de toucher conjugalement sa femme.)

219. CLEAVER, ROBERT. A godly forme of houshold government for the
ordering of private families, according to the direction of Gods word.
Whereunto is adjoyned in a more particular manner, the severall
duties of the husband towards his wife; and the wives dutie towards
her husband: the parents dutie towards their children; and the childrens towards their parents: the masters dutie towards his servants;
and also the servants dutie towards their masters. First gathered by
R. C. and now newly perused, amended, and augmented by John Dod
and Robert Cleaver. London, Thomas Man, 1630. (Also 1588; 1598;
1600; 1603; 1612; 1614.)

220. A closet for ladies and gentlewomen. (Also 1608; 1611; 1614; 1630; 1632; 1635; 1636. Recipes of all kinds.)

221. COCCIO, FRANCISCO (Trans.). Della nobilta et eccellenza delle donne, nuovamente dalla lingua francese nelle italiano tradotto. Vinegia, Gabriel Giolito, 1544. (Written on title page of Harvard copy, "Sum Ben Jonsonii.")

222. ‡COIGNAC, JOACHIM DE. Le bastillon & rampart de chasteté à l'encontre de Cupido & de ses armes, avec plusieurs epigrammes. Lyon, François & Claude Marchants freres, 1550. (Du Verdier. Verse.)

223. COLET, CLAUDE. L'oraison de Mars aux dames de la court, ensemble la response des dames à Mars par Cl. Colet de Rumilly en Champaigne, nouvellement reveuë et corrigee oultre la precedente impression. Plus y sont adjoustés de nouveau aulcuns aultres oeuvres dudict autheur. Paris, Chrestien Wechel, 1548-9. (Ded. dated 1544. Arguments for and against war. Verse.)

224. COLONNA, EGIDIO (Archbishop of Bourges.). Egidius de regimine principum. Venetiis, per magistrum Bernardinum Vercelensem, 1502. (Also 1473; 1482; 1498; 1607. Eng. trans. by Occleve. Fr. trans. 1st pub. 1899. Ital. trans. 1788. Span. trans. 1494. See lib. I, pt. I, cap. VII–XXIV and pt. II, cap. XX–XXI on what "omnes civis & maxime reges et principes" ought to know about marriage, the nature of women and their control.)

225. ———— L'espositione del Mro. Egidio Colonna Romano degli Eremitani. Sopra la canzone d'amore di Guido Cavalcanti Fiorentino. Con alcune brevi annotationi intorno ad essa. Di Celso Cittadini Accademico Sanese. Insieme con una sua succinta descrittion della vita, e con le rime di esso Cavalcante. Siena, Salvestro Marchetti, 1602.

226. ‡Le combat de Maladvisé avec sa dame par amours, sur le jeu de paume, cartes, dez & tablier, monstrant comme tels jeux, joinct celuy des femmes, font aller l'homme à l'hospital. Avec plusieurs autres rondeaux & dixains presentez au puis de risee. Lyon, 1547. (Du Verdier.)

227. (Complaint). S'ensuyt la complainte du nouveau marie nouvellement imprime a Paris.

228. Le conseil du nouveau marie. A deux personnaiges. Cestassavoir. Le mary. Et le docteur. Lyon, Barnabe Chaussard, 1547.

229. CONTARINO, LUIGI. Il vago, et dilettevole giardino, ove si leggono gli infelici fini de molti huomini illustri. I varii, & mirabili essempi de virtù, & vitii de gli huomini. I fatti, & la morte de' profeti. Il nome, & l'opere delle dieci Sibille. Il discorso delle Muse. L'origine, & l'imprese delle Amazone. I meravigliosi essempii delle donne. Gli inventori di tutte le scientie, & arti. L'origine delle religione, & de' cavallieri.

L'eccellenza, & virtù de molti naturali. Alcune ordinationi de' Santi Pontefici. Le belle, & vaghi pitture delle gratie, d'amore, & del vero amico. Le sette meraviglie del mondo. Raccolto dal Padre Luigi Contarino Crucifero. Con licenza de' Superiori. Di nuova ristampato, et ampliato. Vicenza, gli heredi di Perin Libraro, 1589. (Also 1586; 1597–1596; 1604?; 1607; 1619.)

230. ‡Conti, Anton Marie de'. M. Antonii Maioragii orationes et praefationes omnes ... Venetiis, apud Angelum Bonfadium, 1582. (See XXII, *De amore.*)

231. Le contreblason de faulces amours intitule le grant blason damours spirituelles & divines avec certain epigramme & servantoys dhonneur fait et compose a la louenge du treschrestien roy de France/comme icy embas pour commencement peult clerement apparoir/et veoir. Nouvellement imprime a Paris en la rue neufve nostre dame/a lenseigne de lescu de France. Paris. (Verse. See Alexis, Guillaume.)

232. Copland, Robert. The seven sorowes that women have when theyr husbandes be deade. Compyled by Robert Copland. London, William Copland, 1560? (Verse.)

233. Coquillart, Guillaume. Sensuyvent les droits nouveaulx: avec le debat des dames/et des armes lanqueste entre la simple/et la rusee/avec son plaidoye. La complaincte de Echo a Narcisus et le reffus quil luy avec la mort diteluy narcissus. Et le monologue coquillart avec plusieurs autres choses fort joyeuses. Compose par maistre Guillaume coquillart Officiel de Reims les Champaigne. Paris, Jehan Trepperel. (Also 1493; 1532; 1723.)

234. ———— Les presomptions des femmes. Rouen, Abraham Cousturier.

235. Corbeil, Pierre de. Remedium contra concubinas et conjuges, per modum abrevationis libri Matheoli a Petro de Corbolio. (Bib. Nat. Rés. Z. 856. See Motis.)

236. ‡Coringer, F. L'eloge des tetons. (The thirty qualities of beauty necessary to the complete woman. See Costume for such a list.)

237. ‡Corio, Bernardino. De amore, dialogus, 1502.
Corrozet, Gilles. *See* La Perrière.

238. Corso, Rinaldo. Dialogo del ballo di Rinaldo Corso. Bologna, Anselmo Giaccarello, 1557. (Also 1555.)

239. Cortese, Giovambattista. Il selvaggio de M. Giovambattista Cortese de Bagnacavallo, in cui si trattano innamoramenti, battagli, et altre cose bellissime con somma diligenza ridotto, et nuovamente stampato ... Vinegia, G. A. di Nicolini, 1535.

240. Cortese, Isabelle. I secreti de la Signora Isabella Cortese. Ne' quali si contengono cose minerali, medicinali, arteficiose, & alchimiche, & molte de l'arte profumatoria, appartinenti a ogni gran signora.

Venetia, Giovanni Bariletto, 1561. (Also 1565. Toilet preparations including creams, waters, dyes. Ded. to Molto Reverendo Monsignore il Signor Mario Chaboga Dignissimo Archidiacono di Ragusi because of his interest in uncovering the secrets of nature, a praiseworthy way of avoiding idleness.)

241. COSTANUS, ANTONIUS GUIBERTUS. Antonii Guiberti Costani Tolosatis Jurisconsulti, de dotibus & earum jure commentarii. Lugduni, apud Carolum Pesnot, 1556. (Also 1561.)

242. El costume delle donne incomenzando da la pueritia per fin al maritar: la via el modo che se debbe tenere a costumarle e amaistrarle secondo la condition el grado suo. Et similmente de i fanciulli: et e uno spechio che ogni persona doverebbe haverlo: & maxime quelli che hanno figlie & figlioli over aspettano di haverne. Con un capitolo de le trentatre cose che pervien alla donna a esser bella. Stampata novamente. Paulo Danza, 1523? (Also 1552, 4 leaves.)

243. COUSIN, GILBERT. Οἰκέτης, sive de officio famulorum per Gilbertum Cognatum. Parisiis, ex off. C. Wecheli, 1535. (Also 1539. French trans. Du Verdier says by author, 1561; 1562 in *Opera*. Eng. trans. see below.)

244. —————— (Eng. trans.). Of the office of servauntes, a boke made in Latine by one Gylbertus Cognatus and newely Englyshed. Londini, in officina Thomae Berthe., 1543. (Trans. by Sir Thomas Chaloner at request of Sir Henry Knyvet—"In many places I found the same as a glasse to see myne owne fautes in.")

COVERDALE, MILES. *See* Bullinger.

245. CRENNE, HÉLISENNE DE. Les angoysses douloureuses qui procedent d'amours: Contenantz troys parties: laquelle exhorte toutes personnes à ne suyvre folle amour. Paris, Denys Janot, 1538. (Also in *Oeuvres*, 1543, 1560.)

246. —————— Les oeuvres de ma dame Helisenne qu'elle a puis nagueres recogneues et mises en leur entier. Cest ascavoir les angoisses douloureuses qui procedent d'amours. Les epistres familieres et invectives, le songe de ladicte dame, le tout mieulx que par cy devant redigées au vray, et imprimées nouvellement par le commandement de ladicte dame de Crenne. Paris, Charles Langelier, 1543. (Also 1560; *Epistres familieres et invectives, 1539*.)

247. CRETIN, GUILLAUME. Le debat de deux dames sur le passe-temps de la chasse des chiens et oyseaulx, faict et compose par feu Guillaume Cretin, tresorier de la chapelle du Bois de Vincennes. Paris, Antoine Couteau, 1526. (Also 1528, with *Le loyer des folles amours*; in an undated collected edition of his works by his adopted son, François Charbonnier.)

248 CROCE, GIULIO CESARE. Dialogue galante, frà una madre compassionevolo, & una figlia inferma per amor. Alla quale dopò havere

esaminato minutamente il suo male, porge il rimedio uguale alla sua infirmità, con farla sposa. Bologna, gl'heredi del Cochi, 1623. (Also 1631.)

249. ———— La gloria delle donne. Alla Illustriss. & Excellentiss. Sig. Marchesa di Massa. Bologna, l'erede del Cochi, 1635?

250. ———— Otave morali essemplari, e ridicolose di Giulio Ces. Croce. Cioè sopra la vitoria, e pace, imagine dell' ira, ignoranza, giovine nobile, giovane nobile, fede del marito, e della moglie. Ambitione della donna vana. Per l'ingratitudine, ruffiana bastonata, barcha di topino, questione delle pulci, e la vecchia. Bologna, l'erede del Cochi, 1600.

251. ———— I parenti godevoli, opera piacevolissima nella quale s'introduce un riduto di gentilhuomini, e gentildonne à metter ceppo insieme e à cavar la ventura, secondo, che s'usa in Bologna, le feste di natale. Sogetto giocoso, e di nobile trattenimento del Croce. Bologna, l'erede del Cochi, 1605. (Also 1620. The making of impresas.)

252. ———— Scherzi overo motti giocosi sopra l'apresentarsi mazzoli di fiori, fruti, erbe, fronde, piante, animali, oro, gemme, & altri nobili favori. Fra gli amanti d'honest' amore Innamorati di Giuglio Cesare Croce. Bologna, l'erede del Cochi, 1607. (Also 1622; 1626?; 1632; 1637; 1690?)

253. CURIO, COELIUS SECUNDUS. De quatuor Caelii Secundi Curionis filiarum vita atque obitu pio et memorabili epistolae aliquot unà cum diversorum epitaphiis. Basilae, 1565.

254. CYNTHIO, ERCOLE. Opera nova che insegna cognoscere le fallace donne, e quelle insegna amare, composta per Hercule Cynthio.

255. DANEAU, LAMBERT, Traite des danses, auquel est amplement resolue la question, asavoir s'il est permis aux Chrestiens de danser. Seconde edition. 1580. (Also 1579; 1582.)

256. ‡DARCIE, ABRAHAM. The honour of ladies: or, a true description of their noble perfections. London, T. Snodham, 1622.

257. DARDANO, LUIGI. La bella e dotta difesa delle donne in verso, e prosa, di Messer Luigi Dardano gran cancelliero dell' Illustrissimo Senato Vinitiano, contra gli accusatori del sesso loro, con un breve trattato di ammaestrare li figlivoli. Vinegia, Bartholomeo detto l'Imperatore, 1554.

258. DAVIES, SIR JOHN. Orchestra, or a poem of dancing, judicially proving the true observation of time and measure, in the authentical and laudable use of dancing. London, J. Roberts for N. Ling, 1596.

259. DAWSON, THOMAS. The good huswifes jewell. Wherein is to be found most excellend and rare devises for conceites in cookery, found out by the practise of Thomas Dawson. Whereunto is adjoyned sundry approved receits for many soveraine oyles, and the way to distill many precious waters, with divers approved medicines for many diseases.

Also certain approved points of husbandry, very necessary for all husbandmen to know. Newly set foorth with additions. London, for Edward White, 1596. (Also 1587; 1610.)

260. —————— The second part of the good hus-wives jewell. Where is to be found most apt and readiest wayes to distill many wholsome and sweet waters. In which likewise is shewed the best maner in preserving of divers sorts of fruits, & making of sirrops. With divers conceits in cookerie with the booke of carving. London, E. Allde for Edward White, 1597. (Also 1585; 1606.)

261. (Debate). Cy finist le debat des deux seurs disputant damours tres utille & prouffitable pour instruire jeunes filles a marier. Nouvellement imprime en la rue neufue Nostre dame a lenseigne de lescu de france. (Bib. Nat. Rés. Ye. 2938.)

262. ‡Debili, Ermolao dei. Il ricettario sopra le diverse aposteme d'amore, del M. Eccellen. fisico, et naturale filosofo, delle cose secrete d'amore famoso Messere Ermolao dei Debili ad utilità, et sanità di donne, et huomini: giovani, vecchi, et vecchie. Verona, Sebastiano et Francesco dalle Donne Fratelli, 1593.

263. The deceyte of women, to the instruction and ensample of all men, yonge and olde, newly corrected. London, Abraham Vele, 1560. (Also 1561?)

264. Decker, Thomas. The batchelars banquet: or a banquet for batchelars: wherein is prepared sundry daintie dishes to furnish their table, curiously drest, and seriously served in. Pleasantly discoursing the various humours of women, their quicknesse of wittes, and unsearchable deceits, London, T. C., 1603. (Also 1604, 1630; 1631; 1651; 1677. Stories to illustrate humors, taken from *The Fifteen joys of marriage*. See La Sale.)

265. Decor puellarum. Questa sie una opera la quale si chiama decor puellarum: zoe honore del le donzelle: laquale de regola formae modo al stato de le honeste donzelle per magistrum Nicolaum Jenson. 1461. (Bib. Nat. Rés. D. 7276.)

266. La defensione delle donne d'autore anonimo. Scrittura inedita del sec. XV ora pubblicata a cura di Francisco Zambrini. Bologna, 1876.

267. (Definition). La diffinition & perfection d'amour. Le Sophologe d'amour. Traictez plaisantz & delectables oultre l'utilité en iceulx contenue. Paris, Gilles Corrozet, 1542. (Bib. Nat. Rés. p. R. 377.)

268. ‡De Gaillar. Le bouclier des femmes.
Delectable demaundes, and pleasant questions, etc. *See* Chartier.

269. ‡Delphinus, Joannes Antonius. Joan. Antonii Delphini, e Casali maiore conventualis franciscani, De matrimonio & coelibatu libri duo, quorum primus juxta regulas methodi universum negotium de matrimonio tractat; mox alter de coelibatu sacris initiatorum: & de monas-

ticis votis: adeòque de regularium institutis agit. Eiusdem de salutari omnium rerum ac praesertim hominum progressu libri quinque, quorum primus est de rerum eventu: alter de praedestinatione: tertius de originali peccato: de libero arbitrio. Quartus & quintus de justificatione. Camerini, apud Antonium Giciosum, 1553.

270. DESCHAMPS, EUSTACHE. Le mirour de mariage. Reims, P. Tarbé, 1865. (Previously unpublished; written before 1416. Usual diatribe against women and marriage. Last part legends.)

271. ‡DÉSIRÉ, ARTUS. L'origine et source de tous les maux de ce monde, par l'incorrection des pères et mères envers leurs enfans et de l'inobédience d'iceux. Ensemble de la trop grande familiarité et liberté donnée aux servans et servantes, avec un petit discours de la visitation de Dieu envers son peuple chrestien, par affliction de guerre, peste et famine. Par M. Artus Désiré. Paris, J. Dallier, 1571.

272. DESMARINS, BERTRAND. Le rousier des dames sive le pelerin damours nouvellement compose par messire Bertrand desmarins de masan. (Verse.)

273. DESPORTES, PHILIPPE. Stances du mariage par Philippes des Portes, 1573. Rep. 1908. (See Blanchon, Le Gaygnard, and Rouspeau, who defend marriage against this attack.)

274. DES ROCHES, CATHERINE AND MADELEINE. Instruction pour les jeunes dames, par la Mere et Fille d'alliance. Paris, sur la copie imprimée à Lyon par J. Dieppi, 1597. (Unacknowledged trans. See Piccolomini, *Dialogo*. For another unacknowledged trans. see Romieu.)

275. —————— Les oeuvres de mes-dames Des Roches de Poitiers mere et fille. Seconde edition. Corrigee & augmentee de la Tragi-comedie de Tobie & autres oeuvres poëtiques. Paris, pour Abel l'Anglier, 1579. (Also 1578; 1604. See *Epistre aux dames; Epistre a ma fille; Au Roy; Les oeuvres de la mère*—Ode I, Ode III, etc.; *Les oeuvres de la fille—Epistre à sa mere*, etc.—on learning for women, love, beauty.)

276. —————— Les secondes oeuvres de mes-dames Des Roches de Poictiers, mere & fille. Poictiers, pour Nicolas Courtoys, 1583. (Also 1604. See dialogue between Placide and Severe on the management of daughters.)

277. DES RUES, FRANÇOIS. Les fleurs du bien dire, premiere partie recueillies és cabinets des plus rares esprits de ce temps, pour exprimer les passions amoureuses, tant de l'un comme de l'autre sexe. Avec un nouveau recueil de traicts plus signalez, redigez en forme de lieux communs, dont on se peut servir en toutes sortes de discours amoureux. Lyon, prins sur la coppie imprimee à Langres par P. Roche, 1595. (Also 1603; 1604; 1609; and, with *Les marguerites françoises*, 1612; 1614; 1620?; 1625; 1626.)

278. —————— Les marguerites des lieux communs, et excellentes sen-

tences. Avec plusieurs comparaisons & similitudes sur une partie d'icelles. Ausquels sont comprins les plus beaux traits dont on peut user en amour, & en autres discours. Lyon, pour Simon Rigaud, 1605. (Also 1604; 1626.)

279. ———— Les marguerites françoises, ou seconde partie des fleurs du bien-dire: recueilles des plus beau discours de ce temps, & mises selon l'ordre alphabetique, par François Des-ruës, Constançois. Lyon, jouxte la coppie imprimee à Saumur, par Pierre Colle, 1605. (Also, with *Les fleurs du bien dire*, 1603; 1612; 1614; 1625.)

280. (Dialogue). Dialogue apologetique excusant ou defendant le devot sexe femenin: introduict par deulx parsonnaiges: lun a nom Bouche maldisant: lautre Femme deffendant: auquel (pour excuser ou deffendre le dict sexe) est alleguee la saincte scripture: les docteurs de leglise comme sainct Jherosme/ sainct Ambroise/ Sainct Gregoire/ sainct Augustin/Sainct Bernard, et plusieurs auctorites des philosophes. Paris, F. d'Egmont, 1516.

281. ———— A dialogue between the commune secretary & jalousye, touchynge the unstableness of harlottes. 1560? (Ascribed to Edward Gosynhill.)

282. ‡———— Dyalogue defensyve for women, against malicious detractoures. London, 1542.

283. Discorso intorno alla maggioranza dell' huomo, e della donna fatto dall' Accademico Bramoso dell'Accademia de' solleciti di Trevigi . . . . Trevigi, Angelo Mazzolini, 1589.

284. A discourse of the married and single life. Wherein, by discovering the misery of the one, is plainly declared the felicity of the other. London, Jonas Man, 1621.

285. Disputatio nova contra mulieres, qua probatur eas homines non esse. Frankfort, 1595. (Satire on methods of argument used by Socinians. Attributed to Valens Acidalius but denied by him as current long before. Taken seriously by some; see Gedik. Pub. also along with Gedik's answer, 1638; 1641; 1644; 1690; 1695. French trans. 1744 by Meunier de Querlon with title *Probleme sur les femmes*. See his preface for occurrence of the same idea. Ital. trans. 1647.)

286. ‡A dissertation of the nature of love, of philtres, and on the lovers pulse, 1611.

287. Le doctrinal des bon serviteurs. (Bib. Nat. Rés. Ye. 1208. Eng. trans. see below.)

288. ‡———— (Eng. trans.). Doctrynall of good servants. (Trans. by John Butler.)

289. ‡Le doctrinal des femmes mariés.

290. Le doctrinal des filles. A elles tresutile. Lyon, Jacques Maillet, 1490? (Also 1510? Bib. Nat. Rés. Ye. 337.)

291. Le doctrinal des nouveaux mariez. Lyon, 1504. (Bib. Nat. Rés. Ye. 336.)
292. Le doctrinal des nouvelles mariees. Paris?, 1500?
293. Dodeci avvertimenti che deve dare la madre alla figlivola quando la manda a marito. 1300? (First pub. 1847.)
294. DOLCE, LODOVICO. Dialogo della pittura di M. Lodovico Dolce, intitolato L'Aretino. Nel quale si ragiona della dignità di essa pittura, e di tutte le parti necessarie, che a perfetto pittore si acconvengono: con esempi di pittore antichi, & moderni: e nel fine si fa mentione delle virtù e delle opere del Divin Titiano. Vinegia, Gabriel Giolito, 1557. (Ital. and French 1735. Eng. trans. 1769 by W. Brown, ded. to George III as great patron of the arts.)
295. ————— Dialogo di M. Lodovico Dolce della institution delle donne. Secondo il tre stati, che cadono nella vita humana. Vinegia, Gabriel Giolito, 1545. (Also 1547; 1553; 1560. Span. trans. 1584.)
296. ————— Dialogo di M. Lodovico Dolce, nel quale si ragiona della qualità, diversità, e proprietà de i colori. Venetia, Gio. Battista, et Marchio Sessa, Fratelli, 1565.
297. ————— Dialogo piacevole di messer Lodovico Dolce: nelquale Messer Pietro Aretino parla in difesa d'i male aventurati mariti. Curtio Troiano d'i Navò, 1542. (Cuckoldom no disgrace.)
298. ————— Paraphrasi nella sesta satira di Giuvenale, nella quale si ragiona delle miserie de gli huomini maritati. Dialogo in cui si parla di che qualita si del tor moglie, & del' modo, che vi si ha a tenere. Lo epithalamio di Catullo nelle nozze di Peleo di Theti. Venegia, Curtio Navo e fratelli, 1538.
299. ‡DOLCI, FRANCESCO. I due paradosse d'amore. 1612.
300. DOMENICHI, LODOVICO. Dialoghi di M. Lodovico Domenichi; cioè, D'amore, De'rimedi d'amore, Dell' amor fraterno, Della fortuna, Della vera nobiltà, Dell' imprese, Della corte, et Della stampa. Vinegia, Gabriel Giolito, 1562.
301. ————— La donna di corte, discorso di Lodovico Domenichi. Nel quale si ragiona dell' affabilità & honesta creanza da doversi usare per gentildonna d'honore. Lucca, per il Busdrago, 1564. (Unacknowledged trans. of Nifo's De re aulica, lib. II.)
302. ————— La nobilta delle donne di M. Lodovico Domenichi. Corretta, & di nuovo ristampata. Vinetia, Gabriel Giolito e fratelli, 1558 or 1552 (blurred). (Also 1549; 1551. For discussion of Domenichi's indebtedness to Agrippa and Capella see Bond, Introduction to rep. of Bercher, pp. 74–77.)
303. ‡DOMINICI, GIOVANNI, CARDINAL. Regola del governo di cura familiare. Written 1400–1405. (1472?; 1477; 1483; 1496. Contains attack on the revival of ancient learning.)

304. DONDI DALL' OROLOGI, GIUSEPPE. L'inganno dialogo di M. Gioseppe
     Horologgi. Vinegia, Gabriele Giolito, 1562. (Deceit of women in trying
     to make themselves appear more beautiful than they are, pp. 127–145.
     Speakers Ruscelli and Dolce.)

305. ‡A dredge for defenden of women's apparel. London, John Case, 1551.

306. Les droicts nouveaux establis sur les femmes. Paris. (Allowing women
     to do as they please. Verse. Bib. Nat. Rés. Ye. 3905. See Coquillart.)
     DRUSAC, SEIGNEUR DE. See Du Pont.

307. DU BOSC, JACQUES. La femme heroique ou les heröines comparées
     avec les heros, en toute sorte de vertus: et a la fin de chaque compari-
     son, plusieurs reflexions morales. Par le R. P. du Bosc, Religieux
     Cordelier, Conseiller et Predicateur ordinaire du Roy. Paris, Antoine
     de Sommaville, et Augustin Courbe, 1645. (Also 1632 with title
     L'honneste femme; 1633; 1634; 1635; 1636; 1639–1640; 1643; 1658;
     1665; 1766 with title Elise ou l'idee d'une honnête femme. Containing
     from one to three parts. Eng. trans. 1639 with title, The compleat
     woman; 1753 with title, The accomplish'd woman. Ital. trans. 1742 with
     title, La donna onesta.)

308. DU FAUR, GUY, SEIGNEUR DE PIBRAC. Cinquante quatrains, conte-
     nant preceptes et enseignemens utiles pour la vie de l'homme, com-
     posez à l'imitation de Phocylides, d'Epicharmus & autres anciens
     poëtes Grecs, par le Sieur de Pyb. Rouen, Martin le Mesgissier, 1574.
     (Also with successive additions up to 126 quatrains 1575; 1576; 1583;
     1586; 1596; 1597; 1602; 1606; 1615–1619; 1629; 1634; 1640; 1646;
     1659; 1660; 1667; 1674; 1700. Eng. trans. see below. Germ. trans.
     1642. Greek trans. 1642. Latin trans. 1585; 1666; 1668. Latin and
     Greek trans. 1584; 1607; 1621. Intended for both sexes.)

309. ——————— (Eng. trans.). Τετραστικα; or, the quadrains of Guy de
     Faur, Lord of Pibrac. Translated, by Joshua Sylvester. London,
     Humfrey Lownes, 1605.

310. DU PONT, GRATIAN, SEIGNEUR DE DRUSAC. Les controversses des
     sexes masculin et femenin. Tholose, Jacques Colonnies, 1534. (Also
     1536; 1539; 1540; 1541. Verse.)

311. ‡DUPRES, JEAN. Le palais des nobles dames auquel a treze parcelles
     ou chambres principales: en chacune desquelles sont declarees plu-
     sieurs histoires tant Grecques, Hebraiques, Latines que Francoises.
     Ensemble fictions & couleurs poëtiques concernans les vertus &
     louanges des dames. (Du Verdier. Verse.)

312. ‡DURAND DE CHAMPAGNE (end of 13th, first of 14th cent.). Speculum
     dominarum. (Manuel of Christian morality for women in general but
     especially for queens and princesses. Trans. into French for Jeanne de
     Navarre, queen of Philippe le Bel, and again in 16th century for Mar-

guerite de Navarre. Not published. See Piaget, Introduction to rep. of *Miroir aux dames*, pp. 6–7.)

DU REFUGE, EUSTACHE. *See* Refuge.

313. ‡EBERARTUS, JOACHIMUS. Bonus mulier Rhod. 1617; 1627.

314. ELYOT, THOMAS. The defence of good women, devised and made by Sir Thomas Elyot knyght. London, in aed. T. Bertheleti, 1545.

315. En Amanieu de Sescas. Ensenhamen de la donzela. (Aragon, last quarter of 13th cent. Service at Court. Verse.)

316. ENZINAS, JUAN DE. Dialogo de amor. Intitulado Dorida en que se trata, de las causas por donde puede justamente un amante (sin ser notado de inconstante) retirarse de su amor. Nuevamente sacado a luz, corregido y enmendo por Juan de Enzinas . . . Burgos, Philippe de Junta y Juan Baptista Varesio, 1593.

317. ‡Epistre à la louange des dames, addressante à une Dame Tholosaine composee en rime par un sien serviteur pour l'amour de son maistre Pierre Servati. Tholose, 1545. (Du Verdier.)

318. EQUICOLA, MARIO. Libri di natura d'amore di Mario Equicola, novamente stampato, et con somma diligentia corretto. Vinegia, Francesco di Alessandro Bindoni & Mapheo Pasini, 1531. (Also 1525; 1526; 1536; 1554; 1562; 1563; 1583; 1587; 1607. French trans. 1584; 1597.)

319. ERASMUS, DESIDERIUS. Christiani matrimonii institutio, per Des. Erasmum Roteradamum, opus nunc primum & natum, & excusam. Basileae, apud Joannem Frobenium, 1526. (Also 1540; 1650; 1703–1706. French trans. 1714.)

320. ———— Des. Erasmi Rote. opus de conscribendis epistolis, ex postrema autoris recognitione emendatius aeditum. Cum annotationibus marginalibus, quae partim artificium, partim authorum locos explicant. Additus est copiosus rerum index. Antverpiae, Joannes Crinitus, 1546. (Ded. by Erasmus dated 1522, a youthful work begun some thirty years before, pirated and put out in a mutilated form. Repub. almost every year with varying titles until 1558 and then every few years into the 18th cent. See for *Laus et vituperatio matrimonii*; pp. 163–185—*Exemplum epistolae suasoriae*; pp. 185–189—*De genere dissuasorio*. Printed also in Domenici *Baudii amores*, 1638, pp. 241–278. Eng. trans. of *Laus matrimonii* see below.)

321. ———— (Eng. trans.). A ryght frutefull epystle devysed by the moste excellent clerke Erasmus in laude and prayse of matrymony translated in to Englyshe by Rychard Tavernour which translation he hathe dedicate to the ryght honorable Mayster Thomas Cromwel most worthy Counseloure to our soverayne lorde kyng Henry the eyght. London, Robert Redman, 1530?

322. ———— Enchiridion militis christiani, ab Erasmo compositum,

saluberrimus praeceptis refertum . . . et ratio quaedam veri christian-
ismi. Lovanii, opera Theodorici Martini, 1517. (Also 1518; 1519; 1522;
1523; 1535; 1538; 1541; 1563; 1641; 1662; 1685. Eng. trans. see below.
French trans. n.d., Span. trans. 1528.)

323. —————— (Eng. trans.). A booke called in latyn enchiridion militis
christiani and in englyshe the manuell of the christen knyght re-
plenyshed with moste holsome preceptes made by the famous clerke
Erasmus of Roterdame to the whiche is added a newe and mervaylous
profytable preface. London, Wynken de Worde, 1533. (Also 1518;
1534; 1538; 1540?; 1541; 1544; 1548; 1550?; 1576. See cap. XIIII,
bringing up of children; cap. XXXII, foolish love.)

324. —————— Familiarium colloquiorum des Erasmi Roterodami, liber
multis nominibus utilissimus, nuper diligentissime excusus, cum
aliquot, colloquiorum eiusdem autoris accessione. Additus est insuper
index per utilis recens ad legentium usum excogitatus. In fine vero,
loca quaedam in quibus lector non admodum peritus haerere poterat,
sunt brevissimis scholiis explicata. Florentiae, haeredes Philippi
Juntae, 1531. (Also 1527; 1529; 1530?; 1550; 1556; 1564; 1631; 1636;
1638; 1639; 1643; 1650; 1655; 1656; 1657; 1658; 1662; 1664; 1666;
1670; 1676; 1677; 1679; 1681; 1683; 1686; 1690?; 1693; 1697; 1698;
1709; 1712; 1713; 1717; 1723; 1729; 1740; 1747; 1754; 1760; 1773.
Eng. trans. 1671; 1712; 1721; 1725; 1733. French trans. 1720. Germ.
trans. 1663; 1684. Ital. trans. 1545; 1549. Several dialogues on marriage
and on learning for women, with obvious titles.)

325. —————— A mery dialogue, declaringe the propertyes of shrowde
shrewes and honest wives, not onelie verie pleasaunte, but also not a
lytle profitable: made by the famous clerke D. Erasmus Roterodamus.
Translated in to Englyshe. London, Anthony Kytson, 1557. (French
trans. from Latin, 1708. Germ. trans. 1524; 1578; 1591; 1597; 1607;
another trans. 1748. Thought to be a description of More's way with
his first wife.)

326. ‡—————— Modest means to marriage pleasantly set foorth. Tr.
N. L[eigh?]. London, H. Denham, 1568. (Is this the same as above?)

327. —————— Vidua christiana per Des. Erasmum Roterodamum ad
serenissimam pridem Hungariae Booemiaeque reginam, Mariam,
Caroli Caesaris, ac Ferdinandi regis sororem. Opus recens natum, &
nunc primum excusum . . . . Basileae, in officina Frobeniana, 1529.
(Polish trans. 1595. Dutch trans. 1607.)

328. ‡Ercole, Filogenio. Dell eccellenza della donna. Fermo, 1538.

329. Ermengaud, Matfre. Lo breviari d'amor. c. 1288. (Pub. Soc. Arch.
Scient. et Litt. de Béziers, by M. G. Azaïs. See ll. 30,220–31,082,
counsels on love addressed to young married women of the nobility.
For summary see Intro. pt. I, pp. LXVIII–XCII.)

330. ERONDELLE, PIERRE. The French garden: for English ladyes and gentlewomen to walke in. Or, a sommer dayes labour. Being an instruction for the attayning unto the knowledge of the French tongue: wherein for the practise thereof, are framed thirteene dialogues in French and English, concerning divers matters from the rising in the morning till bed-time. Also the historie of the centurion mencioned in the Gospell: in French verses. Which is an easier and shorter methode then hath beene yet set forth, to bring the lovers of the French tongue to the perfection of the same. By Peter Erondelle Professor of the same language. London, printed for Edward White, 1605.

331. ESPINOSA, JUAN DE. Dialogo en laude de las mugeres. Intitulado Ginaecepaenos. Diviso en V. partes. Interloqutores. Philalithes, y Philodoxo. Compuesto por Joan de Spinosa, gentilhomre de la Magestad Catholica . . . y su indice copioso. Milan, Michel Tini, 1580.

332. ESTIENNE, ANTOINE. Remonstrance charitable aux dames et damoyselles de France, sur leurs ornemens dissolus, pour les induire à laisser l'habit du paganisme, et prendre celuy de la femme pudique et Chrestienne. Avec une elegie de la France se complaignant de la dissolution desdictes damoyselles. par F. A. E. M. Pour la quatriesme edition. Paris, Sebastien Nivelle, 1585. (Also 1527, Du Verdier; 1581.)

333. ‡ESTIENNE, CH. Que l'excellence de la femme est plus grande que celle de l'homme. 1554. (See *Femmes*, vol. XLIV.)

334. ‡ESTIENNE, H. Carmen de senatulo foeminarum. 1596.

335. ESTIENNE, NICOLE. Les misères de la femme mariée, où se peuvent voir les peines et tourmens qu' elle recoit durant sa vie, mis en forme de stances par Madame Liebault, Paris, Pierre Menier. Rep. 1855, Fournier, *Variétés historiques et littéraires*, III, 321–331. (Note from Du Verdier: "Nicole Estienne Parisienne fille à feu Charles Estienne, femme de M. Jean Liebault medecin à Paris a escrit en prose une apologie pour les femmes contre ceux qui en mesdisent. Non imprimae. Plus contrestances pour le mariage c'est à dire Responces aux stances que Philippe des Portes a fait contre le mariage.")

336. Les Evangiles des quenouilles. Lyons, Jean Mareschal, 1493. (Du Verdier.)

337. Exhortation aux dames vertueuses, en laquelle est demonstré le vray point d'honneur. Avec l'Hecatonphile de M. Leon Baptiste Albert, contenant l'art d'aymer. Mis en deux langues pour ceux qui desirent conferer la langue Italienne avec la Françoyse. Paris, Lucas Breyel, 1597.

338. EXIMENIZ, FRANCESCH (1350–1409). Le libre de la dones. Barcelona, 1495.

339. ‡EYBE, ALBRECHT VON. De laudibus clarissimarum foeminarum oratio, numero septimo decima, ex. 30. per Albertum de Eybe collectis.

340. ———— Ehebüchlein. 1472. Rep. by Max Hermann, 1890.

341. ‡FALARETE, PRODOCOGENE. Difese delle donne. Padove, 1558.

342. ‡FALOTICO, ACADEMICO DELLA CONGREGADE' ROZZI. Il ricorso de' villani alle donne contro i calumniatori, recitato in Siena l'anno 1576. Firenze, il Tosi, 1577.

343. FARRA, ALLESSANDRO. Tre discorsi d'Alessandro Farra Academico Affidato. Il primo de' miracoli d'amore, all' illustrissimo, & eccellentissimo Signor Marchese di Pescara. Il secondo della divinità dell' huomo, al molto Ill. S. Allessandro Foccaro. L'ultimo dell' ufficio del capitano, al molto Illust. S. Hestorre Visconte. Pavia, Girolamo Bartoli, 1564. (Also 1561. Chiefly philosophical—love produces peace, tranquillity, etc.)

344. FAUSTO DA LONGIANO, SEBASTIANO. Delle nozze trattato del Fausto da Longiano, in cui si leggono i riti, i costumi, gl'instituti, le cerimonie, et le solennità di diversi antichi popoli, onde si sono tratti molti problemi; & aggiuntivi, i precetti matrimoniali di Plutarco. Alla Illustrissima S. Virginia S. Di Piombino. Venetia, Plinio Pietrasanta, 1554.

345. ‡FENNER, DUDLEY. Arts of logic and rhetoric. 1584. (Also 1588. Pt. III, *The order of household*.)

346. FENTON, SIR GEOFFREY. A forme of Christian pollicie gathered out of French by Geffray Fenton. A worke very necessary to al sorts of people generally, as wherein is contayned doctrine, both universall, and special touching the institution of al Christian profession: and also convenient perticularly for all magistrates and governours of common weales, for their more happy regiment according to God. Also, this booke may serve for preachers, and curates, when they advertise every estate of his perticular dutie. London, H. Middleton, 1574. (See bk. V and VI on marriage and the bringing up of children.)
———— Monophylo. *See* Pasquier.

347. FERRAND, JACQUES. Traité de l'essence et guérison de l'amour, ou de la mélancholie érotique, par M. Jacques Ferrand, . . . Toulouse, de Vve. J. et R. Colomiez, 1610. (Also 1623. Eng. trans. see below.)

348. ———— (Eng. trans.). Ερωτομανία, or a treatise discoursing of love. Oxford, L. Lichfield, 1640. (Also 1645. Trans. by E. Chilmead. Medical point of view.)

349. ‡FERRERS, RICHARD. The worth of women; a poem. London, 1622.

350. ‡FETHERSTONE, CHRISTOPHER. A dialogue agaynst light, lewde and lascivious dauncing. London, T. Dawson, 1582. (Also 1595.)

351. FICINO, MARSILIO. Il comento di Marsilio Ficino sopra il Convito di Platone et esso Convito tradotti in lingua toscana per H. Barbarasa da Terni. Venetia, 1544. (Highly philosophic.)

352. ‡FIERVILLE (or FERVILLE). Caco-gynie. Caen, 1617. (Also 1618; 1650, with title *Méchanceté des femmes*.)

353. FILARETO, pseud. Breve raccolto di bellissimi secreti, trovati in servizio, e ornamento delle donne, nuovamente riprovati e posti in luce. Fiorenza, G. Marescotti, 1573. (Recipes for the toilet.)

354. FILIRIACO, ONOFRIO. Vera narratione dell' operationi delle donne. Al signor Alessandro Pollegra, Onofrio Filiriaco. Nuovamente poste in luce. Padova, Lorenzo Pasquali, 1588. (Attack on women.)

355. ‡FILOGENIO, ERCOLE, pseud. (Ercole Marescotti, sen.). All' illustrissima ed eccellentissima la signora Flavia Peretti-Orsina dell' eccellenza della donna, discorso di ec. Fermo, Sertorio Monti, 1589.

356. FILOGENIO, TELEFILO, pseud. (Girolamo Borro). Ragionamento di Telefilo Filogenio della perfettione delle donne. Alla Illustrissima Signora la Signora Donna Isabetta Cibo dalla Rovere, Marchesana di Massa. Lucca, Vincenzo Busdragho, 1561.

357. FIRENZUOLA, AGNOLO. Dialogo della bellezze delle donne. In Prose di M. Agnolo Firenzuola Fiorentino. Fiorenza, Bernardo di Giunta, 1548. (Also in *Prose*, 1552; 1562; 1622; 1723. French trans. 1578.)

358. ——— Epistola in lode delle donne. A Messer Claudio Tolomei nobile Sanese. In Prose di M. Agnolo Firenzuola Fiorentino. Fiorenza, Bernardo di Giunta, 1548. (Also in *Prose*, 1552; 1562; 1622; 1723.)

359. ——— Ragionamenti amorosi. In Prose di M. Agnolo Firenzuola Fiorentino. Fiorenza, Bernardo di Giunta, 1548. (Also in *Prose*, 1552; 1562; 1622; 1723. Dialogue carried on by women—definitions of love, why should a woman not love a woman and escape blame, married woman and lover, love and friendship.)

360. ‡FITZHERBERT. Prologue for the wyves occupacyon.

361. FOCLIN, ANTOINE. La rhetorique francoise d'Antoine Foclin de Chauny en Vermandois, a tresillustre Princesse Madame Marie Royne d'Ecosse. Paris, André Wechel, 1555. (See dedication for an account of her Latin oration before the French court on the subject of the suitability of learning for women. This oration seems not to have been preserved.)

362. FONTAINE, CHARLES. La contr' amye de court: par Maistre Charles Fontaine Parisien. Lyon, chez Sulpice Sabon: pour Antoine Constantin, 1543. (Also 1544; 1547, in *Opuscules d'amour, par Heroet, La Borderie, et autres divins poetes*, pp. 148–200. See Heroët.)

363. ‡FONTANA, ERCOLE. Amorose fiamme di Ercole Fontana in lode delle illustri gentildonne Bolognesi. Bologne, 1574.

364. FORCADEL, ETIENNE. Henrico III. Francorum et Poloniae regi, relata gratia, Stephano Forcatulo jurisconsulto autore. Primo libro continetur, Valesiorum Franciae Regum, origo splendida, invictum

robur, & prosperum imperium. Secundo, Quod foeminae illustres regnis gubernandis, ac legibus ferendis, commodissimae ubique fuerint. Tertio, ampliores gratias regi agens autor, salubria quaedam Gallis detegit: & quare discessum cogitet. Parisiis, apud Guillielmum Chaudiere, 1579.

365. FORESTI, JACOPO FILIPPO. Opus de claris selectisque plurimis mulieribus a fratre Jacobo Philippo Bergomense editum; revisum et castigatum per magistrum Albertum de Placentia et fratrem Augustinum de Casali majori. Ferrariae, opera L. de Rubeis, de Valentia, 1497. (Also 1521. See Ravisius.)

366. ‡Le fort baston de madame verité, pour chastier male-bouche àtousmal disans des dames. Né, trouvé & nourry és terres, forests & boscages du seigneur de Labedan Vicomte de Chasteaubon en la comté de Bigorre. Avec l'honneur, louange & tresor des dames. Tholose, 1534. (Du Verdier.)

367. FRACHETTA, GIROLAMO. La spositione di Girolamo Frachetta sopra la canzone di Guido Cavalcanti: Donna mi prega, etc. All' Illustriss. Signor Scipione Gonzaga. Venetia, i Gioliti, 1585. (See Cavalcanti for similar expositions.)

368. FRANC, MARTIN. Le champion des dames. Livre plaisant copieux & habondant en sentences. Contenant la deffence des dames, contre malebouche & ses consors, & victoire dicelles. Compose par Martin Franc, ... & nouvellement imprime. Paris, Pierre Vidove, 1530. (Also 1485? Attack on Matheolus. Verse.)

369. FRANCO, GIACOMO. Nuova inventione di diversi mostre così di punto in aere come di retticelle hoggi di usate per tutte le parte del mondo, con merletti, mostrette da colari, e da maneghiti, et merli per cantoni da fazoletti. Venetia, 1596. Venezia, F. Ongania, 1878.

370. FRANCO, NICOLÒ. Dialogo di M. Nicolo Franco. Dove si ragiona delle bellezze ... Alla eccellentissima Marchesana del Vasto. Difficile est satyram non scribere. Venetiis, apud Antonium Gardane, 1542.

371. ‡Frauenbiechlein, zum rum und breyse allen tugendsamen auch erberen weybern ist dieses tractetlein auss vorschrifft des hayligen wortt gotes zusammengebracht und verfasset. Da entgegen auch zu straffetlicher halsstoriger und bosshaftiger weyber etwas aus der hayligen geschrifft gezogen. (See Hentsch, p. 228: Writes to aid women to remain in the good way. Not addressed to women shut in cloisters against the will of God instead of fulfilling their vocation and the divine law by being subject to a man and having children. Second part against bad women, warning to his dear sons.)

372. FREGOSO (or FULGOSO), BATTISTA. Baptistae C. Fulgosi anteros.

Mediolani, per Leonardum Pachel, 1496. (French trans., 1581. Two dialogues, attack and defense.)

373. ————— Baptistae Fulgosi de dictis factisque memorabilibus collectanea a Camillo Gilino latina facta. In que quicquid hystoriarum a mundi exordio usque ad hec tempora scitu dignum invenitur/quid diligentissime congestum est. Parrhisii in aedibus Gallioti du Pre, 1518. (Nine books containing chapters under various headings including virtues. Examples unorganized, men and women.)

374. FRISCHLIN, NICODEMUS. Nicodemi Frischlini, viri incomparabilis methodus declamandi (posthuma) in laudatione, thesi de laudibus mulierum demonstrata: cui praetereà annexe sunt eiusdem epistolae et praefationes; in quibus non solùm optimorum ultriusque linguae authorum vitae, laudes, rerum, quas tractant, usus praestantiàque, aut etiam methodus indicantur: verùm etiam suorum ipsius scriptorum, hactenus aliquot vicibus sine praefationibus in lucem denuo emissorum, ratio, consilium & artificium ab authore ipso dextrè ac utiliter explicantur. Cum triplici indice omnium ferè ipsius elucubrationum, quae comparari quidem potuerunt. In eloquentia studiosorum gratiam cuncta edita. Argentinae, typis Johannis Catoli, 1606.

FULGOSO, See Fregoso.

375. FUSCO, HORATIO. La vedova del Fusco. Roma, i Dorici, 1570.

376. G., I. An apologie for women-kinde. London, Edw. Allde, 1605.

377. ‡La garand des dames soubs la protection d'honneur contre les calomniateurs de la noblesse feminine. Lyon. (Du Verdier.)

378. GARAY, BLASCO. Dos cartas: en que se contiene: como sabiendo una sennora que un su servidor se queria confessar: le escrive por muchos refranes: para atra elle a su amor. Y el estando en su buen proposito: respondela que se de al servicio de dios. Hechas por Blasco de garay y corregidas agora de nuevo. Toledo, 1541. (Also 1553, see Ulloa; 1569; 1608; 1614; 1619; 1621; 1634.)

379. GARBO, DINO DEL. Guidonis de Cavalcantibus de natura et motu amoris venerei cantio cum enarratione Dini de Garbo. Venetiis, apud Octavianum Scotum, 1498. (Title taken from Villani's *Vita di Guido*, note 8 by il Conte Mazzuchelli. Read in the Italian trans. apparently made in 14th century, and first pub. 1813, Cavalcanti's *Rime*, pp. 73–115. See Cavalcanti for similar expositions.)

380. GARIN (or GUÉRIN), FRANÇOIS. Les complaintes et enseignemens de Francoys Garin marchant de lyon envoyees a son fils pour soy scavoir regir et gouverner parmy le monde. Paris, Guillaume Mignart, 1495. Rep. 1832. (Second part, advice to son, marriage briefly included. Third part, attack on celibacy.)

381. GARZONI, TOMASO. Le vite delle donne illustri della Scrittura Sacra.

Nuovamente descritte dal R. P. D. Tomaso Garzoni da Bagnacavallo, Canonico Regolare Lateran. Predicatore. Con l'aggionta delle vite delle donne oscure, & laide dell' uno, & l' altro Testamento; et un discorso in fine sopra la nobiltà delle donne. Alla Sereniss. Sig. Duchessa di Ferrara Madama Margarita Estense Gonzaga. Venetia, Gio. Domenico Imberti, 1588.

382. GAURICO, POMPONIO. Pomponii Gaurici Neapolitani tractatus de symmetriis, lineamentis & physiognomia, eiusque speciebus, etc. Third item in a volume with title beginning *Johannis ab Ingine introductiones.* Ursellis, apud Cornelium Sutorium, Impensis Lazari Zetzneri, 1603. (Ded. letter dated 1542.)

383. GEDIK (Gedicus), SIMON. Defensio sexus muliebris, opposita futilissimae disputationi recens editae, qua suppresso authoris & typographi nomine blasphemè contenditur, mulieres homines non esse. Simon Gedicus Sacrosanctae & Theol. Doct. etc. Lipsiae, Michael Lantzenberger, 1595. (Also 1690, with title *Mulier homo.* Printed with *Disputatio* in The Hague 1638; 1641; 1644; 1693; Amsterdam 1744; Cracow 1766. See *Disputatio.*)

384. GELLI, GIOVANBATTISTA. Il Gello Accademico Fiorentino. Sopra que due sonetti del Petrarcha che lodano il ritratto della sua M. Laura. Fiorenza, 1549. (Also in *Lettioni,* 1551, 1555. "Per mirar Polycleto a pruova fiso," and "Quando giunse a Simon l'altro concietto." To show the learning of Petrarch, who in the first praises the portrait after the fashion of Plato, and in the second after that of Aristotle.)

385. ——————— Il Gello sopra un sonetto di M. Franc. Petrarca. Firenze, 1549. (Also in *Lettioni,* 1551, 1555. "O tempo o ciel volubil che fuggendo." Also read in the Academy to show the learning of Petrarch.)

386. ——————— Lettioni fatta da Giovan Battista Gelli, nella Accademia Fiorentina, sopra varii luoghi di Dante & del Petrarca. Firenze, 1555. (Also 1551. Contains the above expositions and others on Petrarch.)

387. GERSON, JEAN. Tractatus Magistri Joannis Gerson contra Romantium de Rosa, qui ad illicitam venerem et libidinosum amorem utriusque status homines quodam libello excitabat. *Opera,* 1606, col. 922-935.

GIAMBELLI, CIPRIANO. *See* Bramoso.

388. GIAMBULARI, BERNARDO. El sonaglio delle donne, composto da Bernardo Giambullari Fiorentino. Dove descrive la condizione, & costumi delle donne, & conforta gli huomini che potendo star senza esse, non debbino mai pigliar moglie, per le loro perverse nature. Con somma diligentia nuovamente ristampato. Fiorenza, 1530? (Also 1500?; 1650? Verse.)

389. GIBSON, ANTHONY. A womans woorth, defended against all the men in the world. Prooving them to be more perfect, excellent and absolute in all vertuous actions, then any man of what qualitie soever. Written by one that hath heard much, seene much, but knowes a great deale more. London, John Wolfe, 1599. (Ded. letter to Elizabeth Countess of Southampton: "A translated apologie of womens faire vertues, written in French by a Lord of great reckoning, given by him to a very honorable Duchesse: since, translated by a fellow and friend of myne now absent, who gave me trust to see it should not wander in the world unregarded." Another ded. to the Maids of Honor, "Mistress Anne Russell, Mis. Margaret Ratcliffe, Mis. Mary Fitten, etc.," with sonnets to the three named. Pp. 62–70, "An other defence of womens vertues, written by an honorable personage, of great reckoning in Fraunce, and therefore thought meete to be joyned with the former discourse." See Pont-Aymerie.)

390. GIRALDI, GIOVANNI BATTISTA. Discorso di M. Gio. Batista Giraldi Cinthio. . . . intorno a quello che si conviene a giovane nobile & ben creato nel servire un gran principe. Pavia, Girolamo Bartoli, 1569. (See ff. 42a–74, honest love at court.)

391. Le Girofflier aux dames. Ensemble le dit des sibiles. Paris, Michel le Noir. (Against *The Romance of the Rose*. Bib. Nat. Rés. Ye. 215.)

392. ‡ GIUDOCCIO, GIACOMO. Dialogo d'amore di Giacomo Giudoccio . . . Padova, Paulo Megetti, 1589.

393. GIUSSANO, GIOVANNI PIETRO. Instruttione a' padri, per saper ben governare la famiglia loro, opera quale fù santamente, & piamente desiderata dal Beato Carlo Borromeo, Card. di S. Prassede, & Arcivescovo di Milano. Con un' altra breve instruttione, per i giovanetti, quali la prima volta hanno da ricevere la Santissima Communione; alle quali s' è aggiunto in principio quella de' Sacerdoti Curati, per le congregationi hanno da fare d'essi padri de famiglia, in essecutione de' Concilii Provinci e Diocesani di Milano. Scritte dal Sig. Pietro Giussano, Sacerdote, & Patritio Milanese, con i ricordi del sudetto B. Carlo Card. Borromeo, spettanti à questa materia, con gl' indici de' capitoli, e delle cose più notabili. Milano, Tini & Filippo Lomazzo, 1603.

GLOVER, ROBERT. *See* Milles, Thomas.

394. GODDARD, WILLIAM. Satirycall dialogue or a sharplye—invective conference, betweene Allexander the great, and that trulye woman-hater Diogynes. Imprinted in the Lowcountryes for all such gentlewomen as are not altogether idle nor yet well. Dort?, 1616? (Diatribe against women, wives, marriage. Verse.)

395. GODOFREDUS, PETRUS. Dialogus de amoribus. Lugduni, apud T. Paganum, 1552. (Also 1548. General, religious in character.)

396. GOSSON, STEPHEN. Pleasant quippes for upstart newfangled gentlewomen. London, Richard Jones, 1596. (Verse.)

397. GOSYNHILL, EDWARD. The prayse of all women called Mulierum Pean. Very fruytfull and delectable unto all the reders. Loke & rede who that can. This boke is prayse to eche woman. London, Wyllyam Myddylton, 1542? (Also 1560? The author has himself addressed in a vision by a number of ladies: "Awake, they sayde, slepe nat so fast, Consyder our grefe, and how we be blamed, And all by a boke that lately is past, Whyche, by reporte, by thee was fyrst framed, The Scole of Women, none auctor named: In print it is passed, lewdely compyled, All women wherby be sore revyled." But priority is confused. See below. An unreserved eulogy of women.)

398. ———— Here begynneth the Scole house of women: wherein every man may reade a goodly prayse of the condicyons of women. London, John Kyng, 1560. (Also 1541 [1561 in colo.]; 1572. See Edward More for answer to this attack. The usual diatribe, occasioned, the first lines say, by *The prayse of all women*. Priority thus claimed by both books.)

399. ———— The vertuous scholehous of ungracious women. (Erroneously attributed to Gosynhill. See Schoolhouse.)

400. GOTTIFREDI, BARTOLOMEO. Specchio d'amore, dialogo di messer Bartolomeo Gottifredi, nel quale alle giovani s' insegna innamorarsi: con una lettera piacevole del Doni in lode della chiave e la risposta del Gottifredi. Fiorenza, il Doni, 1547. Rep. 1912.

401. GOUGE, WILLIAM. Of domesticall duties eight treatises. I. An exposition of that part of Scripture out of which domesticall duties are raised. II. 1. A right conjunction of man and wife. 2. Common-mutuall duties betwixt man and wife. III. Particular duties of wives. IV. Particular duties of husbands. V. Duties of children. VI. Duties of parents. VII. Duties of servents. VIII. Duties of masters. By William Gouge. London, John Haviland, 1622. (Also 1626; 1634; 1639.)

402. GOUJON, JEAN. Le tresor de lamitie parfaicte. Par M. J. Goujon advocat a Lyon. Lyon, Nicolas Jullieron, 1626. (Brought out after his death by his son, François.)

403. GOURNAY, MARIE DE. Les advis, ou, les presens de la demoiselle de Gournay. Paris, Toussainct du Bray, 1634. (Also 1626; 1641. Contents: 1. *De l'education des enfans de France; 2. Naissance de Messeigneurs les enfans de France; 3. Abregé d' institution, pour le prince, souverain,* 4. *Egalité des hommes & des femmes.* 5. *Grief des dames. Les griefs des dames* pub. 1612; *L'egalite des hommes et des femmes* pub. 1604; 1622.)

404. GOZZI, NICOLÒ VITO DI. Dialogo d'amore detto antos, secondo la mente

di Platone. Composto da M. Nicolò Vito di Gozze, gentilhuomo Ragugeo. Nuovamente poste in luce. Venetia, Francesco Ziletti, 1581.

405. ———— Dialogo della bellezza detto Antos, secondo la mente di Platone. Composto da M. Nicolò Vito di Gozze, gentilhuomo Ragugeo. Nuovamente posto in luce. Venetia, Francesco Ziletti, 1581.

406. ———— Governo della famiglia, di M. Nicolò Vito di Gozze, . . . Nel quale brevemente, trattando la vera economica, s'insegna, non meno con facilità, che dottamente, il governo, non pure della casa tanto di città, quanto di contado; ma ancora il vero modo di accrescere, & conservare le ricchezze. Venetia, Aldo, 1589.

407. Granucci, Nicolò. La piacevol notte, et lieto giorno, opera morale. Di Nicolao Granucci. . . . Venetia, Jacomo Vidali, 1574. (See f. 58, dialogue on equality of men and women.)

408. ———— Specchio di virtù, nel quale brevemente si descrive la buona amicitia, la grandezza, e principio del matrimonio; e di quanta eccellenza sia nelle feminine la castità con molti notabilissimi essempi secondi i soggetti, da' quali ciascuno potra prender materia, & ammaestramento di ben vivere. Di nuovamente raccolta da Nicolao Granucci, Luchese. Lucca, il Busdrago, 1566.

409. Greene, Robert. Morando the Tritameron of love: the first and second part. Wherein certaine pleasant conceites, uttered by divers worthie personages, are perfectly discoursed, and three doubtfull questions of love, most pithely and pleasantly discussed: shewing to the wise how to use love, and to the fond, how to eschew lust: and yeelding to all both pleasure and profit. By Robert Greene, Maister of Artes in Cambridge. London, John Wolfe, 1587. (Also 1586.)

410. ———— Penelopes web. Where, in a christall mirrour of feminine perfection represents to the view of every one those vertues and graces, which more curiously beautifies the mind of women, then eyther sumptuous apparell, or jewells of inestimable value: the one buying fame with honour, the other breeding a kinde of delight, but with repentance. In three severall discourses also are three speciall vertues, necessary to be incident in every vertuous woman, pithely discussed: namely obedience, chastity, and sylence: interlaced with three severall and comicall histories. By Robert Greene Master of Artes in Cambridge. London, for John Hodgers, 1601. (Also 1587.)

411. Grévin, Jacques. Cinq livres de l'imposture et tromperie des diables: des enchantements et sorcelleries: pris du latin de Jean Wier, medecin du Duc de Cleves & faits françois. Par Jaques Grevin de Clermont en Beauvoisis, medecin à Paris. Paris, Jacques du Puys, 1567. (See liv. II, ch. 52, on recipes, and ch. 53, on love philtres and enchantments. Bib. Nat. R. 54027.)

412. GRINGORE, PIERRE. Le chateau d'amours. Paris, 1500. (Also 1525?; 1533. Against "amour folle" and in behalf of true love. Verse.)

413. ——— La complainte de trop tard marie. Paris, 1505. (Defense of wife and marriage against Theophrastus, Jean de Meun, and Matheolus.)

414. ——— Les fantaisies de Mere Sote. Paris, 1516. (Mixture, virtues, and faults of men and women illustrated.)

415. ‡GROSNOT (or GROGNET), PIERRE. (Priest, died before middle of 16th cent.) La louange des femmes.

416. ‡——— Bonne doctrine pour les filles.

417. Grund-und probierliche Beschreibung Argument und Schluss-Articul, sampt bengefuegten ausssuehrlichen Beantwortungen: Belangend die Frag ob die Weiber Menschen senn oder nicht? Meisten theils aus heiliger Schrifft das obrige aus andern Scribenten und der Experientz selbsten zusamen getragen. Zuvor Teutsch im Truck nie gesehen: Anjetzo aber zumercklicher guter Nachrichtung. Bevorab dem weib-lichen Geschlecht zu gebürlicher Verantwortung Gesprechsweiss lustig verfasset und publicirt, durch einen besondern liebhaber der Lieb und Bescheidenheit Anno 1617. 1618. (Also 1721. Dialogue between a Benedictine and a Jesuit.)

418. GUASCO, ANNIBAL. Ragionamento del Sig. Annibal Guasco ad Lavinia sua figlivola, della maniera del governarsi ella in corte; andando, per dama alla Serenissima Infante D. Caterina, Duchessa di Savoia. Turino, l'herede del Bevilacqua, 1586. (B. M. copy imperfect, ff. 25–28 missing. Copy in Biblioteca Communale di Bologna.)

419. GUAZZO, STEFANO. La civil conversatione del Signor Stefano Guazzo. . . . divisa in quattro libri. Nel primo si tratta in generale de' frutti, che si cavano dal conversare, & s'insegna a conoscere le buone dalle cattive conversationi. Nel secondo si discorre primieramente delle maniere convenevoli a tutte le persone nel conversar fuori di casa, & poi delle particolari, che debbono tenere conversando insieme i giovani, & i vecchi; i nobili, & gl' ignobili; i prencipi, & i privati; i dotti, & gl' idioti; i cittadini, & i forestiere; i religiosi & i secolari; gli huomini, & le donne. Nel terzo si dichiarano particolarmente i modi, che s'hanno a serbare nella domestica conversatione; cioé tra marito, & moglie; tra padre, & figlivolo; tra fratello, & fratello; tra patrone, & servitore. Nel quarto si rappresenta la forma della civil conversatione, con l'essempio d'un convito fatto in casale, con l'intervenimento di dieci persone. Vinegia, Enea de Alaris, 1574. (Also 1575; 1579; 1580; 1581; 1586; 1593; 1596; 1600; 1611; 1621; 1628. Eng. trans. see below. French trans. by G. Chappuys, 1579; 1580; by F. de Belleforest 1579; 1582.)

420. ——— (Eng. trans.). The civile conversation of M. Steven Guazzo written first in Italian, and nowe translated out of French by

George Pettie, devided into foure bookes. In the first is conteined in generall, the fruites that may bee reaped by conversation, and teaching howe to knowe good companie from yll. In the second, the manner of conversation, meete for all persons, which shall come in any companie, out of their owne houses, and then of the perticular points which ought to bee observed in companie betweene young men and olde, gentlemen and yeomen, princes and private persons, learned and unlearned, citizens and strangers, religious and secular, men & women. In the third is perticularly set foorth the orders to bee observed in conversation within doores, betweene the husband and the wife, the father and the sonne, brother and brother, the maister and the servant. In the fourth, the report of a banquet. London, Richard Watkins, 1581. (Also 1586.)

421. ———— Dialoghi piacevoli del Sig. Stefano Guazzo, . . . Dalla cui famigliare lettione potranno senza stanchezza, & satietà non solo gli huomini, ma ancora le donne raccogliere diversi frutti morali, & spirituali. Nella quali si tratta I Della prudenza de Ré congiunta con le lettere. II Del prencipe della Valacchia maggiore. III Del giudice. IIII Della elettione de' magistrati. V Delle imprese. VI Del paragone dell' arme, & delle lettere. VII Del paragone della poesia Latina, & della Thoscana. VIII Della voce fedeltà. IX Dell' honor universale. X Dell' honor delle donne. XI Del conoscimento di se stesso. XII Della morte. Venetia, Gio. Antonio Bertano, 1586. (Also 1587; 1604; 1610.)

422. GUEVARA, ANTONIO DE. Libro llamado relox de principes enel qual va encorporado el muy famoso libro de Marco aurelio auctor del un libro y del otro: que es el muy reverendo padre fray Antonio de guevara. . . . Valladolid, Nicolas Tierri, 1529. (Also 1531; 1532; 1534; 1535?; 1537; 1543; 1550; 1557; 1650; 1651; 1658; 1675; 1698. Eng. trans. see below. French trans. 1540; 1550; 1552; 1566; 1576; 1592. Germ. trans. 1771. Ital. trans. 1556; with 4th book added 1562 and 1584. Latin trans. 1601; 1611. See lib. II, on marriage, bringing up children, learning needed by princesses and great ladies.)

423. ———— (Eng. trans.). The dial of princes, compiled by the reverend father in God, Don Anthony of Guevara, Byshop of Guadix, Preacher, and chronicler to Charles the fifte, late of that name emperour. Englished out of the Frenche by T. North, sonne of Sir Edward North Knight, L. North of Kytheling. And now newly revised and corrected by hym, refourmed of faultes escaped in the first edition: with an amplification also of a fourth booke annexed to the same, entituled The favored courtier, never heretofore imprinted in our vulgar tongue. Right necessarie and pleasaunt to all noble and vertuous persones. London, Richard Tottill, and Thomas Marshe, 1568.

(Also 1557; 1582; 1619. See bk. II on marriage, upbringing of children, learning needed by princesses and great ladies. Letter XI, a diatribe against women; for French trans. see Pantagruel.)

424. ‡GUIART. Art d'amours. (Du Verdier.)

425. ‡GUIDI, BENEDETTO (Monk, 16th cent.). De laudibus mulierum. Venetiis.

426. GUIDICCIOLO, LEVANTIO DA. Antidoto della gelosia, distinto in doi libri, estratto dall' Ariosto per Levantio da Guidicciolo Mantovano. Con le sue novelle, e la tavola, si de' capitoli, come delle principal materie. Venetia, Francesco Rampazetto, 1565.

GUITTONE D'AREZZO. See Viva.

H., T. A curtaine lecture. See Heywood.

427. HABERT, FRANÇOIS. L'histoire de Titus, et Gisippus, et autres petiz oeuvres de Beroalde de latin, interpretés en rime françoyse, par Francoys Habert d'Yssouldun en Berry. Avec l'exaltation de vraye & perfaicte noblesse. Les quatre amours, le nouveau Cupido, et le tresor de vie. De l'invention dudict Habert. Le tout presenté à Monseigneur de Nevers. Paris, Michel Fezandat & Robert Granion, 1551. (Les quatres amours—delightful love, profitable love, married love, charitable love. First two condemned. Verse.)

428. ——————— La nouvelle Venus, par laquelle est entendue pudique amour, presentee à Madame la Daulphine, jointe une epistre à Monseigneur le Daulphin. Nouvellement composee par François Habert. Lyon, Jean de Tournes, 1547. (Largely religious.)

429. Haec-vir: or the womanish-man: being an answere to a late booke intituled Hic-Mulier. Exprest in a briefe dialogue betweene Haec-Vir the Womanish-Man, and Hic-Mulier the Man-Woman. 1620. (Woodcut portraits of the two. See Hic-Mulier, Muld sacke, and Austin.)

HAEDUS, PETRUS. See Cavretto.

430. HAKE, EDWARD. A touchstone for this time present, expressly declaring such ruines, enormities, and abuses as trouble the Churche of God and our Christian common wealth at this daye. Whereunto is annexed a perfect rule to be observed of all parents and scholemaisters, in the trayning up of their schollers and children in learning. Newly set forth by E. H. London, Thomas Hacket, 1574. (Also 1579. Complaint against women, ff. C4-D3a.)

431. HANNAY, PATRICK. A happy husband or, directions for a maide to choose her mate as also a wives behaviour towards her husband after marriage. By Patrick Hannay, Gent. To which is adjoyned the Good Wife: together with an exquisite discourse of epitaphs, including the choysest thereof, ancient and moderne. By R[ichard] B[rathwait] Gent. London, for Richard Redmer, 1618. (Also 1622. Verse.)

432. HARRINGTON, WILLIAM. In this boke are conteyned the comendacions

of matrymony/the maner & fourme of contractyng solempnysynge and lyvyng in the same. With declaracyon of all suche impedymentes as dothe let matrymony to be made. And also certayne other thynges which curates be bounden by the lawe to declare oftentymes to theyr parysshe. Imprynted at the instaunce of mayster Polydore Vergyl archedeaken of Welles. London, John Skot, 1528.

433. HEALE, WILLIAM. An apologie for women. Or an opposition to Mr. Dr. G[ager] his assertion. Who held in the Act at Oxford. Anno. 1608. That it was lawful for husbands to beate their wives. By W. H. of Ex. in Ox. Oxford, Joseph Barnes, 1609.

434. HEINSIUS, DANIEL. Domenici Baudii epistolarum centuriae duae. Accedunt epistolae clarorum virorum ad D. Baudium, et prolixa Dan. Heinsii inter Baudianas reperta, in qua agitur: an, & qualis literato viro uxor sit ducenda. Item ejusdem D. Baudii comentariolus de Foenore. Lugdini Batavorum, apud Godefridum Basson, 1615. (Heinsius dated 1607, pp. 249–309. Also 1616 in extremely fine print, with title *Dissertatio epistolica;* 1638 in *Dominici Baudii amores.*)

435. ‡——— Emblemata aliquot amatoria D. Heinsii cum additamente aliorum nunc primum in lucem edito. Amsterdam?, 1610? (Also 1612; 1613.)

436. HERMAN V (Archbishop and Elector of Cologne). A briefe and a plaine declaration of the duety of maried folkes, gathered out of the holy scriptures, and set forth in the Almaine tongue by Hermon Archbishop of Colaine, which willed all the housholdes of his flocke to have the same in their bedchambers as a mirror or glasse dayly to looke in, whereby they might know and doo their dueties eche unto others, and leade a godly, quiet and loving life togethers. And newlye translated into the English tongue by Haunce Dekin. London, by J. C., 1588? (Also 1550?)

437. HEROET, ANTOINE. Le mespris de la court, avec la commendation de la vie rustique, nouvellement traduict d'Espaignol en Francois. L'amye de Court. La parfecte amye. L'androgyne de Platon. L'experience de l'amye de court contre la contr'amye. L'honneste amant. Le nouvel amour. Avec plusieurs epistres, elegies, & dizains, au propos que dessus. Paris, Annet Briere, 1556. (Also 1568.)

438. ——— Opuscules d'amour, par Heroet, La Borderie, et autres divins poetes. Lyon, Jean de Tournes, 1547. (Also 1544. Containing: 1. *La parfaicte amye, composee par Antoine Heroët, dict la Maison noeuve,* pp. 3–68. 2. *L'amye de court, inventee par le Seigneur de Borderie,* pp. 111–145, an attack on love. 3. *La contr' amye de Court, responsive a l'amye precedente, par Maistre Charles Fontaine Parisien,* pp. 151–200, a defense of love. 4. *L'experience de M. Paul Angier Carentennois, contenant une brefve defence en la personne de l'honnest*ᵉ

Amant pour l'amye de court contre la contr' amye, pp. 201–234. For other editions of some see below.)

439. ————— La parfaicte amye, nouvellement composée par Antoine Heroet, dict, la Maison neufue. Avec plusieurs aultres compositions dudict autheur. Troyes, Nicole Paris, 1542. (Also 1543; 1544; 1547; 1555; 1556; etc.)

440. Heywood, Thomas. A curtaine lecture: as it is read by a countrey farmers wife to her good man. By a countrey gentlewoman or lady to her esquire or knight. By a souldiers wife to her captain or lieutenant. By a citizens or tradesmans wife to her husband. By a court lady to her lord. Concluding with an imitable lecture read by a Queene to her Soveraigne Lord and King. London, Robert Young, 1637. (Also 1638. Address to reader signed T. H. Stories about country and city quarrels between husbands and wives.)

441. ————— Γυναικειον: or, nine bookes of various history. Concerning women; inscribed by the names of the nine muses. Written by Thom: Heywoode. London, Adam Islip, 1624. (Also 1657.)

442. Hic mulier: or, the Man-Woman: being a medicine to cure the coltish disease of the staggers in the masculine-feminines of our times. Exprest in a briefe declamation. 1620. (See *Haec-Vir*, *Muld Sacke*, and Austin.)

443. Hoby, Sir Thomas. The courtyer of Count Baldesar Castilio, divided into four bookes. London, W. Seres, 1561. (Also 1565; 1571; 1577; 1585; 1593; 1603; 1612. Ital., French, and Eng. in parallel columns, 1588. Lat. trans. by Bartholomew Clerke, 1571. See Castiglione, B.)

444. Hondorff, Andreas. Theatrum historicum illustrium exemplorum ad honeste, pie, beateque vivendum mortale genus informantium, ex antiquissimis simul ac novissimis sacrarum et prophanarum historiarum monumentis constructum, & in decem classes secundum Mosaicae legis praecepta distinctum. Initio quidem à Reverendo viro, D. Andrea Hondorffio, coelestis doctrinae praecone & propugnatore strenuo, idiomate Germanico conscriptum: iam vero, labore et industria Philippi Loniceri, propter insignem utilitatem, ex illius lectione ad Christianum lectorem redundantem, Latinitate donatum, multisque in locis auctum, & illustratum. Francofurti ad Moenum, apud Georgium Corvinum, impensis Sigismundi Feierabend, 1575. (Also 1586; 1598; 1607; 1616. Germ. trans., 1568; 1579; 1580; 1586; 1595. For examples of women see parts 4, 6, 9, 10. See also Ireneus.)

445. Huarte Navarro, Juan De Dios. Examen de ingenios para las sciencias. Donde se muestra la differencia de habilidades que ay en los hombres, y el genero de letras que à cada uno responde en particular. Es obra donde el que leyere con attencion hallatà la manera de su ingenio, y saura escoger la sciencia en que mas ha de aprovechar: y

si por ventura la vivere ya professado, entendera si ativò à la que
pedia su habilidad natural. Compuesta por el doctor Juan Huarte
natural de sant Juan del piè del Puerto. Al Rey Don Philippe II.
Pamplona, Thomás Porralis, 1578. (Also 1591; 1593; 1596; 1603; 1640;
1652; 1662; 1668. Eng. trans. see below. French trans. 1598; 1619;
1645; 1661; 1668. Germ. trans. 1785. Ital. trans. 1582; 1586; 1590;
1600. Lat. trans. 1637. See ch. XVII, "The begetting of wise children.")

446. ————— (Eng. trans.). Examen de ingenios. The examination of
mens wits in which, by discovering the varietie of natures, is shewed
for what profession each one is apt, and how far he shall profit therein.
By John Huarte. Translated out of the Spanish tongue by M. Camillo
Camilli. Englished out of his Italian, by R[ichard] C[arew] Esquire.
London, Adam Islip for Richard Watkins, 1594. (Also 1596; 1604;
1616; 1698 trans. by Ed. Bellamy. See ch. XVII, "In what manner
Parents may beget Wise children and of a Wit for Learning.")

447. ‡An hundreth poyntes of evell huswifrye. 1565–1566.

448. INDIA, FRANCESCO. Discorsi della bellezza et della gratia, di Francesco
India, medico, & filosofo Veronese. Verona, Girolamo Discepolo,
1597.

449. Invectiva cetus feminei contra mares, cum tractatulo de remedio contra concubinas et conjuges. Paris, 1520?

450. IRENEUS, JOHANNES pseud. (Johannes Freder). Lob und Unschuldt
der Ehefrauwen. Und Widerlegung der Sprüch, damit die Weibsbilder,
durch die Philosophos oder Weltweise Heyden, und etliche vermeynte
Christen geschmehet werden. Gott und dem heyligan Ehestande, zu
Ehren geschrieben an die Durchleuchtigste, Hochgeborne Fürstin,
Frauwen Dorothea, Königen zu Dännmark, etc. Anno 1543. Durch
M. Johannen Ireneum. Jetzt auss Pommerischer Sprach in Meissni-
sche gebracht, und mit etlichen schönen Historien und Exempeln
gemehrt. Durch Andream Hondorff. Franckfurt am Mayn, in Verlag:
Hieronymi Feyerabends, 1569. (Also 1543; 1568. Lat. trans. 1544.)

451. IVRY, JEAN D'. Les secretz et loix de mariage composez par le secretaire
des dames. (Verse.)

452. JAMYN, AMADIS. Les oeuvres poetiques d'Amadis Jamyn. Reveuës,
corrigees & augmentees pour la troisieme impression. Paris, Mamert
Patisson, 1577. (Also 1579. See liv. V, ll. 225–228, Le mysogame, ou
qui hayt le mariage.)

453. Le jardin d'honneur, contenant plusieurs apologies, proverbes, & ditz
moraux, avec les histoires & figures. Aussi y sont ajoustez plusieurs
ballades, rondeaux, dixains, huitains, & trioletz fort joyeux. Reveu
& corrigé outre les precedantes impressions. Paris, Estienne Groulleau,
1549. (Various illustrations of wives, lovers.)

454. Le jardin de plaisance et fleur de rethorique. Paris, Michel Lenoir, 1505? (Also 1501; 1503?; 1515; 1525; 1527. Contents: *Allegory of love, with a defence of women and marriage against their detractors, especially Jean le Meung and Matheolus.* Verse.)

455. JOCELINE, ELIZABETH. The mothers legacie, to her unborn childe. By Elizabeth Jocelin. London, John Haviland, 1624. (Also 1625; 1684; 1724. Germ. trans. 1748. Chiefly religious.)

456. JONES, JOHN. The arte and science of preserving bodie and soule in al health, wisdome, and catholike religion: phisically, philosophically, and divinely devised: by John Jones phisition. Right profitable for all persones: but chiefly for princes, rulers, nobles, byshoppes, preachers, parents, and them of the Parliament house. London, Ralph Newberie, 1579. (In the first part, on bringing up and education, some attention is paid to women—proper behavior, occupations. Chiefly notable for attention to English customs and English authorities, among others, Elyot, Lawne, Hake, Ascham, Barnabe Rich, Humphrey.)

457. KINGSMILL, ANDREW. A viewe of mans estate, wherein the great mercie of God in mans free justification by Christ, is very comfortably declared. By Andrewe Kingsmill. Divided into chapters in such sorte as may best serve for the commoditie of the reader. Where unto is annexed a godly advise given by the author touching mariage. London, H. Bynneman, 1576. (Also 1574; 1580.)

458. KNOX, JOHN. The first blast of the trumpet against the monstruous regiment of women. 1558. (See Aylmer.)

459. LABÉ, LOUISE. Oeuvres de Louize Labé Lionnoize. Lion, Jan de Tournes, 1555. (Also 1556; 1762. See ded. to Mlle Clémence de Bourges urging women to devote themselves to studies.)

460. LA BOËTIE, ESTIENNE DE. La mesnagerie de Xenophon, les reigles de mariage de Plutarque. Le lettre de consolation de Plutarque à sa femme. Avec quelques vers latins & François de son invention. Paris, Federic Morel, 1571. (Also 1600. See introductory and dedicatory letters by Montaigne.)

461. LA BORDERIE,—— DE. Opuscules d'amour, par Heroet, La Borderie, et autres divins poetes. Lyon, Jean de Tournes, 1547. (Also 1542; 1544. Pp. 111–145, *L'amye de court, inventee par le Seigneur de Borderie.* See Charles Fontaine for counterblast.)

462. ‡LA BORIE DE VALOIS, FRANÇOIS. Antidrusac, ou livret contre Drusac, faict à l'honneur des femmes nobles, bonnes & honnestes; par maniere de dialogue. Interlocuteurs Euphrates & Gymmisus. Tholose, Jaq. Colomies, 1564. (Du Verdier. See Du Pont.)

463. ‡LA BRYERE, LE SIEUR DE. Replique à l'anti-malice ou défense des femmes du sieur Vigoureux, autrement dict Brye-Comte-Robert,

par le sieur de la Bryère, . . . Paris, 1617. (See Vigoureux and Olivier. Attack on women.)

464. LA CERDA, JUAN DE. Libro intitulado, vida politica de todos los estados de mugeres: en el qual se dan muy provechosos y Christianos documentos y avisos, para criarse y conservarse devidamente las mugeres en sus estados. Dividese este libro en cinco tratados. El primero es, del estado de las donazellas. El segundo, de las monjas. El tercero, de las casadas. El quarto, de las buidas. El quinto, contiene diversos capitulos de mugeres en general. Con un indice alphabetico muy copioso de materias, que sirven de lugares comunes. Compuesto por el P. F. Juan de la Cerda, natural de Tendilla, de la Orden de S. Francisco, y de la Provincia de Castilla. Dirigido a su Alteza de la Infanta Donna Margarita de Austria, Monja en el santo Monesterio de las Descalças de Madrid. Alcala de Henares, Juan Gracian, 1599.

465. LA MARCHE, OLIVIER DE. Le parement et triumphe des dames/Est appelle ce plaisant nouveau livre/Prenez le en gre ainsi que je le livre/pour recepvoir salut de corps & dames. Ce present livre digne de memoire/dit & intitule Le parement et triumphe des dames dhonneur. Auquel sont contenus et declarez tous les habitz/paremens/vestures/triumphes/& aornemens qui appartiennent a toutes nobles dames et femmes dhonneur. A este nouvellement redige additionem & impresse en rigme & prose pour honnorables hommes Jehan petit Michel lenoir/libraires jurez en luniversite de Paris demourans en la grant rue sainct Jacques. 1492? (Also 1510; 1520 Du Verdier. Each garment likened to a virtue in verse, followed by an example of the virtue in prose.)

466. ‡———— Instruction aux princes, aux dames, et aux serviteurs des dames. Paris, 1580.

467. ‡LANCI, CORNELIO. Gli essempi delle virtù delle donne del Cavalier C. L. Firenzi, Francesco Tosi, 1590.

468. LANDI, ORTENSIO. Lettere della molto illustre sra donna Lucretia Gonzaga da Gazuolo, con gran diligentia raccolte & à gloria del sesso femminile nuovamente in luce poste. Vinegia, G. Scotto, 1552.

469. ———— Lettere di molte valorose donne, nelle quali chiaramente appare non esser ne di eloquentia ne di dottrina alli huomini inferiori. Vinegia, Gabriel Giolito, 1548. (Also 1549. Mentioned by Bronzini, *Della dignità*, 1625, pp. 40 ff.)

470. ———— Oracoli de moderni ingegni si d'huomini come di donne, ne quali, unita si vede tutta la philosophia morale, che fra molti scrittori sparsa si leggeva. Venetia, Gabriel Giolito e fratelli, 1550. (Ff. 64–87, *Oracoli o vero saggi detti di moderne donne*.)

471. ———— Varii componimenti di M. Hort. Lando. Nuovamente

venuti in luce. Quaesiti amorosi, con le risposte. Dialogo intitolato Ulisse. Ragionamento occorso tra un cavalliere, et un'huomo soletario. Alcune novelle. Alcune favole. Alcuni scroppoli, che sogliono occorrere nella cottidiana nostra lingua ... Vinegia, Gabriel Giolito e fratelli, 1552. (Also 1556, as *Quatro libri di dubbi*.)

472. LANTERI, GIACOMO. Della economica trattato di M. Giacomo Lanteri ... Nel quale si demostrano le qualità, che all'huomo e alla donna separatamente convengono pel governo della casa. Venetia, Vincenzo Valgrisi, 1560.

473. LA PERRIÈRE, GUILLAUME DE. Les cent considerations damour, composées par Guillaume de la Perriere, Tholosan. Avec une satire contre fol amour. [Par Gilles Corrozet.] Lyon, Jaques Berion, 1548.

474. ‡LA PRIMAUDAYE, PIERRE DE. Academie Francoise, en laquelle il est traitte de l'institution des moeurs et de se qui concerne le bien & heureusement vivre, etc. Paris, Guil. Chaudiere, 1577. (Also 1580; 1581; 1584; 1587; 1598; 1613. Eng. trans. see below. Germ. trans. 1594. Ital. trans. 1610.)

475. ———— (Eng. trans.). The French academie, wherin is discoursed the institution of maners, and whatsoever els concerneth the good and happie life of all estates and callings by preceptes of doctrine, and examples of the lives of ancient sages and famous men: by Peter de la Primaudaye Esquire, ... and newly translated into English by T. B. London, Edmund Bollifant, 1586. (Also 1589; 1594; 1601–1614; 1602–1605; 1618. See chs. 45–48, on women.)

476. LA SALE, ANTOINE DE. Les quinze joyes de mariage, Lyon, 1480–1490. (Also another ed. before 1499; 1595; 1596; 1606; 1607; 1620; 1726; 1734. Eng. trans. 1694; 1760. See Decker. One of the most readable satires on marriage.)

477. LA TAYSONNIÈRE DE CHANEINS, GUILLAUME DE. L'attiffet des damoizelles premiere et plus importante piece de leur embellissement par G. de la Tayssoniere ... Paris, Federic Morel, 1575. (Du Verdier, "C'est l'institution de la belle creance ou nourriture d'une fille de grande maison.")

478. LA TOUR, BERENGER DE. Choreïde, autrement, louenge du bal: aux dames. Par B. de la Tour d'Albennas. Lion, Jan de Tournes, 1556. (And other poems. Against the detractors of the dance.)

479. LA TOUR LANDRY, GEOFFREY DE. Le livre du Chevalier de la Tour Landry pour l'enseignement de ses filles. 1854. (Eng. trans. see below. Germ. trans. 1493; 1495; 1682.)

480. ———— (Eng. trans.). Here begynneth the book whiche the knyght of the toure made, and speketh of many fayre ensamples and thensygnementys and techyng of his doughters (translated out of Frenssh in to ... Englysshe by W. Caxton). Westmynstre, W. Caxton, 1484.

481. LAURO, PIETRO. De le lettere di M. Pietro Lauro Modonese. Il primo libro. Con la tavola de i summarii di ciascuna lettera. Venetia, 1553. (See letters, pp. 7, 18, 87, 99, 121, 158, 185, 192, 212, 214, on such subjects as marriage, children, virginity, choosing a wife, beauty, modesty more desirable in a wife than kindness.)

482. ———— Delle lettere di Messer Pietro Lauro. Libro secondo. Con la tavola de i summarii di ciascuna lettera. Vinegia, 1560. (See letters, ff. 48a, 64, 75, 98, 113, on marriage.)

483. ‡LAUTHEURDE. Les paradoxes. (Cited by Billon, *Le fort inexpugnable*, 1555, p. 14. Pub. a few years before. Detraction of women.)

484. LAUZE, F. DE. Apologie de la danse et la parfaicte methode de l'enseigner tant aux cavaliers qu' aux dames. Par F. de Lauze. 1623.

485. ‡LAWNE, PETER. Dignitie of marriage.

486. LAWSON, WILLIAM. A new orchard and garden. Or the best way for planting, grafting, and to make any ground good, for a rich orchard: particularly in the north parts of England: generally for the whole kingdome, as in nature, reason [sic], scituation, and all probability, may and doth appeare. With the country housewife's garden for hearbes of common use, their vertues, seasons, profites, ornaments, variety of knots, models for trees, and plots for the best ordering of grounds and walkes. As also The husbandry of bees, with their severall uses and annoyances, all grounded on the principles of art, and precepts of experience, being the labours of forty eight yeares of William Lawson. London, Bar. Alsop for Roger Jackson, 1618. (Separate title page for *The countrie housewifes garden*, dated 1617. Ded. to Sir Henry Belosses. Also 1626; 1631; 1648; 1653; 1657; 1660; 1668; 1676; 1683; 1695. Also *The countrie housewifes garden* separately 1623.)

487. ‡LE BERMAN, SIEUR DE LA MARTINÈRE. Le bouclier des femmes.

488. LE CARON, LOUIS. La claire, ou de la prudence de droit, dialogue premier. Plus, la clarté amoureuse, par Lois le Caron, Droit conseillant Parisien au souverain et advocat, Senat des Gaulles. Paris, Guillaume Cavellat, 1554. (The dialogue begins with argument to prove women's capacity for learning and the practice of law and government.)

489. ‡LE CONTE, MICHEL. Le mariage de procez & de la femme. Paris, Denis du Pré, 1579. (Du Verdier. Verse.)

490. LE DELPHYEN. Deffense en faveur des dames de Lyon: avec un bref discours de l'excellence et beauté de la femme. Par Le Delphyen, leur tres-humble serviteur. Lyon, Pierre Michel, 1596. (Verse.)

491. LE FÈVRE, JEAN. Le rebours de Matheolus. Paris, Michel le noir, 1518. (Colophon: "Cy finist le resolu en marriage," under which title it was reproduced early in the 17th century. Rep. 1892 with the Latin text of Matheolus and Le Fèvre's French trans.)

492. LE FOURNIER, ANDRÈ. Le décoration d'humaine nature et aornement des dames/ compile et extraict des très excellens docteurs/ et plus expers medecins/ tant anciens que modernes par Maistre Andre le fournier, docteur regent en la faculte de medecine. . . . Nouvellement imprime et non veu par cy devant. Paris, Jehan Sainct—Denys et Jehan Longis, 1530. (Also 1531; 1537; 1547; 1582. Recipes for soaps, powders, toilet waters, etc.)

493. LE FRANC, MARTIN. Le champion des dames. Paris, Galiot du Pré, 1530. (Also 1485.)

494. LE GAYGNARD, PIERRE. Le contre-mariage de celuy de Desportes par Pierre Le Gaygnard, 1585. Rep. 1908. (See Desportes, Blanchon, Rouspeau.)

495. LE GRAND, JACQUES. Here begynneth the table of a book intytuled the book of good maners. London, Caxton, 1487. (Also 1494; 1500; 1507; 1515?; 1594. Bk. IV, cap. V–IX, marriage, wives, virginity, widowhood, servants.)

496. LEIGH, DOROTHY. The mothers blessing: or, the godly counsaile of a gentlewoman, not long since deceased, left behind her for her children: contayning many good exhortations, and godly admonitions profitable for all parents, to leave as a legacy to their children. By Mrs. Dorothy Leigh. The seventh edition. London, for John Budge, 1621. (Also 1616; 1618; 1627, 10th ed.; 1629; 1630, 15th ed.; 1636; 1656; 1663; 1707; 1718.)

497. LE LOYER, PIERRE. Erotopegnie ou passetemps d'amour. Ensemble une comedie du Muet insensé. Par Pierre Le Loyer, Sieur de la Brosse, Angevin. Paris, Abel l'Angelier, 1576. (See Second livre, ff. 30–40a, *Premier bocage de l'art d'aimer;* ff. 41–53a, *Second bocage de l'art d'aimer.* How to play the game and get any woman by the usual arts of protestations, sighs, tears, gifts, letters, etc. Verse.)

498. LEONE EBREO. (Abravanel, Judah). Dialogi d'amore di maestro Leone medico Hebreo. Roma, Antonio Blado, 1535. (Also 1541; 1545; 1549; 1552; 1558; 1565; 1572; 1586; 1607. French trans. 1551; 1564; 1577; 1580; 1595. Span trans. 1564; 1568; 1590; 1598. Latin trans. 1564; 1587.)

499. LE ROY, FRANÇOIS. Le livre de la femme forte et vertueuse declaratif du cantique de salomon es proverbes au chapitre final qui ce commence. Mulierem fortem quis inveniet. Laquelle exposition est extraicte de plusieurs excellens docteurs utile et prouffitable a personnes religieuses et autres gens de devotion. fait & compose par ung religieux de la reformation de lordre de fonteurault: a la requeste de sa seur religieuse reformee dudict ordre. Imprime pour Symon Vostre Libraire. Paris, Philippe Pigouchet, 1501. (Two other editions. Virgin the realization of this type, etc.)

500. L'Escale, Le Chevalier de. Le champion des femmes. Qui soustient qu'elles sont plus nobles, plus parfaites, & en tout plus vertueuses que les hommes. Contre un certain Misogynés Anonyme auteur & inventeur de l'imperfection & malice des femmes. Par le Chevalier de l'Escale. Paris, la veufue M. Guillemot, 1618.

501. ‡L'Escale, Pierre de. La defense des femmes. 1612. (Analyzes Marguerite de Navarre's book of letters "pour defendre son sexe contre d'injustes mépris," now lost.)

502. ‡Leslie, John (Bishop of Ross). De illustrium foeminarum in repub. administranda, ac ferendis legibus authoritate, libellus, etc. Rhemis, J. Fognaeus, 1580. (Reply to John Knox.)

503. Lesnauderie, Pierre de. La louange du mariage et recueil des hystoires des bonnes: vertueuses: et illustres femmes: compose par maistre Pierre de lesnauderie lors scribe des privileges de luniversite de Caen. Et est divise et departy par sept chapitres comme plus aplain sera veu en la table de cedict livre. Gentilz lecteurs contemplatifz espritz/Qui des femmes voulez scavoir le pris/Tournez icy de voz yeulz lescripture./Vous trouverez comme de bon couraige/On doibt louer lestat de mariage./Vous trouverez le chapitre second/De prudence de femmes bien fecond./Vous trouverez pareillement au tiers/Quelles ont leu les escriptz et psaultiere/Et ont eu don de parfaict science./Au quart aussi verrez leur patience:/Leur charite ou mainte sest amorse./Au cinquiesme est leur grant vertu et force/Leur preux maintien assez manifeste./Au sixiesme lamour et chastete./Et au dernier et septiesme pour somme/Sont contenues troys heritiers de lhomme/Et troys sortes et manieres damer/Dont il ny a goust ne saveur damer. Paris, pour Pierre sergent. (Also 1523; 1525 Du Verdier.)

504. ‡La letra deval scrita feu lo marques de Villena e compte de Ribagorça, qui après fo intitulat duc de Gandia per dona Johana, filla sua, quant la marida ab don Johan, fill del Compte de Cardova, per la qual li scrivi castich e bons nodriments. Printed in Mem. de la Ac. de buenas let. de Barcelona, II.

505. ‡Lettera di un gran personaggio chiamato Paolino, scritta in lingua Francesca, ad una sua nepote magiore, nelle quale biasma le sue vanità particolarmente nel portar il petto scoperto. Plaisance, 1602. (Conatu dall' opera del Pauolo Barry della compagnia di Giesù intitolata: Arte d'imparare a ben morire.)

506. ‡Libro degli adornamenti delle donne.

507. Liburnio, Nicolò. Le occorrenze humane per Nicolo Liburnio composte. Vinegia, de' Figlivoli di Aldo, 1546. (Also 1547. See *Dialogues*, VII, XIV, XVIII, etc., beauties of women, virtues, learned women, etc.)

508. Liébault, Jean. Trois livres de l'embellissement et ornement du

corps humain. Pris du latin de M. Jean Liebaut Docteur medicin a Paris & faict François. Paris, Jacques du Puys, 1582. (Also 1585. B. M. Cat. note: the Latin work of Liebault compiled from Marinelli's *Ornamenti delle donne*. Aids to beauty of hair, complexion, etc.)

509. ‡LIONI, LUIGI DI. Trattato della perfetta maritata del R. P. M. F. Luigi di Lione, dell' ordine di Santo Agostino, tradotto di lingua spagnuola in toscana del Cavaliere fra Giulio Zanchini da Castiglionchio. Venetia, Gio. Battista Ciotti, 1595.

510. ‡Le livre de l'amy fidele. Avec plusieurs discours amoureux en vers & en prose par un gentilhomme Picard. Paris, Jean de l'Astre, 1578. (Du Verdier.)

511. LLOYD, LODOWICKE. The choyce of jewells by Lodowik Lloid Esquire. London, Thomas Purfoot, 1607. (In praise of women.)

512. LOMBARDELLI, ORAZIO. Dell' uffizio della donna maritata. Capi incento ottanta. D'Orazio Lombardelli Senese Accademico Humoroso. Fiorenza, Giorgio Marescotti, 1583. (Ded. letter dated 1574. Letter at end on his wife's death, dated 1577. Directions to his young wife as to her wifely duties.)

513. ‡A looking-glass for ladies.

514. LORINI, NICOLÒ, DEL MONTE. Elogii delle piu principali S. Donne del sacro calendario, e martirologia Romano, vergini, martiri, et altre. Messi insieme con molti vigilie. Dal M. R. P. M. e Predicatore Generale F. Niccolò Lorini del Monte; dell' Ordine de' Predicatori, Patrizio Fiorentino, e Predicatore, del Sereniss. G. Duca di Toscana D. Cosimo II. Dedicati alla Serenissima Arciduchessa Maria Maddalena d'Austria, Gran Ducchessa, e consorte del predetto Signore. A' quali si è aggiunto un regionamento in lode de' Santi Martiri di Mugello, S. Cresci, e Compagni. Firenze, Zanobi Pignoni, 1617.

515. LOUIS IX, SAINT. Enseignements à sa fille Isabelle. Pub. by A. M. Chazand, Paris, 1878. In *Enseignements d'Anne de Beaujeu à sa fille Suzanne*, Collection des historiens de France, t. XX, pp. 82–86, 307. (For another set of instructions to either Blanche or Marguerite see vol. XXIII, pp. 131 ff., of the same collection.)

516. ——————— Instructions de Saint Louis Roi de France, a sa famille royale aux persones de sa cour et autres; extraites du recueil des historiens contemporains de sa vie, imprimé par les soins de MM. de la Biblioteque du Roi en 1761, par M. l'Abbé de Villiers, Licentié ez Loix. Paris, 1761. (Also 1766. See *Testament de S. Loys à Phelippe son Filz & son successeur, reporté par Sire de Joinville*, p. 154; *Testament de Sainz Loys à Phelippe son filz & son successeur, extrait des Annales de Guillaume de Nangis*, p. 284; *Enseignement escrit de la main de Sainz Loys à Phélipe son filz qui régna apres lui, extrait de la vie de Saint Loys par*

le Confesseur de la Royne, p. 330; *Lettre d'enseignement escrite par saint Loys à Madame Isabel sa fille Royne de Navarre*, p. 326.)

LOWTH. *See* Battus.

517. (LOYALTY). La grand loyaulte des femmes. Lyons, 1510? (Diatribe against women.)

518. LUCRETIA ROMANA. Ornamento nobile per ogni gentil matrona, dove si contiene bavari, frisi d'infinita bellezza. 1620.

519. LUIGINI, FEDERIGO. Il libro della bella donna, composto da Messer Federigo Luigini da Udine. Venetia, Plinio Pietrasanta, 1554. (Also 1569.)

520. LUJAN, PEDRO DE. Coloquios matrimoniales del licenciado Pedro de Luxan. Enlos quales se tracta, como se han de aver entresi los casados: y conscruar la paz. Criar sus hijos y governar su casa. Tocanse muy agradables sentencias, dichos y hechos, ley es y costumbres antiguas. Acabaronsea, Domenico Robertis, 1550. (Also, 1552; 1553; 1555; 1589. See Tilney.)

521. LUNA, ALVARO DE . Libro de las claras y virtuosas mugeres por el Condestable de Castilla Don Alvaro de Luna. 15th cent. Rep. 1909.

522. LUTHER, MARTIN. De constituendis scholis Martini Lutheri liber donatus latinitate. Anno MD. XXIIII. In *Opera*, Wittemberg, 1558, vol. VII, ff. 438–447. (Considers both sexes; see f. 445a.)

523. —————— A fruteful predication or sermon of D. Mart. Luth. concernynge matrimony, upon this texte, in the Epistle to the Hebrewes, in the XIII chapiter. Wedlocke is to be had in honour, amonge all men, and the bedde undefyled. As for hoorekepers and advouterers, God shall judge them. (Bound with *Vertuous scholehous of ungracious women*, ff. H1a-L7.)

524. LYLY, JOHN. Euphues. The anatomy of wyt. Very pleasant for all gentlemen to reade, and most necessary to remember: wherin are contained the delights that wyt followeth in his youth by the pleasauntnesse of love, and the happynesse he reapeth in age, by the perfectnesse of wisedom. By John Lylly Master of Arte. Oxon. London, Gabriell Cawood, 1578? (Also 1579; 1581; 1613; 1631; 1716, modernized. With *Euphues and his England*, 1592; 1597; 1607–1606; 1617; 1623; 1631; 1636.)

525. —————— Euphues and his England. Containing his voyage and adventures: mixed with sundry prettie discourses of honest love, the description of the countrie, the court, and the manners of the Isle. Delightfull to be read, and nothing hurtfull to be regarded: wherein there is small offence by lightnesse given to the wise, and lesse occasion of loosenesse proffered to the wanton. By John Lyly Maister of Art. London, Gabriell Cawood, 1597. (Also 1580; 1592; 1609. With *Euphues. The anatomy of wyt*, see above.)

526. MAGGIO, VINCENZO. Un breve trattato dell' eccellentia delle donne, composto dal prestantissimo philosopho (il Maggio) & di latina lingua, in Italiano tradotto. Vi si poi aggiunto un' essortatione a gli huomini perche non si lascino superar dalle donne, mostrandogli il gran danno che lor e per sopravenire. Brescia, Damiano de Turlini, 1545.

527. MAGISTRI, YVES. Mirours et guydes fort propres pour les dames et damoiselles de France, qui seront de bonne volonté envers Dieu & leur salut, tout ainsi que ont esté les tresillustres princesses, madame Janne de France, & Marguarite de Loraine, les vies des quelles seront mises au present volume pour par le moyen d'icelles lesdictes Dames & damoiselles pouvoir mirer leurs vies, & guyder leurs sentes par le destroict de ceste vallée de misere. Le tout mis en lumiere par le R. P. F. Yves Magistri .... Bourges, Pierre Bouchier, 1585.

528. MALICE. ‡Malice des femmes. 1530?

529. ———— Le malicie de le donne. Venice?, 1520? (Verse.)

530. ———— Le malicie & sagacita de le donne: narrando tutti li lor belletti/& aque stilate/solimati/biondi/polvere/e gli impiasti/ciroti che usano per farse belle. Et el consiglio de un philosopho dato a quelli che se voleno maridare: & la via che debeno tenere cosa nova con un capitolo de una cortisana tirata in caretta. (Verse.)

531. ‡———— Novemila novecento novantanove malizie delle donne delle quali si tratta gl'inganni astuzie falsità . . . e pelamenti che usano far ... per gabbare i giovani, che di loro s'innamorano. Naples? 1815. (Verse. Is this the *Nuova nava di novemila*, etc. mentioned by Bronzini?)

532. MANFREDI, MUZIO. I cento artificiosi madrigali del Sig. Mutio Manfredi Il Fermo Academico Olimpico, etc. Fatti per la Sig. Hippolita dalla Penna, cognominata Benigna, sua moglie. Da lei alla Illustrissima, & Eccellentiss. Principessa della Mirandola, dedicati. E più corretti ristampati. Venetia, Roberto Meglietti, 1606.

533. ———— Cento donne cantata da Mutio Manfredi Il Fermo Academico Innominato di Parma. Al Serenissimo Principe di Mantua. Parma, Erasmo Viotti, 1580.

534. ———— Cento madrigali di Mutio Manfredi, Il Fermo Academico Innominato, Invaghito, e di Ferrara. A' Donna Vittoria Principessa di Molsetta, sua Signora, da lui dedicati. Con gli argomenti del medesimo à ciascun madrigale, per esser tutti di straordinari soggetti. Mantova, Francesco Osanna, 1587.

535. ———— Cento sonnetti di Mutio Manfredi, Il Fermo Academico Informe, etc. In lode di Donne di Ravenna. Alla Serenissima Duchessa d'Urbino, dedicati. Ravenna, per gli Heredi di Pietro Giovannelli, 1602. (Mentioned by Bronzini.)

536. ———— Madrigali di Mutio Manfredi Il Fermo Academico Olim-

pico, etc. Sopra molti soggetti stravaganti composti, nè men di tre, nè piu di cinquanta sono per ciascun soggetto. All' Illustriss, e Reverendissimo Monsignor Luigi Capponi Tesorier generale di NS. Venetia, Roberto Meglietti, 1606.

537. ————— Per donne Romane rime di diversi raccolte, & dedicate al Signor Giacomo Buoncompagni da Mutio Manfredi. Bologna, Alessandro Benacci, 1575.

538. Il Manganello. Rep. Paris, 1860. (Two eds. known, without title page, first around 1530. Mentioned in *Cicalamenti del Grappa*, Mantova, 1545. Haym notes a book entitled *Riprensione contra Manganello per Bertocco*. Violent satire against women.)

539. MANSO, GIOVANBATTISTA. Errocallia overo dell' amore e della bellezza dialoghi XII di Gio. Battista Manso . . . con gli argomenti à ciascun dialogo del Cavalier Marino. Et nel fine un trattato del dialogo dell' istesso autore. Con tre tavole, l'una de' capitoli marginali, l'altra delle materie morali naturali, e metafisiche trattate secondo la dottrina Peripatetica, Platonica, e teologica; l'ultima de' diversi autori, e luoghi di scrittura esposti. Venetia, Evang. Deuchino, 1628. (A small part published 1608 as *I paradossi*. See below.)

540. ————— I paradossi overo dell' amore dialogi di Gio. Battista Manso. Milan, Girolamo Bordoni, 1608. (Pirated edition, see letter to the author by G. B. Marino, in extended 1628 ed., ff. a2 ff.)

541. MANTOVA, MARCO (Benavides). Discorsi sopra i dialoghi di M. Speron Sperone, ne' quali si ragiona della bellezza & della eccellenza de lor concetti, d'incerto autore. Venetia, Rampazetto, 1561.

542. Le manuel des dames composé par ung jeune celestin . . . . Paris, Antoine Verard, 1509? (Addressed to novices.)

543. MARCONVILLE, JEAN DE. De la bonte et mauvaistie des femmes par Jean de Marconville. Paris, Jean Dallier, 1571. (Also 1564; 1566; 1568; 1586.)

544. ————— De l'heur et maleur de mariage, ensemble les lois connubiales de Plutarque traduictes en françois. par Jehan de Marconville Gentilhomme Percheron. Paris, pour Jehan Dallier, 1564. (Also 1571; 1578.)

545. MARINELLA, LUCREZIA. La nobilta e eccellenza delle donne: e i diffetti e mancamenti de gli huomini. Discorso di Lucretia Marinella. Venetia, Giovan Battista Ciotti, 1600. (Also 1601; 1621.)

546. MARINELLI, GIOVANNI. Le medicine partenenti alla infirmità delle donne. Venetia, 1563. (Also 1610.)

547. ————— Gli ornamenti delle donne, tratti dalle scritture d'una Reina Greca per M. Giovanni Marinello, & divisi in quattro libri, con due tavole, una de' capitoli, e l'altra d'alcune cose particolari. Opera utile, & necessaria ad ogni gentile persona. Venetia, Francesco de'

Franceschi, 1562. (Also 1574; 1610. Recipes and measures to increase the beauty of each part of the body, which is not so perfect in any woman that it may not be made more so. See Liébault.)

548. MARKHAM, GERVASE. Country contentments, in two bookes: the first, containing the whole art of riding great horses in very short time, with the breeding, breaking, dyeting and ordring of them, and of running, hunting and ambling horses, with the manner how to use them in their travell. Likewise in two newe treatises the arts of hunting, hawking, coursing of greyhounds with the lawes of the leash, shooting, bowling, tennis, baloone etc. By G. M. The second intituled, the English huswife: containing the inward and outward vertues which ought to be in a compleate woman: as her phisicke, cookery, banqueting-stuffe, distillation, perfumes, wooll, hemp, flaxe, dairies, brewing, baking, and all other things belonging to an houshold. A worke very profitable and necessary for the generall good of this kingdome. London, J. Beale for R. Jackson, 1615. (The second book also in 1623; 1631 with title *A way to get wealth;* 1633–1637; 1653; 1660; 1675, "Now the 8th time much augmented, purged, and made most profitable for all men"; 1683.)

549. MAROT, JEAN. Recueil des oeuvres Jehan Marot illustre poëte Francoys, contenant rondeaulx, epistres, vers espars, chantz royaulx. Lyon, Francoys Juste, 1537. (Also 1723, Les Oeuvres, see *Le doctrinal des princesses et nobles dames, faict & deduict en XXIIII rondeaux.*)

550. MARTELLI, LODOVICO (D. 1527, Florentine). Lode delle donne. (See Rubbi, A., *Parnaso Italiano,* 1784, t. 10, pp. 129–161.)

551. MARTIAL D'AUVERGNE. Devotes louanges a la Vierge Marie. Paris, 1509. (Typical of a large number of such eulogies, which bear some relation to the secular treatises, but, I believe, a very remote one.)

552. MARTIN, THOMAS. A traictise declaryng ... that the pretensed marriage of priestes, and professed persones is no marriage but altogether unlawful, and in all ages, and al countreies of Christendome, bothe forbidden, and also punyshed. Herewith is comprised in the later chapitres, a full confutation of Doctour Poynettes boke entitled a defense for the marriage of priestes. Londini, in aedibus Roberti Calii, 1554. (See Poynet and Parker.)

553. MARTINEZ DE TOLEDO, ALFONSO. El arcipreste de Talavera, que fabla de los vicios de las malas mugeres e complexiones de los hombres. Sevilla, Meynardo yngut aleman & Stanislao polono, 1498. (Also 1500; 1529. See *Corvacho ó reprobación del amor mundano.*)

554. MARY, QUEEN OF SCOTS. Latin themes of Mary Stuart, Queen of Scots published, for the first time, from the original manuscript in her own handwriting, now preserved in the Imperial Library, Paris. Edited by Anatole de Montaiglon. London, for the Warton Club, 1855. (Brantôme records that at the age of thirteen she delivered a

Latin discourse to the court on the subject that it was fitting for women to learn languages and the liberal arts. See *Oeuvres*, Paris, 1787, vol. II, discourse 3. See also Foclin.)

555. MASSINONI, GIOVANTONIO. Il flagello delle meretrici, et la nobiltà donnesca ne' figlivoli del Signor Gio. Antonio Massinoni Dottor di Leggi. Nuovamente posta in luce da Giacomo Massinoni. Venetia, Giacomo Antonio Somaschio, 1599. (Also 1605.)

556. MATHEOLUS. Le livre de Matheolus. Lyons?, 1492. (French translation by Jean Le Fèvre. Also 1500?; 1510?; 1540? Rep. 1892 with text of Latin original. A haphazard collection of verses from Matheolus and the *Rebours* of Le Fèvre appears in Robert de Balsat's *Le nef des princes et des batailles de nobless*, 1502, ff. XLVa–XLVII, under title *De la malice des femmes*, reprinted by Montaiglon, 1855, *Recueil de poesies françoises*, vol. 5, see under Champier. See Le Fèvre.)

557. ‡MAURO. Discorso della donna. 1593.

558. ‡MELLEMAN, A. F. Oratio de matrimonio letterati. Berlin, 1588. (Also 1593; 1651; 1714 in a collection by Gottfried Wagner, *Centuria eruditorum coelibum.*)

559. ‡MELLINI, DOMENICO. Trattato di Dominico Mellini intitolato visione dimostratrice della malvagità del carnale amore. Fiorenza, Giunti, 1566.

560. Le menagier de Paris, traité de morale et d'économie domestique composé vers 1393, par un bourgeois parisien; contenant des préceptes moraux, quelques faits historiques, des instructions sur l'art de diriger une maison, des renseignemens sur la consommation du roi, des princes et de la ville de Paris, à la fin du quatorzième siècle, des conseils sur le jardinage et sur le choix des chevaux; une traité de cuisine fort étendu, et un autre non moins complet sur la chasse à épervier. Ensemble: L'histoire de Griseldis, Mellibée et Prudence par Albertan de Briscia (1246), traduit par frère Renault de Louens; et le Chemin de Povreté et de Richesse, poëme composé, en 1342 par Jean Bruyant, notaire au Châtelet de Paris; publiée pour la première fois par la Société des bibliophiles françois. Paris, Imp. de Crapelet, 1846.

561. ‡MERMET, CLAUDE. Le temps passé de Claude Mermet, . . . contenant le bon droict des femmes, la pierre de touche du vray amy, la consolation des mal mariez, de nouveau augmenté de la lamentation de la vieille remariée, de l'advis de mariage et autres poëmes sentencieux et récréatifs, reveu et corrigé par l'autheur mesme. Lyon, B. Bouguet, 1585. (Also 1601. See Trissino, *La consolation des mal mariez.*)

562. MEURIER, GABRIEL. La guirlande des jeunes filles, en françois et flamen, par Gabriel Meurier . . . revue et de plusieurs sentences illustrée par le meme. Anvers, Jean Waesberghe, 1587. (Conversations

among school girls, dedicated to the mistress of a school. Rising, dressing, going to church, eating, household tasks, going to bed, etc. Usual virtues of women listed.)

563. MEXIA, HERNAN. Comiençan las obras de Hernan mexia-Otras suyas en que descubre los defetos dlas condiciones dlas mugeres por mandado de dos damas y en dereça a ellas estas primeras. In Castillo, H., *Cancionero general*, ff. 51a–52a.

564. MEXIA, VICENTE. Saludable instrucion del estado del matrimonio. Compuesto por el doctissimo padre F. Vicente mexia . . . Cordova, Juan Baptista Escudero, 1566.

565. MEYNIER, HONORAT DE. La perfection des femmes. Avec l'imperfection de ceux qui les mesprisent. Par. H. D. M. Provençal. Paris, Julian Jacquin et Nicolas Alexandre, 1625.

566. ‡MILAN, LUIS. Libro demotes de damas y cavalleros: intitulado el juego de mandar. Compuesto por don Luys Milan. Dirigido a las damas. Valencia, Francisco Diaz, 1525. (Pub. 1535.)

567. MILLS, THOMAS. The catalogue of honor or trasury of true nobility, peculiar and proper to the Isle of Great Britaine; that is to say: a collection historicall of all the free monarches aswel kinges of England as Scotland (nowe united togither) with the Princes of Walles, Dukes, Marquises and Erles; their wives, children, alliances, families, descentes, & achievementes of honor. Wherunto is properly prefixed: a speciall treatise of that kind of nobility which soverayne grace, and favor, and contryes customes, have made meerly politicall and peculiarly civill (never so distinctly handled before). Translated out of Latyn into English. London, William Jaggard, 1610. (From Robert Glover, Milles' uncle.)

568. MINTURNO, ANTONIO SEBASTIANI. Panegirico in laude d'amore. Composto dal Signore Antonio Minturno. Venetia, Francesco Rampazetto, 1559.

569. MINUT, GABRIEL DE. De la beaute, discours divers. Pris sur deux fort belles facons de parler, desquelles l'Hebrieu & le Grec usent l'Hebrieu . . . Tob, & le Grec καλὸν κ'αγαθὸν, voulans signifier, que ce qui est naturellement beau, est aussi naturellement bon. Avec la Paulegraphie, ou description des beautez d'une Dame Tholosaine, nommee La Belle Paule. Par Gabriel de Minut . . . Lyon, Barthelemi Honorat, 1587.

570. Le miroir des femmes, qui fait voir d'un côté les imperfections de la méchante femme, et qui montre de l'autre les bonnes qualités de la femme sage, tiré, pour la meilleure partie, des livres de la Sagesse. Premiere édition. Troyes, chez la veuve Oudot, 1717. (16th cent. Verse.)

571. MISOGYNE, ANDRÉ. Épistre de messire André Misogyne gentilhomme

florentin, envoyee au seigneur Pamphile, Theliarche, qui luy avoit
demandé conseil sus le propos de se marier. Traduite d'italien en françois. Pub. with pantagruel, *La louenge des femmes*, Lyon, J. de Tournes,
1551. (Against marriage. See Pantagruel.)

572. MIZAUD, ANTOINE. Secrets de la lune. Opuscule non moins plaisant que
utile, sur le particulier consent, & manifeste accord de plusieurs choses
du monde, avec la lune: comme du soleil, du sexe feminin, de certaines
bestes, oyseaux, poissons, pierres, herbes, arbres, malades, malidies,
& autres de grande admiration & singularité. Par Antoine Mizauld,
medecin et mathematicien. Paris, Federic Morel, 1571. (See ch. II,
*Le sexe feminin en beaucoup de choses symboliser, s'accorder & consentir
avec la lune, aussi feminine*. Begs the natural and sworn enemies of
women not to infer that therefore women are inconstant and variable.)

573. MODERATA FONTE, pseud. (Pozzo, Modesta). Il merito delle donne,
scritto da Moderata Fonte in due giornate. Oue chiaramente si scuopre
quanto siano elle degne, e più perfette de gli huomini. Venetia, Domenico Imberti, 1600.

574. MODIO, GIOVANNI BATTISTA. Il convito di M. Gio. Battista Modio
overo del peso della moglie. Dove ragionando si conchiude, che non
puo la donna dishonesta far vergogna à l'huomo. Roma, Valerio e
Luigi Dorici, 1554. (Also 1558.)

575. MOLINO, ANTONIO. Dialogo, over contrasto d'amore di messer Antonio Molino, cognominato Burchiella . . . . Vinegia, Comin da Trino,
1548. (Antiphilo and Philerio alternately condemn and defend love.
Verse.)

576. MONALDI, MICHELE. Irene, overo della bellezza. Del Signor Michele
Monaldi. Con altri due dialoghi; uno dell' havere, e l'altro della meta-
fisica. Venetia, Francesco Bariletto, 1599.

577. ‡MONTIFIQUET, RAOUL DE. Le guidon & gouvernement des gens
mariez. Lyon, Olivier Arnoullet. (Du Verdier. Verse.)

578. MORATO, FULVIO PELLEGRINO. Del significato de colori e de mazzolli.
Operetta di Fulvio Pellegrino Morato Mantovano nuovamente
ristampata. Vinegia, 1545. (Morato's dedication dated 1522, Ferrara.
Also 1556; 1558; 1559; 1564; 1569; 1593; 1595. For the use of lovers in
sending secret messages.)

579. MORE, EDWARD. A lytle and bryefe treatyse, called the defence of
women, and especially of Englyshe women, made agaynst the Schole
howse of women. London, John Kynge, 1560. (See Gosynhill.)

580. MORE, MARGARET. A devout treatise upon the Pater noster/made
fyrst in latyn by the moost famous doctour mayster Erasmus Rotero-
damus/and tourned in to englisshe by a yong vertuous and well lerned
gentylwoman of XIX yere of age. London, Thomas Berthelet, 1524.
(See Introduction by Richard Hyrde, on education for women.)

581. MORE, SIR THOMAS. Correspondence of Sir Thomas More, ed. E. F. Rogers, 1947, no. 63, letter to William Gonell, tutor to his children, 1518? (Eng. trans. Appendix to *Hints on Education; or directions to mothers in the selection and treatment of a governess*, 1821.)

582. ————— Epigrammata clarissimi divertissimique viri Thomae Mori Britanni ad emendatum exemplar ipsius autoris excusa. Basileae, apud Joannen Frobenium, 1520. (See letter to his children, pp. 110–111.)

583. ————— Thomae Mori Angli qualis uxor deligenda. (Printed 1638 in *Dominici Baudii amores*, pp. 279–288. Verse.)

584. MORI, ASCANIO. Giuoco piacevoli. Ristampato piu corretto . . . con la giunta d'alcune rime, et d'un ragionamento . . . in lode delle donne. 3 pt. Mantova, G. Ruffinello, 1580.

585. ————— Ragionamento d'Ascanio de Mori da Ceno in lode delle donne. Mantove, Giacomo Ruffinello, 1580. (Pub. also same year with *Giuoco piacevole*.)

586. MORO, MAURITIO. Giardino terzo de' madrigali del Costante Academico Cospirante. Mauritio Moro Vinetiano. Et il ritratto delle cortigiane. Al molto illustre il Signor Antonio dalla Vecchia. Venetia, Nicolò Moretti, 1602. (See *Il ritratto delle cortigiane*, pp. 185–234.)

587. MOTIS, JOHANNES. Tractatuli duo metria breves quorum primus continet recommendationem seu defensionem mulierum contra viros seu mares. Secundus remedium virorum contra concubinas atque coniuges, etc. (Also two other undated eds., and one of the first treatise dated 1511, which differs considerably in detail. Subtitles: 1. *Invectiva cetus feminei contra mares edita per magistrum Johem Motis neopolitanensem sancte sedis apostolice secretarium. 2. Remedium contra concubinas & coniuges per modum abbreviationis libri matheoli a petro de Corbolio Archidiacono.* See Corbeil.)

588. MULCASTER, RICHARD. Positions wherin those primitive circumstances be examined, which are necessarie for the training up of children, either for skill in their booke, or health in their bodie. Written by Richard Mulcaster, master of the schoole erected in London anno. 1561. in the parish of Sainct Laurence Powntneie, by the worshipfull companie of the merchaunt tailers of the said citie. London, Thomas Vautrollier, 1581. (See ch. 36, 38, 39.)

589. Muld sacke: or the apologie of Hic Mulier: to the late declamation against her. Exprest in a short exclamation. London, for Richard Meighen, 1620. (See *Hic-mulier* and *Haec-Vir*.)

590. ‡MUNDA, CONSTANTIA. The worming of a mad dogge; or a soppe for Cerberus the Jaylor of Hell. No confutation but a sharp redargution of the bayter of women. By Constantia Munda. 1617. (Attack on Swetnam. See Swetnam.)

591. MUNDAY, ANTHONY. A courtly controversie, between loove and learning. Pleasauntlie passed in disputation, betweene a ladie and a gentleman of Scienna. Wherein is no offence offered to the vertuous, nor any ill motion to delight the vicious. London, John Charlewood, f. Henrie Carre, 1581.

592. ‡MURHON. Discours en faveur des femmes.

593. MURRELL, JOHN. A daily exercise for ladies and gentlewomen. Whereby they may learne and practise the whole art of making pastes, preserves, marmalades, conserves, tartstuffs, gellies, breads, sucket-candies, cordiall waters, conceits in sugar-workes of severall kindes. As also to dry lemonds, orenges, or other fruits. Newly set forth, according to the now approved receipts, used both by honourable and worshipfull personages. By John Murrel professor thereof. London, for the widow Helme, 1617. (See below for another ed.)

594. ——————— A new booke of cookerie. Wherein is set forth a most perfect direction to furnish an extraordinary, or ordinary feast, either in summer or winter. Also a bill of fare for fish-dayes, fasting-dayes, ember-weekes, or Lent. And likewise the most commendable fashion of dressing, or soweing either flesh, fish, or fowle: for making of jellies, and other made-dishes for service, to beautifie either noble-mans or gentlemans table. Together with the newest fashion of cutting up any fowle. Hereunto also is added the most exquisite English cookerie. All set forth according to the now, new, English and French fashion. By John Murrell. London, for John Browne, 1617. (Also 1615; and with the preceding 1621; 1638, 5th ed.; 1641; 1650.)

595. MUSIUS, CORNELIUS. Institutio foeminae Christianae, ex ultimo capite Proverbiorum Solomonis, per Cornelium Musium Delphum, carmine reddita. Eiusdem Odae, & Psalmi aliquot. Omnia nunc primum & data & excusa. Pictavii, ex officina Marnesiorum fratrum, 1536.

596. MUZIO, GIROLAMO. Operette morali del Mutio Justinopolitano. Vinegia, Gabriel Giolito, 1550. (Also 1553; 1571 extended. See *Trattati di matrimonio*, and in 1571 cd. *Instit. della sposa eccelente*.)

597. NANNIUS, PETRUS (Nanninck, Pieter). Dialogismi heroinarum, autore Petro Nannio, Alecmariono, . . . Libellus nunc primum & natus & editus, lectuque dignissimus. Parisiis, apud Christianum Wechelum, 1541. (Also 1544. French trans. 1550, Du Verdier.)

598. NASH, THOMAS. Anatomie of absurditie, contayning a breefe confutation of the slender imputed prayses to feminine perfection, with a short description of the severall practices of youth and soundry follies of our licentious times; by Thomas Nash. London, 1589 .

599. NEGRI, CESARE. Le gratie d'amore di Cesare Negri, milanese, detto Il Trombone, professore di ballare, opera nova, et vaghissima, divisa in tre trattati. Al Potentissimo & Catholico Filippo terzo re di Spagna,

... Milano, per l'herede del quon. Pacifico Pontio, et Gio. Battista Piccaglia Compagni, 1602. (Also 1604, with title *Nuove inventioni di balli*.)

600. NEVIZZANO, GIOVANNI. Sylva nuptialis bonis referta non modicis/ Hunc te lector obnixe rogat/ut se aspicias: deinde quod scriptum est legas/Et protinus visis opusculi annotamentis/cum indice alphabetico contentorum narrativo letaberis guadio maximo. Parrhisiis, apud Joannem Kerver, 1521. (Also 1526; 1540; 1545; 1549; 1556; 1572; 1573; 1602; 1647.)

601. NEWMAN, ARTHUR. Pleasures vision: with deserts complaint, and a short dialogue of a woman's properties, betweene an old man and a young. By Arthur Newman. London, G. E., 1619. (Old man attacks, young man defends. Verse.)

602. NEWSTEAD, CHRISTOPHER. An apology for women: or womens defence. Pend by C. N. late of Albane Hall in Oxon. London, E. Griffin, 1620.

603. ‡NICCHOLES, ALEXANDER. A discourse of marriage and wiving. 1620. (Is this Tasso's?)

604. NIFO, AGOSTINO. Augustini Niphi medicis libri duo, de pulchro, primus. De amore, secundus. Lugduni, apud Godefridum & Marcellum Beringos, 1549. (Also 1641; 1645, *Opuscula moralia et politica*.)

605. ———— De re aulica ad Phausinam libri duo, per Augustinum Niphum Medicem. Neapoli, Joannes Antonius, 1534. (Ital. trans. see below. See lib. II, *De muliere aulica*.)

606. ———— (Ital. trans.). Il cortegiano del Sesso. Genova, Antonio Belloni, 1560. (Trans. by F. Baldelli. See lib. II, *Della donna cortigiana*. Domenichi's *La donna di corte* is another trans. of lib. II, though unacknowledged.)

607. ———— Eutychi Augustini Niphi medices philosophi Suessani libellus de his: quae ab optimis principibus agenda sunt: ad' Ludovicum atque Elveriam Ferdinandos a Corduba Principes Suessanos. Florentiae, per haeredes Phillippi Juntae, 1521. (Also 1645, *Opuscula moralia et politica*. See cap. 29, the virtues belonging to queens and noble women.)

608. NOBILI, FLAMINIO. Trattato dell' amore humano dell' eccelente Signor Flaminio Nobili. Con alcuni discorsi del medesimo sopra le piu importanti quistioni in materia d'honore. Da i quali si vede come un vero cavagliero si debba regolare nelle sue attioni. Con due tavole, delle cose notabili, che in essi si contengono. All' Illustriss. et Eccelentiss. Signor Marchese Boncompagno. Bologna, Pellegrino Bonardo, 1580. (Also 1550; 1558; 1567. French trans. 1588.)

609. The northren mother's blessing. The way of thrift. Written nine yeares before the death of G. Chaucer. London, Robert Robinson, 1597. Pub. with separate title-page in Certaine worthye manuscript poems of

great antiquitie reserved long in the studie of a Northfolke Gentleman. And now first published by J. S. The The statly tragedy of Guistard and Siskeond. The Northren mothers blessing. The way to thrifte. London, for R. D., 1597.

610. NOSTREDAME, MICHEL DE. Excellent et moult utile opuscule à tous nécessaire qui désirent avoir connoissance de plusieurs exquises receptes divisé en deux parties. La premiere traicte de diverses façons de fardemens et senteurs pour illustrer et embelir la face. La seconde nous monstre la façon et maniere de faire confitures de plusieurs sortes, tant en miel, que sucre, et vin cuict, le tout mis par chapitres, comme est faict ample mention en la table. Nouvellement composé par Maistre Michel de Nostredame docteur en medicine de la ville de Salon de Craux en Provence, et de nouveau mis en lumiere. Lyon, Ant. Volant, 1555. (Also 1572, Du Verdier.)

611. NUNEZ, NICULAS. Quel era mejor amar ala donzella/o casada/o buida/ o beata/o monja. In Castillo, H., *Cancionero general.*

612. ‡Nuova nave di novemila novecento novantanove malizie delle donne. (Mentioned by Bronzini.)

613. OBRECHT, GEORGES. Disputatio de patrimonio mulierum; qua frequens et utilis dotium materia brevi methodo conscripta continetur: in inclyta Argentoratensium Academia publicè proposita à Georgio Obrechto IC. Respondente Adamo Huenerero Argentoratensi. Argentorati, Antonius Bertramus, 1590?

614. OLIVIER, JACQUES. Alphabet de l'imperfection et malice des femmes. Dedié à la plus mauvaise du monde. Paris, Jean Petit-Pas, 1617. (Also 1619; 1623; 1626; 1628; 1630; 1631; 1636; 1640; 1643; 1658; 1666; 1683; 1685; 1730. See Vigoureux.)

615. ————— Responce aux impertinences de l'aposté Capitaine Vigoureux: sur La défense des femmes. Par Jacques Olivier, Licencier aux Lois, & en Droit Canon: autheur de l'Alphabet de la malice des mauvaises femmes. Paris, Jean Petit-Pas, 1617. (Seen only in the imperfect copy of the Bibliothèque Nationale, pp. 123–142 missing.)

616. ‡OLIVIER, JEAN. Pandora. Lugduni, apud S. Doletum, 1541. (Also 1542; 1618. French trans. 1542. Diatribe against women.)

617. ORADINI, LUCIO. Due lezzioni di M. Lucio Oradini, lette publicamente nell'Accademia Fiorentina. Fiorenza, Lorenzo Torrentino, 1550. (On two of Petrarch's sonnets: "Quanta invidia ti porto, avara terra," and "Se mai foco per foco non si spense.")

618. Oratione dell' humile invaghito in difesa, et lode delle donne. Mantova, Giacomo Roffinello, 1571. (Same academy addressed by Pusterla, 1568, on the other side.)

OROLOGI, GIUSEPPE. *See* Dondi.

619. OSTAUS, GIOVANNI. Modo bellissimo di trattenere le sue figlivole in

opera come faceva la casta Lucretia Romana le sue damigella, così come da Tarquinio insieme col suo marito Collatino fu trovato in mano d'esse a lavorare. Nel libro primo delle Deche di T. Livio, di 40 tavole incise. 1557. Fac., Venezia, 1878. (Also 1584; 1591. Cross-stitch patterns.)

620. ‡PAGANI MATTIO. La gloria et l'honore de ponti tagliati, e ponti in aere. Venetia, Mathio Pagan, 1558.

621. ‡———— L'onesto esempio del vertuoso desiderio che hanno le donne di nobil ingegno circa lo imparare i punti tagliati a fogliami. Per Mattio Pagan in frezzeria. 1540. (Also 1550. Fac. rep. 1878.)

622. ‡———— Opera nova composta da Domenico da Seva, detto il Franciosino, dove s'insegna a tutte le nobili et leggiardre giovanette di lavorare d'ogne sorte di punti; cucire, recamare et far tutte quelle belle opere, che si appartengono alle virtuose fanciulle; e quai si dilettano di far con le sue mani alcuna gentilezza et ancora molto utile agli tessadri che sogliono lavorare di seta. 1546. Fac. rep. 1878. (The first ed.)

623. ‡———— Il spechio di pensieri delle belle et virtudiose donne, dove si vede varie sorte di punti. Per Mathio Pagan. 1548.

624. ‡PAGANINO, ALEX. Libro primo de rechami per el quale se impara in diversi modi l'ordine e il modo di recamare, cosa non mai più fatta ne stata mostrata el qual modo se insegna al lettore voltando la carta. Fac. rep. 1878. (One of the first.)

625. PALMIERI, MATTEO. Libro della vita civile composto da Mattheo Palmieri cittadino Fiorentino. Firenze? Giunti? 1528? (Also 1529. French trans. by C. Des Rosiers, 1557. Composed c. 1450. See lib. IV on domestic economy.)

PANDOLFINI, AGNOLO. Il governo della famiglia. (See note to Alberti, *Della famiglia*.)

626. PANTÀGRUEL (pseud.). La louenge des femmes. Invention extraite du commentaire de Pantagruel sus l'Androgyne de Platon. Lyon, J. de Tournes, 1551. (Also 1552. Contents: 1. *Le blason de la femme*. 2. *Épistre de messire André Misogyne, gentilhomme florentin, envoyee au seigneur Pamphile, Theliarche, qui luy avoit demandé conseil sus le propos de se marier. Traduite d'italien en françois*. 3. *Description d'amour, par dialogue*. 4. *Epigrammes touchant tous les moeurs, conditions, et natures des femmes*. Added to 1552 ed.: *Enigme ou blason du cou. Responce sur la question faicte par aulcunes dames, dou quant & parqui on esté faites les premieres femmes selon ladvis de plusieurs nations*—a trans. of Guevara, *Relox de principes*, liv. II, letra XI. All against women, love, and marriage.)

627. PARABOSCO, GIROLAMO. Libro primo delle lettere amorose di M. Giro-

lamo Parabosco. Con alcune altre di nuove aggiunte. Venetia, Domenico Farri, 1581. (Also 1545; 1548; 1549; 1561; 1568; 1569. French trans.
1556.)

628. PARADIN, GUILLAUME. Le blason des danses par Guillaume Paradin.
Beaujeu, pour Justinian et Philippes Garils, 1556.

PARASOLE, ELISABETTA CATANEA and ISABELLA CATANEA. *See*
Catanea.

629. ‡PARIS, MICHEL T. L'art et instruction de bien dancer.

630. PARKER, MATTHEW. A defence of priestes mariages, stablysshed by
the imperiall lawes of the realme of Englande, agaynst a civilian,
namyng hym selfe Thomas Martin doctour of the civile lawes, goyng
about to disprove the saide mariages, lawfull by the eternall worde of
God, & by the hygh court of parliament, only forbydden by forayne
lawes and canons of the Pope, coloured with the visour of the Churche.
Whiche lawes & canons, were extynguyshed by the sayde parliament,
and so abrogated by the convocation in their Sinode by their subscrip-
tions. Herewith is expressed, what moderations and dispensations
have ben used heretofore in the same cause, & other like, the canons
of the Churche standyng in full force. Whereby is proved, these constitutions to be but positive lawes of man temporall. London, Richarde
Jugge, 1556?

631. PARTRIDGE, JOHN. The treasurie of commodious conceites, and hidden
secrets. Commonly called, The good huswives closet of provision, for
the health of her houshold. Meete and necessarie for the profitable use
of all estates. Gathered out of sundry experiments lately practised by
men of great knowledge: and now the fourth tyme corrected, and
inlarged, with divers necessary and new additions. London, Richard
Jhones, 1584. (Also 1586.)

632. ‡———— The widowes treasure, plentifully furnished with sundry
precious and approoved secretes in phisicke, and chirurgery for the
health and pleasure of mankinde. Hereunto are adjoyned, sundrie
pretie practises and conclusions of cookerie: with many profitable and
holesome medicines for sundry diseases in cattell. London, Edward
Alde, 1588.

633. PASQUALIGO, LUIGI. Delle lettere amorose del Mag. M. Alvise Pasqualigo. Libri quattro. Ne' quali sono maravigliosi concetti si contengono tutti gli accidenti d'amore. Novamente con somma diligenza
ristampate. Vinegia, Antonio Bertano, 1573. (Also 1564; 1567; 1570;
1581; 1587.)

634. PASQUIER, ETIENNE. Le monophyle. Par Estienne Pasquier, Parisien.
Paris, I. Lougis, B. Prevost pr., 1555. (Also 1554 Du Verdier; 1566;
1578; 1619; 1723. Eng. trans. see below.)

635. —————— (Eng. trans.). Monophylo, drawne into English by Geffray Fenton. A philosophicall discourse, and division of love. London, Wylliam Seres, 1572.

636. —————— Les oeuvres meslees d'Estienne Pasquier. Contenans plusieurs discours moraux, lettres amoureuses, & matieres d'estat, comme aux deux precedens volumes. Tome troisieme. Paris, Jean Petit-Pas, 1619. (*Le Monophile. Colloques d'amour. Lettres amoureuses.*)

637. —————— Ordonnances generalles d'amour, envoyees au seigneur Baron de Myrlinques Chancelier des Iles hyeres, pour faire estroictement garder par les vassaulx dudict Seigneur, en sa Jurisdiction de la Pierre au laict, et aultres lieux de l'obeissance dudict seigneur. Vallezergnes, par l'auctorite du prince d'Amour, 1564. (Also 1574; 16018 [*sic*].)

638. —————— Recueil des rymes et prose de E. P. Paris, en la boutique de Charles L'Angelier, 1555. (See Dialogues I, II, debates on questions of love.)

639. PASSERAT, JEAN. Le premier livre des poemes de Jean Passerat. Paris, Mamert Patisson, 1597. (Also 1602. See *Stanzes sur la difference de jalousie, & d'amour.*)

640. PASSI, GIUSEPPE. Dello stato maritale trattato di Giuseppe Passi Ravennate nell' Academia de' Signori Informi di Ravenna l'ardito. Nel quale con molti essempi antichi, e moderni, non solo si dimostra quello, che una donna maritate deve schivare, ma quello ancora, che fare le covenga, se compitamente desidera di satisfare all' ufficio suo. Opera non meno utile, che dilettevole à ciascheduno. Con una tavola copiosissima delle cose più notabili, che nell' opera si contengono. Venetia, Jacomo Antonio Somascho, 1602. (Latin trans. 1612; 1617.)

641. —————— I donneschi diffetti. Nuovamente formati e posti in luce da Giuseppe Passi. . . . Venetia, Jacobo Antonio Somascho, 1599. (Also 1601, 2nd ed.; 1605, 5th ed. In 1600 appeared his *Discorso del ben parlare, per non offendere persona alcuna. . . . Fatto da lui in occasione d'esser stato calunniato, per haver recitato una sua lettione nella detta Academia*, de' Signori Informi di Ravenna.)

642. —————— La monstruosa fucina delle sordidezze de gl' huomini nuovamente formata, e posta in luce. Da Giuseppe Passi Ravennate nell' Academia de' Signori Informi di Ravenna l'Ardito. Con tre tavole, la prima de i discorsi contenuti nell' opera, la seconda de gl'autori, la terza delle cose notabili . . . Venetia, Jacobo Antonio Somascho, 1603. (No reference to women. A sort of counterpart to the preceding.)

643. ‡PASTARINO. Instruttione sopra la universal peste, et frenetico morbo d'amore. A gli innamorati giovanni Bolognese il Pastarino. Bologna, Gio. Rossi, 1584.

644. PAZZI, ANTONIO DE'. Stanze inedite di Antonio de' Pazzi e di Torquato

Tasso in biasimo ed in lode delle donne edizione fatta per le nozze Mulazzani—Cappadoca. Venezia, Tipografia Picotti, 1810. (Mentioned by Bronzini. Pazzi blames, Tasso defends women, in stanzas built alike.)

645. PELLET, JEAN. Discours de la beaute des dames, prins de l'italien du Seigneur Ange Firenzuola Florentin. Par J. Pallet Saintongeois. A belles, & vertueuses Damoiselles, Jane, & Isabeau de Piarrebuffiere. Paris, 1578. (See ded. for defense of himself for spending time on such a trifling subject.)

646. PEREZ DE MOYA, JUAN. Varia historia de sanctas e illustres mugeres en todo genero de virtudes. Recopilado de varios autores, por el Bachiller Juan Perez de Moya, natural de la villa de Sant Estevan del Puerto. Dirigido al a S. C. R. M. de la Emperatriz donna Maria Infanta de España. Madrid, Francisco Sanchez, 1583.

647. PERKINS, WILLIAM. Christian oeconomie: or, a short survey of the right manner of erecting and ordering a familie, according to the Scriptures. First written in Latine by the author M. W. Perkins, and now set forth in the vulgar tongue for more common use and benefit, by Tho. Pickering. London, Felix Kyngston, 1609.

648. PESCIA, SIMONE DELLA BARGA DA. Nuova spositione del sonetto che comincia "In nobil sangue vita humile e' queta" ne la quale si dichiara qual sia stata la vere nobiltà di madonna Laura. Per M. Simone de la Barba da Pescia Academico Fiorentino. Firenze, 1554.

649. PETRARCA, FRANCESCO. De remediis utriusque fortunae. In Opere quae extant omnia. Basileae, per Sebastianum Henricpetri, 1581. (Also 1613; 1649. Eng. trans. see below. French trans. 1667. Ital. trans. 1607.)

650. ———— (Eng. trans.). Phisicke against fortune, aswell prosperous, as adverse, conteyned in two bookes. Whereby men are instructed, with lyke indifferencie to remedie theyr affections, aswell in tyme of the bryght shynyng sunne of prosperitie, as also of the foule lowryng stormes of adversitie. Expedient for all men, but most necessary for such as be subject to any notable insult of eyther extremitie. Written in Latine by Frauncis Petrarch, a most famous poet, and oratour. And now first Englished by Thomas Twyne. London, Richard Watkyns, 1579. (See *Dialogues* LXV–LXXXIV, on marriage, wives, children.)

651. PICCOLOMINI, ALLESANDRO. Della institutione di tutta la vita dell' huomo nato nobile, et in citta libera. Libri diece in lingua Toscana, dove et Peripateticamente, & Platonicamente, intorno alle cose dell' etica, & iconomica, & parte della politica, è raccolta la somma di quanto principalmente può concorrere alla perfetta, et felice vita di quello. Composti dal S. Alessandro Piccolomini, à benefitio del nobilissimo fanciullino Alessandro Colombini, pochi giorni innanzi nato,

figlivolo della immortale Mad. Laudomia Forteguerri. Al quale, havendolo egli sostenuto a battesimo, secondo l'usanzi de' compari; de i detti libri fa dono. Di nuovo con somma diligentia corretti, & ristampati. Vinegia, Giovanmaria Bonelli, 1552. (Date of Epistle 1542. Also 1543; 1545. For later enlarged edition see below.)

652. ———————— Della institutione morale di M. Allesandro Piccolomini. Libri XII. Ne' quali egli levando le cose soverchie, & aggiugnendo molte importanti, ha emendato, & à miglior forma & ordine ridotto tutto quello, che già scrisse in sua giovanezza della institutione dell' huomo nobile. Venetia, Giordano Ziletti, 1560. (Also 1569; 1575; 1582; 1583; 1594. French trans. 1581. See lib. IX, cap. II, difference between love and friendship; lib. X, love—kinds, definition, signs, loss and cure, fears, preservation, necessity; lib. XI, advice on marriage.)

653. ———————— Della nobilta et eccellenza delle donne [by H. C. Agrippa], dalla lingua francese nella Italiana tradotto. Con una oratione di M. Alesandro Piccolomini in lode delle medesime. Vinegia, Gabriel Giolito, 1549. (Also 1545.)

654. ———————— Dialogo, nel quale si ragiona della bella creanza delle donne, opera veramente degna di esser letta da ogni gentile spirito. All' Illustre Sig. Giovan Francesco Affaetato Prencipe di Chistella. Venetia, Domenico Farri, 1562. (Also 1539; 1540; 1541; 1557; 1558; 1560; 1574; 1622; 1750, London, which brought a confutation by Ubaldo Montelatici, 1755. Eng. trans. 1693. French trans. more or less close, acknowledged or unacknowledged, 1573; also 1597 and 1607, by Marie de Romieu, unacknowledged. Another 1577, with title *Notable discours en forme de dialogue, touchant la vraye et parfaite amitié, ouvrage dans lequel les dames sont deuëment informées du moyen qu'il faut tenir pour bien et honnestement se gouverner en amour.* Another 1581, also 1583, with title *Dialogues et devis des demoiselles, pour les rendre vertueuses et bien heureuses en la vraye et parfaite amitié.* Another without date, entitled *Instruction aux jeunes dames, en forme d' dialogue, écrite premièrement en italien, par laquelle elles sont apprises, comme il se faut bien gouverner en amour.* This is a dialogue between Margherita and the old woman Raffaella who teaches her the delights of love and persuades her to take a lover, already aspiring, because her husband neglects her.)

655. PICO DELLA MIRANDOLA, GIOVANNI. Opere di Girolamo Benivieni Firentino novissimamente rivedute et da molti errori espurgate con una canzone dello amor celeste & divino, col commento dello Ill. S. Conte Giovanni Pico Mirandolano distinto in libbri III et altre frottole di diverse auttori. Venezia, Gregorio de Gregori, 1524. (Also 1519; 1522; 1731. Eng. trans. 1651. French trans. 1598. For comparison of Benivieni's canzone with Cavalcanti's see lib. III, cap. III.)

656. PIETRO, ARETINO. Dialogo di M. Pietro Aretino, nel quale la Nanna, il primo giorno, insegna a la Pippa sua figliola a esser puttana; nel secondo gli conta i tradimenti che fanno gli huomini a le meschine che gli credano; nel terzo et ultimo la Nanna et la Pippa sedendo nel orto ascoltano la comare et la balia che ragionano de la ruffiania. Torino, 1536. (Also 1540; 1584; 1660, as *La seconda parte* of the *Ragionamenti*.)

657. ———— Opera nova del divo & unico signor Pietro Aretino: la qual scuopre le astutie: sclerita, frode, tradimenti, assassinamenti, inganni, truffarie, strigarie, calcagnarie, robarie et le gran fintion, & dolce paroline ch' usano le cortigiane o voi dir tapune per ingannar li semplici giovani, per laqual causa i poverelli per cio restano appesi come uccelli al vischio. Et al fin con vituperio & dishonor posti albasso con la borsa leggiera. Et chi questa opra leggera gli sera uno especchio da potersi schiffar dalle lor ingannatrice mani. Neopoli, 1534. (Also 1535; 1584; 1660, in the *Ragionamenti, la prima parte, la terza giornata*. French trans. 1580; 1595; 1610. Latin trans. 1623; 1660; 1750. Span. trans. 1548; 1549; 1607; 1750.)

658. ———— Ragionamento della Nanna e della Antonia, fatto in Roma sotto una ficaia, composto dal divino Aretino per suo capricio a correttione de i tre stati delle donne. Parigi, 1534. (Also 1536, bound with *Le Dialogo della Nanna*; 1539, bound with *Le raggionamento del Zoppino*; 1584, in the *Ragionamenti, la prima parte*. For ed. of *La terza giornata* alone see above, *Opera nova*. The three states are "Le Monache," "Le maritate," "Le puttane.")

659. ———— Ragionamento del Zoppino fatto frate, a Lodovico puttaniere dove contiensi la vita e genealogia di tutte le cortigiane di Roma. Venetia, Francesco Marcolino, 1539. (Also 1584, in the *Ragionamenti, la seconda parte*, added to *La terza giornata*; 1660.)

660. ‡PIGRO OLIMPICO, pseud. (Buonagente, Annibale). Discorso d'amore fatto dal Pigro Accademico Olimpico. Vincenza, gli eredi di Pierin Libraro, 1595.

661. ‡PIROLON. Lettres nouvelles contenantes le privilege et auctorite d' avoir deux femmes. Papagosse, 1536.

662. ‡———— Lettres nouvelles pour maniere de provision a tous ceux qui desirent d'estre mariez deux fois en acomplissant ce que Nostre Seigneur a dict: crescite et multiplicamini et replete terram. Romme, 1523.

663. PISAN, CHRISTINE DE. Les epistres sur le Roman de la Rose von Christine de Pizan. Nach 3 Pariser Handschriften bearbeitet und zum ersten Male veröffentlicht von Friedrich Beck. Neuberg, 1888. (Written 1402.)

664. ———— Le livre de la cité des dames. (Unpublished MS. Com-

posed 1404. Eng. trans. see below. Defense of women occasioned by
reading Matheolus.)

665. ———— (Eng. trans.). Here begynneth the boke of the cyte of
ladyes/the whiche boke is devyded into III partes. The fyrste parte
telleth howe and by whom the walle and the cloystre aboute the cyte
was made. The seconde parte telleth howe and by whom the cyte was
buylded within and peopled. The thyrde parte telleth howe and by
whom the hyghe battylmentes of the towres were parfytely made/and
what noble ladyes were ordeyned to dwell in the hyghe palayces and
hyghe dongeons. And the fyrst chapytre telleth howe and by whom
and by what movynge the sayd cyte was made. London, Henry Pep-
well, 1521. (Trans. Bryan Ansley.)

666. ———— Le livre de pollicie. (Unpublished MS. Eng. trans. see
below.)

667. ———— (Eng. trans.). Here begynneth the booke whiche is called
the body of polycye. And it speketh of vertues and of good maners/and
the sayd boke is devyded in thre partyes. The fyrst party is adressed
to prynces. The seconde to knyghtes and nobles and the thyrde to the
unyversal people. The fyrste chapytre speketh of the descrypcyon of
the body of polycye. London, John Skot, 1521. (See first and last
chapters where Christine excuses herself for meddling with high
matters.)

668. ———— Le livre du chemin de long estude par Cristine de Pizan.
Publié pour la première fois d'après sept manuscrits de Paris, de
Bruxelles et de Berlin par Robert Püschel. Berlin & Paris, 1881. (Also
1887. Written 1403. French prose trans. see below. Occasionally of
autobiographical interest. Verse.)

669. ———— (French prose trans.). Le chemin de long estude de dame
Cristine de Pise. Ou est descrit le debat esmeu au parlement de Raison,
pour l'ellection du Prince digne de gouverner le monde. Traduit de
langue Romanne en prose françoyse, par Jan Chaperon, dit lassé de
Repos. Paris, Estienne Groulleau, 1549.

670. ———— Oeuvres poétiques de Christine de Pisan. 1886, etc. (See
vol. I, *Cent balades*, XXXVI, LXIV, LXVIII; *Virelays*, XII; *Autres
balades*, IV, VIII. Vol. II, *L'epistre au dieu d'amours*—Eng. trans. by
Thos. Occleve, printed 1721 in Chaucer's works, with title *The letter
of Cupid to lovers*, printed in France in 17th cent. as *Contre Romant de
la Rose; Le dit de la rose; Le debat de deux amans; Le livre des trois
jugements; Le dit de Poissy; Le dit de la pastoure; Epître à Eustache
Morel*. Vol. III, *Oraisons; Enseignements et proverbes moraux; Le livre
du duc des vrais amants; Les cents ballades d'amant et de dame*.)

671. ———— Le tresor de la cité des dames, selon Dame Christine de la
cité de Pise, livre tresutile et prouffitable pour l'introduction des

roynes, dames, princesses, & autres femmes de tous estatz, auquel elles pourront veoir la grande & saine richesse de toute prudence, saigesse, sapience, honneur, & dignité dedans contenues. Paris, Denys Janot, 1536. (Also 1497; 1503. Portuguese trans. 1518. Written 1405. Summary 1912, by M. Laigle. Also known as *Le livre des trois vertus*. One of the very few books of these centuries that differentiate the lady from the woman.)

672. ———— La vision—Christine. Published for the first time, with an introduction by Sister Mary Louis Towner, The Catholic University of America, Wash., D. C., 1932. (Bk. III autobiographical.)

673. ‡PITHOU, NICOLAS. Institution du mariage chrestien. livres deux, divisez par chapitres. Lyon, à la Salamandre, 1565. (Du Verdier.)

674. PIUS II (Aeneus Sylvius Piccolomini). De amoris remedio. Romae, Theobaldus Schencbecher, 1473? (Also 1475?; 1485?; 1490. French trans. 1533? Germ. trans. 1536.)

675. ———— De pravis mulieribus. Paris, A. Bonnemere, 1507? (Also 1470?)

676. ———— Pii secundi pontificis maximi contra luxuriosos & lascivos. . . . Tractatus de amore incipit. . . . 1467? (Also 1509. Four leaves, warning against love.)

PLATINA. *See* Sacchi.

677. PLATT, SIR HUGH. A closet for ladies and gentlewomen, or the art of preserving, conserving, and candying. With the manner howe to make divers kinds of syrops: and all kinds of banqueting stuffs. Also divers soveraigne medicines and salves, for sundry diseases. London, for Arthur Johnson, 1608. (Also 1611; 1614; 1630; 1632; 1635; 1636; 1638. Mostly medicines.)

678. ———— Delightes for ladies, to adorne their persons, tables, closets and distillatories: with beauties, banquets, perfumes and waters. London, Peter Short, 1602. (Also 1599; 1605?; 1608; 1609; 1611; 1615; 1627; 1630; 1632; 1635; 1636; 1647; 1651; 1654.)

679. POLIZIANO (Angelo Ambrogini). Illustrium virorum epistolae ab Angelo Politiano partim scriptae, partim collectae, cum Sylvianis commentariis & Ascensienis scholiis, non parum auctis & diligenter repositis. Addidit enim Sylvius omnium fere argumenta, &, quae duodecim chartis etiam integris capi nequeant, expositiones optimas. Paris, 1523. (See letter numbered XVII—numbering of pages and letters badly mixed—to "Cassandrae Edeli Venetae puellae doctissimae," praising learned women, chiefly examples from ancients.)

680. ‡Le pompe, opera nova di recami dove trovansi varie mostre di punto in aere. Venezia, 1557.

681. PONT-AYMERIE, ALEXANDRE, Paradoxe apologique, ou il est fidelement demonstré que la femme est beaucoup plus parfaicte que l'homme

en toute action de vertu. Dedié a tres-illustre & vertueuse Dame Madame la Duchesse de Reths. Par Alexandre de Pontaymerie Seigneur de Focheran. Paris, Hubert Velu, 1596. (Also 1594; 1599, with title *Apologie des femmes*. Eng. trans. see Gibson.)

682. ‡Porro, Pietro Paolo. L'eris d'amore.

683. ‡Portius, Simon. De coloribus aculorum. Florentiae, 1550. (Ital. trans. 1551 by G. B. Gelli.)

684. Postel, Guillaume, pseud. (Elias Pandocheus). Les tres-merveilleuses victoires des femmes du nouveau monde, et comment elles doibuent à tout le monde par raison commander, & même à ceulx qui auront la monarchie du monde vieil. A Madame Marguerite de France. A la fin est adjoustée: La doctrine du siècle doré, ou de l'evangelike Régne de Jesus Roy des Roys. Par Guillaume Postel. Paris, Jehan Ruelle, 1553.

685. Poynet, John. A defence for mariage of priestes, by Scripture against aunciente writers. London, R. Wolff, 1549. (Also 1562? See Martin, and Parker.)

Pozzo, Modesta. *See* Moderata Fonte, pseud.

686. La presumption des femmes; avecques le testament de Lucifer. Paris, 1520?

687. ‡Prevost, Anthoine. L'amant deconforté, cherchant confort parmy le monde, contenant le mal et le bien des femmes, avec plusieurs preceptz et documentz contre l'amour: faict et compilé par Anthoine Prevost. Lyon, c. 1530.

688. ‡Dos privilegios et prerogativos que ho genero femino ten por dereito comun et ordonançoes do reyno mais que ho genero masculino. Ulyssiponae, Joh. Barrerius, 1557.

689. The proude wyves Pater Noster that wolde go gaye and undyd her husbonde and went her waye. London, John Kynge, 1560.

690. Le purgatoire des mauvais marys/avec lenfer des mauvaises femmes. Et le purgatoire des joueurs de dez et de cartes/& de tous autres jeux. Paris, c. 1530. (Bib. Nat. Rés. Y² 2714. Also c. 1480. Rés. Y² 244.)

691. Pusterla, Giovanni Francesco. Oratione del S. Gio. Francesco Pusterla detto l'assicurato academico invaghito. In biasmo del la crudelta della donna. Mantova, 1568. (See *Oratione*.)

692. Puttenham, George. The arte of English poesie. Contrived into three bookes: the first of poets and poesie, the second of proportion, the third of ornament. London, Richard Field, 1589. (See bk. I, ch. XXVI, *The maner of rejoysings at mariages and weddings*.)

693. Pyrrye, C. The praise and dispraise of women, very fruitfull to the well disposed minde, and delectable to the readers therof. And a fruitfull shorte dialogue uppon the sentence, know before thou knitte. C. Pyrrye. London, William How, 1569?

694. Questions et demandes recreatives pour resjouyr les espritz melencoliques, propres pour deviner & y passer le temps honestement. Avec les responses subtilles, & autres propos joyeux pour rire. Paris, Anthoine Houie, 1573.

695. ‡Questions naturelles, questions morales, questions d'amour, etc. Lyon, Gabriel Cotier. (Du Verdier.)

696. ‡Ragionamente de sei nobile fanciulle genovesi, le quali con assai bella maniera de dire discorrono di molte cose allo stato loro appartenenti. Opera non meno utile che dilettevole, di nuovo data in luce dall' illustrissimo Sig. Ottavio Imperiale. Pavia, Girolamo Bartoli, 1585.

697. RATCLIFFE, AEGREMONT. Politique discourses, treating of the differences and inequalities of vocations, as well publique, as private: with the scopes or endes whereunto they are directed. Translated out of French, by Aegremont Ratcliffe, esquire. London, for Edward Aggas, 1578. (See bk. I, ch. XIX, bk. II, ch. II, XI on the "domesticall vocation of marriage.")

698. RAVISIUS, JOANNES (Editor). De memorabilibus et claris mulieribus: aliquot diversorum scriptorum opera. Parisiis, ex aedibus Simonis Colinaei, 1521. (Contents: 1. *De claris mulieribus—Plutarchi philosophi de virtutibus mulierum traductio, per Alamanum Ranutinum, civem Florentinum. 2. Opus Jacobi Philippi Bergomensis, de claris mulieribus. 3. Aliud de illustribus foeminis opusculum, incerto authore.*)

699. ‡Recueil des exemples de la malice des femmes et des malheurs, survenus à leur occasion, ensemble les exécrables cruautés exercées par icelles. Lyon, 1596.

700. REFUGE, EUSTACHE DE. Traicte de la cour ou instruction des courtisans. Nouvelle edition, e beaucoup enrichie, comme il se verra au fueilles suivant. Et illustrée de plus: de nottes & interpretations, comme il se verra à la fin. Paris, Abraham Saugrain, 1619. (Also 1617; 1618; 1622. Eng. trans. see below. Latin trans. by J. Pastorius 1642; 1644. See pt. II, ch. 38, *Of the favor of Princes toward women.*)

701. ———— (Eng. trans.). A treatise of the court. Digested into two bookes. Written in French by the noble and learned jurisconsult, and councellor of estate, Monsieur Denis De Refuges. Done into English by John Reynolds. II bookes. London, Aug. Matthewes for William Lee, 1622.

702. ‡ REGNAUD, NICOLAS. Les chastes amours, contenans 66. sonnets. Ensemble les chansons d'amour, La fable du pin, l'orenger. Paris, Thomas Brumen, 1560. (Du Verdier.)

703. RENIERI, ANTONIO. Di M. Antonio Renieri da Colle Auzzo intronato, vero soggetto d'amore. Lucca, Vincenzo Busdraghi, 1566.

704. Le renoncement damours. Paris, Jehan Trepperel, 1510? (Debate on love.)

705. RICH, BARNABY. The excellency of good women. The honour and estimation that belongeth unto them. The infallible markes whereby to know them. By Barnabe Rych souldier servant to the King's most excellent Majestie. London, Thomas Dawson, 1613.

706. ————— My ladies looking glasse. Wherein may be discerned a wise man from a foole, a good woman from a bad: and the true resemblance of vice, masked under the vizard of vertue. By Barnabe Rich. London, for Thomas Adams, 1616. (Also 1606, with title *Faultes faults*, etc.)

707. RICHARD DE FOURNIVAL. Le bestiaire d'amour par Richard de Fournival suivi de la reponse de la dame enrichi de 48 dessins graves sur bois publies pour la premiere fois d'apres le manuscrit de la Bibliotheque Imperiale par C. Hippeau. Paris, 1860. (Composed last half 13th cent.)

708. ‡RIDOLFI, GIOVANNI. Giuditio sopra la falsa narratione de le operationi de le donne di Giovanni Ridolfi. Padova, Lorenzo Pasquati, 1588.

709. RIDOLFI, LUC' ANTONIO. Aretifila, dialogo, nel quale da una parte sono quelle ragioni allegate, lequali affermano, lo amore di corporal bellezza potere ancora per la via dell' udire pervenire al quore: et dall' altra, quelle che vogliono lui havere solamente per gl' occhii l'entrata sua: colla sentenza sopra cotal quistione. Lione, Guliel. Rovillio, 1560. (Also 1562?)

710. RINGHIERE, INNOCENZIO. Cento giuochi liberali, et d' ingegno, novellamente da M. Innocentio Ringhiere ... ritrovati, & in dieci libri discritti. Bologna, Anselmo Giaccarelli, 1551. (Also 1553; 1580. French trans. of part—see below.)

711. ————— (French trans.). Cinquante jeus divers d'honnete entretien, livre premier. Tr. H. P. de Villiers. Lyon, C. Pesnot, 1555.

712. ‡ROBERT, NICOLAS. De l'estat & maintien du mariage vrayement Chrestien, où sont contenues toutes les loix & reigles que doivent tenir & observer par ensemble le mary & la femme. Plus une consolatoire sur la mort des enfans ou amis. Lyon, Jean Saugrain, 1565. (Du Verdier.)

713. ROBERT DE BLOIS. Le chastiement des dames. Pub. by Etienne de Barbazon, *Fabliaux et contes*, etc., Paris, 1808, vol. 2, pp. 184–219. (Poem of the 13th cent., introduced with minor changes into *Le jardin de plaisance*, 1501, by L'Infortune, under title, *Le livre des dames à icelles baillé au jardin de plaisance pour les instruire et doctriner en quelle manière elle se doivent tenir et contenir*.)

714. RODRIGUEZ DEL PADRON (or DE LA CAMARA), JUAN. Diez mandamientos de amor. In Castillo, *Concionero*, 1535.

715. ———— Triunfo de las donas. In *Obras*, 1884. (French trans. 1460; 1530? Fifty reasons why women should be loved more than men.)

716. ROIG, JAUME. Libre de consells: fet per lo magnifict mestre Jaume roig/los quals son molt profitosos y saludables axi per al regiment y orde d ben vivre com pera augmentar la devocio ala puretat y concepcio dela sacratissima verge Maria. Valencia, Francisco Diaz, 1531. (Also 1561, with title *Comença lo llibre de les dones;* 1735. Verse.)

717. ROMEI, ANNIBALE. Discorsi del Conte Annibale Romei Gentilhuomo Ferrarese di nuovo ristampati, ampliati, e con diligenza corretti. Divisi in sette giornate, nelle quali tra dame e cavaglieri ragionando, nella prima si tratta della bellezza, nella seconda dell'amor humano, nella terza dell' honore, nella quarta dell' iniquità del duello, del combattere alla macchia; e del modo d'accomodar le querele, e ridur à pace le inimicitie private. Nella quinta della nobiltà, nella sesta della richezze, nella settima della precedenza dell' arme, e delle lettere. Con la risposta a tutti i dubbii, che in simil materie proponer si sogliono. Alla Sereniss. Sig. la S. D. Lucretia da Este Duchessa d'Urbino. Ferrara, Vittorio Baldini, 1586. (Also 1585; 1591; 1594; 1604. Eng. trans. see below. French trans. 1595.)

718. ———— (Eng. trans.). The courtiers academie: comprehending seven severall dayes discourses: wherein be discussed, seven noble and important arguments, worthy by all gentlemen to be perused. 1. Of beauty. 2. Of humane love. 3. Of honour. 4. Of combate and single fight. 5. Of nobilitie. 6. Of riches. 7. Of precedence of letters or armes. Originally written in Italian by Count Haniball Romei, a gentleman of Ferrara, and translated into English by J[ohn] K[epers]. London, Valentine Sims, 1598.

719. ROMIEU, MARIE DE. Instruction pour les jeunes dames, dans laquelle elles sont apprises comme il faut se bien gouverner en amour. Lyon. (Also 1583; 1597. Unacknowledged trans. See Piccolomini. For another unacknowledged trans. see Des Roches.)

720. ———— Les premieres oeuvres poetiques de mademoiselle Marie de Romieu Vivaroise, contenant un brief discours, que l'excellence de la femme surpasse celle de l'homme non moins recreatif que plein de beaux exemples. Paris, pour Lucas Breyer, 1581.

721. ROSCIO, J. L., pseud. (John Lowin). Conclusions upon dances. London, f. J. Orphinstrange, 1607. (Also 1609.)

722. ROSSO, PAOLO DEL. Al gran Cosmo Medici. . . . Comento sopra la canzone di Guido Cavalcanti. Di F. Paolo del Rosso Cavaliere de la Religione di S. Gio. Battista, & Accademico Fiorentino. Fiorenza, Bartolomeo Sermatelli, 1568. (See Cavalcanti.)

723. ROUSPEAU, YVES. Quatrains spirituels de l'honneste amour, avec les

stances des louanges du S. Mariage opposees a celles de Philippes Desportes. Nouvellement mis en lumiere par Yves Rouspeau Saintongeois. Pons, Thomas Portau, 1593. (Also 1594; 1584 and 1586 without Desportes' stanzas. See Desportes, Blanchon, Le Gaygnard.)

724. ROVERE, GIROLAMO DELLA. Ad commendationem sexus muliebris. Oratio. Habita Ticini, per Hieronymum Ruvere, puerulum annum agentis decimum. Ticini, apud Joan. Mariam Simonetam, 1540.

725. ‡ROVIGLIONI, GIACOMO. Discorso intorno alla dignità del matrimonio, fatto, e recitato nell' academia degli Illustrati di Casale li 23 gennaro 1594. dal Sig. Giacomo Roviglioni academico detto l'Inviato. Con alcune conclusioni raccolte da lui in esso discorso, et sostenute dal Sig. Carlo Natta Academico detto l'Adombrato. Casale, Bernardo Grasso, 1595.

726. ‡———— Discorso intorno alla essenza d'amore fatto e recitato nell' Academia degl' illustrati di Casale li 4 di agosto 1594. Dal sig. Giacomo Roviglioni Academico detto l'Inviato. Casale, Bernardo Grasso, 1595.

727. ‡RUMPOLT, MARX. Ein new Kochbuch, . . . Auch ist darinnen zu vernemmen, wie man herrliche grosse Panncketen, sampt gemeinen Gastereyen, ordentlich anrichten und bestellen soll, . . . Durch M. Marxen Rumpolt, Churf. Meintzischen Mundtkoch . . . Franckfort am Mayn, Johann Feyerbendts, 1546.

728. RUSCELLI, GIROLAMO. Lettura di Girolamo Ruscelli, sopra un sonetto dell' illustriss. signor marchese della Terza alla divina signora marchesa del Vasto. Ove con nuove et chiare ragioni si pruova la somma perfettione delle donne; & si discorrono molte cose intorno alla scala platonica dell' ascendimento per le cose create alla contemplatione di Dio. Et molte intorno alla vera bellezza, alla gratia, & alla lingua volgare ove ancora cade occasione di nominare alcune gentildonne delle piu rare d'ogni terra principal dell' Italia. Venetia, Giovan Grifo, 1552.

729. ‡S., RS. A briefe instruction for all families. London, f. W. Ponsonby, 1583.

730. SABADINO, GIOVANNI DEGLI ARIENTI. Gynevera de le clare donne di Joanne Sabadino de li Arienti. Bologna, 1888. (Written 1483.)

731. SACCHI, BARTHOLOMEUS, DE PLATINA. Dialogus Platinae contra amores et amatorculos. Erphurdiae, ex officina litteraria Stribelitae, 1510. (Also 1481; 1530 with other works; 1646. French trans. pub. with Fregoso's L'anteros.)

732. ———— Libellus platine de honesta voluptate ac valitudine. Bononiae, per Joannem antonium platonidem, 1499. (Also 1475; 1480; 1485?; 1498; 1499; 1503; 1517; 1529; 1530; 1537; 1538; 1541. French trans. 1505; 1530; 1548; 1560; 1571; 1586. Germ. trans. 1530; 1542. Ital. trans. 1487; 1494.)

733. SADOLETO, JACOPO. Jac. Sadoleti de liberis recte instituendis, liber. Venetiis, per Jo. Antonium et fratres de Sabio, 1533. (Also 1534; 1538; 1541. French trans. 1537. Ital. trans. 1745.)

734. SAINT-GELAIS, OCTOVIEN DE. La chasse et le depart damours. Faict et compose par reverend pere en dieu messire Octovien de sainct gelaiz, evesque dangoulesme et par noble homme blaise dauriol, . . . Paris, Anthoine Verard, 1509.

735. SAINTE-MARTHE, SCÉVOLE DE, THE ELDER. Scaevolae Sammarthani Paedotrophiae libri tres. Ad Henricum III. Galliae et Poloniae regem. Lutetiae, apud Mamertum Patissonium, 1584. (Also 1587; 1698 with French prose trans.; 1708. Eng. trans. into verse by Nicholas Rowe 1710; another 1797. Proper care of children by mothers. Verse.)

736. SALTER, THOMAS. A mirrhor mete for all mothers, matrones, and maidens, intituled the Mirrhor of modestie, no lesse profitable and pleasant, then necessarie to bee read and practised. London, f. Edward White, 1579. (Proper bringing up. See Bruto.)

737. ‡SANCHEZ, THOMAS. Disputationum de sancto matrimonii sacramento libri tres; auctore Thoma Sanchez e Societate Jesu. Antverpiae, apud Martinum Nutium, 1607. (Also 1602–1605; 1617; 1620; 1621; 1623; 1626; 1637; 1652; 1656; 1669; 1689; 1693; 1712; 1739.)

738. SANDYS, EDWIN, ARCHBISHOP. Sermons made by the most reverende Father in God, Edwin, Archbishop of Yorke, etc. London, Henrie Midleton, 1585, rep. Parker Society, 1841. (Also 1616. See Sermons 11, 16, duties of husbands and wives.)

739. SAN PEDRO, DIEGO DE. Carcel de amor. Burgos, Fadrique Aleman de Basilea, 1496. (Also 1523; 1525; 1526; 1540; 1553; with *Question de amor*, 1556; 1576; 1598. Eng. trans. see below. French trans. with Span. 1526; 1552; 1567; 1616. Ital. trans. 1515; 1518; 1525; 1530; 1533; 1537; 1546. Germ. trans. 1660; 1675. See end for attack and defense of women.)

740. ————— (Eng. trans.). The castell of love. Tr. J. Bourchier. London, R. Wyer f. R. Kele, 1540? (Also 1549?; 1560.)

741. ————— Question de amor de dos enamorados: al uno era muerta su amiga: el otro sirve sin esperança de galardon. Disputan qual delos dos sufre mayor pena. Entrexeren se enesta contraversia muchas cartas y enamorados razonamientos. Introduze se mas una caça: un juego de cañas; una egloga; ciertas justas: & muchos cavalleros y damas con diversos y muy ricos atavios; con letras & invenciones. Concluye con la salida del señor viso rey de napoles donde los dos enamorados al presente se hallavan para socorrer al santo padre: donde se cuenta el numero de agguel luzido exercito & la contraria fortuna de ravena. La mayor parte dela obra es istoria verdadera. Compuso la un gentil hombre que se hallo en todo. Valencia, Diego de gumiel, 1513. (Also

1533; 1545; 1553, with Boccaccio's thirteen questions from *Filocopo* added in trans.; with *Carcel de amor*, 1556; 1576; 1598. French trans. 1541, *Le debat des deux gentilzhommes Espagnolz*. The two lovers named Flamiano and Vasquiran.)

742. SANSOVINO, FRANCESCO. Delle lettere amorose di diversi huomini illustri. Libri novi. Nelle quali si leggono nobilissimi, & leggiadri concetti, in tutte le materie occorrenti ne' casi d'amore, da i più eccellenti ingegni de' tempi nostri scritti, & per la maggior parte non più stampate, ò vedute. Venetia, Jacomo Cornetti, 1584. (Also 1563; 1567; 1587; 1591; 1599; 1606.)

743. ———— Ragionamento di M. Fran. Sansovino. Nel quale brevemente s'insegna a giovani huomini la bella arte d'amore. Mantova, Mad. Gasparina, 1545.

744. SAPET, P. Les enthousiasmes ou eprises amoureuses de P. de Sapet. Paris, Jehan D'allier, 1556. (Only XVII–XXIII concern lover, his pains and dangers.)

745. SARDI, ALESSANDRO. Discorsi del S. Alessandro Sardo. Della bellezza. Della nobiltà. Della poesia di Dante. De i precetti historici. Delle qualità del generale. Del terre moto. Di novo posti in luce. Venetia, J. Giolito, 1586.

746. SAVONAROLA, GIROLAMO. Copia duna epistola laquale manda el reverendo padre frate Hieronymo da Ferrara dellordine de frati predicatori a madonna Magdalena Contessa della mirandola/laquale volea intrare in monasterio. Fiorenza, Lorenzo Morgiani, 1497? (Also 1500?; 1520? Severe requirements of such a life.)

747. ———— Libro della vita viduale. Fiorenza, Bartolomeo de'Libri, 1495?

748. ‡SCALA, BARTHOLOMEUS. An viro sapienti ducenda uxor?

749. SCALIGER, JULIUS CAESAR. Julii Caesaris Scaligeri viri clarissimi poemata in duas partes divisa. Apud Petrum Santandreanum, 1591. (See pp. 358–384, *Julii Caesaris Scaligeri heroinae*, ancients; pp. 458–471, *Julii Caesaris Scaligeri sidera*, moderns.)

750. (Schoolhouse). The vertuous scholehous of ungracious women. A godly dialogue or communication of two systers. The one a good and vertuous wedowe, oute of the land of Meissen. The other, a curst ungracious, froward and brawlinge woman, oute of the mountaynes. To the honour and prayse of all good women. And to the rebuke and instruccion of suche as be unpacient. London, W. Lynne?, 1550? (A prose work. Wrongly assigned to Edward Gosynhill by *Short Title Catalogue*, as earliest ed. of *Schole house of women*.)

751. ‡SERA, DOMENICO DE. Le livre de lingerie, composé par Maistre Dominique de Séra, Italien, enseignant le noble & gentil art de l'esguille, pour besongner en tous points: utile & profitable à toutes

dames & damoyselles, pour passer le temps, & eviter oysiveté. Nouvellement augmenté, & enrichi, de plusieurs excelens & divers patrons, tant du point coupé, raiseau, que passement, de l'invention de M. Jean Cousin peintre à Paris. Paris, Hierosme du Marnef & la veufue de Guillaume Cavellat, 1584. (Also 1546.)

752. SERAFINI, MICHELANGIOLO. Michelagniolo Serafini academico fiorentino sopra un' sonetto della gelosia di m. Giovanbatista Strozzi. Firenza, Lorenzo Torrentino, 1550.

753. SERDONATI, FRANCISCO. Libro di M. Giovanni Boccaccio delle donne illustri. Tradotto di Latino in volgare per M. Giuseppe Betussi, con una giunta fatta dal medesimo, d'altre donne famose. E un' altra nuova giunta fatta per M. Francesco Serdonati, d'altri donne illustri, antiche e moderne. Con due tavole una de nomi, e l'altra delle cose piu notabili. Fiorenza, Filippo Giunti, 1596. (Contributions of the three distinguished in text and index. Serdonati, pp. 479–676.)

754. SERENA. Opera nova di recami nella quale si ritrova varie et diverse sorte di punti in stuora et punti a filo etc. Venetia, Domenico de Franceschi, 1564. Facsimile, Venezia, 1878.

755. ‡SESCAS, HENNIEU DE. Ensenhamen de la donzela. Last quarter 13th cent. (For summary see Hentsch, p. 94. Advice to young girl in service of a châtelaine. Verse.)

756. SIBILET, THOMAS. Art poetique françois. Pour l'instruction des jeunes studieux, & encor' peu avancez en la poësie Françoyse. Avec le Quintil Horatian, sur la defense & illustration de la lange Françoise. Reveu, & augmenté. Paris, par la vuefue Jean Ruelle, 1573. (Also 1548; 1556. See ch. X, pp. 126–127, *Du blason, & de sa definition & description*.)

757. ‡SIMEONI, GABRIEL. Le III parti del campo de primi studii di Gabriel Symeoni fiorentino. Vinegia, Comino da Trino, 1546. (See *Della qualita del buon marito*.)

758. Les singeries des femmes de ce temps descouvertes. 1623. (Bib. Nat. Rés. Y² 3516.)

759. SMITH, HENRY. A preparative to mariage. The summe whereof was spoken at a contract, and inlarged after. Whereunto is annexed a treatise of the Lords supper: and another of usurie. By Henry Smith. Newly corrected and augmented by the authour. London, J. Charlewood for Thomas Man, 1591.

760. SMITH, SIR THOMAS. De republica Anglorum. The maner of governement or policie of the realme of England, compiled by the honorable Thomas Smyth, Doctor of the civil lawes, knight, and principall secretarie unto the two most worthie princes, King Edwarde the sixt, and Queene Elizabeth. London, Henrie Midleton, 1583. (Also 1584; 1589; 1594; 1601; 1609; 1612; 1621; 1633; 1635; 1640. Latin

trans. 1610?; 1625; 1630; 1641. See bk. III, ch. 6 on liberty of English wives.)

761. SNAWSEL, ROBERT. A looking glasse for maried folkes. 1610. (Dialogue between four women and one man on the treatment wives owe their husbands.)

762. SOCIO, NOBILE. Le miserie de li amanti di messer Nobile Socio. Vinegia, Bernardino de' Vitali, 1533.

763. ‡SORANZO, GIOVANNI. Il Coppino, o vero dell'eccell. delle donne. (Mentioned by Bronzini.)

764. SORBOLI, GIROLAMO. Lettioni sopra la definitione d'amore posta dal gran filosofo Platone nel libro chiamato il convito, di Girolamo Sorboli da Bagnacavallo theologo, & medico fisico di Brescello. Modona, Paolo Gadaldino, 1590.

765. SORDELLO (c. 1200–1270). L'ensenhamens d'onor. Pub. 1886–7, *Le poesie inedite di Sordello*, vol. V, Ser. VI, p. 1471–1509. (Verses 1069–1270 addressed specially to women.)

766. SOWERNAM, ESTHER, pseud. Esther hath hang'd Haman; or an answere to a lewde pamphlet, entituled the Arraignment of Women; with the arraignment of lewd, idle, froward and unconstant men and husbands. . . . Written by Ester Sowernam, neither maide, wife, nor widdowe, yet really all, and therefore experienced to defend all. London, 1617. (See Swetnam and Specht.)

767. SPECHT, RACHEL. A mouzell for Melastomus, the cynicall bayter of, and foule mouthed barker against Evahs sex. Or an apologeticall answere to that irreligious and illiterate pamphlet made by Jo. Sw. and by him intituled, The arraignement of women. By Rachel Specht. London, Nicholas Okes, 1617. (See Swetnam and Sowernam.)

768. SPERONI, SPERONE. Dialoghi del Sig. Speron Speroni nobile Padovano, di nuovo ricorretti; a' quali sono aggiunti molti altri non più stampati. E di più l'apologia de i primi. Venetia, Roberto Meietti, 1596. (Also 1542; 1543; 1544; 1546; 1550; 1552; 1558; 1560. See in *Prima parte, Dialogo dell' amore, Dialogo della dignità delle donne, Dialogo della cura famigliare;* in *Seconda parte, Dialogo delle lodi delle donne.*)

769. SPIFAME, MARTIN. La louenge du mariage contre Des-portes. In *Les premieres oeuvres poetiques*, Paris, pour le vefue Luscas Breyer, 1583. (Ff. 28–30a.)

770. ‡Lo splendore delle virtuose giovani dove si contengono molte, et varie mostre à fogliami, cioè ponti in aere, & punti tagliati bellissime, & con tale artificio, che li punti tagliati servino alli punti in aere, et da quella ch'è sopragasi far si possono, medesimamente molte altre. Vinegia, Iseppo Foresto, 1558.

771. SPONTONE, CIRO. Hercole difensore d'Homero. Dialogo del sig. cavalliere Ciro Spontone; nel quale oltre ad alcune nobilissime materie;

si tratta de' tiranni, delle congiure contro di loro, della magia naturale; & dell' officio donnesco. Verona, Girolamo Discepolo, 1595.

772. ‡Spositione d'un sonetto Platonica fatto sopra il primo effecto d'amore, che è il separare l'anima dal corpo de l'amante, dove si tratta de la immortalità de l'anima secondo Aristotile, e secondo Platone. Fiorenza, 1554.

773. Stiblinus, Gasparus. Coropaedia, sive de moribus et vita virginum sacrarum, libellus planè elegans, ac saluberrimis praeceptis refertus: Gasparo Stiblino autore. Eiusdem de Eudaemonensium republica commentariolus. Basileae, per Joannem Oporinum, 1555.

774. Suarez. Comiençan las obras de Suarez. Y esta primera es una que hizo en satisfacio de las quexas que las mugeres tienen de sus servidores. In Castillo, *Cancionero*, 1535.

775. Swetnam, Joseph. The arraignment of lewd, idle, froward, and inconstant women: or the vanitie of them, choose you whether. With a commendation of wise, vertuous and honest women. Pleasant for married men, profitable for young men, and hurtfull to none. London, for Thomas Archer, 1616. (Also 1615; 1617; 1619; 1620; 1622; 1628; 1629; 1633; 1637; 1699; 1702; 1707; 1738. Dutch trans. 1641; 1645? See Sowernam, Specht, Munda, and below.)

776. ———— (Counter-attack.). Swetnam, the woman-hater arraigned by women. A new comedie, acted at the Red Bull, by the late Queenes Servants. London, for Richard Meighen, 1620.

777. Swinburne, Henry (Lawyer, c. 1590). A treatise of spousals, or matrimonial contracts: wherein all the questions relating to that subject are ingeniously debated and resolved. By the late famous and learned Mr. Henry Swinburne, author of the Treatise of wills and testaments. London, S. Roycroft for Robt. Clavell, 1686. (Also 1711. Long unprinted.)

778. ‡T., G. An apologie for womankinde. 1605.

779. ‡Tabourot, Jehan. Orchesographie: traité pour apprendre et practiquer l'honnête exercice des dances. Langres, 1588.

780. Tagliente, Giovantonio. Esemplario nuovo che insegna a le donne a cuscire, a raccamare, & a disegnare a ciascuno. Et anchora e di grande utilita ad ogni artista, per esser il disegno a ognuno necessario. Vinegia, G. A. et i fratelli da Sabbio, 1531. Facsimile Venezia, 1879.

781. ———— Opera amorosa che insegna a componer lettere, & a rispondere a persone d'amor ferite, over in amor viventi, in toscha lingua composta, con piacer non poco, & diletto di tutti gli amanti, laqual si chiama il rifugio di amanti. Vinegia, Franchesco Bindoni & Mapheo Pasini, 1533. (Also 1535; 1537.)

782. Tahureau, Jacques. Les dialogues de feu Jacques Tahureau, gentilhomme du Mans, non moins profitables que facetieus. Ou les vices

d'un châcun sont repris fort âprement, pour nous animer davantage à les fuir & suivre la vertu . . . Paris, Gabriel Buon, 1565. (Also 1566; 1568; 1570; 1574; 1576; 1580; 1583; 1585; 1589; 1602—14 times in all before 1600. See *Le Democritie, & Le Cosmophile*, attacking and defending love.)

783. TAILLEMONT, C. DE. Le discours des champs faez, a l'honneur, et exaltation de l'amour et des dames. Contenant plusieurs chansons, quatrains, dialogues, complaintes, & autres joyeusetez d'amours. Par C. de Taillemont Lyonnois. Paris, Richard Roux, 1557. (Also 1553; 1571.)

784. ‡TALAVERA, HERNANDO DA (1428–1507). Como se ha de occupar una señora de cada dia. (Poem against women.)

785. ‡————— Reprobacion del amor mundano, o Corbacho.

786. TASSO, BERNARDO. Le lettere di M. Bernardo Tasso. Vinegia, V. Valgrisi, 1551. (Also 1557; 1561; 1562; 1564; 1570; 1580; 1603; 1733–1751. French trans. 1554. See *Lettera 199*, pp. 342–350, "a la Signora Portia sua," teaching his young wife how she ought to bring up her children, Cornelia and Torquato. Trans. in full by Du Verdier, pp. 121–124.)

787. TASSO, ERCOLE. Dello ammogliarsi piacevole contesa fra i due moderni Tassi, Hercole, cioè, & Torquato, gentilhuomini Bergamaschi, novamente in più luoghi al confronto de' loro originali corretta. Bergamo, Comin Ventura, 1595. (Also 1593; 1594. Eng. trans. see below.)

788. ————— (Eng. trans.). Of mariage and wiving. An excellent, pleasant, and philosophicall controversie, betweene the two famous Tassi now living, the one Hercules the philosopher, the other, Torquato the poet. Done into English by R. T. gentleman. London, Thomas Creede, 1599.

789. TASSO, TORQUATO. Il Cataneo, ovvero conclusiones. 1578. (Dialogue on love.)

790. ————— Il cavaliere amante e la gentildonna amata. In *Parte terza delle rime e prose*, Vinegia, Vasalini, 1583. (Also 1584; 1585; 1589; 1738.)

791. ————— Conclusioni amorose. In *Parte prima delle rime*, Vinegia, Aldo, 1581. (Also 1585; 1612; 1738.)

792. ————— Dello ammogliarsi piacevola contesa, etc., see Ercole Tasso.

793. ————— Dialogo dei casi d'amore di Torquato Tasso. First pub. 1894. (Attributed to Tasso.)

794. ————— Discorso della gelosia. In *Aggiunta di rime e prose*, Vinegia, Aldo, 1585.

795. ————— Discorso della virtu femenile, e donnesca, del Sig. Torquato Tasso. Venetia, Bernardo Giunti, 1582. (Also in *Parte terza delle rime e prose*, 1582.)

796. ————— Discorso in lode del matrimonio e un dialogo d'amore. Milan, Tini, 1586. (Also 1594; 1595; 1738; 1796. The second part pub. 1587, with title *Il Molza* in *Parte V e VI delle rime et prose.*)

797. ————— Discorso sopra due questioni amorose. In *Parte quarta della rime e prose*, Venetia, Vasalini, 1586. (Also 1612; 1738.)

798. ————— Il forestiero napoletano o vero della gelosia. In *Parte quarta delle rime e prose*, Venetia, Vasalini, 1586. (Also 1738. Dialogue.)

799. ————— Il padre di famiglia dialogo del Sig. Torquato Tasso. Nel quale brevemente trattando la vera economia, s'insegna, non meno con facilità, che dottamente, il governo non pur della casa, tanto di città quanto di contado; ma ancora il vero modo di accrescere, & conservar le richezze. Con la tavola delle cose più notabili. In *Delle rime, et prose*, Ferrara, Simon Vasalini, 1585. (Also 1583. Eng. trans. see below. Here is described Tasso's experience on his second or third flight from Ferrara to Vercelli, after the middle of October, 1578.)

800. ————— (Eng. trans.). The householders philosophie. Wherein is perfectly and profitably described, the true oeconomica and forme of housekeeping. With a table added thereunto of all the notable thinges therein contained. First written in Italian by that excellent orator and poet Signior Torquato Tasso, and now translated by T[homas] K[yd]. Whereunto is anexed a dairie booke for all good huswives. London, by F. C. for Thomas Hacket, 1588.

801. ————— Stanze inédite . . . in lode delle donne. (Pub. 1810 with Pazzi's verses to the opposite effect, exactly duplicating the stanza form and rhymes. Written when Tasso was very young.)

802. Les tenebres de mariage. Rouen, Abraham Cousturier. (Printer's dates, 1582–1628. Verse.)

803. TERRACINA, LAURA. Discorso sopra tutti li primi canti d'Orlando Furioso fatti per La Signora Laura Terracina. Vinetia, Gabriel Giolito, 1550. (Also 1564; 1565; 1613. Verse.)

804. THIERRY, JOHANNES. Speculum impudicarum mulierum per Jo. Thierry jurium doctorem minimum ad vitiorum suffocationem compilatum. Rome?, in calcographia honesti viri Marcelli Silber alias Franck, 1523.

805. ‡ THOMAGIN, GIOVANNI DAVID. Dell' eccellentia de l' huomo sopra quella de la donna libri tre compositione dello eccellente jurisconsulto M. Giovanni David Thomagin ridotta in tre dialoghi. Venetia, Giovanni Varisco, e Compagni, 1565.

806. TILLIER, FRANÇOIS. Le premier et second livre du Philogamie ou amy des nopces. A Monsieur. Par François Tillier, Tourangeois. Paris, pour Jean Poupy, 1578.

807. TILNEY, EDMUNDE. The flower of friendship. A briefe and pleasaunt

discourse of duties in mariage. London, Henry Denham, 1568. (Also 1571; 1577. Seems to be taken in part at least from Lujan.)

808. TIRAQUEAU, ANDRÉ. Andreae Tiraquelli Fontiniacensis judicis ex commentariis in Pictonum consuetudines sectio de legibus connubialibus: diligenter recognita & tersa erasis videlicet spurcitiis nuper per dolum fraudemque insertis. Vaenemdatur rursus in aedibus Ascensianis, 1515. (Also 1513; 1524; 1546. Considered antagonistic to women. See Bouchard for answer.)

809. ————— De nobilitate et jure primogeniorum, tertia hac, eademque postrema editione, ab autore ipso diligentissime recogniti, & tertia amplius parte locupletati. Lugduni, apud Guliel. Rovillium, 1566. (See ch. XV and XVIII on nobility as it concerns women.)

810. ‡TIRON, ANTOINE. Recueil de plusieurs plaisantes nouvelles, apophthegmes & recreations diverses. Anvers, Henry Heyndrick, 1578. (Du Verdier.)

TOFTE, ROBERT. See Varchi, Blazon of jealousie.

811. TOMMASINO DI CIRCLARIA. Der Wälsche Gast des Thomasin von Zirclaria. Zum ersten Mal herausgegeben mit sprachlichen und geschichtlichen Anmerkungen von Dr. Heinr. Rüchert. Quedlinberg & Leipzig, 1852. (For article and summary with some extracts see *Early German courtesy-books*, Eugene Oswald, *E. E. T. S.*, Ex. Ser. VIII, 1869, pp. 77–140. Rules of courtesy of first book published with trans. into modern German by Max Müller, *The German Classics*, Longman, 1864, pp. 212 ff., notice of Tommasino, p. xvii.)

812. TORELLI, POMPONIO. Trattato del debito del cavalliero, di Pomponio Torelli, Conte di Montechiarugolo, nell' Academia de' Signori Innominati di Parma, Il Perduto. Parma, Erasmo Viotti, 1596. (Beauty that is appropriate to men, ff. 91a–99; love and music as honest recreations, ff. 171–180.)

813. TORRELLAS, PEDRO DE. Mal dezir de mugeres. In Castillo, *Cancionero*, 1535.

814. Tractatus de bonitate et malitia mulierum. Pub. Paul Heyse, *Romanische inedita auf italiänischen Bibliotheken*, Berlin, 1856, pp. 63–71.

815. (Traité). Le traicte di lutilite et honneste de mariage. Et sil est licite aux prestres de soy marier. Argentine, Jehan Prüss, 1527.

816. ————— Cy commence le traittie intitule les evangiles des quenoilles faittes a lonneur & exancement des dames. (Two undated editions. Bib. Nat. Rés. Ye. 93, Rés. Y² 919. Satire on women.)

817. ————— Cy commence un petit traittie intitule labuse en court fait nagaires et compose par treshault et trespuissant prince rene roy de secile de naples et de iherusalem. Bruges, Cobard Mansion. (How to live well in court.)

818. (Treatise). ‡Here begynneth a lyttell treatyse cleped la conusaunce damours. London, R. Pynson.

819. ————— Here foloweth a lytell treatyse of the beaute of women, newly translated out of Frenshe into Englyshe. London, R. Fawkes, 1525? (Also 1540?)

820. ‡————— A neawe treatys: as concernynge the excellency of the nedle worcke spânisshe stitche and weavynge in the frame, very necessary to al theym wiche desyre the perfect knowledge of seamstry, quiltinge and brodry worke, conteinynge a CXXXVIII figures or tables, so playnli made & set out in portrature, the whiche is difficyll; and nat only for craftsmen but also for gentlewomen & yonge damosels that therein may obtayne greater conynge delyte and pleasure. Antwerp, Willem Vorsterman. (Dates of Vorsterman, 1514–1542.)

821. ‡Le triomphe des dames, par P. D. B. Rouen, Osmont, 1599.

822. ‡Trissino, Giovanni Giorgio. La consolation des mal mariez par quatrains. Lyon, Leonard Odet, 1583. (Du Verdier says a trans. from Trissino by Claude Mermet. See Mermet, *Le temps passe.*)

823. ————— Epistola del Trissino de la vita, che dee tenere una donna vedova. Roma, Lodovico de gli Arrighi Vincentino, e Lautitio Perugino, 1524.

824. ————— I ritratti del Trissino. Roma, Lodovico de gli Arrighi Vincentino e Lautitio Perugino, 1524. (Also 1531; 1729. Dialogue on beauties of women, inside and out. Bembo chief speaker.)

825. Trotto, Bernardo. Dialoghi del matrimonio, e vita vedovile del signor C. A. Bernardo Trotto. Turino, Francesco Dolce, 1578. (Also 1580; 1583.)

826. Tuke, Thomas. A treatise against painting and tincturing of men and women: against murther and poysoning: pride and ambition: adulterie and witchcraft. And the roote of all these, disobedience to the ministery of the word. Whereunto is added the picture of a picture, or, the character of a painted woman. By Thomas Tuke, minister of Gods Word at Saint Giles in the Fields. London, Tho. Creed, 1616.

827. Tunstall, Cuthbert. Cuthberti Tonstalli in laudem matrimonii oratio habita in sponsalibus Mariae Potentissimi regis Angliae Henrici octavi filiae/et Francisci Christianissimi Francorum regis primogeniti. Londini, per Richardum Pynson, 1518. (Also 1519.)

828. ‡Twill, D. Asylum veneris. 1616.

829. Tyler, Margaret. The mirror of princely deedes and knighthood, 1599–1583–1601. (Trans. of Diego Ortuñez de Calahorra, *Espejo de principes y cavalleros.* See ded. on women as writers.)

830. Tyndale, William. The obedience of a Christen man, and how Christen rulers ought to governe, wherein also (if thou marke dili-

gently) thou shalt find eyes to perceave the craftie conveyaunce of old jugglers. Set forth by William Tyndale. 1528. Parker Society, 1848. (Vol. 48, pp. 171–172.)

831. ULLOA, ALFONSO DE. Processo de cartas de amores que entre dos amantes passaron; con una carta del author para un amigo suyo pidiendole consuelo, y una quexa y aviso contra amor. Assimesmo hay eneste libro otras excellentissimas cartas que allende de su dulce y pulido estilo, estan escriptas en reffranes traydos a proposito. Y al cabo se hallara un dialogo muy sabroso que habla de las mugeres. Todo con diligentia nuevamente corregido. Venetia, Gabriel Giolito, 1553. (Subtitles: 2nd, *Cartas de reffranes de Blasco de Garay con otras de nuevo annadides;* 3rd, *Dialogo que habla delas condiciones delas mugeres. Son interlocutores Alethio que dize mal de mugeres: y Fileno que las defiende. Va nuevamente corregido de algunas cosas mal sonantes: que en otras impressiones solian andar.* See Garay.)

832. VALERIO, AGOSTINO, CARDINAL. Instruttione delle donne maritate. Venetia, Bolognino Zaltino, 1575. Rep. 1744. (Also 1577. In *Augustini Valerii . . . opusculum numquam antehac editum de cautione adhibenda in edendis libris,* . . . Patavia, 1719, appears an *Index opusculorum quae scripsit Augustinus Valerius* with the following items: *LVI, De virginitate liber, ad Donatam sororem, quae apud Jo. Aloysium fratrem suum cum laude vivabat; LVII, De institutione, et recta disciplina feminarum quae matrimonio junctae sunt, ad Laura sororem, quae Georgio Gradenico, erudito viro, et praesenti Senatori, nupserat; LVIII, De viduitate, ad Hadrianani Contarenam juniorem, viduam.* All in Italian.)

833. ‡VANDENBUSCHE, ALEXANDRE. Recueil des dames illustres en vertu, ensemble un dialogue de l'amour honneste. Paris, Nicolas Bonfons, 1576. (Du Verdier.)

834. VARCHI, BENEDETTO. Della bellezza, e della grazia. In *Lezzioni,* 1590.

835. ———— Della pittura d'amore. Lezione una. Dichiarazione sopra que' versi del Trionfo d'amore, i quali incominciano: Quattro destrier via più che neve ecc., letto nello studio Fiorentino. In *Opere,* Milano, s.d., vol. 2, pp. 489–496.

836. ———— Lezzione di M. Benedetto Varchi, sopra il sonetto di M. Francesco Petrarca, il quale incomincia. "S'amor non è, che dunque è qual ch' io sento?" Letta da lui publicamente nell' Accademia Fiorentina, la terza Domenica di Quaresima. L'anno 1553. In *Lezzioni,* 1590.

837. ———— Lezzione di M. Bendetto Varchi sopra un sonetto del molto Reverendo, & virtuosissimo Mons. M. Giovanni della Casa, dove si tratta della gelosia. Con alcune quistioni dal medesimo authore nuovamente aggiunte. Lione, Gulielmo Rovillio, 1560. (Ded. dated 1550. Also 1545; 1590. Eng. trans. see below. Sonnet—"Cura, che di

timor ti nutri e cresci." Read many years before in Padua, before
Academia della infiammatti, see ded.)

838. ————— (Eng. trans.). The blason of jealousie. A subject not
written of by any heretofore. First written in Italian, by that learned
gentleman Benedetto Varchi . . . and translated into English, with
speciall notes upon the same; by R[obert] T[ofte] Gentleman. London,
by T. S. for John Busbie, 1615.

839. ————— Lezzioni sul Petrarca. I. Sulle tre canzoni degli occhi.
Lezioni otto. Lezione prima letta privatamente nello studio Fiorentino
il quarto Giovedì d'Aprile 1545. In *Opere*, Milan, vol. 2, pp. 439–486.

840. ————— La seconda parte delle lezzioni di M. Benedetto Varchi
nella quale si contengono cinque lezzioni d'amore, lette da lui publicamente nell' Accademia di Fiorenza, e di Padova. Nuovamente stampate. Fiorenza, I Giunti, 1561. (Also 1566; 1590; 1659.)

841. ————— Sopra sette dubbi d'amore. Lezione una. Letta publicamente nell' Accademia Fiorentina, 1554. In *Opere*, Milano, vol. 2, pp.
525–531.

842. ————— Sur un sonetto del Bembo. Leziona una. 1540. In *Opere*,
Milano, vol. 2, pp. 562–568. (Sonnet: "A questa fredda tema, a questo
ardente.")

843. VASOLO, SCIPIONE. La gloriosa eccellenza delle donne, e d'amore. . . .
Opera del Capitan Scipione Vasolo. Fiorenza, Giorgio Marescotti,
1573.

844. VAUGHAN, ROBERT. A dyalogue defensyve for women/agaynst maly-
cyous detractoures. London, Robert Myer, 1542.

845. VAUGHAN, WILLIAM. The golden-grove, moralized in three bookes:
a worke very necessary for all such, as would know how to governe
themselves, their houses, or their country. Made by W. Vaughan,
Master of Artes, and graduate in the civill law. The second edition,
now lately reviewed and enlarged by the author. London, Simon
Stafford, 1608. (Also 1600. See bk. II, marriage.)

846. VAUQUELIN DE LA FRESNAYE JEAN (1530–1607). Les diverses poesies
du Sieur de la Fresnaie Vauquelin. Caen, Charles Macé, 1612. (See
Satyres francoises, pp. 347–367 on marriage.)

847. ‡VAVASSORE, GIO. ANDREA. Essemplario novo di più di cento variate
mostre di qualunque sorte bellissime per cusire intitolato: Fontana
degli essempli. Presso Vavassore detto Guadagnino. Venezia, 1550.

848. ‡————— Opera nuova universale intitulata Coronna di racammi
dove le venerande donne e fanciulle trovarono di varie opere per far
colari di camisiola, etinelle di cuscini, shufioni cendali di più sorte, et
molte opere per recamatore, di 40 tavole incise 1546. Facsimile,
Venezia, 1878.

849. VECELLIO, CES. Corona delle nobile e virtuose donne, libri quattro nei

quali si mostra in 114 disegni tutte le sorti di mostre, di punti tagliati di fregi, merli, ecc. 1600. Facsimile, Venezia, 1876. (Pt. V pub. 1620 under title *Ornamento nobile*, facsimile 1876.)

850. VEGIO, MAFFEO. Maphei Vegii patria Laudensis divinarum scripturarum cum primis peritissimi/oratoris item & poete celeberrimi Martini pape quinti Datarii. De educatione liberorum et eorum claris moribus libri sex. Elegantia non minus quam sententie gravitate redolentes. Primus autem liber continet XX capitula. Secundus XX. Tertius XV. Quartus XIII. Quintus IV. Sextus vero & ultimus VI. Dyalogus veritatis insuper adjungitur eiusdem Maphei vegii & Phalalithis ad Eustachium fratrem. Parisiis, per magistrum Bertholdum Rembolt/& Johannem Waterloes, 1511. (Also 1491; 1508; 1513. French trans. 1513. See lib. III, cap. XII, XIII, XIV, on the education of girls after the pattern of Santa Monica.)

851. VERMIGLI, PIETRO. A briefe treatise, concerning the use and abuse of dauncing. Collected oute of the learned workes of the most excellent Devine Doctour, Peter Martyr, by Maister Rob. Massonius: and translated into English by I. K. London, John Jugge, 1580?

852. VIDA, GIROLAMO. Il Sileno dialogo di Hieronimo Vida Justinopolitano. Nelquale si discorre della felicità de' mortali, & si conclude, che tra tutte le cose di questo mondo l'amante fruisca solo la vera, & perfetta beatitudine humana. Insieme con le sue rime, & conclusioni amorose. Et con l'interpretatione del Sig. Ottonello de' Belli Justinopolitano sopra il medesimo dialogo. Vicenza, Giorgio Greco, ad instanza di Alciato de' Alciati, & Pietro Bertelli, 1589.

853. ‡———— Dubii amorosi di Gieronimo Vida justinopolitani.... Venetia, Gio. Battista Vaglierino, 1636.

854. VIERI, FRANCESCO DE'. Discorsi di M. Francesco de' Vieri, detto Il Verino Secondo, Cittadino Fiorentino. Delle maravigliose opere di Pratolino, & d'amore. Firenze, Giorgio Marescotti, 1586. (Also 1587.)

855. ———— Discorso delle bellezze, fatto da M. Francesco de' Vieri citadino Fiorentino, cognominato il secondo Verino. E recitato da esso nell' Academia de gli Suegliati in Pisa, al Consolato del Sig. Cammillo Berzighelli. Firenze, Sermartelli, 1588.

856. ———— Discorso della grandezza, et felice fortuna d'una gentilissima, & graziosiss. donna; qual fù M. Laura, di M. Francesco de' Vieri.... Fiorenza, Giorgio Marescotti, 1580.

857. ———— Lezzione di M. Francesco de' Vieri Fiorentino, detto il Verino Secondo. Per recitarla nell' Accademia Fiorentina, nel consulato di M. Federigo Strozzi l'anno 1580. Dove si ragiona delle idee, et delle bellezze.... Fiorenza, Giorgio Marescotti, 1581. (The beauties of Laura.)

858. VIGOUREUX, LE SIEUR, CAPITAINE DU CHASTEAU DE BRYE-COMTE-

ROBERT. La defense des femmes, contre l'alphabet de leur pretendue malice & imperfection. Par le Sieur Vigoureux, Capitaine du Chasteau de Brye Comte-Robert. Paris, Pierre Chevalier, 1617. (See Olivier. Bib. Nat. Rés. 24100.)

859. VILLENA, ENRIQUE DE ARAGON, MARQUES DE. Los doze trabajos de ercules copilados por don enrrique de villena. Aplicolos alos doze estados del mundo. Es asaber: estado de principe: estado de perlado: estado de cavallero: estado de religioso: estado de cibdadano: estado de mercader: estado de labrador: estado de oficial: estado de maestro: estado de discipulo: estado de solitario: estado de mujer. Burgos, Juan de burgos, 1499. (Also 1482; 1502. In the last, Alcmena is held up as a model of virtue for women.)

860. VINCENT DE BEAUVAIS. Tractatum de eruditione filiorum regalium venerabilis patris Vincentii beluacensis. Basilea, I. de Amerbach, 1481. (See cap. XXXVII, XLII–LI for the bringing up of girls— virtues, duties in marriage, widowed state, virginity.)

861. VINCENZO DA BOLOGNA. Preclara operetta dello ornato delle donne, et de alquante cose de conscienza circa el matrimonio. Bologna, 1530?

862. VITI, NICCOLAO. Lezione della gelosia letta nella Academia Fiorentina. Orvieto, Baldo Salviami, 1585.

VITO DI GOZZI. See Gozzi.

863. VIVA, GUITTONE DEL (Guittone d'Arezzo). Sonetti. In Rime di diversi antichi autori toscani in dieci libri raccolte. Di Dante Alaghieri lib. IIII. Di M. Cino da Pistoia libro I. Di Guido Cavalcanti libro I. Di Dante da Maiano libro I. Di Fra Guittone d'Arezzo libro I. Di diverse canzone e sonetti senza nome d'autore libro I. Vinegia, Jo. Antonio, e Fratelli da Sabio, 1532. (Twenty-four sonnets form a kind of art of love. Mentioned by Equicola.)

864. VIVES, JUAN LUIS. Joannis Lodovici Vivis Valentini de institutione feminae Christianae, ad inclytam d. Catharinam Hispanam, Angliae reginam, libri tres. Ab autore ipso recogniti, aucti, & reconcinnati, unà cum rerum ac verborum locupletissimo indice. Basileae, per Robertum Winter, 1538. (Also, alone or with other works, 1523; 1540; 1541; 1614; 1650. Eng. trans. see below. French trans. 1542; 1543; 1545—4 times; 1549, 1579—3 times; 1580; 1587; 1614. Germ. trans. 1544; 1566. Ital. trans. 1546; 1561. Span. trans. 1528; 1529; 1530; 1539; 1545; 1555; 1584; 1792; 1793.)

65. ———— (Eng. trans.). A very frutefull and pleasant boke called the instruction of a Christen woman/made fyrst in Laten/and dedicated unto the quenes good grace/by the right famous clerke mayster Lewes Vives/and turned out of Laten into Englysshe by Rycharde Hyrd. Which boke who so redeth diligently shall have knowledge of many thinges/wherin he shal take great pleasure/and specially

women shall take great commodyte and frute towarde thencreace of vertue & good maners. London, Thomas Berthelet, 1540. (Also 1529?; 1541; 1547; 1557; 1585; 1592.)

866. —————— Joannis Ludovici Vivis Valentini de officio mariti liber unus. De institutione foeminae Christianae libri tres. De ingenuorum adolescentum ac puellarum institutione libri duo. Omnes ab autore ipso recogniti, aucti ac reconcinnati, unà cum rerum ac verborum locupletissimo indice. Basileae. (Also *De officio mariti*, alone or with other works, 1529; 1538; 1540; 1541; 1614. Eng. trans. see below. French trans. with *De institutione* 1542; 1543; 1545—4 times; 1549; 1579—3 times; 1580; 1614. Germ trans. 1566. Ital. trans. 1546; 1561; 1580.)

867. —————— (Eng. trans.). The office and duetie of an husband, made by the excellent philosopher Lodovicus Vives, and translated into Englyshe by Thomas Paynell. London, John Cawood, 1553?

868. —————— De ratione studii puerilis. Published with *De officio mariti* above under title *De ingenuorum adolescentium ac puellarum institutione libri duo*. (Also under various other titles with various works, 1524; 1527; 1531; 1532; 1536; 1537; 1538; 1539; 1540; 1541; 1543; 1544; 1545; 1546; 1547; 1551; 1555; 1556; 1562; 1572; 1586; 1593; 1594; 1600; 1614; 1618; 1619; 1640; 1644; 1670; 1692. Lib. II, advice addressed to Queen Catherine, Oxford, Oct. 2, 1523, for the use of the tutor of her daughter Mary.)

869. W., A. A booke of cookerie. Verie necessarie for all such as delight therein. Gathered by A. W. And nowe newly enlarged, with the serving in of the table. And the proper sauces to each dish of meate convenient. London, Edward Allde, 1594. (Also 1584; 1587; 1591.)

870. ‡W., R. Order of matrimony. London, 1580.

871. Watriquet de Couvin. Li mireoirs as dames. 1324. (Rep. 1868, *Dits de Watriquet de Couvin.*)

872. ‡Whately, William. A bride-bush. 1619. (Also 1623.)

873. Whetstone, George. An heptameron of civill discourses. Containing: the Christmasse exercise of sundrie well courted gentlemen and gentlewomen. In whose behaviours, the better sort, may see, a representation of their own vertues: and the inferiour, may learne such rules of civil government, as wil rase out the blemish of their basenesse: wherin, is renowned, the vertues, of a most honourable and brave mynded gentleman. And herein, also, [as it were in a mirror] the unmaried may see the defectes which eclipse the glorie of mariage: and the wel maried, as in a table of housholde lawes, may cull out needefull preceptes to establysh their good fortune. A worke, intercoursed with civyll pleasure, to reave tediousnesse from the reader: and garnished with morall noates to make it profitable, to the regarder. The reporte,

of George Whetstone, Gent. London, Richard Jones, 1582. (Also 1593, with title *Aurelia*.)

874. The widdowes treasure. Plentifully furnished with sundry precious and approved secrets in phisicke and chirurgery, for the health and pleasure of mankinde. Heereunto are adjoyned, sundry prittie practises and conclusions of cookerie, with many profitable and wholsome medicines, for sundrie diseases in cattell. London, J. Roberts for Edward White, 1595. ("To the courteous reader"—written not many years before for the private use of a gentlewoman in the country.)

875. WIER, JOHANN. De praestigiis daemonum, et incantationibus & veneficiis, libri V. recogniti, & valde aucti. Authore Joanne Wiero Graviano, illustrissimi Ducis Cliviae, Juliae, etc. medico. Praeter locupletem accessionis cumulum, ut lectoris memoriae consuleretur, in capita quoque jam sectus est quilibet liber: cuius argumentum in praefatione comperies. Accessit index amplissimus. Basileae, per Joannem Oporium, 1564. (Also 1563; 1566; 1568; 1577; 1583. French trans. by Grévin, 1567, 1569, see there cap. 52, 53; another trans. 1579. Germ. trans. 1575; 1586. See *Liber secundus*, cap. 46. *Memoranda historia de malefica muliere, quae trium virorum capita palam ferire voluit;* cap. 47. *De philtris, hippomanes, & reliquis amatoriis quisquiliis;* cap. 48, *Quòd amatoria pocula, hippomanes, & quaecunque id genus alia, citius furorem inducant, quàm amorem concilient.*)

876. Die Winsbekin. Leipzig. 1845. (13th cent. Advice of the Lady of Winsbeke to her daughter.)

877. ‡Women's worth defended. 1599.

878. WYCLIF, JOHN. Of weddid men and wifis and of here children also. (Attributed to Wyclif, included by Arnold in *Select English Works of John Wyclif*, 1869–1871, vol. 3, pp. 188–201.)

879. XIMENEZ, FRANCESCH. Le libre de les dones. Barcelone, 1495. (Also 1542, trans. into Castilian from Catalan.)

880. ZAMPESCHI, BRUNORO. L'innamorato dialogo del S. Brunoro Zampeschi. Bologna, Giovanni Rossi, 1565.

881. ZARRABINI, ONOFRIO. Della nobilta civile; et Christiana libri quattro. Et de gli stati verginale, maritate, et vedovile; del M. R. D. Onofrio Zarrabini da Cotignola. Canonico Regolare della Congregatione del Salvatore, dell' ordine di S. Agostino. Venetia, Francesco de' Franceschi Senese, 1586.

882. ZINANO, GABRIELE. L'amante, overo sollevatione dalla bellezza dell' amata alla bellezza di Dio. Reggio, Hercoliano Bartholi, 1591? (Also 1627.)

883. ———— L'amante secondo. Over l'arte di conoscere gli adulatori. Di Gabriele Zinano. Parma, Erasmo Viotto, 1591. (Contains also: *Conclusioni amorose; Delle cagioni naturali d'amore.*)

884. ——————— L'amata, overo della virtù heroica. Di Gabriele Zinano. Reggio, Hercoliano Bartholi, 1591.

885. ——————— L'amata seconda. Over delle cagioni naturali d'amore. Parma, E. Viotto, 1591.

886. ——————— L'amico, over del sospiro. Di Gabriele Zinano. Reggio, Hercoliano Bartholi, 1591. (Kinds, causes, and significance of sighs.)

887. ——————— Conclusioni amorose. Di Gabriele Zinano. . . . Parma, E. Viotti, 1591.

888. ZOPPINO (Nicolo d'Aristotile). Esemplario di lavori dove le tenere fanciulle et altre donne nobile potranno facilemente imparare il modo di lavorare, cusire, reccamare, finalemente far tutte quelle gentilezze et lodevili opere le quali po fare ma donna virtuosa con laco in mano, con li suoi compassi et misure. Venezia, 1530. Facsimile Venezia, 1878. (Also 1529.)

889. ——————— Gli universali dei belli recami antichi e moderni ne i quali un pellegrino ingegno, si di huomo come di donna potrà in questa nostra età con l'ago virtuosamente esercitarsi. Non anchora da alcuni altri dati in luce. Per Nicolò d'Aristotile detto Zoppino. Venezia, 1537. Facsimile Venezia, 1877.

890. ZOPPIO, MELCHIORRE. Psafone trattato damore del Caliginoso Gelato Il S. Melchiorre Zoppio, nel quale secondo i poeti, e filosofi, ethnici, e profani scrittori, platonici, & altri, si discorre sopra le principali consideratione occorrenti nella materia dell' amore humano, ragionevole, e civile. In libro non fui fatto da vecchio, ne per vecchi. Bologna, Sebastiano Bonomi, 1617. (Written thirty years before.)

891. ZUCCOLO, VITALE. Discorsi del molto R. Padre D. Vitale Zuccolo sopra le cinquante conclusioni del Sig. Torquato Tasso. Di nuovo dati in luce dal Sig. Camillo Abbioso. Bergamo, Comino Ventura, 1588. (Love.)

SUPPLEMENTARY BIBLIOGRAPHICAL LIST FOR
THE GENTLEMAN

1. ABARCA, JUAN FERNANDES. Discorso de las partes y calidades con que se forma un buen secretario, con catorze capitulos, que debe guardar para su entereza con una recopilacion de el numero que ay de cartas misibas para su exercicio. Y de los generos que son, y las que tocan a cada uno. Y un tratado, de las partes quean de tener los criados, que an de servir en las casas de los señores. Compuesto por Juan Fernandes Abarca, . . . dirigido a don Juan de Mendoza, . . . Lisboa, P. Craesbeeck, 1618.

2. ACOSTA, CHRISTOVAL. Tratado en contra y pro de la vida solitaria, con otros dos tratados, uno de la religion y religioso, otro contra los hom-

bres que mal viven . . . por Christoval a Costa. . . . Venetia, G. Cornetti, 1592.

3. ADAM, NATHANAËL. Le secretaire françois. Par Nathanaël Adam, Secretaire de Madame de Mortemart. Derniere edition, reveuuë corigée & de beaucoup augmentée. Paris, Anthoine du Brueil, 1616. (Model letters for various occasions, chiefly personal, preceded by a chapter on the honorable office of secretary and general requirements. At the end a section of *Lettres amoureuses*.)

4. ALBERGATI, FABIO. Dei discorsi politici di Fabio Albergati libri cinque, nei quali viene riprobata la doctrina politica di Gio. Bodino, e difesa quella d'Aristotile . . . Roma, L. Zanetti, 1602. (Also 1603; 1664.)

5. ————— Le morali del sig. Fabio Albergati. . . . Bologna, V. Benacci, 1627. (Also 1664.)

6. ————— La republica regia del sig. Fabio Albergati. . . . Bologna, V. Benacci, 1627. (Also 1664.)

7. ALBERTI, LEON BATTISTA. Cena di famiglia. *Opere volgari*, Firenze, 1844. (Vol. I, pp. 165–183; three brothers, Francesco, Leon Battista, and Matteo explain on what the greatness of their family rests— solidarity, honest upbringing, etc.)

8. ALBERTI, ROMANO. Trattato della nobilta della pittura . . . da Romano Alberti, . . . Roma, F. Zannetti, 1585.

9. ALDANA, COSME DE. Discorso contro il volgo . . . dell' illustre sig. Cosimo Aldana, . . . Fiorenza, G. Marescotti, 1578.

10. ALDOBRANDINI, PIETRO. De perfecto principe . . . apophthegmata Card. P. Aldobrandini . . . ab Henrico Farnesio, . . . in librum unum congesta, . . . Ticini, ex typ. A. Viani, 1600. (Also 1608, see Sacchi.)

11. ALESMIUS, FRANCISCUS. Verae nobilitatis controversia, autore Francisco Alesmio, . . . Oratio Claudio Ptholomei, . . . ad Henricum . . . secundum, . . . latina facta, autore eodem Alesmio. Dialogus de pacis commodo et calamitate belli . . . Burdigalae, apud F. Morpanium, 1557.

12. ALLEGRI, FRANCESCO DEGLI. Tractato nobilissimo della prudentia et justitia laqual debba havere chadanno justo signore. . . . Venetia, Melchior Sessa, 1508.

13. ALONSO DE CARTAGNA. Doctrinal de los cavalleros, por don Alonso de Cartajena, obispo de Burgos. Burgos, Fadrique Aleman, 1487.

14. AMBOISE, MICHEL D'. Le guidon des gens de guerre ouquel est contenu l'art de scavoir mener et conduyre gens de cheval, et de pied, assieger villes, les assaillir, et deffendre, faire rampars, bastillons, trenchées, batailles, bataillons, scoyadrons, entreprises, courses, et autres choses appartenantes à la guerre, utile et necessaire à tous capitaines, et autres desirans suyvre le mestier des armes. Faict et composé par

Michel D'amboise Escuyer, seigneur de Chevillon, dict l'Esclave fortuné. Paris, Galliot du Pré, 1543.

15. AMOREVOLI, BATTISTA. Desio d'honore et zelo d'amicitia, abbatimento nuovo successo in Parigi, tra sei illustri cavalieri de la corte, i di 26 d'Aprile 1578, composto per M. Battista Amorevoli . . . Parigi, 1578.

16. ANGLEBERME, JEAN PYRRHUS D'. Institutio boni magistratus, ubi ad jurisprudentiam nonnulla maxime conducentia. Elegans interpretatio L. Contractus, de Regu. jur. ff. tota poene contractuum causa agitur. Author Pyrrhus Anglebermeus . . . Aureliae, in aedibus J. Hoys et ejus generi.

ANHALT. See Christian II.

17. ANTONIUS, PETRUS, FINARIENSIS. De dignitate principum liber. Heidelbergae, 1602.

18. AQUILAR, PEDRO DE. Tratado de la cavalleria de la gineta. Malaga, I. Rene, 1600.

19. ARBUSANUS, AURELIUS. Dialogus de solitudine. Venetiis, 1545.

20. ARRIGHI, PAOLO. Perutilis tractatus de bonitate principis vel uniuscujusque dominantis regnis, provinciis et civitatibus necnon familiis et suae propriae vitae F. Pauli Arrighii, . . . Florentiae, in off. G. Marescoti, 1578.

21. ATANAGI, DIONIGI. Ragionamento di M. Dionigi Atanagi de la eccellentia et perfettion de la historia. Venetia, D. et C. de' Nicolini, 1559.

22. AUDIGUIER, VITAL D', SIEUR DE LA MÉNOR. Le vray et ancien usage des duels confirmé par l'exemple des plus illustres combats et deffys qui se soient faits en la chrestienté . . . par le sieur d'Audiguier. Paris, P. Billaine, 1617.

23. AUGE, DANIEL D'. Deux dialogues de l'invention poetique, de la vraye cognoissance de l'histoire, de l'art oratoire, et de la fiction de la fable: tres utiles à un chascun désirant bien faire, dire et delibérer, ainsi qu' en on traicté les anciens, par Daniel d'Auge. Paris, R. Breton, 1560.

24. AUGER, EMOND. Le pédagogue d'armes, pour instruire un prince chrétien à bien entreprendre et heureusement achever une bonne guerre, pour estre victorieux de tous ennemis de son estat et de l'eglise catholique, dedié au Roy par M. Emond, de la Compagnie de Jesus. Paris, J. Nivelle, 1568.

25. AUGUSTINO DA SIENA. Opera del reverendo Padre Don Augustino da Sciena, . . . nella quale s'insegna a scrivere varie sorti di lettere, tanto cancellaresche quanto mercantesche, con varie sorti di lettere todesche, con diverse sorti di alphabetti bellissimi et con alcune dechiarationi del temperar della penna et una recetta per far l'inchiostro negrissimo . . . Venetia, F. de Tomaso di Salo, 1573.

26. BADUEL, CLAUDE. De officio et munere eorum qui juventutem eru-

diendam suscipiunt, epistola Claudii Baduelli, . . . Lugduni, apud S. Gryphium, 1544.

27. BAÏF, JEAN-ANTOINE DE. Epistre au Roy, sous le nom de la Royne sa mère, pour l'instruction d'un bon roy, par J. Antoine de Baif. Paris, F. Morel, 1575.

28. BAIRO, PIETRO. Lixoperita perpetue questionis et annexorum solutio. De nobilitate facultatum per terminos utriusque facultatis, utrum medicina et philosophia sint nobiliores utroque jure, scilicet civili et canonico, et qui doctores earumdem facultatum nobiliores ac digniores existant, quomodove incedere ac invicem precedere debeant. Taurini, per magistrum Franciscum de Sylva, 1512.

29. BALMFORD, JAMES. A shorte and plaine dialogue concerning the unlawfulness of playing at cards or tables, or any other game consisting in chance, . . . London, Richard Boile, 1593. (Also 1623.)

30. BALSAC, ROBERT DE. La nef des princes et des batailles de noblesse, avec aultres enseignemens utilz et profitables à toutes manières de gens pour congnoistre à bien vivre et mourir dediqués et envoyés à divers prelas et seigneurs ainsi qu'on pourra trouver cy après, composés par noble et puissant Robert de Balsat. . . . Lyon, 1502.

31. BARET, MICHAEL. An hipponomie or the vineyard of horsemanship. Wherein is plainely set forth how to apply both hunting and running horses to the true grounds of this art, both in trayning, dieting and riding. Being more truely purged from errors then any heretofore published hath beene. By Michael Baret Practitioner in the same art. London, George Eld, 1618.

32. BARON, STEPHEN. Incipit tractatulus eiusdem venerandi patris de regimine principum ad serenissimum regem anglie henricum octavum.

33. BARRES, JOANO DE. Aphorismos y exemplos politicos y militares, sacados de la primera decada de Juan de Barros, . . . Lisboa, P. Craesbeeck, 1621.

34. BEAUPOIL DE SAINTE-AULAIRE DE LA RENODIE, FRANÇOIS DE. Bref discours sur la louange de la chasse . . . réimprimée sur l'édition originale de 1619. Louviers, 1888.

35. BELLARMINO, ROBERTO, SAINT. De officio principis christiani libri tres, auctore Roberto S.R.E. card. Bellarmino, . . . Romae, B. Zannetti, 1619. (French trans. 1625. Ital. trans. 1620.)

36. BELLEFOREST, FRANÇOIS DE. Harangues militaires et concions de princes, capitaines, ambassadeurs et autres, manians tant que guerre que les affaires d'estat . . . recueillies et faites françoises par François de Belle-Forest,. . . reveu, corrigé, augmenté et enrichi de plusieurs belles harangues de nostre temps pour la seconde édition. Paris, P. Ménier, 1588. (Also 1595.)

37. BELLUGA, PETRUS. Speculum principum ac justitiae . . . Petri Bellugae, quo regalium amortizationum, fiscalium usurarum . . . omnesque quotidianae materiae, nusquam antea ita enucleatae, irrefragabiliter deciduntur, cum repertorio alphabetico . . . Richardi Sancti Martini . . . Parisiis, vaenundatur a G. Pratensi, 1530.

38. BENOIST, RENE. Instruction pour tous estats, etc. Paris, Nicolas Chesneau, 1564. (Du Verdier.)

39. BERLAYMONT, PHILIPPUS DE. Paradisus puerorum, in quo primaevae honestatis totiusque pueritiae recte informatae reperiuntur exempla . . . per R. P. Philippum de Berlaymont, . . . Duaci, J. Bogardi, 1618.

40. BERNAERTS, JAN. Johannis Bernatii de utilitate legendae historiae libri duo. Antverpiae, ex officina Plantiniana, apud viduam et J. Moretum, 1593.

41. BERRETTARI, ELPIDIO. Elpidii Berrettarii . . . tractatus de risu. Florentiae, apud C. Juntam, 1603.

42. BETHUNE, PHILIPPE DE. Le conseiller d'estat; ou recueil des plus grandes considerations servans au maniement des affairs publiques. Divisé en trois parties. La I. contient les moyens d'establir un estat. La II. les moyens de la conserver. La III. les moyens de l'accroistre. Par un des anciens conseillers des Roys tres-chrestiens Henry IV. & Louys XIII. 1632. (Eng. trans. see below.)

43. ———— (Eng. trans.). The counsellor of estate. Contayning the greatest and most remarkeable considerations serving for the managing of publicke affairs. Divided into three parts. The first contaynes the meanes to settle an estate. The second, the meanes to preserve it. And the third, the meanes to encrease it. Written in French by one of the ancient counsellors to the most Christian Kings, Henry the Fourth, and Lewis the thirteenth. Translated by E. G. London, Nicholas Okes, 1634.

44. BEURER, JOHANN JACOB. Synopsis historiarum et methodus nova . . . auctore Joanne Jacobo Beurero, . . . Hanoviae, apud G. Antonium, 1594.

45. BEZ, FERRAND DE. Institution puerile, a Charles d'Alouville, Jean & Christophle de Thou freres, Christophle Bouguier, & Gaspar Viallet ses disciples. (Du Verdier. Verse.)

46. BIESIUS, NICOLAUS. Nicolai Biesii . . . de republica libri quatuor, quibus universa de moribus philosophia continetur . . . Antverpiae, apud M. Nutium, 1556. (Also 1564 with *Ejusdem oratio pro bonis litteris*.)

47. BILICERUS, MATHIAS. Diatriba politica gemina; prior, de conversatione civili, privata et publica (M. Bilicerus respondebat); altera, quomodo adolescentes, antequam ad academias ablegantur sint

praeparandi (G. Mendelius respondebat) . . . Editio secunda. Franco-furti, typ. W. Richteri, 1603.

48. BIONDO, MICHELANGELO. Ad christianissimum regem Galliae. De canibus et venatione libellus, authore Michaele Angelo Biondo, in quo omnia ad canes spectantia morbi et medicamina, continentur . . . Romae, apud A. Bladum, 1544.

49. ————— Michaelis Angeli Biondi Veneti speculum juventutis. Neopoli, per Mathiam Canze, 1534. (39 brief dialogues on the characteristics, faults, temptations, and proper behavior of youth.)

50. BIZZARI, PIETRO. Petri Bizzari varia opuscula, quorum indicem sequens pagina demonstrabit. Venetiis, Aldus, 1565. (De optimo principi, De bello & pace, etc.)

51. BODEGEMIUS, BARTHOLOMAEUS. De gloria libri quinque, de nobilitate civili et christiana libri totidem . . . Rothomagi, 1616. (Ed. Osorio, Hieronymo.)

52. BOFFLES, SIRE DE. Les douze vertus de noblesse, extrait du registre secret du sire de Boffles, seigneur de Souchez (Artois), au XVIe siècle, par le Cte Achmet d'Héricourt. Paris, 1863.

53. BONAVENTURA, FEDERICO. Della ragion di stato et della prudenza politica libri quatro di Federico Bonaventura, . . . Urbino, A. Corvini, 1623.

54. BONNER, EDMUND. An honest godlye instruction, and information for the tradyng and bringinge up of children, set furth by the Bishoppe of London. Commaundyng all scholemaisters and other teachers of youthe within his Diocese, that they neither teach, learne reade, or use anye other maner of ABC, Cathechisme or rudimentes, then this made for the first instruction of youthe. London, Robert Caly, 1555.

55. BONOURS, CHRISTOPHLE DE. Eugeniaretilogie, ou discours de la vraye noblesse, par Christophle de Bonours. Liège, L. Streel, 1616. (Also 1619.)

56. BORNITIUS, JACOBUS. Jacobi Bornitii, . . . Aerarium, sive tractatus politicus de aerario sacro, civili, militari, communi, et sacratiori . . . Francofurti, impensis G. Tampachii, 1612.

57. ————— Jacobi Bornitii, . . . tractatus duo. I. De majestate politica et summo imperio ejusque functionibus . . . II. De praemiis in republica decernendis . . . Lipsiae, apud H. Grosium seniorem et T. Schürerium, 1610.

58. BOTTRIGARO, HERCOLE. Il desiderio, overo de' concerti di varii strumenti musicali dialogo del m. ill. sig. cavaliere Hercole Bottrigaro, . . . Bologna, Y. B. Bellagamba, 1599.

59. BOUCHET, JEAN. Epistres morales & familieres du traverseur. Poictieurs, Jacques Bouchet, 1545. (Pt. II consists of epistles to kings, courtiers, gentlemen, soldiers, lawyers, subjects, etc.)

60. ———— Le panegyric du Chevallier sans reproche. Poictiers, Jacques Bouchet, 1527.

61. BOUGONYN, SIMON. L'espinette du jeune prince conquérant le royaulme de bonne renommée. Paris, pour Anthoyne Vérard, 1508. (Also 1514. Allegorical—advice on love, the three estates.)

62. ———— L'homme juste et l'homme mondain, nouvellement composé et imprimé à Paris. Paris, pour Anthoine Vérard, 1508.

63. BOURBON, NICOLAS. Nicolai Borbonii Vandoperani opusculum puerile ad pueros de moribus sive ΠΑΙΔΑΓΩΓΕΙΟΝ. Lugduni, apud Seb. Gryphium, 1536.

64. BOZIO, TOMMASO. De imperio virtutis sive imperia pendere a veris virtutibus, non a simulatis, libri duo adversus Machiavellum, auctore Thoma Bozio . . . Romae, ex typographia B. Bonfadini, 1593. (Also 1594.)

65. BRACCINI, GIULIO CESARE. Reppublica e politica cristiana. Venetia, 1619. (Trad. Giovanni di Santa Maria.)

66. BRAGACCIA, GASPARO. L'ambasciatore, del dottore Gasparo Bragaccia . . . libri sei, opera nella quale si hanno avvertimenti politici et morali per gli ambasciatori, et intorno quelle cose, che sogliono accadere all' ambasciare . . . Padova, F. Bolzetta, 1626. (Also 1627.)

67. BRANDT, JOHANN, D'ANVERS. Joannis Brantii . . . Senator, sive de perfecti et veri senatoris officio libri duo. Antverpiae, ex officina Plantiniana, 1633.

68. BRASSAVOLA, ANTONIO MUSA. Antonii Musae Brasavoli Ferrariensis. Ad Magnificam & Illustrem Dianam Estensem contrariam, de hominum aequalitate, & quare alter alterum excellat. Venetiis, in officina S. Bernardini, 1537. (Concerns nobility.)

69. BRÈCHE, JEAN. Manuel royal, ou opuscules de la doctrine et condition du prince, tant en prose que rhyme françoyse. Commentaire de Plutarque, autheur grec, de la doctrine du prince, translaté en françoys. Les octante préceptes d' Isocrates, du régime et gouvernement du prince et de la république, aussi tournez en françoys. Le tout par J. Brèche, de Tours. Tours, Mathieu Chercelé, 1541.

70. ———— Premier livre de l'honneste exercise du prince, à Madame la princesse de Navarre, par Jehan Brèche, de Tours. Paris, 1544. (Verse.)

71. BRETON, ROBERT. Roberti Britanni, . . . agriculturae encomium. Parisiis, apud C. Wechelum, 1539.

72. ———— Rob. Britanni de instituenda juventute ad honestatem dialogus. Parisiis, apud L. Grandinum, 1543.

73. ———— Roberti Britanni de optimo statu réipublicae liber, huic adjuncta est scripta Gul. Langei Bellaii comitis ac legati regis deploratio. Parisiis, ex. off. C. Welcheli, 1543.

74. —————— Rob. Britanni de ratione consequendae eloquentiae liber, cui adjunctum est jocosum, fictis introductis personis et rerum simulachris, de virtute et voluptate et paterno amore in liberos colloquium, studiosis discendi adolescentibus perutile. Parisiis, apud L. Grandinum, 1544.

75. BREUL, HEINRICH. De militia politica duplici, togata et armata, in cuius priori parte de advocatis, procuratoribus et notariis, in altera vero de vere armatis et martialibus militibus tractatur, per Henricum Breulaeum, . . . Francofurti ad Moenum, ex off. N. Bassaei, 1593.

76. BRUCIOLI, ANTONIO. De l'office d'un cappitaine. Poictiers, E. de Marnef, 1551.

77. BRUNELLUS, JOANNES. Tractatus de dignitate et potestate legati, nec non de primaria cardinalium origine atque institutione, in quo obiter etiam de materia beneficiali agitur, editus a Joanne Brunello, . . . Aureliae, J. Hoys, 1519.

78. BRUNFELS, OTTO. Aphorismi institutionis puerorum Othone B. Moguntino Carthusiano, autore, frugi adulescentibus, atque iis qui illos probe erudire velint adprime conducibiles. Jo. Sapidi Selestad. paedonomi. Qua ratione puer primis formetur ab annis, iste bona plenus fruge libellus habet. Hanc tibi sememtem fecit Brunnefelsius Ottho, qui suus est candor, lector ut ipse metas. Argentorati, apud Joannem Scotum, 1519.

79. —————— De disciplina et institutione puerorum Othonis Brunfelsii paraenesis. Item, institutio puellarum ex epistola divi Hieronymi ad Laetam. Argentorati, Joannes Schuebelius, 1525. (Also 1527; 1538; 1541; 1542; 1556.)

80. BRY, THÉODORE, JEAN-THÉODORE ET JEAN-ISRAEL DE. Emblemata nobilitate et vulgo scitu digna, singulis historiis symbola adscripta et elegantes versus historiam explicantes. Accessit galearum expositio et disceptatio de origine nobilitatis. Omnia recens collecta, inventa, et in aes incisa a Theodoro de Bry, . . . Francofurti ad Moenum, 1592.

81. —————— Jani Jacobi Boissardi, . . . Emblematum liber. Ipsa emblemata, a Theodoro de Bry sculpta et nunc recens in lucem edita. Francofurti ad Moenum, 1593. (German and Latin texts.)

82. Das Buechlein saget von bewerter ertzeney der pferd. Erffort, 1500.

83. BUIS, PAUL. Illustrium disquisitionum politicarum liber, quo quaestiones politicae, seu eius quae est de gerendae reipublicae ratione, septendecim disputationibus explicantur, publice in Academia Franckerana, ductu Pauli Busii, . . . propositis et discussis. Franckerai, apud U. Balck, 1613.

84. BULLAEUS, ANTONIUS. Operae horarum subcisivarum, sive discursuum academicorum, tam ex jure publico quam privato desumtorum decas miscellanea complectens in se . . . materias de majestate imperatoria,

jure nobilitandi, pacto successorio, causis singulare horum constituentibus . . . auctore Antonio Bullaeo, . . . Bremae, typis T. Villeriani, 1621.

85. CABOSSE, JEAN. Le mirrouer de prudence, par Maistre Jehan Cabosse. Paris, D. Janot, 1541. (The four virtues.)

86. CABRERA DE CORDOVA, LUIS. De historia, para entenderla y escrivirla . . . Luis Cabrera de Cordova, . . . Madrid, L. Sanchez, 1611.

87. CACCIALUPI, GIAMBATTISTA. De dignitate et praerogativa monachorum. Lugduni, 1552. (Also 1581.)

88. CALEFATTI, PIETRO. Specchio di dignita, nobiltà et honore, di Piero Calefati, . . . Lucca, il Busdrago, 1564. (Latin version bound with it.)

89. ———— Tractatus aureus et quotidie practicalibus aequestris dignitatis et de principibus, . . . Petri Calefati, . . . Mediolani, apud M. Tinum, 1581.

90. CALVIAC, C. La civile honesteté pour les enfants, avec la manière d'apprendre à bien lire, prononcer et escrire qu'avons mise au commencement. Paris, R. Breton, 1560.

91. CAMERARIUS, JOACHIM KAMMERMEISTER. Symbolorum et emblematum ex re herbaria desumtorum centuria una, collecta a Joachimo Camerario, . . . Noribergae, impensis J. Hofmanni et H. Camoscii, 1590. (Also 1661.)

92. CAPACIO, GIULIO CESARE. Gli apologi del Signor Giulio Cesare Capaccio Gentil' huomo del Serenissimo Signor Duca d'Urbino; con le dicerie morali ove quasi con vivi colori al modo cortegiano l'humana vita si dipinge, la malignità si scopre, la bizzarria de' cervelli si castiga, la frode si scaccia, la mattezza si punisce, al poco saper de gli huomini si provede, e di tutti i civili costumi si fà paragone. Al molto illustre, & eccellentissimo Signore Il Signior Cesare Ottato. Venetia, Barizzo Barrezzi, 1619.

93. CAPELLO, GIROLAMO. De disciplinis ingenuis, urbe libera liberoque juvene dignis, per compendium in capita resolutis, libri sex a Hieronymo Capello editi . . . Patavii, L. Pasquatus, 1570.

94. CARBONARIO DA TERNI, MEZENTIO. Il governatore politico e christiano di Mezentio Carbonario de Terni, . . . nel quale si discorre del mondo, che deve tener ciascun che governa, tanto in stato pacifico, quanto inquieto . . . distinto in sei libri. Fabriano, C. Scaccioppa, 1619.

95. CARDANO, GIROLAMO. H. C., . . . de propria vita liber. Adjecto hac secunda editione de praeceptis ad filios libello. Amstelaedami, 1654.

96. ———— H. C., . . . Liber de libris propriis. Lugduni, 1557. (Also 1562; 1585.)

97. ———— H. C., . . . Proxeneta seu de prudentia civili liber. Lugduni Batavorum, ex officina Elzeviriana, 1627. (Also 1630; 1635. French trans. 1652; 1661.)

98. CARNEVALI, LUIGI. Ragionamente de' titoli di Gioseppe Carnevale, . . . ove si mostra che cosa sia la nobiltà. Napoli, G. G. Carlino et A. Pace, 1592.

99. CASTORI, BERNARDINO, S. J. Institutione civile e christiana per uno che desideri vivere, tanto in corte quanto altrove, honoratamente e christianamente, del P. Bernadino Castori, . . . Roma, A. Zannetti, 1622.

100. CAVICEO, GIACOMO. Libro del peregrino, diligentemente in lingua toscha correcto, et novamente stampato et historiato. Venetia, Georgio Rusconi, 1520. (Also 1527; 1538; 1559. French trans. 1527; 1528; 1529; 1535; 1540. Span. trans. 1548.)

101. CENTORIO DEGLI HORTENSII, ASCANIO, pseud. Discorsi di guerra, del signor Ascanio Centorio, divisi in cinque libri, nel primo si contiene l'officio d'un generale di essercito, nel secondo, l'ordine del medesimo per expugnare una provincia, nel terzo si tratta della qualità del maestro di campo, nel quarto del modo che deve tenere una città ch' aspetta l'assedio, e nel quinto sotto diversi capi si contengono molte cose appertenenti all' arte della militia. Venegia, G. Giolito, 1559–1566. (Also 1567. Pts. 1–3, 1557–1558.)

102. CERMENATA, GIOVANNI PIETRO DA. Rapsodia Jo. Petri Cermenati de recta regnorum ac rerumpublicarum administratione, deque principum moribus . . . ex optimis . . . authoribus collecta. Lugduni, L. & C. Penot, 1561. (French trans. of extract, 1561.)

103. CERNOTI, LEONARDO. De optimo principe oratio Leonardi Cernotii, . . . Venetiis, 1592.

104. CERUTI, FEDERICO. Dialogi duo, quorum alter de comedia, alter de recta adolescentulorum institutione inscribitur, a Federico Ceruto, . . . conscripti . . . Veronae, apud H. Discipulum, 1593.

105. CERVIO, VINCENZO. Il trinciante di M. Vincenzo Cervio, ampliato et a perfettione ridotto dal cavalier Reale Fusoritto da Narni, gia Trinciante dell' Illustrissimo, & Reverendissimo Signor Cardinal Farnese, & al presente dell' Illustriss, Signor Cardinal Mont' alto. Con diverse aggiunte fatte dal cavalier Reale, et dall' istesso, in questa ultima impressione, aggiuntovi nel fine un breve dialogo detto Il Mastro di casa [di Cesar Pandini], per governo d'una casa di qual si voglia principe con li offitiali necessarii, utile et giovevole à ogni cortigiano. Roma, stampa del Gabbia, 1593.

106. CHABODIE, D. Le petit monde où sont represantées au vrai les plus belles parties de l'homme, par D. Chabodie, . . . Paris, D. Guillemot et E. Roland, 1604.

107. CHAMPIER, SYMPHORIEN. Le fondement et origine des tiltrez de noblesse et excellens estatz de tous nobles et illustres, quant à la différence des empires, royaulmes, duchez, contez et aultres seigneuries.

Petit dialogue de noblesse auquel est déclaré que c'est de noblesse et les inventaires d'icelles. Paris, 1535. (Also 1544; 1547.)

108. CHAPPELL, BARTHOLOMEW. The garden of prudence. 1595.

109. CHAPPUZEAU, CHARLES. Le devoir général de l'homme en toutes conditions, envers Dieu, le Roy, le public, son prochain et soy-mesme . . . divisé en six livres, par Charles Chappuzeau. Paris, 1617.

110. ———— De la société, de la vie humaine, des alliances et ambassades des princes et devoir des ambassadeurs . . . par Charles Chappuzeau . . . Paris, P. Rocollet, 1623.

111. ———— Les personnes que les roys et princes doivent apeler et choisir pour leurs commensaux, domestiques, serviteurs, conseillers de leurs maisons et ministre de leurs estats, quel le devoir d'iceux et leur récompense . . . Paris, E. Estienne, 1620.

112. CHEFFONTAINES, CHRISTOPHE DE (Archbishop). Chrestienne confutation du poinct d'honneur sur lequel la noblesse fonde ses querelles. 2 pts. Paris, C. Fremy, 1568. (Also 1586.)

113. CHIODINUS, JOANNES BAPTISTA. Disputationes quinquagenta de nobilitate civili et salutis . . . per mag. Jo. Bapt. Chiodinum, . . . Venetiis, A. et B. Dei, 1614.

114. CHRISTIAN II, PRINCE D'ANHALT. De officio principis orationes tres publice habitae ab illustriss. ac generosiss. principibus Anhaltinis D. Johanne Casimiro, D. Christiano et D. Friderico Mauricio, patruelibus, etc. in Academia Genevensi. Lipsiae, M. Lautzenberger, 1610. (Also 1618.)

115. CHYTRAEUS (DAVID KOCHHAFF). De ratione discendi et ordine studiorum in singulis artibus recte instituendo. David Chytraeus. Witebergae, 1564.

116. CIECO, VENTURA. De conscribenda historia dialogus, Ventura Caeco authore . . . Bononiae, J. Rubeus, 1563.

117. CIGOGNA, GIOVAN MATTHEO. Il primo libro del trattato militare di Giovan Mattheo Cigogna, Veronese . . . Venetia, G. Bariletto, 1567.

118. CINUZZI, IMPERIALE. La vera militar disciplina antica e moderna del capitano Imperiale Cinuzzi, Sanese. Siena, S. Marchetti, 1604. (Also 1620.)

119. CLAMORGAN, JEAN DE. La chasse du loup, nécessaire à la maison rustique, par Jean de Clamorgan, . . . Paris, J. Du Puys, 1574. (Also 1566; 1583; 1640. Germ. trans. n. d.)

120. CLAPMARIUS (ARNOLD CLAPMAIER). Arnoldi Clapmarii de Arcanis rerum publicarum libri sex . . . Bremae, in officina typographia J. Wesselii, 1605. (Also 1611; 1624; 1641; 1644; 1665; 1668.)

121. CLEMENTE, AFRICO. Trattato dell' agricoltura di M. Africo Clemente, . . . Venetia, 1572. (Also 1623; 1692.)

122. CLÈVES, PHILIPPE DUC DE. Instruction de toutes manières de guer-

royer, tant par terre que par mer, et des choses y servantes, rédigée par escript, par Messire Philippe duc de Clèves . . . Paris, G. Morel, 1558.

123. COBHEAD, THOMAS. A briefe instruction for the exercise of youth. London, T. Newton, 1579.

124. COGNIÉRES, PIERRE DE. Le Pasquil de la cour, composé nouvellement par Maistre Pierre de Cognières resuscité, jadis advocat en la Cour de Parlement à Paris. 1561.

125. COLA DA BENEVENTO. Del governo della corte d'un signore in Roma . . . Roma, F. Priscianese, 1543.

126. COLET, JOHN. The governance of kings and princes. 1511.

127. ———— A right fruitfull monicion concernynge the order of a good Cristen mannes lyfe. London, 1534. (Also 1577.)

128. COLLADO, LUYS. Platica manual de artilleria, en la qual se tracta de la excelencia de el arte militar, y origen de ella, y de las máquinas con que los antiquos començaron à usarla, de la invencion de la polvora y artilleria . . . y à la fin un muy copioso, y importante examen de artilleros . . . por Luys Collado, . . . Milan, P. G. Poncio, 1592. (Ital trans. 1606; 1641.)

129. ———— Practica manuale di artiglieria, nella quale si tratta della inventione di esse, dell' ordine di condurla . . . fabricar mine, da far volar in alto le fortezze, spianar le montagne . . . far fuochi artificiali, etc. Venetia, 1586. (Different work from the preceding.)

130. COLLE, GIOVANNI FRANCESCO. Refugio, over ammonitorio de gentilhuomo, composto per Jo. Francesco Colle . . . 1532.

131. COLLENUCCIO, PANDOLFO. Educatione usata da li antichi a levare li loro figlioli, et come partivano il tempo ad insignarli le doctrine et le scientie de le litere et altre cose da pelegrini ingegni et animi generosi, composte dal magnifico cavaliero meser Pandolpho Collenuti, . . . Romae, A. Blado, 1535.

132. COLLI, HIPPOLYT VON. Hippolyti a Collibus, princeps, consilarius, palatinus sive aulicus et nobilis, editio postrema . . . Hanoviae, G. Antonius, 1598. (Also Consilarius, 1596, 1643, 1646; Palatinus, 1615; Princeps, 1668.)

133. Colloquiorum familiorium incerto autore libellus Graece & Latine, non pueris modo sed quibusvis, in cotidiano colloquio, graecum affectantibus sermonem, impendio futurus utilis. Lovanii, apud Theodorum Martinum, 1517.

134. COLLURAFI, ANTONIO. L'idea del gentil'huomo di republica nel governo politico, ethico ed economico, ovvero il nobile veneto del cavalier Collurafi, . . . Venetia, P. Baglioni, 1633. (Also 1623.)

135. COLOMBRE, AGOSTINO. I tre libri della natura de i cavelli et del modo de medicar le loro infermità, composti da maestro Agostino Columbre, . . . Vinegia, F. Fanfani, 1547. (Also 1622.)

136. COMHERTIUS, THEODORO. Emblemata moralia et oeconomica. Arnhemi, 1609.

137. CONCENATIUS, JACOBUS. . . . Dialogus Jacobi Concenatii de vita aulica, deque literarum studiis memoriae prodendis. Lugduni, apud F. Frellonium, 1556. (See Giribaldi.)

138. CONTZEN, ADAM. Politicorum libri decem, in quibus de perfectae reipub. forma, virtutibus et vitiis . . . tractatur, authore R. P. Adamo Contzen, . . . Moguntiae, B. Lippus, 1620.

139. CORLIEU, FRANÇOIS DE. Briefve instruction pour tous estats, en laquelle est sommairement déclairé comme chacun en son estat se doit gouverner et vivre selon Dieu. Paris, Philippe Danfrie et Richard Breton, 1558. (Also 1559.)

140. CORNAZZANO, ANTONIO. Cornazano de re militari, novamente impresso. Venetia, Alexandro de Bindoni, 1515. (Also 1536.)

141. ————— Opera nova de miser Antonio Cornazano in terza rima, la qual tratta. De modo regendi. De motu fortune. De integritate rei militaris: & qui in re militari imperatores excelluerunt. Novamente impressa: & hystoriata. Venetia, Nicolo Zoppino et Vincentio Campagni, 1518.

142. CORTESE, GIOVAMBATTISTA. Il selvaggio de M. Giovambattista Cortese de Bagnacavallo, in cui si trattano innamoramenti, battagli, et altre cose bellissime, con somma diligenza ridotto, et nuovamente stampato . . . Vinegia, G. A. di Nicolini, 1535.

143. COTES, WILLIAM. Short questions betweene the father and the sonne. 1585.

144. The counsell of a father to his sonne. c. 1620.

145. The court of good counsell. 1607.

146. CRESCENZI, PIETRO DE. Opus ruralium commodorum, auctore Petro de Crescentiis. Augsbourg, 1471. (Also 1474; 1486; 1500; etc.)

147. CRINITO, PIETRO RICCIO. Petri Criniti commentarii de honesta disciplina. Florentiae, per Philippum Juntam, 1504–1505. (Also 1508; 1510; 1518; 1520; 1525; 1532; etc.)

148. CRISPOLTI, CESARE. Idea dello scolare che versa negli studi affine di prendere il grado del dottorato, del signor Cesare Crispolti, . . . Perugia, V. Columbara, 1604.

149. CROCE, FLAMINIO DELLA. L'essercitio della cavalleria et d'altre materie, del capitano Flaminio della Croce, . . . Anversa, H. Aertsio, 1625.

150. CROGERUS, NICOLAUS. Monomachia, in qua misanthropos et philanthropos de honoribus, oneribus, sylvanni et oppidani, armis logicis, theologicis, arcem veritatis impugnant, non expugnant, caduceatoribus bellum allaborantibus transigere, frustratis, rex basilice dispensano crisin promulgat aeropagiticam . . . concinnata per Nicolaum Crogerum, . . . Francofurti, e collegio musarum Paltheniano, 1608.

151. CROWLEY, ROBERT. The voyce of the laste trumpet, blowen by the seventh angel (as is mentioned in the eleventh of the Apocalips) callyng al estats of men to the ryght path of theyr vocation, wherin are conteyned. XII. lessons to twelve several estats of men, which if thei learne and folowe, al shall be wel, and nothing amis. London, Robert Crowley, 1550. (Verse.)

152. DADONVILLE, JACQUES. L'honneur des nobles, blason et propriété de leur armes en général blasonnées et comprinses soubz ung seul escu d'armes cy desoubz pourtraict, invention très singulière, avecques ung petit livre de bonne grâce très exquis. Le tout nouvellement composé par Dadonville. 15—.

153. DANEAU, LAMBERT. Politicorum aphorismorum silva, ex optimis quibusque tum graecis, tum latinis scriptoribus . . . collecta, per Lambertum Danaeum . . . Antverpiae, ex off. C. Plantini, 1583. (Also 1591; 1612; 1620; 1623; 1638; 1652.)

154. DANTI, ANTONINO, DA SANTA MARIA IN BAGNO. Osservationi di diverse historie et d'altri particolari degni di memoria: con un cumulo di sententie notabili di molti huomini famosi: & con una raccolta di lettioni sententiose & pie, tolte da piu auttori illustri. Per Antonino Danti da Santa Maria in Bagno . . . Venetia, Matteo Boselli, 1573.

155. DARELL, WALTER. A short discourse of the life of servingmen. Hereunto is also annexed a treatise, concerning manners and behaviours. London, f. R. Newberie, 1578.

156. DAVIDSON, JOHN. Dialog between a clerk and ane courteour. Edinburgh, R. Lekpreuik, 1573.

157. DELFINO, GIOVANNI ANTONIO. De nobilitate, Jo. Antonius Delphinus, . . . ejusdemque auctoris de varia provinciae Marchiae nomenclatura brevis ac dilucida narratio . . . edita . . . per F. Horatium Civallum . . . Perusiae, apud P.-P. Orlandum, 1590.

158. DELIUS, MATTHAEUS. De arte jocandi libri quatuor scripti carmine a Mattheo Delio, filio Matthei Delii gubernantis studia doctrinae in inclyta urbe Hamburga cum praefatione Philippi Melanthonis de tribus virtutibus in sermone, veritate, comitate, et εὐτραπελία. Witebergae, ex off. V. Creutzer, 1555.

159. DÉSIRÉ, ORTUS. Les batailles du chevalier celeste contre le chevalier terrestre. Paris, Magdaleine Boursette, 1553. (Also 1557; 1570.)

160. ————— Le desordre & scandale de France par les estats masquez & corrompus, contenant l'eternité des peines deuës pour les pechez: & de la retribution des eleuz & des predestinez de Dieu. Paris, Guillaume Julien, 1577. (Du Verdier.)

161. DICK, LEOPOLD. De optima studiorum ratione, idque in omni facultatum genere, methodus, Leopoldo Dickio, . . . autore. Ejusdem christianae et civilis vitae compendium . . . 1564.

162. DILLINGHAM, FRANCIS. Christian economy or houshold government. London, J. Tapp, 1609.

163. A display of duty. 1589.

164. Dispute, qu'il est necessaire a un grand prince, sçavoir les lettres, & que par ce moyen la vertue se peult apprendre. Paris, Chrestien Wechel, 1548.

165. Le donat de noblesse en rime. Lyon, Olivier Arnoullet. (Du Verdier.)

166. DONI, ANTONIO FRANCESCO. I marmi del Doni, academico Peregrino. Cioè ragionamenti introdotti a farsi da varie conditioni d'huomini a'luoghi di honesto piacere in Firenze. Ripieno di discorsi in varie scienze, & discipline. Molti arguti, istorie varie, proverbii antichi, & moderni, sentenze morali, accidenti & novellettes morali. Diviso in quattro libri. Opera giovevole à persone d'ogni stato, per il correggimento de' costumi; & per ogni professione d'huomini ... Venetia, G. B. Bettoni, 1609.

167. DROIT-DE-GAILLARD, PIERRE. Methode qu'on doit tenir en la lecture de l'histoire, vray miroir & exemplaire de nostre vie. Où les principaux poincts des sciences morales & politiques rapportez à la loy de Dieu, & accommodez aux moeurs de ce temps, sont contenus, & illustrez des plus beaux exemples tirez des histoires, tant sacrees que prophanes. Par P. Droit de Gaillard Advocat à la cour. Avec deux tables, l'une des chapitres, & l'autre des choses memorables contenues en ce livre. Paris, Pierre Cavellat, 1579. (Also 1580; 1604.)

168. DUBREUIL, CLAUDE. Quod utilius sit rempublicam a rege gubernari quam a populo vel ab optimatibus, ... oratorio secunda. Parisiis, 1548.

169. DU CHOUL, JEAN. Dialogue de la ville et des champs. Epistre de la sobre vie. Par J. Du Chol, ... Lyon, 1565.

170. DU FAUR, GUY, SEIGNEUR DE PIBRAC. Cinquante quatrains, contenant preceptes et enseignemens utiles pour la vie de l'homme, composez à l'imitation de Phocylides, d'Epicharmus, & autres anciens poëtes Grecs, par le Sieur de Pyb. Rouen, Martin le Mesgissier, 1574. (Also 1592; 1596; 1602; 1613; 1615–1619; 1621; 1634; 1667. Eng. trans. see below. Successive additions up to 126 quatrains.)

171. ———— (Eng. trans.). Τετραστικα; or, the quadrains of Guy de Faur, Lord of Pibrac. Translated, by S. Sylvester. 1605. London, Humfrey Lownes, 1605. (Accompanied by the French text.)

172. DU GUÉ, CLAUDE. Doctrina, sive institutio scholarum, in duas partes distributa ... auctore Claudio Du Gué, ... Parisiis, G. Chaudière, 1577.

173. EBERLIN, GEORG. Illustris et perspicua in titulum digestorum de origine juris et omnium magistratuum et successione prudentium explicatio,

... auctore Georgio Eberlino, ... Henricopoli, C. Horn, 1592. (Also 1595; 1613; 1616.)

174. ECK, JOHANN MAIER. Epistola Johan. Eckii, ... de ratione studiorum suorum, scripta anno 1538, nunc vero primum aedita ... Ingoldstadii, A. Weisenhorn, 1543.

175. EDMONDS, CLEMENT. Observations upon Caesars Commentaries setting forth the practise of the art militaric in the time of the Romaine Empire for the better direction of our moderne warrs, by Clement Edmonds ... London, M. Lownes, 1604. (Also 1655. Trans. of Caesar with observations.)

176. EGUILUZ, MARTIN DE. Milicia, discurso y regla militar, del capitan Martin de Eguiluz, ... Anvers, P. Bellero, 1595.

177. EHINGER, BURCKHARDUS. Hanc collegii politici classis posterioris disputationem octavam, de legatis, et item de republica augenda, praside Du. Christophoro Besoldo, ... discutiendam proponit Burckhardus Ehinger. Tubingae, typis J. A. Cellii, 1614.

178. EMERICUS. Emerici Panonii Colosvarini oratio de vera et populari, constanti atque usitata ratione et via tradendarum tractandarumque disciplinarum atque artium, habita Parisiis 1552. Lutetiae, apud M. Vascosanum, 1552. (Incomplete.)

179. ENENKEL, GEORGIUS ACACIUS. De privilegiis juris civilis libri tres, auctore Georgio Acacio Enenkelio, barone Hohenheimensi, ... Prostat in nobili Franckfurti Paltheniana, 1606.

180. ———— Georgii Acacii Enenkelii, baronis Hoheneccii, de privilegiis militum et militiae libri duo et de privilegiis veteranorum liber unus ... Francofurti, e collegio Musarum Paltheniano, 1607.

181. ———— Georgii Acacii Enenkelii, baronis Hoheneccii, de privilegiis parentum et liberorum tractatus ... Tubingae, J. A. Cellius, 1618.

182. ———— Georgii Acacii Enenkellii, d. baronis Hoheneccii, Sejanus, seu de praepotentibus regum ac principum ministris commonefactio. Argentorati, haeredes L. Zetzneri, 1620.

183. ENGERD, JOHANN, Ed. Methodus de liberalibus pueritiae et adolescentiae studiis recte ordinandis: a viro quodam excellenti atque doctissimo nuper conscripta: nunc autem in usum literariae iuventutis, opera M. Joannis Engerdi, P. L. ac poësios in alma Ingolstadiensi Academia Professoris ordinarii, etc. in lucem edita. Huic praefixum est eiusdem Carmen Protrepticum de ratione studii puerilis; accessit verò tum sententiarum utilium ex Joannis Ludovici Vivis Introductione ad veram sapientiam excerptarum, tum aureorum Pythagorae carminum expositio metrica. Ingolstadii, ex officina typographica Davidis Sartorii, 1583.

184. ENOCH, LOUIS. De puerili graecarum literarum doctrina liber, Lodoico Enoco authore. Parisiis, oliva R. Stephani, 1555.

185. ERNAUD, LOYS. Discours de la noblesse et des justes moyens d'y parvenir, par Loys Ernaud, seigneur de Chantores. Caen, B. Macé, 1584.

186. ESCALANTE, BERNARDINO DE. Dialogos del arte militar, de Bernardino de Escalante. Brusellas, R. Velpio, 1595.

187. ESPENCE, CLAUDE D'. Deux notables traictez, composez par feu Monsieur Despence, . . . l'un desquels monstre combien les lettres et sciences sont utiles et proufitables aux rois et princes, l'autre contient une forme de devis et discourse à la louange des trois lys de France. Paris, G. Auvray, 1575.

188. ———— Institution d'un prince chrestien, par M. Claude d'Espence, . . . Lyon, J. de Tournes, 1548.

189. ESPINOSA DE SANCTAYANA, RODERIGO DE. Arte de retórica, en el qual se contienen tres libros: el primero enseña el arte generalmente, el segundo particularmente el arte de hystoriador, el tercero escrivir epistolas y dialogos . . . Madrid, G. Drouy, 1578.

190. EVITASCANDALO, CESARE. Dialogo del maestro di casa, nel quale si contiene di quanto il maestro di casa deve essere instrutto, et a ciascun' altro, che voglia essercitare officio in corte deve sapere et operare, utile a tutti li padroni, cortegiani, officiali e servitori della corte, di Cesare Evitascandalo, . . . Roma, G. Martinelli, 1598. (Also 1620.)

191. L'exercise & discours politiques de l'homme vertueux, contenant plusieurs notables exemples & enseignemens appartenans tant à la police & gouvernement du public, qu'au particulier, ordonné par chapitres & lieux communs tirez des sainctes escritures & des prophanes. Paris, Nicolas Chesneau, 1581. (Du Verdier.)

192. FARNESIUS, HENRICUS (HENRI DU FOUR). De simulacro reip. sive de imaginibus politicae et oeconomicae virtutis. Henrici Farnesii Eburonis J. C. Et artis oratoriae interpraetis regii. Panegyrici lib. IIII. absoluti. In quibus quam imperii faciem adumbrent quaedem illustrium familiarum insignia: apologi: emblemata: fabulae: adagia: hieroglyphica: breviter ostenditur. Huc accedunt mores: leges: ritus antiquorum: synonyma virtutum; paradoxa disputantium: exemplorum testimonia, ac denique orationes pro arte imperandi quinque. Papiae, ex officina haeredum Hieronymi Bartoli, 1593.

193. ———— Diphtera Jovis, sive de antiqua principis gloria. Ex qua olim Aegyptiorum reges Trimegisti ter maximi optimi: Sapientiss. ac potentiss. sunt appellati. Henrici Farnesii Eburonis J. C. & artis oratoria interpretis regii, atque in strenua, & augusta intentorum Palestra Academici Intenti Conspirantis. Libri III. Quorum primus est de virtute: alter de sapientia: ultimus de potentia armati principis,

singuli verò omnes centum tenentur absoluti elogiis, quae ad Aegyptiacam disciplinam, naturae monimentis, poëtarumque commentis, primùm figurata: deinde exemplorum testimoniis colorata, faciem repraesentant antiquam regiae virtutis, & gloriae. Mediolani, apud Hieronymum Bordonum, & Petrum Martyrem Locarnum, 1607.

194. FARRA, ALESSANDRO. Discorso dell'ufficio del capitano, d'Alessandro Farra, . . . Pavia, G. Bartoli, 1564.

195. FAUCHET, CLAUDE. Origines des chevaliers, armoires, et heraux. Paris, I. Perier, 1600.

196. FAUCON, ISABEAU? Le livre du faulcon. Paris, P. Le Rouge?, 1490? (Also 1520?)

197. FELIX, MAGNO. Los quarto libros del cavallero Felix Magno. Sevilla, S. Trugillo, 1549.

198. FENARIO, PANFILO. Discorsi di Panfilo Fenario sopra i cinque sentimenti . . . con un trattato del medesimo delle virtù morali, dove con brevità si dichiara quale sia il vero loro fine . . . Venetia, G. B. Somascho, 1587. (Also 1605.)

199. FENNER, DUDLEY. A short and profitable treatise of lawfull and unlawfull recreations. Midleburgh, R. Schilders, 1587?

200. FERNENDEZ DE ANDRADA, PEDRO. Libro de la gineta de España. Sevilla, A. de la Barrera, 1599.

201. FERRARIUS, JOHANNES, MONTANUS. A woorke of Johannes Ferrarius Montanus, touchynge the good orderynge of a common weale: wherein as well magistrates, as private persones, bee put in remembraunce of their dueties, not as the philosophers in their vaine tradicions have devised, but according to the godlie institutions and sounde doctrine of christianitie. Englished by William Bavande. London, John Kingston, 1559.

202. FIGON, JEAN. La peregrination de l'enfant vertueux. Oeuvre contenant le sommaire des disciplines qui conduisent à plus haute vertue. Avec trois chants royaux parmy la prose. Lyon, François Arnoullet, 1584. (Du Verdier.)

203. FILLATRE, GUILLAUME. Le premier volume de la toison d'or, composé par révérend père en Dieu Guillaume . . . jadis évesque de Tournay, . . . auquel soubz les vertus de magnanimité et justice appartenans à l'estat de noblesse sont contenus les haulx, vertueux et magnanimes faicts tant très chrestiennes maisons de France, Bourgongne et Flandres que d'autres roys et princes de l'Ancien et Nouveau Testament, nouvellement imprimé à Paris . . . Le second volume de la toison d'or, traictant de la vertu de justice et des autres vertus qui d'elle dependent et procédent. Paris, F. Reynault, 1517. (Also 1530.)

204. FINETTI, OTTAVIO. Dell' uficio de' figlivoli verso il padre, e come

s'habbi a reggere il padre verso i figlivoli per vivere tranquillamente nelle private case, e a mantenimento e grandezza del politico governo, opera di Ottavio Finetti. Venetia, G. de Salis, 1615.

205. FISTON, WILLIAM. The schoole of good manners. 1595.

206. FLORIO, GISMONDO. Istoria morale di Gismondo Florio, . . . nella quale si discorre di materie di stati, et di diverse attioni de' prencipi, tanto antichi quanto del nostro tempo . . . Trevigi, E. Dehuchino, 1599.

207. Le fondement & origine des tiltres de noblesse & excellents estats de tous nobles & illustres, comtez & autres seigneuries, & la maniere comment elles ont esté erigees pour la defense & gouvernement de la chose publique. Avec la maniere de faire les royes d'armes, heraux & poursuivans. Ensemble le secret des armoiries. Et l'instruction de faire les combats contenant la difference d'iceux. Paris, Denis Janot, 1535. (Also 1547.)

208. FORGET, GERMAIN. Les plaisirs et félicitez de la vie rustique, par M. Germ. Forget, . . . Paris, A. Drouard, 1584.

209. FORREST, SIR WILLIAM. Poesye of princely practice. 1548.

210. FORSET, EDWARD. A comparative discourse of the bodies natural and politique, . . . by Edward Forset. London, J. Bill, 1606.

211. FOSSOMBRONE, TOMASO ATTIO DA. Discorsi nuovi delle prerogative de' curiali antichi et moderni cortegiani, e di titoli di qualunque persona, posti per ordine insieme . . . dell' ecc^no signor Tomaso Attio da Fossombruno, . . . Venetia, heredi di M. Sessa, 1600.

FRANÇOIS, DE SAINT-THOMAS. *See* Simeone.

212. FRATTA, GIOVANNI. Della dedicatione de' libri, con la correction dell' abuso in questa materia introdotto, dialoghi del sig. Giovanni Fratta, . . . Venetia, G. Anglieri, 1590.

213. FREYBERGK, WILHELM LUDWIG VON. Disputationem . . . de constitutione politices et societate civili in genere . . . defendet ac propugnabit . . . Guilielmus Ludovicus a Freybergk, . . . praeside Joanne Crugerio, . . . ad d. 24. maii ann. 1609. Giessaz, typis Chemlinianis, 1609.

214. ———— Disputatio . . . de remediis contra corruptiones rerumpubl., cuius positiones . . . in . . . academia giessena . . . defendet . . . Guilielmus Ludovicus baro a Freybergk, praeside Joanne Crugerio, . . . ad d. 28 Julii. Giessas, typis Chemlinianus, 1609.

215. FRIEDRICH, ANDREAS. Emblemata nova, das ist New Bilderbuch, . . . durch . . . Andreas Friedrichen. Francoforti, J. de Zetter, 1617. (French trans. 1617.)

216. FRITZE, PETER. Petri Fritzii, . . . Conclusiones de nobilitate politica sive civili, eiusque praerogativis et privilegiis, quas . . . in Academia jenensi . . . publice proposuit et propugnavit. Jenae, sumptibus J. V. Mohro, 1614.

217. FROYDEVILLE, EYMAR DE. Dialogues de l'origine de la noblesse, où est déclaré que c'est d'icelle et ses inventeurs . . . Composé par Eymar de Froydevile de Viers, . . . Lyon, B. Honorati, 1574.

218. FULBECKE, WILLIAM. A direction or preparative to the study of the lawe. 1600.

219. FUNGERUS, JOHANNES. De puerorum disciplina et recta educatione liber, per Joannem Fungeri. Lugduni Batavorum, apud F. Raphelengium, 1586.

220. FUSTEL, MARTIN. Les sentences memorables en order alphabetique, contenans preceptes et enseignemens utiles pour l'instruction de la jeunesse. Avec plusieurs reigles generales, diversement expliquees, touchant la vraye supputation & forme de compter au brief, nouvellement composé: par Martin Fustel, escrivain juré, & arithmeticien, à Paris. Paris, Guillaume Chaudiere, 1577.

221. GALATEUS, ANTONIUS. De educatione.

222. GALLO, AGOSTINO. Le dieci giornate della vera agricoltura e piaceri della villa, di M. Agostin Gallo, in dialogo. Vinegia, D. Sarri, 1565. (Also with title Le vinti giornati, 1569, 1575. French trans. 1571.)

223. GAMBARO, PIETRO ANDREA. Tractatus de officio atque auctoritate legati de latere, per R. Petrum Andream Gambarum . . . ab Augustino Ferentillo . . . recognitus . . . Venetiis, apud V. Valgrisium, 1572.

224. GARIMBERTO, GIROLAMO. Concetti divinissimi di Girolamo Garimberto e d'altri degni autori, raccolti da lui per iscrivere e ragionar familiarmente, di nuovo . . . corretti e emendati con la gionta. Venetia, C. da Trino, 1562. (Also 1582; 1596; 1609. French trans. 1604; 1610; 1685.)

225. GARZONI, THOMASO. La piazza universale di tutte le professioni del mondo nuovamente ristampata & posta in luca da Thomas Garzoni. Venetia, Vincenzo Somasco, 1595. (Also 1585; 1587; 1599; 1616; 1617; 1619; 1638; 1651; 1665. Germ. trans. 1626; 1641.)

226. GASSION, JACQUES DE. Ἀναλυσις πολιτική, in qua de prima civitatum origine, de praestantiori illarum statu seu administratione, denique de ultimo illarum fine seu summo bono . . . disputatur, authore Jacobo Gassiono, . . . Burdigalae, apud S. Millangium, 1591.

227. GAST, JEAN. Convivalium sermonum liber, meris jocis ac salibus refertus. 1549. (4th ed.)

228. GEBHARDI, HEINRICH. De principiis et dignitate jurisprudentiae tractatus philosopho-juridicus . . . compositus . . . ab Heinrico Gebhardi, . . . cui adjecta ejusdem de usucapionibus tractatio methodica . . . [et oratio de . . . problemate: literarumne an vero armorum gloria illustrior et utrorumnam praestantior usus?]. A typographo ruthengerano, 1613.

229. GENTILLET, INNOCENT. Discourse upon the meanes of wel governing against N. Macchiavelli. 1602.

230. GIANUTIO, HORATIO. Libro nel quale si tratta della maniera di giuocar a scacchi, con alcuni sottilissimi partiti, nuovamente composto da Horatio Gianutio. Torino, A. de' Bianchi, 1597.

231. GIRIBALDI, MATTEO. Matthaei Gribaldi, ... de methodo ac ratione studendi libri tres novis accessionibus ... locupletati. His nunc primum accessit dialogus Jacobi Concenatii de vita aulica, deque literarum studiis memoriae prodendis. Lugduni, apud F. Frellonium, 1556. (Also 1541; 1544; 1553; 1559.)

232. GOCLENIUS, L'ANCIEN (Rudolf Göcke). Rodolphi Goclenii, ... exercitationes et disquisitiones ethicae et politicae ... Marpurgi, typis P. Egenolphi, 1614.

233. GOUYN, OLIVIER. Le mepris & contennement de tous jeux de sort, composé par Olivier Gouyn de Poictiers. Paris, Charles l'Angelier, 1550.

234. GRAMIGNA, VINCENZO. Del governo tirannico e regio libri due, di Vincenzo Gramigna ... Napoli, T. Longo, 1615.

235. ————— Il segretario, dialogo, di Vincenzo Gramigna ... Firenze, P. Cecconcelli, 1620.

236. GRATIUS FALISEUS. De venatione liber I. Lugduni, 1537.

237. GREGOIRE, PIERRE. De republica libri sex et viginti, in duos tomos distincti, authore D. Petro Gregorio, ... emendati et additionibus aucti. Lugduni, J. Pillehotte, 1609. (Also 1642, 3rd ed.)

238. GRILLANDARI, GIOVANNI BATTISTA. Travaglio della corte et riposo della villa, tradotto di franzese in toscano, dal cap. Gio. Battista Grillandari, ... Modona, gli haeredi C. Gadaldini, 1563.

239. GRIMALDI ROBIO, PELEGRO DE. Discorsi di messer Pelegro de Grimaldi Robio, ... nei quali si ragiona compiutamente di quanto far debbono i gentilhuomini ne' servigi de' lor signori per acquistarsi la gratia loro ... Genoa, A. Bellono, 1543.

240. GRIMAUDET, FRANÇOIS. De la puissance royalle et sacerdotale, opuscule politique. 1579.

241. ————— Les opuscules politiques de Françoys Grimaudet advocat du Roy ... Paris, Gabriel Buon, 1580. (Also Ital. trans. of part, 1604. Duties of governors and magistrates.)

242. GRISALDI, PAOLO. Oratio de vera nobilitate in laudem ... D. Marci Antonii Venerii ac totius familiae Veneriae, Rev. P. F. Pauli Grysaldi, ... Venetiis, ex officina D. Guerraci et J. B. fratrum, 1586.

243. GRYNDALL, WILLIAM. Hawking, hunting, fouling, and fishing. 1596.

244. GAULTHERUS, MARCUS. Dialogi de schola libri duo in quorum primo dilucide asseritur scholarum dignitas ... altero ostenduntur partim emolumenta, partim incommoda eorum, qui in scholasticis functio-

nibus versantur, addita etiam in fine conjectanea quaedam philologa, authore Marco Gualthero, . . . Franicae, V. D. Balck, 1613.

245. GUARDIOLA, JUAN BENITO. Tratado de nobleza. Madrid, Viuda de A. Gomez, 1591.

246. GUÉROULT, GUILLAUME. Le premier libre des emblèmes composé par Guillaume Guéroult. Lyon, B. Arnoullet, 1550.

247. GUIDANI, FRANCESCO. Discorso del sig. Francesco Guidani, nel quale brevemente si ragiona della vera nobilità . . . Venetia, G. B. Sessa et fratelli, 1574.

248. GUIDI, CIPRIANO. Speculum peregrinarum quaestionum. Venetia, 1597.

249. GUTIERREZ DE LOS RIOS, GASPAR. Noticia general para la estimacion de las artas y de la manera en que se conocen las liberales de las que son mecanicas y serviles . . . por el L. Gaspar Gutierrez de Los Rios, . . . Madrid, P. Madrigal, 1600.

250. H., W. The reformed travailer. 1606.

251. HABERT, PIERRE. L'histoire de Titus, et Gisippus, et autres petiz oeuvres de Beroalde de latin, interpretés en rime françoyse, par Françoys Habert d'Yssouldun en Berry. Avec l'exaltation de vraye & perfaicte noblesse. Les quatre amours, le nouveau Cupido, et le tresor de vie. De l'invention dudict Habert. Le tout presenté à Monseigneur de Nevers. Paris, Michel Fezandat & Robert Granion, 1551.

252. ———— Le chemin de bien vivre et miroir de vertu, avec le stille de composer toutes sortes de lettres missives. Paris, C. Micard, 1571. (Also 1574?; 1587.)

253. ———— L'institution de vertu. Paris, I. Ruelle, 1597.

254. HAKE, EDWARD. A touchstone for this time present. 1574.

255. HALE, GEORGE. The private schoole of defence. London, f. J. Helme, 1614.

256. HALL, JOSEPH. Quo vadis? a just censure of travell as it is commonly undertaken by gentlemen. London, E. Griffin, 1617.

257. HAUDENT, GUILLAUME. Le variable discours de la vie humaine, nouvellement traduict de latin en rithme françoyse, par M. Guillaume Haudent. Paris, N. Buffet, 1545.

258. HEGENDORFF, CHRISTOPHLE. Christiana studiosae juventutis institutio, per Christophorum Hegendorphinum. De disciplina & institutione puerorum Othonis Brunfelsii Paraenesis. Parisiis, ex officina Roberti Stephani, 1541. (Also 1542; 1556. Outline.)

259. ———— Dialogus pueriles Christophori Hegendorphini XII Lepidi aeque ac docti. Parisiis, ex officina Roberti Stephani, 1528.

260. HELUÏS, JEAN. Le miroüer du prince chrétien posé sur les deux colonnes roïalles de piété et justice, . . . par Jean Heluïs, . . . Paris, Thomas Brumen, 1566.

261. HERMAN IV (Archibishop of Cologne). The governement of all estates. London, H. Denham, 1565? (Trans. N. Boorman.)

262. HÉROARD, JEAN. De l'institution du prince, par Jean Heroard, sieur de Vaulgrigneuse. Paris. J. Jannon, 1609. (Lat. trans. 1617.)

263. ——————— Hippostologie, c'est a dire, discours des os du cheval. Par M. Jehan Heroard Conseiller, Medecin ordinaire et secretaire du roy. Paris, Mamert Patisson, 1599. (From the dedication to the King: "Commanded by King Charles, who took particular pleasure in the veterinary art, to put down some instructions to marshals and others who work without reason or knowledge on the diseases of horses, to the great regret often of those who lose their favorite horses.")

264. HERRERA, GABRIEL ALONSO DE. Libro de agricultura que es de la-brança y criança, y de muchas otras particularidades y provechos de las cosas del campo, compilado por Gabriel Alonso de Herrera ... nuevamente corregido y añadido en muchas cosas muy necessarias y pertenescientes al presente libro por el mismo autor ... Alcala, Joan de Brocar, 1539. (Ital. trans. 1568; 1577.)

265. HEYDEN, SEBALD. Musicae, id est, artis canendi libri duo. Autor Se-baldus Heyden. Norimbergae, apud J. Petreium, 1537. (Also 1540.)

266. ——————— Paedonomia scholastica pietatis, studii literarii ac morum honestatis praecepta continens. Auctor Sebaldus Heyden. Norim-bergae, in off. J. Montani et U. Neuber, 1546.

267. HOCKENHAFFEN, JOHANN. Axiomata disciplinae moralis, hoc est ethi-cae, oeconomiae, politicae ... Francofurti, 1595.

268. HONDORFF, ANDREAS. Theatrum historicum illustrium exemplorum ad honeste, pie, beateque vivendum mortale genus informantium ... initio quidem a. D. Andrea Hondorffio, idiomate germanico conscrip-tum, jam vero labore ... Phillipi II. Loniceri, ... latinitate donatum ... Francofurti ad Moenum, S. Feierabend, 1575. (Also 1586; 1598; 1607.)

269. HOROZCO Y COVARRUVIAS, JUAN. Emblemas morales de Don Juan de Horozco y Covarruvias, ... Segovia, J. de la Cuesta, 1589. (Also 1604.)

270. IBARRA, MARTIN. De puerorum moribus disticha ... Barcinone, 1526. (Also 1539; 1557; 1560; 1570.)

271. INDIA, FRANCESCO. L'heroe, overo della virtù heroica, dialogo di Francesco India. Verona, G. Discepolo, 1591.

272. ISOLANO, ISIDORO, O. P. De regum principumque omnium institutis liber frater Isidori Isolani, ... Mediolani, ex officina magistri Petri Martyris et fratrum de Mantegatiis, 1520?

273. Le jardin d'honneur. Paris, E. Groulleau, 1549.

274. Jo. Friderici & Jo. Wilhelmi, fratrum illustrium principum juniorum Saxonia declamationes 4. quarum prima est, De boni principis officia.

2. de divo Georgio. 3. de dignitate legum conservanda. 4. Gratulatio, qua patrem suum clem. Jo. Frid. Du. Sax. Electo. victorem à Brunsing redeuntem excepit. Witembergae, 1583. (Du Verdier.)

275. JONAS PHILOLOGUS, pseud. (Johann Günther). Jonae Philologi dialogi aliquot lepidi ac festivi, in studiosae juventutis informationem nunc primum et nati et aediti, quibus accessit adulationis et paupertatis dialogus pulcherrimus, quo juventus monetur, ne vel ulla necessitudine devicta, a bonis literis animum inflectat. Moguntiae, J. Schoeffer, 1529. (Also 1530; 1540.)

276. JONES, JOHN. The arte and science of preserving bodie and soule in healthe, wisedome, and catholike religion: phisically, philosophically and divinely devised: by John Jones Phisition. Right profitable for all persons: but chiefly for princes, rulers, nobles, byshoppes, preachers, parents, and them of the Parliament house. London, Henrie Bynneman, 1579.

277. JUNIUS (ADRIAN DE JONGE). Hadriani Junii, . . . emblemata . . . Ejusdem aenigmatum libellus . . . Antverpiae, ex officina C. Plantini, 1565. (Also 1556; 1569; 1575; 1585; 1596. French trans. 1570.)

278. ———— Hadr. Junii epistolae, quibus accedit ejusdem vita et oratio de artium liberalium dignitate. Dordrechti, apud V. Caimax, 1552.

279. JUVIGNY, SAMSON DE SAINT-GERMAIN, SIEUR DE. Traitté d'estat, contenant les points principaux pour la conservation des monarchies. Au roy par le sieur de Juvigny, . . . Paris, P. Des Hayes, 1618.

280. KETH, W. W. Keth his seeing glasse unto the nobilitie and jentlemen of Englande.

281. LA BIGNE, GACES DE. Des desduiz de la chasse des bestes sauvages et des oyseaux de proye. Paris, Antoine Verard, 1507?

282. LA FAYE, ANTOINE DE. Emblemata et epigrammata miscellanea, selecta ex stromatis peripateticis Antonii Fayi. Genevae, P. & J. Chouet, 1610.

283. LA GESSÉE, JEAN DE. La philosophie morale et civile du sieur de la Jessée. Paris, F. Morel, 1595. (First ed.)

284. LA JAILLE, HARDOUIN DE. Traitez et advis de quelques gentilshommes françois sur les duels et gages de bataille, assçavoir de Messire Olivier de La Marche, Messire Jean de Villiers, Messire Hardoiun de La Jaille et autres escrits sur le mesme sujet. Paris, J. Richer, 1586.

285. L'ALOUËTE, FRANÇOIS DE. Des affaires d'estat, des finances, du prince et de sa noblesse, par le présid. de Lalouette, . . . reveu et augmenté de nouveau en ceste seconde édition, par l'auteur même, de plusieurs belles remarques. Metz, J. d'Arras, 1597.

286. LA MADELEINE, JEAN DE. Discours de l'estat et office d'un bon roy, prince ou monarque pour bien et heurueusement régner sur la terre et

pour garder et maintenir ses subjectz en paix, union et obéissance, par maistre Jehan de La Madeleyne. Paris, Lucas Brayer, 1575. (Also 1597.)

287. La Marche, Oliver de. The resolved gentleman. London, R. Watkins, 1594. (Trans. Lewes Lewkenor.)

288. L'Ancre, P. de. Le livre des princes, contenant plusieurs notables discours, pour l'instruction des roys, empereurs et monarques, par P. de Lancre . . . Paris, N. Buon, 1617.

289. Landi, Ortensio. Varii componimenti di m. Hort. Lando. Nuovamente venuti in luce. Quaesiti amorosi, con le risposte. Dialogo intitolato Misse. Ragionamente occorso tra un cavaliere, et uno homo soletario . . . . Vinegia, Gabriel Giolito, 1552. (Also 1556.)

290. ————— La Sferza de' scrittori antichi et moderni di M. Antonio di Utopia, alla quale è dal medesimo aggiunta una essortatione allo studio delle lettere. Vinegia, 1550.

291. L'Anglois, Pierre. Discours des hieroglyphes aegyptiens, emblemes, devises, et armoiries. Paris, A. L'Angelier, 1584. (Also 1583.)

292. La Place, Pierre de. Du droict usage de la philosophie morale avec la doctrine chrestienne, par Pierre de la Place . . . Paris, F. Morel, 1562. (Also 1658.)

293. ————— Traitté de la vocation & maniere de vivre à laquelle chacun est appellé, par Pierre de la Place, . . . Paris, Federic Morel, 1561. (Also 1574; 1578.)

294. Larivey, Pierre de. Deux livres de filosophie fabuleuse, le premier prins des discours de M. Ange Firenzuola, Florentin, par lequel, souz le sens allégorie de plusieurs belles fables, est monstrée l'envie, malice et trahison d'aucuns courtisans: le second extraict des traitez de Sandebar, indien philosophe moral, traictant soubs pareilles allégories de l'amitié et choses semblables, par Pierre de La Rivey, . . . Lyon, B. Rigaud, 1579. (Also 1620.)

295. Lauder, William. Ane compendious and breve tractate, concernyng ye office of kyngis. St. Andrews, J. Scot, 1556.

296. Lauterbach, Johann. Tractatus novus de armis et literis, quo de praecedentia militis et doctoris affatim disseritur, Johanne Lauterbach, . . . Witebergae, typis M. G. Mullerii, 1595.

297. Le Breton, François. La fontaine d'honneur & de vertue, ou est monstré comme un chacun doit vivre en tout aage, en tout temps, & en tout lieu envers Dieu & envers les hommes. Lyon, Jean de Tournes, 1555. (Du Verdier. Trans. from Latin.)

298. Le Caron, Louis. Les dialogues. Paris, V. Sertenas, 1556.

299. Legrand, Jean-Mathieu. Joannis Mathaei Magni de literata nobilitate. Orationes quinque. Ad nobilissimum, & omnibus virtutum, ac

literarum ornamentis praestantissimum virum D. Philippum Hurault
. . . Parisiis, ex typographia Dionysii à Prato, 1588. (Arms or letters.)

300. LE GUILLARD, PIERRE DE. L'epenopetie, ou la loüange du jeu des dez.
Caen, Pierre le Chandelier. (Du Verdier.)

301. LE JAY, FRANÇOIS. De la dignité des rois et princes souverains, du
droict inviolable de leurs successeurs légitimes et du devoir des peuples
et subjectz envers eux. Tours, M. Le Mercier, 1589.

302. LE MAIRE, JEAN. Le temple dhonneur & de vertus. Paris, A. Lotrian
et D. Janot, 1535?

303. LE MASLE, JEAN. Le breviaire des nobles, contenant sommairement
toutes les vertues & perfections requises à un gentilhomme pour bien
entretenir sa noblesse (Prose.) Plux deux discours en rime traictans
de l'origine du droict & de la noblesse. Paris, Nicolas Bonfons, 1578.
(Du Verdier.)

304. ———————— Les nouvelles recreations poetiques de Jean Le Masle,
Angevin. Contenans aucuns discours, non moins recreatifs & plaisans,
que sententieuz & graves. Au premier desquels est traite, des loüanges
du droit et loix civiles, ensemble de leur origine. Au second, de l'origine & excellence de la noblesse. Et au troisieme, de l'origine des
Gaulois: ensemble des Angevins et Mauceaux. Avec plusieurs sonnets,
odes et autres oeuvres dudict Le-Masle. Paris, Guillaume Bichon,
1586.

305. LESNAUDERIE, PIERRE LEMONNIER DE. Opusculum de doctoribus et
privilegiis eorum Petri de Lesnauderie, legum doctoris, nuper emacu-
latissime impressum, in lucem felici sydere prodit. Parhisiis, expensis
Francisci Regnault, 1517.

306. LEYSER, CHRISTOF. Orationes quinque de certo genere vitae homini
nobili deligendo, exercitii causa a quinique adolescentibus [Enrico a
Gera, Christophoro Leysero, Philippo Theodorico Böcklino, Benedicto
a Qualen, Wolffgango Esurico Jagenreuthero] scriptae . . . Argentorati,
A. Bertramus, 1586.

307. Libro della natura delli cavalli. 1537.

308. LICETI, GIOSEPPE. La nobilità de principali membri dell' huomo, dialogo di Gioseppe Liceto, . . . Bologna, G. Rossi, 1590.

309. LIEB, CHRISTOPHORUS JACOBUS. Gebissbuch oder Kurtzer und
Gründlicher Bericht, von Gebiss und Zeumung der Pferd, sampt
deroselben unterschiedlichen Wurckung, auch wie dieselben nütz-
lich und nach gelegenheit der Pferdt zugebrauchen sein. Allen Hohen
und Nieders Standes Personen, und dieser Kunst Liebhabern zu sonderbahren Ehren auffs kürtzte verfast, und in offnen Druck gegeben,
durch Christoff. Jacob Lieb. . . . Dressden, Gimel Bergen, 1616.

310. ———————— Practica et arte di Cavalleria. Ubung und Kunst des

Reitens, in welcher der Bereuter, die Pferd nach jhrer Art und Natur zu unterweisen und abzurichten, erfahren und geübt sein sol. Auch wie, und uff was weise dieselben in solcher handlung und abrichtung, zu schönen wolstendigen Geberden und guten Tugenden sollen gewehnet und gezogen werden. Allen Liebhabern, und dieser Adelichen Ritterlichen Kunst zugethanen, zu sonderbahren Ehren und gefallen, uffs kürtzte in zwey Theil verfast, und in offnen Druck gegeben. Durch Christoff. Jacob Lieb. Mit Rom. Käy ... Dressden, Gimel Bergen, 1616.

311. LINDSAY, DAVID (BISHOP). De potestate principe aphorismi. Edinburgi, T. Finlason, 1617.

312. LINDSAY, SIR DAVID. A dialogue betweene experience and a courtier. London, T. Purfoote, 1581.

313. Le livre du roy Modus. 1328. (On the chase.)

314. LOBERA DE AVILA, LUIS. Libro de las quatro enfermedades cortesanas que son catarro, gota, arthetica, sciatica, mal de piedra y de riñones e brijada, e mal de buas y otras cosas utilissimas, nuevamente compuesto por el excellentissimo doctor Luys Lobera de Avila, ... 1544. (Also Ital. trans. 1558.)

315. ————— Vanquete de nobles cavalleros e modo de bivir desde que se levantan hasta que se acuestan, y habla de cada manjar que complexion y propiedad tiene e que daños y provechos haze, e trata de regimiento, curativo e preservativo de las fiebres pestilenciales e de la pestilencia e otras cosas utilissimas ... nuevamente compuesto por el doctor Luys de Avila, ... Augustae Vindelicorum, per H. Stainerum, 1530. (Also 1542. Germ. trans. 1531; 1551.)

316. A looking glasse for eche degree. 1595.

317. LOPEZ DE SIGURA, RUY. Libro de la invención liberal y arte del juego del axedrez ... Compuesta ... por Ruy López de Sigura, ... Alcala, A. de Angulo, 1541. (French trans. 1615, 2nd ed.; 1636; 1674. Ital. trans. 1584.)

318. LORKYN, THOMAS. Recta regula & victus ratio pro studiosis & literatis. Londini, 1562.

319. LOTINI, FRANCISCO. Avvedimenti civili, di M. Giovan Francesco Lottini da Volterra, ne' quali si contengono molti ammaestramenti utili, così per la vita politica, come per le consulte, & per li governi de gli stati. Al Sereniss. D. Francesco Medici Gran Duca di Toscana. Venetia, Jacomo Leonzini, 1575. (Also 1582; 1583; 1588; 1598; 1608. French trans. 1584.)

320. LOUIS IX. Les preceptes du Roy S. Louys a Philippes III son fils, pour bien vivre & regner: tirez des histoires de France, & des registres de la Chambre des Comptes. Avec les discours sur chacun d'iceux de Me. A. Theveneau Advocat en Parlement. Sont raportez, et inter-

pretez plusieurs ordonnances touchant la police, tant spirituelle, que temporelle. Paris, Jean Petit-Pas, 1627. (Eng. trans. 1662. A slighter and different set of precepts was published in 1766.)

321. LUCHINI, PAOLO, O. S. A. Due brevi ragionamenti, uno del modo del parlare senza errare, e l'altro del consigliarsi bene, per non cadere in pericolo nelle cose importanti & per non restare ingannato, composti dal R. P. Maestro in Theologia Fra Paolo Luchini . . . Urbino, Bartholomeo Ragusii, 1588.

322. ———— Eptamerone overo eptalogi della nobiltà mondana, del M. R. P. F. Paolo Luchini da Pesaro, . . . nuovamente stampati e corretti per opera del P. F. Nicola Zacconi da Pesaro, . . . Pesaro, G. Concordia, 1599.

323. LUCINGE, RENÉ DE. De la naissance, durée et cheute des estats, où sont traittées plusieurs notables questions sur l'establissement des empires et monarchies . . . par René de Lusinge, . . . Paris, M. Orry, 1588. (Eng. trans. see below.)

324. ———— (Eng. trans.). The beginning, continuance and decay of estates, wherein are handled many notable questions concerning the establishment of empires and monarchies, written in French by R. de Lusing, . . . and translated into English by J[ohn] F[inett]. London, J. Bill, 1606.

325. ———— La manière de lire l'histoire . . . par René de Lusinge, sieur des Alymes. Paris, T. Du Bray, 1614.

326. LUGO, PEREGRINUS DE. Principia seu introductiones in via doctoris subtilles. London, R. Pynson, 1508?

327. LYSTER, JOHN. A rule how to bring up children. London, T. East, 1588.

328. MACCIUS, SEBASTIANUS. Sebastiani Macii, . . . de historia libri tres . . . Venetiis, A. & B. Dei, 1613.

329. MAGO, AGOGO. Opera nobilissima composta per lo excellente Maestro Agogo Mago. De tutte le passion vien a falconi astori e sparaveri. Venezia?, 1523.

330. MANÇANAS, EUGENIO. Libro de enfrenamientos de la gineta, por Eugenio Mançanas, . . . Toledo, P. Rodriguez, 1583.

331. MANRIQUE, GOMEZ. Regimento de principes.

332. MARCHANT, CLÉMENT. Remonstrance aux Francoys, sur les vices qui de ce temps regnent en tous estats, avec le remède à iceux, par M. Clément Marchant. Paris, N. Chesneau & J. Poupy, 1576. (Also 1586; 1587; 1588.)

333. C'est li mariages des filles au Diable. Jubinel, Nouveau recueil, Paris, 1839. (T. I. pp. 283–292. The evil doings of all estates and what each ought to be.)

334. MARKHAM, GERVASE. A schoole for young soldiers. 1616.

335. MARNIX, JEAN DE. Résolutions politiques et maximes d'estat du Sr.

Jean de Marnix, ... Rouen, J. Pain, 1620. (Also 1621; 1622; 1624; 1627; 1631; 1632.)

336. MARY QUEEN OF SCOTS. Royal advice to her son. The institution of a prince. (French verse.)

337. MASTRILLO, GARSIA. De magistratibus, eorum imperio et jurisdictione, tractatus in duas partes distinctus, Don Garsia Mastrillo, ... authore, ... Lugduni, A. Pillehotte, 1621. (Also 1667.)

338. MATEROT, LUCAS. Les oevres de Lucas Materot, ... où l'on comprendra facilement la manière de bien et proprement escrire toute sorte de lettre italienne selon l'usage de ce siècle. Avignon, J. Bramereau, 1608.

339. MATTEACI, GIUSEPPE. Ragionamenti politici di Giuseppe Mattheacci, ornati de dottrina civile et militare, con essempi antichi e moderni, da Pietro, suo figlivolo, raccolti ... Venetia, Santo-Grillo e fratelli, 1613.

340. MAUGIN, JEAN. Le parangon de vertu contenant 36. chapitres pour l'institution de tous princes. Lyon, Guillaume Rouille, 1556. (Also 1573. Du Verdier.)

341. MAURICE, MATHURIN. De l'origine de vraye noblesse & nourriture d'icelle pour les enfans genereux. Paris, Nicolas Chrestien, 1551. (Du Verdier.)

342. MAZZELA, SCIPIONE. La dechiratione dell' imprese, motti e versi. Napoli, 1584.

343. MELANCTHON, PHILIP. Philippi Melanchthonis de arte dicendi declamatio. Parisiis, ex officina Roberti Stephani, 1527. (Argument for study of the arts.)

344. ———— Philippi Melancthonis de corrigendis studiis sermo. Rodolphi Agricolae de formandis studiis epistola doctiss. Parisiis, ex officina Roberti Stephani, 1527.

345. MENAGUERRA, PONZ DE. Lo cavaller. Valenda, 1532. Facsimile, 1880? (Riding, military training.)

346. MESCHINOT, JEAN. Les lunettes des princes, par Jehan Meschinot ... Nantes, E. Larcher, 1493. (Also 1495; 1501; 1528; 1539.)

347. MEXIA, FRANCISCO, O.P. Dialogo del soldado, compuesto por el Reverendo Padre Fray Francisco Mexía, ... Valencia, J. Navarro, 1555.

348. MEXIA, HERNANDO. Libro de la nobleza. Sevilla, Pedro Brun, 1492.

349. MEYNIER, HONORAT DE. Les reigles, sentences et maximes de l'art militaire, et les remarques du sieur de Meynier sur le devoir des simples soldats et de leurs supérieurs. Paris, Vve. de M. Guillemot, 1617.

350. MICHAULT, PIERRE. Le doctrinal de court, divisé en douze chapitres selon orde (sic) du doctrinal de maistre Alexandre, composé par

maistre Pierre Michault . . . Genesve, Jacques Vivian, 1522. (Also 1466.)

351. MIGNAULT, CLAUDE. De liberali adolescentum institutione in academia parisiensi declamationes contrariae, quarum summa quaestio est, an sit commodius adolescentes extra gymnasia quam in gymnasiis ipsis institui. Harum argumentum duobus . . . suis auditoribus [Lazaro de Selve et Jacobo Thomas] proponebat Claudius Minos, . . . Parisiis, apud J. Richerium, 1575.

352. MILAN, LUIS. Libro intitulado el cortesano, dirigido a la Catholica, Real, Magestad, del Invictissimo Don Phelipe . . . Compuesto por Don luys Milan. Donde se vera lo que deve tener por reglas y practica. Repartido por iornadas. Mostrando su intincio por huyr prolixidad debaxo esta brevedad. Sirviendo de prologo, y direction, y utilidad, esta presente carta. Valencia, Joan de Arcos, 1561.

353. MONTBOURCHER, PAUL DE. Traicté des cérémonies et ordonnances appartenans à gage de bataille et combats en camp-clos, selon les institutions de Philippes de France, donné au Roy par Paul Demontbourcher, sieur de La Rivaudière.—Advis au Roy touchant le restablissement du gage de bataille en camp-clos . . . Paris, G. Marette, 1608.

354. MONTE, HIERONYMUS DE. Tractatus de finibus regendis civitatum, castrorum, ac praediorum . . . D. Hieronymo de Monte, Brixiano . . . auctore . . . Venetiis, ex officina J. Zilleti, 1556. (Also 1562; 1573; 1574; 1590.)

355. MONTENAY, GEORGETTE DE. Emblèmes ou devises chrestiennes, composées par damoiselle Georgette de Montenay. Lyon, J. Marcorelle, 1571. (Latin trans. 1584. Belgian, Eng., Germ., Ital., Latin, Span. trans. 1619.)

356. MONTLUC, BLAISE DE. Commentaires de messire Blaise de Monluc, . . . où sont descris les combats, rancontres . . . avecque plusieurs autres faicts de guerre signalez et remarcables, esquels ce grand et renommé guerrier s'est trouvé . . . ensemble diverse instructions qui ne doivent estre ignorées de ceux qui veulent parvenir par les armes à quelqu' honneur . . . Blasii Monluci . . . Tumulus. Bordeaus, S. Millanges, 1592. (Also 1593; 1594; 1607; 1626; 1641; 1661; 1746.)

357. MONZON, FRANCISCO DE. Libro primero d'l espejo del principe christiano. Lisboa, L. Rodriquez, 1544. (Also 1571.)

358. MORE, GEORGE. Principles for yong princes: collected out of sundry authors. London, N. Okes, 1611.

359. MORTIER, RUMOLD. Rumoldi Mortierii oratio de querimoniis professionis litterariae . . . Parisiis, S. Prevosteau, 1600.

360. MOSCATELLO, GIOVANNI BERNARDINO. De doctoratus dignitate, decore

ac auctoritate, in cujus fine recensentur similitudines antiquorum Romanorum magistratuum cum supremis magistratibus nostri temporis in regno Neap., auctore Jo. Bernardino Muscatello... Ejusdem judicium inter utramque militiam. Neapoli, apud J. Carlinum, 1579.

361. MOSELLANUS, PETRUS, pseud. (Peter de Schade). Paedologia Petri Mosellani Protegensis in puerorum usum conscripta et aucta. Dialogi XXXVII. Parisiis, ex officina Roberti Stephani, 1528.

362. MOUILHET, PIERRE DE. Discours politique au Roy, par P. D. M. Paris, 1618.

363. MOULERE, DE. Vida y muerte de los cortesanos, compuesta por el señor de Moulere. Paris, G. Robinot, 1614.

364. MOUNDEFORD, THOMAS. Vir bonus. Q. Vir bonus est quis? R. Qui consultat patrum, qui leges juraque servat temperentiae, prudentiae, justitiae, fortitudinis... authore Tho. Moundeford,... Londini, per F. Kingstonum, 1622.

365. MUNDAY, ANTHONY. A banquet of daintie conceits. Furnished with verie delicate and choyse inventions, to delight their mindes, who take pleasure in musique, and there-withall to sing sweete ditties, either to the lute, bandora, virginalles, or anie other instrument. Published at the desire of bothe honorable and worshipfull personages, who have had copies of divers of the ditties heerein contained. Written by A. M. servaunt to the Queenes most excellent Majestie. London, by J. C. for Edwarde White, 1588.

366. MUSSET, LOUIS. Discours sur les remonstrances et réformations de chacun estat, et déclaration de l'obéissance du peuple aux roys et. princes... par M. Louys Musset,... Paris, N. Chesnau, 1582.

367. MUTIO, GASPARO. Fonte di nobilità di Gasparo Mutio della Stella... Genova, A. Bellone, 1570.

368. NAALDWYCK, PETRUS à. Libri duo philippicorum sive de equorum natura, electione, educatione, disciplina et curatione. Authore Petro à Naaldwyck,... Lugduni Batavorum, apud Andream Cloucquium, 1531.

369. NATTA, MARCANTONIO. Marci Antonii Nattae Astensis volumina quaedam nuper excusa, numero & ordine, qui subiicitur. De libris suis quibusdam nunc primum in lucem editis & argumentis eorum. De principum doctrina, libri IX in quibus plurima de veterum heroum, regum, imperatorum gestis & regimine continentur. In funere Jo. Francisci Nattae patruelis, oratorio. In obitu illust. Hieronimi Aedurini laudatio, seu consolatio. Pro se & fratribus, seu pro familiarum dignitate. Quum suscepit Mantuae magistratum Rotae, oratorio. Post absolutionem gesti magistratus alia oratio. De Christianorum eloquentia liber. Venetiis, in officina Aldi, 1562.

370. NAUSEA, FRIEDRICH GRAU. Friderici Nauseae, . . . de puero literis instituendo consiliorum liber primus. Coloniae, J. Gymnicus, 1536.

371. NEUGEBAUER, SALOMON. Tractatus de peregrinatione methodo naturali conscriptus, ac historicis, ethicis, politicisque exemplis illustratus, studio Salomonis Neugebaueri, . . . cum indice rerum et exemplorum. Basileae, per S. Henricpetri, 1605.

372. NIGER, FRANCISCUS. Ars epistolandi Francisci Nigri. Daventriae, 1491. (Also 1496; three others undated but before 1500; 1502.)

373. NOLDEN, JOSAIS. Josiae Nolden . . . de statu nobilium civili synoptica tractatio, in qua nobilium jura, privilegia, immunitates, dignitates . . . explicantur . . . Gissae Hessorum, typis Hampelii, 1623.

374. NORDEN, JOHN. England; an intended guyde for English travailers. 1625.

375. —————— The fathers legacie; with precepts and prayers. London, f. J. Marriot, 1625.

376. Il nuovo cortegiano de vita cauta et morale. Con gratia et privilegio. Nessuno ardisca stampare il presente volume sotto le pene che ne privileggiisi contengono.

377. OBICIUS, HIPPOLYTUS. De nobilitate medici contra illius obtrectatores, dialogus tripartitus in quo . . . comprobatur medicum jurisprudente esse nobiliorem; postea de omnibus scientiis artibusque compendiosus habetur tractatus, auctore Hippolyto Obicio, . . . Venetiis, apud R. Mejettum, 1605. (Also 1619.)

378. OFFREDI, PIETRO. La politica saviezza fondata sopra le quattro virtù morali . . . data in luce dal sign. capitano Pietro Offredi. Fiorenza, P. Cecconcelli, 1624.

379. OLIVIERO, ANTONIO FRANCESCO. La Alamanna di M. Antonio Francesco Oliviero, . . . Venetia, V. Valgrisi, 1567. (See t. II, L'origine d'amore. Verse.)

380. An order whych a prince in battayll must observe and kepe, yf he entende to subdewe or passe thoroughe his enemyes landes. London, Thomas Raynold and William Hyll, 1548?

381. PALAZZO, GIOVANNI ANTONIO. Discorso del governo e della ragion vera di stato, di Gio. Antonio Palazzo, . . . diviso in quattro libri . . . Venetia, G. A. & G. de' Franceschi, 1606. (French trans. 1611. Latin trans. 1637.)

382. PALMIERE, LORENZINO. Perfette regole et modi di cavalcare di Lorenzino Palmieri, . . . et sieme si tratta della natura de' cavalli, si propongono le loro infermità; e s'additano gli remedi per curarle . . . Venezia, B. Barezzi, 1625.

383. PARAVICINO, BASILIO. Discorso del riso, vera proprietà dell' huomo . . . composta da M. Basilio Paravicino, . . . Como, H. Frova, 1615.

384. PARUTA, PAOLO. Discorsi politici di Paolo Paruta, . . . nei quali si

considerano diversi fatti illustri . . . di principi e di republiche antiche
e moderne; divisi in due libri aggiontovi nel fine un suo soliloquio,
nel quale l'authore fa un breve essame . . . della sua vita. Venetia,
D. Nicolini, 1599. (Also 1600; 1602.)

385. PASQUIER, ETIENNE. Des recherches de la France livre premier. Plus,
un pourparler du prince. Le tout par Estienne Pasquier, advocat en
la cour de Parlement de Paris. Paris, Vincent Sertenas, 1560. (See the
Pourparler, a dialogue particularly on the question of the prince's
learning.)

386. PASQUIER, NICOLAS. Le gentilhomme, par Nicolas Pasquier. Paris,
J. Petit-Pas, 1611. (Wrongly attributed in the original bibliography to
Etienne, the father of Nicolas.)

387. PASSI, GIUSEPPE. Discorso del ben parlare, per non offendere persona
alcune, nuovamente formato e poste in luce da Gioseppe Passi, nell'
Academia de' Signore Informi di Ravenna, l'Ardito, fatto da lui in
occasione d'esser stato calumniato, per haver recitato una sua lettione
nello detta academia. Venetia, G. A. Somasco, 1600.

388. PELLETIER, THOMAS. La nourriture de la noblesse, ou sont repre-
sentées, comme un tableau, toutes les plus belles vertus, qui peuvent
accomplir un jeune gentilhomme . . . Par le sr. Pelletier. Paris, Vve.
M. Patisson, 1604. (Also 1610.)

389. PERCY, HENRY, EARL OF NORTHUMBERLAND. Letters to his son Alger-
non, 1595 or 1596; 1609. Pub. by G. B. Harrison, 1930. (2nd letter,
pub. in *Archaeologia*, vol. 27 (1838), pp. 306–358.)

390. PEREZ, ANTONIO. L'art de gouverner discours addressé à Philippe III
(1598) publié pour la première fois en espagnol et en français . . . Paris,
1867. Facsimile.

391. PEREZ DEL BARRIO ANGULO, GABRIEL. Dirección de secretarios de
señores, y las materias cuy dados y obligaciones que les tocan . . . por
Gabriel Perez del Barrio Angulo. Madrid, A. M. de Balboa, 1613.
(Also 1645; 1667.)

392. A perfect booke for keping of sparhawkes or goshawkes. Written about
1575. Now first printed from the original MS. on vellum with introduction and glossary by J. E. Harting. London, Bernard Quaritch, 1886.

393. PERSICO, PANFILO. Del segretario del sig. Panfilo Persico libri quattro,
. . . Venetia, l'heredi di D. Zenaro, 1620. (Also 1656; 1670.)

394. PERUSCUS, MARIUS. De studiis ac literarum laudibus, oratio, in aedibus divi Eustachii, a Mario Perusco, Julii filio, habita. Romae, apud
J. de Angelis, 1571.

395. PESCETTI, ORLANDO. Dell' onore, dialoghi tre d'Orlando Pescetti, nel
primo de' qual si distrugge l'onore innato del Conte Annibal Romei.
Nel secondo si porta l'opinione dell' autore, e con molte ragioni si prova
le richezze essere di maggior valore, e per consequenza di maggior onor

degne della virtù. Nel terzo si risolvono alcuni dubbi nati dalle cose dette, e reprovansi molte opinioni del Romei, e dell' Albergati... Verona, Angelo Tamo, 1624.

396. ———— Orazione d'Orlando Pescetti dietro al modo dell' instituire la gioventù, alla magnifica, et inclita città di Verona... Verona, Girolamo Discepolo, 1592.

397. PESCI, RUGGIERO. Delle imprese, discorso del Sonnacchio havuto nell' academia della notte di Bologna. Dedicato all' illustriss. signor Bartolomeo Lupari. Bologna, N. Tebaldini, 1624.

398. PETRAEUS, NICOLAUS. Enchiridion politicum, praeceptis, sententiis, historiis et controversiis methodice dispositis adornatum, opera Nicolai Petraei, ... Argentinae, 1625.

399. PHARETRATUS, MICHAEL. M. Michaelis Pharetrati tractatus de nobilitate in honore et precio habenda, cui accessit stemma nobilium Brandensteiniorum... Lipsiae, ex officina Grosiana, 1622.

400. PHILIPPE DE LEYDE. De republica cura et sorte principatis a reverendissima universitate et felici collegio doctorum et scolarium studii Aurelianensis missus... potenti duci Wilhelmo de Bavaria, ... Philippi de Leyden, ... Tractatus. Ejusdem de formis et semitis republice utilius et facilius gubernande... Leydis, in aedibus J. Severini, 1516.

401. PHILOTHEUS, MONACHUS BRIXIANUS. Theophili Brixiani de vita solitaria & civili. Ad invictissimum principem Guidonem Ubaldum monferetrium Urbini ducem Carmen lepidum atque familiare. Colonie, per Martinum de Werdena, 1510. (Also 1496.)

PIBRAC, SEIGNEUR DE. See Du Faur.

402. PICCOLOMINI, FRANCESCO. Breve discorso della instituzione di un principe. First pub. 1858.

403. PIETRE, ROLAND. Le premier livre des considérations politiques de Roland Pietre, ... Paris, R. Estienne, 1566.

404. PIETRO ARETINO. Ragionamento nel quale M. Pietro Aretino figura quattro suoi amici, che favellano de le corti del mondo, e di quella del cielo. Francesco Marcolino, 1539. (Also 1538; 1541; 1589.)

405. PILORCIUS, ROCCHUS. Rocchi Pilorcii, ... de scribendi rescribendique epistolas ratione liber... Antverpiae, ex officina C. Plantini, 1577.

406. PITHOU, JEAN. Instruction pour tous estats, en laquelle est sommairement declaré comme chacun en son estat se doit gouverner & vivre selon Dieu. Lyon, Jean Saugrain, 1566. (Du Verdier.)

407. PITSILLIUS, MARCUS ANTONIUS. M. Ant. Pitsillii, ... commentariorum de instruendo principe imago... Neapoli, ex typ. J. B. Subtilis, 1603.

408. PIUS II (Aeneus Sylvius Piccolomini). Tractatus de liberorum educatione ad Ladislaum Ungariae & Bohemiae regem. In *Opera quae extant omnia*, 1571. (Pp. 965–992.)

409. ———— Tractatus pulcherrimus Enee Silvii sive Pii Pape II de curialium miseria feliciter incipit. 1475.

410. Porteus of noblenes. Tr. A. Cadion. Edinburgh, W. Chemian and A. Millar, 1508.

411. PRATO, ANTONIO. Discorso del M. R. D. Antonio Prato dottor theologo, sopra il saggio reggimento del prencipe. Scritto al molt' Illustre Signor Emanuel Filiberto di Negro Marchese di Mullazzano. Et da esso signore tradotto nella lingua volgare. Genuae, apud Hieronymum Bartolum, 1590.

412. PRICE, DANIEL. The creation of the prince. A sermon. London, G. Eld f. R. Jackson, 1610.

413. PROCTER, THOMAS. Of the knowledge and conducte of warres. Londini, in aed. R. Totteli, 1578.

414. PRUDENT LE CHOYSELAT. A discourse of housbandrie, etc. Tr. R. Eden? London, J. Kyngston f. M. Jennynges, 1577. (Also 1580.)

415. QUIXADA DE REAYO, JUAN. Doctrina del arte de la cavalleria, ordenado por Juan Quixada de reayo vezino dela villa de Olmedo hombre de armas de la capitania del muy illustrissimo señor el duque de Alburguerque a fin de dar course jo a un hijo suyo como mas viejo en las guardas delos reyes passados de gloriosa memoria. So correction de otros cavalleros que lo saben mejor bazer y dezir. Medina, Pedro de Castro, 1548. Facsimile 1880?

416. RAPIN, NICOLAS. Les plaisirs du gentilhomme champestre, augmenté de quelques nouveaux poèmes et épigrammes, par N. R. P. Paris, Vve. L. Breyer, 1583.

417. REGIUS, URBANUS. A comparison betweene the olde learnyge & the newe. 1537. (Also 1538; 1548. Trans. W. Turner.)

418. RINGELBERGIUS, JOACHIMUS FORTIUS. Ratio studii. Lyon, 1523. (Also 1531; 1541; 1556; 1622; 1645; 1792.)

419. RINUCCINI, ANNIBALE. Quatro lezzioni di M. Annibale Rinuccini Fiorentino. Lette publicamente da lui nell' Academia Fiorentina. Firenze, Lorenzo Torrent, 1561. (Honor, friendship.)

420. RIVAULT, DAVID DE FLURANCE. Les estats, esquels il est discouru du prince, du noble, & du tiers estat, conformement a nostre temps, . . . par D. D. R. de Flurance. Lyon, B. Rigaud, 1596. (Also 1595.)

421. ———— Minerva armata de conjungendis literis et armis, lectio habita a D. Rivaldo a Flurantia, . . . in celeberrima humoristarum academia, Romae, 28 Februarii . . . 1610. Romae, apud S. Paulinum, 1610.

422. ROGERS, THOMAS. Anatomie of the minde. 1576. (Bk. II, *Of morall vertues.*)

423. ROLLENHAGEN, GABR. Nucleus emblematum selectissimorum . . . studio singulari undique conquisitus . . ., venustis inventionibus auctus, additis carminibus, illustratus a Gabr. Rollenhagio. Coloniae,

ex museo caelatorio Crisp. Passaei, 1611–1613. (Also 1615. French trans. 1611.)

424. RONSARD, PIERRE DE. Institution pour l'adolescence du Roy, tres chrestien Charles neufiesme de ce nom. Par P. de Ronsard Vandomois. Paris, Gabriel Buon, 1563.

425. ROSCIO, LUCIO VITRUVIO. De docendi studendique modo, ac de claris puerorum moribus, libellus planè aureus. L. Vitruvio Roscio Parmensi autore, cui adiecimus etiam alios ejusdem argumenti libellos aliquot, nunc primum summa diligentia in studiosorum gratiam editos. Quorum catalogum proxima statim à praefatione pagella indicabit. Basileae, ex officina Roberti Winter, 1540. (Also 1541. Contents: 1. *L. Vitruvii Roscii Parmensis de docendi studendique modo, ac de claris puerorum moribus, libellus. 2. Jacobi Comitis Purliliarum de generosa liberorum educatione opusculum. 3. Maphei Vegii Laudensis de educatione liberorum, & claris eorum moribus lib. VI. Eiusdem Maphei Vegii vita. 4. Petri Pauli Vergerii Justinopolitani de ingenuis moribus ac liberalibus studiis libellus. 5. Praecepta vitae puerilis, Joachimo Camerario Pabergensi autore. 6. Praecepta honestatis atque decoris puerilis, eodem autore. 7. De gymnasiis, sive ludis puerorum, dialogus, eodem autore. 8. Jani Anysii sententiae, iambicis metris comprehensae, totius philosophiae moralis veluti promptuarium quoddam oratio matutina ad omnipotentem deum, Decio Ausonio autore.*)

426. ROWLAND, DAVID. A comfortable ayde for scholars. London, H. Wykes, 1568. (Also 1578.)

427. ROY, WILLIAM. A proper dyalog betwene a gentillman and a husbandman. 1530.

428. RUSH, ANTHONY. A president for a prince. 1566.

429. RUSTO, GIORDANO. Il dotissimo libro non piu stampato delle mascalzie del cavallo del Signor Giordano Rusto Calaurese. Dove con bellissimo ordine da' conto di conoscere tutte le cose pertinenti al cavallo, e tutte le sorti d'infirmità, & da che nascano, con i rimedi di quelle. Di puj, vi s'è aggionto un trattato di Alberto Magno dell' istessa materia, tradotto dal latino in questa nostra volgar lingua. Et alcuni altri belli secreti di diversi autori non piu stampati per l'adietro. Con tre tavole appartate poste per ordine delle cose continenti in detto libro. Bologna, Giovanni de' Rossi, 1561.

430. S., T. A jewell for the gentrie. 1614.

431. SACCHI, BARTHOLOMEUS, DE PLATINA. Dialogus Platyne de vera nobilitate. Erphordiae, in aedit. Stribelitae, 1510.

432. ————— Principis Διατύπωσις. Baptistae Sacci Platinae, viri, omni virtutum et doctrinarum genere clarissimi, tractatus utilissimus, continens, quae principi vero, qui perfectus esse velit, cum pacis tum belli tempore, facienda, sint quaeque fugienda. Ubi de pii principis virtutibus, disciplinaque aulica & militari, cum cohaerentibus hisce,

perpulchrè differitur; vitiorumque dehortatio obiter interspergitur. Opusculum, ex probatissimis autoribus concinnatum, imperatorum, regum & sapientissimorum heroum exemplis illustratum, & iam primum editum. Cui, ob materiae affinitatem, Cardinalis P. Albodrandini Apophthegmata, De perfecto principe, artem imperandi complectentia, adiecimus. Francofurti, apud Nicolaum Hofmannum, impensis Egenolphi Emmelii, 1608.

433. Sainct Fere, Jean. La republique Chrestienne, divisee en deux parties, contenant le vray miroir & institution d'un prince Chrestien, pour bien & heureusement conduire ses meurs & actions en l'administration & gouvernement d'un royaume, comme aussi de tous ceux qui ont charge & manyement des affaires du public, & pareillement de toutes autres personnes qui desirent vivre selon les vertues morales & intellectives, & conformer leur vie aux preceptes d'icelles. Illustre de la doctrine & innumerables exemples des histoires anciennes & modernes, prises tant de la saincte escriture & ancient peres de l'eglise, que des autheurs prophanes. Paris, Jean Poupy, 1578. (Du Verdier.)

434. Saint-Gelais, Octavien de. Le sejour dhonneur. Paris, A. Verard, 1519.

435. ———— Le vergier dhonneur. Paris, P. Le Noir, 1520?

436. Salel, Hugues. Chasse royalle, contenant la prise du Sanglier Discord, par tres haultz & trespuissans princes, Lempereur Charles cinquiesme, et le Roy, Francoys Premier de ce nom. In *Les oeuvres*, Paris. 1539. (Hunting terms used for a political allegory.)

437. Salvadori, Andrea. Heroica instituzione di principe. 1620–1630.

438. Sarpi, Paolo. The free true school of warre. 1625.

439. Scazzo, Giovanni. Institutio principum.

440. Schoonhovius, Florentius. Emblemata, partim moralia, partim etiam civilia, cum latiori eorumdem interpretatione: accedent et alia quaedam poematia. Goudae, 1618. (Also 1626; 1648.)

441. Schottenius, Hermann. Vita honesta, sive virtutis: quomodo quisque vivere debeat, omni aetate, omni tempore, & quolibet loco, erga Deum & homines. Hermanus Schottennio Hesso authore. Huic novissimè adjecimus institutionem Christiani hominis, per Adrianum Barlandum aphorismis digestam. Hic accessit, formula honestae vitae, sive de quatuor virtutibus, consarcimatio. Martino Episcopo Dumiensi, authore. Liber planè aureus, hactenus Senecae falsò adscriptus. Lugduni, sub Scuto Coloniensi, 1545.

442. Scott, Patrick. Omnibus et singulis, affording matter profitable for all men, alluding to a fathers advice or last will to his sonne. 1619.

443. ———— A table-booke for princes. 1621.

444. Scott, Thomas. Four paradoxes: of arte, of lawe, of warre, of service. London, f. T. Bushell, 1602.

445. Simeone, Gabriele. Cesar renouvellé. Par les observations mili-

taires du S. Gabriel Symeon, Floren. Paris, Jean Longis, 1558. (Also 1569, revised by Francoys de S. Thomas, with title *La vraye forme de bien et heureusement vivre et gouverner un royaume ou monarchie* ...)

446. SORBIN, ARNAUD. Exhortation a la noblesse pour les dissuader et destourner des duels, & autres combats, contre le commandement de Dieu, devoir & honneur deus au prince. Par M. Arnauld Sorbin, dict de S. Foy, Predicateur du Roy. Paris, Guillaume Chaudiere, 1578.

447. STOCKWOOD, JOHN. A Bartholomew Fairing for parentes. 1589.

448. SULPITIUS, JOANNES. Libellus de moribus in mensa servandis, Joanne Sulpitio Verulano authore. Cum familiarissima et rudi juventuti aptissima elucidatione Gallicolatina Gulielmi Durandi. Lugduni, apud Stephanum Doletum, 1542. (Also 1560.)

449. TALPIN, JEAN. La police Chrestienne: au Roy. Livre tresutile & salutaire à tous governeurs de republiques, pour heureusement les regir & gouverner selon Dieu: & autant necessaire à toutes manieres de gens, de quelque estat ou vocation qu' ils soyent, à cause qu'il contient la doctrine non seulement generale, mais aussi speciale, pour l'instruction de toute particuliere & chrestienne profession. De la doctrine duquel aussi les curez & predicateurs se pourront servir quand ils voudront advertir chacun estat de son particulier devoir. Par M. Jean Talpin, Docteur & Chanoine Theological a Perigueux. Paris, Nicolas Chesneau, 1568.

450. TAPIA ALDANA, JACOBUS. Dialogus de triplici bono et vera hominis nobilitate. Salmantiae, C. Bonardus, 1588.

451. TOMAGNI, GIO. Dell' eccellenza dell' huomo.

452. TOMMASI, FRANCESCO. Reggimento del padre di famiglia di F. T. Firenze, Giorgio Marescotti, 1580.

453. TURNER, RICHARD. Youth know thy selfe. 1624.

454. TYNDALE, WILLIAM. The obedience of a Christen man, and how Christen rulers ought to governe, wherein also (if thou marke diligently) thou shalt find eyes to perceave the craftie conveyaunce of old jugglers. Set forth by William Tyndale. 1528. Parker Society, 1848. (Vol. 48, pp. 154–155, the difference between Aristotle and the Scriptures.)

455. TYPOTIUS, JACOBIUS. Symbola divina et humana, pontificum Arnhemi, 1609. (Also 1601–1606.)

456. VAENIUS, OTHO. Amorum emblemata, figuris Aeneis incisa, studio Othonis Vaenii. Anvers, 1607. (Also 1608; 1611; 1618.)

457. VALERA, DIEGO DE. Le gouvernement des princes. Le tresor de noblesse. 1497. (Trans. from Span.)

458. VALLA, LORENZO. Laurentius Valla de libero arbitrio. Apologia ejusdem adversus calumniatores, quando super fide sua requisitus fuerat. Item, contra Bartoli libellum, cui titulus, de insignis & armis, epistola.

Ubi acutissimi viri iudicium acerrimum & raram variamque eruditionem probabit lector. Basileae, apud And. Crat., 1526. (The ignorance and bad Latin of Bartolus and of jurisconsults in general.)

459. VALLAMBERT, SIMON. Cinq livres de la manière de nourrir et governer les enfans de la naissance. Poictiers, 1565.

460. VEILROC, FRANÇOIS. Briefue instruction pour tous estats. Paris, P. Danfrie et R. Breton, 1558. (Also 1559.)

461. VENTURA, COMINO. Trésor politique . . . contenant les relations, instructions, traictez et divers discours appartenans à la parfaicte intelligence de la raison d'estat . . . Paris, 1608. (Trans. Nicola Du Fossé.)

462. VERREPAEUS, SIMON. Sinonis Verrepaei institutionum scholasticarum libri tres. Primus agit de qualitate, delectu & officio tum praeceptorum tum discipulorum: ac de tota docendi ratione generatim II. exhibet facilem instituendi modum in humanioribus literis III. ostendit qua ratione & modo sit educanda iuventus in pietate & Christiana ac Catholica religione. Antverpiae, apud Joan. Bellerum, 1573. (Du Verdier.)

463. VIGGIANI, ANGELO. Trattato dello schermo. Nel quale discorre intorno all' eccellenza dell' arani & delle lettere, & intorno all' offesa & difesa. . . . Bologna, 1588. (Also 1575.)

464. VIRET, PIERRE. The schoole of beastes, intituled, the good housholder, etc. London, 1585.

465. WALSINGHAM, SIR FRANCIS. Anatomizing of honesty, ambition, and fortitude: written in the year 1590. 1672.

466. WATRIQUET DE COUVIN. Dits de Watriquet de Couvin, edit, Aug. Scheler, Bruxelles, 1868. (X. Li dis de haute honneur. Comment li peres enseigne au filz. XI. Li enseignemens du Jone fil de Prince. XVI. Li dis du preu chevalier. 1319. XVII. Li mireoirs aus princes. 1327.)

467. WHIGHT, NICHOLAS. The commendation of musick. C. 1562–1563.

468. WILSON, GEORGE. The commendation of cockes and cockfighting. London, f. H. Tomes, 1607.

469. WRIGHT, L. A display of dutie, dict with sage sayings, pythie sentences, and proper similes. London, 1589.

470. WYATT, SIR THOMAS. Letters to his son.

471. YATES, JAMES. The castell of courtesie, whereunto is adjoyned the holde of humilitie. 1582.

472. ZINANO, GABRIELE. Il soldato, over della fortezza. Reggio, H. Bartholi, 1591.

473. ———— Il viandante, overo della precedenza dell' armi, et delle lettere. Di Gabriele Zinano. Reggio, Hercoliano Bartholi, 1590.

INDEX TO TREATISES ON THE LADY

SUPPLEMENTARY INDEX TO TREATISES

ON THE GENTLEMAN

CLASSIFIED ACCORDING TO NATIONALITY OF AUTHOR

(Numbers refer to items in Bibliography, not pages.)

INDEX TO TEXT AND NOTES